"I Studied Inscriptions from before the Flood"

Sources for Biblical and Theological Study

General Editor:
David W. Baker
Ashland Theological Seminary

1. *The Flowering of Old Testament Theology: A Reader in Twentieth-Century Old Testament Theology, 1930–1990*
   edited by Ben C. Ollenburger, Elmer A. Martens, and Gerhard F. Hasel

2. *Beyond Form Criticism: Essays in Old Testament Literary Criticism*
   edited by Paul R. House

3. *A Song of Power and the Power of Song: Essays on the Book of Deuteronomy*
   edited by Duane L. Christensen

4. *"I Studied Inscriptions from before the Flood": Ancient Near Eastern, Literary, and Linguistic Approaches to Genesis 1–11*
   edited by Richard S. Hess and David Toshio Tsumura

"I Studied Inscriptions from before the Flood"

Ancient Near Eastern, Literary, and Linguistic Approaches to Genesis 1–11

edited by

Richard S. Hess
and
David Toshio Tsumura

Eisenbrauns
Winona Lake, Indiana
1994

Printed in the United States of America.

Library of Congress Cataloging-in-Publication Data

I studied inscriptions from before the flood : ancient Near Eastern, literary, and linguistic approaches to Genesis 1–11 / edited by Richard S. Hess and David Toshio Tsumura.

p. cm. — (Sources for biblical and theological study ; 4)

Includes bibliographical references and index.

ISBN 0-931464-88-9 (alk. paper)

1. Bible. O.T. Genesis I–XI—Historiography. 2. Middle Eastern literature—Relation to the Old Testament. 3. Myth in the Old Testament. 4. Genealogy in the Bible. 5. Bible. O.T. Genesis I–XI—Comparative studies. 6. Bible. O.T. Genesis I–XI—Criticism, interpretation, etc. 7. Creation—Comparative studies. 8. Deluge—Comparative studies. I. Hess, Richard S. II. Tsumura, David Toshio. III. Series.

BS1235.5.I35 1994

222′.1106—dc20 94-37707

CIP

The paper used in this publication meets the minimum requirements of the American National Standard for Information Sciences—Permanence of Paper for Printed Library Materials, ANSI Z39.48-1984.♾

CONTENTS

Indexes

SERIES PREFACE

Old Testament scholarship is well served by several recent works which detail, to a greater or lesser extent, the progress made in the study of the Old Testament. Some survey the range of interpretation over long stretches of time, while others concern themselves with a smaller chronological or geographical segment of the field. There are also brief *entrés* into the various subdisciplines of Old Testament study included in the standard introductions as well as in several useful series. All of these provide secondary syntheses of various aspects of Old Testament research. All refer to, and base their discussions upon, various seminal works by Old Testament scholars which have proven pivotal in the development and flourishing of the various aspects of the discipline.

The main avenue into the various areas of Old Testament inquiry, especially for the beginner, has been until now mainly through the filter of these interpreters. Even on a pedagogical level, however, it is beneficial for a student to be able to interact with foundational works firsthand. This contact will not only provide insight into the content of an area, but hopefully will also lead to the sharpening of critical abilities through interaction with various viewpoints. This series seeks to address this need by including not only key, ground-breaking works, but also significant responses to these. This allows the student to appreciate the process of scholarly development through interaction.

The series is also directed toward scholars. In a period of burgeoning knowledge and significant publication in many places and languages around the world, this series will endeavor to make easily accessible significant, but at times hard to find, contributions. Each volume will contain essays, articles, extracts, and the like, presenting in a manageable scope the growth and development of one of a number of different aspects of Old Testament studies. Most volumes will contain previously published material, with synthetic essays by the editor(s) of the individual volume. Some volumes, however, are expected to contain significant, previously unpublished works. To facilitate access to students and scholars, all entries will appear in English and will be newly typeset. If students are excited by the study of Scripture and scholars are encouraged in amicable dialogue, this series would have fulfilled its purpose.

DAVID W. BAKER, *series editor*
Ashland Theological Seminary

Publisher's Note

Articles republished here are reprinted without alteration, except for minor matters of style not affecting meaning. Page numbers of the original publication are marked with double brackets (⟦267⟧, for example). Other editorial notes or supplementations are also marked with double brackets, including editorially-supplied translations of foreign words. Footnotes are numbered consecutively throughout each article, even when the original publication used another system. No attempt has been made to bring transliteration systems into conformity with a single style.

EDITORS' PREFACE

Probably no other section of the Hebrew Bible has enjoyed more discussion and reflection than Genesis 1–11. We all share a fascination with stories about humanity's origins and earliest history. The quotation in the book's title suggests that this fascination is not only a modern phenomenon: it is taken from the writings of Ashurbanipal, king of Assyria (seventh century B.C.). His personal "library" included editions of creation and flood accounts. Discovery of these documents in the nineteenth century revolutionized the study of Genesis 1–11 and provided the raw material for many of the articles included here.

In preparation for this volume, we did not attempt to survey and select from all of the literature on the subject. Instead, we narrowed the field to two disciplines that have made contributions: ancient Near Eastern studies, and literary and linguistic approaches that discuss all or part of these texts. We chose these areas with several groups of readers in mind.

First, we felt that it would be helpful for students beginning the study of Genesis 1–11. If the comparative approach—reading the Primeval History in conjunction with the relevant texts from the Levant—initiates the student to the world outside the text, literary and linguistic studies introduce the reader to the world within the text. The emphasis is on the meaning of Genesis 1–11 within its present context. Why were these stories included in the Bible? Is there any rhyme or reason to such a diverse collection? What do these stories have to teach the reader?

A second reason for our inclusion of comparative and literary/linguistic approaches was to provide a ready tool for lecturers and teachers of Genesis 1–11. Good translations of many of the relevant ancient Near Eastern texts already exist, and our purpose was not to duplicate these, although a few articles do present new translations. Instead, we have included studies that provide seminal or classic interpretations of these texts. Again, we have not attempted to collect the latest works on the literary/linguistic interpretation of Genesis 1–11, nor have we sought to represent every methodology in this section. Instead, the studies selected are those that we have found most helpful in the interpretation of the texts. Some are from obscure sources in journals or festschriften. Others are translated from French or German. It is our hope that their presentation here will ease access for others who wish better to understand these texts from Genesis in the light of some significant literary interpretations.

There is a third group of potential readers: those who minister the message of these biblical texts to faith communities, as well as those who seek to understand them better for their own sake. Many of the articles discuss the theological themes of Genesis 1–11, considering who the creator God is and the nature of God's relationship with humanity. Literary studies often address these questions, but they also have a special significance for ancient Near Eastern comparisons. They raise questions about what is special to the biblical account and what is common to other accounts from the same culture. Although the work is published in an academic series, we have tried to keep in mind those with little background in the rarified air of ancient Near Eastern philology and Hebrew linguistics.

Three introductory chapters survey the field and consider some of the most important discussions. These chapters also introduce the rest of the articles in the book. By reading them first, an interested individual may gain acquaintance with the contribution of each of the later studies to the interpretation of Genesis 1–11, as well as a sense of the contents of these studies. We hope that those with little or no prior background will find here some items of interest and feel invited to dip further into this vast and wonderful "ocean" of research.

Finally, we must confess that our aims included satisfying our personal interests in these exciting fields. It has been our privilege to learn from the scholars represented here as well as from many others whom we (sadly) could not include. If this volume succeeds in its goals, it will be because the writers of these articles communicated their interest and love of the study of Genesis 1–11. We would like especially to thank Prof. W. G. Lambert for writing a postscript to his article in this volume. For the opportunity to continue our own explorations in these fascinating texts we thank the series editor, David Baker, and the publisher, James Eisenbraun. Last, we thank the Genesis 1–11 Project of Tyndale House, Cambridge, under whose auspices we worked during the initial stages of preparation of this volume.

RICHARD S. HESS
Glasgow Bible College

DAVID T. TSUMURA
Japan Bible Seminary

Abbreviations

General

AH	Atrahasis Epic
Akk.	Akkadian
AKL	Assyrian King List
Eg.	Egyptian
ET	English translation
Heb.	Hebrew
JB	Jerusalem Bible
KJV	King James Version
KN	King name
LXX	Septuagint
MA	Middle Assyrian
MT	Masoretic Text
NA	Neo-Assyrian
NAB	New American Bible
NB	Neo-Babylonian
NEB	New English Bible
NIV	New International Version
(N)JPS(V)	(New) Jewish Publication Society (Version)
NT	New Testament
OT	Old Testament
PN	Personal name
RS	Field numbers of tablets excavated at Ras Shamra
RSV	Revised Standard Version
SB	Standard Babylonian
SKL	Sumerian King List

Books and Periodicals

AB	Anchor Bible
ABAT	*Altorientalische Bilder zum Alten Testament*
ABL	R. F. Harper, *Assyrian and Babylonian Letters*
AEL	E. W. Lane, *Arabic-English Lexicon*

AfO	*Archiv für Orientforschung*
AH	W. G. Lambert and A. R. Millard, *Atra-Ḫasīs: The Babylonian Story of the Flood*
AHw	W. von Soden, *Akkadisches Handwörterbuch*
AJBI	*Annual of the Japanese Biblical Institute*
AJSL	*American Journal of Semitic Languages and Literature*
AnBib	Analecta Biblica
ANEP	J. B. Pritchard (ed.), *Ancient Near East in Pictures*
ANET	J. B. Pritchard (ed.), *Ancient Near Eastern Texts Relating to the Old Testament* (3d ed.)
AO	Tablets in the collections of the Musée du Louvre
AOAT	Alter Orient und Altes Testament
AOS	American Oriental Series
ARM	Archives royales de Mari
ArOr	*Archiv orientální*
AS	Assyriological Studies
ATAT	*Altorientalische Texte zum Alten Testaments*
AUSS	*Andrews University Seminary Studies*
BA	*Biblical Archaeologist*
BASOR	*Bulletin of the American Schools of Oriental Research*
BASORSS	Bulletin of the American Schools of Oriental Research Supplement Series
BDB	F. Brown, S. R. Driver, and C. A. Briggs, *Hebrew and English Lexicon of the Old Testament*
BE	Babylonian Expedition of the University of Pennsylvania, Series A: Cuneiform Texts
BHS	Biblia Hebraica Stuttgartensia
Bib	*Biblica*
BibOr	Biblica et Orientalia
BiOr	*Bibliotheca Orientalis*
BJRL	*Bulletin of the John Rylands University Library of Manchester*
BK	*Bibel und Kirche*
BKAT	Biblischer Kommentar: Altes Testament
BR	*Biblical Research*
BS(ac)	*Bibliotheca Sacra*
BSO(A)S	*Bulletin of the School of Oriental (and African) Studies*
BZ	*Biblische Zeitschrift*
BZAW	Beihefte zur *ZAW*
CAD	*The Assyrian Dictionary of the Oriental Institute of the University of Chicago*
CAH	*Cambridge Ancient History*
CBQ	*Catholic Biblical Quarterly*
CBQMS	Catholic Biblical Quarterly Monograph Series
CBS	Tablets in the collections of the University Museum of the University of Pennsylvania, Philadelphia
CML[2]	J. C. L. Gibson, *Canaanite Myths and Legends* (2d ed.)

CRRA(I)	Compte rendu de la Rencontre assyriologique internationale
CT	Cuneiform Texts from the British Museum
CTA	A. Herdner, *Corpus des tablettes en cunéiformes alphabétiques*
DT	Tablets in the collections of the British Museum
ERC	Éditions recherche sur les civilisations
EvQ	*Evangelical Quarterly*
EvT	*Evangelische Theologie*
ExpTim	*Expository Times*
FBBS	Facet Books, Biblical Series
GKC	*Gesenius' Hebrew Grammar*, ed. E. Kautzsch, trans. A. E. Cowley
HKAT	Handkommentar zum Alten Testament
HSM	Harvard Semitic Monographs
HTR	*Harvard Theological Review*
IB	*Interpreter's Bible*
ICC	International Critical Commentary
IDB	G. A. Buttrick (ed.), *Interpreter's Dictionary of the Bible*
IDBSup	*Supplementary volume to IDB*
Int	*Interpretation*
JANES	*Journal of the Ancient Near Eastern Society of Columbia University*
JAOS	*Journal of the American Oriental Society*
JBL	*Journal of Biblical Literature*
JCS	*Journal of Cuneiform Studies*
JJS	*Journal of Jewish Studies*
JNES	*Journal of Near Eastern Studies*
JRT	*Journal of Religious Thought*
JSOT	*Journal for the Study of the Old Testament*
JSOTSup	Journal for the Study of the Old Testament Supplement Series
JSS	*Journal of Semitic Studies*
JTS	*Journal of Theological Studies*
KAR	Keilinschrifttexte aus Assur religiösen Inhalts
KB	L. Koehler and W. Baumgartner, *Lexicon in Veteris Testamenti libros*
KD	*Kerygma und Dogma*
KTU	M. Dietrich, O. Loretz, and J. Sanmartín, *Die keilalphabetische Texte aus Ugarit*
LAPO	Littératures anciennes du Proche-Orient
MAD	Materials for the Assyrian Dictionary
MAOG	*Mitteilungen der Altorientalischen Gesellschaft*
MDOG	*Mitteilungen der deutschen Orient-Gesellschaft*
MLC	del Olmo Lete, *Mitos y leyendas de Canaan segun la tradicion de Ugarit* (Madrid: Ediciones Cristiandad, 1981)
MMEW	A. Livingstone, *Mystical and Mythological Explanatory Works of Assyrian and Babylonian Scholars* (Oxford: Clarendon, 1986)
NFT	*Nouvelles Fouilles de Tello* (Paris, 1910)
NICOT	New International Commentary on the Old Testament
OECT	Oxford Editions of Cuneiform Texts
OLZ	*Orientalische Literaturzeitung*

Or	*Orientalia*
OTL	Old Testament Library
PBS	Publications of the Babylonian Section, University Museum, University of Pennsylvania
PEQ	*Palestine Exploration Quarterly*
RA	*Revue d'assyriologie et d'archéologie orientale*
RB	*Revue biblique*
RelS	*Religious Studies*
RlA	*Reallexikon der Assyriologie*
RSP	L. R. Fisher (ed.), *Ras Shamra Parallels*
SAHG	*Sumerische und akkadische Hymnen und Gebete*
SBH	F. I. Andersen, *The Sentence in Biblical Hebrew*
SAOC	Studies in Ancient Oriental Civilization
SBLSP	SBL Seminar Papers
SNTSMS	Society for New Testament Studies Monograph Series
SSN	Studia Semitica Neerlandica
ST	*Studia Theologica*
SVT	Vetus Testamentum Supplements
TAPA	*Transactions of the American Philological Association*
T(h)Z	*Theologische Zeitschrift*
TO	*Textes Ougaritiques, tome 1: Mythes et légendes* (LAPO 7; du Cerf, 1974)
TRE	*Theologische Realenzyklopädie*
TRS	*Textes religieux sumeriens du Louvre*
TynBul	*Tyndale Bulletin*
UET	Ur Excavations, Texts
UF	*Ugarit-Forschungen*
Ug.	*Ugaritica*
UM	Tablets in the collections of the University Museum of the University of Pennsylvania, Philadelphia
USQR	*Union Seminary Quarterly Review*
UT	C. H. Gordon, *Ugaritic Textbook*
UVST	J. Huehnergard, *Ugaritic Vocabulary in Syllabic Transcription* (HSS 32; Atlanta: Scholars Press, 1987)
VAT	Tablets in the collections of the Staatliche Museen, Berlin
VT	*Vetus Testamentum*
VTSup	Vetus Testamentum Supplements
WBC	Word Biblical Commentary
WMANT	Wissenschaftliche Monographien zum Alten und Neuen Testament
WO	*Die Welt des Orients*
WTJ	*Westminster Theological Journal*
WZKM	*Wiener Zeitschrift für die Kunde des Morgenlandes*
YOR	Yale Oriental Series, Researches
ZA	*Zeitschrift für Assyriologie*
ZAW	*Zeitschrift für die Alttestamentliche Wissenschaft*
ZDMG	*Zeitschrift der deutschen morgenländischen Gesellschaft*
ZTK	*Zeitschrift für Theologie und Kirche*

Introduction

One Hundred Fifty Years of Comparative Studies on Genesis 1–11: An Overview

RICHARD S. HESS

The Earliest Evidence

The first attempts to compare material in Genesis 1–11 with documents from the ancient Near East apparently date from the Hellenistic Period. B. Z. Wacholder has observed the interest Jewish and other scholars of this period had in synchronizing early biblical texts with those containing the mythologies and chronologies of the surrounding world.[1] For example, in the second century B.C.E., Eupolemus, who may also appear as a Maccabean envoy to Rome, attempted a number of synchronizations, which were referred to and elaborated by later authors.[2] A fragment identified by its presumed "author" Pseudo-Eupolemus states that Babylon was the first city built after the Flood. Pseudo-Eupolemus says

Author's note: The author has benefited from conversations with A. R. Millard and the comments of W. G. Lambert and D. T. Tsumura on this paper.

1. "Biblical Chronology in the Hellenistic World Chronologies," *HTR* 61 (1968) 451–81; repr. in B. Z. Wacholder, *Essays on Jewish Chronology and Chronography* (New York: KTAV, 1976) 106–36.

2. Idem, *Eupolemus: A Study of Judaeo-Greek Literature* (Cincinnati: Hebrew Union College–Jewish Institute of Religion, 1974).

that it was originally named Belus and built by the Sons of God who had escaped the Flood.[3] W. G. Lambert has argued that the designation of Babylon as the first city must come from Berossus' history of Babylon, rather than from a non-Babylonian source.[4] Lambert observes that although cuneiform writing would have constituted an initial barrier to Jewish scholars' examination of this material, the activities of a Babylonian scholar such as Berossus, who in the first half of the third century B.C.E. translated the material into Greek, would have made it accessible. Assigning the Pseudo-Eupolemus material to Eupolemus, Lambert goes on to suggest that here is evidence of the use of Babylonian sources by Jewish scholars.[5] He further identifies a hebraized version of Berossus that includes a "doublet" concerning origins. The first is the origin of the world by water alone, following Babylonian tradition. The second is also the beginning of the world, with both water and darkness, which Lambert compares with Genesis.[6] This may be the earliest evidence for written studies comparing ancient Near Eastern sources and Genesis 1–11. Berossus, along with material from the sixth-century C.E. scholar Damascius, remained the primary source of such comparisons for all later commentators and scholars, including Josephus and the Church Fathers.

The Nineteenth-Century Discoveries

It was only in the last half of the nineteenth century that the combined efforts of the new sciences of archaeology and Semitic philology (new only in its study of Assyriology) provided the materials for additional comparisons between the Hebrew and Babylonian sources. In 1847 the work of Austin Henry Layard at the mound of Kouyunjik near Mosul brought to light the first of thousands of cuneiform tablets and fragments, many belonging to what was identified as Ashurbanipal's library of the seventh century B.C.E. In a preliminary examination of the texts, Henry Rawlinson observed some points of similarity between Genesis and these accounts. However, it was the careful collation and joining of the tablets by George Smith that brought to the world for the first time a Flood story in Akkadian, a story which would later be identified as tablet XI of the "Gilgamesh Epic." In a paper read in London to the Society

3. Wacholder ("Biblical Chronology," 458–59), who refers to quotations from Eusebius.

4. W. G. Lambert, *The Background of Jewish Apocalyptic* (Ethel M. Wood Lecture; London: University of London, 1978) 13–15.

5. Lambert also refers to Alexander Polyhistor and others who made use of Berossus.

6. Ibid., 15.

of Biblical Archaeology on 3 December 1872, he provided the first published report of this discovery:[7]

> A short time back I discovered among the Assyrian tablets in the British Museum, an account of the flood; which, under the advice of our President, I now bring before the Society.
>
> For convenience of working, I had divided the collection of Assyrian tablets in the British Museum into sections, according to the subject-matter of the inscriptions.
>
> I have recently been examining the division comprising the Mythological and Mythical tablets, and from this section I obtained a number of tablets, giving a curious series of legends and including a copy of the story of the Flood. On discovering these documents, which were much mutilated, I searched over all the collections of fragments of inscriptions, consisting of several thousands of smaller pieces, and ultimately recovered 80 fragments of these legends; by the aid of which I was enabled to restore nearly all the text of the description of the Flood, and considerable portions of the other legends. These tablets were originally at least twelve in number, forming one story or set of legends, the account of the Flood being on the eleventh tablet.
>
> Of the inscription describing the Flood, there are fragments of three copies containing the same texts; these copies belong to the time of Assurbanipal, or about 660 years before the Christian era, and they were found in the library of that monarch at Nineveh.

Smith went on to argue that the texts possessed much greater antiquity. He related some of their contents and compared them with the accounts of Berossus and of Genesis. His concluding remarks were as follows:

> All these accounts, together with considerable portions of the ancient mythologies have, I believe, a common origin in the Plains of Chaldea. This country, the cradle of civilisation, the birthplace of the arts and sciences, for 2,000 years has been in ruins; its literature, containing the most precious records of antiquity, is scarcely known to us, except from the texts of the Assyrians, but beneath its mounds and ruined cities, now awaiting exploration, lay, together with older copies of this Deluge text, other legends and histories of the earliest civilisations in the world.

These words were to prove prophetic. In a second paper read to the same society almost three years later (2 November 1875), Smith furthered a discovery already announced to the *Daily Telegraph* on 4 March

7. George Smith, "The Chaldean Account of the Deluge," *Transactions of the Society of Biblical Archaeology* 2 (1873–74) 213–34, quoting from p. 213; repr. in *The Flood Myth* (ed. A. Dundes; Berkeley: University of California Press, 1988) 29–48.

of the same year.[8] He had located and now presented copies of two tablets dealing with the Babylonian account of the Creation.[9] Smith subsequently departed on an ill-fated journey to the Middle East, from which he never returned. He left a legacy that subsequently appeared in a popular volume providing translations and commentary on the texts.[10] Both the newspaper account and the volume left no doubt as to Smith's own views on the relationship of this material to Genesis. On pp. 13–14, in a reprint of the newspaper account, we read:

> Whatever the primitive account may have been from which the earlier part of the Book of Genesis was copied, it is evident that the brief narration given in the Pentateuch omits a number of incidents and explanations—for instance, as to the origin of evil, the fall of the angels, the wickedness of the serpent, &c. Such points as these are included in the Cuneiform narrative . . .

Cuneiform copies of these texts were published by F. Delitzsch.[11] In 1883, an additional text, part of the important fourth tablet of the Creation account (known by the first two words of the account, "Enuma Elish"), was discovered by H. Rassam.[12] Studies and publications of these texts proceeded in German, French, and English. Ten years later G. A. Barton prepared a transliteration and translation with commentary of what had then been published of the first, fourth, and fifth tablets.[13]

Comparative Studies before World War I

Although much more could be written concerning the contribution of many Assyriologists to comparative studies, the matter came to a focus in 1895 with the appearance of H. Gunkel's *Schöpfung und Chaos in Urzeit*

8. He mentions in this announcement that the *Daily Telegraph* had provided the funding for the expedition.

9. George Smith, "On Some Fragments of the Chaldean Account of the Creation," *Transactions of the Society of Biblical Archaeology* 4 (1875–76) 363–64 + 5 plates. In addition to the tablets of the Creation account, Smith also included a copy of a tablet related to the "Fall." This was later reinterpreted as not containing such an account.

10. The lengthy but revealing title of Smith's book was *The Chaldean Account of Genesis. Containing the Description of the Creation, the Fall of Man, the Deluge, the Tower of Babel, the Times of the Patriarchs, and Nimrod; Babylonian Fables, and Legends of the Gods; from the Cuneiform Inscriptions* (London: Sampson Low, Marston, Searle, and Rivington, 1876). Before the year was out this volume was in its third printing.

11. F. Delitzsch, *Assyrische Lesestücke* (Leipzig, 1876).

12. First announced by E. A. Wallis Budge in a communication in the *Proceedings of the Society of Biblical Archaeology* 6 (1883–84) 5–9.

13. G. A. Barton, "Tiamat," *JAOS* 15 (1893) 1–27.

und Endzeit.[14] Gunkel, with the help of the Assyriologist H. Zimmern, systematically compared the Babylonian Creation myths and the Gilgamesh fragment concerning the Flood to Genesis 1–11. He argued that Genesis 1–11 displayed extensive dependence on the mythological tradition of Babylonia. He also argued that this dependence had begun in the earliest period of Israel's history. This view, with extensive support in detailed philological and formal study, formed the basis of his form-critical approach, which was expressed in his influential commentary on Genesis.[15] It is not necessary to detail the subsequent history of publication of "Enuma Elish" and the "Gilgamesh Epic."[16] It is sufficient to observe that with the appearance of the fragments of these epics in the late nineteenth century, interest in comparing the ancient Near Eastern documents and traditions with the accounts of Genesis 1–11 reemerged.

The turn of the century also saw the emergence of the pan-Babylonian school of thought and the "Babel and Bible" controversy, both led by Friedrich Delitzsch and his students.[17] These developments reflected a common assumption, the antiquity and superiority of Babylonian culture to Israelite culture. On a broader scale, they shared with Gunkel's approach and that of many Assyriologists an optimism concerning the use of "Enuma Elish," the "Gilgamesh Epic,"[18] and other cuneiform literature for interpreting the biblical text.

During this period Assyriology and Hebrew Bible studies enjoyed a close relationship. The two were tied together, as the publications of

14. H. Gunkel, *Schöpfung und Chaos in Urzeit und Endzeit: Eine religionsgeschichtliche Untersuchung über Gen 1 und Ap Joh 12* (Göttingen: Vandenhoeck & Ruprecht); for an abridged English translation by C. A. Muenchow of the portion of the book relevant to Genesis 1, see *Creation and the Old Testament* (ed. B. W. Anderson; Issues in Religion and Theology 6; Philadelphia: Fortress/London: SPCK, 1984) 25–52.

15. H. Gunkel, *Genesis übersetzt und erklärt* (HKAT 3/1; Göttingen: Vandenhoeck & Ruprecht, 1901). The introduction was translated into English by W. H. Carruth and has been reprinted with an introduction by W. F. Albright as *The Legends of Genesis: The Biblical Saga and History* (New York: Schocken, 1974).

16. For a convenient summary of the important publications, see R. Borger, *Handbuch der Keilschriftliteratur* (Berlin: de Gruyter, 1967–) 1.225–26, 555–57; 2.126–27, 292–94.

17. On the pan-Babylonian school of thought, see pp. 96–112 in O. Carena, *History of the Near Eastern Historiography and Its Problems: 1852–1985. Part One: 1852–1945* (AOAT 218/1; Kevelaer: Butzon & Bercker/Neukirchen-Vluyn: Neukirchener, 1989). On Babel and Bible see the summary by H. B. Huffmon, "*Babel und Bibel*: The Encounter between Babylon and the Bible," in *Backgrounds for the Bible* (ed. M. P. O'Connor and D. N. Freedman; Winona Lake, Ind.: Eisenbrauns, 1987) 125–36. See also the forthcoming study by R. G. Lehmann, *Friedrich Delitzsch und der Babel-Bibel-Streit.*

18. On the study of Gilgamesh, much of which concerns matters unrelated to the Flood epic, but which nevertheless have a bearing on the history of religion and thought, see the useful collection of important essays edited by K. Oberhuber, *Das Gilgamesch-Epos* (Wege der Forschung 215; Darmstadt: Wissenschaftliche Buchgesellschaft, 1977).

Assyriologists in biblical studies reveal. Indeed, it may be for this reason, in addition to the infancy of the discipline, that the early decades of this century were such a fruitful time for comparative studies between sources from the ancient Near East and Genesis 1–11. In addition to the studies on the Creation and Flood accounts, the period leading up to World War I saw the appearance of studies on other parts of Genesis 1–11. Studies compared the king lists of the Babylonians and Assyrians with the genealogies of Genesis 4, 5, 10, and 11.[19] There also were attempts to introduce comparative materials from other cuneiform languages, especially Sumerian.[20]

The Effect of Assyriology as an Independent Discipline

The experience of a world war shattered optimistic visions about the inevitable evolutionary progress of humanity and may have had the same effect on the view of the increasing significance of ancient Near Eastern studies for biblical understanding. If we take the early work of W. F. Albright as an example this seems to have been the case. In an important article of 1924, "Contributions to Biblical Archaeology and Philology,"[21] Albright argues that, although the syntax of the initial phrase in Genesis 1 (and biblical Creation material in general) "has been stylistically influenced from Mesopotamia," in terms of the actual ideas of Genesis 1 with its general rejection of an ancient Near Eastern mythological world view, "P's mind was an enlightened product of the sixth century B.C.; we must consider his world-view in connection with the philosophy of contemporary Ionia, and of other cultured lands of the eastern Mediterranean, instead of comparing it directly with Mesopotamian myths which

19. E.g., H. Zimmern, "Urkönige und Ur Offenbarung," in *Die Keilinschriften und das Alte Testament* (ed. E. Schrader; 3d ed.; Berlin: Reuther & Reichard, 1905) 530–43. Although Zimmern comments on other figures in Genesis as well, J. C. VanderKam found his work to be an essential starting point for his study of the ancient Near Eastern material related to Enoch (*Enoch and the Growth of an Apocalyptic Tradition* [CBQMS 16; Washington, D.C.: Catholic Biblical Association, 1984]). Commenting on Zimmern's work, VanderKam observes: "The pages are the logical starting point for a survey of research on this topic for two reasons: in them Zimmern made readily available to commentators the most important cuneiform text for understanding the background of Jewish traditions about Enoch, and his comments about Enochic passages became highly influential and proved to be correct in most cases" (p. 11).

20. See S. Landersdorfer, *Sumerisches Sprachgut im Alten Testament* (Leipzig: Hinrichs, 1916).

21. W. F. Albright, "Contributions to Biblical Archaeology and Philology," *JBL* 43 (1924) 363–93.

were fully developed by at least 2000 B.C."[22] Albright's own application of the cuneiform sources to Genesis 1–11 focused on the significance of comparative phonology and lexicography, including the study of personal names and place-names. While this latter emphasis continues the line of some of the scholars of the preceding two decades, Albright's early published work veered away from the assumptions of some of the early Assyriologists and biblical scholars, who applied the cuneiform accounts of Creation and Flood stories to the biblical ones *in toto.*

A change was also taking place within Assyriology itself. With the great increase in the number of texts available for study and with the surge of archaeological projects in the ancient Near East, we find the discipline gradually extricating itself from dependence on biblical and theological studies. In the United States, for example, the Oriental Institute at the University of Chicago was founded in 1919. Two years later it initiated the massive *Chicago Assyrian Dictionary* project, which does not make reference to Biblical Hebrew.[23] There was a similar philosophical outlook evident elsewhere in major universities in America and Europe.

In his 1926 inaugural lecture at Leipzig, B. Landsberger advocated the perception of the Babylonian world through a study of its own language and the categories inherent in it.[24] Although not concerned directly with issues of the comparative approach, he did address the assumption of an originally common Semitic world view for East and West Semitic, an assumption that underlay every comparison between the literary form and ideas of cuneiform and biblical mythology:

> The study of ancient civilization, however, does not confirm this hypothesis, at least, not its purely formal version, for no matter whether we deal with language, custom, law, society, or even economics, everywhere, even in the oldest available documents we encounter extraordinarily subtle differentiations and an abundance of concepts and formations.[25]

Throughout the article, Landsberger's concern with demonstrating that Akkadian is distinct from Hebrew broke with some earlier studies of the cuneiform language in which, "after a superficial look at the individual

22. Ibid., 364, 396.

23. C. W. Meade, *Road to Babylon: Development of U.S. Assyriology* (Leiden: Brill, 1974) 90–104.

24. Published as "Die Eigenbegrifflichkeit der babylonischen Welt," *Islamica* 2 (1926) 355–72; trans. T. Jacobsen, B. Foster, and H. von Siebenthal, with an introduction by T. Jacobsen, and a postscript by B. Landsberger, as *The Conceptual Autonomy of the Babylonian World* (Monographs on the Ancient Near East 1/4; Malibu, Cal.; Undena, 1976).

25. *Conceptual Autonomy,* 10.

language every phenomenon was immediately projected onto the Semitic plane and thereby lost all colour and shape."[26] Inasmuch as he connected language with the whole world view of the culture it reflected, he reflected the prevailing movement, which was separating the disciplines of Assyriology and biblical studies. Henceforth greater restraint would be exercised in making parallels, and although many would not observe the cautions set forth by these and other scholars, the optimistic use of ancient Near Eastern materials to fill "gaps" in the biblical texts and virtually to reinterpret them would no longer find acceptance in either field.

Meanwhile, many biblical scholars continued to stress shared features. The effect of comparative studies on the scholarly world may be represented by the ways in which two of the major Genesis commentaries of the period dealt with "Enuma Elish." The International Critical Commentary on Genesis was authored by J. Skinner.[27] It appeared in 1910, and appeared in a second edition, with few changes, in 1930. Skinner provided a ten-page excursus on comparative cosmogonies, including a summary of the contents of "Enuma Elish," as well as similarities and differences. Skinner concluded, "In view of these parallels, it seems impossible to doubt that the cosmogony of Gn. 1 rests on a conception of the process of creation fundamentally identical with that of the *Enuma elîš* tablets."[28] The important German commentary of P. Heinisch, which appeared in 1930, followed a similar line. There are too many similarities to reject a common source to the form, but the theological content is distinctive to Israel.[29]

A. Heidel's publication by the University of Chicago Press of two volumes analyzing "Enuma Elish" and the "Gilgamesh Epic" represents perhaps the most important attempt to bridge the gap between Assyriology and English readership. Each volume provides a translation of the work with a discussion of its background, its structure, and any Old Testament parallels. The discussion of the Creation account appeared in 1942,[30] while the volume on the "Gilgamesh Epic" first appeared in 1946.[31]

26. Ibid.

27. J. Skinner, *A Critical and Exegetical Commentary on Genesis* (ICC; Edinburgh: T. & T. Clark).

28. Ibid., 47.

29. P. Heinisch, *Das Buch Genesis Übersetzt und Erklärt* (Die Heilige Schrift des Alten Testaments 1/1; Bonn: Peter Hanstein, 1930) 109. Heinisch quotes A. Jeremias (*Das Alte Testament im Lichte des Alten Orients* [3d ed., 1916] 35: "Ihm kommt es auf die Darstellung religiöser Gedanken an, und er erfüllt alte Formen mit neuem Inhalt."

30. A. Heidel, *The Babylonian Genesis: The Story of Creation* (Chicago: University of Chicago Press, 1942). A second edition appeared in 1951.

31. A. Heidel, *The Gilgamesh Epic and Old Testament Parallels* (Chicago: University of Chicago Press, 1946).

Both works assume a "close" relationship with the biblical texts, whether the Creation or the Flood story. Both also ask which came first, Genesis or the cuneiform text. The option that seems to be preferred is that of a common origin, but the author is noncommittal. This attitude is characteristic of the comparative approach in biblical studies in the years following World War II.

New and Refined Methods: The Post-War Era

Significant advances in the 1950s and early 1960s were made in the analysis of Akkadian lexicography and studies on specific place and personal names. A model essay in this regard was S. Gevirtz's study, "Lamech's Song to His Wives."[32] The author demonstrated the value of comparative biblical and ancient Near Eastern literature for understanding the onomastic, poetic, and philological components of this ancient poem. The increasing unruliness of the couplets may be compared not only with the pride and murderous rebellion of Lamech, but also with the moral decline characteristic of the line of Cain and culminating in the judgment of the chaos of the Flood. J. Heller's attempt to find a Hurrian etymology for the name *Eve* may be cited as an example of onomastic studies of the period.[33] G. Castellino summarized the literary parallels between Mesopotamian myths and Genesis 2–4.[34] G. Wallis published an important study on both the genealogy of Genesis 4 and the narrative of chap. 11, entitled "Die Stadt in den Überlieferungen der Genesis."[35] Studies of individual verses appeared. Of special note is R. Borger's study of Gen 4:1, which used Akkadian personal names composed of *itti* with the meaning 'from' to demonstrate such an interpretation for the particle *ʾt*, in Eve's enigmatic exclamation at the birth of Cain.[36]

D. Neiman's article on the cursing of Canaan in Genesis 9 represented his own interesting method, which incorporated early Greek traditions, as well as those of the Near East.[37] He attempted to relate the text to the Conquest period. The study asserts that "rash promises to the

32. S. Gevirtz, "Lamech's Song to His Wives," in this volume, 75–95.

33. J. Heller, "Der Name *Eva*," *ArOr* 26 (1958) 636–56.

34. G. Castellino, "Les origines de la civilisation selon les textes bibliques et les textes cunéiformes," appearing in this volume as "The Origins of Civilization according to Biblical and Cuneiform Texts," 75–95.

35. G. Wallis, "Die Stadt in den überlieferungen der Genesis," *ZAW* 78 (1966) 133–48.

36. R. Borger, "Gen. iv 1," *VT* 9 (1959) 85–86.

37. D. Neiman, "The Date and Circumstances of the Cursing of Canaan," in *Biblical Motifs: Origins and Transformations* (ed. A. Altmann; Philip W. Lown Institute of Advanced Judaic Studies: Studies and Texts 3; Cambridge: Harvard University Press, 1966) 113–34.

Philistines" by the Israelites are the central theme of the poetry assigned to Noah.

The structure of Genesis 10 received special scrutiny in the works of J. Simons and D. J. Wiseman.[38] Simons attempted to fit the divisions of the Table of Nations into geographical distinctions. Wiseman argued that a context from the early second millennium B.C.E. is to be found in the Table of Nations. Although some of the particular observations concerning the peoples and places mentioned would now require modification, the work remains important for its analysis of the arrangement of Genesis 10 and for its discussion of problems with later dates for the list. On specific names in the Table of Nations, I. J. Gelb's brief but technical note on Babylon's etymology is one of the most interesting.[39]

Parallel to the studies of comparative ancient Near Eastern material was an increased focus on the literary constitution of the text. While not yet directly related (except in works such as that of Gevirtz) to comparative studies, the emphasis of this literary research on the unity and sense of the present text and its attempt to fit it into a historical context set the stage in the 1960s for a relationship with the ancient Near Eastern materials. One of the most valuable contributions was a study of wisdom themes in Genesis 2–3 by L. Alonso-Schökel.[40] Aside from the important emphasis on the fact that these chapters of Genesis have their source in wisdom traditions, this essay represents a serious attempt to wrestle with the questions of genre that surround this text. In what sense is this material myth? In what sense is it history? Responding to Roman Catholic claims for the historical reality of this text, Alonso-Schökel introduced the principle of "triangular ascent." This approach allowed the author to draw from the contemporary experience of humanity and, resting firmly inside the Hebrew wisdom tradition, to retroject back to the historical reality of which that tradition is a reflection.

Another innovator in this area of study was W. Brueggemann. In a series of articles beginning in 1968, Brueggemann approached Genesis using a variety of methods. In his 1968 essay,[41] he sought to build on the

38. J. Simons, "The 'Table of Nations' (Genesis 10): Its General Structural and Meaning," in this volume, 234–53; D. J. Wiseman, "Genesis 10: Some Archaeological Considerations," in this volume, 254–65.

39. I. J. Gelb, "The Name of Babylon," in this volume, 266–84. Of course, Babylon actually does not appear in the Table of Nations but occurs in Gen 10:10 in the gloss concerning Nimrod.

40. L. Alonso-Schökel, "Motivos sapienciales y de alianza en Gn 2–3," *Bib* 43 (1962) 295–315; translated as "Sapiential and Covenant Themes in Gen 2–3," *TD* 13 (1965) 3–10; and reprinted in *Studies in Ancient Israelite Wisdom* (ed. J. L. Crenshaw; Library of Biblical Studies; New York: KTAV, 1976) 468–80.

41. W. Brueggemann, "David and His Theologian," *CBQ* 30 (1968) 156–81.

work of von Rad and to relate Genesis 2–11 more closely to the period of the Monarchy. Brueggemann attempts to compare the narrative of David's rise to power in 2 Samuel 9–10 and 1 Kings 1–2 with Genesis 2–11 by identifying similar traits and themes in the two stories. A strong impression of similarity is created, despite the lack of parallel phrases and word pairs. In a later essay he followed the method of analysis of Wolff on the theology of J, E, and DtnG, suggesting that the five verbs in Gen 1:28 are the central theme for P: be fruitful, multiply, fill, subdue, and have dominion.[42] This theme is traced through the remainder of Genesis as well as the Conquest material. Indeed, it seems to have most relevance during the first (Joshua) and second (Babylonian) entrances into the Promised Land.

Some of these literary/theological studies focused on the first chapters of Genesis and especially on the question of the image of God in 1:26. In the 1950s an interesting work by D. T. Asselin combined anthropological and literary study along with a clear style, relating the whole of Genesis 1–3 to what follows.[43] Perhaps the most useful work on Gen 1:26 was an article by D. J. A. Clines, "The Image of God in Man."[44] Clines provided an overview of the scholarship of the 1950s and 1960s on this question, thereby covering the impact of the Biblical Theology movement. Clines himself defends the *beth essentiae* approach, that is to say, humanity is created "as the image of God." A year later, J. Barr published a study that proposed an alternative method for the study of the meaning of *the image of God*.[45] He uses various approaches to the literary context and the semantic range of the Hebrew word for 'image'. Barr points out the significance of this word's appearance in Gen 1:26–27. His results modify theological presuppositions often placed on this text and offer new directions for the study of words and word pairs.

The 1960s also saw the appearance in English of two important commentaries on Genesis. The first was the work of U. Cassuto, whose two volumes on Genesis 1–11 had appeared some years earlier in Hebrew.[46] Although mentioning the Creation and Flood epics, Cassuto's major

42. Idem, "The Kerygma of the Priestly Writers," *ZAW* 84 (1972) 397–414. See also idem, "From Dust to Kingship," *ZAW* 84 (1972) 1–18. This article applies to Genesis 2 the understanding of dust as a metaphor for the position of a "nobody."

43. D. T. Asselin, "The Notion of Dominion in Genesis 1–3," *CBQ* 16 (1954) 277–94.

44. D. J. A. Clines, "The Image of God in Man," *TynBul* 19 (1968) 53–103.

45. J. Barr, "The Image of God in the Book of Genesis: A Study of Terminology," *BJRL* 51 (1968–69) 11–26.

46. U. Cassuto, *A Commentary on the Book of Genesis, Part I: From Adam to Noah, Genesis I–VI 8* (trans. I. Abrahams; Jerusalem: Magnes, 1961; originally published in Hebrew, 1944); *Part II: From Noah to Abraham, Genesis VI 9–XI 32, with an Appendix: A Fragment of Part III* (trans. I. Abrahams; Jerusalem: Magnes, 1964; originally published in Hebrew, 1949).

comparative contribution is the study of similar Ugaritic words and phrases for the understanding of the biblical material.

The second commentary was written by E. A. Speiser for the Anchor Bible commentary series and appeared in 1964.[47] Many of Speiser's original ideas on the interpretation of various passages in Genesis 1–11 had already appeared during the preceding decade in a series of important articles scattered throughout many publications. These included articles on אֵד in Genesis 2, on ידון in Gen 6:3, on the identification of the rivers in Genesis 2, on the identification of Nimrod with Tukulti-Ninurta I, and on "Mesopotamian Motifs in the Early Chapters of Genesis." Of these, the first four have been reprinted in Speiser's collected works.[48]

New Texts and Their Study: The Last Twenty-Five Years

Text Editions and Discoveries, 1960–1989

Fragments of the Creation and Gilgamesh epics continued to appear. The occasional king list fragment or lexical analysis also found publication. However, there was almost a complete absence of such materials in the discoveries of cuneiform texts at Ugarit, Alalakh, Nuzi, and Mari. These were texts with a language and sites with populations that were either West Semitic or close enough to the biblical world to raise the possibility of parallels. Yet, with one exception, that of a small and broken Akkadian fragment from Ugarit that deals with the Flood,[49] none of the published texts from these sites revealed narratives of Creation or the Flood. However, Ugarit has produced an abundance of themes and concepts related to the earlier chapters of Genesis.[50] Of course, this does not deny the presence of cosmogonies in Ugaritic mythology, as noted by L. R. Fisher, F. M. Cross, and R. J. Clifford.[51] They are found

47. E. A. Speiser, *Genesis* (AB 1; Garden City, N.Y.: Doubleday, 1964).

48. Idem, "*ᵓEd* in the Story of Creation," *BASOR* 140 (1955) 9–11; "*YDWN*: Gen. 6:3," *JBL* 75 (1956) 126–29; "The Rivers of Paradise," in this volume, 175–82; "In Search of Nimrod," in this volume, 270–77; "Mesopotamian Motifs in the Early Chapters of Genesis," *Expedition* 5 (1962) 18–19, 43; *Oriental and Biblical Studies: Collected Writings of E. A. Speiser* (ed. J. J. Finkelstein and M. Greenberg; Philadelphia: University of Pennsylvania Press, 1967) 19–52.

49. J. Nougayrol, *Ugaritica 5: Textes suméro-accadiens des archives et bibliothèques privées d'Ugarit* (Mission de Ras Shamra 16; Paris: Imprimerie Nationale, 1968) 300–304. An edition of this text also appears in Lambert and Millard, *Atra-Ḫasīs: The Babylonian Story of the Flood* (Oxford: Clarendon, 1969) 131–33.

50. See, however, the negative assessment of A. S. Kapelrud, "Creation in the Ras Shamra Texts," *ST* 34 (1980) 1–11.

51. L. R. Fisher, "Creation at Ugarit and in the Old Testament," *VT* 15 (1965) 313–24; F. M. Cross, *Canaanite Myth and Hebrew Epic* (Cambridge: Harvard University Press, 1973) 41–43; R. J. Clifford, "Cosmogonies in the Ugaritic Texts and in the Bible," *Or* n.s. 53 (1984) 183–201.

in conflicts between Baal and Mot and in the building of Baal's palace. However, the related biblical texts are not in the first eleven chapters of Genesis.

W. G. Lambert, in an important essay that appeared in 1967, addressed the question of Mesopotamian influences on the Hebrews and called for a reexamination of the entire matter in the light of evidence from the Ugaritic texts.[52] The study thus served as a polemic against the tendency to rely on generalizations of scholarly conclusions that cannot withstand the scrutiny of new evidence. In arguing that the Amarna Age of the fourteenth century was the only time of cultural borrowing from Mesopotamia into the West Semitic world of the Hebrew text of Genesis, Lambert suggested that influences on the Israelites was relatively late and that they did not borrow from the Amorites or earlier West Semitic peoples.

In the decade of the 1960s important new materials for comparative studies appeared, in particular, a new edition of a Flood story and a volume containing two essays that discussed some texts and their applications. Both works brought to light a range of new materials.

(1) In 1965 W. G. Lambert and A. R. Millard published a collection of tablets and fragments on the "Atra-Ḫasīs Epic."[53] Four years later the two scholars brought out a critical edition with transliteration, translation, and philological notes.[54] The work also included a new section of the Sumerian Flood story prepared by M. Civil (pp. 138–45). These works brought together for the first time the relevant sources for this story of the Flood, whose main copy dates from the reign of Ammiṣaduqa, great-great-grandson of Hammurapi. The implications of the this newly edited material were brought to the attention of biblical scholars by A. R. Millard in another important essay in 1967.[55] The "Atra-Ḫasīs Epic" includes both an account of the creation of humanity and an account of the Flood. Millard compared and contrasted "Atra-Ḫasīs" with the Genesis narrative. Similarities in general narrative framework, but not in intention or purpose, suggest only a limited borrowing at most. Millard's study thus served to establish a comparable structure between Genesis 1–9 and a Mesopotamian work of literature from the second millennium B.C.E.

(2) Volume 88 of the *Journal of the American Oriental Society* appeared in 1968 as a memorial to E. A. Speiser. As such it contained two articles

52. W. G. Lambert, "A New Look at the Babylonian Background of Genesis," in this volume, 96–113.

53. Lambert and Millard, *Cuneiform Texts from Babylonian Tablets in the British Museum*, part 46 (London: Trustees of the British Museum, 1965).

54. Lambert and Millard, *Atra-Ḫasīs.*

55. A. R. Millard, "A New Babylonian 'Genesis' Story," in this volume, 114–28.

related to Genesis 1–11 that explored for the first time new comparative data from the ancient Near East.[56] A. Malamat, in one of the essays, "King Lists of the Old Babylonian Period and Biblical Genealogies,"[57] provided the classic analysis of the relationship between the king list of Hammurapi's dynasty, which had been published by J. J. Finkelstein several years earlier,[58] and the genealogies of the Hebrew Bible. As the king list of an Amorite dynasty, the cuneiform text's comparison with the West Semitic genealogies of Israel's traditions may have particular interest. Although focusing on the similarities more than the differences and on biblical genealogies that lie outside of Genesis 1–11, this study provides a summary of many of the essential comparisons between the two forms of literature. Another essay should be mentioned here as well, the publication by E. Reiner of a tablet describing the *apkallu*, antediluvian sages, seven in number, who were not kings but were each associated with a ruler.[59] This study, combined with some of the earlier ones on other texts, provided important material for comparison with the biblical accounts of Cain's genealogy and its cultural founders.

The second article was S. N. Kramer's study of a portion of a Sumerian epic, which he compared and contrasted to the narrative of the Tower of Babel in Gen 11:1–9.[60]

The following decade brought further texts to light. Four major areas are particularly worthy of note.

(1) In a 1974 article, R. Borger provided a comprehensive summary of the known cuneiform texts that relate to the *apkallu*, the wisdom figures already mentioned, who are associated with the antediluvian kings of the Sumerian King List and sometimes are related to the "cultural hero" line of Cain in Genesis 4.[61] With the discovery of some additional text fragments, Borger finds among these figures the ancient Near Eastern parallel to Enoch and his journey to heaven.

56. A third, T. Jacobsen's ("The Battle between Marduk and Tiamat," 104–8) comparison of the struggle of the storm-god at Ugarit with the "Enuma Elish" contest between Marduk and Tiamat, which posits an etymology for Marduk as "son of the storm," is not directly relevant to Genesis 1–11 but does have interest for the debate over the presence of a conflict motif at Ugarit and its relation to Creation.

57. Reprinted in this volume, 183–99.

58. J. J. Finkelstein, "The Genealogy of the Hammurapi Dynasty," *JCS* 20 (1966) 95–118.

59. E. Reiner, "The Etiological Myth of the 'Seven Sages,' " *Or* n.s. 30 (1961) 1–11.

60. S. N. Kramer, "The 'Babel of Tongues': A Sumerian Version," reprinted in this volume, 278–82.

61. R. Borger, "Die Beschwörungsserie *Bīt Mēseri* und die Himmelfahrt Henochs," *JNES* 33 (1974) 183–96; appearing for the first time in English in this volume, "The Incantation Series *Bīt Mēseri* and the Ascension of Enoch," pp. 224–33.

(2) The discovery of the ninth/eighth-century Aramaic/Akkadian bilingual inscription at Tell Fekheriye[62] has led to some interesting observations related to lexical matters in Genesis 1–11, both in terms of the possible etymology and meaning of Eden[63] and in light of the usage in the inscription of cognates for the Hebrew expressions translated 'image' and 'likeness' in Gen 1:26.[64]

(3) In 1981 T. Jacobsen published a paper in which he argues for the reconstruction of a Sumerian myth from three disparate fragments.[65] He argues for a date similar to that of the "Atra-Ḫasīs Epic" and proceeds to use the resulting myth as a source for comparison with the Genesis account. The problem remains that there is no evidence for the existence of this text in the form reconstructed by Jacobsen. Whereas Jacobsen focused on what he considered to be the P account of creation, P. D. Miller, in a subsequent article, pointed out similarities in form that extend to include J as well, in other words, the whole of Genesis 1–11.[66] Miller was also helpful in presenting the theological distinctives of Genesis in comparison with the relevant ancient Near Eastern cuneiform documents. A further contribution to the study of this material was made by J. van Dijk.[67]

(4) A remark should be made concerning the materials from Ebla because of the initial publicity of the texts. The discovery of this third-millennium archive in the mid-seventies gave rise to much hope concerning the possibility of materials for comparison with the biblical text. As of this writing the progress of publishing the texts and interpreting them is moving forward. However, there is little that may be drawn upon at present for comparison with Genesis 1–11. Given the initial rush to compare and the manner in which many similar parallels dissolved before

62. A. A. Assaf, "Die Statue des HDYS^{c}Y, König von Guzana," *MDOG* 113 (1981) 3–22; A. A. Assaf, P. Bordreuil, and A. R. Millard, *La statue de Tell Fekherye et son inscription bilingue assyro-araméenne* (ERC; Paris: ADPF, 1982); S. A. Kaufman, "Reflections on the Assyrian-Aramaic Bilingual from Tell Fakhariyeh," *Maarav* 3 (1982) 137–75.

63. A. R. Millard, "The Etymology of Eden," *VT* 34 (1984) 103–6. He finds the meaning 'to enrich, make abundant' demonstrated by the Akkadian equivalent of the Aramaic verb, whose root is identical to that for Eden.

64. P.-E. Dion, "Image et ressemblance en araméen ancien (Tell Fakhariyah)," *Science et esprit* 34 (1982) 151–53; R. S. Hess, "Eden—A Well-Watered Place," *Bible Review* 7/6 (1991) 28–33.

65. T. Jacobsen, "The Eridu Genesis," in this volume, 129–42. Jacobsen discusses his sources on pp. 129–130.

66. P. D. Miller, "Eridu, Dunnu, and Babel: A Study in Comparative Mythology," 143–68 in this volume.

67. J. van Dijk, *LUGAL UD ME-LÁM-BI NIR-GÁL: Le Récit épique et didactique des travaux de Ninurta, du déluge et de la nouvelle création, Tome 1: Introduction, texte composite, traduction* (Leiden: Brill, 1983).

interested readers' eyes, we are well cautioned to proceed slowly and carefully. The one area that does seem to have received a certain amount of study and reflection and that might have a bearing on Genesis 1–11 is that of proper names. A collection of essays edited by A. Archi attempts to put this study into an ancient Near Eastern and biblical context.[68] Of the papers, including several touching on relations to West Semitic environments, only that of C. H. Gordon touches on matters related to Genesis 1–11.[69] He observes the divine name Adam at Ebla and notes some other similarities with the structure and elements found in personal names in Genesis, including the explanation of Eve in 4:1.

Comparative and Literary Studies, 1970–1990

The remainder of this section is a survey of some of the comparative studies that have appeared in the last twenty years. I will proceed section by section through Genesis 1–11, beginning with general surveys of the whole. Some of the literary analyses are also noted.

A useful historical survey of the comparative material is found in chapter two of K. A. Kitchen's *Bible and Its World.*[70] Pages 26–36 provide a tightly packed but competent historical overview. In 1980, W. G. Lambert published an encyclopedia article in which he surveyed the major sources and issues involved in relating cuneiform studies to Genesis.[71] While it is probable that the older and more prestigious culture of Babylon influenced Israel and not vice versa, that influence was clearer in nonreligious items and ideas, such as the names of the months. In an additional article on the subject of comparative materials, Lambert discussed the possibility of Amorite sources behind the material from Ebla. He also provided a list of shared features among myths from regions between the Mediterranean and India.[72] Much of what is mentioned in the genealogies of Genesis 4–10, such as the long lives of the pre-Flood figures, is similar to cuneiform king lists and the wisdom figures associ-

68. *Eblaite Personal Names and Semitic Name-Giving: Papers of a Symposium Held in Rome, July 15–17, 1985* (ed. A. Archi; Archivi reali de Ebla studi 1; Rome: Missione archeologica italiana in Siria, 1988).

69. C. H. Gordon, "Notes on Proper Names in the Ebla Tablets," ibid., 153–58. See also his "Eblaitica," in *Eblaitica: Essays on the Ebla Archives and Eblaite Language* (ed. C. H. Gordon, G. A. Rendsburg, and N. H. Winter; Eblaitica 1; Winona Lake, Ind.: Eisenbrauns, 1987) 19–28; and the cautions in the review of W. G. Lambert, *BSO(A)S* 52 (1989) 115–16.

70. K. A. Kitchen, *The Bible in Its World: Archaeology and the Bible Today* (Exeter: Paternoster, 1977) 26–36.

71. W. G. Lambert, "Babylonien und Israel," *TRE* 5 (1980) 67–79.

72. W. G. Lambert, "Old Testament Mythology in Its Ancient Near Eastern Context," in *Congress Volume, Jerusalem 1986* (ed. J. A. Emerton; VTSup 40; Leiden: Brill, 1988).

ated with them. The source material suggested by the Genesis genealogies would have entered Israelite tradition before the first millennium, probably during the international period of the Amarna age.

In the area of literary studies, it is difficult to know where to begin. One should mention the study of P. D. Miller, which examines specific passages.[73] More recently the works of I. M. Kikawada and A. Quinn, G. Rendsburg, and T. L. Thompson attempt to provide a unified reading for the text of Genesis 1–11.[74] D. J. A. Clines' 1976 essay provides an example of the weaknesses and strengths of several approaches to reading the text as it presently stands.[75] Whether or not the historical setting proposed by Clines is accepted by his readers, the analysis of the chapters reveals a sensitivity to the meanings and implications found there.

Along with these studies, mention should be made of two major commentaries that appeared during this time. The first was the enormous work by C. Westermann that was published in 1974.[76] Westermann provides the reader with the most comprehensive bibliography and review of literature on Genesis 1–11 to be found in print. The work incorporates innumerable comparative discussions. Rather than tracing origins and influences, Westermann is concerned to record the similarities and differences in the material. He does note other views but is not in a hurry to incorporate them into an interpretation of the text. See, for example, his discussion of the cursing of Canaan, which he refuses to interpret in any other way than as a literal family quarrel, within the context of the narrative following the Flood story.[77]

The second commentary was written by G. Wenham. Wenham also interacts with much of the material in his bibliographies. He incorporates the research into his own understanding of the issues and makes ready use of comparative studies.[78]

In the study of material on Genesis 1–3, consideration should be given to G. F. Hasel's essays on the methodology and problems of applying the comparative approach to the first chapter of Genesis. In few

73. P. D. Miller, *Genesis 1–11: Studies in Structure and Theme* (JSOTSup 8; Sheffield: JSOT Press, 1978).

74. I. M. Kikawada and A. Quinn, *Before Abraham Was: The Unity of Genesis* (Nashville: Abingdon, 1985); G. Rendsburg, *The Redaction of Genesis* (Winona Lake, Ind.: Eisenbrauns, 1986); T. L. Thompson, *The Origin Tradition of Ancient Israel, Vol. I: The Literary Formation of Genesis and Exodus 1–23* (JSOTSup 55; Sheffield: Sheffield Academic Press, 1987), esp. 61–80.

75. D. J. A. Clines, "Theme in Genesis 1–11," reprinted in this volume, 285–309.

76. C. Westermann, *Genesis, I: Teilband Genesis 1–11* (BKAT 1/1; Neukirchen-Vluyn: Neukirchener, 1974); translated by J. J. Scullion as *Genesis 1–11: A Commentary* (London: SPCK, 1984).

77. Ibid., 657–58, following the view expressed by B. Jacob.

78. G. Wenham, *Genesis 1–15* (WBC 1; Waco, Tex.: Word, 1987).

other passages of the Bible have so many facile comparisons been made with ancient Near Eastern myths and so many far-reaching conclusions posited. Hasel provides observations on fundamental distinctions in the creation accounts, with a strong focus on an antimythological apologetic for Genesis.[79] A radical distinction between "Enuma Elish" and Genesis 1 is also argued in an article by A. W. Ultvedt.[80] One of several comparisons and contrasts between Adam and the cuneiform myth of Adapa is found in a paper by N.-E. Andreasen.[81] Of interest from the perspective of specific problems in Genesis 1 are articles by L. M. Pasinya, who developed a study of three verbs that constitute essential elements in the creation process,[82] and by M. Weinfeld, who argued for common liturgical themes in biblical, Mesopotamian, and rabbinic literature: Creation, temple, and Sabbath.[83] Though theological in emphasis, P. A. Bird's study of Gen 1:26–27 is invaluable.[84] Her approach draws from and critiques theological (especially feminist) interpretations of the texts, utilizing literary and comparative methods. As a balanced approach that places careful limits on what can be concluded from the text, the study represents a model for work done in such a controversial area of biblical theology.

I. M. Kikawada has written an interesting study relating the two Creation accounts in Genesis 1–3.[85] He compares several other Mesopotamian accounts of the creation of humanity and argues that each forms a doublet. Å. W. Sjöberg has produced a provocative essay on Genesis 2–3.[86] He presents a collection of assumptions often accepted by biblical scholars but questioned by Assyriologists, and he suggests new directions for further research. J. Van Seters compares the Creation

79. G. F. Hasel, "The Significance of the Cosmology in Genesis 1 in Relation to Ancient Near Eastern Parallels," *AUSS* 10 (1972) 1–20; "The Polemic Nature of the Genesis Cosmology," *EvQ* 46 (1974) 81–102.

80. A. W. Ultvedt, "Genesis 1 og dens literaere kilder," *Nederlands Theologisch Tijdschrift* 81 (1980) 37–54. I thank Mr. G. Erikson for calling this article to my attention.

81. N.-E. Andreasen, "Adam and Adapa: Two Anthropological Characters," *AUSS* 19 (1981) 179–94.

82. L. M. Pasinya, "Las cadre littéraire de Genèse 1," *Bib* 57 (1976) 225–41.

83. M. Weinfeld, "Sabbath, Temple and the Enthronement of the Lord: The Problem of the Sitz im Leben of Genesis 1:1–2:3," in *Mélanges bibliques et orientaux en l'honneur de M. Henri Cazelles* (ed. A. Caquot and M. Delcor; AOAT 212; Kevelaer: Butzon & Bercker/ Neukirchen-Vluyn: Neukirchener, 1981) 501–12.

84. P. A. Bird, " 'Male and Female He Created Them': Genesis 1:27b in the Context of the Priestly Account of Creation," in this volume, 329–61.

85. I. M. Kikawada, "The Double Creation of Mankind in *Enki and Ninmah, Atrahasis* I 1–351, and *Genesis* 1–2," in this volume, 169–74.

86. Å. W. Sjöberg, "Eve and the Chameleon," in *Essays on Ancient Palestinian Life and Literature in Honor of G. W. Ahlström* (ed. W. B. Barrick and J. R. Spencer; JSOTSup 31; Sheffield: JSOT Press, 1984) 218–25.

account of Genesis 2–3 with a neo-Babylonian text recording a separate creation of mortals in general and of a king in particular.[87] Van Seters argues that these two separate acts of creation have been combined in the biblical text.

Genesis 2–3 forms a key text for testing new literary approaches, and the literature is immense. Only three or four items may be mentioned here. The 1977 article of J. T. Walsh displayed a mastery of several of the traditional aspects of exegetical method.[88] The result is a structural unity outside and inside the Garden, ordering and reordering the relationships of the characters involved. The literary and theological conclusions provide a point of departure for comparison with more recent literary approaches. A study important for its identification of a key set of themes in the text, intimacy and alienation, is found in an article by A. J. Hauser.[89] He demonstrates the close relationship of these themes to the vocabulary and narrative flow of the text.

The 1980 issue of *Semeia* (18) is entitled, *Genesis 2 and 3: Kaleidoscopic Structural Readings.* Fourteen scholars contributed structuralist readings, and reactions were provided by colleagues. In a follow-up to this issue, one of the contributors, D. Jobling, provided an evaluation of the method to date, with his own interpretation of its effect on understanding Genesis 2–3.[90] By using a deconstructionist method and positing "the-man-to-till-the-soil" model in order to explain some aspects of the narrative untouched by the "creation-and-fall" model, Jobling proceeds toward fresh observations and conclusions concerning guilt, fallenness, and feminist interpretations. G. J. Wenham, in a paper that expands on some themes in his commentary, argues for parallels between the description of Eden and that of Israel's sanctuaries.[91]

When considering the genealogies of Genesis 1–11, I find R. R. Wilson's 1977 study, *Genealogy and History in the Biblical World,* to be an essential volume.[92] An abbreviated summary of this work appeared two

87. J. Van Seters, "The Creation of Man and the Creation of the King," *ZAW* 101 (1989) 333–42. The text that Van Seters refers to is that of W. R. Mayer, "Ein Mythos von der Erschaffung des Menschen und des Königs," *Or* n.s. 56 (1987) 55–68.

88. J. T. Walsh, "Genesis 2:4b–3:24: A Synchronic Approach," in this volume, 362–82. The criticism of ahistoricity (H. N. Wallace, *The Eden Narrative* [HSM 32; Atlanta: Scholars Press, 1985] 16) is one to which structural studies are subject.

89. A. J. Hauser, "Genesis 2–3: The Theme of Intimacy and Alienation," in this volume, 383–98.

90. D. Jobling, "Myth and Its Limits in Genesis 2.4b–3.24," in *The Sense of Biblical Narrative: Structural Analyses in the Hebrew Bible, II* (JSOTSup 39; Sheffield: JSOT Press, 1986) 17–43.

91. G. J. Wenham, "Sanctuary Symbolism in the Garden of Eden," in this volume, 405–15.

92. R. R. Wilson, *Genealogy and History in the Biblical World* (Yale Near Eastern Researches 7; New Haven: Yale University Press, 1977).

years earlier.[93] Wilson provides a survey of the most important research, including an extensive critical evaluation of Malamat's method and conclusions. The essay represents the first attempt at a systematic incorporation of anthropological data into the discussion of Old Testament genealogies. Among several later contributions, J. M. Sasson's is of interest for positing a special significance to the fifth and seventh place in ancestor lists.[94] R. B. Robinson treats genealogies from a literary perspective.[95] Rather than resolving the tension between the genealogies and the narratives that surround them, Robinson focuses on the distinction and the way the two types of literature interact with one another to create tension, interest, and purpose in the text. The freewill/deterministic paradox that Robinson identifies is, like much of the essay, programmatic in its value. Further survey of the modern discussion on genealogies is provided in my essay, which seeks to identify functional and formal distinctions between the genealogies of Genesis 1–11 and comparative ancient Near Eastern literature.[96]

Borger's study on the Cainite genealogy of Genesis 4 has already been noted.[97] In addition, J. F. A. Sawyer's article on the line of Cain should be mentioned.[98] He attempts to settle some of the figures of Genesis 4 in a West Semitic geographical environment, the Arabah. The biblical and archaeological associations of this region with Kenites/metal smiths provide a balance to the study of Mesopotamian traditions associated with this genealogy.

Study of the "Atra-Ḫasīs Myth" has continued to result in articles discussing its implications for Genesis 6–11. R. A. Oden's 1981 article listed thirty-three studies since the publication of Lambert and Millard's work.[99] Oden's own study disputes the assumption that the reason for the flood in the "Atra-Ḫasīs Epic" was overpopulation, an interpretation suggested by A. D. Kilmer and W. L. Moran.[100] Such hubris is condemned through Genesis 1–11, suggesting a similarity between it and the "Atra-

93. Idem, "The Old Testament Genealogies in Recent Research," reprinted in this volume, 200–223.

94. J. Sasson, "A Genealogical 'Convention' in Biblical Chronography?" *ZAW* 90 (1978) 171–85.

95. R. B. Robinson, "Literary Functions of the Genealogies of Genesis," *CBQ* 48 (1986) 595–608.

96. R. S. Hess, "The Genealogies of Genesis 1–11 and Comparative Literature," in this volume, 58–72.

97. See n. 61 above.

98. J. F. A. Sawyer, "Cain and Hephaestus: Possible Relics of Metalworking Traditions in Genesis 4," *Abr-Nahrain* 24 (1986) 155–66.

99. R. A. Oden, "Divine Aspirations in Atrahasis and in Genesis 1–11," *ZAW* 93 (1981) 197–216; n. 4.

100. A. D. Kilmer, "The Mesopotamian Concept of Overpopulation and Its Solution as Reflected in Mythology," *Or* n.s. 41 (1972) 160–77; W. L. Moran, "Atrahasis: The Babylonian

Ḫasīs Epic." Moran, on the other hand, has attempted to reaffirm the overpopulation explanation.[101] He argues that condemnation for overly ambitious mortals would have to be read into the text. It is not there, and the clearest reading of the text affirms overpopulation as the cause.

There are two literary studies that point out distinctive aspects to the narrative of Genesis 6–9 in comparison with other ancient Near Eastern Flood stories. G. J. Wenham analyzes these chapters as part of a long and complex chiasm, whose focus lies in God's remembering of Noah.[102] An example of literary sensitivity and contextual study is B. W. Anderson's study of these chapters in an article, "From Analysis to Synthesis: The Interpretation of Genesis 1–11."[103]

The study of chap. 10 of Genesis has prompted the writing of articles devoted to identifying particular proper names in the list. A recent technical study was authored by R. Zadok, who uses comparative Semitic phonology and textual data to propose a new location for Shinar.[104] F. V. Winnett's analysis and identification of the Arabian genealogies in Genesis has proven to be a consistently helpful guide to dealing with the many uncertainties surrounding these names.[105] Mention should also be made of B. Oded's attempt to identify the three divisions of the Table of Nations in sociocultural terms; for example, Shem represents nomads, Ham urban peoples, and Japheth is associated with sea merchants.[106]

Genesis 11 is illuminated by J. M. Sasson, who suggests a literary rationale for the episode of vv. 1–9 and its location after the Table of Nations but before the narrative of Abram.[107]

This survey of comparative and literary studies of Genesis 1–11 over the past twenty years has no more than touched the surface here and there in a vast field. However, it has demonstrated several points.

Story of the Flood," *Bib* 52 (1971) 51–61. For further discussion, see D. T. Tsumura, "Genesis and Ancient Near Eastern Stories of Creation and Flood: An Introduction," in this volume, 27–57.

101. W. L. Moran, "Some Considerations of Form and Interpretation in *Atra-ḫasīs*," in *Language, Literature, and History: Philological and Historical Studies Presented to Erica Reiner* (ed. F. Rochberg-Halton; AOS 67; New Haven: American Oriental Society, 1987) 251–55.

102. G. J. Wenham, "The Coherence of the Flood Narrative," in this volume, 436–47. This and other attempts at a unified literary interpretation have been recently challenged by J. Emerton, "An Examination of Some Attempts to Defend the Unity of the Flood Narratives in Genesis," part I, *VT* 27 (1987) 401–20; part II, *VT* 28 (1988) 1–21.

103. In this volume, 416–35.

104. R. Zadok, "The Origin of the Name Shinar," *ZA* 74 (1984) 240–44.

105. F. V. Winnett, "The Arabian Genealogies in the Book of Genesis," *Translating and Understanding the Old Testament* (ed. H. T. Frank and W. L. Reed; Nashville: Abingdon, 1970) 171–96.

106. B. Oded, "The Table of Nations (Genesis 10): A Socio-Cultural Approach," *ZAW* 98 (1986) 14–31.

107. J. M. Sasson, "The 'Tower of Babel' as a Clue to the Redactional Structuring of the Primeval History (Gen. 1:1–11:9)," in this volume, 448–57.

(1) There is a continuing interest in the comparative application of cuneiform materials to the study and interpretation of Genesis 1–11. Just as traditional literary criticism did not push aside the comparative method but adopted it to its own ends,[108] so the modern literary methods and approaches have not cast aside the comparative method. On the contrary, the incorporation of such methods into the comparative task has now become a part of the interpretation of the biblical texts. The role of literary criticism in the interpretation of ancient Near Eastern myths has yet to be explored with the same fervor, but the introduction of the methods from biblical and literary studies seems inevitable.

(2) The literary study of the Bible is enhanced by the comparative method, not diminished. If we are to understand the biblical text in terms of its own message, the comparative approach is necessary to show parallels and points of incongruence. But the literary approaches, with their concern for context and/or contextualization, are also valuable as means by which the full implications of the text are made known within and in contrast to its Near Eastern environment.

(3) The increasing demands of understanding, let alone making use of, the literature and issues in Hebrew Bible and in Assyriology mean that working in both fields with credibility will become increasingly difficult. However, as the literature demonstrates, this difficulty has not stopped scholars from trying. Certainly there need to be quality controls on the work being done. But there also must be encouragement to continue to work in both fields, an encouragement that appropriately manifests itself in (a) the continuing interest of biblical and assyriological journals and publishers in cross-disciplinary works; (b) the continuing cultivation of cross-disciplinary study in universities; and (c) a controlled means of popularizing the results of the research so that public understanding, support, and enthusiasm grow for this field of research central to humanity's cultural heritage.

Directions for the Future

It seems certain that the future will find scholars producing a steady stream of articles and monographs on comparative studies. By way of example, I would point out the lexical and thematic comparisons of

108. For an interesting reversal, in which, rather than trying to "prove" the Bible by using the cuneiform evidence an attempt is made to "prove" source criticism by using ancient Near Eastern texts, see J. H. Tigay, "An Empirical Basis for the Documentary Hypothesis," *JBL* 94 (1975) 329–42; and his subsequent volume, *The Evolution of the Gilgamesh Epic* (Philadelphia: University of Pennsylvania Press, 1982). ⟦See also D. W. Baker, "Reverse Archaeology—Deconstruction of Texts: A Critique of Jeffrey Tigay," *Proceedings, Eastern Great Lakes and Midwest Biblical Societies* 9 (1989) 34–48.⟧

Genesis 2–3 in H. N. Wallace's *Eden Narrative* (see n. 88 above). D. T. Tsumura's monograph *The Earth and the Waters in Genesis 1 and 2* provides a comparative and contextual study of several of the disputed lexical items in those chapters.[109]

Most important for this essay have been the actual cuneiform texts that form the basis of continued comparative work. Many remain unedited, and there is much additional work to be done on those that have been studied. For Genesis 1–11 the most important texts are the Creation and Flood epics,the study of which requires continually returning to the great archives of the Mesopotamian empires in the heart of the Assyriological world. The comparative approach to Genesis 1–11 will be able to flourish with new stimuli, but the unfinished texts must continue to be identified, edited, and published. That they are present is not doubted. The work remains to be done.[110]

Since this manuscript was written, numerous studies have appeared with relevance to both comparative and literary approaches to Genesis 1–11. Although selective, a few should be mentioned.[111] In ancient Near Eastern and biblical studies, Van Seters' higher critical study of the book of Genesis draws together Neo-Babylonian and Hellenistic parallels to these chapters.[112] Some of this work contains revisions of material published earlier.[113] My work on the personal names of Genesis 1–11 attempts to place these names in their Near Eastern setting.[114] It suggests that, as a whole, the personal names (that are not also place-names) most closely resemble Amorite names from the early second millennium B.C. C. Meyers has applied anthropological and archaeological data to contextualize the story of the Garden of Eden in the agrarian world of early Israel.[115] Her study includes the reprint of her analysis of

109. D. T. Tsumura, *The Earth and the Waters in Genesis 1 and 2* (JSOTSup 83; Sheffield: Sheffield Academic Press, 1989), part of which is now reprinted in this volume, 310–28.

110. In this regard, it is encouraging to see the appearance of a recent edition of cuneiform texts by S. Dalley, *Myths from Mesopotamia: Creation, the Flood, Gilgamesh, and Others* (Oxford: Oxford University Press, 1989).

111. For further discussion of recent comparative literature discussing the creation narratives, see the two postscripts to Lambert's article, in this volume, 110–13.

112. J. Van Seters, *Prologue to History: The Yahwist as Historian in Genesis* (Louisville: Westminster/John Knox, 1992).

113. Cf. my review of his comparison of Genesis 10 with the Greek Catalogue of Women in "The Genealogies of Genesis 1–11 and Comparative Literature," in this volume, 69–70.

114. R. S. Hess, *Studies on the Personal Names of Genesis 1–11* (AOAT 234; Kevelaer: Butzon & Bercker/Neukirchen-Vluyn: Neukirchener Verlag, 1993). A second part of the book also examines the functions of the names in the wordplay of the Genesis texts.

115. Carol Meyers, *Discovering Eve: Ancient Israelite Women in Context* (Oxford: Clarendon, 1988).

Gen 3:16, which translates God's judgment as requiring toil and the bearing of children, rather than as pain in childbirth. Of the many literary studies one may cite the examples of E. van Wolde's semiotic study of Genesis 2–3, H. White's application of narrative analysis to the text of Genesis, and A. Brenner's collection of feminist studies.[116] Two English-language commentaries have appeared that apply comparative studies to understanding Genesis 1–11.[117]

116. E. J. van Wolde, *A Semiotic Analysis of Genesis 2–3: A Semiotic Theory and Method of Analysis Applied to the Story of the Garden of Eden* (SSN 25; Assen/Maastricht: Van Gorcum, 1989); H. C. White, *Narration and Discourse in the Book of Genesis* (Cambridge: Cambridge University Press, 1991); A. Brenner (ed.), *A Feminist Companion to Genesis* (Feminist Companion to the Bible 2; Sheffield: Sheffield Academic Press, 1993). Cf. also van Wolde's study, *Words Become Worlds: Semantic Studies of Genesis* (Biblical Interpretation Series 6; Leiden: Brill, 1994).

117. N. Sarna, *Genesis* (JPS Torah Commentary; New York: Jewish Publication Society, 1989); V. Hamilton, *The Book of Genesis Chapters 1–17* (NICOT; Grand Rapids: Eerdmans, 1990).

Genesis and Ancient Near Eastern Stories of Creation and Flood: An Introduction

David Toshio Tsumura

Creation

Creation has been one of the most interesting and intriguing subjects in the Old Testament. In modern biblical scholarship a number of new interpretations of the early chapters of Genesis have been suggested, especially in the areas of comparative study and literary analysis.

Genesis 1–2

Double Creation Stories? A theory has long been advocated that the early chapters of Genesis contain a "doublet" of creation stories and that these stories, characterized by the distinctive divine names, Elohim and YHWH, are of different origins with two independent, and even opposing, cosmologies. According to this traditional critical theory, the former is the priestly account (P source) of creation from the postexilic period, while the latter is an earlier Yahwistic account (J source). Hence, it is usually assumed that there exist some discrepancies or contradictions between the two accounts.[1]

1. For a useful summary of recent critical discussions, see G. J. Wenham, *Genesis 1–15* (WBC 1; Waco, Tex.: Word, 1987) xxv–xlii; idem, "Genesis: An Authorship Study and Current Pentateuchal Criticism," *JSOT* 42 (1988) 3–18; R. N. Whybray, *The Making of the Pentateuch: A Methodological Study* (JSOTSup 53; Sheffield: Sheffield Academic Press, 1987) 17–131.

Recently, however, it has been emphasized by scholars like Alter that whatever their origins may be, "the two accounts are complementary rather than overlapping, each giving a different *kind* of information about how the world came into being." According to him, "the two different creation stories," i.e., the P and J stories, constitute a "composite narrative" that encompasses "divergent perspectives" by placing in sequence "two ostensibly contradictory accounts of the same event," such as two stories of the creation of woman.[2]

When one takes a closer look at both stories, it is evident that they are not two "parallel" versions of the same or similar "creation" stories, since the theme and purpose of the two are certainly different. Castellino distinguishes Genesis 1, "un vrai recit de creation" ⟦'a true creation account'⟧, from Genesis 2, which is in a strict sense not a creation story but "un texte d'organisation" ⟦'an organizational text'⟧ and serves as an "introduction" to Genesis 3.[3] A story without any reference to the sun, the moon and the stars, or the sea is certainly not a true cosmological myth. Genesis 2 and following, therefore, should not be treated as the same literary genre as Genesis 1, which locates the creation of humankind at the grand climax of the creation of the cosmos,[4] while the former is concerned with the immediate situation of mankind on the earth.

However, as I recently demonstrated, both chapters do reflect essentially the same cosmology. In Gen 1:2, the initial situation of the "world" is described positively in terms of the still unproductive and uninhabited (*tōhû wābōhû*)[5] "earth" totally covered by "ocean-water," while in 2:5–6 the initial state of the "earth" is described negatively in terms of the not-yet-productive "earth" in more concrete expressions, "no vegetation" and "no man." And the underground-water was flooding out to inundate the whole area of the "land," but not the entire earth as in Gen 1:2.[6]

2. R. Alter, *The Art of Biblical Narrative* (New York: Basic Books, 1981) 141–47. As an example of contradiction between Genesis 1 and 2, he notes that in Genesis 1 the woman was created "at the same time and in the same manner" as the man (p. 145). However, in Gen 1:27, which constitutes a three-line "parallelism," the human being is simply described as being created as male and female. The text does not necessarily imply the simultaneous creation of both sexes.

3. G. Castellino, "Les origines de la civilisation selon les textes bibliques et les textes cunéiformes," *Congress Volume: Strasbourg, 1956* (VTSup 4; Leiden: Brill, 1957) 116–37; this article has now been translated and appears for the first time in this volume as "The Origins of Civilization according to Biblical and Cuneiform Texts," pp. 75–95.

4. For the literary structure of Genesis 1, see below, pp. 31–35.

5. See below, p. 33.

6. D. T. Tsumura, *The Earth and the Waters in Genesis 1 and 2* (JSOTSup 83; Sheffield: Sheffield Academic Press, 1989) 168. This conclusion is entirely different from the traditional critical view, represented by von Rad that the nature of the earth-waters relationship

Thus, Genesis 1 describes an earlier stage in the one creation process in which the waters cover the earth, Genesis 2a a later stage (in 1:9–10) in which the waters have separated and the dry land has appeared.

The Double Creation of Mankind? The Genesis account as it stands mentions the creation of mankind twice, in 1:27 and 2:7. Kikawada hence suggests that there are two creations of mankind in Genesis, comparing Genesis 1–2 with the myth of Enki and Ninmah and the "Atra-Ḫasīs Epic" (I 1–351).[7] According to him, Genesis 1 refers to "the first creation of mankind," while Genesis 2 refers to "the second creation of mankind," namely the creation of the specific persons Adam and Eve, and these two biblical creation accounts are parallel to each other.

It should be noted, however, that in Genesis those "double creation stories" deal with the same topic, the origin of humankind (*ʾādām*), and do not necessarily *refer* to "two" separate creative actions regarding human creation. The debate is whether the reason for this twofold description is (1) that there were actually two independent creation stories of the same event or (2) that there were actually two separate creation acts or (3) that a technique of narrative discourse was used that recounts one and the same event from two different viewpoints. To this third possibility I now turn.

Discourse Grammar.[8] It has been noted by scholars such as U. Cassuto[9] that Genesis 1 gives a general description of mankind in the framework of the entire creation of the world and Genesis 2 gives a detailed

---

in 1:2 ('watery chaos') is totally different from that in 2:5–6 ('dry chaos'). See G. von Rad, *Genesis* (OTL; Philadelphia: Westminster, 1961) 76–77; also B. Otzen, "The Use of Myth in Genesis," in *Myths in the Old Testament* (ed. B. Otzen, H. Gottlieb and K. Jeppesen; London: SCM, 1980) 40–41.

7. I. M. Kikawada, "The Double Creation of Mankind in *Enki and Ninmah, Atrahasis* I 1–351, and *Genesis* 1–2," below, pp. 169–74; I. M. Kikawada and A. Quinn, *Before Abraham Was: The Unity of Genesis 1–11* (Nashville: Abingdon, 1985) 39ff.

8. For recent works on the discourse analysis of Genesis, see R. E. Longacre, *Joseph: A Story of Divine Providence, a Text Theoretical and Textlinguistic Analysis of Genesis 37 and 39–48* (Winona Lake, Ind.: Eisenbrauns, 1989); F. I. Andersen, "On Reading Genesis 1–3," in *Backgrounds for the Bible* (ed. M. P. O'Connor and D. N. Freedman; Winona Lake, Ind.: Eisenbrauns, 1987) 137–50. For a brief summary of discourse analysis with bibliographies see W. R. Bodine, "Linguistics and Philology in the Study of Ancient Near Eastern Languages," in *"Working with No Data": Semitic and Egyptian Studies Presented to Thomas O. Lambdin* (ed. D. M. Golomb; Winona Lake, Ind.: Eisenbrauns, 1987) 39–54.

9. U. Cassuto, *A Commentary on the Book of Genesis, Part One: From Adam to Noah* (trans. Israel Abrahams; Jerusalem: Magnes, 1961) 89–92; also K. A. Kitchen, *Ancient Orient and Old Testament* (Chicago: InterVarsity Press, 1966) 116–17.

description of humankind and their immediate context on the earth.[10] From a discourse grammatical point of view, this relationship between Genesis 1 and Genesis 2 may be explained as a generic-specific relationship[11] and the two constitute a "hyponymous"[12] parallelism, so to speak.

This feature might also be explained as a phenomenon of what Grimes calls a "scope change" in narrative discourse, which is a phenomenon of "zooming in from an overall perspective to a closeup, with a corresponding shift in reference."[13] This is the way I have described the nature of the relationship between the two "creation" stories of Genesis elsewhere;[14] they have different scopes or viewpoints by which the author or narrator describes one and the same creation of mankind, first with relation to the cosmos, and then with a narrower focus on the man's relationship with the woman, the animals, and the environment in the second story. Therefore, the flow of discourse runs from Genesis 1 to Genesis 2 and following, not vice versa, as assumed by the traditional source critics.

As for 2:4, whose two halves constitute a chiastic parallelism, Wenham takes this verse as serving "both as a title to 2:5–4:26 and as a link with the introduction 1:1–2:3."[15] In another context I have suggested that it serves as a link between the two stories and that this linkage is a kind of transitional technique that according to Parunak points to a surface pattern of repetition or similarity that joins successive textual units together.[16] Genesis 1–2 could thus be explained as Parunak's A/aB pattern; in 2:4a (a) the narrator repeats the keywords of Gen 1:1–2:3 (A) and initiates a new section of story, 2:4b–4:26 (B).

10. For this "general-detailed pattern" in Ugaritic, Akkadian and Egyptian literatures, see D. T. Tsumura, "The Problem of Childlessness in the Royal Epic of Ugarit: An Analysis of Krt [KTU 1.14:1]: 1–25," in *Monarchies and Socio-Religious Traditions in the Ancient Near East* (ed. T. Mikasa; Wiesbaden: Harrassowitz, 1984) 18–19 n. 37. The same pattern appears also in Japanese narrative stories such as the initial section of "Suma" in *The Story of Genji*; see D. T. Tsumura, "Ugaritic Studies (3): On the Prologue of Keret Epic," *Studies in Language and Literature* 9 (1984) 77 n. 64 [in Japanese]. For the pattern in the genealogical doublets, see R. S. Hess, "Genesis 1–2 in Its Literary Context," *TynBul* 41 (1990) 146–47.

11. Cf. R. E. Longacre, *The Grammar of Discourse* (New York: Plenum, 1983) 119 and 122.

12. On this term, see D. T. Tsumura, "A 'Hyponymous' Word Pair, *ʾrṣ* and *thm(t)*, in Hebrew and Ugaritic," *Bib* 69 (1988) 258–60.

13. J. Grimes, *The Thread of Discourse* (The Hague: Mouton, 1975) 46–47.

14. Tsumura, "Evangelical Biblical Interpretation: Towards the Establishment of Its Methodology," *Evangelical Theology* 17 (1985) 47–50 (in Japanese, with an English summary, pp. 169–71).

15. For the chiastic structure of 2:4, see Cassuto, *From Adam to Noah*, 98–99; Wenham, *Genesis 1–15*, 55.

16. Tsumura, "Evangelical Biblical Interpretation," 48. See H. van Dyke Parunak, "Transitional Techniques in the Bible," *JBL* 102 (1983) 525–48.

Genesis 1

Genesis 1 and "Enuma Elish." Ever since H. Gunkel's famous book *Schöpfung und Chaos in Urzeit und Endzeit* (1895), scholars have taken it for granted that the Hebrew *tĕhôm* in Gen 1:2 has its mythological background in the ancient Babylonian goddess Tiamat of the "creation" myth "Enuma elish," in which the storm-god Marduk fights with and wins over the sea dragon Tiamat, establishing the cosmos.[17] I have thoroughly reexamined the problem from a linguistic point of view, and it is now clear that it is phonologically impossible to conclude that *tĕhôm* 'ocean' was borrowed from *Tiamat*. The Hebrew *tĕhôm* 'ocean' together with the Ugaritic *thm*, the Akkadian *tiāmtu*, the Arabic *tihāmat*, and the Eblaite *ti-ʾà-ma-tum* /tihām(a)tum/ is simply a reflection of a common Semitic term *tihām-.[18]

While the Hebrew and Akkadian terms refer to the "primeval" water, as Lambert notes, "the watery beginning of Genesis in itself is no evidence of Mesopotamian influence."[19] He also notes that while the horizontal division of the cosmic water in Gen 1:6–8 has its parallel description in Ee IV 135–V 62, "the case for a battle as a prelude to God's dividing of the cosmic waters is unproven." In other words, "neither on the Hebrew side nor on the Mesopotamian is there any clear proof that a battle is necessarily tied to the dividing of the waters." So, Genesis 1 and "Enuma elish," which was composed primarily to exalt Marduk in the pantheon of Babylon,[20] have no direct relation to each other. Not only is the creation by divine fiat in Genesis unique in the ancient Near East, the creation of light as the first creating act appears only in Genesis.[21] Thus the creation in the Genesis story is quite different

17. For a useful translation and discussion of this text, see A. Heidel, *The Babylonian Genesis* (3d ed.; Chicago: University of Chicago Press, 1963); also E. A. Speiser's translation in "The Creation Epic," *ANET*, 60–72. The most recent translation can be found in S. Dalley, *Myths from Mesopotamia: Creation, the Flood, Gilgamesh, and Others* (Oxford: Oxford University Press, 1991) 233–74.

18. See Tsumura, *The Earth and the Waters*, 45–52.

19. W. G. Lambert, "A New Look at the Babylonian Background of Genesis," below, 103.

20. W. G. Lambert ("Babylonien und Israel," *TRE* 5 (1980) 71–72) discusses the nature of "Enuma elish," which is "in reality occupied with the ascent of Marduk in the pantheon" and whose "creation account takes only a subordinate position within the whole." The myth, according to him, was probably composed around 1100 B.C.E. and it is "extremely eclectic." In "A New Look" (100 below), he concludes similarly: "The *Epic of Creation* is not a norm of Babylonian or Sumerian cosmology. It is a sectarian and aberrant combination of mythological threads woven into an unparalleled compositum."

21. Lambert, "Babylonien und Israel," 71; idem, "A New Look," 96–109.

from the idea of "order out of chaos," though the latter is also often called "creation."[22]

It is not correct to say that "Enuma elish" was adopted and adapted by the Israelites to produce the Genesis stories. As Lambert holds, there is "no evidence of Hebrew borrowing from Babylon."[23] Sjöberg accepts Lambert's opinion that "there was hardly any influence from that Babylonian text on the Old Testament creation accounts."[24] Hasel thinks rather that the creation account of Genesis 1 functions as an anti-mythological polemic in some cases (e.g., with the "sun," the "moon," and *tnnm* ('sea monsters'?), etc.).[25] One thing is clear with regard to the religious nature of the creation story of Genesis: in Genesis 1 and 2 no female deity exists or is involved in producing the cosmos and humanity. This is unique among ancient creation stories that treat of deities having personality.

Canaanite Background to Genesis 1? According to Jacobsen, "the story of the battle between the god of thunderstorms and the sea originated on the coast of the Mediterranean and wandered eastward from there to Babylon."[26] Along the same line, Sjöberg as an Assyriologist warns Old Testament scholars that "it is no longer scientifically sound to assume that all ideas originated in Mesopotamia and moved westward."[27]

Recently Day asserted that Gen 1:2 was a demythologization of an original *Chaoskampf* ⟦'chaos-battle'⟧ myth from ancient Canaan.[28] However, the conflict of the storm-god Baal with the sea-deity Yam in the Ugaritic myth has nothing to do with a creation of cosmos like that of Marduk with Tiamat in "Enuma elish." Kapelrud notes that "with the existing texts and the material present so far we may conclude that they have no creation narrative."[29] Also de Moor recently demonstrated that Baal in Ugaritic literature is never treated as a creator-god.[30] I have noted elsewhere that if the Genesis account were the demythologization of a

22. See D. J. McCarthy, "Creation Motifs in Ancient Hebrew Poetry," *CBQ* 29 (1967) 393–406.

23. Lambert, "A New Look," below, 105.

24. Å. W. Sjöberg, "Eve and the Chameleon," in *In the Shelter of Elyon: Essays on Ancient Palestinian Life and Literature in Honor of G. W. Ahlström* (Sheffield: JSOT Press, 1984) 217.

25. E.g., G. F. Hasel, "The Polemic Nature of the Genesis Cosmology," *EvQ* 46 (1974) 81–102.

26. T. Jacobsen, "The Battle between Marduk and Tiamat," *JAOS* 88 (1968) 107.

27. Sjöberg, "Eve and the Chameleon," 218.

28. J. Day, *God's Conflict with the Dragon and the Sea: Echoes of a Canaanite Myth in the Old Testament* (Cambridge: Cambridge University Press, 1985) 53.

29. A. S. Kapelrud, "Creation in the Ras Shamra Texts," *Studia Theologica* 34 (1980) 9.

30. J. C. de Moor, "El, the Creator," in *The Bible World: Essays in Honor of Cyrus H. Gordon* (ed. G. Rendsburg et al.; New York: KTAV, 1980) 171–87.

Canaanite dragon myth, we would expect the term *yām* 'sea', which is the counterpart of the Ugaritic sea-god Yam, in the initial portion of the account. However, the term *yām* does not appear in Genesis 1 until v. 10. It is difficult to assume that an earlier Canaanite dragon myth existed in the background of Gen 1:2.[31]

Chaos in Genesis 1:2? (a) *tōhû wābōhû.* The expression *tōhû wābōhû,* which is traditionally translated in English as "without form and void" (RSV) or the like, is often taken as signifying the primeval "chaos," in direct opposition to "creation." I have demonstrated, however, that the phrase *tōhû wābōhû* has nothing to do with primeval chaos; it simply means 'emptiness' and refers to the earth in a "bare" state, without vegetation and animals as well as without humans. This "unproductive and empty, uninhabited" earth becomes productive with vegetation and inhabited by animals and humankind by God's fiats.[32]

I have also pointed out that in Gen 1:2 *hāʾāreṣ* and *tĕhôm* are a "hyponymous" word pair and hence the 'ocean' (*tĕhôm*) is a part of the 'earth' (*hāʾāreṣ*), since the term *hāʾāreṣ,* which constitutes an antonymous word pair with *haššāmayim* 'the heavens' in Gen 1:1, must refer to everything under the heaven.[33] However, vv. 6ff. suggest that the water of *tĕhôm* in Gen 1:2 covered all the 'earth'.[34] This water-covered earth is described in this passage by a pair of expressions, *tōhû wābōhû // ḥōšek,* not yet normal, that is to say, not yet productive or inhabited and without light. But it was not chaotic. It should be noted that even in "Enuma elish" the initial mingling of Apsu and Tiamat (Ee I 5) was orderly, not chaotic.[35]

(b) *rûaḥ ʾĕlōhîm.* Albright, who rejected the "world egg theory" (Gunkel) and the view that "the *rûaḥ* corresponds to the winds which Marduk sends against Tiâmat," suggested as the most probable view that "*rûaḥ ʾĕlōhîm* means 'spirit of God', but is substituted for an original *rûaḥ,* 'wind', in order to bring the personality of God into the cosmogony

31. For a detailed discussion, see Tsumura, *The Earth and the Waters,* 62–65. I also note that if any comparison with Gen 1:2 should be drawn from Ugaritic materials, it would be with the Canaanite god El's residence at the source of 'two oceans' (*thmtm*). This association of a creator-god with his watery abode or domain can be seen also in the case of Ea, one of the Mesopotamian triad deities. This motif of a watery beginning appears also in Egyptian, Anatolian, and Greek myths. For a detailed discussion, see chapter 8 of *The Earth and the Waters.*

32. Below, 326–28.

33. The cosmology in vv. 1–2 is bipartite, not tripartite, describing the entire world in terms of "heavens and earth."

34. Tsumura, *The Earth and the Waters,* 78–79.

35. Ibid., 60 n. 70.

from the beginning." Albright, however, thinks that "the *rûaḥ ʾĕlōhîm* was evidently still thought of as exercising a 'sexual' influence upon the *tehôm.*" The verb *rāḥap* ('hovered'), according to him, suggests that "the *rûaḥ ʾĕlōhîm* was conceived of originally in the form of a bird."[36]

Recently DeRoche suggested that just as the *rûaḥ* 'wind' in Gen 8:1 and Exod 14:21 "leads to the division within the bodies of water, and consequently, the appearance of dry land," so "the *rûaḥ ʾĕlōhîm* 'wind or spirit of God' of Gen 1:2c must also be a reference to the creative activity of the deity."[37] However, he holds, *rûaḥ ʾĕlōhîm* is not "a wind sent by God," that is to say, a creature, but "a hypostasis for *ʾĕlōhîm.*" He does not think that it is "part of the description of chaos." According to him, "It expresses Elohim's control over the cosmos and his ability to impose his will upon it. As part of v 2 it is part of the description of the way things were before Elohim executes any specific act of creation."[38]

Man as the Image of God. Clines offers a thorough discussion of "The Image of God in Man," reviewing the history of interpretation. He concludes that "Genesis 1:26 is to be translated 'Let us make man as our image' or 'to be our image'. . . . according to Genesis 1 man does not have the image of God, nor is he made *in* the image of God, but is himself the image of God."[39] As for the image itself, Clines observes, with K. H. Bernhardt, that "in the ancient Near East the primary function of the image was to be the dwelling-place of spirit or fluid which derived from the being whose image it was." He also notes that in the ancient Near East the king is "the image of God," and "the image of the god is associated very closely with rulerhood. The king as image of the god is his representative. The king has been created by the god to be his image."[40]

In her recent treatment of the specification of human sexual distinction, P. A. Bird, like Clines, asserts that the *ṣelem ʾĕlōhim* 'image of God' in Genesis 1 is "a royal designation, the precondition or requisite for rule"[41] and concludes that "the genius of the formulation in Gen 1:26 may be seen in its use of a common expression and image of Mesopotamian (-Canaanite) royal theology to counter a common image of Mesopota-

36. W. F. Albright, "Contributions to Biblical Archaeology and Philology," *JBL* 43 (1924) 368 and n. 10.

37. M. DeRoche, "The *rûaḥ ʾĕlōhîm* in Gen 1:2c: Creation or Chaos?" in *Ascribe to the Lord: Biblical and Other Studies in Memory of Peter C. Craigie* (JSOTSup 67; ed. L. Eslinger and G. Taylor; Sheffield: Sheffield Academic Press, 1988) 314–15.

38. Ibid., 318.

39. D. J. A. Clines, "The Image of God in Man," *TynBul* 19 (1968) 53–103.

40. Ibid., 80–85.

41. P. A. Bird, "'Male and Female He Created Them': Genesis 1:27b in the Context of the Priestly Account of Creation," 341 below.

mian (-Canaanite) anthropology, viz., the image of humanity as servant of the gods."[42]

Bird suspects a polemical intention also in the blessing of v. 28, "Be fruitful and multiply." For, since "the power of created life to replenish itself is a power given to each species at its creation," it is "not dependent upon subsequent rites," that is to say, the fertility cult, "for its effect." However, the "word of sexual differentiation [in v. 27] anticipates the blessing" since "sexual constitution is the presupposition of the blessing of increase." Verse 27 as a whole, she holds, signifies that "*unlike* God, but *like* the other creatures, *adam* is characterized by sexual differentiation." In other words, "*adam* is created *like* (i.e., resembling) God, but *as* creature, and hence male and female."[43]

Genesis 2–3

Adam and Adapa. Shea lists "principal parallels" between the "Adapa Epic"[44] and the account of Adam in Genesis 2–3: "(1) Both subjects underwent a test before the deity, and the test was based upon something they were to consume. (2) Both failed the test and thereby forfeited their opportunity for immortality. (3) As a result of their failure, certain consequences passed upon mankind. (4) Both subjects qualify as members of the first generation of mankind. (5) Their names can be equated linguistically."[45]

However, among the differences Shea notes are these: (1) "Adapa was tested with bread and water while Adam and Eve were tested with the fruit." (2) Though both were sentenced to death and "this sentence is even given in rather similar terms," these terms have "quite different meanings in their respective contexts." (3) Adapa's choice was made in obedience to Ea, but Adam made his own free choice contrary to correct instructions. (4) "Adapa's offense, in essence, was that he upset the course of nature, while Adam's offense was moral in nature." In conclusion, Shea suggests that "it is possible to view these two separate sources

42. See below, p. 345. Note that the idea "that man was created to relieve the gods of hard labour by supplying them with food and drink was standard among both Sumerians and Babylonians"; see the opening section of the "Atra-Ḫasīs Epic." Cf. W. G. Lambert and A. R. Millard, *Atra-Ḫasīs: The Babylonian Story of the Flood* (Oxford: Clarendon, 1969) 15. Note also that, according to Miller, this royal status of *ʾādām* has "an echo in the Eridu Genesis expression about humankind: 'their kingship, their term, has been uprooted' (col. iv 10). However, kingship in Genesis is 'democratized' " (see P. D. Miller Jr., "Eridu, Dunnu, and Babel: A Study in Comparative Mythology," below, p. 160).

43. Bird, " 'Male and Female He Created Them,' " 351.

44. For an English translation, see Speiser's in *ANET,* 101–3.

45. W. H. Shea, "Adam in Ancient Mesopotamian Traditions," *AUSS* 15 (1977) 39.

as independent witnesses to a common event."[46] Niels-Erik Andreasen also thinks that "parallels do indeed exist between Adam and Adapa, but they are seriously blunted by the entirely different contexts in which they occur."[47] However, the view that "the name Adapa is a secondary development from Adam" is not conclusive.

As for the etymology of the word *Adam*, recently Sjöberg suggested that the Sumerian a_2-dam, which refers exclusively to people, is "a 'Canaanite', West-Semitic loanword in Sumerian," since it has no "Sumerian" etymology.[48] The nearest cognate of the Hebrew "ʾadam is, so far, the Ugaritic *adm* which appears in an epithet of the god El, i.e., *ab adm* 'Father of man.' "[49]

Creation of Man. "The most important single witness to Babylonian speculation on the origins and nature of man is," as Moran says, "the description of his creation in the first tablet of the "Atra-Ḫasīs Epic," especially lines 192–248."[50] In 1967, Millard first noted that the "Atrahasis Epic is more specific on [the making of man] than any other Babylonian Creation account." In the "Atra-Ḫasīs Epic" I 221ff., "Man was created from the flesh and blood of a slaughtered god mixed with clay. . . . Man's earthy constituency is emphasized by both Babylonian and Hebrew [i.e., Gen 2:7] narratives, and his divine part equally. . . . No hint of the use of dead deity or any material part of a living one is found in Genesis."[51]

In 1969, Lambert and Millard discussed the account of man's creation in the "Atra-Ḫasīs Epic" in detail. "The author used what was the generally accepted view . . . that man was formed from clay mixed with the blood of a slain god. . . . 'Clay' in this context is the material substance of the human body. This can be learnt from a number of passages that speak of death as a 'returning to clay'. Exactly the same conception is shown in the Hebrew account of man's creation . . . (Genesis 3:19)."[52] As for the "blood," Lambert and Millard speculate that "in all probability the Babylonians conceived of man as matter ('clay') activated by the addition of divine blood," while on the other hand "the Hebrew account of

46. Ibid., 28–35, 41.

47. N.-E. Andreasen, "Adam and Adapa: Two Anthropological Characters," *AUSS* 19 (1981) 192.

48. Sjöberg, "Eve and the Chameleon," 223.

49. See R. S. Hess, "Splitting the Adam: The Usage of ʾādām in Genesis i–v," in *Studies in the Pentateuch* (VTSup 41; ed. J. A. Emerton; Leiden: Brill, 1990) 1–15; idem, *Studies in the Personal Names of Genesis 1–11* (AOAT 234; Neukirchen-Vluyn: Neukirchener, 1993) 14–19, 59–65; Andreasen, "Adam and Adapa," 181 n. 9.

50. W. L. Moran, "The Creation of Man in Atrahasis I 192–248," *BASOR* 200 (1970) 48. For the most recent translation of this epic, see Dalley, *Myths from Mesopotamia*, 9–35.

51. A. R. Millard, "A New Babylonian 'Genesis' Story," below, p. 120.

52. Lambert and Millard, *Atra-Ḫasīs*, 21; see also Lambert, "Babylonien und Israel," 73.

creation in Gen 2 explains that God imparted 'the breath of life' into man, and so animation began."[53]

Eden Story. For a long time the Eden story has drawn much scholarly attention[54] and has recently been treated thoroughly by Wallace in his monograph.[55] Here, however, I would like to focus on comparative materials with respect to this story.

(a) *Enki and Ninhursag.* The story has been compared with Sumerian myths such as Enki and Ninhursag, a Sumerian paradise story.[56] Kramer summarizes it as follows:

> Dilmun is a land that is "pure," "clean," and "bright," a "land of the living" which knows neither sickness nor death. What is lacking, however, is the fresh water so essential to animal and plant life. The great Sumerian water-god, Enki, therefore orders Utu, the sun-god, to fill it with fresh water brought up from the earth. Dilmun is thus turned into a divine garden, green with fruit-laden fields and meadows.[57]

Kramer thinks that there are "numerous parallels" between this "divine paradise" myth and the Eden story. He suggests that the Biblical paradise, "a garden planted *eastward* in Eden," may have "originally" been identical with Dilmun, "a land somewhere to the east of Sumer." He also compares the "fresh water brought up from the earth" in Dilmun with the *ʾēd*-water in Gen 2:6. He notes that "the birth of the goddesses without pain or travail illuminates the background of the curse against Eve that it shall be her lot to conceive and bear children in sorrow; Enki's eating of the eight plants and the curse uttered against him for his misdeed recall the eating of the fruit of the tree of knowledge by Adam and Eve and the curses pronounced against each of them for this sinful action."[58]

Kramer holds that this Sumerian literary background would explain why Eve, "the mother of all living," was fashioned from the rib of Adam. In the present myth one of Enki's sick organs is the rib (Sumerian *ti*); the goddess created for healing his rib was called in Sumerian Nin-ti

53. Lambert and Millard, *Atra-Ḫasīs*, 22.

54. For bibliographical references, see Westermann, *Genesis 1–11*, 178–81; Wenham, *Genesis 1–15*, 41–44.

55. H. N. Wallace, *The Eden Narrative* (HSM 32; Atlanta: Scholars Press, 1985).

56. For a translation and discussion see S. N. Kramer, "Enki and Ninhursag: A Paradise Myth," in *ANET*, 37–41; idem, *The Sumerians: Their History, Culture, and Character* (Chicago: University of Chicago Press, 1963) 147ff. For a recent translation, see P. Attinger, "Enki et Ninḫursag̃a," *ZA* 74 (1984) 1–52.

57. Kramer, *The Sumerians*, 147–48.

58. Ibid., 148–49.

'the Lady of the rib'. But the Sumerian *ti* also means 'to make live'. The name Nin-ti may thus mean 'the Lady who makes live' as well as 'the Lady of the rib'. Through the wordplay, these two designations were used for the same goddess. It is this "literary pun," according to Kramer, that explains Eve's title and her being fashioned from Adam's rib.[59]

(b) *Eden's Four Rivers.* Speiser,[60] following F. Delitzsch,[61] holds that the term *Cush* (Gen 2:13) is "the eponym of the Kassites" rather than the name for the region of the Upper Nile and "only a Kassite context can accord with the phrase 'in the east' of Gen 2:8."[62] Then Speiser, in search of the Garden of Eden refers to Dilmun, "the land of living," which lay near the head of the Persian Gulf and tries to identify the Pishon and the Gihon with actual rivers not far from the mouths of the Tigris and the Euphrates.[63]

Speiser contends that "the original narrator . . . has to be visualized as looking from the Persian Gulf inland" and hence "the 'four heads' (v. 10) are meant to be viewed upstream rather than down." However, this view has been aptly criticized by Wenham, who holds that "the general setting as described in vv. 5–8 favors a Mesopotamian site." As Wenham says, "the greatest difficulty with this [Speiser's] view is that, according to Genesis, the rivers as they flow from Eden split into four, whereas on Speiser's location they flow toward Eden to converge there."[64]

Westermann holds that "the intention of the author in inserting 2:10–14 was not to determine where paradise lay, as the majority of interpreters hold, but rather to point out that the 'life-arteries' of all lands of the earth have their source in the river that watered paradise."[65] He thus denies any attempt to identify the source of the four rivers geographically. On the other hand, Wenham holds that "in Eden a great river rises, and after leaving the garden, splits up into four rivers including the Tigris and Euphrates. On this basis alone we should conclude that Eden lies somewhere in Armenia near the sources of the Tigris and Euphrates. And this is a long-established, widely held view."[66]

59. Ibid., 149. For recent studies on Eve, see I. M. Kikawada, "Two Notes on Eve," *JBL* 91 (1972) 33–37; also see Lambert, "Babylonien und Israel," 72–73.

60. E. A. Speiser, "The Rivers of Paradise," below, 175–82.

61. F. Delitzsch, *Wo lag das Paradies?* (Leipzig, 1881).

62. Speiser, "The Rivers of Paradise," 177. Note that Westermann (*Genesis 1–11*, 210–11) takes מִקֶּדֶם as meaning 'to the east of the narrator, not to the east of Eden' and explains that the intention of this phrase is "not to fix the area geographically but to push the scene of the event into the far, unknown distance."

63. Speiser, "The Rivers of Paradise," below, 178–82. For the etymologies of the words *Tigris* and *Euphrates*, see Tsumura, *The Earth and the Waters*, 137–39.

64. Wenham, *Genesis 1–15*, 66.

65. Westermann, *Genesis 1–11*, 216.

66. Wenham, *Genesis 1–15*, 66.

(c) Sumerian Origin? According to Miller, the picture of creation set forth in the initial section of the "Harab Myth"[67] may be compared with Genesis 2–4:

1. "In the Harab myth, the re-creation state is 'wasteland' (*harab*), not unlike the picture in Genesis 2 of a time with no plant or herb, no rain, nor anyone to till the earth."
2. "Both stories give primacy to the need to work or till the earth."
3. "As in Genesis 2, the first thing that is done in the creation is the creation of water, though in Genesis 2 it is sweet water to water the plants (*ʾēd*) and in Harab it is sea (Tamtu). But in the Harab myth, river, i.e., Idu (= Heb. *ʾēd*), comes in the next generation as daughter of sea (Tamtu)."
4. Farming and shepherding appear in the creation "in a *genealogical sequence*" in both stories.
5. In both, the first city tradition (Gen 4:17 Irad // Eridu) comes between creation and flood.[68]

But there are also differences between the two, as Miller notes. In the Genesis account, there exists a clear distinction between the divine world and the human world, and the tilling of the earth and the ruling and shepherding of the animals as well as the building of cities are human tasks.[69] We might add that in Genesis 2–3 Yahweh is the sole divine agent and is significantly without any female consort.

Until recently, the Sumerian connection of the Eden story has been supported almost unanimously. However, according to Sjöberg, who recently reexamined Sumerian connections with regard to the "tree of life," there is "no evidence" for such a tree in Mesopotamian myth and cult. He says, "The identification of different trees on Mesopotamian seals as a Tree of Life is a pure hypothesis, a product of pan-Babylonianism. . . . There is no Sumerian or Akkadian expression 'Tree of life.' "[70] Wallace collects "a wide range of material which has some pertinence for the study of the tree of life in Gen 2–3," including the tree symbolism of Asherah. He carefully avoids equating this Asherah symbol with the tree of life in Genesis 2–3, which "concerns eternal life and not the fertility of womb and field."[71] However, it must be admitted that those references outside of the Bible are indirect.

67. For a translation, see T. Jacobsen, *The Harab Myth* (Sources from the Ancient Near East 2/3; Malibu: Undena, 1984) 7 and 9; cf. Miller, "Eridu, Dunnu, and Babel," below, 165–66.

68. Miller, "Eridu, Dunnu, and Babel," below, 155–56.

69. Ibid., 156.

70. Sjöberg, "Eve and the Chameleon," 219–21.

71. Wallace, *The Eden Narrative*, 114.

Etymology of ᵓēd. The term *ᵓēd* in Gen 2:6 has been rendered as 'spring'/'fountain' (e.g., LXX: πηγῆ) or as *ᶜănānāᵓ* '(rain-)cloud' or 'vapor, mist' (targum). Modern versions translate it 'mist' (KJV, RSV, NEB note, NIV note), 'flood' (RSV note, NEB), 'water' (JB), or 'streams' (NIV). However, there has been no satisfactory Semitic etymology.

Recently I investigated the etymology of *ᵓēd* thoroughly.[72] I have shown that Albright's view that the Hebrew *ᵓēd* is a Sumerian loanword via Akkadian *id* 'river'[73] is less convincing than Speiser's view that *ᵓēd* is connected to the Akkadian *edû* 'flood', which is a Sumerian loanword from e$_4$-dé-a.[74] While it is possible that *ᵓēd* is a shortened form of *ᵓēdô* in Job 36:27, as a result of the loss of a final vowel when or after Akkadian *edû* was borrowed into Canaanite, I have made the following suggestions:

1. *ᵓēd* (Gen 2:6) is a loanword directly borrowed from Sumerian e$_4$-dé;
2. *ᵓēdô* (Job 36:27) is a loanword from Sumerian via Akkadian *edû*.

Both *ᵓēd* and its allomorph *ᵓēdô* mean 'high water' and refer to the water flooding out of the subterranean ocean.[75]

Etymology of ᶜēden. In the light of the new information from Fekheriyeh, Millard, Greenfield, and others have recently suggested that the term *ᶜēden* means 'a well-watered place'.[76] This fits the context of Genesis 2 very well. There are three theoretically possible explanations for the etymology of the Hebrew *ᶜēden*:

(a) *Sumerian Loanword Directly into West Semitic.* The Sumerian edin 'plain', has been suggested as its origin. But since Sumerian presumably has no phoneme /ᶜ/, it is not likely that the Sumerian edin was borrowed directly into Canaanite as *ᶜēden* or the like. Also, the meaning 'plain, steppe', or uncultivated land, does not fit the context of Genesis well.

(b) *Sumerian Loanword via Akkadian into West Semitic.* It has been suggested that the Sumerian edin was borrowed through Akkadian *edinu.* While this has been a common view for the etymology, Hebrew *ᶜēden* cannot be a loanword from or via Akkadian *edinu,* since Akkadian has no

72. Tsumura, *The Earth and the Waters,* 93–116.

73. W. F. Albright, "The Babylonian Matter in the Predeuteronomic Primeval History (JE) in Gen 1–11," *JBL* 58 (1939) 102–3.

74. E. A. Speiser, "*ᵓEd* in the Story of Creation," *BASOR* 140 (1955) 9–11.

75. Tsumura, *The Earth and the Waters,* 115.

76. A. R. Millard, "The Etymology of Eden," *VT* 34 (1984) 103–6; J. C. Greenfield, "A Touch of Eden," in *Orientalia J. Duchesne-Guillemin Emerito Oblata* (Hommages et Opera Minora 9; Leiden: Brill, 1984) 219–24. Also Wallace, *The Eden Narrative,* 84.

phoneme /ᶜ/ either. Also *edinu* might be simply a semitized reading of the Sumerian edin and not used as an actual Akkadian word.

(c) *Common West Semitic.* The root *ᶜdn, which appears in the Fekheriyeh Inscription, in a Ugaritic text, in the divine epithet *hᶜdn* in Old South Arabic, as well as in the Arabic verb *ᶜadana,* probably has the literal meaning 'to make abundant in water supply'. Hence, the Hebrew *ᶜēden* probably means 'a place where there is an abundant water supply' (see Gen 13:10). The term *ᶜeden (pl. *ᶜădānîm* in Ps 36:9), which means 'pleasure, luxury', has the same etymology as *Eden,* though the MT seems to distinguish *ᶜēden* from *ᶜeden.[77]

Two Waters. I compare the two waters in Gen 2:5–6, 'rain' and 'flooding water' (*ᵓēd*), with the two *thmt*-waters in a Ugaritic expression that seems to refer to the waters above in heaven and the waters below under the earth, as in Gen 7:11 and 8:2, and to "an ancient tradition about the separation of heaven-water and ocean-water as reflected in the Genesis Creation story, not in 1:2, but in 1:6ff."[78] This upper *thmt*-water is probably associated or identified with the god "Heaven," while the lower *thmt*-water may well correspond to the goddess "Ocean" in Ugaritic religion.[79]

In various parts of the ancient Near East a rain-god such as Ada, Hadad, and Baal is called "a giver of abundant water-supply." In the Fekheriyeh Inscription, for example, he is described not only as a rain-giver but also as the "water-controller of all rivers." Similarly, as I have noted before, the Lord God of Genesis 2 is presumably understood as a rain-giver and as the controller of the subterranean waters. When he planted a garden in a well-watered place (2:8ff.), he apparently drained the *ᵓēd*-water there. Thus, he is also a controller of both rain and the subterranean water. However, the Lord God is more than a water-controller. He is the maker of the total universe, of 'earth and heaven' (*ᵓereṣ wĕšāmāyim,* 2:4).[80]

Canaanite Background. Soggin suggests that the account in Genesis 3 "contains an Israelite attack on syncretism as it existed between Israelite and Canaanite religion." According to him, "the origin of the story seems to have been Canaanite, that is, it came from the very milieu that the story was intended to oppose." Thus Soggin assumes that "an original Canaanite account disclosing the rites of fertility was taken over

77. Tsumura, *The Earth and the Waters,* 123–37.
78. Ibid., 151–52.
79. Ibid., 122.
80. Ibid., 141–42.

by Israel and turned completely around as a direct polemic against those same rites, accusing them of producing not life and fertility, but death and sterility.[81] Recently Wyatt, following F. F. Hvidberg,[82] also advocated that "the story is intended as a polemic against Canaanite religion," though he suggests that "it is the cult of El and Ašerah and not that of Baᶜal which is attacked."[83] According to Wyatt's conjecture, "the tree of knowledge is an allusion to the cult of El," while the tree of life refers to Ašerah, who appears as the consort of El in the Ugaritic texts and whose Ašerah-pole was "undoubtedly a surrogate tree (of life)."[84] However, these hypotheses are highly speculative.

Mullen, following Clifford and Cross,[85] compares "Eden, the garden of God" (Ezek 28:13) with El's abode[86] at the 'source of the two rivers' (*mbk nhrm*) // 'in the midst of the streams of the two *thmt*-waters' (*qrb apq thmtm*) or 'in the assembly of the two *thmt*-waters' (*bᶜdt thmt*) in the Ugaritic literature. He comments, "While it is most common to associate the biblical Eden with the Mesopotamian 'land of the living' and the Sumerian Dilmun, the Canaanite and biblical evidence points to the fact that the 'garden of God' (Ezek 28:13), which is equivalent to the 'mountain of God' (Ezek 28:16; cf. v. 14), is to be located in the North, the *yarkətê ṣāpôn* (Isa 14:13), the meeting place of the heavenly assembly."[87] The abode of El was probably located at the farthest horizon where "heaven" and "ocean" meet together.

Based on two Ugaritic texts, de Moor suggests the existence of "a Canaanite tradition about the Garden of Eden."[88] According to KTU 1.100, a divine She-ass and her son were "among the *first living creatures.* Only the sun, heaven, primordial Flood, spring and stone precede them. So the story seems to be situated close to the origin of the inhabited world." In KTU 1.107, a rather broken text that de Moor thinks precedes 1.100, "the premature death of the first man was eventually prevented by invoking the help of all the great gods against the offspring of the god

81. J. A. Soggin, "The Fall of Man in the Third Chapter of Genesis," *Old Testament and Oriental Studies* (BibOr 29; Rome: Pontifical Biblical Institute, 1975) 88–111.

82. F. F. Hvidberg, "The Canaanite Background of Gen. I–III," *VT* 10 (1960) 285–94.

83. N. Wyatt, "Interpreting the Creation and Fall Story in Genesis 2–3," *ZAW* 93 (1981) 19.

84. Ibid., 17. For various interpretations of the "tree of knowledge," see Oden, "Divine Aspirations in Atrahasis and in Genesis 1–11," *ZAW* 93 (1981) 211–13.

85. R. J. Clifford, *The Cosmic Mountain in Canaan and the Old Testament* (HSM 4; Cambridge: Harvard University Press, 1972) 35–57; F. M. Cross, *Canaanite Myth and Hebrew Epic: Essays in the History of the Religion of Israel* (Cambridge: Harvard University Press, 1973) 37–38.

86. For this subject, see also Tsumura, *The Earth and the Waters*, 150–53.

87. E. T. Mullen Jr., *The Divine Council in Canaanite and Early Hebrew Literature* (HSM 24; Chico, Cal.: Scholars Press, 1980) 153; followed by Wallace, *The Eden Narrative*, 94, et al.

88. J. C. de Moor, "East of Eden," *ZAW* 100 (1988) 106.

of the serpents, Horonu the Devil. Therefore the latter had to give in, as related in KTU 1.100."[89] Hence, de Moor suggests that "the Israelite tradition about the enmity between the seed of man and the seed of the serpent[90] (Gen 3:15) would have been derived from this myth under abolition of all references to a divine power next to God."[91]

It must be admitted, however, that de Moor's suggestion is based on the reconstructed text of KTU 1.107:27–41, and his theory remains highly hypothetical.

Literary Approaches. In recent years a great number of literary analyses of the Eden story have appeared, and it is almost impossible to review all of them even briefly. The following is an inexhaustive sample.[92]

Structure. Walsh divides Gen 2:4b–3:24 into a series of seven scenes "principally by shifts in *dramatis personae* and changes in literary form," and for each scene, he discusses the literary structure, or framework, and its unity.[93] He also notes discourse grammatical features such as narrative and speech, monologue and dialogue, paraphrase, deliberation, transition or link, as well as the importance of "narrative *wayyiqtōl*s,"[94] operative words, or motif words for structural understanding.

"The basic structural principle of the Eden account," according to Walsh, is "the concentric arrangement of its scenes. The pattern involves *dramatis personae*, themes, and in some cases, internal structural elements of each scene." He then argues that there are major structural divisions in the narrative: "Introduction (scenes 1–2), action (scenes 3–6), and epilogue (scene 7)." He concludes thus:

> Analysis reveals that the apparently "artless" story of man and woman in the garden of Eden has in fact structures and intricate patterns of organization that involve even minor details of the text. Moreover, the patterns so interlock that the deletion of any part of the text (except, perhaps, 2:10b–14) would have significant repercussions for the whole passage.[95]

89. See J. C. de Moor, *An Anthology of Religious Texts from Ugarit* (Leiden: Brill, 1987) 146–56, for his full translation of KTU 1.100.

90. Cf. Sjöberg ("Eve and the Chameleon," 222–23), who suggests that "it was a chameleon that seduced Eve to eat the apple and thereby deprived her and her husband Adam of a pleasant, eternal life in the Garden of Eden"!

91. De Moor, "East of Eden," 109.

92. For structuralist approaches to Genesis 2–3, see D. Patte (ed.), *Genesis 2 and 3: Kaleidoscopic Structural Readings* (Semeia 18; Chico, Cal.: Scholars Press, 1980).

93. J. T. Walsh, "Genesis 2:4b–3:24: A Synchronic Approach," in this volume, 362–82.

94. For Longacre's view that "the storyline or the backbone of a discourse in Biblical Hebrew is conveyed by use of clauses that begin with a *waw*-consecutive verb," see *Joseph: A Story of Divine Providence*, 64ff.; also see Tsumura, *The Earth and the Waters*, 119 n. 9.

95. Walsh, "Genesis 2:4b–3:24," below, p. 375.

Intimacy and Alienation. Hauser aims to analyze the "writer's development of the two-dimensional theme of intimacy and alienation," for he thinks that "they clearly express a major motif the writer has used to focus and integrate his narrative." In Genesis 2 "the writer weaves several components into an intimate picture of harmony, with all revolving around man, the first and central element in the created order."[96] However, in Genesis 3, Hauser explains, the "world of harmony and intimacy becomes a world of disruption and alienation."

Sanctuary Symbolism. Wenham, in his recent article, contends that:

> The garden of Eden is not viewed by the author of Genesis simply as a piece of Mesopotamian farmland, but as an archetypal sanctuary, that is a place where God dwells and where man should worship him. Many of the features of the garden may also be found in later sanctuaries particularly the tabernacle or Jerusalem temple. These parallels suggest that the garden itself is understood as a sort of sanctuary.[97]

There are certainly many other aspects of the creation stories in Genesis. The above are just samples in the areas of comparative study and literary analysis, but they are basic and significant materials for the theological understanding of the earliest chapters of the Bible.

Flood

Creation and Flood

Until recently, the *Creation* and the *Flood* have often been treated as separate units. One of the reasons for this may be that initially discovered ancient Mesopotamian documents provided either a Creation myth without the Flood story ("Enuma elish" and others) or the Flood story without a Creation motif ("Gilgamesh Epic," tablet XI), all in seventh-century neo-Assyrian copies from the Nineveh of Ashurbanipal's time.[98] Therefore, scholars were busy comparing Genesis 1 with "Enuma elish," and Genesis 6–8 with "Gilgamesh" XI, without integrating these two sections of Genesis.

96. A. J. Hauser, "Genesis 2–3: The Theme of Intimacy and Alienation," in this volume, 383–84.

97. G. J. Wenham, "Sanctuary Symbolism in the Garden of Eden Story," below, 399–404.

98. The best introductions to these Mesopotamian stories are still A. Heidel, *The Babylonian Genesis* and idem, *The Gilgamesh Epic and Old Testament Parallels* (2d ed.; Chicago: University of Chicago Press, 1949). See also Speiser's translations of "The Creation Epic" ("Enuma elish") and "The Epic of Gilgamesh" (in *ANET,* 60–99) and the most recent translations by Dalley (*Myths from Mesopotamia,* 109–20 ["Gilgamesh" XI]; 233–74 ["Enuma elish"]).

However, we now have some evidence that the "continuous narrative of the first era of human existence" in the ancient Near East covered both the Creation and the Flood, as Millard and others have noted.[99] For example, the "Atra-Ḫasīs Epic" from the Old Babylonian Period (ca. 1630 B.C.E.), which Lambert and Millard presented in 1969 in a thorough study, with the text and its translation,[100] covers the history of man from his creation to the Flood. This history was widely known in ancient Mesopotamia, and a similar tradition with the same overall structure was known in the early second millennium B.C.E.

Recently Jacobsen suggested the existence of a Sumerian version of such a tradition. According to him, the Sumerian Deluge Tablet from Nippur, which gives not only an account of the Flood but also a list of five cities before the Flood like those in the Sumerian King List,[101] may be combined with another Sumerian fragment from Ur and a later bilingual fragment from Nineveh. This combined text, which he names the "Eridu Genesis,"[102] comprises: (1) the creation of man, (2) the institution of kingship, (3) the founding of the first cities and (4) the great Flood. While Jacobsen's reconstruction of two Sumerian fragmentary texts (ca. 1600 B.C.E.) and one Sumerian-Akkadian bilingual fragment (ca. 600 B.C.E.) from three different places remains hypothetical, it seems that an overall tradition linking Creation, early kings, and the Flood existed in Babylonia from early times.[103]

Comparative Approach. Biblical scholars have accepted the view that a similar tradition, which links Creation and the Flood, is also reflected in the overall literary structure of Genesis 1–11. Coats, following Clark, notes that in the Sumerian King List and the "Atra-Ḫasīs Epic," "various narrative elements are set together in something of the same series as the OT primeval saga."[104] According to Clark, "in his total outline P is influenced by the King List tradition which had now (in some editions) incorporated the flood narrative." As for "J," he proposes that "J is basically dependent on the tradition of the Atrahasis epic for his outline of the primeval history including the sequence of creation, repeated sin,

99. Millard, "A New Babylonian 'Genesis' Story," 116 below.

100. Lambert and Millard, *Atra-Ḫasīs.* See also Dalley, *Myths from Mesopotamia,* 9–35.

101. For a critical edition of the text, see T. Jacobsen, *The Sumerian King List* (AS 11; Chicago: University of Chicago Press, 1939) 69ff.

102. T. Jacobsen, "The Eridu Genesis," in this volume, 129–30. See Miller, "Eridu, Dunnu, and Babel," below, 144–46, for the appropriateness of the label *"Eridu Genesis."*

103. Millard, "A New Babylonian 'Genesis' Story," 125 below.

104. G. W. Coats, *Genesis, with an Introduction to Narrative Literature* (The Forms of the Old Testament Literature 1; Grand Rapids: Eerdmans, 1983) 38.

punishment, and divine grace culminating in the flood."[105] It is not so simple, however, to divide the Mesopotamian traditions exactly between the King List, "priestly" tradition, and the "Atra-Ḫasīs" "epic" tradition. In fact the latter played important roles in the priestly tradition. For example, it is reported that a Babylonian incantation priest cited a part of the "Atra-Ḫasīs Epic" to advise a late-Assyrian king on a drought.[106]

A number of scholars have made a thorough study of "Atra-Ḫasīs" and its relevance to Genesis research.[107] For example, Kikawada, who abandons the source analysis of Genesis, studied the structural similarities between "Atra-Ḫasīs" and Genesis 1–11 as a whole. According to him, both compositions used the same literary convention, "a five point outline," consisting of (1) creation: man, (2) first threat, (3) second threat, (4) final threat: flood, (5) resolution, "narrating primaeval history up to the time of a great flood, followed by a solution to the problem that persisted throughout the pre-flood history," namely "increase of population." While "Atra-Ḫasīs" gives "the urban solution," birth control, to this problem of population growth, "Genesis offers dispersion, the nomadic way." Kikawada, following Kilmer's view of "overpopulation,"[108] suggests that "Genesis 1–11 may be a polemic against urban life and its solution to over-population, birth control."[109] Similarly, Moran and Frymer-Kensky hold that Gen 9:1ff. is "a conscious rejection" of the "Atra-Ḫasīs Epic."[110]

However, Oden rejects the overpopulation hypothesis. He holds that "the primary theme of Atrahasis is the development and then the maintenance of the boundary between the gods and humans." According to him, the key to the interpretation of the "Atra-Ḫasīs Epic" is in the human activity, indicated by the "noise" and the "tumult" that "rob Enlil of sleep and prompt him to command the plague, droughts, and then the

105. W. M. Clark, "The Flood and the Structure of the Pre-Patriarchal History," *ZAW* 83 (1971) 187–88.

106. Lambert and Millard, *Atra-Ḫasīs*, 27–28. For other examples, see A. Livingstone, *Mystical and Mythological Explanatory Works of Assyrian and Babylonian Scholars* (Oxford: Clarendon, 1986) chap. 4: "Works in Standard Babylonian explaining state rituals in terms of myths." Note also C. H. Gordon's view that the genealogies of Genesis, which are usually attributed to P, "should not be detached from the narrative," as indicated by Homeric epic (*The Common Background of Greek and Hebrew Civilizations* [New York: Norton, 1965] 284).

107. Oden ("Divine Aspirations," 197–98) gives "a fairly comprehensive list" of studies in "Atra-Ḫasīs" and its relevance to the Old Testament.

108. A. D. Kilmer, "The Mesopotamian Concept of Overpopulation and Its Solution as Reflected in Mythology," *Or* 41 (1972) 160–77.

109. I. M. Kikawada, "Literary Convention of the Primaeval History," *AJBI* 1 (1975) 3–21, esp. 12–13.

110. W. L. Moran, "Atrahasis: The Babylonian Story of the Flood," *Bib* 52 (1971) 51–61; T. Frymer-Kensky, "The Atrahasis Epic and Its Significance for Our Understanding of Genesis 1–9," *BA* 40 (1977) 147–55.

flood." The "crime" was that of "scheming humans noisily planning ways to alter the divinely established order so that their status might become something more than workers for the gods."[111] Oden therefore holds that the Tower of Babel tale (Gen 11:1–9), in which human aspirations to divine status are so transparent, seems to be "the visual equivalent of the auditory assault of Atrahasis."[112]

Whether overpopulation or the guilt of man brought the Flood is still a lively issue in interpreting the epic, as Moran recently pointed out.[113] The similarities between the Genesis account and the "Atra-Ḫasīs Epic" do not support the idea that Genesis is a direct borrowing from the Mesopotamian but do indicate that Mesopotamian materials could have served as models for Genesis 1–11, as Jacobsen holds.[114] P. D. Miller also admits that "there were Mesopotamian models that anticipate the structure of Genesis 1–11 as a whole."[115] K. A. Kitchen notes a similar outline, namely "creation–flood–later times," and a common theme, namely "creation, crisis, continuance of man," of the "primeval proto-history" in the "Atra-Ḫasīs Epic," the Sumerian Flood story, and the Sumerian King List, as well as in the Genesis account. He recognizes here "a common literary heritage, formulated in each case in Mesopotamia in the early 2nd millennium BC."[116]

However, there are also many differences between the Mesopotamian traditions and the Genesis account, in addition to the basic concepts of divine-human relationship. According to Jacobsen, the P source of Genesis has a rather pessimistic view of existence, introducing moral judgment on man's sinfulness, while the "Eridu Genesis" holds "an affirmative and optimistic view."[117] Whether the Genesis viewpoint is pessimistic or not,

111. Oden, "Divine Aspirations," 200, 204. He summarizes three views of the "noise" of humans, on pp. 206–7:

1. G. Pettinato: the noise of their rebellious activity. Human rebellion consisted of not submitting to the divinely established order, and this lack of submission made the gods, particularly Enlil, restless.
2. A. D. Kilmer, also Moran: behind the noise made by humans lay simply the problem of too many humans. In other words, the epic deals with the problem of overpopulation.
3. Von Soden: the crime that occasioned the Flood was not simply human rebellion, as Pettinato argued, but more precisely the human tendency to reach ever higher and to approach ever closer to the gods.

112. Oden, "Divine Aspirations," 210–11.

113. W. L. Moran, "Some Considerations of Form and Interpretation in *Atra-Ḫasīs*," in *Language, Literature, and History: Philological and Historical Studies Presented to Erica Reiner* (ed. F. Rochberg-Halton; AOS 67; New Haven, Conn.: American Oriental Society, 1987) 251–55.

114. Jacobsen, "The Eridu Genesis," 141.

115. Miller, "Eridu, Dunnu, and Babel," 150.

116. K. A. Kitchen, *The Bible in Its World* (Exeter: Paternoster, 1977) 31.

117. Jacobsen, "The Eridu Genesis," below, 142.

however, depends on the way scholars treat Genesis 1–11 as a literary whole, a subject to which I will return later.

Jacobsen takes the "Eridu Genesis," as well as the biblical account (P), neither as a history nor as a myth; he assigns them to a "mytho-historical" genre, since they both have a chronological arrangement along a line of time, with a chain of cause and effect, and show interest in numbers and chronology.[118] Miller is supportive of Jacobsen's view, since the "Eridu Genesis" and "the full shape of Genesis 1–11" (not just the P account) share both "substantial content with typical myths of the ancient Near East" and "features that remind one more of historical chronicles."[119]

Before discussing the theme of primeval protohistory, I should like to turn our attention to the other literary aspect, namely the structure of Genesis 1–11 as a whole.

Literary Structure. Not only does comparative evidence point to the adequacy of treating both the *Creation* and the *Flood* together as a unified literary work, but the recent emphasis on the holistic approach[120] to "the text in its final form"[121] or "the text as it stands"[122] leads us to investigate the literary theme and structure of Genesis 1–11 as a whole. Before one seeks the theme of Genesis 1–11, one must decide its structure. For this, the *toledot*-formula of Genesis is indicative of the narrative structure in the mind of the author/editor. Thompson's recent study of the *toledot*-structure of Genesis is in this regard very important, though his view of a sharp break between Genesis 1–4 and Genesis 5ff. ("The Book of the Toledoth of Adam") is rather overemphasized.[123] Thompson's view was most recently challenged by Hess, who argued that "the literary form of Genesis 1–2 is intended to parallel the genealogical doublets of chapters 4–5 and 10–11."[124]

The major problem in deciding the theme and structure of Genesis 1–11 is determining the precise terminus of the "primeval history." The following suggestions have been made.

Creation → Flood (1:1–9:29). In the light of the literary structure of "Creation-Rebellion-Flood" in the "Atra-Ḫasīs Epic," some scholars have suggested that the primeval history in Genesis stretches from the crea-

118. Ibid., 140–141.

119. Miller, "Eridu, Dunnu, and Babel," below, 148.

120. E.g., M. Greenberg, *Ezekiel 1–20* (AB 22; New York: Doubleday, 1983) 18–27; M. Weiss, *The Bible from Within: The Method of Total Interpretation* (Jerusalem: Magnes, 1984).

121. Cf. D. J. A. Clines, "Theme in Genesis 1–11," in this vol., 285.

122. Oden, "Divine Aspirations," 211.

123. T. L. Thompson, *The Origin Tradition of Ancient Israel, 1: The Literary Formation of Genesis and Exodus 1–23* (JSOTSup 55; Sheffield: Sheffield Academic Press, 1987) chapter 3.

124. R. S. Hess, "Genesis 1–2 in Its Literary Context," *TynBul* 41 (1990) 150 n. 23.

tion story through the end of the Flood story, namely Genesis 1–9, rather than Genesis 1–11.[125] Since the end of chap. 9 follows up the description of Noah in 5:31 and completes the full description of him in the same manner that the other nine patriarchs are described in chap. 5, it is likely that the Flood story in chaps. 6–9 is meant to be a part of a larger literary unit that begins at 5:1, that is, "The Book of the *Toledot* of Adam." The Flood story is, so to speak, a detailed description of Noah and his life inserted into the framework of the genealogy of Genesis 5.[126]

Creation → *Babel* (1:1–11:9). J. M. Sasson recently explained the Tower of Babel story as "a clue to the redactional structuring" of Genesis 1–11. According to him, Gen 1:1–11:9 is divided into two parts, "from Creation to Noah (10 generations)" and "from the Flood to Abram (10 generations)"; just as the Nephilim story (6:1–8) serves as a concluding remark for the first part, the Babel story (11:1–9) comes at the end of the second part.[127] This division at the end of 6:8 accords with the biblical *toledot*-structure; up to that verse the section is "The Book of the *Toledot* of Adam," while the section after 6:9 is "The *Toledot* of Noah." Coats also thinks that the primeval saga ends with the tale about the tower, since the tale "binds off the series of narratives about the people of the world."[128] For a different reason, Oden also considers the conclusion of the primeval history to be Gen 11:1–9, where "human aspirations to divine status are so transparent."[129]

However, the end of the second part, 11:9, does not accord with the end of "The *Toledot* of Noah" (9:29), though 6:8 does accord with the end of "The *Toledot* of Adam." Also, in Sasson's scheme, the reason for placing Abram in the tenth generation is not clearly demonstrated, since his structure lacks both the genealogical list (11:10–26) and the *toledot* of Terah (11:27ff.), which refer to Abram himself. Before these sections Abram's name does not even appear.

Creation → *Terah* (1:1–11:26).[130] Some recognize the "Creation-list–Flood-list" pattern in Genesis 1–11 and note that just as Noah is the tenth generation from Adam in the first list, the genealogy in Gen 5:1–32, so Abram is the tenth generation from Noah in the second list (11:10–26).

125. E.g., Clark, "The Flood and the Structure of the Pre-Patriarchal History," 205–6.

126. In Thompson's terminology, it is "an expanded genealogical narrative" (*The Origin Tradition of Ancient Israel*, 83).

127. J. M. Sasson, "The 'Tower of Babel' as a Clue to the Redactional Structuring of the Primeval History (Genesis 1:1–11:9)," in this volume, 456.

128. Coats, *Genesis*, 36.

129. Oden, "Divine Aspirations," 211.

130. E.g., B. W. Anderson, "From Analysis to Synthesis: The Interpretation of Genesis 1–11," below, 416–35.

According to Malamat, "the ante- and postdiluvian lines (i.e., of Adam and of Shem, respectively), symmetrically arranged to a ten-generation depth, are undoubtedly the product of intentional harmonization and in imitation of the concrete genealogical model."[131] Thus the ten-generation scheme of the ancient Near Eastern genealogies might be taken as a formulaic pattern for the Genesis account of the primeval history.

Nevertheless, in the *toledot* of Shem, 11:10–26, there are only nine patriarchs listed with a full description, though Abram, the tenth one, is referred to as one of the Terah's sons. Also, strictly speaking, the genealogy in Gen 11:10–26 does not follow the same pattern as that in Genesis 5. In fact, in the second list there is no description of the death of the patriarchs, while all ten individuals of the first list have after the life span the final comment, "and he died" (cf. 9:29 for Noah) or "and he was not" (v. 24 for Enoch).

Creation → Abram (1:1–11:32). The phrase *and he died* appears together with the life-span for the description of Terah in 11:32 for the first time since it appeared with Noah in 9:29. This might well suggest that 11:32 is the terminus of the primeval history. This position seems to be supported by Y. T. Radday's analysis of Genesis based on the computerized statistics, according to which Gen 5:1–32 and 11:10–32 stand out as "very distinct" within Genesis.[132] Thompson notes that 11:27–32 is a genealogical entry that is expanded with an extended narrative and serves with 11:10–26 as a "link" between the tradition of Gen 1:1–11:9 and the traditions about Abra(ha)m.[133]

Creation → Abraham's Call (1:1–12:3). According to von Rad, "The story of the Tower of Babel ends without grace, and therefore . . . the main question which the primeval history raises for the reader is that of the further relationship of God to the nations."[134] Therefore, "the end of the Biblical primeval history is . . . not the story of the Tower of Babel; it is the call of Abraham in Gen. XII. 1–3: indeed, because of this welding of primeval history and saving history, the whole of Israel's saving history is properly to be understood with reference to the unsolved problem of Jahweh's relationship to the nations."[135] Thus, von Rad set the terminus of the primeval history at Gen 12:3 for theological reasons.

131. A. Malamat, "King Lists of the Old Babylonian Period and Biblical Genealogies," in this volume, 188.

132. Wenham, "Genesis: An Authorship Study," 13. Wenham notes here the observations made by Y. T. Radday et al., *Genesis: An Authorship Study in Computer Assisted Statistical Linguistics* (AnBib 103; Rome: Pontifical Biblical Institute, 1985).

133. Thompson, *The Origin Tradition of Ancient Israel,* 83.

134. G. von Rad, *Old Testament Theology* (New York: Harper & Row, 1962) 1.163.

135. Ibid., 164. Later, however, in his commentary on Genesis, he ends his discussion of the biblical primeval history with 12:9, taking 12:1–9 as a "transitional paragraph" like 6:5–8 (*Genesis: A Commentary* [rev. ed.; OTL; Philadelphia: Westminster, 1972] 165).

However, from the literary point of view, Gen 12:1–3 is better taken as a "link" between Genesis 1–11 and the following story of the patriarchs. This is what Parunak calls a "transitional technique" A/aB, which is used to link the Patriarchal story (B) with the primeval history (A), by recapitulating the universal relationship of God with the nations at the beginning (a) of the new section, in this case, 12:1ff. (B).[136]

Thus, Genesis 1–11 seems to have been written with the historical purpose of introducing Abram on the stage, and hence its narrative continues "from the stories of origins on down into later times, that is, to the present, the time when the narrative came into being." Hence Miller concludes: "The sense of a single story from the creation to the present may have existed in Mesopotamia as well as Israel."[137] Kitchen, who believes that "each component in the population of early second millennium Mesopotamia (Sumerians, Babylonians, Western Semites) contributed its formulation of inherited traditions," namely a common literary heritage, concludes that "whenever it reached its present form within the entire book of Genesis, that unit Gen 1–11 best finds its literary origins in the early second millennium B.C."[138]

Literary Theme. Many suggestions for a unifying theme of Genesis 1–11 as a whole (rather than of P or J, as proposed by von Rad,[139] Brueggemann,[140] etc.), which Clines rightly distinguishes from "a recurrent motif in the primeval history,"[141] have been made, such as the "spread of sin," "creation–uncreation–re-creation," and so on. Clines suggests the following two possible themes for Genesis 1–11, one negative or *pessimistic,* and the other positive or *optimistic*:

1. Mankind tends to destroy what God has made good.
2. God's grace never fails to deliver man from the consequences of his sin.

But he prefers the latter theme to the former, "if the patriarchal history unfolds the fulfillment of the blessing promise (12:2–3)."[142] On the

136. Parunak, "Transitional Techniques in the Bible," 525–48.

137. Miller, "Eridu, Dunnu, and Babel," 151 below.

138. Kitchen, *The Bible in Its World,* 35.

139. Von Rad (*Old Testament Theology,* 1.163) discusses "the growth of sin" depicted by the Jahwist and explains thus: "God punished these outbreaks of sin with increasingly severe judgments. Nevertheless there is also to be seen . . . a saving and sustaining activity on the part of God. . . . As sin waxed, grace waxed the more."

140. W. Brueggemann, "The Kerygma of the Priestly Writers," *ZAW* 84 (1972) 397–414; idem, "David and His Theologian," *CBQ* 30 (1968) 156–81.

141. Clines, "Theme in Genesis 1–11," 291 below.

142. Ibid., 304–5.

other hand, Oden explains the theme differently: "Rather than an ascending cacophony of wickedness, Gen 1–11 is a collection of several instances of the human propensity to trespass upon the divine sphere."[143]

The Flood Story

As Heidel commented, "The most remarkable parallels between the Old Testament and the entire corpus of cuneiform inscriptions from Mesopotamia . . . are found in the deluge accounts of the Babylonians and Assyrians, on the one hand, and the Hebrews, on the other."[144] After forty years the situation remains the same, with even more information about the story of the Flood being available from ancient Mesopotamia, though in recent years literatures from ancient Syria, especially from Ugarit and Ebla,[145] have been providing enormous amounts of material in other topics for comparative studies.

Mesopotamian Flood Stories. (a) *"Gilgamesh" XI.*[146] About 120 years ago, in 1872, George Smith of the British Museum read the paper "The Chaldean Account of the Deluge" before the Society of Biblical Archaeology. There for the first time he presented a translation and a discussion of a number of fragments of the "Gilgamesh Epic," especially of tablet XI, where the Flood story is narrated. This was so similar to the biblical Flood story that it created immediate enthusiasm for studies in parallels between the two stories.[147] Certainly, as Millard says, "No Babylonian text provides so close a parallel to Genesis as does the Flood story of Gilgamesh XI."[148]

Thorough comparisons have been made between the Flood stories of Genesis and the "Gilgamesh Epic," tablet XI, and their interrelationship and priority have been discussed. Heidel discusses the problem of dependence and summarizes three main possibilities that have been suggested: (1) the Babylonians borrowed from the Hebrew account, (2) the Hebrew account is dependent on the Babylonian, (3) both are descended from a common original. The first explanation, according to him, finds "little favor among scholars today," while "the arguments which have been advanced in support of [the second view] are quite indecisive." As for the

143. Oden, "Divine Aspirations," 211.

144. Heidel, *The Gilgamesh Epic and Old Testament Parallels,* 244.

145. For a useful introduction to these materials, see P. C. Craigie, *Ugarit and Old Testament* (Grand Rapids, Mich.: Eerdmans, 1983), which has a section on Ebla (chap. 6).

146. For English translations of the Flood story in the "Gilgamesh Epic," tablet XI, see Speiser's in *ANET,* 93–95; Heidel, *The Gilgamesh Epic and Old Testament Parallels,* 80–88.

147. Ibid., 1ff.

148. Millard, "A New Babylonian Genesis Story," below, 123.

third way of explanation, Heidel thinks that "for the present, at least, this explanation can be proved as little as the rest."[149]

According to Lambert, who is extremely careful with regard to the Mesopotamian influence on the Genesis Creation story and does not admit the Hebrew borrowing from the Babylonian "Creation" story, "Enuma elish," too easily, "the flood remains the clearest case of dependence of Genesis on Mesopotamian legend. While flood stories as such do not have to be connected, the episode of the birds in Gen 8:6–12 is so close to the parallel passage in the XIth tablet of the Babylonian *Gilgamesh Epic* that no doubt exists."[150] Thus, Lambert holds the second position with regard to the problem of dependence.

(b) *Earlier Mesopotamian Flood Stories.* The "Gilgamesh Epic," as is well known, is a seventh-century neo-Assyrian copy of an older original, and the Flood story built into it was taken from a much older independent story of the Flood.[151] We now have several Old Babylonian versions (seventeenth century B.C.E.) of the Flood story, the "Atra-Ḫasīs Epic," as well as the Sumerian Flood story,[152] thus pushing the Mesopotamian Flood tradition back at least a thousand years earlier than "Gilgamesh" XI. From Ugarit, a fourteenth-century copy of the Flood story, "the only version of the Babylonian Flood story found outside Mesopotamia so far," has been unearthed.[153]

The Flood itself is also mentioned in other Mesopotamian literature such as the Sumerian King List, which lists kings both from before the Flood and from after the Flood, thus dividing the history into two eras, pre- and post-Flood.[154] The King List, after giving a summary of the antediluvian era as "5 cities were they; 8 kings reigned there 241,200 years" (col. i 36–38), refers to the Flood: "The Flood swept thereover. After the Flood had swept thereover, when the kingship was lowered from heaven the kingship was in Kish" (col. i 39–42).[155] Lambert and Millard note other allusions to the Flood in eight cuneiform texts and the mentions of antediluvian kings in texts such as "a list of seven sages," omens, and incantations.[156]

149. Heidel, *The Gilgamesh Epic and Old Testament Parallels*, 260–67.

150. Lambert, "A New Look," 101 below.

151. See J. H. Tigay, *The Evolution of the Gilgamesh Epic* (Philadelphia: University of Pennsylvania Press, 1982) chap. 12.

152. See M. Civil's translation and discussion of this story in Lambert and Millard, *Atra-Ḫasīs*, 138–45.

153. Ibid., 131–33.

154. For the biblical tradition, see D. T. Tsumura, "'The Deluge' (*mabbûl*) in Psalm 29:10," *UF* 20 (1988) 351–55.

155. Jacobsen, *The Sumerian King List*, 77.

156. Cf. Lambert and Millard, *Atra-Ḫasīs*, 25–27.

Similarities and Differences. Thus the Flood tradition has a long history in ancient Mesopotamia, and it is not simply enough to compare the Flood story in "Gilgamesh" XI and the Genesis story on literary grounds. It is essential to place each of the Mesopotamian stories in the history of Flood traditions before its historical interdependence and priority are discussed in relationship with the Genesis account. Recent comparison is therefore made in terms of the Flood traditions behind the literature, assuming that "the essential narrative is identical" in both Mesopotamian and Hebrew traditions. Cassuto in his commentary lists nineteen parallels and sixteen differences.[157] Kitchen, who unlike Cassuto had access to Lambert and Millard's 1969 *Atra-Ḫasīs*, lists seven similarities and nine differences.

Similarities: "The Common Framework"

1. A divine decision is made to send a punishing Flood;
2. One chosen man is told to save self, family and creatures by building a boat;
3. A great flood destroys the rest of the people;
4. The boat grounds on a mountain;
5. Birds are sent forth to determine availability of habitable land;
6. The hero sacrifices to deity;
7. Mankind is renewed upon earth.[158]

Differences

1. The Mesopotamian gods tire of the noisiness of mankind, while in Genesis, God sees the corruption and universal wickedness of mankind.
2. The Mesopotamian assembly of gods is at pains to conceal their Flood plan entirely from mankind (this is not evident in Genesis at all).
3. In the Mesopotamian epics, the saving of the hero is entirely by the deceit of one god, while in Genesis, God from the first tells Noah plainly that judgment is coming, and he alone has been judged faithful and so must build a boat.
4. The size and type of craft in "Gilgamesh" is a vast cube, perhaps even a great floating ziggurat, while that in Genesis has far more the proportions of a real craft.

157. U. Cassuto, *A Commentary on the Book of Genesis, Part Two: From Noah to Abraham* (Jerusalem: Magnes, 1964) 16–23.

158. Kitchen, *The Bible in Its World,* 28–29.

5. The duration of the Flood differs in the Mesopotamian and biblical accounts. "Atra-Ḫasīs" has seven days and seven nights of storm and tempest, as does the Sumerian version; "Gilgamesh" has six (or seven) days and nights, with subsidence of the waters beginning on the seventh day; none of the Mesopotamian narratives gives any idea of how long the flood-waters took to subside thereafter. In contrast, Genesis has an entirely consistent, more detailed time-scale. After 7 days' warning, the storm and floods rage for 40 days, then the waters stay for 150 days before beginning to sink, and further intervals follow until the earth is dry a year and 10 days from the time the cataclysm began (Gen 7:11, 8:14).
6. In the Mesopotamian versions, the inhabitants of the boat include also a pilot and craftsmen, etc.; in Genesis one finds only Noah and his immediate family.
7. The details of sending out birds differ entirely in "Gilgamesh," Berossus, and Gen 8:7ff.; this is lost in "Atra-Ḫasīs" (if ever it was present).
8. The Mesopotamian hero leaves the boat of his own accord and then offers a sacrifice to win the acceptance of the gods. By contrast, Noah stays in the boat *until* God summons him forth and then presents what is virtually a sacrifice of thanksgiving, following which divine blessing is expressed without regret.
9. Replenishment of the land or earth is partly through renewed divine activity in "Atra-Ḫasīs" but simply and naturally through the survivors themselves in Genesis.[159]

The Problem of Dependence. As Lambert and Millard note, "It is obvious that the differences are too great to encourage belief in direct connection between "Atra-Ḫasīs" and Genesis, but just as obviously there is some kind of involvement in the historical traditions generally of the two peoples." After suggesting "one possible explanation" of such involvement, namely the westward movement of these traditions during the Amarna period (ca. 1400 B.C.E.), Lambert and Millard simply conclude that "the question is very complex."[160]

To this problem of dependence, Wenham explains that there are basically three approaches: (1) minimalists, (2) maximalists, (3) somewhere between:

1. "The minimalists argue that the differences between the Mesopotamian and the biblical accounts are too great to suppose dependence

159. Ibid., 29–30.

160. Lambert and Millard, *Atra-Ḫasīs*, 24.

of the latter on the former. Both must be independent developments of an earlier common tradition.

2. "Maximalists argue that the Genesis editor was in fact familiar with Mesopotamian traditions in something like their present form. . . . The writer seems to be aware of other ancient Near Eastern ideas and to be deliberately opposing or commenting on them.
3. "The truth lies somewhere between the minimalist and maximalist positions."[161]

Kitchen holds that "it is fair to say that the Mesopotamians had a flood-tradition in common, which existed and was transmitted in several versions." Therefore it is out of place to talk of "borrowing the Hebrew from the Babylonian (or Sumerian) or vice-versa." Kitchen explains that "parallel traditions about some ancient event in common Mesopotamian memory would be a simpler and more satisfying answer." He then notes that Gen 6:9–8:22, whose 60 verses "might be roughly equal to 120 lines of Sumerian or Akkadian text," was "probably the simplest and shortest of all the ancient versions, possibly originating as early as they, and was certainly not a secondary elaboration of them."[162]

Similarities among these traditions seemingly show that at least for the ancient Mesopotamians, the Flood was a once-and-for-all cosmic event that happened a long time ago. Kitchen explains it thus: "The Sumerians and Babylonians of *c.* 2000/1800 BC believed so firmly in the former historical occurrence of such a flood that they inserted it into the Sumerian King List."[163]

Literary Unity. Wenham lists seventeen points in common between the Genesis account and the Mesopotamian traditions, the "Atra-Ḫasīs Epic," the Ras Shamra version, the epic of "Gilgamesh" tablet XI, and the Sumerian "Eridu Genesis" version. According to him, "These lists underline the very close parallels between the Mesopotamian and biblical accounts of the flood." He notes that "this is particularly striking in the case of the combined (J + P) version of the flood in Genesis. . . . It is strange that two accounts of the flood so different as J and P, circulating in ancient Israel, should have been combined to give our present story which has many more resemblances to the "Gilgamesh" version than the postulated sources." Therefore, Wenham suggests two alternatives as assumptions, preferring the second to the first: (1) "The J and P versions of the flood story were in their original form much closer to each other than

161. Wenham, *Genesis 1–15*, 163.
162. Kitchen, *The Bible in Its World*, 30.
163. Ibid.

the relics of these sources now suggest." (2) "Only one source was used by the writer of Genesis, a source presumably similar to the Mesopotamian flood story."[164] Thus, the J and P distinction is illusory, at least in the Flood story. The recent emphasis on the literary unity of the story by Andersen ("chiasmus"), Wenham ("palistrophe"), Anderson, and Longacre is noteworthy, despite Emerton's dissent.[165]

164. G. J. Wenham, "The Coherence of the Flood Narrative," in this volume, 443; also idem, *Genesis 1–15*, 163–64.

165. F. I. Andersen, *The Sentence in Biblical Hebrew* (Janua Linguarum, Series Practica 231; The Hague: Mouton, 1974) 123–26; Wenham, "The Coherence of the Flood Narrative," below, 433–38; Anderson, "From Analysis to Synthesis," below, 412–31; R. E. Longacre, "The Discourse Structure of the Flood Narrative," in *Society of Biblical Literature 1976: Seminar Papers* (SBLSP; ed. G. MacRae; Missoula: Scholars Press, 1976) 235–62; J. A. Emerton, "An Examination of Some Attempts to Defend the Unity of the Flood Narrative in Genesis: Part I," *VT* 37 (1987) 401–20; idem, "An Examination of Some Attempts to Defend the Unity of the Flood Narrative in Genesis: Part II," *VT* 38 (1988) 1–21. Emerton in these articles criticizes "five attempts to defend the unity of the flood narrative against those who believe it to be composed out of two sources," i.e., the attempts of Umberto Cassuto, Eduard Nielsen, F. I. Andersen, G. J. Wenham, and Y. T. Radday.

The Genealogies of Genesis 1–11 and Comparative Literature

RICHARD S. HESS

⟦241⟧ Approaches making use of anthropological, literary, and comparative Ancient Near Eastern data have been applied to the study of the genealogies in Genesis 1–11.[1] There has been a tendency to make

Reprinted with permission from *Biblica* 70 (1989) 241–54.

Research for this paper was done as part of the Genesis 1–11 Project, Tyndale House, Cambridge, England. I thank A. R. Millard and D. T. Tsumura for reading and commenting on it. A draft of this paper was read at the Society of Biblical Literature Annual Meeting, Chicago, 21 November 1988.

1. Recent studies include J. Gabriel, "Die Kainitengenealogie," *Bib* 40 (1959) 409–427; D. Neiman, "The Date and Circumstances of the Cursing of Canaan," *Biblical Motifs: Origins and Transformations* (ed. A. Altmann; Studies and Texts 3; Cambridge; MA, 1966) 113–134; ibid., "The Two Genealogies of Japhet," *Orient and Occident: Essays Presented to Cyrus H. Gordon on the Occasion of His Sixty-Fifth Birthday* (ed. H. A. Hoffner, Jr.; AOAT 22; Kevelaer/ Neukirchen-Vluyn, 1973) 119–126; A. Malamat, "King Lists of the Old Babylonian Period and Biblical Genealogies," *JAOS* 88 (1968) 163–173; ⟦183–99 in this volume⟧; M. D. Johnson, *The Purpose of the Biblical Genealogies with Special Reference to the Setting of the Genealogies of Jesus* (SNTSMS 8; Cambridge, 1969); F. V. Winnett, "The Arabian Genealogies in the Book of Genesis," *Translating and Understanding the Old Testament* (eds. H. T. Frank and W. L. Reed; Nashville/New York, 1970) 171–196; T. C. Hartman, "Some Thoughts on the Sumerian King List and Genesis 5 and 11b," *JBL* 91 (1972) 25–32; J. M. Miller, "The Descendants of Cain: Notes on Genesis 4," *ZAW* 86 (1974) 164–174; C. Westermann, *Genesis. I. Teilband Genesis 1–11* (BKAT I/1; Neukirchen-Vluyn, 1974) 8–24; R. R. Wilson, "The Old Testament Genealogies in Recent Research," *JBL* 94 (1975) 169–189; ⟦200–223⟧; G. F. Hasel, "The Genealogies of Gen 5 and 11 and Their Alleged Babylonian Background," *AUSS* 16 (1978) 361–374; J. M. Sasson," A Genealogical 'Convention' in Biblical Chronography?" *ZAW* 90 (1978) 171–185; R. R. Robinson, "Literary Functions of the Genealogies of Genesis," *CBQ* 48 (1986) 595–608; D. T. Bryan, "A Reevaluation of Gen 4 and 5 in Light of Recent Studies in Genealogical Fluidity," *ZAW* 99 (1987) 180–188.

the assumption that it is possible to characterize a genre of literature or of communication and to call it genealogy, without sufficient attention to the question of what constitutes a genealogy.[2] The problem with this approach is that it too easily groups ⟦242⟧ together examples from various cultures on the basis of some similarities but tends to ignore the differences which may well be just as important. This is significant because it will be argued here that none of the comparative Ancient Near Eastern examples proposed by scholars actually have a precise parallel with any of the genealogical forms found in Genesis 1–11. Further, it will be argued that the primary functions of the biblical genealogies are significantly different from those found in the Ancient Near Eastern examples. This is not to suggest that useful comparisons cannot be made and inferences drawn concerning the sort of environment in which the biblical genealogies emerged. In fact, the contrasts between the biblical and Ancient Near Eastern texts will provide a means for better understanding the former. It is, however, important to maintain that the differences require any specific conclusions about their value and purpose to be controlled by the contextual data rather than the comparative.[3] Some consideration will also be given to recent comparisons made between Genesis 10 and Greek genealogies. Similar conclusions will be argued for these studies.

Formal Characteristics of the Genealogies of Genesis 1–11

The method used to study genealogies in Genesis 1–11 will examine those texts where proper names are found and kinship relationships are noted between the name bearers. Although any such notice may technically constitute something of a genealogy, the focus will be on notices of kinship relations which occur more than once in a predictable pattern. Such constructions provide the dominant means of expressing genealogical relations and form a basis for comparison with repeated patterns of kinship relations which may be found in Ancient Near Eastern texts.

2. One study on the subject which provides a working definition of the term genealogy is that of R. R. Wilson, *Genealogy and History in the Biblical World* (Yale Near Eastern Researches 7; New Haven/London, 1977) 9: "a written or oral expression of the descent of a person or persons from an ancestor or ancestors." His distinction of segmented genealogies and linear genealogies will be used throughout the essay. Segmented genealogies are those with more than one line of descent, whereas linear ones have only one line of descent. Wilson's work is by far the most thorough and useful analysis of the anthropological and Ancient Near Eastern data presently available. See also Hasel, "The Genealogies of Gen 5 and 11," 368, for a similar definition of a biblical genealogy.

3. See the review of Wilson, *Genealogy*, by W. G. Lambert, *JNES* 39 (1980) 75–77.

Genealogical forms which are repeated occur in Genesis 4, 5, 10, and 11. In each of these chapters there is one form which recurs in a predictable pattern, and each of these four forms is distinct.

In Genesis 4 the only recurrent form is found in v. 18: PN$_1$ יָלַד אֶת-PN$_2$ "And PN$_1$ begot PN$_2$."[4] This form appears three times in a linear genealogy covering four generations. Scholars also find a second (J) genealogy in 4:25–26.[5] However, there is no repetitive form to the Sethite genealogy in 4:25–26. In fact, it records a total of three generations, less than half of any of the other linear genealogies in Genesis 1–11. Further, half of these two verses is taken up with notices which are not genealogical. Finally, the obvious parallel of the first part of v. 25 with that of v. 1 suggests that we have here a ⟦243⟧ notice which brings to an end the record of the immediate offspring of Adam. Therefore, it would seem that, if this is to be understood as a genealogy, it is a segmented one beginning with v. 1 and interrupted by lengthy notes. If this is the case, then one should regard all of Genesis 1–11 as a segmented genealogy. Such may indeed be true. The point here, however, is that 4:25–26 should not be considered as a genealogy in itself but rather as part of a larger genealogy if it is to be studied with reference to its form as a genealogy. This is not true of the genealogy in 4:18 which may stand on its own, with a repeated pattern of a genealogical relationship which does not appear elsewhere.

This example illustrates the problem of identifying the genre of genealogy. Even within the biblical text of Genesis 1–11 there is a great variety in the form of what may be identified as genealogy. For purposes of this discussion it was therefore felt best to limit the consideration of the forms of genealogies to those clearly repetitive patterns which serve as links between generations.

The form in Genesis 5 recurs, with some interruptions and modifications in the narratives of Enoch and Lamech,[6] in vv. 3–31:

וַיְחִי-PN$_1$ x שָׁנָה וַיּוֹלֶד אֶת-PN$_2$
וַיְחִי-PN$_1$ אַחֲרֵי הוֹלִידוֹ אֶת-PN$_2$ y שָׁנָה
וַיּוֹלֶד בָּנִים וּבָנוֹת
וַיִּהְיוּ כָּל־יְמֵי-PN$_1$ x + y שָׁנָה וַיָּמֹת

4. For the relationship of this genealogy with the literary context of Genesis 4, see G. Wallis, "Die Stadt in den Überlieferungen der Genesis," *ZAW* 78 (1966) 133–141. For a suggestion as to its relationship with Genesis 6, see Gabriel, "Die Kainitengenealogie," 422–427.

5. Westermann, *Genesis*, 439; Wilson, *Genealogy*, 138–148.

6. For these modifications as part of the narrative form used to place this genealogy within the context of Genesis 1–11, see T. L. Thompson, *The Origin Tradition of Ancient Israel. I. The Literary Formation of Genesis and Exodus 1–23* (JSOTSup 55; Sheffield, 1987) 74.

And PN_1 lived x years and begot PN_2
And PN_1 lived, after he begot PN_2, y years
And he (PN_1) begot sons and daughters
And all the days of PN_1 were x + y years and he died.

This form appears nine times in a linear genealogy covering ten generations. It is interrupted in the first, seventh, and ninth appearances.

In Genesis 10 a segmented genealogy occurs. There is much variation.[7] However, there is one form which dominates. It appears eight times in vv. 2, 3, 4, 6, 7 (twice), 22, and 23: PNx. . PN_2 PN_1 (וּ)בְנֵי "(And) the sons of PN_1 were PN_2. . PN_x" [where x is the number of descendants plus one]. The conjunctive *waw* is missing between the second and third name of the descendants in the form which appears in v. 4. The initial waw appears in all occurrences of the form except the first (Japheth) and the sixth (Shem). The number of descendants in each form may number anywhere from two to ⟦244⟧ seven. The form is used for each of the three sons of Noah and may or may not be used in the subsequent generation. It is not used for any figure more than two generations removed from Noah.

The form in Genesis 11 recurs without interruption but with a minor variation in vv. 12–15:

וַיְחִי-PN_1 x שָׁנָה וַיּוֹלֶד אֶת-PN_2
וַיְחִי-PN_1 אַחֲרֵי הוֹלִידוֹ אֶת-PN_2 y שָׁנָה
וַיּוֹלֶד בָּנִים וּבָנוֹת

And PN_1 lived x years and begot PN_2
And PN_1 lived, after he begot PN_2, y years
And he (PN_1) begot sons and daughters.

The variation appears in vv. 12 and 14 where the first two occurrences of the form replace the initial verb with the verbal form חַי, and position this after the initial PN_1. This form appears seven times in a linear genealogy covering eight generations. Its similarity with the form in Genesis 5 is obvious, although Genesis 11 omits the final statement totaling the number of years and recording the death of PN_1. It should also be

7. For comments on the overall structure of this chapter, see J. Simons, "The 'Table of Nations' (Gen. X): Its General Structure and Meaning," *Oudtestamentische Studien* 10 (1954) 154–184 ⟦reprinted in this volume, 234–53⟧; D. J. Wiseman, "Genesis 10: Some Archaeological Considerations," *Journal of the Transactions of the Victoria Institute* 87 (1955) 14–24 ⟦reprinted in this volume, 254–65⟧; Westermann, *Genesis*, 665–670; B. Oded, "The Table of Nations (Genesis 10)—A Socio-cultural Approach," *ZAW* 98 (1986) 14–31.

noted that Gen 11:10–11 has a form similar to the one which recurs in vv. 12–25, but there are variations and additions.

With these forms of the biblical genealogies noted, we may now turn to the Ancient Near Eastern genealogies which also have repetitive forms, and observe the similarities and differences.

Genesis 1–11 and Ancient Near Eastern King Lists

Formal Comparisons

Sumerian and Akkadian king lists have provided the major sources for comparative study. Thus the Sumerian King List is often examined.[8] But here there are no regular genealogical notices. Those which do appear are sporadic, and their form tends to use the relational term "son," which does not appear in the forms of the biblical genealogies. The list of the rulers of Lagash adds no new examples to those found in the Sumerian King List.[9] The Assyrian King List[10] texts include sections with a formal statement of a ⟦245⟧ relational nature following each name. The relational term used is always that of "son." That this king list is clearly composed of earlier lists which were separate is demonstrated by the lack of common form except in certain sections of it. The Babylonian King List[11] also seems to be composed of several dynasties, which were contemporaneous historically. Sporadic genealogical notices here as well use only relational terms denoting sonship.

The genealogy of the Hammurabi dynasty is considered to be of special importance.[12] This is because, of all the Sumerian and Akkadian king lists, this list preserves a record of the early rulers in the line which

8. Wilson, *Genealogy*, 73–83. See Hartman, "Some Thoughts, 25–32. Hartman draws additional distinctions between the Sumerian King List and the genealogies of Genesis on the basis of differences in purposes and of the ten-generation genealogical pattern for West Semitic genealogies. For the former, Hartman refers to B. Mazar, "The Historical Background of the Book of Genesis," *JNES* 28 (1969) 73–83. For the latter, see Malamat, "King Lists," 163–173 ⟦183–99 in this volume⟧.

9. T. Jacobsen, *The Sumerian King List* (Oriental Institute of the University of Chicago Assyriological Studies 11; Chicago, 1939); E. Sollberger, "The Rulers of Lagaš," *JCS* 21 (1967) 279–291; Hartman, "Some Thoughts"; Wilson, *Genealogy*, 83–86.

10. I. J. Gelb, "Two Assyrian King Lists," *JNES* 13 (1954) 209–230; B. Landsberger, "Assyrische Königsliste und 'Dunkles Zeitalter,'" *JCS* 8 (1954) 31–45, 47–73, 106–133; Wilson, *Genealogy*, 86–101. See also the discussion of the Old Assyrian king list below under note 23.

11. *ANET*, 271–272; Wilson, *Genealogy*, 101–107.

12. The original publication is that of J. J. Finkelstein, "The Genealogy of the Hammurapi Dynasty," *JCS* 20 (1966) 95–118. See also W. G. Lambert, "Another Look at Hammurabi's Dynasty," *JCS* 22 (1968) 1–2; Malamat, "King Lists," 163–173 ⟦183–99⟧; Wilson, "The Old Testament Genealogies," 173–177, 185–188 ⟦204–7, 218–22⟧; ibid., *Genealogy*, 108–114.

preceded Hammurabi and his Amorite dynasty in Babylon. Because the Amorites are thought to have been related to the West Semitic peoples of whom the Hebrews were one, it is thought to have the closest relation with the Hebrew genealogies of any of the genealogies from these cuneiform sources. The form of this king list involves the listing of names of each of the rulers with no intervening comment, no expression of kinship.[13] Correspondences in the names with the Assyrian King List and with the Babylonian King List confirm that this is a list of kings although there are discrepancies concerning the order and some names are conflated. It is clear from these comparisons that this king list is a composite. The comments which follow the list of names suggest that this text was used in a cultic context and designed for invoking or honoring these royal ancestors of the present ruler.[14]

Wilson has provided a convenient catalog of other Ancient Near Eastern genealogies.[15] These include those royal genealogies found in cuneiform inscriptions. Of these, there are none whose form resembles any found in the biblical examples noted above. They are linear and tend to begin with the latest generation. The relational terms tend to be "son" and "grandson." Non-royal genealogies which are only one or two generations, as well as those priestly genealogies which can be much longer, employ relational formulas which use kinship terms describing sonship or descent. This is true of the short genealogical notices found at Ugarit, of the longer Phoenician and Punic genealogies, and of those kinship notices which can be found in ⟦246⟧ genealogies from Hebrew, Moabite, Aramaic, Egyptian, and Pre-Islamic Arabic sources.

Of additional interest for comparison are the *apkallu*, cultural founders who appear in Mesopotamian tradition.[16] They are associated

13. Wilson, "The Old Testament Genealogies," 185 ⟦218⟧, observes the lack of kinship terms in this text disqualify it from the designation, genealogy, according to his definition.

14. W. G. Lambert, "The Seed of Kingship," *Le palais et la royauté (archéologie et civilisation): XIXe R.A.I. Paris, 21 juin–2 juillet 1971* (ed. P. Garelli; Paris, 1974) 427–440; argues that the Amorites introduced the use of king lists to establish legitimacy to the throne. The third millennium king lists were not used for this purpose. For additional discussion of this ritual, see below.

15. *Genealogy*, 57–72, 114–132.

16. H. Zimmern, "Urkönige und Uroffenbarung," *Die Keilinschriften und das Alte Testament* (ed. E. Schrader; Berlin, ³1903) 530–543; E. Reiner, "The Etiological Myth of the 'Seven Sages,'" *Or* NS 30 (1961) 1–11; R. Borger, "Die Beschwörungsserie *Bīt Mēseri* und die Himmelfahrt Henochs," *JNES* 33 (1974) 183–196 ⟦reprinted in this volume, 224–33⟧; Westermann, *Genesis*, 341–342; Wilson, *Genealogy*, 150–158; J. C. VanderKam, *Enoch and the Growth of an Apocalyptic Tradition* (CBQ Monograph Series 16; Washington, D.C., 1984) 45–51. Various Mesopotamian cities seem to have possessed their own set of seven *apkallu*. See H. and J. Lewy, "The Origin of the Week and the Oldest West Asiatic Calendar," *HUCA* 17 (1942–1943) 40–41.

particularly with kings before the flood. The relationship is such that one *apkallu* is associated with each king.[17] They are not portrayed as genealogically related, either to each other or to the kings with whom they are associated. Thus there is no genealogy of *apkallu*. On the other hand many of the kings in the king lists which are often used for comparison also have no genealogical association. There are seven *apkallu* occupying seven generations before the flood. The genealogy of Gen 4:17–22 also includes seven generations.

Some of the *apkallu* have names which are similar to the kings to whom they correspond in the Sumerian King list. Thus, in the same king list, there are two simultaneous lists, those of the antediluvian kings and those of their corresponding *apkallu*. There is no evidence that both lists derive from the same original list. The two serve different functions and include names that are clearly distinct. Thus it is not satisfactory to assume that Genesis 4 and 5 preserve two variations of the same genealogy simply because some of the names in each of the chapters are similar in their spelling.[18] In fact, it is consistent with the Mesopotamian account to note that two groups of antediluvian figures exist, each with a representative for each generation, and that ⟦247⟧ these groups are understood to preserve the names of different individuals, despite the similarities of names between the groups.[19]

17. These relationships are not attested before the Neo-Assyrian period. For a historical survey of the development of the tradition, see, in addition to the references above, W. W. Hallo, "Antediluvian Cities," *JCS* 20 (1970) 62.

18. This point has also been made by, among others, J. J. Finkelstein, "The Antediluvian Kings: A University of California Tablet," *JCS* 17 (1963) 50, n. 41; Hallo, "Antediluvian Cities," 63; Hartman, "Some Thoughts," 28, n. 10; and Bryan, "A Reevaluation," 180–188. These comparisons must be treated with caution, however. As Finkelstein observes, only three of the seven antediluvian *apkallu* have parts of names which sound like those of the corresponding kings, and only one of these three has a name (Enmegalamma) which sounds like the entire name of the corresponding king (Anmegalanna). Even here the correspondence is not exact. In the Genesis genealogies of chapters 4 and 5, however, all of the six names in the genealogy of chapter 4 correspond to ones in chapter 5 in terms of sounding similar. Of these, two (Enoch and Lamech; Adam too if we count the common ancestor) have names which are spelled exactly alike. Thus the similarities are much greater and include the same spellings, a phenomenon not found with the *apkallu*.

19. It may be useful here to note Wilson's (*Genealogy*, 28–37, 46–55) observations on fluidity, which he finds to be particularly a trait of oral genealogies. Fluidity in genealogies is something which may be controlled by a secret group or, in most societies, the lineage elders, who openly discuss it. They cannot invent their own genealogy but choose one of the existing variants on the basis of what information they can remember, and on the basis of contemporary social relations. Three major types of changes may occur: 1. Change in relationship of the names. 2. Change in structure of the lineage, including the addition of names or segments. 3. Disappearance of names and telescoping. Such fluidity does not occur in the Hebrew biblical text of Genesis 1–11 in a demonstrable way. The argument that

Formal Contrasts

This study has brought out a number of significant distinctions between the form of written genealogies found throughout the Ancient Near East and those found in Genesis 1–11. The first contrast to be made is that segmented genealogies are quite rare, and so nothing on the order of the Table of Nations in Genesis 10 is found for comparison.[20]

The second contrast is that almost all the longer genealogies of the Ancient Near East are concerned with the succession of office holders, usually kings but also priests and scribes. This is in contrast to the lists of Genesis 4, 5, and 11. Political offices or land holdings do not seem to be involved in the genealogies of Genesis 1–11. The one exception may be Genesis 10 where various tribes seem to inhabit specific areas of the world. The degree to which this ⟦248⟧ was used to justify the habitation of these areas is unknown, however. Religious functions do not apply here in so far as they concern individuals or guilds and the genealogies of Genesis 1–11 lead ultimately to tribes and nations. The possibility of an ancestor cult may be suggested by the genealogies but that may be called into question with the observation that as many negative features

Eve and Adam have Cain as their eldest son in Genesis 4 and Seth in Genesis 5 has no basis in any statement in the text. It rests on the assumption that linear genealogies must involve the eldest son—an assumption which cannot be proven for Genesis. Unfortunately, Wilson's preoccupation with putative source critical assumptions in the genealogies of Genesis 4 and 5 has caused him to overlook the implications of this similarity in names and instead to opt for a discussion of fluidity between the lists which allows him to incorporate assumed parallels with his anthropological findings. See also Miller, "The Descendants of Cain," 171–173, who, noting similarities between parts of the Hammurabi and the Assyrian king lists, argues for a "stock genealogy" as the common source of the similar genealogies of the J and P writers in Genesis 4 and 5. The facts that (1) two different sets of similar names have been identified, those of the *apkallu* and the Sumerian King List and those of the Hammurabi and Assyrian king lists, and that (2) each of these similarities reflects a different origin (the former in at least two separate sources; the latter in a single common source) implies the need to exercise reserve in using either approach to demonstrate the origins of the similarities in Genesis 4 and 5. There is something of a fluidity when the names in the MT are compared with those in LXX and other versions as well as in the NT. For example, we see the addition of a name, Kenan, in Genesis 11. For an explanation of this phenomenon as an attempt to reckon Abraham as twenty-first from Adam, see Sasson, "A Genealogical 'Convention,' " 177.

20. This is not true for genealogies in other biblical texts, where segmented examples are common. See A. Malamat, "Tribal Societies: Biblical Genealogies and African Lineage Systems," *Archives européennes de sociologie* 14 (1973) 126–136; T. J. Prewitt, "Kinship Structures and the Genesis Genealogies," *JNES* 40 (1981) 87–98. For the implications of Genesis 10 as unique in terms of its universal outlook, see Hasel, "The Genealogies of Gen 5 and 11," 369–370.

as positive ones are portrayed in the ancestors named in these chapters. In contrast to the Ancient Near Eastern genealogies, those of Genesis 1–11 are uniformly concerned with ancestral lines which involve relationships that are only those of kinship, i.e., of father and son or of father and descendant.[21]

Tied closely with the matter of office is that of status. A purpose of Ancient Near Eastern genealogies, as well as those from other cultures, is to give a certain status to a leader or official. This is not true within Genesis 1–11. There each genealogy seems to end with figures who perform acts which bring about condemnation not status. Thus Genesis 4 ends with Lamech's murders. Genesis 5 ends with the condemnation of humanity in the Flood. Although Noah receives special notice as righteous, even his story terminates in Genesis 9 with the curse of his offspring. Genesis 10 seems to include the ancestry of the entire known world so that the figures here receive no special status in so far as status is some sort of favorable distinction in comparison with other persons. Genesis 11 is unique in that it leads to Genesis 12 and the unqualified promise of blessing to Abram. Yet Genesis portrays Abraham himself as part of a genealogy which consummates in the ancestors of Israel. Thus a nation rather than an individual ultimately receives status by the genealogies.

Third, although some of the king lists include numbers recording lengths of reign and although these numbers are incredibly large, the length of years lived and the age at which the next figure named was begotten "is never recorded in the Ancient Near Eastern king lists. This is in contrast to the biblical genealogies for whom the only purposes in using numbers seems to be that of recording the lifespan of each name bearer and the age at which he begot the next name bearer. However these numbers are to be understood, they play a significantly different role in the two sets of genealogies.[22]

Finally, there is a fundamental difference in the orientation of the genealogies in the Ancient Near East and those in Genesis, particularly chapters 4, 5, and 11. In the former the use of the kinship term "son" in describing the relation between generations (and this is only occasionally used) gives the genealogies an impression of direction that moves

21. For the focus of Genesis upon people, rather than gods and kings, see Westermann, *Genesis*, 11–12. Westermann, 472, also notes this and the remaining differences. See further, Hasel, "The Genealogies of Gen 5 and 11," 365–367. Unlike the present study, which centers around the form of the genealogy, Hasel compares and contrasts the king list-flood-king list sequence of the Sumerian King list with that of Genesis 5–11.

22. This is true despite a common decline in lengths of reign for some of the figures on the Sumerian King List and for the lengths of lifespan in Genesis. See Hartman, "Some Thoughts," 30–31.

from the latest generation ⟦249⟧ to the earliest.[23] In the biblical genealogies of Genesis 4, 5, and 11, no such term as "son" is ever used in the formulas to describe the kinship relations between each generation. It only appears in Genesis 5 and 11 to describe the birth of additional sons and daughters. But the focus in relations between generations is one of the father begetting the son.[24] This means there is a genealogical movement from the earliest ancestor to the latest, the opposite of that of the other genealogies in the Ancient Near East.

Functional Implications

These distinctions reflect different functions in the biblical genealogies as compared with those of the Ancient Near East. The biblical emphasis upon the figures as human beings, with the functions of begetting and eventually dying, suggests that no ancestral cult is to be found here.[25]

23. This impression may exist even where the overall genealogy moves forward in time. For example, the Old Assyrian king list is a composite of several lists, with each list intended as the chronological successor to the previous one. The first list is a group of names with no comment other than "total of 17 kings who dwelled in tents." The second list of names has each name followed by "son of" (DUMU) and the name of the previous king on the list (plus a note as to how many years the figure ruled). Thus the list moves chronologically backwards from the latest king to the earliest. After another list, primarily of names only, the remaining king lists are structured so that (usually) each name is followed by "son of" (DUMU) and the name of the previous king on the list (plus a note as to how many years the figure ruled). Thus the king list moves forward with each new name succeeding the previous ruler. However, the expression "son of PN" has an effect of always pulling the reader back to the previous generation before moving forward. Although "x son of y" may be a customary means of identification here serving to establish a legitimacy to the throne, the cumulative effect of these repetitions is to always push the reader's attention to the earlier generation, even while moving forward in time. For the text and translation, cf. Gelb, "Two Assyrian King Lists," 209–230.

24. Although the verb, "to beget," and the Toledot expressions share a common root, their usages in Genesis have become distinct, with the latter appearing at turning points in the overall story (Scharbert) and implying divine blessing (Weimar). See J. Scharbert, "Der Sinn der Toledot-Formel in der Priesterschrift," *Wort-Gebot-Glaube: Walter Eichrodt zum 80. Geburtstag* (eds. H. J. Stoebe, J. J. Stamm, and E. Jenni; Abhandlungen zur Theologie des Alten und Neuen Testaments 59; Zürich, 1970) 45–56; F. M. Cross, *Canaanite Myth and Hebrew Epic. Essays in the History of the Religion of Israel* (Cambridge, MA, 1973) 302–305; P. Weimar, "Die Toledot-Formel in der priesterschriftlichen Geschichtsdarstellung," *BZ* NF 18 (1974) 65–93; J. Schreiner, "יָלַד *jālad*," *TWAT* III 4/5 (1980) 633–639; S. Tengström, *Die Toledotformel und die literarische Struktur der priesterlichen Erweiterungsschicht im Pentateuch* (Coniectanea Biblica Old Testament Series 17; Uppsala, 1981).

25. This function is tied closely with the two West Semitic king lists which have been discovered from the second millennium B.C., the Hammurabi genealogy already mentioned above and the king list from Ugarit. For the latter, see K. A. Kitchen, "The King List of Ugarit," *UF* 9 (1977) 131–142. On the tablets of both of these lists there appears a ritual which

The absence of ⟦250⟧ any reference to a common office or profession moves these genealogies away from functions involving royal cults or guilds. The movement from earlier to later in the biblical genealogies is one which separates the perceptions which the keepers and readers of these genealogies held of themselves. Is this because the king lists and genealogies of the Ancient Near East directed their readers to seek in the past for the ideal and for the sources of help? Did they find meaning in the present by repeating the past? If so, there is a contrast with the biblical genealogies which saw no ideal among their past members. To the contrary, the narrative notes and sections reveal failure as much or more than they reveal success. So the genealogies push the reader forward in history,[26] recognizing that the past must be learned from, but that the challenges of the present require that former failures not be repeated. Finally, whatever else the Table of Nations in Genesis 10 should emphasize, it is clear from its context in Genesis 1–11 that it points to the common humanity of all peoples, who share in the failures and hopes of a common ancestry, and ultimately in a common creation in the image of God.[27]

It seems in order to conclude with the observations made at the beginning of this essay. In addition to questions which may arise from literary studies in terms of identifying where genealogies may be found in Genesis 1–11 and where they begin and end; there is also the problem of attempting to compare what are primarily Ancient Near Eastern king

---

has been associated with the honoring of the dead kings and with reverencing them as divine. For discussion of the kispu ritual in general as well as its presence in the text from Ugarit, see, in addition to Finkelstein, "The Genealogy," 95–118; Malamat, "King Lists," 163–173 ⟦183–99⟧; Wilson, "The Old Testament Genealogies," 174, 186 ⟦206, 219⟧; ibid., *Genealogy,* 108–114; also W. T. Pitard, "The Ugaritic Funerary Text RS 34.126," *BASOR* 232 (1978) 65–75; J. F. Healey, "The Immortality of the King: Ugarit and the Psalms," *Or* NS 53 (1984) 245–254; ibid., "The Ugaritic Dead: Some Live Issues," *UF* 18 (1986) 272–32; A. Tsukimoto, *Untersuchungen zur Totenpflege* (kispum) *in alten Mesopotamien* (AOAT 216; Kevelaer/Neukirchen-Vluyn, 1985); K. Spronk, *Beatific Afterlife in Ancient Israel and in the Ancient Near East* (AOAT 219; Kevelaer/Neukirchen-Vluyn, 1986) 139–236.

26. For the forward movement of the genealogies as part of their literary function in the context of the narratives of Genesis, see D. J. A. Clines, "Theme in Genesis 1–11," *CBQ* 38 (1976) 491–494 ⟦293–97⟧; M. Fishbane, *Text and Texture: Close Readings of Selected Biblical Texts* (New York, 1979) 27–39; Robinson, "Literary Functions," 595–608. Johnson, *The Purpose of the Biblical Genealogies,* 3–36, discusses the genealogies within the confines of the sources J and P. Does the use of qal and niphal verbal forms of ילד in the genealogy of chapter 4, as opposed to the predominance of hiphil forms in Genesis 5 and 11 (see Gabriel, "Die Kainitengenealogie," 421), reflect a value judgment upon the two genealogies? But see Westermann, *Genesis* 23–24, 465–467, for the relation of this movement to the commission and blessing of Gen 1:28, "Be fruitful and multiply," and for a positive evaluation of Gen 4:17–26.

27. Westermann, *Genesis,* 704–706.

lists with the genealogies. The differences in the form and function of these two collections of texts suggest that attempts to make comparisons proceed with caution and that the context of the texts themselves, within their particular literary and cultural world, be the controlling factor in interpretation. ⟦251⟧

Genesis 1–11 and the Greek Catalogue of Women

Recent publications have drawn attention to formal similarities between the biblical genealogies and a Greek work known as the Catalogue of Women.[28] Although attributed to Hesiod, the critical analysis of M. L. West has found the final redaction to date from the sixth century B.C. with ancient (oral) sources reaching back well before the eighth century B.C. As reconstructed, the Catalogue describes the unions of male deities and mortal women. It traces these lines, with the addition of narrative glosses, as far as the Trojan War at which point events take place which separate the demigod offspring from the mortals. What remains, however, provides the background for the names of cities and regions throughout the Greek-speaking world and beyond.

Although parallels between this material and various parts of Genesis have been noted,[29] the interest of this study lies primarily with Genesis

28. M. L. West, *The Hesiodic Catalogue of Women. Its Nature, Structure, and Origins* (Oxford, 1985) 13; J. Van Seters, "The Primeval Histories of Greece and Israel Compared," *ZAW* 100 (1988) 1–22.

29. Van Seters, "The Primeval Histories," 9–15, on the basis of the similarities with narrative inclusions in the Catalogue and the reference to divine-human unions, argues for a sixth-century J source whose narratives in chapter 6, 9, and 11, as well as much of chapter 10 and a Shem-to-Abram genealogy, were joined with Genesis 12ff. to form a unity. This coherence reflects the unique "Western antiquarian tradition" with its emphasis on the migration and settlement of ancestors who become nations; something not found in Ancient Near Eastern primeval histories (ibid., 19). Two observations may be in order. First, the interdependence of J and P, with J as the primary source and P as editorial comment, which (as van Seters observes) has been argued by Tengström, *Die Toledotformel*, 25–31, requires a reconsideration of the whole process. See also C. Savasta, "Alcune considerazioni sulla lista dei discendenti dei figli de Noè," *RivB* 17 (1969) 89–102, 337–363. Note, however, F. H. Cryer, "The Interrelationships of Gen 5,32; 11,10–11 and the Chronology of the Flood (Gen 6–9)," *Bib* 66 (1985) 241–260. See G. J. Wenham, *Genesis 1–15* (Word Biblical Commentary 1; Waco, TX, 1987) 214–215, who here and elsewhere in Genesis posits J as drawing together an earlier P and other sources. Thus Wenham can argue (as does van Seters) that all of 10:1 belongs to J. Second, the observation on the unique Western tradition of migration and settlement of ancestors who become nations requires qualification. One need go no farther than West's own comparative discussion to find other nations (e.g., Armenian and African, *The Hesiodic Catalogue*, 21, 25–26) whose genealogies include accounts of migration and settlement by ancestors. The practice seems instead to reflect perceived origins of peoples and their ways of life. In the case of Greek traditions, this is associated

10 and the formal similarities observed between it and the Greek Catalogue. Four such similarities have been noted. First, both are segmented.[30] Second, both have an international scope.[31] Third, "both contain genealogies of geographic and ethnic eponyms, the major ancestral line (or lines) of the people as a whole, and the heroic stories, all within a unified genealogical ⟦252⟧ structure."[32] Fourth, numbers, especially threes and sevens, recur in counting brothers, sons, and chiefs.[33]

While important formal similarities appear to be present here, the following observations should be taken into consideration. First, as to genealogical segmentation, it is significant that West's reconstruction demonstrates the existence of several different genealogies with independent starting points or ancestors.[34] Thus these genealogies are not so much segmented as they are separate. This is unlike Genesis 10 which explicitly traces all ancestry back to Noah.

Second, as to the international scope of the Catalogue, it embraces, other than the Greeks, "Egyptians, Phoenicians, Arabs, Scythians, Ethiopians, Libyans, and Pygmies, not to mention various mythical peoples."[35] Dated to the sixth century B.C. and primarily confined to one genealogy (Inachid), the functions of these international notices are: (1) to justify attachments between the Greek communities who lived in these lands and their neighbors; and (2) to trace elements of Greek civilization from the East. In comparison with Genesis 10 it should be observed that the Greek Catalogue is much more restrictive in the number of nations mentioned, in their location, and in their general confinement to one genealogical branch. Genesis 10 includes many more names of peoples and cities. Its geography extends farther south and east, without diminishing reaches to the north and west comparable to the Catalogue. Genesis 10 "scatters" these nations through all branches of its genealogy. So varied is this dispersion that, while some patterns may be observed,[36] enough exceptions remain to call into question attempts to identify a single pattern of distribution. Also, Genesis 10 has not yielded any ethnic group clearly identifiable as mythical. Although there is reason to date many parts of

---

with seafaring. In the case of Israelite traditions, it is grounded (at least partially) in nomadic wanderings on land. In Mesopotamian tradition, it is based in urban culture.

30. West, *The Hesiodic Catalogue*, 13, uses the term "multilinearity."

31. Ibid., 13–15.

32. Van Seters, "The Primeval Histories," 11.

33. West, *The Hesiodic Catalogue*, 27–29.

34. Ibid., 29.

35. Ibid., 131.

36. See Simons, "The 'Table of Nations' "; Wiseman, "Genesis 10"; Oded, "The Table of Nations."

the chapter much earlier, even a sixth century date would not justify a comparable function of serving to attach Jewish communities of the Diaspora to their neighbors. To the contrary, the post-exilic period was one in which the biblical authors identified Judaism through separation rather than integration. Finally, Genesis 10 is concerned primarily with other nations. The line from Shem to Abram is traced only so far as is necessary to include these. Not until Genesis 11 is that genealogical line completed. On the other hand, the Catalogue is concerned almost exclusively with Greek-speaking peoples. Only in a minor way does it mention other nations.

This leads to the third point which is posited as shared by both texts; the unified genealogical structure including eponyms and the major ancestral line of the people. The contrast has already been noted between the Catalogue, which contains separate genealogies unrelated by their origins, and Genesis 10 with its common ancestry in Noah. Also observed has been the lack of a complete ancestral line from Shem to Abram in Genesis 10. To these formal ⟦253⟧ distinctions, a textual observation might be added. Genesis 10 exists as a complete document well attested in manuscripts of the book. The Catalogue does not. The most recent critical edition provides a collection of 245 fragments gathered together in 120 pages with no fragment reaching five pages in length.[37] No complete text is attempted, either in Greek or in transliteration. Thus, despite West's careful and insightful reconstruction,[38] the text is fragmentary, its reconstruction hypothetical, and its gaps numerous.

The fourth point of comparison, appearances of groups of three and seven, also occurs in the genealogies of other peoples, as West has already noted.[39]

Thus the comparisons between the Greek Catalogue of Women and the biblical Table of Nations are not as significant, formally or functionally, as might be supposed. Indeed, given the derivative and composite nature of the Catalogue, its primary focus upon the Greek peoples, and its secondary focus upon narratives and other nations, a better biblical comparison might be made with 1 Chronicles 1–9.

37. R. Merkelbach and M. L. West, eds., *Fragmenta Hesiodea* (Oxford, 1967) 1–120.

38. Including a structural comparison with the later *Bibliotheke* of Apollodorus (*The Hesiodic Catalogue*, 44).

39. Ibid., 28. This confirms the existence of such structuring devices but denies it as something unique in biblical or West Semitic genealogies (see Sasson, "A Genealogical 'Convention' "), perhaps in contrast to the number ten (see Malamat, "King Lists"; Hartman, "Some Thoughts").

* * *

This essay has attempted to demonstrate the distinctions which exist between the genealogies of Genesis 1–11 and the king lists of the Ancient Near East as well as other types of literature which have been compared. While useful comparisons can be drawn between the forms of literature, the fact remains that these basic forms are different and that this difference is reflected in the purposes of the literature; purposes which thrust the lists of generations in two different directions. The king lists consistently suggest a backward movement in time, while the biblical genealogies move forward in time. This would suggest a different purpose for the two forms of literature. This also seems to be the case with the Table of Nations which remains distinct in terms of its breadth of scope.

It may be an oversimplification to see here evidence of a unique view of history and of racial equality at some point in ancient Israel. What is clear is that the comparative study of ancient literature forms only one part of the answer. Even the formal study of the biblical genealogies is not completely adequate. It is at once too broad and too narrow. It is too broad in that it ignores the basic components which form the genealogies, the personal names themselves. It is too narrow in that it fails to examine the narrative context of Genesis 1–11 and how the genealogies fit therein. A full consideration of the significance of these texts requires three additional items: (1) a study of the ⟦254⟧ personal names in terms of their place in the onomastic environment of the Ancient Near East; (2) a study of the purpose which the narrative elements of Genesis 1–11 serve; and (3) a comparison of the relation between the names, the genealogical forms, and the narratives. Broadening the method to include comparative and contextual study of the onomastica as well as the narratives will provide the optimum perspective from which to view the place of the genealogies in Genesis 1–11.

Part 1

Ancient Near Eastern and Comparative Approaches

The Origins of Civilization according to Biblical and Cuneiform Texts

G. CASTELLINO

⟦116⟧ The first chapters of Genesis present numerous problems for the exegete. Some of these can be considered to have been resolved. Others still await a solution, or rather, the solutions that have been proposed for them are not entirely satisfactory.

If we now approach these chapters in the hope of reaching more certain solutions, even after the original and important work of such commentators as H. Gunkel and P. Humbert (citing only two names among those who are authorities), it is in order to follow somewhat newer paths and to use some texts, especially Sumerian texts, that were only made available to the public in the last few years.

In doing this we have no intention of tracing the narratives of Genesis back to purported cuneiform prototypes or of denying the real differences between the two literatures. Our goal is limited to drawing from these texts help in clarifying the vocabulary, structure, and genre of the biblical narratives. Consequently, we will not again compare the biblical world with the Mesopotamian world. Also, although we will deal with some "origins," we will leave aside all comparison between *Enūma eliš* and the first chapter of Genesis, since others have already done that well

Translated and reprinted with permission from "Les Origines de la civilisation selon les textes bibliques et les textes cuneiformes," *Volume du Congrès Strasbourg* 1956 (Supplements to Vetus Testamentum 4; Leiden: Brill, 1957) 116–37. Translation by David W. Baker.

enough. Similarly, the ante- and postdiluvian genealogies will not detain us here. This definition of the subject matter will also have the advantage of allowing us to study the texts with greater ease and to await conclusions that may shed a bit of light on aspects of the texts we are forced to leave aside.

Biblical and Cuneiform Texts

The Texts To Be Examined

(a) ⟦117⟧ *The Genesis texts* that command our attention are the following: most importantly, chaps. 2–3, which make up the core of our study; then chap. 4, concerning the origin of material culture and in particular 4:2–4 and 12, dealing with the beginnings of agriculture and pastoral life (Cain and Abel); in addition, 4:17–22 helps us with the birth of the first city (4:17), nomadic life with tents (4:20), the first endeavors in music (4:21), and the art of the smith (4:22).

(b) *Sumero-Akkadian texts.* As we have mentioned, we are going to study the Genesis chapters with the aid of certain Mesopotamian texts. These can be organized into two series: (1) Sumerian texts that deal with origins. These were published several years ago by S. N. Kramer in his book *Sumerian Mythology* (cited as *SM*),[1] in numerous articles scattered among different journals and publications and finally in a popular volume.[2]

The "Myths of Origins" form the most important part of his book (pp. 30–75), followed by the myths of Kur, and finally some special myths. From among all of these texts we are only considering those that may lend themselves to comparison with the biblical texts, in particular:

1. "Enki and Ninmah" (*SM*, 68–72 and 117 n. 71): creation of humanity;
2. "Lahar and Ašnan" (*SM*, 53–54 and 115 n. 53): gods of livestock and of grain;
3. "The Creation of the Pickax" (*SM*, 51–53 and 114 n. 52): the creation of the pickax, a tool for agricultural work;
4. "Gilgamesh, Enkidu and the Nether World" (*SM*, 30–39 and 113 n. 35);
5. "Enki and Ninhursag" (*SM*, 54–59; BASORSS 1): the myth of "Dilmun," previously (1918) published by S. Langdon with the attractive

1. S. N. Kramer, *Sumerian Mythology* (American Philosophical Society Memoirs 21; Philadelphia, 1944). See also the important critical review by T. Jacobsen in *JNES* 5 (1946) 128–52.

2. S. N. Kramer, *From the Tablets of Sumer* (Indian Hills, Colorado: Falcon's Wing Press, 1956).

title "Sumerian Epic of Paradise, the Flood and the Fall of Man"[3] [[118]];
6. "Enki and Sumer" or "Enki and the World Order" (*SM*, 59–62 and 116 n. 69; *HTR* 49, 55): describes the organization of the land of Sumer and her neighbors;
7. "The Flood" (*SM*, 97–98): the text starts, in the preserved section, with the creation of humanity and the founding of the antediluvian cities;[4]
8. "Enki and Eridu" (*SM*, 62–63 and 116 n. 60);[5]
9. "Marriage of Martu" (*SM*, 98–101; Chiera, *Sumerian Religious Texts*, 15–23).

A second series comprises a small number of Sumerian texts with Akkadian translations, and Assyro-Babylonian texts.

1. KAR (= *Keilinschriften aus Assur religiösen Inhalts*) no. 4: the colophon marks it as a "secret" text; in the first column it contains cryptographic marks that have intrigued Assyriologists who have attempted an explanation. This is the most important text of this series.
2. CT (= *Cuneiform Texts*) XIII 35–37; a long, bilingual introduction to an incantation;
3. CT VI 5, 1–27: a difficult, damaged text concerning the creation of humanity;
4. F. Thureau-Dangin, *Rituels accadiens* (Paris: Ernest Leroux, 1921), 46, 24–40;
5. CT XIII 34 (= DT 41): a small tablet of about a dozen lines concerning creation.[6]

For anyone setting out to examine chaps. 2–3 of Genesis, the first question is: what is the relationship between chap. 2 and chap. 1? In

3. PBS = *Publication of the Babylonian Section* X/1, and translated into French, *Le Poème Sumérien du Paradis, du Déluge et de la Chute de l'Homme* (Paris, 1919).

4. A. Poebel, PBS V/1; transcription and translation in PBS IV/1; translation in S. N. Kramer, *From the Tablets of Sumer*, 177.

5. German translation by A. Falkenstein, in *Sumerische und Akkadische Hymnen und Gebete* (Zurich: Artemis, 1953), no. 31.

6. A recent English translation of the second series, with a bibliography, is found in A. Heidel, *The Babylonian Genesis* (Chicago: University of Chicago Press, 1942); a French translation in E. Dhorme, *Choix de textes religieux assyro-babyloniens* (Paris, 1907); C. Jean, *La Littérature des Babyloniens et des Assyriens* (1924); a German translation is in A. Ungnad, *Die Religion der Babylonier und Assyrer* (1921); H. Gressmann, *Altorientalische Texte* (2d ed., 1926); an Italian translation in a little book by G. Furlani, *Poemetti mitologici babylonesi e assiri* (Florence, 1945). See also J. B. Pritchard, *ANET.*

both there is a creation narrative, of the heavens and the earth, of humanity, of the animals, of the plants, and so on. Yet there are also contrasts and differences that separate the two chapters, putting one narrative in opposition to the other. Exegetes have generally concluded from this that chap. 2 is also a ⟦119⟧ creation account but completely independent from chap. 1 and deriving from the Yahwistic document.

If one compares chaps. 2 and 3, the difficulties and problems appear to multiply. Indeed, one sees in these two chapters repetitions, unevenness of style and content, and even contradictions. In order to resolve these it has been thought necessary to admit the presence of two different sources that were the basis of the two independent narratives, sources that were melded together by a redactor. Thus there is a narrative or "myth" of creation consisting of 2:4b–7, 9a, 15, 18–24 and 3:20; and a narrative or "myth" of Paradise contained in 2:8, 9b, 16, 17, 25; 3:1–19, 21, and 24. This is the division proposed by P. Humbert, but it was already formulated with only very minor differences by H. Gunkel.[7] With Gunkel,[8] P. Humbert considered 2:10–14 to be a scholarly gloss.[9]

Analysis of the Narratives

Now let us look at the texts. The narrative of chap. 2 opens with a temporal indicator: *bĕyôm* 'the day when, when', announcing the circumstances of the creation of the heavens and the earth. It speaks of the condition of the earth—"arid," "without plants and without herbs"—and

7. P. Humbert, *Études sur le récit du Paradis et de la chute dans la Genèse* (Neuchâtel, 1940); H. Gunkel, *Genesis* (1901) 23–24.

8. Ibid., 7.

9. H. Schmidt (*Die Erzählung vom Paradies und Sündenfall*, 1931) had found three different sources. For the entire critical question, see J. Coppens, *La Connaissance du bien et du mal et le Péché du Paradis* (Louvain, 1948) appendix I, "L'analyse littéraire de Genèse II–III: Le Problème des documents ou sources littéraires (pp. 49–72); and my article "Storicità dei capi 2–3 del Genesi," in *Salesianum* (1951) 334–60, in particular pp. 353ff. Gunkel recognized a difference in style between chap. 2 and 3. In chap. 3, he thought, one has a connected, compact narrative that forms a very distinct unit; in chap. 2, on the other hand, he saw different themes, almost without interrelationship, concerning: (1) the primordial condition of the earth and the water; (2) the creation of humanity; (3) [the plants]; (4) animals and the woman. Then, in chap. 2 he notices some *Unzuträglichkeiten*, some incompatibilities: the announcement of the creation of the herbs and plants in 2:5, but in 2:9a only the plants are created. According to 2:5, the earth's fecundity depends on the rain, whereas according to 2:6 it derives from the presence of the *ʾēd* ⟦'spring'⟧. According to 2:5 again, humanity was created to cultivate the fields, but according to 3:23 it is only after he has been expelled from Paradise that he begins to cultivate the "field." Finally, from the context of chap. 2 one concludes that all of the animals are found in the "garden," and it is not said anywhere that they were driven out with man. Their presence in the real world thus rests on air!

gives the reason for the aridity: "God had not yet brought rain upon the earth." Here a new person, agricultural man, enters the scene ⟦120⟧, but only in order to indicate the absence of agriculture. Then, in complete contrast to the primordial aridity, a "spring" (?) that irrigates the entire surface of the earth is introduced. There follows the creation of humanity in great detail.

Two remarks should be made on these three and one-half verses (4b–7): (1) the complexity of the arrangement of the phrases (it appears that all of this only makes up one period; we will return to it after having studied the exegesis of the parts); (2) at the center, the presence of the *ʾēd*, which irrigates *all* of the surface of the earth, in contrast with the original aridity. The commentators have noted this contrast, but they have not fully appreciated it. Some have thought to explain it by distinguishing three different periods: the primordial aridity; then the irrigation by the *ʾēd*, still without Yahweh; and finally the creation of humanity.[10]

However, while the contrast is indeed real, one must not seek the solution in a distinction between time periods, but rather in a distinction between geographical regions! It is the author who bids us do so.

The section contains three different terms with geographical-spatial value: (1) above all we have the *ʾereṣ* 'earth', which, in opposition to the *šāmayim* 'heavens', has a very general significance, "all the surface of the earth"; (2) then follows the *śādeh* 'field', a specification of the earth that properly designates the uncultivated land, unworked but able nevertheless to produce herbs and plants spontaneously when rain unexpectedly falls; in a word, "the steppe"; (3) third comes the *ʾădāmâ* 'ground', which is specifically the part of the earth that is the province of humanity (*ʾādām*), who cultivates and works it. This is the significance of the word in our context. Although watered by the *ʾēd*, the *ʾădāmâ* 'soil' does not produce crops because humanity is not there to make use of the presence of the water. To clarify this, imagine the conditions in Mesopotamia, especially the southern part. Verse 6a is tied to that which precedes it. The initial *waw* must therefore be translated as the concessive 'although'.

⟦121⟧ The two scenes can, therefore, exist side by side. On the one side is the whole earth, without vegetation for lack of rain. (In Mesopotamia and Arabia, in the spring and autumn, the rain makes the desert flower.) On the other side is the *ʾădāmâ* 'soil', humanity's realm, also

10. Gunkel, *Genesis*, 5: "Ursprünglich war die Erde trocken, dann, noch unabhängig von Jahve, ward das Land durch einen *ʾēd* getränkt; jetzt erst tritt Jahve auf und schaft seine Geschöpfe aus feuchter Erde." ⟦'Originally the earth was dry, then, still independently of Yahweh, the earth was watered by an *ʾēd*; then Yahweh first appeared and created his creatures out of moist earth'.⟧

sterile notwithstanding the presence of water. It is sterile because the human (*ʾādām*) is not there to regulate the canals and irrigation, thus making the *ʾădāmâ* 'ground' fertile.[11] Consequently, *śādeh* 'field' and *ʾădāmâ* express the same opposition as "the desert and the sown." This opposition results quite clearly from Gen 4:2–3, 12. Cain cultivates the *ʾădāmâ*, and after the crime of fratricide, he is expelled from the *ʾădāmâ* into the *ʾereṣ* 'earth' (4:12). If he cultivates it, it will not provide him crops and he will be "a wanderer and a fugitive on the earth (*bāʾāreṣ*)." In contrast, in 2:6, although *ʾereṣ* 'earth' and *ʾădāmâ* 'soil' are found side by side, the same opposition does not exist. Here *ʾereṣ* simply signifies 'soil': the *ʾēd* would arise from the soil and water the entire surface of the *ʾădāmâ*.[12]

The geographical distinctions that we have just proposed also correspond to the cuneiform texts. To the biblical *ʾereṣ* 'earth' correspond the Akkadian *erṣetu* and the Sumerian ki.[13] The Hebrew *ʾădāmâ* finds its correspondence in the Sumerian kalam 'cultivated and fertile land' and the Akkadian *mātu*.[14] Living beings (zi.sa.gal) are found in the kalam.[15] The same opposition between ki=*erṣetu* and kalam=*mātu* is found in KAR 4.1ff., 24, rev. 7. Just as *ʾădāmâ* may signify 'land' or 'nation', so also may kalam and *mātu*. The Hebrew *śādeh*, on the other hand, translates Sumerian edin and Akkadian *ṣēru*, about which we will speak in a moment.

It is common knowledge that the term *ʾēd* is found in Job 36:27, where it signifies 'cloud' or 'mist'. The context of Genesis 2 does not favor this meaning, and so scholars have drawn a parallel with the Akkadian *edû* 'high water' and the Sumerian id 'canal, stream, river'. W. F. Albright took a stand for the Sumerian id,[16] but more recently E. A. Speiser[17] entered into the debate in favor of the Akkadian *edû*. But perhaps the arguments in favor ⟦122⟧ of a Sumerian derivation have not been entirely exhausted. From the point of view of phonetics, *ʾēd* can more easily come from id than from *edû* (which Speiser also admits). Philologically, id appears very often in Sumerian myths of origins.[18]

11. This is the situation described for us in KAR 4.5ff.; 34ff.; rev. 6ff.

12. For *ʾereṣ* as 'soil', see Gen 1:26, 30; 18:2; 33:3; Exod 4:3; 1 Sam 4:5; 17:49 (Goliath, struck on the forehead by David's pebble, falls *ʾorṣâ*), etc.

13. See the beginning of the following texts: "Gilgamesh, Enkidu and the Nether World," lines 7–12; "The Creation of the Pickax," 4–5; KAR 4.1–4; CT XIII 34.11.

14. For kalam, see "Lahar and Ašnan," 56–57.

15. Ibid., 54.

16. W. F. Albright, *JBL* 58 (1939) 102–3 n. 25.

17. E. A. Speiser, *BASOR* 140 (1935) 9–11.

18. See, for example, "Dilmun," 33–35, 45ff.; "Enlil and Ninlil," 4–5, etc.

In the Paradise section (2:8–17), the style becomes ordinary narrative. Only two points concerning Paradise merit our attention. The first is the value of the terms *gan* 'garden' and *ᶜēden* 'Eden'. The word *ᶜēden* has been identified etymologically with Sumerian e d i n, entering into Akkadian as *edenu* and corresponding to *ṣēru* 'open country, steppe'. The Sumerian term has recently been explained by the Sumerologist Thorkild Jacobsen of the Oriental Institute of Chicago. Apart from the ordinary meaning 'desert, steppe', e d i n indicates the region between the Tigris and Euphrates, just as the Arabic term *gezirah* does today. "It was the pasturing ground of the Sumerian shepherds—as it is of the shepherds of today—and all the chief centers of the shepherd-god Dumuzi, Zabalam, Umma, Bad-tibira, and Uruk, lie clustered in a half circle around it. The cultivated area on its southeastern edge toward Telloh was called from ancient times the 'border of Edin' (G ú - e d i n - n a) and its higher-lying northern part, the 'high Edin' (A n - e d i n) was, as we know, near Bseikh (Zabalam)."[19]

The term *ᶜēden* is therefore a specification of the *ᵓădāmâ* 'ground'. As one represents a delimitation of the earth as a region of humanity's natural province, so the *ᶜēden* is a part of the *ᵓădāmâ.*[20] The other term *gan* 'garden' is a part of the *ᶜēden.* Etymologically it is again the Sumerian g a n, passed to Akkadian (*ganū*) *gannat* (and also to Arabic *ǧannat* and Ethiopic *gannat*). It is a term that has traveled, since the *Etymology M* (223:45) has: γάνος . . . ὑπὸ δὲ κυπρίων παράδεισος ⟦' "ganos" from the Cypriot for garden'⟧.[21] There we have the specific value of the term in Genesis, in contrast to Sumerian, where the term signifies 'field'. For the idea 'garden', Sumerian has k i r i$_6$ (GIŠ.ŠAR), properly a garden with trees, which one finds in the myth "Gilgamesh, Enkidu and the Nether World."[22] ⟦123⟧ Thus the sacred scribe gradually delimited the space in which the principal drama was to be enacted. From the *earth,* which embraced the entire horizon, he passed on to the *ᵓădāmâ,* then to the *plain* (the *ᶜēden*), to finish at the *gan* destined for humanity. That the garden should be planted with trees was only logical for the Mesopotamian world.[23]

19. T. Jacobsen, *Archaeology* 7 (1954) 54 B. In CT XV 27.21–23 the 'high edin' and the 'low edin' are mentioned together.

20. See also H. Zimmern, *Akkadische Fremdwörter,* 43. In the OT, it is derived from the root *ᶜdn* 'delight' (LXX: *paradeisos tēs truphēs*).

21. See ibid., 40.

22. Line 34. See also CT XIII 35.29 [k i r i$_6$ ^{giš}]t i r = *ki-ra-tu u qi-ša-tu* 'garden and trees'.

23. In Ezek 31:8ff., the "western" nature of the trees—cedar, cypress, plane-tree—corresponds to the "western" development of the conception of Paradise. See in this regard the previously cited article: "Storicità," 356–57.

The last element to characterize the 'garden' is the statement about the four rivers. From the slightly more concise style of the narration and from conclusions incorrectly drawn from the context (mention of the sources[?] of the Tigris and Euphrates; the double use of *nahar* 'river' in 2:10 and *ʾēd* 'spring?, river?' in 2:6), H. Gunkel, among others, deduced that the whole section 10–14 is to be considered "ein alter Zusatz," an ancient addition.[24]

The geographical horizon of the narrative, which had narrowed itself down from the 'earth' to the *gan* 'garden', is reextended with the mention of the four rivers, and now covers some regions far removed from Mesopotamia: Havila and Cush (commonly understood as Ethiopia). In the face of the geographical importance and the riches of the regions touched by the Pishon and the Gihon, the Tigris and the Euphrates have an almost puny appearance. From a stylistic point of view, the geographical precision or instructional elements that the author provides for the four rivers makes the text so ponderous that the equilibrium of the construction, impeccable up to this point, is suddenly destroyed. But the unified geographical horizon and the structural equilibrium are immediately restored if one omits the explanations concerning the names of the rivers that cause the overload. One should attribute the additions to the western development of the Paradise idea. We shall return to this subject below.

However, the *nāhār* 'river' of v. 10 should not be passed over in silence. How could one think of a garden without water? In the Dilmun myth it is expressly stated that, in spite of the abundance of water, there is a lack of sweet water, and this causes a persistent craving.[25] The *nāhār* is not a useless repetition of the *ʾēd* of 2:6. The *ʾēd* corresponds to the *ʾădāmāh,* and the *nāhār* is for the *gan,* reflecting two distinct entities. Thus, we do not need to position the garden at the ⟦124⟧ northern sources of the Tigris and Euphrates. The geography of the myths is not scientific geography, not even that of the Sumerians. The remaining two rivers, the Pishon and Gihon, which have no credible identification in the Mesopotamian myths, must be considered as western elements added to the narrative.[26]

The Man and the Woman

Let us now investigate the ways that the man and the woman are introduced into this "scenario." The man is first mentioned in v. 5d of the

24. Gunkel, *Genesis,* 7.
25. Lines 45ff. See also my thoughts in "Storicità," 354.
26. See ibid., 354, 356–57.

second chapter in order to note his absence. The question immediately arises: is he tied to that which precedes, and should his absence be considered a second cause for the earth's barrenness? This supposition seems to be demanded by the distinction that could be made between *śîaḥ* 'undergrowth', every plant that grows wild, and *ᶜēśeb*, which could well be grasses and plants resulting from man's cultivation.[27] The rain would cause the underbrush to grow, while the labor of man would be responsible for the plants and herbs. This proposal, although justifiable from the point of view of vocabulary, should be abandoned. In fact, the author gives to *śîaḥ* 'undergrowth' as much as to *ᶜēśeb* 'grass' the specification of *śādeh* 'field', which is really the steppe, where man's labor does not intervene.

Consequently we are led to link the mention of the man with that which follows, the *ᵓēd* 'spring?'. Having thus brought out the need for the man to regulate the canals and to make the *ᵓădāmâ* 'ground' fertile, the author with vigorous, essential strokes presents us with the creation of humanity from the mud of the earth (*ᵓădāmâ*) and his vital inspiration by Yahweh. After the preparation of the garden, man is transported to it and receives the double charge to guard and cultivate it.

Now comes the woman's turn. She is to be the drama's principal character and is therefore introduced with solemnity. As with the creation of the man, hers is preceded by deliberation and is ⟦125⟧ demanded by Adam's failure to find a correspondent worthy of him after the analysis of the nature (*šēm* 'name') of each animal and bird. Drawing attention to what is nonexistent requires the production and creation that follows. This is also the process in the Mesopotamian texts cited below.

Although the animals do not meet the needs of the man, their failure justifies and requires a new creation, the woman.[28] Therefore, the creation of the man, his transfer to the garden, the creation of the animals

27. See Exod 9:25; 10:15; Amos 7:2; etc., often with *pĕrî* 'fruit'.

28. Leaving aside the "speculations" that the late Prof. S. Langdon proposed in his interpretation of the myth of Dilmun but that have fallen under their own weight by the simple progress of science, in regard to the creation of Eve, it is sufficient to mention here the following analogies: (1) the correspondence of the spring that must water Dilmun with the *ᵓēd* of 2:6, which we treated above; (2) the double correspondence of Eve's being taken from a rib and being called "mother of living things" with the goddess Nin-ti's being called "goddess of the rib" and "goddess who causes to live." The Sumerian ti means at the same time 'rib' and 'life', 'to live' in the causative, 'to make live'. The first to point out this comparison seems to have been P. Scheil (*Comptes Rendus* [1915] 534ff.). Then it was taken up by many others. We cite only C. J. Gadd (*Ideas of Divine Rule in the Ancient East* [Schweich Lectures, 1945; London, 1948] 4 [5]), who emphasized several new details, and Kramer (*From the Tablets of Sumer*, chap. 17, 169–75).

and of woman, and the drama of the Fall are tied together and constitute the different parts of a whole that holds together very well.[29]

Grammatical Structure of 2:4b–7

Before addressing the more general question of literary genre, it remains for us to study the arrangement of the phrases at the beginning of the narrative (2:4b–7) in order to grasp the grammatical structure. Even an expert such as U. Cassuto thought that, taking all of the passage as one complete sentence, "one makes of it something grossly complicated, completely foreign to the genius of the Hebrew language and without comparison. The initial formulae of the Babylonian cosmologies, with their long enumerations of things which as yet did not exist, are very distant from such a complicated syntax."[30]

Is this really so? One needs only to arrange the passage in stichs to grasp the interrelationships of the phrases and the organic character of the whole ⟦126⟧:

Protasis

	1. time:	*<u>bĕyôm</u> ʿăśôt* Yhwh *E. ʾereṣ wĕšāmayim*
a.	2. condition:	*wĕkōl śîaḥ haśśādeh ṭerem yihyeh bāʾāreṣ*
(*ʾereṣ*)	(negative)	*wĕkol ʿēśeb haśśādeh ṭerem yiṣmāḥ*
	3. explanation:	*kî lōʾ himṭîr* Yhwh *E. ʿal hāʾāreṣ*
b.	1. explanation:	*wĕʾādām ʾayin laʿăbōd ʾet hāʾădāmâ*
(*ʾădāmâ*)	2. condition:	*wĕʾēd yaʿăleh min-hāʾāreṣ*
	(positive)	*wĕhišqâ ʾet kol pĕnê hāʾădāmâ*

Apodosis:

	3. first	*wayy îṣer* Yhwh *E. ʾet hāʾādām*
c.	creation	*ʿāpār min hāʾădāmâ*
(*ʾādām*)		*wayyippaḥ bĕʾappāw nišmat ḥayyîm*
		wayĕhî hāʾādām lĕnepeš ḥayyâ

In this collection, 4b–5abc forms the first scene; *wĕ . . . ṭerem* ⟦'but . . . not yet'⟧ of 5a and 5b tie the phrases to 4b; and the *kî* of 5c gives the explanation of 5ab. Verses 5d and 6ab form the second scene, grammatically tied to the first by the initial *waw* of 5d, *wĕʾādām* ⟦'and humanity'⟧; and 6a is tied to 5d by a concessive *waw* 'although'. We therefore reach the principal proposition of 7a: *wayyîṣer* ⟦'and he created'⟧ . . . , continued by two clauses introduced by the *waw* as follows: "*and* he breathed

29. For the division and the arrangement of the different parts, see Castellino, "Storicità," 356.

30. U. Cassuto, *La question e della Genesi* (1934) 270–71.

out . . . ; *and* the man was [became] a living being." Verse 4b is therefore a protasis that is subordinate to a principal verb, the *wayyîṣer* of 7a. One notes that along with the threefold division of the three scenes there is also a threefold structure of the phrases. Again, the mention of the man ties together the second and third scenes.

Everyone acknowledges that the sentence is overloaded and that it is not an ordinary Hebrew construction. But it is not, on the other hand, without parallel. We have another like it at the beginning of chap. 5.[31] In the extrabiblical ⟦127⟧ texts one can note that the opening of *Enūma eliš* is also quite complicated, compared to the ordinary construction in the rest of the poem. This is one of the stylistic laws of ancient Semitic languages. It is necessary to capture the attention of the reader and to alert him to the importance of what one desires to present by means of a solemn and extraordinary opening.[32]

This goal is attained by means of special grammatical constructions. In Hebrew the protasis is introduced by *bĕyôm* ⟦'when'⟧ followed by an infinitive construct, and the apodosis, or the principal clause, is picked up by the initial *waw*, the *waw* of the apodosis:[33] *wayyiṣer* . . . 'then [Yahweh] formed. . . .' In Akkadian this construction ordinarily corresponds to *enūma* 'when, on the day when' at the start, and then *-ma* as a verbal suffix in the principal clause:

31. *bĕyôm bĕrōʾ ʾĕlōhîm ʾādām*
bidmût ʾĕlōhîm ʿāśâ ʾōtô
zākār ûnĕqēbâ bĕrāʾām
wāyĕbārek ʾōtām
wayyiqrāʾ ʾet šĕmām ʾādām
bĕyôm hibbārĕʾām (Gen 5:1b–3)

Here also a protasis opens the pericope, being of the same type as that found in 2:4b: *bĕyôm bĕrōʾ ʾĕlōhîm ʾādām* ⟦'when God created humanity'⟧, to compare with *bĕyôm ʿăśôt* YHWH *E. ʾereṣ wĕšāmāyim* ⟦'when Yahweh God made earth and sky'⟧. That is to say, the statement has four elements: a temporal description, infinitive construct, subject, and complement. The first statement is followed by two others, which form a triptych in which the verb *ʿśh* ⟦'make'⟧ alternates with *brʾ* ⟦'create'⟧. We note in passing that this is the same alternation as that between *banû* ⟦'build'⟧ and *epēšu* ⟦'do'⟧ in the Akkadian texts, or further, between dù and dím of the Sumerian texts. For these two word pairs, see CT XIII 35–37.1ff. Then follows yet another triptych, of which two stichs introduced by *waw* form two statements, coordinated and closed in their turn by a third, which recalls the first stich by the verb and the construction.

32. For the New Testament, one should remember the opening of the Gospel of St. Luke and that of the Epistle to the Hebrews, with the classical parallels that one usually cites in order to explain the figures and the balanced phrases.

33. Concerning the *waw* of the apodosis, see P. Joüon, *Grammaire de l'hébreu biblique*, §176, 529ff.

enūma eliš la nabû šamāmu . . .
⟦'when above the heavens were not named'⟧
. . . .
ibbanûma ilû qerebšun.
⟦'then the gods were formed within them'.⟧

Here *-ma* comes after 9 lines! The same construction occurs in DT 41.1–9 (= CT XIII 34); the *-ma* on the apodosis is missing in *Rituels accadiens* 46.24ff., but the text is not completely preserved.

There are many different constructions in Sumerian. Very often the phrase is contained in a temporal clause marked by u_4 'the day when, when' at the start, and the suffix -a of the relative at the end. The main clause, in its turn, is introduced by u_4.ba (or u_4.bi) 'on that day, then', which picks up the u_4 of the protasis. This is the pattern that most closely resembles that of the Akkadian and the Hebrew. One also has the protasis with u_4 at the beginning and -a at the end. For example, the myth of "Lahar and Ašnan" begins thus

ḫur.sag an.ki.bi.da.ke_4
u_4 an.ne ^{d}a.nun.na im.tu.dè.eš.a.ba

After which, on the mountain of the Heaven and the Earth,
An begat the Anunnaki . . .

There follows a long series of negative clauses (lines 3–31), closed ⟦128⟧ by the main clause introduced by u_4.ba . . . (line 25) and taken up again a few lines later by another verbal clause. The negative clauses serve to underscore the nonexistence of the different things that will be created later on, in order to make their necessity evident. The same negative schema occurs in Prov 8:22ff. and 4 Esdr 6:1ff. Instead of negative clauses, there are at times affirmative clauses that aim to describe a factual situation that prepares for or anticipates the development of the action.

Organization versus Creation

The Literary Genre

We now possess all of the elements necessary to proceed from a higher and more general point of view to an analysis of the literary genre of the narratives that have been the object of our scrutiny to this point. These Sumerian myths can be divided into two categories: myths of "organization" and myths of "action." The first have as their goal a description of the times and of the means by which culture was introduced; in other words, the organization of social life in cities, including humanity's common occupations: trades, agriculture, and cattle breeding. The others aim to narrate events that have deities for actors and that assume a determinative importance in the origin of a city or a region. The two categories have this in common: the texts almost invariably start with an introduction that follows one or the other of the following patterns.

1. In a series of positive clauses, the author describes or announces the creation that interests him. The narrative is fixed in a temporal framework, the form of which we have presented above: "when . . . then" or "after which . . . then" (u_4.a.ba . . . ; u_4.ba). This is the simplest form. See, for example, the introduction to the hymn to the temple É-engurra ("Enki and Eridu").
2. A second form of introduction is made up of three motifs: (a) a temporal indicator, by which the author refers to the origin of things (the same pattern as the first form); (b) a series of negative clauses that enumerate the things that do not as yet exist; (c) finally, there appears a positive element, or new creation (see the myth "Lahar and Ašnan").
3. The third form of introduction opens with an array of negative and positive clauses, putting the things that existed at ⟦129⟧ the outset in opposition to that which did not exist. This is the case with the introduction of the text concerning the "Marriage of Marduk."

These introductions are of interest because of their parallels with the Genesis narratives. The later bilingual or Babylonian texts of creation or organization also merit our attention.

If introductions of the first type lend themselves chiefly to comparisons of style or literary genre, introductions of the second type offer the most points of contact regarding style and content with the Genesis texts.[34]

The myths of "organization" continue and develop the content of the introduction in the main body of the myth. In the myths of "action," on the other hand, the introduction can give the impression of an *hors d'oeuvre,* having no tie with what follows. An introduction forms an integral part of any myth. As we ascertain the types of myths, it can help us to identify the style or literary genre of each myth.

In Genesis 2–3 we have an introduction similar to introductions in Babylonian myths. Genesis 2 can, in effect, correspond to the introduction

34. For a synthetic survey of the cosmogonic ideas of the Sumerians, see Kramer, *From the Tablets of Sumer,* chap. 12, 71–96.

and Genesis 3 to the body, or the "action." Though the analogy between the "action" of Genesis 3 (the Fall) and the "action" of the myths is completely external and purely formal, one cannot say the same thing concerning Genesis 2. Here the analogies are more direct and lend themselves to comparison. This analogy between the construction of Genesis 2–3 and that of the Sumerian texts allows us to draw a conclusion. This structural relationship between Genesis 2 and 3 means that one should not assume that the two chapters have their origins in independent sources.

A second observation bears on the beginning of the myths of creation and of action. Mention of the creation of heaven and earth is among the formulas that reappear in the opening of several other texts. For example, the myth of "Gilgamesh, Enkidu and the Nether World," after several fragmentary lines, continues as follows ⟦130⟧:

> After the Heaven had been separated from the Earth,
> the Earth had been delimited by the Heaven,
> the name of humanity had been established;
> after An had carried away the Heaven,
> after Enlil had carried away the Earth,
> and (the Earth) had been given as a gift to Ereškigal in the underworld . . . [35]

Likewise, in the myth of "The Creation of the Pickax":

> The lord had really produced that which was fitting (for government)
> the lord whose decisions cannot be altered,
> Enlil, in order to bring out from the ground the seed of mankind,
> was truly eager to separate the Heaven from the Earth,
> was truly eager to separate the Earth from the Heaven,
> in order that the "producer of the flesh" could impel the origin (of humanity),
> and he bound for it (the Earth) the "bond of the Heaven
> and the Earth", the hole (made by the pickax).[36]

The same construction and idea is found in KAR 4.1ff.:

35. Note, for lines 4–6, the Sumerian construction: u_4 An.né an ba.an.túm.a.ba / ^{d}en.líl.le ki ba.an.túm.a.ba / ^{d}ereš.ki.gál.la.ra kur.ra sag.rig$_7$.ga.šè im.ma.ab.rig$_7$.ga.a.ba.

36. For this translation, see Jacobsen, *JNES* 5 (1946) 137.

After the Heaven was separated from the Earth, the two
    faithful twins far away,
the mother of the goddesses was produced,
after the Earth was founded, the Earth was fashioned. . . .

Finally we will cite two additional Akkadian texts:

When the gods in their assembly created [everything]
made the firmament exist, and tie[d together the solid
    Earth] . . . (CT XIII 34).

When Anu created the Heaven,
when Nudimmud created the abyss (of the waters), his
    habitation,
Ea took in the abyss a pinch of clay
and created Kulla for the restoration [of the temples]
    (*Rituels accadiens*, 46 24ff.).[37]

All of these texts, having begun with the origin of heaven and the earth, omit further mention of heaven and concentrate exclusively on the earth. The author's intent is not to focus on the creation of the world, but ⟦131⟧ to take this as a point of departure. Its purpose is to introduce the organization of the earth. Consequently we call these texts narratives of "organization" rather than "creation."

In Genesis 2, the creation of the heavens and the earth is followed by a description, in negative terms, of the primordial situation. Comparison with Sumerian texts permits us to see a literary process here. In the myth "Lahar and Ašnan," the negative description carries on for about 20 lines and includes domesticated animals, different types of wheat, and vegetation in general. The myth of "Dilmun" also, after having outlined the condition of the region, passes (in lines 13–30) to a long enumeration of things that were absent. However, the analogy with Genesis 2 is here purely formal, the content being completely distinct.

The introduction to the incantation in CT XIII 35ff. also reveals, by use of negative terms, that at that time there did not yet exist any temples of the gods, construction material, reeds and bricks, houses and cities (lines 1–9). The author concludes the enumeration by declaring that all areas were water and that at the center there was a stream of water.

37. Note the grammatical structure of the two texts:
    <u>*enūma*</u> *ilāni ina puḫrišunu ibnū* [*kullatum*]
    <u>*enūma*</u> ^{d}*Anu ibnū šamē* . . .

Order and Object of Creation

In the positive parts of the introduction, one generally comes upon the following items: (1) vegetation and rivers, (2) animals, (3) cities, and (4) humanity. The order of the creation or appearance of the different classes is not fixed. Thus the myth "Lahar and Ašnan" has the animals created after humanity. The same thing happens in the story of the Flood.[38] Here it is humanity who ought to take an interest in augmenting and increasing the domestic animals and the birds. Just the opposite happens in the little Akkadian creation text, CT XIII 34ff.: the animals are made before humanity. The creation of humanity almost always serves as either the final event or as the climax to the story.

The Sumerians and the Babylonians had neither unique doctrine nor coherent traditions concerning the modality of the creation of humanity. Sometimes humanity's creation is announced with general expressions. Thus, the text of "Gilgamesh, Enkidu and the Nether World" restricts itself to saying: "After . . . the name of mankind was established" (mu nam.lú.lu$_6$ ba.gar.ra.ba, line 9). Likewise, "Lahar ⟦132⟧ and Ašnan": "then (in that day) humanity came into existence" (u$_4$.ba nam.lú.lu$_6$ in.ši.íb.gál, line 35). An original concept (although not without analogy elsewhere) is that man sprouts from the earth like a plant—one could say a kind of "hologenesis." We encounter it in the brief introduction to the hymn on the temple É-engurra:

> When (or "after") the destiny of all created things was established
> (when) in a bountiful year which An produced,
> humanity, like the plant, pushed through the cracks of the earth . . .
>
> a.ri.a nam.ba.tar.ra.ba
> mu.ḫé.gál an ù.tu.da
> ukù.e [ú]šim.gin ki in.dar.ra.ba. . . .[39]

The same concept reappears in the myth of the "Creation of the Pickax." In line 3 there is the announcement that the human "seed" must sprout from the earth, and further on (line 17ff.) we are given the

38. PBS V 1.15′; CT XIII 35ff., 22, 27ff.; KAR 4 rev. 13ff.

39. By reading line 2, mu.ḫé.gal ana ù.tu.da, one can translate, 'in a year of abundance produced by An', as Jacobsen did (*JNES* 5 [1946] 136). Outside of Mesopotamia, compare the birth of Gayōmart 'from the earth', like the plant. (Cf. Sven Hartman, *Gayōmart* [Uppsala, 1953] 40, and the sources cited by him there. According to one document, Gayōmart and his wife 'resembled [even materially] the plant'.)

details: the god Enlil thrusts the pickax into the uzu.è and from the hole so formed, the firstfruits of humanity come to light while going up toward Enlil. The uzu.è (literally 'the place from which the flesh comes out') is to be associated with the uzu.mú.a ('the place where the flesh sprouts or increases'), of which the text KAR 4.24 speaks. This locates it in Dur.an.ki, the sacred quarter of Nippur. The text that we have just cited provides us yet another view of the origin of humanity. Mankind is made from the blood of the two Lamga gods (KAR 4 25–26). This is the idea in *Enūma eliš* VI.

Finally, a third tradition, much more compatible with that of Genesis, has mankind fashioned by a goddess (or a god) from some clay. One could cite first of all the myth "Enki and Ninmah," which expressly deals with the creation of humanity.[40] Compare also the legend of "Ea and Atrahasis" (col. IV) and the "Gilgamesh epic" (I 30, 33–35) in the same sense.

⟦133⟧ In the *šiptu*, or incantation, of CT XIII 35ff., 20ff., it is Marduk, aided by the goddess Aruru (the goddess of creation), who fashions humanity.[41] The two traditions of "blood" and "clay" are united in the text CT VI 5.22–27: a god must be sacrificed and then from his sinews, his blood, and some clay, humanity is fashioned.

According to the narrative of Genesis, mankind is destined to cultivate the *ʾădāmâ* ⟦'soil'⟧ (2:5) or the garden (2:15). This same purpose is assigned the creation of man in the Sumerian and Babylonian texts. At first glance this purpose seems contradictory, or at least different from the purpose that is assigned to humanity in *Enūma eliš*, that is, to serve the gods. In reality, serving the gods constitutes the ultimate purpose. Agriculture, breeding, and procuring abundance are the intermediate purposes, which are justifiable only in light of the final goal.[42]

It is here that one notices one of the really vivid differences between Genesis and the Sumero-Babylonian myths. The spiritual and monotheistic conception of God (the anthropomorphisms should not deceive us) could not permit the notion that God had need of material help from humanity.

40. That humanity is here created from silver one can only deduce from the context, since the relevant portion of the text is not preserved. Earlier on, the text reported a kind of dispute between Enki and Ninmah that pitted the two in creating defective beings with silver; the opponent was to establish an appropriate destiny for these beings. See, for this interpretation, Jacobsen, *JNES* 5 (1946) 143.

41. See further *Rituels accadiens*, 46.26ff.; CT XIII 34.9; but the latter text is not entirely preserved.

42. See, for example, "Lahar and Ašnan," lines 25–35; KAR 4 27–31, rev. 1ff., where the two goals are reunited.

The Origins of Organized Life

Leaving aside for the moment the secondary points of comparison, it is appropriate to say yet another word concerning the allusions in Genesis (chap. 4) to the origins of organized life.

The two brothers Cain and Abel pursued two different occupations, which since the Neolithic period have been the basis of all social life: agriculture and pastoral life. These are the two forms of life one sees in the south of Babylonia, the first favored by the network of canals and streams that aid the land's fertility. It is completely natural that they are also documented in the texts we are now examining, especially under the category of "organizational myths." See for example the myth "Lahar and Ašnan," the chief goal of which is to depict these two types of life. Lines 3–23 lament ⟦134⟧ their absence; after the creation of humanity, the reader witnesses their organization, which is described in the most minute detail (lines 36–70). Finally the real dispute begins between Lahar (pastoral life) and Ašnan (agriculture).

Again, in the myth "Enki and the World Order," the introduction of which is only preserved in a fragmentary state, one witnesses the organization of the different regions of Sumer as well as regions outside Sumer's frontiers, such as Meluhha. One reads of agricultural implements, the plow and the yoke, and fields and vegetation. Stalls, fields, animals, and plants have their part, and the pastoral god Dumuzi has the direction and responsibility for their prosperity. The "Myth of the Pickax" (lines 26ff.) lists uses of the pickax, as well as the benefits of the pickax to agriculture and gardening. Finally, one can cite KAR 4, where it is said that humanity was created in order to regulate and control the canals and the waters of the Tigris and Euphrates (which were created prior to humanity), to establish field boundaries, to cultivate, and to oversee the increase of animals, stalls, flock, fish, and birds. The goddess Nisaba received authority for their supervision and direction. All of this functioned for the service of the gods (see particularly rev. 1–24).

Alongside the pastoralists and the peasants, social life was comprised of the occupations and crafts of the artisans. The allusion to the founding of the first town, for instance, in Gen 4:17, has its correspondence in the myths of organization that touch upon the origins of one or several towns. The "Marriage of Marduk" starts in the following way:

> The (city o)f Nisaba existed, Kiri_{x}.tab[43] did not exist. . . .

43. For the probable reading of this name, formerly read ŠID.tab, then Ak.tab (A. Poebel, *JAOS* 57, 359ff.), see *ZA* N.S. 17, 74.74.

But the creation of the historical cities of Sumer is presented to us in the Sumerian narrative of the Flood (II 14′ff.): Eridu, Bad-tibira, Larak, Sippar, and Šuruppak were created before the Flood. The incantation of CT XIII 35–37 mentions Nippur, Uruk, Eridu . . . Babylon, and the temples Ekur, Eanna, Esagil, and, preceding the cities, construction of the temples and the houses, with the construction material, reeds, and bricks (lines 1–9, 15ff., 35ff.).

No mention, so it seems, is made in the Mesopotamian creation texts of musical art. But music was certainly ⟦135⟧ used in preparation for the festivals of the gods, and these are mentioned, for example, in KAR 4 rev. 8–10.[44]

As for smiths (Gen 4:22), we have mention of the different crafts that were utilized in construction and the implements that came from smiths.[45] Again, Sumer possessed an important center for smiths in the city of Bad-tibira (one of the cities founded before the Flood). In fact *Bad-tibira* means 'center of the smiths'.

Let us add a final observation. Genesis attributes the origin of the different occupations and crafts to individual people. In the Mesopotamian texts, the prerogative of invention reverts to the gods, who assign arts and crafts to humanity and thereafter stay in control, maintaining the responsibility for good running order.

In "Lahar and Ašnan," apart from Lahar and Ašnan, Uttu (the goddess of weaving) and the god Sumugan are mentioned. In "Enki and the World Order" there is a whole series of chief administrators: Enbilulu is supposed to preside over the Tigris and Euphrates; the son of Keš over the fish; Sirara, the sea; Iškur, the winds; Sumugan, the plain; Muš-damma "the great builder of Enlil," the construction of houses; Dumuzi, stalls and sheepfolds; and so on.[46]

In the myth of Oannes, of which Berossus speaks,[47] the half-fish, half-human being comes out from the sea every day to teach arts and crafts to mankind and then retires for the night. This creature is a prototype of the "cultural hero" of ethnology. But this opens new perspectives that we are unable to treat here. It is enough to indicate the possibilities.

44. For music and dance in religious festivals, see, for example, the hymn of *Sumerian Religious Texts* No. 36.26–27. A translation of it was provided by R. Jestin in *RA* 44, 45ff., and a new translation by Castellino will appear in *Scritti in onore di G. Furlani.*

45. See "Creation of the Pickax" 1.26ff.; "Enki and Sumer"; and the mention of the gašam=Akkadian *ummānu* 'artisans' in KAR 4 rev. 19–20.

46. See also CT XIII 35ff.

47. See Eusebius, *Chron. liber prior* (ed. Schoene), p. 14; further the article *Oannes-Ea* in Roscher, *Lexicon of Greek and Roman Mythology* III, cols. 577–78.

Summary and Conclusion

First of all, the analysis of vv. 4b–7 of chap. 2 allowed us to distinguish three scenes that mark a progression in delimiting the geographical horizon and to concentrate on the principal creation, humanity. An analysis of the spatial terms [[136]] used by the author, *ʾereṣ* 'earth', *śādeh* 'field', *ʾădāmâ*, gave us the key to eliminate the apparent contradiction between the aridity of the 'earth' in v. 5 and the presence of the water provided by the *ʾēd* 'spring?' of v. 6. The cuneiform texts served to provide proof that our interpretation was not by any means subjective and arbitrary but was founded on convincing evidence.

Through the aid of cuneiform texts we were better able to determine the meaning of the two words *gan* 'garden' and *ʾēden* 'Eden' in the section on Paradise (2:8–17). By that means we were led to see how Paradise represents the ultimate delimitation of the "scenario" in which the "action" of chap. 3 unfolded. A subsequent philological and literary analysis showed us the "occidental" character of the names of two rivers (out of the four) and the possible nonoriginality of the instructive elements that accompany the mention of the rivers, as many critics have already noted. We have retained the mention of the rivers as necessary for the garden, and for all the places and the times of interest in the biblical narratives. Here again the cuneiform texts have provided useful confirmation. The creation of animals and of the woman allowed an explanation of the role the animals played in the relationship between Adam and Eve.

In addition, the distinction we made between texts of "organization" and texts of "action" and an analysis of the relationship between the introduction and the body of the myths have led us to establish a parallel between Genesis 2 and the introduction to the Babylonian myths on one hand, and between Genesis 3 and the body or the action of the myths on the other. One can express it all by means of an equation: Genesis 2 is to Genesis 3 as the introduction of the myths is to their core.

Passing on to the literary analysis of the same texts, we have stated the difference that exists between them and *Enūma eliš*. Whereas this poem is really *the* poem of "creation," the texts we studied are texts concerning the organization of the earth and civilized life. One cannot therefore put them in the same schema. Again, one recognizes a correspondence with Genesis 1 and 2 in this regard. Though Genesis 1 constitutes a real creation narrative along the lines of *Enūma eliš*, Genesis 2 is strictly an organizational text. It does not perform double duty with Genesis 1, and one should not place the two narratives in opposition to each other. This allows one to do justice to the two chapters and at the same time facilitates exegesis.

Finally, the comparison of the introductions of the cuneiform texts with [[137]] Genesis 2–3a allows a reiteration of the differences and similarities, either referring to the literary methods of style and construction, or to content. With the aid of the cuneiform documents, we made several clarifications of the origin of civilized life in cities, as well as the origin of other social structures and activities of humanity such as one sees presented in chap. 4 of Genesis.

A New Look at the Babylonian Background of Genesis

W. G. Lambert

⟦287⟧ My subject arose in the first place from study of the cuneiform tablets from Ashurbanipal's library in Nineveh, which had been dug up for the British Museum in the 1850's. The most important discoveries were published in the 1870's by George Smith: first, in 1872, a Babylonian version of the flood story was made known,[1] and three years later a Babylonian account of creation was announced,[2] translations of the pieces being given in Smith's book, *The Chaldean Account of Creation*, which appeared in the following year, 1876.

The attention of Old Testament scholars was now assured.[3] Even the most sceptical had to yield when confronted with the passage in the Babylonian text which described how three birds were sent out of the ark as the waters were subsiding. With the creation account the similarities were not so great. Although the Babylonian cosmology began with a primaeval Tiāmat, which is the etymological equivalent of *t^ehôm*, 'the deep',

Reprinted with permission from *Journal of Theological Studies* 16 (1965) 287–300.

A paper read to the Society for Old Testament Study on 2 January 1964 at King's College Hostel, London.

1. In a paper read to the Society of Biblical Archaeology on 3 December 1872, which was printed in the *Transactions* of the Society the following year.

2. In a letter to the *Daily Telegraph*, 4 March 1875.

3. Criticisms of George Smith's work, however, were more severe than is often realized today. A writer in the *Athenaeum* spoke of "the melancholy death of Mr. Smith just as all European scholars were most anxious that his earlier and, in some cases, hasty conclusions should derive the advantage of his calmer and better informed judgement" (July to December, 1877, p. 864).

in Genesis 1, the major item of the Babylonian text, the battle between Marduk and Tiāmat, does not appear in the Hebrew accounts of creation. The German scholar Gunkel supplied the missing link in his book *Schöpfung und Chaos in Urzeit und Endzeit* (1895). He drew attention to a series of passages in the poetic books of the Old Testament in which a battle between Yahweh and the sea, or sea monsters, is alluded to. On this basis it could be affirmed that a conflict had existed in Hebrew traditions of creation, but had been washed out of the monotheistic formulation of Genesis 1. Gunkel was not in fact the first to propound this idea. Our own Cheyne, in the year in which this book appeared, took the author to task in the *Critical Review* for not acknowledging that as far back as 1877 he himself had been advancing such views.[4] ⟦288⟧ Cheyne had in fact mentioned the battle with Tiāmat as a possible parallel to the poetic allusions, whereas Gunkel was asserting that all the references to Rahab, Leviathan, etc., were but borrowed versions of Marduk's fight. However, another scholar had much greater claim to have been plagiarized. George A. Barton, a young American, had read a paper in 1890 in which he cited the main passages about Rahab, Leviathan, etc., and the dragon of the Book of Revelation, and drew the conclusion that these were direct reflections of the Babylonian myth. This paper was published in 1893[5] and was known to Gunkel in the preparation of his book, since he quoted it on various minor points.

Whoever first propounded the idea (Barton seems to have the better claim), he provided the justification for assuming a direct connexion of some kind between the Babylonian and Hebrew accounts of creation. By the turn of the century the idea of dependence on a Babylonian original in the two cases of creation and flood was an accepted opinion in critical circles, so much so that strong assertions usually covered up the differences in the case of the former. Few thought it necessary even to admit of any problem, as did S. R. Driver in his commentary on Genesis, where he says about the creation narratives:

> In estimating these similarities, it must further be remembered that they do not stand alone: in the narrative of the Deluge we find traits borrowed unmistakably from a Babylonian source; so that the antecedent difficulty which might otherwise have been felt in supposing elements in the Creation-narrative to be traceable ultimately to the same quarter is considerably lessened. *The Book of Genesis*[6] (1907) 30.

4. *Critical Review* 5 (1895) 256–66.
5. *JAOS* 15, pp. 1ff.

This amounts to saying that even though the case for the creation narrative is dubious, the better case of the flood can be used to prove it, a very debatable procedure. It should be added that another factor involved in the acceptance of this opinion by the turn of the century was the date assigned to the Babylonian texts. While the copies then available were not earlier than 750 B.C., the texts were believed to go back to at least 2000 B.C., well before the earliest possible date for Genesis.

The last sixty years have witnessed vast increases in knowledge of the various factors involved in this problem. It is no longer possible to talk glibly about Babylonian civilization. We now know that it was composed of three main strands. First, it inherited much from the Sumerians, who built up the first great civilization in Southern Mesopotamia. A second element was derived from a group of Semites who probably came down the Euphrates valley in the middle of the third millennium B.C. Thirdly, it owed something to the Amorites, who likewise came down the ⟦289⟧ Euphrates valley, but at the end of the third millennium, and took over the country. The Sumerians were the most original and dynamic in cultural matters, and the other two groups owed something to them even before they had settled down. Consequently it is often difficult to know if a particular item of Babylonian civilization originated with one of these three groups or was a new creation. More is known of the Amorites than of the earlier Semitic migrants, and their influence can be found in works of Babylonian literature. In my opinion the *lex talionis* in the Code of Hammurabi depends on an Amorite legal tradition, since it was an innovation in Mesopotamian law. Also the location of the Sumero-Babylonian pantheon on Mount Hermon in the Babylonian *Epic of Gilgamesh* is certainly Amorite in conception.[6] Thus Babylonian civilization was a highly composite thing, and it is no longer scientifically sound to assume that all ideas originated in Mesopotamia and moved westwards. This is pan-babylonism. Parallels to Genesis can indeed be sought and found there, but they can also be sought and found among the Canaanites, the ancient Egyptians, the Hurrians, the Hittites, and the early Greeks. When the parallels have been found, the question of dependence, if any, has to be approached with an open mind.

Another qualification which is often overlooked in comparative studies of this kind is the inner diversity of so large and so long-lasting a

6. See W. G. Lambert, *Babylonian Wisdom Literature* (1960) 12–13. The American scholar A. T. Clay between 1908 and his death in 1925 countered the opinion that Hebrew religion derived much from Babylon by asserting the influence of the Amorites. In detail much that he wrote has proved wrong, and was indeed never generally accepted, but his main thesis has been vindicated in some measure, as stated by the present holder of his Yale chair, Albrecht Goetze, in *The Yale University Library Gazette* 36 (1962) 133–7.

civilization as the Babylonian. Our remoteness often causes the inquirer to attach an exaggerated importance to whatever fragment from this vast complex he happens to be working on. The doctrine of one text may be carelessly styled '*the* Babylonian view', as though it were proved to have been held by all Babylonians of all periods and areas. More systematic study reveals what could very well have been conjectured, that a great variety of ideas circulated in ancient Mesopotamia. Sumerian religion crystallized in city states, each with its particular gods and cults. Mutual tolerance was manifested in a generally accepted hierarchical order of the chief gods from the different cities. While Hammurabi welded the same cities into a single Babylonian state, religion continued its city-bound organization, though quite substantial changes gradually took place in the official hierarchy. And in all matters the 1,100 years between Hammurabi and Nebuchadnezzar II witnessed tremendous development. Yet, to the end, despite the political ⟦290⟧ unity based on the city of Babylon, matters of thought still reflected local attachments. In the first millennium B.C. creativity in myth was no longer expressed in literary compositions of epic style. Instead, expository texts and scholarly commentaries of a highly esoteric character were compiled. The distinction between those expounding the myths of Nippur and those the myths of Babylon, for example, is easily discerned.

One matter can be disposed of very quickly. The recovery of the Ugaritic texts has shown that the allusions to Yahweh's battle with Leviathan and the *tannîn*, but not Rahab, are derived from Canaanite Baal myths, and these show no signs of dependence on Mesopotamian sources.[7] Accordingly, one of the main supports for assuming the dependence of Genesis on Babylonian myths has gone, and the whole question needs reconsideration. Yet not all Old Testament scholars have really faced the facts. The following random quotations of recent opinion illustrate the position. Kaufmann in his *Religion of Israel* does indeed assert the Canaanite rather than Babylonian origin of the poetic allusions to battles with monsters.[8] Similarly Hans-Joachim Kraus in his commentary on the Psalms refers to the Babylonian epic only as a parallel, and insists on the prior relevance of the Ugaritic material.[9] Contrast this with Eissfeldt's article on Genesis in the *Interpreter's Dictionary of the Bible*, which

7. The two main passages, Andrée Herdner, *Corpus des tablettes en cunéiformes alphabétiques* (1963), no. 3.3.33–44 and no. 5.1.1–3, are conveniently quoted with translation by Otto Kaiser, *Die mythische Bedeutung des Meeres* (*ZAW*, Beiheft 78) 74–75. The other passages can be found in the glossaries of C. H. Gordon and G. R. Driver, and in the dictionary of Aistleitner, under *ltn* and *tnn*.

8. Y. Kaufmann, *The Religion of Israel* (English digest by M. Greenberg, 1961) 62.

9. *Biblischer Kommentar, Altes Testament* 15/1 (1960) 518.

repeats essentially what Gunkel said, only modernizing the terminology: instead of Babylonian origin he speaks of "Sumerian-Akkadian prototypes."[10] Von Rad, in his commentary on Genesis, asserts the "unbestreitbare Zusammenhang" ⟦'indisputable connection'⟧ of the Babylonian Tiāmat and *tᵉhôm* in Genesis 1, meaning a mythological and not only a philological connexion.[11] Similarly Orlinsky, in a recently published apologia for the Jewish Publication Society's new translation of the Pentateuch, asserts: "Scholars have long recognized that the biblical version of creation has great affinity with what we know of the Mesopotamian versions, that the former—whether directly or indirectly—derives ultimately and in significant measure from the latter."[12]

On the Sumero-Babylonian side matters are hardly more satisfactory. New editions of *Enūma Eliš*, or the *Babylonian Epic of Creation* as it is ⟦291⟧ commonly called, have been made by merely adding new material to the old editions, with all their inevitable and, in their cases, excusable faults. L. W. King's excellent edition of 1902[13] was the last truly critical edition based on first-hand study of all the textual evidence. In addition to this major and several minor texts, there is a mass of allusions and other secondary material comparable with the allusions in Hebrew poetry, which no one has hitherto collected, much less studied. The greatest failure, however, has been in the general interpretation of the major epic. Views put out as plausible conjectures at the end of the last century have, by frequent repetition, become endowed with canonical status, and are now asserted in such terms as "it is generally admitted"[14] (which means that no one has ever proved) and "there is no convincing reason against"[15] (which patently confesses the lack of conclusive reasons for). Under these circumstances I have tried to get to the bottom of the various questions and to assemble neglected material. Some of my results, for what they are worth, must be used in the following notes.[16]

The first major conclusion is that the *Epic of Creation* is not a norm of Babylonian or Sumerian cosmology. It is a sectarian and aberrant combination of mythological threads woven into an unparalleled compositum.

10. Ed. G. A. Buttrick (1962), 2, p. 375.

11. *Das Alte Testament Deutsch*, Teilband 2, p. 38.

12. *JBL* 82 (1963) 256.

13. L. W. King, *The Seven Tablets of Creation.* The writer is engaged on a new critical edition. For the moment one of the best, and the most convenient English translation, is that of A. Heidel, *The Babylonian Genesis*[2] (Third [corrected] Impression, 1963).

14. A. Heidel, op. cit., 12.

15. E. A. Speiser apud J. B. Pritchard, *ANET* ([1]1950, [2]1955) 60.

16. Where possible, reference is given to a published source, but in some cases, such as where unpublished materials are used, this has not been practicable.

In my opinion it is not earlier than 1100 B.C. It happens to be the best preserved Babylonian document of its genre simply because it was at its height of popularity when the libraries were formed from which our knowledge of Babylonian mythology is mostly derived. The various traditions it draws upon are often perverted to such an extent that conclusions based on this text alone are suspect. It can only be used safely in the whole context of ancient Mesopotamian mythology. With this introduction let us turn to the matter in hand.

The flood remains the clearest case of dependence of Genesis on Mesopotamian legend. While flood stories as such do not have to be connected, the episode of the birds in Gen 8:6–12 is so close to the parallel passage in the XIth tablet of the Babylonian *Gilgamesh Epic*[17] that no doubt exists. The only other Babylonian testimony to ⟦292⟧ these birds is that of the priest Berossus, some 300 B.C. That edition of the *Gilgamesh Epic* which contains the flood story is the latest; no copies earlier than 750 B.C. are known, though it was a traditional text, and the late form may well have been put in shape between 1200 and 1000 B.C. Parts of earlier editions survive, for its origins go back, at least in Sumerian, to the third millennium, but none of them is known to have contained any flood narrative. In the late edition it is a digression, and was inserted from another Sumero-Babylonian epic, known in its later forms from the hero of the flood, Atra-ḫasīs. The Sumerian prototype, of which one incomplete copy of about 1800 B.C. alone survives, is very concise and its account of the flood has no mention of birds.[18] The first Babylonian edition known, from copies of about 1600 B.C., is incomplete, but so far there is nothing about birds. The late Babylonian editions are similarly incomplete.[19] Thus the only surviving testimony to the most telling parallel happens to be later than the Biblical account, but nevertheless I hold that there is certain dependence of the Hebrew writers on a Mesopotamian tradition. First, there is no dispute that the late Mesopotamian forms of the flood story are local developments of the earlier Sumerian accounts, and these we know from copies of about 1800 B.C. This virtually excludes any possible Amorite influence in the initial formation of the Mesopotamian tradition. Thus priority rests on the Mesopotamian

17. The most recent translations are: A. Schott and W. von Soden, *Das Gilgamesch-Epos* (1958); E. A. Speiser apud J. B. Pritchard, *ANET*[2] (1955) 72–99; A. Heidel, *The Gilgamesh Epic and Old Testament Parallels*[2] (1949).

18. The only translations of this are by A. Poebel, *Historical Texts* (1914) 17–20; and by S. N. Kramer apud *ANET*, 42–44.

19. See provisionally W. G. Lambert, "New Light on the Babylonian Flood," *Journal of Semitic Studies* 5 (1960) 113–23. A new edition based on much new material is being prepared by the present writer and A. R. Millard. ⟦now published as Lambert and Millard, *AH*, 1969⟧.

side, where floods are an annual phenomenon. Secondly, it is inconceivable that the Hebrews as such influenced the development of Babylonian epics. There seem, then, to be only two ways of escape from acknowledging Hebrew borrowing. The one is to assert that both Sumerians and Amorites held independent flood traditions, and from the latter the episode of the birds passed to both Hebrews and Babylonians. I can think of no refutation of such a view, though it seems most probable to me. Alternatively it could be argued that the Hebrew and Babylonian accounts go back to the event rather than to a common source of tradition. This is unacceptable to me for reasons to be explained later.

Neither in Mesopotamia nor in Palestine did the flood story stand alone. In Berossus ten long-reigning kings precede it.[20] A similar tradition, but of nine kings, occurs in a bilingual fragment from Ashurbanipal's library. Several Sumerian tablets from about 1800 B.C. attest this line of kings, but either eight or ten in number, extending from the ⟦293⟧ beginning of civilization to the flood.[21] The Sumerian prototype of the *Atra-ḫasīs Epic* lacks the kings, but describes the founding of the five cities in which they are said to have reigned. In Genesis the ten long-lived patriarchs from Adam to Noah lead up to the flood. It appears certain to me that this is no coincidence, and since the Sumerian character of this traditional history assures priority on the Mesopotamian side, borrowing on the part of the Hebrews seems certain.

The creation narratives are altogether more difficult. We shall start from the beginning of the first biblical account. Much has been made of the similarity of the Hebrew *tᵉhôm* ⟦'the deep'⟧ and the Babylonian Tiāmat in *Enūma Eliš.* Both are primaeval and watery. The etymological equivalence is of no consequence, since poetic allusions to cosmic battles in the Old Testament use *yām* and *tᵉhôm* indiscriminately. So far as the concept is concerned, the idea of a watery beginning was by no means the only Mesopotamian notion. There were three basic doctrines. According to the most commonly attested, earth came first and all else emerged in some way from this. Less commonly attested is the conception of primaeval water, and thirdly time was considered the source and origin of all things. Earth in this cosmological sense is first attested about 2600 B.C. Water is not known before 2000, and time makes its first appearance about 1700 B.C. Since the evidence for all three is scanty, these dates have no absolute value. In contrast with these different Mesopotamian

20. F. Jacoby, *Die Fragmente der griechischen Historiker* 3C (1958) 373–82.

21. See T. Jacobsen, *The Sumerian King List* (1939), and J. J. Finkelstein and W. W. Hallo, both in *Journal of Cuneiform Studies,* 17 (1963) 39ff. and 52ff. The bilingual fragment has been joined to another previously unpublished piece, see *Cuneiform Texts from Babylonian Tablets in the British Museum,* part 46 (1965), no. 5.

ideas, the ancient Egyptians quite generally acknowledged the god of the primaeval waters Nu (Nun) as the source of all things.[22] In early Greece there were different opinions, as in Mesopotamia, but Ocean is described as the father (γένεσις) of the gods in Homer,[23] and water is the prime element in the cosmologies of Thales and Anaximander. Thus the watery beginning of Genesis in itself is no evidence of Mesopotamian influence.

The activity of the second day is more explicit. God divided the cosmic waters into two parts on the vertical plane. Similarly in *Enūma Eliš* Marduk splits the body of Tiāmat. These seem to be the only two examples of the splitting of a body of water from the area and periods under discussion (apart from Berossus),[24] so a parallel must be acknowledged. However, Gunkel and his followers have wanted to push the ⟦294⟧ matter further. In *Enūma Eliš* a battle precedes the splitting, and since there are poetic allusions to a battle of Yahweh with the sea, it is urged that there is dependence on *Enūma Eliš*, and that a battle did precede the separation of the waters in earlier forms of the tradition recorded in Genesis 1. This involves most intricate problems. This splitting, whether in *Enūma Eliš* or Genesis is, of course, only a variant of the common mythological theme of the dividing of heaven and earth,[25] the only difference being that these two accounts involve water, not a solid mass. This separation of heaven and earth does not necessarily presume a conflict. There are three Sumerian versions,[26] and in none is the matter being cut asunder the body of a monster slain in battle. The whole process is peaceful: a job of work. In a version in the Hittite language a saw is used to do the cutting, not a weapon of war.[27] In Egypt Shu pushes apart Nut, the heaven, and Geb, the earth, without any antecedent battle.[28] The doctrine of the world egg, as found in some forms of Phoenician[29] and Orphic[30] cosmogony, similarly involves a peaceful sundering.

22. See H. Bonnet, *Reallexikon der ägyptischen Religionsgeschichte* (1952) 535–6; and Otto Kaiser, op. cit., 1–39.

23. *Iliad* 14.201.

24. F. Jacoby, op. cit., 370–3.

25. See W. Staudacher, *Die Trennung von Himmel und Erde* (1942) 37; K. Marót, same title, *Acta Antiqua Hungarica* 1 (1951) 35–66; F. K. Numazawa, *Scientia* 47 (1953) 23–35 (last two references provided by R. T. Rundle Clark).

26. S. N. Kramer, *Sumerian Mythology* (1944) 37; T. Jacobsen, *JNES* 5 (1946) 134; E. Ebeling, *ZDMG* 70 (1916) 532; and A. Heidel, op. cit., 68.

27. H. G. Güterbock, *Journal of Cuneiform Studies* 6 (1952) 29, 52–54. The meaning of the Hittite word is not certain, though the translation 'saw' rests on etymology. It is not the name of any known weapon.

28. H. Bonnet, op. cit., 685–9; R. T. Rundle Clark, *Myth and Symbol in Ancient Egypt* (1959) 48–50, 250.

29. See H. W. Haussig (ed.), *Wörterbuch der Mythologie* I. Abteilung, Teil 1, 309–10.

30. W. K. C. Guthrie, *Orpheus and Greek Religion*[2] (1952), ch. 4.

Is there, then, good reason to presume a battle behind the second day of creation in Genesis? The poetic allusions nowhere speak of Yahweh splitting the sea, except for Ps 74:13 in the traditional English rendering: "Thou didst divide the sea by thy strength." However, the meaning of פּוֹרַרְתָּ ⟦'divide'⟧ has been disputed on purely lexicographical evidence, and an Arabic cognate favours rather: "Thou didst set the sea in commotion."[31] Thus the case for a battle as a prelude to God's dividing of the cosmic waters is unproven.

On the Mesopotamian side the matter is very confused. Tiāmat is not uniform in the *Epic of Creation.* At times she is presented as a solid-bodied monster, at other times as a mass of water. The author is conflating two traditions. Berossus combined the two traditions more ⟦295⟧ systematically: he presents Tiāmat advancing against Marduk as a woman yet at the same moment as a body of water so that monsters are swimming inside her![32] To me this is obviously a combination of two ideas. The question is whether the separating of the body of water really belongs to the dragon-slaying episode, or is just hitched on, to the greater glory of Marduk. To answer this question we must survey briefly the Mesopotamian traditions of cosmic water. The only one known from the Sumerians pictured a watery goddess Nammu as the mother of heaven and earth and of all the gods. She, however, was not split and no battle with her is known of. Another view, associated especially with Marduk, makes the primaeval waters a substratum merely on which the earth was placed. In some cases the water was an impersonal passive element, in other cases this sea had to be subjugated before the work of creation could be done on top of it. In either case there is no splitting: all the water stays below. Thus *Enūma Eliš* and Berossus have something unique so far in Mesopotamia. No other tradition of a watery beginning involves the separation.

One other aspect remains, the cultic. Although much that has been written on this subject is altogether wrong, there is good circumstantial evidence that Marduk defeated Tiāmat each New Year in the Akītu house of Babylon.[33] But this only applies to Babylon in the time of the Late Babylonian empire, not to any other Akītu house of any other city. There are only very scrappy hints about the precise conception of Tiāmat involved in this annual rite, but they all savour of underworld connexions, which means that concept of a sea beneath the earth, not of a sea both above and beneath. Too much has been made of the recitation of *Enūma Eliš* in the New Year rites. The epilogue contradicts the suggestion that it

31. So L. Koehler, *Lexicon in Veteris Testamenti Libros* (1953) 782.
32. F. Jacoby, op. cit., 371–2.
33. W. G. Lambert, *Iraq* 25 (1963) 189–90.

was written expressly for use in the month Nisan, and nothing in the formulation of the epic implies a specific cultic use.

We are left, then, with the fact that the sequence of the battle and the splitting of the cosmic waters may be only the result of conflation of no particular antiquity, and it is only one of two traditions associated with a single Mesopotamian god. *Enūma Eliš* is the first testimony to it. Thus neither on the Hebrew side nor on the Mesopotamian is there any clear proof that a battle is necessarily tied to the dividing of the waters. More generally, there is no proof that the conflict of a deity with the sea is of Mesopotamian origin. So far it is only known in the cult and literature of Babylon. It was an Amorite dynasty that made Babylon from an unimportant settlement into the capital of an empire, and it is ⟦296⟧ always possible that they introduced the ideas into Mesopotamia. If so, the Babylonians were as much borrowers as the Hebrews.

To sum up discussion of the second day, there is one close parallel between Genesis and *Enūma Eliš*, but no evidence of Hebrew borrowing from Babylon.

The third day can be dealt with more briefly. God separates the sea from the dry land. My opinion is that the second and third days contain originally unrelated traditions, put in this sequence by the Hebrew author. Three clear poetic allusions refer to Yahweh's pushing back the cosmic waters from the land and defining their limits: Ps 104:6–9, Prov 8:29, and Job 38:8–11. A conflict is definitely involved. The last passage is the most explicit: the section occurs in a cosmological setting, and involves not simply the separation of sea and dry land, but tells of the waters breaking forth "from the womb" and being forced back by God within fixed limits. There is a Mesopotamian parallel for this, connected with Ninurta, the Sumero-Babylonian god of war, who was, incidentally, the dragon-slayer of ancient Mesopotamia. The story goes that "the mighty waters" began to rise and threatened to overwhelm the land, so Ninurta built a stone wall to hold them back until eventually they receded. Thereby Ninurta saved the land. This is part of a composite Sumerian myth first known from copies of about 1800 B.C., though later bilingual copies also survive.[34] There seems to be an allusion to this one episode in Cylinder A of Gudea of Lagash (*c.* 2100 B.C.), who describes how he went into the house of Ninurta and prayed to him, beginning, "Lord, who held back the savage waters. . . . "[35] This Mesopotamian story reads very much like an account of the annual flood projected on to the mythological

34. There is no adequate edition of this myth, but for what it is worth mention may be made of the edition of this particular section by H. Radau, *Sumerian Hymns and Prayers to God Nin-ib from the Temple Library of Nippur* (1911) 66–70.

35. A. Falkenstein and W. von Soden, *Sumerische und akkadische Hymnen und Gebete* (1953) 146.

plane. The parallel with the Hebrew material is striking, since these seem to be the only two narratives of a god holding back savage waters from the ancient Orient. It is true that the water is conceived somewhat differently in the Old Testament: there it is sea, a term not used of Ninurta's exploit. But if the account were of Mesopotamian origin and had been borrowed in Syria and Palestine, where there is no annual flood, it would be very natural for such a change to take place. Since it is a traditional Sumerian myth, it is quite possible that this is the correct explanation of the facts.

For me the seventh day of creation offers a still more convincing case. The sabbath has, of course, been the subject of much study, both the ⟦297⟧ institution and the name. My own position, briefly, is that the Hebrew term *šabbāt*, meaning the completion of the week, and the Babylonian term *šapattu*, meaning the completion of the moon's waxing, that is the fifteenth day of a lunar month, are the same word. But since there is no genuine Sumerian equivalent of, nor Babylonian etymology for, *šapattu*, and it first appears only about 1700 B.C., I believe that Hebrews and Babylonians depend on a similar Amorite source.[36] The attempt to find days of rest in the Mesopotamian calendars has hardly succeeded.[37] There is, however, another approach to the question. The Hebrews left two explanations of the Sabbath. The first is that of Genesis 1–2 and Exodus 20, that it repeats cyclically what God did in the original week of creation. The second, in Deuteronomy 5, regards it as a repeated memorial of the Hebrews' deliverance from Egypt. This divergence suggests that historically the institution is older than the explanations. On this assumption the use of the week as the framework of a creation account is understandable as providing divine sanction for the institution, but unexpected in that God's resting hardly expresses the unlimited might and power that are His usual attributes: "See, Israel's guardian neither slumbers nor sleeps." It is generally assumed that the use of the week as the framework of the account simply required that God rest on the seventh day. But there was no compulsion to have a week of creation at all. Furthermore, this implies that the development of the doctrine of God's rest came from pure, deductive reasoning, which I doubt very much. The authors of ancient cosmologies were essentially compilers. Their

36. The best discussion of this word is still that of B. Landsberger, *Der kultische Kalender der Babylonier und Assyrer* (1915) 131–5.

37. The various Babylonian calendars have *dies fas* ⟦'propitious days'⟧ and *dies nefas* ⟦'unpropitious days'⟧ just like the Roman, but the latter are not really days of rest. The nearest approach to the Hebrew Sabbath is offered by the prohibitions for the king (nothing is said about the people) to be observed on the seventh day of each month, which forbid both secular and religious activities. The best summary of information on this topic is B. Landsberger, op. cit., 92ff.

originality was expressed in new combinations of old themes, and in new twists to old ideas. Sheer invention was not part of their craft. Thus when the author tells us that God rested, I believe he drew on a tradition to this effect. Therefore in seeking parallels to the seventh day, one must look not only for comparable institutions, but also for the idea of deities resting.

Here Mesopotamia does not fail us. The standard Babylonian account of man's creation is not found in *Enūma Eliš*, but in the *Atra-ḫasīs* epic. An earlier form of this myth occurs in the Sumerian *Enki and Ninmaḫ*.[38] ⟦298⟧ The essentials of the story are that the gods had to toil for their daily bread, and in response to urgent complaints man was created to serve the gods by providing them with food and drink. On the last point all the Mesopotamian accounts agree: man existed solely to serve the gods, and this was expressed practically in that all major deities at least had two meals set up before their statues each day. Accordingly, man's creation resulted in the gods' resting, and the myths reach a climax at this point. Even in *Enūma Eliš* this is clear, despite much conflation. At the beginning of Tablet VI Ea and Marduk confer on what is called "the resting of the gods," and thereupon man is created and the gods are declared free from toil. This common Mesopotamian tradition thus provides a close parallel to the sixth and seventh days of creation. Since the particular concept of the destiny of man goes back to the Sumerians, but is unparalleled in other parts of the ancient Near East, ultimate borrowing by the Hebrews seems very probable.

These, in my opinion, are the significant points of similarity between Mesopotamian and Hebrew accounts of origin. Other scholars, from the time of George Smith and onwards, have attached importance to other points, though to me they are inconclusive.[39] No sure Babylonian parallels have yet been found even for the Tower of Babel or the

38. The literature on this myth is given by M. Lambert in *Revue d'Assyriologie* 55 (1961) 186–7, no. 18, but there is no edition of the text.

39. A collection of such material is given by J. Plessis in *Dictionnaire de la Bible, Supplément*, ed. L. Pirot, Tome Premier (1928) 714ff., and detailed comparisons of *Enūma Eliš* and Genesis have been made by A. Deimel, *"Enuma Eliš" und Hexaemeron* (1934), and by A. Heidel, *The Babylonian Genesis*[2] (1963), ch. 3. Among the more recent and reputable suggestions of particular scholars the following may be noted. W. F. Albright in *JBL* 62 (1943) 369, on the basis of the translation of Gen 1:1, "When God began to create . . . ," proposed a definite borrowing from a Sumero-Babylonian "When . . . then . . . " period. S. H. Langdon, in his book *Sumerian Epic of Paradise, the Flood and the Fall of Man* (1915), also in French translation, *Le Poème sumérien du paradis, du déluge et de la chute de l'homme* (1919), tried to relate a Sumerian myth to more than one episode of Genesis, but wrongly. See the altogether more reliable edition of the same text by S. N. Kramer, *Enki and Ninḫursag, A Sumerian 'Paradise' Myth* (*BASOR* Supplementary Studies, no. 1, 1945). On p. 9 of this new edition Kramer suggests a connexion between the word play on the Sumerian homophones *ti* 'life'

kingdom of Nimrod.[40] We are left, then, with the succession of long-lived ⟦299⟧ worthies culminating in the flood, perhaps God's holding back of the primaeval waters, and, more probably, God's rest. So far the similarities have been stressed, but the differences must not be overlooked. The Sumero-Babylonian tradition is of a line of kings from the founding of civilization to the flood, not of a line of patriarchs, the ancestors of the Hebrew nation, from creation onwards. In the one case the names are mostly Sumerian, but Semitic in the other, nor do they bear any kind of relationship to the corresponding name in the other series. The differences are indeed so great that direct borrowing of a literary form of Mesopotamian traditions is out of the question. But if the case for borrowing is to be established, at least a suggestion of the manner and time of transference must be made. The exile and the later part of the monarchy are out of the question, since this was the time when the Hebrew traditions of creation and the early history of mankind were being put in the form in which they were canonized. That the matters spoken of were included in Genesis is proof that they were long established among the Hebrews. Kaufmann has rightly argued that prophetic use of the traditions of Yahweh's battle with the sea implies that these traditions were therefore long established on Hebrew soil. Thus one is forced back at least to the time of the Judges, and even this may be too late. Also, knowledge of this time does not suggest that Babylonian myths and legends would have gained currency then if they were not established earlier. The present writer's opinion is that only the Amarna period has any real claim to be the period when this material moved westwards. This is the period when the Babylonian language and cuneiform script were the normal means of international communication between countries from Egypt to the Persian Gulf. From within this period

---

and *ti* 'rib' and the fashioning of Eve ('Life') from the rib of Adam. In this he was anticipated by V. Scheil, *Comptes rendus de l'Académie des inscriptions et belles-lettres* (1915) 534–5. The relevance of this Sumerian myth for the location of Eden has been maintained by E. A. Speiser, "The Rivers of Paradise," *Festschrift J. Friedrich* (1959) 473–85 ⟦in this volume, 175–82⟧. The name Eden itself has often been derived from the Sumerian *ᶜedin*, 'open country, desert', though the *ᶜayin* is inexplicable, and the meaning unsuitable. Also the *ʾēd* (of unknown meaning) in Gen 2:6 has been given at least two Mesopotamian etymologies, on which see most recently E. A. Speiser, *BASOR* 140 (1955) 9–11. J. J. A. van Dijk in *Acta Orientalia* 28 (1964) 40–44, has pointed out a Sumerian parallel to the content of this part of Genesis.

40. E. A. Speiser, in "Word Plays on the Creation Epic's Version of the Founding of Babylon," *Orientalia*, n.s., 25 (1956) 317–23, put forward an ingenious theory of a literary derivation of the biblical episode of the Tower of Babel from the Babylonian *Enūma Eliš*. Also, in *Eretz-Israel* 5 (1958) 32*–36*, ⟦270–77⟧, he proposed that the biblical Nimrod is a dim reflection of the Assyrian king Tukulti-Ninurta I (*c.* 1240–1200 B.C.). The present writer prefers the more usual opinion that the Sumero-Babylonian war god Ninurta is meant.

the Hittite capital in Asia Minor has yielded a large quantity of fragments of Mesopotamian literature, both Sumerian and Babylonian, including the *Gilgamesh Epic.* A smaller quantity of similar material has been yielded by Ras Shamra, including a piece of the *Atra-ḫasīs Epic.*[41] Megiddo has given up a piece of the *Gilgamesh Epic,*[42] and Amarna itself several pieces of Babylonian literary texts. This spread of Babylonian writings at this period of history is not only the result of the use of ⟦300⟧ cuneiform writing for international communication, but also is owed to the cultural activities of the Hurrians, for they were great borrowers from all the peoples in which they moved and settled, so much so that they were rapidly absorbed and lost their identity. Thus in the Amarna age the Hittites not only had Babylonian and Sumerian literature in addition to native texts, but also works translated from West Semitic.[43] Cultural barriers were indeed broken down in Syria and adjacent lands at this time. Nor was knowledge of borrowed Mesopotamian works restricted to the small number of scribes competent in cuneiform. Among the Hittites the *Gilgamesh Epic* was available in both Hittite and Hurrian translations. Also that version of *Nergal and Ereshkigal* from Amarna is so completely different from the traditional Mesopotamian one in its wording as to give the impression that oral tradition alone will explain it.[44]

Earlier borrowing of the material is ruled out, in the present writer's opinion, because Genesis shows no knowledge of Mesopotamian matters prior to 1500 B.C., a point of considerable importance. The description of Nimrod's kingdom and the account of the Tower of Babel both presume a period when legends were clustering around the city of Babylon. Up to the sudden and unexpected rise of Babylon under Hammurabi (*c.* 1750 B.C.) it was an utterly unimportant and obscure place. One must surely allow a century or two before it could become the centre of legends about early times, as indeed it did in Mesopotamia by about 1200 B.C. Negatively the case is equally strong: Genesis shows no knowledge of Mesopotamian matters prior to about 1500. The very existence of the Sumerians is nowhere hinted at. While the borrowing may have been something altogether more involved and complex than we have suggested, all the known facts favour the idea that the traditions moved westwards during the Amarna period and reached the Hebrews in oral form.

41. To be published by J. Nougayrol in a forthcoming volume of *Le Palais royal d'Ugarit*; see *Comptes rendus de l'Académie des inscriptions et belles-lettres* (1960) 170–1.

42. A. Goetze and S. Levy, *ʿAtiqot* 2 (1959) 121–8.

43. H. G. Güterbock in S. N. Kramer (ed.), *Mythologies of the Ancient World* (1961) 143 and 155.

44. See O. R. Gurney, *Anatolian Studies* 10 (1960) 107.

Postscript

While generally the writer has not changed his approach nor conclusions since the above was published in 1965, there are two aspects on which he would write differently today.[45] The first concerns the origins of the Amorite culture. It remains clear that their irruption into southern Mesopotamia *c.* 2000 B.C. brought with it a certain cultural impact on Babylonian civilization, but it must now be questioned how much of this ideology was Amorite in origin. The archive from mid-third-millennium Ebla, south of Aleppo in Syria, shows that much of the Ugaritic pantheon was firmly established in Syria long before the Amorites appeared, and they had comparatively little impact on it. The third-millennium texts from Mari favour the same conclusions. The area of roughly the modern Syria and Lebanon was, it seems, more or less homogeneous in religion over the second half of the third millennium. Thus what the Amorites brought down the Euphrates to Babylonia was presumably a mixture of nomadic-Amorite and settled-Syrian ideology. Hammurabi's lex talionis no doubt belongs to the former, the concept of the Babylonian pantheon residing on Mount Hermon presumably to the latter.

The second matter concerns the background of Tiāmat in "Enūma Eliš." The writer is now less inclined to consider this monster and the battle in which it fights as possible Amorite imports in southern Mesopotamia. Since 1965 such a diversity of previously unknown Babylonian myth, with no suspicion of foreign origin, has come to light that lack of cuneiform sources for Tiāmat earlier than "Enūma Eliš" seems less significant than it did before. And the name and person are attested. An exercise tablet from Tell Asmar in the Diyala area east of the Tigris, *c.* 22nd century B.C., preserves the beginning of a Semitic hymn to Tišpak, patron god of the town Ešnunna:

> Steward of Tiāmat, warrior, fierce one, arise!
> Tišpak, steward of Tiāmat, fierce one, arise!
> A. Westenholz, *AfO* 25 (1974/77) 102

Also among the personal names of Assyrians trading in Cappadocia in the 18th century B.C. there occurs: *Puzur*$_4$*-tí-a-am-tim/tí-im*, "Protected-by-Tiāmat," all occurrences apparently referring to one person (H. Hirsch, AfO, Beiheft 13/14 [1961], 34). In neither case is there reason to suspect Amorite influence, and Tiāmat does not so far occur among the thou-

45. This postscript is reprinted with permission from Lambert. It first appeared at the end of this same article when it was reprinted in *Babylonien und Israel: Historische, religiöse und sprachliche Beziehungen* (ed. H.-P. Müller; Darmstadt: Hissenschaftliche Buchgesellschaft, 1991) 94–113.

sands of Amorite personal names known from cuneiform sources, though the god Yam may occur, though this is not certain. Thus the lack of a deity corresponding to Tiāmat in Sumerian mythology no longer directs us to look to the Amorites necessarily. North-Mesopotamian mythology may have handed down the tradition which "Enūma Eliš" took up. The male Ugaritic Yam does not suggest borrowing from the West.

The writer has further elaborated his ideas in three articles: Babylonien und Israel, in: Theologische Realenzyklopädie V (1979), 67–79; Interchange of ideas between southern Mesopotamia and Syria-Palestine as seen in literature, in: H.-J. Nissen and J. Renger (eds.), Mesopotamien und seine Nachbarn (Berliner Beiträge zum Vorderen Orient, 1 [1982]), T. 1, 311–16; Old Testament Mythology in its Ancient Near Eastern context, Supplements to Vetus Testamentum 40 (1988), 124–43.

Second Postscript (September, 1994)

J.-M. Durand, to whom the world of scholarship owes so much for the tremendous resurgence of Mari studies over the last fifteen years, has recently published an important Mari letter alluding to Addu's defeat of Tiāmat (there in the Mari dialect form *têmtum*), in an oracle from Addu, the storm-god, himself:

> [giš]*kakkī*[[meš]] *ša it-ti te-em-tim am-ta-aḫ-ṣú ad-di-na-ak-kum*
>
> I have given you the weapons with which I fought with the Sea / Tiāmat.
> *MARI* 7 (Paris, 1993) 45 3′–4′

The article in question, "Le Mythologème du combat entre le dieu de l'orage et la mer en Mésopotamie" (pp. 41–61) deals cursorily with a wide range of issues and cannot be dealt with in detail here, but will be considered elsewhere. In a context of Pan-Amoritism it is argued that the Babylonian Tiāmat in "Enūma Eliš" was borrowed from the West Semitic Yam. (The shade of A. T. Clay must be stirring.) The present writer still holds that the two are descended from a common prehistoric tradition spread very widely from the Indus Valley to the Aegean, and that borrowing from the known Syrian tradition into the Babylonian world is not proven or probable. Here a few key points alone will be made.

The passage from the Old Akkadian school tablet is reinterpreted by J.-M. Durand as follows:

> *ab parrāk tiʾāmtim qurādum azzum tibi*
>
> O Père! toi dont la tâche est d'être la barrière contre les flots de la Mer, guerrier furieux, attaque!

O Father! You whose work it is to be a barrier against the waves of the Sea, fearsome warrior, attack!

This taking of *a-ba-ra-ak* as *ab parrāk* presumes an endingless vocative (rare in Akkadian, and not found in the following *qurādum azzum*), a sandhi-writing (equally rare), and an otherwise unknown word *parrākum*: three improbabilities on either one or two words. (The uncertainty is emphasized by the offering of an alternative *parrāq*: 'Toi dont le rôle de dépecer' ⟦'You whose role is to dismember, carve up'⟧, an equally unknown word.) The resulting sense is compared with Ninurta's holding back the cosmic waters (not, as stated, in *le Retour de Nin-urta,* but in *Lugal ud me-lám-bi nir-g̃ál* (ed. J. J. A. van Dijk; Leiden, 1983, I pp. 95–96, lines 349–55)). However, this holding back of the cosmic waters is paralleled in the Hebrew Bible, and direct borrowing in either direction is highly improbable, though descent from a very ancient common tradition is very likely. Even on the new interpretation of this Old Akkadian text from the Diyala (in which Amorite influence cannot be suspected) we have an allusion to a struggle between Tišpak, a local warrior god, and the Sea/Tiāmat, enough to form the base of the conflict in "Enūma Eliš" between Marduk and Tiāmat. The tradition of dragon-slaying was strong in Mesopotamia, and new variants easily arose from motifs and local deities.

The reasons for preferring the old reading *a-ba-ra-ak* are: (i) Tišpak was a powerful god in the Diyala region, but that does not mean that he was the most senior and important god. In Sumerian mythology Ninurta was the major dragon-slayer, but he was inferior to his father Enlil. In Ugarit Baᶜal gets into the fights, but his much less active father, El, is the head of the pantheon. In "Enūma Eliš," before everything is changed upon Marduk's victory, a quiescent Anšar is king of the gods, while the inferior Ea and Anu do the fighting and struggling. Thus Tišpak could have been inferior to another deity in rank, even if less is heard of that deity. (ii) There is new evidence of the status of Tiāmat in the Mesopotamian pantheon that has so far not been drawn to attention. One passage alone will be quoted:

a-ab-ba ama dingir-re-e-ne-ke$_4$
ta-am-tú um-mi ilāni^{meš}
Sea/Tiāmat, mother of the gods
E. von Weiher, *Spätbabylonische Texte aus Uruk* II (Berlin, 1983) no. 57, cf. p. 37

This is a bilingual incantation, no doubt composed in southern Iraq. The concept expressed is of course implicit in "Enūma Eliš" but does not receive formal expression there. If this view were current in the Diyala, then

Tišpak would have been inferior to Tiāmat in status and ranking. (iii) The term agrig (Sumerian) or *abarakku* (Akkadian) refers to an official not as lowly as J.-M. Durand implies. Note one meaning in *CAD*: 'chief steward of a private or royal household'. Note also that Sumerian kings contemporary with the school text in question also bear this title. Lugalzaggesi, for example, is "the exalted agrig of the gods." Thus stronger evidence than has been presented would be needed before one can deny that Tišpak could be the *abarakku* of Tiāmat in the Diyala region. Only one text with Diyala mythology exists, apart from the school extract, and in that, Sîn acts as chief god (see CT 13 33–34). We know almost nothing of mythology of this area.

A New Babylonian "Genesis" Story

A. R. Millard

⟦3⟧ Association of the Hebrew accounts of Creation and the Flood with the Babylonian is a commonplace of Old Testament studies. It is now some ninety years since George Smith's discoveries of a Flood story in Akkadian very similar to the story of Noah, and of tales of the creation of the earth.[1] During that time many studies have been made of the interrelationship of the various accounts. The following expression by G. von Rad represents a widespread current view with regard to the Flood of Genesis, "Today . . . the dossier on the relation of the Biblical tradition to the Babylonian story of the Flood as it is in the Gilgamesh Epic is more or less closed. A material relationship between both versions exists, of course, but one no longer assumes a direct dependence of the Biblical tradition on the Babylonian. Both versions are independent arrangements of a still older tradition, which itself stemmed perhaps from the Sumerian. Israel met with a Flood tradition in Canaan at the time of her immigration and assimilated it into her religious ideas."[2] The situation is similar, though less certain, with regard to Creation. Most commentators suggest that the Israelites adopted and adapted the Babylonian story *Enuma elish* as transmitted through Canaanite sources.[3] The few dissentient voices are largely ignored.[4]

Reprinted with permission from *Tyndale Bulletin* 18 (1967) 3–18.

1. See G. Smith, *The Chaldean Account of Genesis*, Sampson Low, London (1876).

2. *Genesis*, SCM Press, London (1961) 120.

3. E.g., C. A. Simpson in *The Interpreter's Bible*, Abingdon Press, New York (1952) I, 195, 445f.; S. H. Hooke in M. Black and H. H. Rowley (eds.), *Peake's Commentary on the Bible*, Nelson, London (1962) §§144, 145; S. G. F. Brandon, *Creation Legends of the Ancient Near East*, Hodder & Stoughton, London (1963) 118–157.

4. Such as A. Heidel, *The Babylonian Genesis*², University of Chicago Press (1954) 139, or J. V. Kinnier Wilson in D. W. Thomas (ed.), *Documents from Old Testament Times*, Nelson, London (1958) 14.

Old Testament scholars have generally concentrated upon ⟦4⟧ the famous *Enuma elish* in considering the Creation stories, neglecting the other Babylonian accounts entirely. In fact, the relevance of *Enuma elish* is considerably less than has normally been thought, as an important paper by W. G. Lambert has recently demonstrated.[5] This conclusion, in part, follows from the dating of the composition of *Enuma elish* at the very end of the second millennium B.C., in part, from a study of Babylonian Creation accounts as a whole. Although *Enuma elish* embodies earlier material, this is clearly turned to the poem's main purpose, the exaltation of Marduk, patron of Babylon. Scrutiny of all Babylonian Creation stories is essential before theories can be erected upon apparent similarities with the Hebrew. The significance of such similarities will only appear when each has been evaluated in its own context.

Fewer complications attend comparison of the Flood stories. A. Heidel's book *The Gilgamesh Epic and Old Testament Parallels*[6] remains the authoritative study of the theme. The Babylonian material to be utilized is found in two compositions only, the Epic of Gilgamesh and the Epic of Atrahasis.

The Epic of Atrahasis

Our present purpose is to add more information concerning the Creation and Flood stories rather than to reconsider the whole of this material. The Epic of Atrahasis provides most of this new material. Until 1965 about one-fifth of the story was known; now four-fifths of the whole can be restored. Briefly, it recounts the events precipitating the creation of man, namely, the refusal of the gods to tend the earth, his disturbance of Enlil, the god ruling the earth, and the attempts to quell the trouble, culminating in the Flood and subsequent reorganization of the earth.[7]

The most complete text belongs to the Old Babylonian period and dates about 1630 B.C. How much earlier it was actually composed cannot yet be said. At that time the poem was contained ⟦5⟧ on three large tablets, consisting together of 1,245 lines of writing. Parts of four copies of the first tablet, two of the second, and one of the third are known at

5. *JTS* NS 16 (1965) 287–300. ⟦in this volume, 96–113⟧.

6. Second edition, University of Chicago Press (1949).

7. The text is mostly published in *Cuneiform Texts* XLVI, The British Museum, London (1965) pls. I–XXVII; an edition of the Epic with translation and discussion by W. G. Lambert and the writer is in preparation; understanding of the text owes much to the acumen of Lambert. Parts of this paper are based upon a thesis submitted to the University of London, 1966, entitled *The Atrahasis Epic and Its Place in Babylonian Literature.*

present. In addition, the Assyrian libraries at Nineveh almost a thousand years later included at least three copies equivalent to the first tablet, two covering parts of the first and second, and two of the third, showing evidence of varying editions. A neo-Babylonian fragment was unearthed at Babylon, and a piece of uncertain date, probably Kassite, at Nippur. The story was thus well known, or, at least, widely available, in ancient Mesopotamia. It circulated further afield, too. A tablet from the Hittite capital, Bogazköy, mentioning the hero Atrahasis, shows that something of the story was known there, about 1300 B.C.[8] At the same period a copy of a form of the Epic was present at Ugarit on the Syrian coast.[9] Thus knowledge of the Epic of Atrahasis was very far flung in the second millennium B.C.

As far as can be observed the significance of this composition for Genesis studies has not been noted by Old Testament scholarship in recent years, although its nature as an account covering both Creation and Flood was clearly demonstrated ten years ago from the material then available.[10] It is the only Babylonian parallel to the Hebrew Genesis in providing a continuous narrative of the first era of human existence.

The import of this is immediately apparent: comparisons of accounts from the two literatures made heretofore have generally treated the Creation and the Flood as separate parts—necessarily so since no all-embracing Babylonian narrative was recognized. Some modification of this statement is necessary, for there is one Sumerian composition covering the ground. That is the Deluge Tablet from Nippur of which about one-third survives. It can be dated about 1700 B.C. A discussion of its place in comparative contexts was published by the Assyriologist L. W. King fifty years ago.[11] It is now evident that this Sumerian narrative belongs to the same tradition as the ⟦6⟧ Atrahasis Epic. It differs from the latter in including before the Flood a list of five cities founded as cult-centres for particular deities. Here an association can be made with the Sumerian King List, for these same five cities (Eridu, Bad-tibira, Larak, Sippar, Shuruppak) are given as the seats of the ante-diluvian kings (incidentally, they were never dynastic centres after the Deluge). The association is not merely a modern one; a small fragment of a neo-Assyrian

8. *Keilschrifturkunden aus Boghazköi* VIII, Staatlichen Museen, Berlin (1924) No. 63; cf. H. G. Güterbock, *Kumarbi*, Europaverlag, Zürich (1946) 30f., 81f.

9. J. Nougayrol, *Comptes rendus de l'Academie des inscriptions et belles lettres* (1960) 170–171.

10. J. Laessøe, *Bibliotheca Orientalis* 13 (1956) 90–102; cf. W. G. Lambert, *JSS* 5 (1960) 113–116.

11. *Legends of Babylonia and Egypt in Relation to Hebrew Tradition*, Schweich Lectures for 1916, Oxford University Press (1918).

tablet lists these kings and then continues with a narrative, using a phrase characteristic of the Atrahasis Epic.[12] As is well known, the King List has a complete break with the coming of the Flood, and a fresh start afterwards. While this may be the result of joining a list of ante-diluvian rulers to the later King List, it establishes that there was a tradition linking Creation, early kings, and the Flood in Babylonia, reaching back to the early second millennium B.C. at least.

It is possible that the Atrahasis Epic was compiled from separate narratives of the two major events, and the Sumerian Deluge Tablet likewise. In their present form, however, neither shows any sign of a conflation of sources. An attempt to isolate literary "strata" in the fragments of the Atrahasis Epic known ten years ago fails completely in the light of the new material.[13]

Comparison with the Hebrew Genesis

The Beginning of the World

No account of the creation of the world is found in the Atrahasis Epic; it is concerned exclusively with the story of Man and his relationship with the gods, and this is hinted at in the incipit "When the gods, man-like, . . . " The introduction does describe the situation at the outset of the story, when the world had been divided between the three major deities of the Sumerian-Akkadian pantheon.

> The gods took one hand in the other,
> They cast the lot, made division.
> Anu went up to heaven ⟦7⟧,
> [Enlil] . . . the earth to his subjects.
> The lock, the bar of the sea,
> They gave to Enki, the prince.

Some interest attaches to the last of these realms. The word for 'sea' is *tiāmtu*, the common noun from which the name Tiāmat was developed. There is no need to consider the identity of this word and תְּהוֹם ⟦'deep' (sea)⟧; theories concerning, or based upon, that equivalence collapse with the demonstration that the words are no more than etymological

12. See T. Jacobsen, *The Sumerian King List*, University of Chicago Press (1939); *Cuneiform Texts* XLVI, pl. XXIII, No. 5.

13. J. Laessøe, *Bibliotheca Orientalis* 13 (1956) 95–96. Similarly, efforts to demonstrate the fusion of two disparate narratives into the Flood story of Gilgamesh XI, based upon "doublets" of names and supposed contradictions or inconsistencies, can be disproved as shown in chapter 7 §i.c of the thesis mentioned in n. 7.

cognates.[14] The texts show that the proper name is certainly not intended in the Atrahasis Epic, nor is there any hint of a battle with the sea as found in *Enuma elish.* Nevertheless, the implication is that the sea is an unruly element in need of control. If a parallel is to be sought in the biblical narrative it may be found in Gen 1:9, "Let the waters from under the heaven be gathered to one place and let the dry land appear." This brief ordinance should be considered along with the other references to God confining the sea and preventing it from overwhelming the land. We may doubt whether it is legitimate to understand any Old Testament passage as depicting a primaeval battle between God and the sea. The Rahab, Leviathan, and Tannin verses do not have this implication,[15] nor do the descriptions of the containing of the sea adduced by H. Gunkel to this end appear really convincing.[16] The words employed in the three major passages (Job 38:8–11, Prov 8:29, Ps 104:6–9) are not those employed elsewhere of conflict; thus they contrast with the Rahab, Leviathan, Tannin texts which clearly describe battle. They do refer to bars and bounds and doors.

Some caution should be present in drawing the parallel of the barring of the sea, as it is found in one other Babylonian Creation story, the bilingual *Marduk Account.* This text relates the creation of man and beast, rivers and vegetation, and then ⟦8⟧ states, "He built up a dam at the edge of the sea." As the next line described the draining of a swamp, this may have been related to that, but mention of the sea suggests that the dam's purpose was to keep the land from sea-floods.[17]

Paradise

The introductory description of the world situation in the Atrahasis Epic depicts the junior gods (the Igigu) labouring at the behest of the senior deities (the Anunnaku):

> When the gods, man-like,
> Bore the labour, carried the load,
> The gods' load was great,

14. A. Heidel, *The Babylonian Genesis* 98–101; W. G. Lambert, *loc. cit.* 293 ⟦102 in this volume⟧; K. A. Kitchen, *Theological Students' Fellowship Bulletin* 44 (1966) 3.

15. K. A. Kitchen, *loc. cit.* 3–5.

16. H. Gunkel, *Schöpfung und Chaos,* Vandenhoeck & Ruprecht, Göttingen (1895) 91–111; W. G. Lambert, *loc. cit.* 296 ⟦105 in this volume⟧ (note that the Ninurta Epic there cited as having a parallel conflict with savage waters is describing the salvation of the land from flooding after Creation; the passage is summarized in S. N. Kramer, *Sumerian Mythology*², Harper and Brothers, New York (1961) 80, 81; all the Old Testament allusions to the raging sea refer to the creation and sustaining of the world order, not to a later catastrophe).

17. *Cuneiform Texts* XIII, Pl. 38, l. 31. A. Heidel, *The Babylonian Genesis* 63.

> The toil grievous, the trouble excessive.
> The great Anunnaku, the Seven,
> Were making the Igigu undertake the toil.

In particular, this task took the form of digging the beds of the waterways, the corvée work later considered a menial occupation. Such work was too much for the gods; they held a meeting and decided to depose their taskmaster, Enlil. So they set fire to their tools and advanced to force Enlil to relieve them. It was night-time and the god slept, but his vizier awoke him, soothed his terror, and advised him to consult with his colleagues upon a means to appease the rebels. The council decided to send a messenger to enquire into the cause of the disturbance. Upon learning the state of the gods, the council further deliberated, eventually deciding to make a substitute do the work, namely Man.

No other Babylonian myth exhibits this theme in this way. The conflicts in *Enuma elish* are put down to the youthful exuberances of the gods (Tablet I:21–28), not the refusal to work, but later it is evident that the followers of Tiāmat were set to work, eventually to be liberated by the creation of Man (Tablet IV:107–121, 127; V:147, 148; VI:152, 153; VII:27–9).[18] A bilingual Creation story dating from at least the late second millennium[19] speaks of the creation of the rivers and canals, although without naming the agent of creation, then concentrates upon the making of man to maintain them. Other ⟦9⟧ Akkadian texts indicate man's purpose as the upholding of earth's order so that there is produce to feed the gods.[20] One Sumerian myth exhibits almost all the features of this episode in the Atrahasis Epic; the introduction to the tale *Enki and Ninmah* clearly belongs to the same tradition as Atrahasis.[21]

The underlying idea of the Atrahasis Epic and the other Babylonian Creation stories, then, is that man was made to free the gods from the toil of ordering the earth to produce their food. The gods instructed the Mother-goddess (Nintu or Mami):

> Create a human to bear the yoke.
> Let him bear the yoke, the task of Enlil,
> Let man carry the load of the gods.

18. Cf. B. Landsberger and J. V. Kinnier Wilson, *JNES* 20 (1961) 178–179.

19. E. Ebeling, *Keilschrifttexte aus Assur Religiösen Inhalts*, J. C. Heinrichs, Leipzig (1919) No. 4, datable by its script to the Middle Assyrian period, *vide* E. F. Weidner, *AfO* 16 (1952–3) 207; A. Heidel, *The Babylonian Genesis* 68–71.

20. A. Heidel, *The Babylonian Genesis* 61–63, 65–66.

21. See S. N. Kramer, *Sumerian Mythology* 69–70; J. J. van Dijk, *Acta Orientalia* 28 (1964) 24–31.

Genesis has something in common with this. "The Lord God took the man, and put him into the garden of Eden to dress it and to keep it" (2:15). However, the garden and, indeed, the rest of the earth had produced vegetation already, without great labour (although it is stated that either rainfall or irrigation was necessary, 2:5), and were at man's disposal. The rivers are named and their courses indicated, but there is no account of their formation. Only after the Fall does man really face the toil of wresting his food from a reluctant soil.

The Making of Man

The Atrahasis Epic is more specific on this matter than any other Babylonian Creation account.

> Let them slaughter one god,
> So that all the gods may be purified by dipping.
> With his flesh and blood
> Let Nintu mix clay.
> So let god and man be mingled
> Together in the clay.
> . . . .
> After she had mixed the clay,
> She called the Anunna, the great gods.
> The Igigu, the great gods,
> Spat upon the clay.
> Mami opened her mouth
> And said to the great gods ⟦10⟧,
> "You commanded me a task
> And I have finished it.
> . . . .
> I have removed your toil,
> I have imposed your load on man."

Man was created from the flesh and blood of a slaughtered god mixed with clay. Various aspects of the slaughter do not concern us, but we note that the clay was provided by Enki, presumably from the Apsu, his realm, and mixed with the corpse by the Mother-goddess. When the mixture was ready the gods spat upon it and, with the task completed, the rejoicing gods conferred upon the goddess the title 'Mistress of the gods'. In an elaborate process of birth, the first human couples then came into being, their substance the god-clay mixture.

Once again there is a theme also known to other Babylonian myths. Slaughter of a god and utilization of his blood is found in *Enuma elish*

(Tablet VI), and in the bilingual account already cited deities are killed. The Sumerian *Enki and Ninmah* may also have the same idea. Allusion to the clay is absent from *Enuma elish* and the bilingual account; it probably appears in another bilingual text from Babylon as the substance of creation, and in references in other texts.[22] The gods participating in the creation of man vary from text to text.

Comparison with Genesis may also be made on this topic. God 'formed man of the dust of the ground, and breathed into his nostrils the breath of life; and man became a living soul' (2:7). Man's earthy constituency is emphasized by both Babylonian and Hebrew narratives, and his divine part equally. It is tempting to equate the breathing of Genesis with the spitting of the Atrahasis Epic, but they are very different actions. The 'breath of life' is peculiar to God and man in the Old Testament;[23] the spitting may have no more significance than preparation of the material for working. Yet we may wonder whether it was the life-giving act, finally preparing the material. No hint of the use of dead deity or any material part of a living one is found in Genesis. ⟦11⟧

The Multiplication of Mankind

From the creation of man the Atrahasis Epic passes to the great increase in his number, with a short, and damaged, account of how he now laboured on earth. No other Babylonian text treats of this phase of human history, so this Epic may be placed alone beside Genesis. God commanded man to multiply and fill the earth (Gen 1:28), and as man multiplied, so did his sin. The narrative relating the increase of man and sin is Gen 6:1–8, and in studies of this passage the Epic of Atrahasis has been mentioned as a "parallel."[24] The Atrahasis Epic recounts that:

> There had not passed twelve hundred years,
> The inhabited land had expanded, the
> people had multiplied,
> The land was bellowing like a wild bull.
> The god was disturbed by their clamour,
> Enlil heard their din.
> He said to the great gods,
> "Grievous has grown the din of mankind,
> Through their clamour I lose sleep. . . . "

22. A. Heidel, *The Babylonian Genesis* 65–66; *Theodicy* 258, 276–278; W. G. Lambert, *Babylonian Wisdom Literature*, Clarendon Press, Oxford (1960) 86–89.

23. As T. C. Mitchell has demonstrated, *VT* 11 (1961) 177–187.

24. E. G. Kraeling, *JNES* 6 (1947) 193–195; A. Heidel, *The Gilgamesh Epic and Old Testament Parallels*[2], University of Chicago Press (1949) 225–226.

To meet the problem Enlil sent a plague to decimate the human race, but this was terminated by the intervention of Enki, the god who had been responsible for creating man. He instructed his devotee, Atrahasis, that he should order the city elders to proclaim a cessation of worship of all the gods except the responsible plague-god, who might be persuaded thereby to lift his hand. The command was duly obeyed; the plague ceased; mankind recovered and began to multiply again. Enlil, disturbed by the increasing noise, instigated a drought. Enki gave the same instructions to Atrahasis and the visitation was ended. The next stage is obscure owing to damaged manuscripts; it is clear that there was another attack in the form of a prolonged dearth. This may have been stopped by Enki and Atrahasis, for the gods are next found planning a destruction, the Flood.

The Epic of Atrahasis reveals a motive on the part of the gods in sending the Flood. This is lacking from the Flood story contained within the Gilgamesh Epic—it was irrelevant there, the simple statement that the gods decided to send the Flood ⟦12⟧ being sufficient to the account of how Uta-napishtim (= Atrahasis) obtained immortality (Gilgamesh XI:14).[25]

Genesis 6 states that: ". . . men began to multiply on the face of the earth" (verse 1); "And God saw that the wickedness of man was great in the earth . . . " (verse 5); ". . . The end of all flesh is come before me; for the earth is filled with violence through them" (verse 13).

In the common analysis of the literary structure of Genesis the first four verses of chapter 6 are detached from the remainder of the chapter. The episode related is treated as an aetiology of the Nephilim and characterized as a pagan myth, its offensive details whittled down until it was just fit to be absorbed into the Hebrew sacred literature.[26] Many of the problems attached to these verses fall beyond this study; a few points do arise in the present context. If parallelism of scheme is allowed between Hebrew and Babylonian traditions of ante-diluvian history, then this section should be accepted as an integral part of the scheme; it presents the "population explosion" theme not found elsewhere in the Hebrew account.

The sin of the promiscuity of the "sons of God" cannot be explained directly from Babylonian texts, but some hint may be found of their nature. A theory recently propounded as to their identity involves Babylonian concepts, and is attractive: the "sons of God" are not divine beings,

25. A. Heidel, *The Gilgamesh Epic* 80; *ANET* 93.

26. Cf. B. S. Childs, *Myth and Reality in the Old Testament*, SCM Press, London (1960) 49–57.

but kings.[27] Support is found in application of the title "son of God" to kings in various ancient texts.[28] The sin of the "sons of God" was, therefore, "the sin of polygamy, particularly as it came to expression in the harem. . . ."[29] Gilgamesh, heroic king of Uruk some time after the Flood, well exemplifies the type of activity described in Gen 6:1ff.[30]

The sin of mankind as a whole was his evil conduct resulting in violence, according to Genesis. While an equation with the "din" of the Atrahasis Epic may appear improbable, the basic ⟦13⟧ idea of disturbing deity is surely common to both narratives as the provocation leading to the decision to send the Flood.[31]

The several attempts to quell man's noise in the Atrahasis Epic have no counterpart in Genesis. It has been suggested that there is a similarity between the one-hundred-and-twenty-year 'period of grace' in Gen 6:3 and the plague, drought, dearth episode in Atrahasis.[32] Certainly, the number 'an hundred and twenty' could have Babylonian undertones from the sexagesimal system, and the intervals between the visitations in the Epic are delimited by the expression "not twelve hundred years had passed." Therein a further theme linking this episode with the Flood sequence may exist.[33]

The Flood

No Babylonian text provides so close a parallel to Genesis as does the Flood story of Gilgamesh XI. Considerable study has been devoted to the accounts in the two languages and to comparison of them. The work of Alexander Heidel is the most comprehensive, the commentary of Umberto Cassuto the most detailed.[34]

In the Atrahasis Epic the Flood is the major topic; at the end the whole composition is apparently referred to as "the Flood." Since the major text of the Epic dates from the seventeenth century B.C. (see above, p. 4 ⟦115⟧), it is thus about a millennium older than the texts of

27. M. G. Kline, *WTJ* 24 (1962) 187–204.

28. It may be noted that an Akkadian god-list identifies several of the ante-diluvian rulers with Dumu-zi, Tammuz; *Cuneiform Texts* XXIV, pl. 19, K4338b; XXV, pl. 7, K7663+11035.

29. M. G. Kline, *loc. cit.* 196.

30. A. Heidel, *The Gilgamesh Epic* 30 (Tablet II.22–37); *ANET* 77–78.

31. J. J. Finkelstein, *JBL* 75 (1956) 329 n. 7 sees an "echo" of Atrahasis in Genesis 6.

32. A. Heidel, *The Gilgamesh Epic* 230–232; M. G. Kline, *loc. cit.* 197.

33. The figure in Gen 6:3 may denote man's life span, not a period of grace at all, so B. S. Childs, *op. cit.* 52–53; cf., however, K. A. Kitchen, *loc. cit.* 6.

34. A. Heidel, *The Gilgamesh Epic*; U. Cassuto, *A Commentary on the Book of Genesis* II, Magnes Press, Jerusalem (1964) 4–24; cf. G. Hilion, *Le Déluge dans la Bible et les Inscriptions akkadiennes et sumériennes*, Geuthner, Paris (1925).

Gilgamesh XI which stem from Ashurbanipal's Library at Nineveh and from neo-Babylonian Babylon. Nevertheless the story is the same. That is not to say that every word is identical, nor even every incident, but the greater part is closely similar where both Epics are preserved. The differences are partly due to editorial redaction when the story was inserted into the Gilgamesh cycle, partly inexplicable with any certainty.

A notable fact is the portrait of the Babylonian Noah, Atrahasis. He is entitled "servant" of Enki and was quite clearly a special devotee of that god. Indeed, it is possible to interpret his name as 'the exceedingly devout' as well as 'exceedingly wise', the common explanation, for the root *ḫss* has the sense of ⟦14⟧ devotion, respect, and care. This describes aptly the character of the hero portrayed in the Flood story, for it was not of his own wisdom that he saved himself, but by obedience to divine instructions. Moreover, the reason given by Enki for revealing the plan to exterminate humanity to one man has more weight when understood as "I caused the exceedingly devout one to see dreams, he heard the decision of the gods" than as "the exceedingly wise one" (Gilgamesh XI:187; not preserved in the extant text of the Atrahasis Epic). His piety then appears clearly as the reason for his survival. In addition to his relationship to his god, he had authority to summon and instruct the city elders, pointing to his high rank, consonant with his representation as a king in the King List tradition, and as a priest in the Sumerian Deluge Tablet.[35] This supports the contention that it was for his piety he was saved from destruction, just as Noah was saved for his righteousness.[36]

Other points of similarity are those already found in the Gilgamesh Flood story and require no new examination at present. The episode of the birds is not present in the Epic of Atrahasis, but it cannot be said definitely that it was never included because the only manuscript is broken at the appropriate point. Agreement between the Atrahasis and Gilgamesh narratives on so much of the story lends weight to the supposition that the incident was included.[37]

After the Flood, Atrahasis made sacrifices to the gods who are depicted as sitting miserably in heaven without food or drink for its duration. The gods, already regretting their action, indulged in further recrimination. Enki made a speech similar to that in Gilgamesh XI which begins "On the sinner lay his sin; on the transgressor lay his transgression" (line 180), but that illuminating line does not occur in the incomplete text of the Atrahasis Epic. Atrahasis' destiny is also unknown

35. Cf. J. J. Finkelstein, *JCS* 17 (1963) 48.
36. A. Heidel, *The Gilgamesh Epic* 228; *contra* U. Cassuto, *op. cit.* 20.
37. W. G. Lambert, *loc. cit.* 292, is noncommittal.

because of damage to the tablets. The gods so ordained society thereafter that there would be some control of the number of mankind.

Observations on the Babylonian and the Hebrew Accounts Compared

The Scheme as a Whole

There can be no doubt that the concept ⟦15⟧ of a history of man from his creation to the Flood is similar both in Babylonian and in Hebrew. Any future consideration of possible origins of the Hebrew story must take this into account, and not treat Creation and Flood separately. Thus it is no longer legitimate to describe the Hebrew Flood story as "borrowed" from a Babylonian "original" without including its complementary Creation account.[38] The objection may be raised that exactly such a separation is made within Akkadian literature; the Flood story is given in Gilgamesh XI without its context. However, that poem itself makes the reason plain: Uta-napishtim related the story of how he gained immortality, and for his purpose the Creation narrative was unnecessary. That it is there a case of literary borrowing cannot be doubted, but the intention is clear and the new context, the account related by the hero, is quite natural.

While the overall scheme, Creation—Rebellion—Flood, is identical, most of the detail is different; on a few points only there is agreement. A summary may help in considering interrelationship.

Man's Constituency. Both the Bible and some Babylonian Creation accounts depict man as created from "the dust of the earth" or "clay." To this is added some divine component, "breath" in Genesis, flesh and blood of a god, and divine spittle in Babylonia. This concept of clay and divine substance mixed is not exclusive to these two literatures. It is found in Egypt in certain traditions, and, further afield, in China.[39] Common ideas need not share a common source. The earthy concept may be placed in the category of a deduction from natural processes which could be made independently. The belief in a divine indwelling "spark" seems to be common to so many faiths and cultures that this also need not be traced to a common origin.

38. As, for example, A. Richardson, *Genesis I–XI,* SCM Press (1953) 97.

39. See S. G. F. Brandon, *Creation Legends of the Ancient Near East,* Hodder & Stoughton, London (1964), and *La Naissance du Monde, Sources Orientales* I, Editions du Seuil, Paris (1959).

Divine Rest. In Babylonian tradition the creation of man relieved the gods of the need to work; they entered a new era of rest. In Genesis God rested after His creation was complete. The actions are very similar, the contexts are quite different. The Hebrew God needed not to labour for His sustenance, nor [[16]] did He tire of His work. The Babylonian gods, on the other hand, were "like a man," toiling and wearying, needing help in the business of keeping alive. Wholly different theologies underlie these two views. Emphasis is often laid on the word שַׁבָּת and its Akkadian cognate *šapattu.*[40] Both words basically denote 'cessation, completion'. However, use of cognate terms does not carry with it identity of practice or of the origins of a practice. In fact, the Akkadian word denotes specifically the full moon, the peak of the lunar cycle on the fifteenth day of the lunar month, and nothing else. Hebrew שַׁבָּת is not used in that way, nor is it used solely of a week's end. An analogy is found in the usages of the cognates תְּהוֹם and Tiāmat. Thus only the idea of divine rest is really similar; no derived Sabbath existed in Babylonia. It may be asked, therefore, whether this similarity is strong enough and striking enough to indicate borrowing.

Man's Task. Again it may be argued that cultivating and tending the earth is so common an occupation that the designation of this as the reason for man's existence could have arisen in two places independently. In fact Genesis does not express this so simply as man's purpose.

Man's Rebellion. While the biblical Fall finds no counterpart in Babylonia, the provocation of deity leading to the Flood is comparable in general terms.

The Flood. Here is the section most similar in the two traditions: the Ark, its passengers, the birds, the grounding on a mountain, and the sacrifice are all basically shared.

Did the Hebrews Borrow from Babylon?

Neither an affirmative nor a negative reply to the question can be absolutely discounted in the light of present knowledge. Reconstructions of a process whereby Babylonian myths were borrowed by the Hebrews, having been transmitted by the Canaanites, and "purged" of pagan elements[41] remain imaginary. It has yet to be shown that any Canaanite

40. W. G. Lambert, *loc. cit.* 296f. [[106–7 in this volume]]

41. E.g., C. A. Simpson in *The Interpreter's Bible* I, Abingdon Press, Nashville (1952) 195, 445–450.

material was absorbed into Hebrew sacred literature on such a scale or in such a way. Babylonian literature itself was known in Palestine at the time of the Israelite conquest, ⟦17⟧ and so could have been incorporated directly. The argument that borrowing must have taken place during the latter part of the second millennium B.C. because so many Babylonian texts of that age have been found in Anatolia, Egypt, and the Levant,[42] cannot carry much weight, being based on archaeological accident. The sites yielding the texts were either deserted or destroyed at that time, resulting in the burial of "libraries" and archives intact.[43] Evidence does exist of not inconsiderable Babylonian scribal influence earlier (e.g., at Alalakh and Byblos).[44]

However, it has yet to be shown that there was borrowing, even indirectly. Differences between the Babylonian and the Hebrew traditions can be found in factual details of the Flood narrative (form of the Ark; duration of the Flood, the identity of the birds and their dispatch) and are most obvious in the ethical and religious concepts of the whole of each composition.[45] All who suspect or suggest borrowing by the Hebrews are compelled to admit large-scale revision, alteration, and reinterpretation in a fashion which cannot be substantiated for any other composition from the Ancient Near East or in any other Hebrew writing. If there was borrowing then it can have extended only as far as the "historical" framework, and not included intention or interpretation. The fact that the closest similarities lie in the Flood stories is instructive. For both Babylonians and Hebrews the Flood marked the end of an age. Mankind could trace itself back to that time; what happened before it was largely unknown. The Hebrews explicitly traced their origins back to Noah, and, we may suppose, assumed that the account of the Flood and all that went before derived from him. Late Babylonian sages supposed that tablets containing information about the ante-diluvian world were buried at Sippar before the Flood and disinterred afterwards.[46] The two accounts undoubtedly describe the same Flood, the two schemes ⟦18⟧ relate the same sequence of events. If judgment is to be passed as to the priority of one tradition over the other, Genesis inevitably wins for its

42. W. G. Lambert, *loc. cit.* 299–300. ⟦108–9 in this volume⟧

43. This is true of almost every large collection of literary texts in cuneiform, not only Amarna, Ugarit, Bogazköy at this period, but also Ur and Nippur earlier, Assur, Nineveh, Nimrud, and Sultantepe at the end of the Assyrian Empire, Babylon and Uruk even later; cf. W. G. Lambert, *Revue d'Assyriologie* 53 (1959) 123.

44. D. J. Wiseman, *Syria* 39 (1962) 181–184 for Alalakh; W. F. Albright, *BASOR* 163 (1961) 45 for Byblos.

45. Most recently stated by K. A. Kitchen, *loc. cit.* 7.

46. Berossus; A. Heidel, *The Gilgamesh Epic* 117.

probability in terms of meteorology, geophysics, and timing alone. In creation its account is admired for its simplicity and grandeur, its concept of man accords well with observable facts. In that the patriarch Abraham lived in Babylonia, it could be said that the stories were borrowed from there, but not that they were borrowed from any text now known to us. Granted that the Flood took place, knowledge of it must have survived to form the available accounts; while the Babylonians could only conceive of the event in their own polytheistic language, the Hebrews, or their ancestors, understood the action of God in it. Who can say it was not so?

Careful comparison of ancient texts and literary methods is the only way to the understanding of the early chapters of Genesis. Discovery of new material requires re-assessment of former conclusions; so the Epic of Atrahasis adds to knowledge of parallel Babylonian traditions, and of their literary form. All speculation apart, it underlines the uniqueness of the Hebrew primaeval history in the form in which it now exists.

The Eridu Genesis

Thorkild Jacobsen

Texts

⟦513⟧ The more or less fragmentary story for which we suggest the name "The Eridu Genesis" has come down to us in bits of related, but variant, versions. It is written in Sumerian and probably took form late, perhaps around 1600 B.C. It deals with the creation of man, the institution of kingship, the founding of the first cities and the great flood. Thus it is a story of beginnings, a Genesis, and, as I shall try to show in detail later, it prefigures so to speak, the biblical Genesis in its structure. The god Enki and his city Eridu figure importantly in the story, Enki as savior of mankind, Eridu as the first city. Thus "The Eridu Genesis" seems appropriate.[1]

Our sources for it are first and foremost the lower third of a clay tablet of Old-Babylonian date (ca. 1600 B.C.) from Nippur inscribed with six columns of Sumerian text.[2] Secondly we have a fragment from Ur,

Reprinted with permission from *Journal of Biblical Literature* 100 (1981) 513–29. Original footnotes 6–11 and 13–16, which deal with the restoration of the Sumerian text, have been eliminated in this edition. For Jacobsen's translation of "The Eridu Genesis," see also pp. 160–64 in this volume. Although parts are reproduced in Jacobsen's article as well, it was thought best to retain both for the reader's convenience.

1. Special abbreviations used are: AS = The Oriental Institute of the University of Chicago, *Assyriological Studies* (Chicago, 1931–). *Atra-ḫasīs* = W. G. Lambert and A. R. Millard, *Atra-ḫasīs, the Babylonian Story of the Flood* (Oxford, 1969). CT = *Cuneiform Texts from Babylonian Tablets in the British Museum* (London, 1896–). GSG = A. Poebel, *Grundzüge der sumerischen Grammatik* (Rostock, 1923). MSL = B. Landsberger, *Materialien zum Sumerischen Lexikon* (Rome, 1937–). PBS = University of Pennsylvania, the University Museum, *Publications of the Babylonian Section* (Philadelphia, 1911–). ŠL = A. Deimel, *Šumerisches Lexikon* (Rome, 1928–1937). UET = *Ur Excavation Texts* (London, 1928–).

2. The tablet was found at Nippur during the third season's work of the Expedition of the University of Pennsylvania (1893–1896) but was not immediately recognized for what it was. The box in which it was kept was labeled "incantation." Thus it was not until 1912,

likewise in Sumerian and of about the same date. It is the left edge of a tablet and ⟦514⟧ preserves only the beginnings of the lines it once had.[3] Third is a bilingual fragment, Sumerian with Akkadian translation, from Ashurbanipal's library in Nineveh. It dates to about 600 B.C.[4]

While all of these fragments of texts can be seen to tell the same story; creation, earliest cities, the flood; they vary a good deal among themselves in explicitness and so must be taken to represent not one, but several different versions, some more some less full in their renderings of the original story.

The first column of the Nippur text sets in, after some 36 lost lines, with a monologue by the goddess of birth, the mother of mankind, Nintur. (Another name for her, which the text uses when she is mentioned as one of the four highest gods who together make all major decisions, is Nin-hursağa(k) "The queen of the foothills.")[5] She has decided to

---

when Arno Poebel went through the tablet collection, that its true nature was discovered. Poebel published it in handcopy in PBS V as no. 1 and furnished a transliteration, translation and penetrating analysis in the companion volume PBS IV (pp. 9–70). He convincingly dated the tablet (pp. 66–69) on epigraphical and other grounds to the latter half of the First Dynasty of Babylon. Little further work of consequence was done on the text for thirty-six years—a detailed bibliography may be found in Rykle Borger, *Handbuch der Keilschriftliteratur* I (Berlin: de Gruyter, 1967) p. 411 to PBS V no. 1—but in 1950 Samuel N. Kramer's translation was published in *ANET* (pp. 42–44), and again, almost twenty years later, Miguel Civil restudied the text in his chapter in *Atra-ḫasīs* (pp. 138–47). The interpretation here offered owes much to our predecessors, far more than would appear from our often very different understanding of the text.

3. Published in UET VI as no. 61. It is in Sumerian and of about the same date as the one published by Poebel in PBS V. Only the beginning of the lines it once had are preserved, but in many cases their stereotype content admits of ready restoration.

4. First published from a copy by F. Geers in AS 11, plate at end of volume, cf. p. 59 n. 113. Republished with an additional fragment which adds remnants of six more lines at the beginning by W. G. Lambert in CT XLVI, pl. xxiii no. 5.

5. For this goddess see Poebel PBS IV pp. 24–34 and our article "Notes on Nintur" in *Orientalia* n.s. 42 (1973) 274–98. We would now hesitate to see her as "in origin two distinct and different deities, not one" (p. 285), for the blend in her of mountain- and birth-goddess becomes understandable once it is realized that she traces straight back to the neolithic precursor of the *potnia theron*, the "Great Goddess of Life, Death and Regeneration" to use Marija Gimbutas's term for her. We hope at some other time to deal with this in more detail. For the time being compare M. Gimbutas, *The Gods and Goddesses of Old Europe 7000–3500 B.C.* (Berkeley and Los Angeles: University of California, 1974) 152–200 and p. 232 figs. 247–50. In Gimbutas's "Sorrowful God" (pp. 230–34), who traces down to the emaciated figures flanking Nintur on a well known Old-Babylonian plaque, we would now—differently from "Notes on Nintur" (p. 285 n. 89)—prefer to see a representation of aged dead and buried people awaiting rebirth in the earth. Ud-ğu$_{10}$-ul in the myth of Enki and Ninmah may be relevant here. For later representations of the figure see Edith Porada, "An Emaciated Male Figure of Bronze in the Cincinnati Art Museum" in *Studies Presented to*

call mankind home from a nomadic, vagrant existence, to have them build cities and temples, and thus become sedentary and civilized. The text reads ⟦515⟧:

> Nintur was paying attention:
> Let me bethink myself of my humankind,
> (all) forgotten as they are;
> and mindful of mine, Nintur's, creatures
> let me bring them back,
> let me lead the people back from their trails.
>
> May they come and build cities and cult-places,
> that I may cool myself in their shade;
> may they lay the bricks for the cult-cities
> in pure spots, and
> may they found places for divination
> in pure spots!
>
> She gave directions for purification, and cries for quarter,
> the things that cool (divine) wrath,
> perfected divine service and the august offices,
> said to the (surrounding) regions: "Let me institute peace
> there!"
>
> When An, Enlil, Enki, and Ninhursağa
> fashioned the darkheaded (people)
> they had made the small animals (that come up) from (out
> of) the earth
> come from the earth in abundance
> and had let there be, as befits (it), gazelles,
> (wild) donkeys, and fourfooted beasts in the desert.

⟦516⟧ Exactly what had preceded this benevolent decision of the goddess is unfortunately lost in the missing lines 1 to 36 at the beginning of the text, but some of it we can guess at with a fair degree of confidence.

We must have been told about the creation of man and of the animals, since their existence is assumed in the section preserved. As creators the text mentions the four highest gods, An, Enlil, Enki and

---

A. Leo Oppenheim (Chicago: University of Chicago, 1964) 159–66 figs. 1–4 and 9, and H. Frankfort, "A Note on the Lady of Birth," *JNES* 3 (1944) 198–200. For survival of the goddess in the Greek world see generally W. K. C. Guthrie, *The Greeks and Their Gods* (Boston: Beacon, 1950) 99. It should be noted that the text PBS V no. 1 seems to treat of Nintur and Nin-hursağa as if they were two different deities and not one. The former is the concerned mother of mankind, the latter a detached authority figure.

Ninhursaĝa but as seen already by Poebel numerous parallels in other myths implicate that only Enki and Ninhursaĝa in her aspect as birth-goddess, in which she is called Nintur, did the actual work of creation. This is clear from Nintur's speaking of mankind as "my creatures" and it explains her and Enki's special concern for man in the story. It is *mutatis mutandis* "parental" protectiveness.

It must also seem likely that the miserable way of life of man, before he had attained to the benefits of civilization, was described in some detail to give point to the goddess' taking pity on him. Here we may, therefore, turn for enlightenment to the text from Ur, which on its obverse seems to have dealt with just these early conditions. The line-beginnings which it preserves can, in large measure, be restored from stereotypes in the introductions to other myths. Thus restored it tells that in those days no irrigation canal had yet been dug, no ditches dredged. The seeder-plow was not used, so no one sowed grain in furrows; it was broadcast. People suffered during years of famine in which nothing was produced. The god of herds, Sumukan, had not yet appeared, so with no wool for weaving into cloth people had to go naked. On the credit side, though, was one fact. There were no dangerous beasts: "In yonder days there was no serpent, no scorpion; and as there was no hyena, no panther, no wolf; as there was no fear of attack, man had no opponent." The last line of the fragment still readable has the word for "king," so it may reasonably be assumed that it told that these early men had no one to guide them, had as yet no king.

⟦517⟧ More difficult is the problem of what may have stood at the beginning of column ii in the lacuna that follows the section telling of the goddess' resolve. Offhand, one would have thought that the carrying out of her intentions would have been related here, but clearly that cannot have been the case, for 36 lines later, when the text again resumes, the cities have still not been built and a deity—apparently still Nintur—is planning to provide mankind with leadership, giving them a king to organize the work and carry out the necessary rites. It would seem, therefore, that what the missing 36 lines must have told about was a first unsuccessful attempt at city building that came to naught for lack of proper leadership, so that Nintur had to add to her earlier benefactions by the instituting of kingship. Be that as it may, when the text is preserved in the lower part of column ii, it reads ⟦518⟧:

> . . . . . and let me have *him* advise;
> let me have *him* oversee their labor,
> and let *him* teach the nation to follow
> unerringly like cattle!

When the royal scepter was coming down from heaven,
the august crown and the royal throne being already down
from heaven,
he (i.e., the king) regularly performed to perfection
the august divine services and offices,
laid the bricks of those cities in pure spots.
They were named by name and allotted half-bushel baskets.

The firstling of those cities, Eridu,
she gave to the leader Nudimmud,
the second, Badtibira, she gave to the Prince and Sacred One
the third, Larak, she gave to Pabilsag,
the fourth, Sippar, she gave to the gallant, Utu,
the fifth, Shuruppak, she gave to Sud.

These cities, which had been named by names,
and been allotted half-bushel baskets,
dredged the canals, which were blocked with purplish
(wind-borne) clay, and they carried water.
Their cleaning of the smaller canals
established abundant growth.

⟦519⟧ That the first cities were given "bushel baskets" is to be understood in the light of the fact that the ancient Mesopotamian economy was a distributional one, not a money economy. All remuneration for work performed was accordingly given in goods, especially edibles such as grain or flour. The "half-bushel baskets" characterize therefore the cities as economical centers, "distribution points," and are to be understood as symbols of that function.

The end of the list of cities is also given, after a long gap, on the reverse of the fragment from Ur. The text of that fragment, however, appears to represent a slightly abbreviated version of the story for it omits the lines about the dredging of the canals and seems to lead directly into the appointment of the first king.

Returning to the Nippur text we have there after the listing of the cities a lacuna of about 34 lines at the beginning of column iii, and what originally was told here is suggested by the bilingual fragment from Ashurbanipal's library. It preserves the end of a listing of the kings who ruled in the cities and their reigns. That listing, furthermore, can be restored from independent tradition as well as from the Sumerian Kinglist, to which it was secondarily added by some ancient copyists.

The fragment from Ashurbanipal's library may be restored as follows:

(1′–5) In Eridu Alulim reigned 36,000 years (1′–4) Alagar ruled 10,800 years (1′–3) ⟦520⟧ 2 kings reigned 46,800 years, Eridu's term. (1′–2) Eridu's term was commuted (shifted) (1′–1) In Bad-tibira Enmenluanna reigned 46,800 years (1′) Enmengalanna reigned 64,800 years (2′) Dumuzi the shepherd reigned 36,000 years (3′) 3 kings reigned 100,000 years, Bad-tibira's term. (4′) Bad-tibira's term was commuted (5′) In Sippar Enmeduranki reigned 64,800 years (6′) one king reigned 64,800 years, Sippar's term. (7′) Sippar's term was commuted (8′) In Larak Ensipadzianna reigned 36,000 years (9′) One king reigned 36,000 years, Larak's term. (10′) Larak's term was commuted (11′). In Shuruppak Ubara-Tutu reigned 28,800 years (12′) Ziudsudra reigned 64,800 years (13′) two kings reigned 93,600 years, Shuruppak's term. (14′) Five individual cities, nine kings reigned 352,800 years, their terms. (15′) Enlil took a dislike to mankind (17′) the clamor of their shouting . . . kept him sleepless.

The reigns listed are notable for their lengths, which run from a relatively modest 10,800 years for one king to as much as 64,800 years for others. An amusing sidelight—at least new to me—falls on their amazing longevity from a text listing kings of the city of Lagash. It makes clear that these ancients not only lived extraordinarily "long" but also, apparently, lived extraordinarily "slowly," they took their time about growing up. The Lagash Kinglist says about the generations immediately after the flood had subsided:

> In those days a child spent a hundred years
> in diapers (lit. "in ⟨bits⟩ of the wash")
> After he had grown up he spent a hundred years
> without being given any task (to perform) ⟦521⟧
> He was small, he was dull witted
> his mother watched over him,
> His straw-bedding was laid down in the cowpen.

A similar slow development from child to man's estate we should probably assume also for the biblical patriarchs. It would, at least, fit in well with the otherwise puzzlingly high age they had to reach before they were able to beget children. Methuselah, for example, was 187 years old when he begat his firstborn Lamech, and Lamech was 182 when he begat Noah. Before leaving this singular concept of slow growing up I should mention a most striking similarity between the Lagash list and Hesiod's silver race, to which Professor John Peradotto drew my attention. Both have the 100 years childhood—the stupidity—and the being watched over by the mother. Hesiod, after telling about the first golden race says:[6]

> Next after these the dwellers upon Olympus made a second race, of silver, far worse than the other. They were not like the golden ones either in shape or spirit. A child was a child for a hundred years, looked after and playing by his gracious mother, kept at home an utter imbecile. . . .

The bilingual text from Ashurbanipal's library follows up, as we saw, the list of kings and reigns with a mention of the noise man made and of the god Enlil, referring, undoubtedly to the reason for the flood: man made such a din that Enlil was kept awake day and night until he finally decided to rid himself of his tormentors by that radical means. The lacuna in the Nippur text presumably also told of this, for when the text resumes in column iii the flood has been decided upon by the gods. After five lines of which only a few signs are left, we hear how ⟦522⟧:

> That day Nintur wept over her creatures
> and holy Inanna was full of grief over their people;
> but Enki took counsel with his own heart.
> An, Enlil, Enki, and Ninhursağa
> had the gods of heaven and earth swear
> by the names An and Enlil.
> At that time Ziusudra was king
> and lustration priest.
> He fashioned, being a seer, (a statue of)
> the god of giddiness (inducing ecstasy)
> and stood in awe beside it, wording (his
> wishes) humbly.
>
> As he stood there regularly day after day he heard
> something that was not a dream appearing: conversation
> a swearing (of) oaths by heaven and earth, a (confirming)
> touching of throats
> and the gods bringing their thwarts up to Ki-ùr.
>
> And as Ziusudra stood there beside it he went on hearing:
> "Step up to the wall to my left and listen! ⟦523⟧
> Let me speak a word to you at the wall
> and may you grasp what I say,
> May you heed my advice!
> By our hand a flood will sweep over
> (the cities of) the half-bushelbaskets, and the country,

6. Translation by John Peradotto.

the decision, that mankind is to be destroyed,
has been made,
a verdict, a command by the assembly,
cannot be revoked,
an order of An and Enlil is not known
ever to have been countermanded,
their kingship, their term, has been uprooted
they must bethink themselves (of that)
Now . . . .
What I have to say to you . . . ."

Here the text breaks off, but there can be little doubt that Enki's advice to Ziusudra was that he should build a boat and with it save himself and a couple of each living thing. Nor that Ziusudra followed the advice conscientiously.

The description of how Enki's warning came to his ward is interesting. It is intimately connected with the king's role as diviner, seer and prophet. This side of kingship was very important in older times; the king was, as priest-king, mediator between the people and the gods, and by discovering the gods' will and obeying it he ensured peace and prosperity.

Ziusudra's priestly status is indicated by his title g u d a - a b z u "lustration priest," that of seer, if we have restored it correctly, by e n s i "diviner." That Ziusudra made a statue of the god of giddiness suggests that he also was able to communicate with the world beyond through ecstasy, and so valued and sought the giddiness that precedes and induces ecstatic trance as it does, for instance, in the whirling dervishes or in ecstasy induced by other means, as normal consciousness recedes.

Ziusudra served the god of giddiness diligently. Thus it comes about that his senses open up to the supernatural and he becomes aware of what is happening in the world of the gods: their arrival to assembly in Ki-ùr in Nippur where the divine place of assembly, Ubshuukkinna, was located, their conversation and swearing of the traditional introductory oath to abide loyally by what the assembly may decide. A homely trait is that, as the gods arrive in their boats, they take the thwarts along with them to sit on in the assembly. One imagines that the thwarts were upholstered.

As Ziusudra senses all of this activity he hears a voice which calls him over to the wall where Enki sits—we would probably say: calls him aside to talk privately with him—and tells him about the catastrophe that has been decided upon and what he must do to save his life.

The beginning of column iv follows directly upon the end of column iii but then comes once more a lacuna, which extends to the beginning of ⟦524⟧ column v. Very obviously though, the text must here have told how Ziusudra built his boat, boarded it with his family and the animals, and how the gods unleashed the elements; for with column v we are in the middle of the great flood:

> All evil winds, all stormy winds gathered into one
> and with them, the Flood was sweeping over (the cities of)
>   the half-bushel baskets
> for seven days and seven nights.
> After the flood had swept over the country,
> after the evil wind had tossed the big boat
>   about on the great waters,
> the sun came out spreading light
>   over heaven and earth.
>
> Ziusudra then drilled an opening in the big boat,
> and the gallant Utu (the sun-god) sent
>   his light into the interior of the big boat.
> Ziusudra, being a king,
> stepped up before Utu kissing the ground (before him).
> The king was butchering oxen, was being lavish with the
>   sheep
> barley cakes, crescents together with . . . .
> . . . . he was crumbling for him
> . . . .
> juniper, the pure plant of the
>   mountains he filled on the fire
> and with a . . . . clasped to
>   the breast he . . . .

At this point of the tale a new lacuna intervenes, so we do not know how the news about Ziusudra's surviving the flood was received by the gods. Most likely Enlil, as in the other versions of the tale that have come down to us, ⟦525⟧ was at first enraged, but was then talked into accepting the situation by the clever Enki.

At the point at which column vi begins we are, as far as one can see, at the end of Enki's convincing argumentation. He says, addressing first the gods among whom he stands, then An and Enlil:

> "You here have sworn by the life's breath of heaven,
>   the life's breath of earth, that he verily is allied with you
>   yourself;

you there, An and Enlil, have sworn by the life's breath
of heaven, the life's breath of earth, that he is
allied with all of you,
He will disembark the small animals
that come up from the earth!"

Ziusudra, being king, stepped up before An and Enlil
kissing the ground,
And An and Enlil did well by him,
were granting him life like a god's,
were making lasting breath of life, like a god's
descend into him.
That day they made Ziusudra,
preserver as king of the name of the small
animals and the seed of mankind,
live toward the east over the mountains
in Mount Tilmun.
. . . .

At this the text again breaks off, but it seems unlikely that there was much more to tell. Mankind and all living things had escaped destruction.

Interpretation

⟦526⟧ In seeking to interpret this tale one may profitably begin by noting that it is formed of three distinct parts, each apparently with its own theme and purport. We can consider them in order. The motif of *the first one* is the well known one of nature versus culture. Unlike other treatments of this widespread theme, however, there is here no tension between these two ways of life; culture is overwhelmingly superior. Because man in his natural state is so pitiful the mother goddess has compassion on him and gives him cities and government, which produces prosperity. The myth thus celebrates—reflecting quite accurately and realistically the economic possibilities of Southern Mesopotamia—the potential of irrigation agriculture and the dependence of the latter on strong governmental organization for its success. It is accordingly—if we would wish to use Malinowski's term—a "charter" for the state, specifically for the city-state.

The second part has to do with the first cities thus founded and their rulers. In style this section is clearly modeled on the great Sumerian Kinglist and its formulaic language and arrangement. As to its import one is somewhat at a loss. It does not particularly seem aimed at conferring special prestige on cities or dynasties prominent in historical times, rather, the cities listed never did play a role politically and their kings are, as far as one can see, quite unpolitical, forms of the dying and reviving god of fertility, Dumuzi, mostly. Thus the closest one can come is probably to credit the inclusion of this section in the tale to pure historical interest on the part of its composer.

Lastly there is the story of the flood; and if the motif of nature versus culture is a widespread one, surely that of the flood is even more so. It is found all over the globe. And one may well wonder why that should be so. What is there about it to make it so universally fascinating? True, the idea of universal destruction, of genocide on an absolute scale, has a kind of morbid attraction comparable, perhaps, to that which makes people go to see "horror films" or read stories like Poe's "The Pit and the Pendulum." But the flood-story, although it deals with an ultimate horror, is not for that really a horror-story. The listener follows and identifies with the survivor, the hero of the story, not with the victims and their sufferings, they are mere background and hardly become real at all. And from the beginning it is clear to all—given the logic of myth and folktale—that the hero will survive. So we must look elsewhere than to "horror" for what the story meant, and for what made it so generally important.

Here a clue would seem to be given with the circumstances under which we first find references to the story in Mesopotamia. It is in a passage describing the appointment by Enlil of king Ishme-Dagān of Isin to restore Enlil's temple and cult in Nippur "after the flood had swept over." As ⟦527⟧ already seen by the editor of that text Willem Römer,[7] "the flood" is used here figuratively for the cataclysmic destruction that befell Sumer at the end of the Third Dynasty of Ur. Barbaric invaders from the eastern mountains, Elam and the Sua people, overran the country bringing the capital Ur to fall, butchering its inhabitants and destroying and looting Nippur and Enlil's temple Ekur, as well as many other major cult-centers throughout the land. The same phrase "after the flood had swept over" that Ishme-Dagān here uses occurs—apart from its use in the flood-story itself—in the Sumerian Kinglist in those copies that include an antediluvian section, to introduce the list of historical dynasties. Similarly used it occurs in the Lagash Kinglist to introduce its series of kings. It may thus be said to carry the implications of a return to normalcy after a near fatal cataclysm—a Greek word, incidentally, that also literally

7. W. H. Ph. Römer, *Sumerische 'Königshymnen' der Isin-Zeit* (Leiden: Brill, 1965) 70 note 348.

denotes "the flood." This gives us, I believe, the key to why the story is so universally popular. It is not really a story of all-embracing catastrophe. It is the story rather of surviving such a catastrophe, and starting life over again. Its "message," if I may use that outdated word, is that man will somehow survive and that the cataclysm will not repeat itself. The gods have learned a lesson. As such it serves to relax anxiety and give hope, especially to a generation of survivors that have experienced the universe suddenly turned viciously inimical and need reassurance badly.

Spread

As mentioned when we explained why we have called the story we are here considering the "Eridu Genesis," there are very striking similarities between it and the biblical account of beginning, particularly one should add, as it is told in the P-source.

Both traditions are tripartite and have in order first the creation of man and animals, second lists of leading figures after creation, in Mesopotamia city-rulers with their reigns, in the Bible, patriarchs with the years they lived, and then the flood. These three parts, moreover, are in both traditions combined simply by arranging them along a line in time and not according to the most usual device for connecting separate tales or myths: grouping them around a single hero as done, e.g., in the Gilgamesh epic or in the Joseph story, Gunkel's "Sagenkränze" ⟦'garland of legends'⟧ In the "Eridu Genesis" moreover the progression is clearly a logical one of cause and effect: the wretched state of natural man touches the motherly heart of Nintur, who has him improve his lot by settling down in cities and building temples; and she gives him a king to lead and organize. As this chain of cause and effect leads from nature to civilization, so a following such chain carries from the early cities and kings ⟦528⟧ over into the story of the flood. The well organized irrigation works carried out by the cities under the leadership of their kings lead to a greatly increased food supply and that in turn makes man multiply on the earth. The volume of noise these people make keeps Enlil from sleeping and makes him decide to get peace and quiet by sending the flood. Now, this arrangement along a line of time as cause and effect is striking, for it is very much the way a historian arranges his data, and since the data here are mythological we may assign both traditions to a new and separate genre as mytho-historical accounts.

Even more remarkable than this close similarity of structure is a similarity of style of a peculiar and unusual character. Both traditions are greatly interested in chronology. In both we are given precise figures for respectively the length of reigns and the lifespans of the persons listed, and in both traditions the figures given are extraordinarily large. It seems too—as we said earlier on—that in both traditions the underlying concept is that these early men grew exceedingly slowly from child to adult and on into old age.

This interest in numbers is very curious, for it is characteristic of myths and folktales that they are not concerned with time at all. They take place "in *illo tempore*" or "once upon a time" and the prince and the princess live happily "ever after" never any stated number of years. No!—interest in numbers of years belongs elsewhere, to the style of chronicles and historiography. In Mesopotamia we find it first in date-lists, lists of reigns, and in the Kinglist, later on in the Chronicles, but to find this chronological list-form combined, as it is here, with simple mythological narrative, is truly unique. It suggests that the "Eridu Genesis" depends directly upon the Kinglist and its style. And that is borne out by the awkward language in which "Eridu Genesis" has Enki announce the decision of the gods to bring on the flood to Ziusudra. He says of mankind, as you may remember: "their kingship, their term, has been uprooted!" That is proper terminology for stating that the term of office of a king and his capital has come to an end by a decision of the gods and is given to another king and city. It does not rightly fit the destruction of all mankind and has clearly been mechanically taken over from the language of changing dynasties. The assignment of the tale to a mytho-historical genre is thus further confirmed.

In the Bible the special interest in chronology with which we are concerned is characteristic of the P-source, generally dated to ca. 500 B.C., and if, as seems likely, P is here influenced by Mesopotamian writings, it is of interest to note that the "Eridu Genesis" tradition was alive and known in Mesopotamia at least as late as the years around 600 B.C., for the bilingual fragment from the library of Ashurbanipal is of that date and had both the list of reigns and the story of the flood.

What form such influence on P may have taken is obviously not easy to say for certain. We should imagine that we are dealing here essentially with a matter of standards set. P—or the circle of writers designated by that ⟦529⟧ name—may have known and admired the precision of Mesopotamian records and they may have been inspired to imitation. The Mesopotamian materials will have served as models rather than having been directly borrowed from.

If we accept—as I think we very clearly must—a degree of dependency of the biblical narrative on the older Mesopotamian materials, we must also note how decisively these materials have been transformed in the biblical account, altering radically their original meaning and import.

The "Eridu Genesis" takes throughout, as will have been noticed, an affirmative and optimistic view of existence; it believes in progress. Things were not nearly as good to begin with as they have become since and though man unwittingly, by sheer multiplying, once caused the gods to turn against him; that will not happen again. The gods had a change of heart, realizing apparently that they needed man.

In the biblical account it is the other way around. Things began as perfect from God's hand and grew then steadily worse through man's sinfulness until God finally had to do away with all mankind except for the pious Noah who would beget a new and better stock.

The moral judgment here introduced, and the ensuing pessimistic viewpoint, could not be more different from the tenor of the Sumerian tale; only the assurance that such a flood will not recur is common to both.

It follows from this, I should think, that one ought to be extremely cautious when one seeks to interpret a myth, for myths are protean. They have no single constant meaning; they change their spots. All is in flux according to place and time. So while it is always tempting, and often correct, to see myths of origin as "normative" or as "charters" one need only contrast Genesis on newly created man: "And God saw everything that he had made, and behold it was very good" with the wretched creature on which Nintur takes pity in the Sumerian tale, to realize that the meaning of myth is relative and changeable, and that accordingly and regrettably all easy generalization perforce is out.

Eridu, Dunnu, and Babel: A Study in Comparative Mythology

Patrick D. Miller Jr.

⟦227⟧ This essay focuses on some themes in two quite different myths from ancient Mesopotamia, one known commonly as the Sumerian Deluge or Flood story, discovered at Nippur and published around the turn of the century by Poebel (1914a and b), the other published much more recently by Lambert and Walcot (1966) and dubbed by Jacobsen (1984) "The Harab Myth" ⟦see appendix, pp. 165–66⟧. The former myth was the subject of some attention at the time of its publication and extensive analysis by Poebel, particularly in King's Schweich Lectures (1918). As Jacobsen notes, it has not been the subject of much further work except for Kramer's translation (Pritchard 1955: 42–44) and Civil's translation and notes in Lambert and Millard (1969: 138–47). More recently, Kramer has given a new translation of the text together with notes (Kramer 1983).

Both texts have now been the subject of major new treatments in the last three or four years by Jacobsen (1978 and 1984), and that is in a large sense the impetus for my turning to them. Indeed, I first became interested in the two texts when Jacobsen delivered a paper on them

Reprinted with permission from *Hebrew Annual Review* 9 (1985) 227–51.

Special abbreviations used are: ARM = *Archives royales de Mari* (texts in transliteration); CAD = *The Assyrian Dictionary of the Oriental Institute of the University of Chicago*; CT = *Cuneiform Texts from Babylonian Tablets in the British Museum*; PBS = *Publications of the Babylonian Section, University Museum, University of Pennsylvania*; TCL = *Musee de Louvre, Departement des antiquites orientales, Textes cuneiforms*; TRS = *Textes religieux sumeriens du Louvre*; UET = *Ur Excavation Texts.*

entitled "Two Mesopotamian Myths of Beginnings" at a symposium on mythology given at Sweetbriar College several years ago. His rationale for dealing with the two of them at that time was that each "in its own way stands apart and it seems to me, raises interesting questions of a more general nature—about composition, interpretation, and what happens when a myth is borrowed from one people to another" (1978: 1). Neither in his original presentation nor in the separate publications has Jacobsen made any association between the two myths other than that they both—like numerous myths—deal with beginnings. His original treatment of them together caught my attention so that I am in part interested in their thematic interrelationship, to the extent that such may be discerned, as well as how these Mesopotamian myths of beginnings compare with the biblical tradition about similar subjects. My primary attention will be devoted to the older text, now dubbed by Jacobsen "The Eridu Genesis" ⟦see appendix⟧; secondarily I want to address the Harab Myth in ⟦228⟧ its relation to the Eridu Genesis. In both cases Jacobsen's reconstruction and translation and his analysis provide the basis for my discussion. For the Eridu Genesis I have examined and used the translation of Civil and Kramer as well as Poebel. There are, naturally, some significant differences in these translations. For the most part they do not affect the analysis given here. I am also indebted to Jo Ann Hackett for bibliographical references and for her detailed notes on the Sumerian text.

I

Jacobsen's reconstruction and translation (1981) of the Sumerian flood story, or the "Eridu Genesis," is based upon three texts (CBS 10675 = PBS V/1 [ca. 1600 B.C.E.]; UET VI 61 [ca. 1600 B.C.E.]; and CT 46.5, a bilingual fragment from Ashurbanipal's library [ca. 600 B.C.E.])[1] all of which are given according to his restorations in the notes to his publication. Elsewhere, he gives the following brief summary of the myth (1976: 114):

1. This text was first published by Jacobsen (1939: 59–60, n. 113). More recently Lambert (1973: 271–75) has published a copy and translation of this text with additional joins, and further sources have been published by I. Finkel (1980). The text is part of the Dynastic Chronicle (or Chronicle 18; Grayson 1975) and, therefore, may not have belonged originally to the Eridu Genesis. Jacobsen is still probably correct, however, when he says that what originally was told in the lacuna at the beginning of col. iii or PBS V 1 "is suggested" by this bilingual fragment (1981: 519 ⟦p. 133 in this volume⟧). For that reason it is included in the appended reproduction of Jacobsen's translation of the Eridu Genesis.

> This myth, the beginning of which is missing, described the creation of man by the four great gods: An, Enlil, Ninhursaga (here called Nintur), and Enki. After Nintur has decided to turn man from his primitive nomadic camping grounds toward city life the period began when animals flourished on earth and kingship came down from heaven. The earliest cities were built, were named, had the measuring cups, emblems of a redistributional economic system, allotted to them, and were divided between the gods. Irrigation culture was developed and man thrived and multiplied. However, the noise made by man in his teeming settlements began to vex Enlil sorely, and, driven beyond endurance, he persuaded the other gods to wipe out man in a great flood. Enki, thinking quickly, found a way to ⟦warn his favorite, one Ziusudra. He told him to⟧ build a boat in which to survive the flood with his family and representatives of the animals. Ziusudra wisely followed Enki's instructions and after the flood had abated Enki was able to persuade the other ⟦229⟧ gods not only to spare Ziusudra but to give him eternal life as a reward for having saved all living things from destruction.

Jacobsen's proposal to call this text "The Eridu Genesis" is appropriate and important. For while it was early recognized that the myth indicated some relationship between creation and deluge (so Poebel and King), the focus of attention was placed largely on the flood story. Partly on the basis of his recognition of the connection of the Ur fragment and the Ashurbanipal bilingual to the Nippur text, and partly on the basis of his analysis and interpretation of the whole, Jacobsen has gone much further in signalling the character of this myth in its full form as being not simply a flood story, but a myth of beginnings on a scope comparable to that of the Primeval History in Genesis 1–11. Indeed, Jacobsen's study should serve the purpose of placing this myth on a par with *Enuma eliš*, Atra-Ḫasīs, and the Gilgamesh Epic among Mesopotamian literary remains that lie behind the biblical tradition. (There is still further reason for insisting on the appropriateness of the label "Eridu Genesis" over the more usual ones, but that will be discussed below.) In addition to the change of name, Jacobsen has underscored the significance of this text in recognizing that its various sources point to a time span for the myth from about 1800 to 600 B.C.E., indicating not only the range of its continuity in the literary tradition of Mesopotamia, but also that it was a living myth or epic throughout the whole course of Israel's history and the history of its literature.

With regard to Jacobsen's interpretation of "The Eridu Genesis" as a whole, a question can be raised about the division of the text into "three distinct parts, each apparently with its own theme and purport" (1981: 526). Particularly with large segments uncertain, that division into nature versus culture (col. i and UET VI 61), the founding of the first cities and their rulers (col. ii and the first part of col. iii, as suggested by CT 46.5 or its like), and the story of the flood (the remainder of col. iii through col. iv) must be held fairly tentative. I wonder if the first part ought to be reduced so easily to the familiar polarity of nature versus culture, particularly when Jacobsen acknowledges that there is no tension here between two ways of life. More appropriate, I think, is his suggestion that this section functions as a charter for the city state. But if that is the case, then the line between the first part and the second part is significantly blurred, and one must ask if they do not serve somewhat the same purpose. The focus of cols. iv, v, and vi is clearly the story of the flood, yet even here there are some important thematic connections to the prior columns in the several references to kingship and the description of the flood sweeping over the kab-du$_{11}$-ga (economic centers or capitals). To this line of continuity I shall return below.

II

⟦230⟧ Before turning to the main line of discussion, I want to identify a point of comparison with the biblical tradition that is not central to Jacobsen's treatment of the "Eridu Genesis," but has to do with a subject that has been of much interest in the investigation of relationships between Mesopotamian and Hebrew literature and religion. In what takes place in the existing portions of cols. iii and iv, we are very close to some of the basic notions and conceptuality underlying Hebrew prophecy, that is, its mythic background in the conceptions of a heavenly assembly. Jacobsen has frequently called attention to the significance of the assembly of the gods as a factor in Mesopotamian mythology and religion. Here we have another instance. The fundamental authority undergirding the prophetic message in ancient Israel is the fact that the prophet has stood in the council of Yahweh, has listened in on the decisions of the heavenly assembly (for example, 1 Kings 22; Jer 23:18–22). The divine government is effected by the decisions of Yahweh in the divine assembly. The prophet has access to the council and is sent to declare the divine decisions. In col. iii the "Eridu Genesis" may provide us with a fairly close conceptual background to this mythopoeic phenomenon.

Dreams as a means of communication from the deity, either as a message or by symbolism, are, of course, common in ancient Near Eastern texts (Oppenheim 1956a). We know that they were frequently a part of the "machinery" of prophetic revelations at Mari. In the Gilgamesh Epic, there is a dream sequence that forms something of an analogue to our text and is regarded by Oppenheim in his survey of ancient Near Eastern dream phenomena as atypical (1956: 196). Enkidu has a dream in which he "sees and hears the great gods deliberate in their heavenly assembly and decide that he is to die" (Oppenheim 1956: 196; cf. *ANET*: 85–86). The appropriate section of the Eridu Genesis goes even further, however. Ziusudra, king and priest, is also a seer (*ensi*; cf. Oppenheim 1956: 221–25), a prophetic type of figure who fashions a statue of *Ṣidanu*, the god of giddiness, according to Jacobsen,[2] and regularly stands by it to induce ecstasy. In ⟦231⟧ the course of doing this, he has an experience that is at least auditory and may be visionary. It is specifically said to be "something that was not a dream appearing." As Jacobsen describes it, Zuisudra's "senses open up to the supernatural and he becomes aware of what is happening in the world of the gods: their arrival to assembly in Ki-ur in Nippur where the divine place of assembly, Ubshukkina, was located, their conversation and swearing of the traditional introductory oath to abide loyally by what the assembly may decide" (1981: 523). That it is not a dream is a way of underscoring the special ecstatic experience that is not like any typical dream experience.[3]

In all of this we are not far conceptually from the phenomena associated with much of Hebrew prophecy. Ziusudra does not stand in the divine council, as did the prophets, but he is given access to the divine assembly on an occasion when it is making decisions, and the decision is communicated to him, albeit privately, by one of the gods, Enki.

There are obvious differences between the phenomena of this text and those of Israelite prophecy, for example, the dual role of king and seer that Ziusudra plays; but the basic experience described here lies close to that which is at the center of the prophetic experience in ancient Israel.

It is also not unlike what one finds in one of the "prophetic" texts from Mari (ARM X 9) where the *āpilum* Qishti-Diritim reports to Shibtu

2. Jacobsen (1981: 522, n. 14) gives a brief explanation of his reading of Ṣidanu on the basis of the Akkadian rendering of *sag nigin* in Šurpu VII.15–16. The word *ṣidanu* refers to a disease, either vertigo (so *CAD* Ṣ 171–72) or epilepsy (so E. Reiner, *Šurpu* 36, ll. 15–16). Jacobsen refers to the appearance of Ṣidanu as one of the companions given to Nergal by Ea in the Amarna version of "Nergal and Ereshkigal" (EA 357.49). There *Ṣidanu* appears in a list of demons of disease. One notes that in the Egyptian story of Wen-Amon where a young man is seized with a divine ecstasy or prophetic frenzy, "the determinative of the word '(prophetically) possessed' shows a human figure in violent motion or epileptic convulsion" (Wilson, *ANET*: 26, n. 13). It should be noted, by the way, that the si of *en-si* is restored by Jacobsen (1981: n. 4, l. 21).

3. Against the reading of Jacobsen and Civil, who see the text referring to something that was not a dream, Kramer (1983: 119) translates line 149: "bringing forth all kinds of dreams, con[versing]." He also does not see any reference to *ki ur* in line 151. It should be noted that in the small fragment of the flood story found at Ugarit, Atra-hasis says that he knew the oath of the great gods "though they did not reveal it to me" (Lambert and Millard 1969: 133).

a vision of the divine assembly where the gods and goddesses under the direction of Ea swear oaths not to go against Mari.[4]

III

In his treatment of the "spread" of the Eridu Genesis, Jacobsen takes up some larger relationships between this work and the traditions of Genesis 1–11. He has suggested that in both the Eridu Genesis and the Priestly source of Genesis 1–11 we have "a new and separate genre" (1981: 528) that he calls mytho-historical. While one needs to be ⟦232⟧ chary of proposing a new literary genre and in such a case must define the proposed genre, mark it off from related types, and give sufficient examples to demonstrate its typicality, Jacobsen has gone a long way toward making his case. On the one hand, both texts deal with matters of beginnings or origins in primeval times and share substantial content with typical myths of the ancient Near East, for example, description of pre-creation state, creation of human beings, and the activity of the gods in creating and shaping the destiny of the human creatures. On the other hand, the two texts also share features that remind one more of historical chronicles. Among them are the continuous chain of cause and effect,[5] the large interest in chronology including precise figures for lengths or reigns and life spans, and stylistic features more characteristic of dynastic chronicles than myths and folk tales. As one such stylistic

4. I am indebted to my colleague, J. J. M. Roberts, for his citation and his translation of the text (cf. Moran 1969: 50–51).

5. Jacobsen summarizes this chain of cause and effect as follows:

> In the "Eridu Genesis" moreover the progression is clearly a logical one of cause and effect: the wretched state of natural man touches the motherly heart of Nintur, who has him improve his lot by settling down in cities and building temples; and she gives him a king to lead and organize. As this chain of cause and effect leads from nature to civilization, so a following such chain carries from the early cities and kings over into the story of the flood. The well-organized irrigation works carried out by the cities under the leadership of their kings lead to a greatly increased food supply and that in turn makes man multiply on the earth. The volume of noise these people make keeps Enlil from sleeping and makes him decide to get peace and quiet by sending the flood. Now, this arrangement along a line of time as cause and effect is striking, for it is very much the way a historian arranges his data . . . (Jacobsen 1981: 527–28 ⟦this volume, 140⟧).

One notes that Atra-hasis seems to have a similar chain of cause and effect from creation through the flood, so this is not peculiar to the Eridu Genesis. But the latter narrative includes elements, such as the settling down in cities and the sequence of cities and kings, that are not a part of Atra-hasis. The scope of the narrative as it is reconstructed seems to be somewhat more comprehensive in its sweep of cosmic and world history.

feature, Jacobsen mentions the way the decision to destroy mankind is expressed: "their kingship, their term, has been uprooted." This is terminology more appropriate to the end of a term of office of a king and his capital city than to the destruction of all mankind. Another stylistic feature that seems to reflect the historical style of the Eridu Genesis was first pointed out by Poebel. This is the comparatively frequent use of *ud-ba* (or *ud-bi-a*), "that day" or "at that time" (UET VI.61, ll. 3′, 11′; PBS V/1, iii:15′; iii:20′; vi:10). According to Poebel, the phrase "directs the attention to bygone days in contradistinction to the present . . . to make historical facts pass in review before the listener" (1914: 66). He indicates this use of *ud-ba* is "a very common feature of historical poetry" and sees an exact parallel in the use of *ʾāz* ⟦'then'⟧ five times in Judges 5 "to introduce some striking incident" (1914: 66). One could add to those examples the use of *ʾāz* in Exod 15:1 and 15.

⟦233⟧ What Jacobsen proposes about the genre of the Eridu Genesis is quite significant for the background of the Genesis materials and sets them more clearly in the context of myth and story-telling in the ancient Near East. One of the ways the early narratives of Genesis have been distinguished from ancient Near Eastern myth is that primeval time in those narratives is not really that. It is simply the beginning of history that continues in a sequence clearly connected and running in an unbroken stream down to the present. But that sequential "historical" character that is basic to the Genesis stories is exactly what Jacobsen discerns in the Eridu Genesis. Thus the divide between the biblical presentation and the Mesopotamian may not be so sharp as we have thought or at least that divide is to be located at another point (i.e., the nature of the divine world).

The particular strand of Genesis 1–11 with which Jacobsen compares the Eridu Genesis is the P source because of its tripartite division into creation of human beings and animals, its list of leading figures after creation, and then the flood, as well as its heavy interest in dates and chronology. One might add to those affinities with P the pious portrait of the flood hero.

When, however, one compares the Eridu and biblical Genesis material closely, there are several places where the affinities with the Yahwistic stratum are as striking as, if not more so than, those with P:

a. Insofar as one can reconstruct the creation section of the Eridu Genesis, it is more truly a narrative and less the formalized, almost theogonic stages of Gen 1:1–2:4a(P). The Priestly material as a whole reveals a paucity of independent literary narrative in contrast to the Eridu Genesis, which has a very strong narrative line.

b. The reconstructed creation section of the Eridu Genesis (UET VI.61), which describes the initial situation in "not yet" terms (that is, no canal, no ditches, no plow, no wool) is much closer in style and formulation to the opening part of the Yahwistic Genesis account. This is particularly true, of course, of the motif of the original nakedness of humankind.
c. The Eridu Genesis has a clear interest in cities. The material in P reflects no sign of this interest whereas at three points in J—Gen 4:17; 10:8–12; and 11:1–9—there is a word about cities (see below).

Now all of this does not take us in another direction from Jacobsen's analysis, but it perhaps needs to be put in another way, that is, in terms of the Priestly tradent building on the J narrative in the light of a Mesopotamian model. This would tend to confirm the direction suggested by F. M. Cross and others toward viewing P not as a separate narrative source but as a framing, systematizing, and supplementing of ⟦234⟧ the JE epic tradition. In any event, one must look at the full shape of Genesis 1–11 against the background of the Eridu Genesis rather than just the strictly P material or supplementation, whether P is source or tradent. What is clear and important is that there were Mesopotamian models that anticipate the structure of Genesis 1–11 as a whole and not simply one or the other of the possible strata or sources.

A further important outcome to this comparison of the Eridu Genesis and the Primeval History of the biblical Genesis is that it tends to reinforce the conclusion reached by others, to wit that the primary structural unity in the opening chapters of Genesis is from the creation through the flood, i.e., Genesis 1–9 rather than Genesis 1–11 (cf. Clark 1971: 205ff., n. 89 and the bibliography cited there). The Babel story in Gen 11:1–9 is not reflected in this Mesopotamian model and is clearly set in its place as a backdrop to the Abraham story (see below). It is a specifically Yahwistic addition that is indebted to themes and motifs of the Mesopotamian accounts of origins but is not reflected there as such.

At the same time, one should note Poebel's analysis of the authorship of the Nippur text of the Eridu Genesis:

> . . . our tablet shows a remarkable affinity to the list of kings which is published as No. 5 of this volume. . . . It seems to me, therefore, sufficiently certain that the two tablets were written by the same hand and probably were intended to form, together with one or two others, a series of tablets on which the scribe wrote an outline of the history of Babylonia from its earliest beginnings down to his own time. As each column of the king list contained the name of about thirty-nine or forty kings, the missing portion of the last column cannot have given the

> names of more than nineteen kings, but in all likelihood much less, as there must have been left some space for the summary and probably a colophon. On a rough estimate the list will thus be carried down to approximately the latter half of the dynasty of Babylon, and this then would likewise be the time when the list as well as the deluge and creation tablet were written (Poebel 1914a: 69).

If Poebel is correct, then the Eridu Genesis would provide an even more extensive analogue to the biblical narrative which, via genealogies (Genesis 10) plus additional stories (i.e., Gen 11:1–9 and beyond) continues from the stories of origins on down into later times, that is, to the present, the time when the narrative came into being. The sense of a single story from the creation to the present may have existed in Mesopotamia as well as Israel.

IV

The other mythological text that has been the focus of a recent major study by Jacobsen is the Harab myth. Neither in his earlier presentation ⟦235⟧ of these two myths (1978) nor in his later separate publication of them did he attempt to relate the two myths to each other. In some very basic ways, of course, they are quite different. There are, however, features of the myths that merit examination and comparison in relation to the biblical tradition.

Both the Eridu Genesis and the Harab myth have to do with beginnings, the former more with the origin of the world and humankind, the latter more with the origin of the world and the gods. They both clearly reflect and are concerned with a movement in time. They depart from each other in that in one case the movement is from the beginning through history down to and past the flood (Eridu Genesis), while in the other case it is a movement through the year (Harab myth). But both start from the beginning and progress from there in one way or another, and the fertility cycle Jacobsen sees in the Harab myth is set within a linear or sequential movement, one that begins with Earth and Sea, ploughing god and herding god, and moves through a theogony from the olden gods until it reaches young gods who are now in charge. The Harab myth is in one sense a succession document, particularly in that it locates all this in the city of Dunnu, and the deities here are also rulers of Dunnu. The figures in the theogony are gods and rulers at one and the same time. Other theogonies (e.g., Sanchunyaton who has Kronos founding the first city Byblos) have some relationship to a city but few, I think, quite as insistently as this one.

In the Harab myth, in typical mythic form where those things that happened at the beginning are repeated at regular intervals, the linear and sequential (i.e., the level of the myth whose components consist of beginning, succession, the rulership of Dunnu, the movement from olden gods to young gods, and the possible moral growth) interacts with the repetitive and cyclical (i.e., the level whose components consist of the god representing dimensions of fertility and agriculture, and the sequence of months, which unlike years indicates repetitive rather than linear movement). But whether one understands the dates as referring to the monthly progress of the agricultural process (Jacobsen 1984) or the days on which offerings were made to the deposed dynast (Lambert and Walcot 1966), one must not be so impressed with the seasonal or festival character of the myth that one misses the origin and succession, i.e., the progressive and linear dimension, a feature that Jacobsen has lifted up more in his published discussion than in his earlier and briefer oral presentation.

All of this suggests that the Eridu Genesis and the Harab myth are similar in type. Jacobsen summarizes his understanding of the Harab myth as follows ⟦236⟧:

> As it stands, the story with which we have been dealing may be described briefly as a *dynastic chronicle* [italics mine] telling how a certain Harab built a city Dunnu, assumed lordship there and founded a dynasty in which son followed father, coming to power in extraordinary patterns of patricide and incest with mother and sister.
>
> A special perspective for interpreting the meaning of this curious chronicle is given, however, with the fact that all the members of the dynasty are gods; we are dealing with a *myth* [italics mine], therefore; and that the line of successive ruling generations seems to lead down to Enlil and his son Ninurta. The lordship of which the story tells would thus seem to be that held by Enlil in the storyteller's own day, that is, lordship over the cosmos as a whole, and the gods and events told about would all antedate Enlil, reaching back into the dark and remote ages before the present generation of gods and the present world order came into being (Jacobsen 1984: 15).

Such a summary, which accurately grasps the myth, leads one to ask if in some sense we do not have here also a kind of mytho-historical text like the Eridu Genesis, with the significant difference that the Harab myth—in what is preserved—does not involve an interaction between gods and human beings. It does, however, reflect a chronological interest and sets this "history" of the gods (i.e., theogony) in the midst of a human city.

V

The above comments point toward the way in which the Eridu Genesis and the Harab myth most clearly intersect and one of the points at which they may be most clearly distinguished from the mythic materials in Genesis 1–11.

In his discussion of the second part of the Eridu Genesis, Jacobsen expresses himself to be somewhat at a loss as to the import of the list of cities and their kings and suggests that this section is in the myth for "pure historical interest" (1981: 526 ⟦p. 139 in this volume⟧). There is more going on than that, however; the establishment and rule of cities is fundamental to both of these texts. The antediluvian cities referred to in col. ii of the Eridu Genesis play a major role in Mesopotamian traditions, as Hallo (1970) has demonstrated. They appear in many contexts. In one of the oldest pieces of Sumerian mythology (AO 4153, NFT 80; see van Dijk 1964–65: 39–44) the pre-creation stage is described as being a time when daylight and moonlight did not shine, Enlil and Nilil did not exist, and Enki and Eridu had not yet appeared.

A later text highlights Eridu and other antediluvian cities (with some changes in the list reflecting the later period). It is a bilingual version of ⟦237⟧ the creation of the world by Marduk, which, according to Hallo, is a part of the mouth-washing ritual (Hallo 1970: 63, n. 80; for a translation see Heidel 1951^2: 61–63). What is most interesting here is that the pre-creation state is described (in summary) as a time or state when there was no holy house, no reed, no tree, no brick, no brickmold, no house, no city, no living creature, Nippur not made and Ekur not built, Uruk not made and Eanna not built, the Apsu not made and Eridu not built, a holy house of the gods not made. Then in lines 12ff., the first act of creation is the establishment of Eridu with its Esagila followed by the establishment of Babylon and the building of its Esagila temple.

Eridu is here explicitly seen in relation to the creation, as is also the case in the Eridu Genesis, so that its founding and indeed the founding of all the antediluvian cities is related both to creation (as in these two cases mentioned) and to the Flood (in the Sumerian King List as well as the Eridu Genesis where the Flood sweeps over the bushel baskets).[6] Further, the antediluvian cities and other cities provide a structure or framework for the Sumerian King List—from Eridu through the antediluvian and postdiluvian cities to Isin. Hallo, Wilson, and others make a strong case for seeing this as the primary function and rationale for the Sumerian King List: "Indeed that List should more properly be called the 'Sumerian City List' in terms of its own summary ('11 cities which

6. Or "capital cities" if that should be the correct understanding of kab-du$_{11}$-ga.

exercised kingship'). In its fullest form, the List begins with (the building of) Eridu and ends with (the destruction of) Isin, that is, it records the entire history of 'The City' " (Hallo 1970: 66). Or as Wilson puts it succinctly: " . . . SKL is primarily concerned with the succession of *cities* (author's italics) through which kingship passed . . ." (Wilson 1977: 81).

According to Jacobsen—and this has been confirmed by more recent discoveries—the antediluvian tradition of the Sumerian King List is not original to that list but has been taken over from the Sumerian epic contained in the Eridu Genesis and put on as a Prologue (Jacobsen 1939: 55–68). If that is the case, two things follow: (a) the antediluvian city and ruler tradition is an important one or it would not be taken over; and (b) the Sumerian King List has to be viewed in terms of that framework, which affects and shifts its focus and intention, as Hallo and Wilson have noted.

In the Harab myth, the antediluvian cities do not appear, but once again the myth has much to do with and in some sense focuses on a city, ⟦238⟧ in this case the city of Dunnu. Jacobsen says with regard to the locale of the myth:

> These findings, that the myth is so closely tied to a provincial town in the Isin kingdom are *certainly surprising* (italics mine) in view of its pretense to universal significance as a story of bygone rulers of all of the cosmos; we can see no other reasonable explanation for this conflict of local and universal than to assume that the story in its origins represents a purely local tradition concerned with Dunnu and the story of the local gods of its tomb-sanctuary, a simple herdsman's cosmogony of limited geographical horizon (Jacobsen 1984: 22).

Here again, as with the Eridu Genesis, Jacobsen does not seem to have taken full account of the centrality of the city both as a cosmogonic motif and as a social institution whose significance is etiologized in various literary traditions, such as the ones under study here. The city was in Mesopotamia a center of power, and, even though kingship and the city or city-state were closely tied together, cities could stand against the power of a king. They were, as Oppenheim has put it, "The institutionalization of the desire for continuity in Mesopotamia" (1964: 79).

A city is the point of continuity in the Harab myth. A particular city, Dunnu, becomes the meeting place of heaven and earth, but in a quite different way from Babylon/Babel with its tower, whether in *Enuma eliš* or in Genesis (see below). Dunnu, therefore, claims its place in the cosmos. The succession of the gods is a succession of the rulers of Dunnu. The olden, dead gods even have their abode in Dunnu, and the building of Dunnu, the "eternal city" (Hallo 1970: 66), or the "city of yore" (so

Jacobsen for *Du-un-nu ṣa-a-te* in l. 6: Jacobsen 1984: 6–7) is a primordial act. It is not only that a city is built, but that it is an act of the creation. It takes place "in the beginning" (l. 1). The god and the goddess Harab and Ersetu build the city as a part of their creative activity. Indeed it is the second (or third) and concluding creation (ll. 1–6).

One can hardly avoid comparison with Genesis 2–4 and the picture or activity of creation set forth there. In the Harab myth, the re-creation state is "wasteland" (*harab*), not unlike the picture in Genesis 2 of a time with no plant or herb, no rain, nor anyone to till the earth. Both stories give primacy to the need to work or till the earth, Harab by doing that as the first creative act, Genesis 2 by describing the re-creation state as the absence of one to till the earth and then the creation of *ʾādām* to do just that.

As in Genesis 2, the first thing that is done in the creation is the creation of water, though in Genesis 2 it is sweet water to water the ⟦239⟧ plants (*ʾēd*) and in Harab it is sea (Tamtu). But in the Harab myth, river, i.e., Idu (= Heb. *ʾēd*), comes in the next generation as daughter of sea (Tamtu). Sumuqan "the shepherd god," is also brought forth in the initial creation, though in Genesis the shepherd does not happen until chapter 4:2. Still, one notes that in Harab we have at the beginning the god of ploughing, the farmer, worker of the earth, and the god of shepherding. Perhaps what is most interesting is that these two human functions and vocations appear in the creation in a *genealogical sequence* in both the Harab myth and in Genesis 2–4. In the former it is a genealogy of the gods; in the latter a genealogy of *humanity* (Adam/Cain and Abel)—an accentuation, I think, again of a feature to which I have called attention before (Miller 1978: 9–26 and 35–36), that being the concern in the biblical primeval history for the distinction between the divine world and the human world, more specifically the guarding of that distinction (cf. Hanson 1977: 214; and Oden 1981: 197–216). The responsibility for tilling the earth (Genesis 2–4) and ruling and shepherding the animals (Genesis 1–2 and 4) is clearly a human responsibility. In some sense it defines humanity. So it is set totally in the sphere of the human. In the Harab myth, however, it is as much a sphere of the gods.

Equally significant is the next step in the creative activity. In the Harab myth it is the building of Dunnu, "the city of yore" conceived as a "pristine, heavenly city," according to a lexical text (Hallo 1970: 66), of which it is also said that Harab gave himself title to the lordship there, Sumuqan "loved" it (*irāmmu*), and the succession of gods was laid to rest there. In Genesis, the next step in the creative work of Yahweh is not, of course, building a city, but the creation of *ʾādām* ⟦'humanity'⟧, who will build the city (Gen 4:17; 10:10–12; 11:1–9). Here, we come to one of the most significant contrasts between the Mesopotamian and the biblical stories of beginnings. In the former, the building or providing of the cities is a divine or a divine and human enterprise, i.e., the responsibility of gods and rulers, if we may take our clues from the Eridu Genesis, the Harab myth, *Enuma eliš*, and the like. In the former, Nintur institutes kingship so that the king may build the cities, a primary desire on the part of the deity (col. i, ll. 40–43), cities which are then given by Nintur to other deities, presumably as cult centers for their worship and service. In the biblical stories of beginnings, the building of cities is a subject of interest three times: Gen 4:17; 10:10–12 (Nimrod); and 11:1–9. All of these references, of course, have to do with the Mesopotamian centers. In all of the cases the building of cities and the interest in cities is a purely human enterprise and, as such, subject to the ambiguity of all human enterprises.

⟦240⟧ The city, or the cities, of Mesopotamia, therefore, play a central role in its literary tradition and quite specifically in the two myths under consideration here. That role is set in a variety of contexts:

a. In relation to *creation* (e.g., the early mythological text that describes pre-creation as a time when Eridu did not exist [van Dijk 1964–65: 39–44]; the Eridu Genesis, which puts the cities where Genesis 1–9 does—between creation and flood; the creation part of the mouth-washing ritual text; *Enuma eliš*, where the building of Babylon and Esagila is the climactic and creative act of the gods to confirm the rule of Marduk and Babylon; and the Harab myth, which has the building of a city, Dunnu, at the earliest creation stages in the beginning of the theogony).
b. In relation to the *divine world* (e.g., the Old Babylonian list of gods in TCL XV 10, which, according to van Dijk's analysis [1964–65: 12ff.] pictures the pre-existence of an embryonic universe in the heart of which live the numina, the chthonic deities; this universe is conceived of as city, the "uru-ul-la", the "city of yore"; from it rises the heaven, An, who becomes "the lord of the city of yore"; heaven unites itself to earth (Uras) in a cosmic hierogamy; at a given moment heaven separates itself from earth; and out of the union of heaven and earth the great gods appear by way of "emersion").[7]
c. In relation to *theogony* (Harab myth and TCL XV 10 = TRS 10 god list—both theogonies).[8]
d. In relation to *economy* (the Eridu Genesis?).

7. For a somewhat different treatment of this text see Jacobsen 1970: 115–117.
8. For discussion and bibliography of TCL XV 10 = TRS 10 see Cross 1976.

e. In relation to *flood* (the Eridu Genesis, the Sumerian King List and the Dynastic Chronicle).
f. In relation to *kingship* (the Sumerian King List, the Eridu Genesis, *Enuma eliš*, the Dynastic Chronicle, and the Harab myth).

All of this fits quite well with what we know of Mesopotamian history and civilization and the central place of the cities and the city states in that history from the third millennium onward. The city and kingship were intimately related, as the Eridu Genesis and Harab myth both underscore. Kings did not exist without cities, nor did the cities have a history apart from kingship. Individual cities might exist in loose relationship to kings or in tension with them. They could effectively challenge the king in various ways. But the builders and rulers of the great cities were remembered in the tradition as either kings, or gods, or both.

VI

⟦241⟧ When we turn to the biblical Genesis with these data and conclusions in mind, we find both a consonance and a dissonance. The antediluvian cities tradition is probably there in Genesis 4, and where we would expect it to be in light of the Mesopotamian models, that is, between creation and flood. It appears, as we have noted, in the Yahwistic stratum and not the Priestly source or supplementation. The tradition of the first cities, however, is quite submerged in the biblical story and present only in the note in Gen 4:17 that tells of the first builder of a city. That builder seems to be Enoch, who named the city after his son, Irad, "a name that is strikingly similar to the name Eridu," as Wilson (1977: 139)—along with others—has noted. The tradition (or text) is so unstable, however, that it can only be discerned by recognizing, as I think one must do even without supporting textual witnesses, a gloss in the text that has made Cain the city builder (despite the clear Yahwistic understanding of him as ground tiller, like his father) and Enoch the city (cf. Hallo 1970: 64; and Wilson 1977: 138–41).[9]

9. The textual reconstruction and reading of Gen 4:17 and 18 is a complex matter. One needs to take account of the relation of the Cainite genealogy to the Sethite genealogy in Genesis 5 (where Yered = Irad is the father of Enoch and not his son) as well as the effects of oral tradition on both lists. A few things may be said in a preliminary fashion about 4:17–18 textually and linguistically:

a. One would expect the subject of *wayĕhî bōneh ʿîr* ⟦'and he founded a city'⟧ and *wayyiqrāʾ* ⟦'and called'⟧ to be the immediately preceding personal antecedent, inasmuch

So in Genesis 1–11, theogonic and cosmogonic elements and structures were remembered and used, as well as the first city tradition, ⟦242⟧ according to Mesopotamian models. But "the tradition of the antediluvian cities remained embedded, and for practical purposes concealed within the context of the primeval history of mankind" (Hallo 1970: 66). That is not the case, however, in Mesopotamian literary traditions early and late where the antediluvian cities, especially Eridu, and other cities were remembered and played a prominent role in both mythology and king lists.

The beginning of the cities is mentioned as a datum of importance in the history of culture described in Genesis 4 and also in the post-flood Yahwistic account of the building of the great Mesopotamian cities, such as Babylon, Erech, Akkad, Calah, and Nineveh, by the mighty Nimrod (Gen 10:10–12). The prominence of the city in the biblical primeval history comes, however, in a quite different way in the structure of the whole, and that is in the story of the building of the city and tower of Babel. When the founding of the city or cities as the center of culture

---

as no separate subject is given for these verbs. For Cain to be the subject, the reader would be required to move back in the sentence past the reference to Enoch and past two feminine verbs.

b. Cain is regularly identified in 4:1–16 *vis-à-vis* his vocation as one who tills the earth (*ᶜōbēd ᵓădāmâ*).

c. Gen 4:17–18a is formulated on analogy with 4:1–2, not on analogy with the rest of the genealogical listings of the rest of v. 18. This has several implications:

1. *ḥănôḵ* ⟦'Enoch'⟧ at the end of v. 17 is a secondary insertion.
2. *wayĕhî bōneh ᶜîr* does not simply say, "He built a city" (*wayyiben ᶜîr*), as one would expect if Cain were the builder. The phrase is identical in form to the vocational notices of Gen 4:2 where the first notice, *wayĕhî heḇel rōᶜēh ṣōᵓn* ⟦'and Abel was a keeper of sheep'⟧, follows immediately after the reference to Abel's birth (*heḇel* ⟦'Abel'⟧ is mentioned as the subject because the sentence is paired with the notice about Cain's vocation). On analogy with this, *wayĕhî bōneh ᶜîr* ⟦'and he founded a city'⟧ in 4:17 clearly refers to *ḥănôḵ* ⟦'Enoch'⟧, not *qayin* ⟦'Cain'⟧. Cain's vocation, *ᶜōḇēd ᵓădāmâ* ⟦'tiller of the ground'⟧, has already been explicitly identified. It makes no sense in context and linguistically to see him as *bōneh ᶜîr* ⟦'founder of a city'⟧ here.
3. The only explanation of the clause *wayyiwālēd laḥănôḵ ᵓet-ᶜîrād* ⟦'to Enoch was born Irad'⟧ that makes sense *in this context* is to see it as an explanation of the name of the city, which has been given before the birth notice. "[Enoch] named the city after his son, for Irad had been born to him." One could even place the second clause in parenthesis.
4. That the first clause is explanatory to the preceding and not simply a standard genealogical note is seen by comparison with the rest of the verse, which proceeds for three generations with the same form: *wĕ*-X *yālad ᵓet* Y ⟦'and X begot Y'⟧. If the reference to the birth of Irad were not a part of the preceding discussion about the naming of a city after a son, one would expect at the beginning of v. 18: *waḥănôḵ yālad ᵓet-ᶜîrād* ⟦'and Enoch begot Irad'⟧.

does emerge as a significant element of the mytho-historical account, it is after the flood and another moment of breakdown in the human story. (Note that the city is founded, Babel = Babylon, is one of the few that carries the epithet "eternal city" in Mesopotamian tradition and is also one that replaces some of the original antediluvian cities in a variety of later systematizations.)

It is clear that the primary focus of the story in Gen 11:1–9 is the city (*ᶜîr*) and the city as cult center (cf. the Eridu Genesis). While the attention of readers early and later is naturally drawn to the great or high *migdāl* ⟦'tower'⟧, the story more properly should be captioned "The City of Babel." The phrase *ᶜîr ûmigdāl* is a heniadys, "city with a tower" or "city crowned by a tower" (cf. Speiser 1964; and Westermann 1984). *Migdāl* ⟦'tower'⟧ appears twice in collocation with *ᶜîr* ⟦'city'⟧ but never by itself. The conclusion of the story focuses only on the city: "They stopped building the city. Therefore, its [i.e., the city's] name is called Babel" (11:9).

So Gen 11:1–9 is about the human plan to build cities and cult places, or, to use Jacobsen's term, "cult cities." But such a move is seen as ⟦243⟧ precisely the opposite of divine plan and divine instruction, in contrast to the way the Eridu Genesis tells of the building of the first cities. Rather than the building of a great city and cult center being seen as the divine intention or plan, it is perceived by the deity as human ambition, the usurpation of divine prerogatives (contrast Gen 11:4 with 12:2 as well as 1 Sam 7:9), again a violation of the distinction or separation between divine world and human world. So the human effort is thwarted by the divine command.

Like the Eridu Genesis, the Babel story in Genesis 11 begins in the movement of a people from their wandering about (*benosᶜām miqqedem* ⟦'migrated from the east'⟧) to settlement in a great city. In the Eridu Genesis, that movement is at the command of the ruler-creator goddess Nintu, or the god Enki, if Kramer (1983: 116) is correct in his interpretation. The building of the cities with bricks is also at the command of the deity under the direction of the king. There the goddess (or god) will put peace. In Genesis 11, such a move is a purely human plan, understood not as a program for divinely created peace and harmony but human unity created out of hubris and the desire for autonomy.

The Primeval History of Genesis 1–11 thus varies from the Eridu Genesis in several ways:

a. The foundation of cities is a purely human enterprise in Genesis 1–11. It is either neutral *vis-à-vis* the divine world (Gen 4:17; 10:10–12) or a negative act, a potential threat to the divine rule (Gen 11:1–9).

b. Kingship is democratized, as indicated by the Priestly description of the human nature and purpose in royal terms in Gen 1:26–28. *ʾādām* is king in the biblical tradition, a feature that has an echo in the Eridu Genesis expression about humankind: "their kingship, their term, has been uprooted" (col. iv 10).
c. The negative act of human effort to build a city is the explicit backdrop to the biblical story of Yahweh's intention to provide a name and blessing not through the creation of cities, but through the wandering movement of an obedient people. Abraham is sent out.

The theme of the city does not, of course, disappear from the biblical tradition. With the monarchy the cities, and one particular city especially, rise to prominence, but the Primeval History of Genesis does not project this back to the beginning. For Israel, in some sense the city was as viable and as ambiguous as kingship, as capable of fulfilling the destiny of God for the human community (Isa 1:26; Zech 8:3–5) as kingship was (e.g., Isa 11:1–9), and as capable of subverting that divine intention as was kingship (Isa 1:21–23; Mic 3:9–12).

Appendix

The Eridu Genesis

(Restored and translated by Thorkild Jacobsen [1981])

⟦244⟧ Thirty-six lines missing from beginning of col. 1 of Nippur text (PBS V). Jacobsen assumes the account of creation of the world and human beings and then the following:

UET VI.61 (as restored and translated by Jacobsen):

Lines 1′–2′	Mankind's trails when forgotten by the gods were in the high (i.e., not subject to flooding) desert.
3′–4′	In those days no canals were opened, no dredging was done at dikes and ditches on dike tops.
5′	The seeder plough and ploughing had not yet been instituted for the knocked under and downed people.
6′	No (one of) all the countries was planting in furrows.
7′–10′	Mankind of (those) distant days, since Shakan (the god of flocks) had not (yet) come out on the dry lands, did

For the convenience of the reader and with the permission of the author and the appropriate editors, Jacobsen's reconstructed translations of the Eridu Genesis and the Harab myth are included as an appendix.

not know arraying themselves in prime cloth, mankind walked about naked.

11′–15′ In those days, there being no snakes, being no scorpions, being no lions, being no hyenas, being no dogs, being no wolves, mankind had no opponent, fear and terror did not exist.

16′–17′ [The people had as yet no] king.

PBS V/1

Col. i Jacobsen's numbering

37 Nintur was paying attention: 1′
38 Let me bethink myself of my humankind, 2′
(all) forgotten as they are;
39 and mindful of mine, Nintur's, creatures 3′
let me bring them back,
40 let me lead the people back from their trails. 4′

41 May they come and build cities and cult-places, 5′
that I may cool myself in their shade;
42 may they lay the bricks for the cult-cities 6′
in pure spots, and
43 may they found places for divination 7′
in pure spots! ⟦245⟧
44 She gave directions for purification, and cries for quarter, 8′
the things that cool (divine) wrath,
45 perfected divine service and the august offices, 9′
46 said to the (surrounding) regions: "Let me institute 10′
peace there!"
47 When An, Enlil, Enki, and Ninhursaga 11′
48 fashioned the darkheaded (people) 12′
49 they had made the small animals (that come up) from (out 13′
of) the earth come from the earth in abundance
50 and had let there be, as befits (it), gazelles, 14′
(wild) donkeys, and fourfooted beasts in the desert.

36-line lacuna at beginning of col. ii

Col. ii

85 . . . and let me have *him* advise; 6′
86 let me have *him* oversee their labor, 7′
87 and let *him* teach the nation to follow unerringly like cattle! 8′

88 When the royal scepter was coming down from heaven, 9′

89 the august crown and the royal throne being already 10′
down from heaven,
90 he (i.e., the king) regularly performed to perfection the 11′
august divine services and offices,
91 laid the bricks of those cities in pure spots. 12′
92 They were named by name and alloted half-bushel baskets. 13′
93 The firstling of those cities, Eridu, 14′
she gave to the leader Nudimmud,
94 the second, Badtibira, she gave to the Prince and Sacred One 15′
95 the third, Larak, she gave to Pabilsag, 16′
96 the fourth, Sippar, she gave to the gallant, Utu, 17′
97 the fifth Shuruppak, she gave to Sud. 18′
98 These cities, which had been named by names, 19′
and been allotted half-bushel baskets,
99 dredged the canals, which were blocked with purplish 20′
(wind-born) clay, and they carried water.
100 Their cleaning of the smaller canals 21′
established abundant growth.

CT 46.5

36-line lacuna at the beginning of col. iii. What originally was told here is suggested by the fragment from Ashurbanipal's library (CT 46.5):

> (1′–5) In Eridu Alulim reigned 36,000 years (1′–4) Alagar ruled 10,800 years (1′–3) 2 kings reigned 46,800 years, Eridu's term. (1′–2) Eridu's term was commuted (shifted) (1′–1) in Bad-tibira Enmenluanna reigned 46,800 years (1′) Enmengalanna reigned 64,800 years (2′) Dumuzi the shepherd reigned 36,000 years (3′) 3 kings reigned 100,000 years, Bad-tibira's term. (4′) Bad-tibira's term was commuted (5′) In Sippar Enmeduranki reigned 64,800 years (6′) one king reigned 64,800 years, Sippar's term. (7′) Sippar's term was commuted (8′) In Larak Ensipandzianna reigned 36,000 years (9′) One king reigned 36,000 years, Larak's term. (10′) Larak's term was commuted (11′). In Shuruppak Ubara-Tutu reigned 28,800 years (12′) Ziusudra reigned 64,800 years (13′) two kings reigned 93,600 years, Shuruppak's term. (14′) Five individual cities, nine kings reigned 352,800 years, their terms. (15′) Enlil took a dislike to mankind (17′) the clamor of their shouting . . . kept him sleepless.

Col. iii
140 That day Nintur wept over her creatures 15′
141 and holy Inanna was full of grief over their people; 16′
142 but Enki took counsel with his own heart. 17′

143 An, Enlil, Enki, and Ninhursaga 18′
144 had the gods of heaven and earth swear 19′
by the names An and Enlil.
145 At that time Ziusudra was king 20′
and lustration priest.
146 He fashioned, being a seer, (a statue of) 21′
the god of giddiness (inducing ecstasy)
147 and stood in awe beside it, wording (his 22′
wishes) humbly.

148 As he stood there regularly day after day he heard 23′
149 something that was not a dream appearing: conversation 24′
150 a swearing (of) oaths by heaven and earth, a (confirming) 25′
touching of throats
151 and the gods bringing their thwarts up to Ki-ur. 1

152 And as Ziusudra stood there beside it he want on hearing: 2
153 "Step up to the wall to my left and listen! 3
154 Let me speak a word to you at the wall 4
and may you grasp what I say,
155 May you heed my advice! 5
156 By our hand a flood will sweep over 6
(the cities of) the half-bushel baskets, and the country,
157 the decision, that mankind is to be destroyed, 7
has been made,
158 a verdict, a command by the assembly, 8
cannot be revoked,
159 an order of An and Enlil is not known 9
ever to have been countermanded,
160 their kingship, their term, has been uprooted 10
they must bethink themselves (of that)
161 Now 11
162 What I have to say to you . . . . . ." 12
Lacuna from here to bottom of column ⟦247⟧.

Col. v
201 All evil winds, all stormy winds gathered into one 1
202 and with them, the Flood was sweeping over (the cities of) 2
the half-bushel baskets
203 for seven days and seven nights. 3
204 After the flood had swept over the country, 4
205 after the evil wind had tossed the big boat 5
about on the great waters,

206 the sun came out spreading light 6
over heaven and earth.
207 Ziusudra then drilled an opening in the big boat, 7
208 and the gallant Utu (the sun-god) sent 8
his light into the interior of the big boat.
209 Ziusudra, being a king, 9
210 stepped up before Utu kissing the ground (before him). 10
211 The king was butchering oxen, was being lavish with the sheep 11
212 barley cakes, crescents together with . . . 12
213 . . . . . . he was crumbling for him 13
214 14
215 juniper, the pure plant of the 15
mountains he filled on the fire
216 and with a . . . clasped to 16
the breast he . . . . .

Lacuna from here to bottom of column.

Col. vi

251 "You here have sworn by the life's breath of heaven, the life's 1
breath of earth, that he verily is allied with you yourself;
252 you there, An and Enlil, have sworn by the life's breath 2
of heaven, the life's breath of earth, that he is allied
with all of you,
253 He will disembark the small animals 3
that come up from earth!"

254 Ziusudra, being king, stepped up before An and Enlil 4
255 kissing the ground, 5
255a And An and Enlil did well by him, 6
256 were granting him life like a god's, 7
257 were making lasting breath of life, like a god's 8
descend into him.
258 That day they made Ziusudra, 9
259 preserver as king of the name of the small 10
animals and the seed of mankind,
260 live toward the east over the mountains 11
in Mount Tilmun.
260 12

Text breaks off near the end ⟦248⟧.

The Harab Myth

(Restored and translated by Thorkild Jacobsen, *The Harab Myth.* Sources from the Ancient Near East 2/3. [Malibu: Undena Publications, 1984], pp. 7 and 9)

Obv.

[Harab,] in the first [beginnings, took Earth to wife,]
[to (found) a f]amily and (exercise) lordship [his heart urged him:]
"We will cut furrows in the wasteland of the country!"
[By] ploughing with their soilbreaking plough they caused Sea to be created,
[the fur]rows by [the]mselves gave birth to Sumuqan.
His stro[nghold,] Dunnu (the city) of yore they built, the two of them.
[Har]ab gave himself clear title to the lordship in Dunnu, but
[Earth] lifted (her) face to Sumuqan, his son,
and said to him: "Come, let me love thee!"
Sumu[qan] took Earth, his mother, to wife, and
Harab, [his father,] he killed, and
in Dunnu, which he loved, he laid [him] to rest;
also, Sumuqan [t]ook over the lordship of his father, and
Sea, his older sister, [he to]ok to wife, but
Gaiu, the son of Sumuqan, came, and
killed Sumuqan, and in Dunnu
in the mausoleum of his father he laid him to rest.
Sea, his mother, he took to wife;
also, Sea murdered Earth, her mother.
In the month of December on the 16th day he took over the lordship and the kingship.
[Gaiu], son of Gaiu took Idu (River), his own sister, to wife;
[Gaiu] senior and Sea, his mother, he killed, and
[in the m]ausoleum he laid them to rest together.
[In the month of January] on the 1st day [he seiz]ed the kingship and the lordship for himself.
[Kush, son of G]aiu to[ok] Ua-ildak (Pasture and Poplar), his sister, to wife,
he made [the verdure] of the earth plenti[ful,]
put it at the [disposal of fold and] pen
[as fo]od for the wildlife and mo[ving (creatures)];
[also,] he p[ut] (all) neces[sities] at [the disposal] of the needs of the gods.

[Gaiu and] Idu (River), his mother, he killed, and
[in the mausoleum] he made them dwell.
[In the month of February on the . . . day] he took over the lordship and the kingship for himself.
[Haharnum, son of Ku]sh, to[ok] Bêlit-ṣêri, his sister, to wife,
⟦249⟧ [Kush and] Ua-ildak (Pasture and Poplar), his mother, he [killed], and
[in the mausoleum] he made them dwell.
[In the month of Ma]rch on the 16th (var. 29th) day [he took over] the kingship (and) lordship.
[Hayashum], son of Haharnum
to[ok X,] his own [si]ster, to wife;

[at New Year] he took over the lordship of his father, but
he did [not k]ill him; al[ive]
he seized him, and ordered his city to hold his father captive, and
he was put in cha[ins.]

(lacuna)
(lacuna)

Rev.

[Nus]ku to . . . . .
[he inf]ormed [them . . .
[say]ing: ["Ninurta will exercise the kingship and the lordship . .]
"Yes" [answered. . . .
and Sharrat-[Nippuri. . . .
saying: [". . . . .
Ninurta [will exercise] the kingship [and the lordship . . .]
and . . . [
Enlil . . . [
Nusku . . . [
in the mi[dst] of the house of . . . [
and Enlil and . . [
Enlil . . . . . . [
Ninurta the Head(?) of . . [
. . . . .
. . . .
[. . . .] the Akitu festival of the mon[th of April . . .]
The (ploughman's) [work-so]ng [let him sound] shrilly [in the country]
Written [according to] a tablet which is a copy from Babylon and Assur and collated.
[(Composition beginning:) "Ha]rab." Complete.

Bibliography

Clark, W. M.
1971 The Flood and the Structure of the Pre-Patriarchal History. *Zeitschrift für die Alttestamentliche Wissenschaft* 83: 184–211 ⟦250⟧.

Cross, F. M.
1976 The "Olden Gods" in Ancient Near Eastern Creation Myths. Pp. 329–38 in *Magnalia Dei: The Mighty Acts of God*, eds. F. M. Cross, W. E. Lemke, and P. D. Miller Jr. Garden City: Doubleday.

Finkel, I. L.
1980 Bilingual Chronicle Fragments. *Journal of Cuneiform Studies* 32: 65–80.

Grayson, A. K.
1975 *Assyrian and Babylonian Chronicles.* Texts from Cuneiform Sources 5. Locust Valley, N.Y.: Augustin.

Hallo, W. W.
1970 Antediluvian Cities. *Journal of Cuneiform Studies* 23: 57–67.

Hanson, P. D.
1977 Rebellion in Heaven: Azazel, and Euhemeristic Heroes in 1 Enoch 6–11. *Journal of Biblical Literature* 96: 195–233.

Heidel, A.
1951 *The Babylonian Genesis.* Chicago: University of Chicago Press.

Jacobsen, T.
1939 *The Sumerian King List.* Assyriological Studies 11. Chicago: University of Chicago Press.
1970 *Toward the Image of Tammuz.* Cambridge: Harvard University Press.
1976 *The Treasures of Darkness.* New Haven: Yale University Press.
1978 Two Mesopotamian Myths of Beginnings. Unpublished.
1981 The Eridu Genesis. *Journal of Biblical Literature* 100: 513–29. Reprinted in this volume, pp. 129–42.
1984 *The Harab Myth.* Sources from the Ancient Near East 2/3. Malibu: Undena.

King, L. W.
1918 *Legends of Babylon and Egypt in Relation to Hebrew Tradition.* London.

Kramer, S. N.
1983 The Sumerian Deluge Myth Reviewed and Revised. *Anatolian Studies* 33: 115–21.

Lambert, W. G.
1973 A New Fragment from a List of Antediluvian Kings and Marduk's Chariot. Pp. 271–80 in *Symbolae Biblicae et Mesopotamicae Francisco Mario Theodoro De Liaghre Bohl dedicatae.* Leiden: Brill.

Lambert, W. G. and Millard, A. R.
1969 *Atra-Ḫasis: The Babylonian Story of the Flood.* Oxford.

Lambert, W. G. and Walcot, P.
1966 A New Babylonian Theogony and Hesiod. *Kadmos* 4: 64–72.

Miller, P. D.
1978 *Genesis 1–11: Studies in Structure and Theme.* Journal for the Study of Old Testament Supplement Series 8. Sheffield: JSOT Press.

Moran, W. L.
1969 New Evidence from Mari on the History of Prophecy. *Biblica* 50: 15–56.

Oden, R. A.
1981 Divine Aspirations in Atrahasis and in Genesis 1–11. *Zeitschrift für die Alttestamentliche Wissenschaft* 93: 197–216 [[251]].

Oppenheim, A. L.
1956a *The Interpretation of Dreams in the Ancient Near East.* Philadelphia: American Philosophical Society.
1964 *Ancient Mesopotamia.* Chicago: University of Chicago Press.

Poebel, A.
1914a *Historical Texts.* Publications of the Babylonian Section, the University Museum 4/1. Philadelphia.
1914b *Historical and Grammatical Texts.* Publications of the Babylonian Section, The University Museum 5. Philadelphia.

Pritchard, J. B., ed.
1955 *Ancient Near Eastern Texts Relating to the Old Testament.* Princeton: Princeton University Press.

Speiser, E. A.
1964 *Genesis.* The Anchor Bible 1. Garden City, N.Y.: Doubleday.

van Dijk, J.
1964–65 Le motif cosmique dans la pensée sumérienne. *Acta Orientalia* 28: 1–59.

Westermann, C.
1984 *Genesis 1–11.* Minneapolis: Fortress.

Wilson, R. A.
1977 *Genealogy and History in the Biblical World.* New Haven: Yale University Press.

The Double Creation of Mankind in *Enki and Ninmah*, *Atrahasis* I 1–351, and *Genesis* 1–2

ISAAC M. KIKAWADA

⟦43⟧ Poetry is built upon two seemingly contradictory literary foundations; one of density or compactness, as the German word *Dichtung* well signifies, and the other of repetition. A poet repeats a word, phrase or motif to condense ideas into a small space.

My purpose in this paper is to suggest that there was in the Ancient Near East a literary convention of telling the story of the origin of mankind in a doublet. The first part of the story relates the creation of mankind in more general and abstract terms, whereas the second part of the story narrates it in more specific and concrete terms. The technique of bringing the two independent parts together into a unified narrative is quite similar to the way in which a bicolon in poetry is composed, namely, by the juxtaposition of two similar materials according to the principle of parallelism of the members. The difference is in the quantity of literary material. For this purpose, I would like to present three examples. A synoptic outline of the Sumerian, Akkadian and Hebrew stories is as follows:

The Sumerian story, *Enki and Ninmah*, describes the creation of man in two parts. These two parts of the story are parallel, being analogous to the two lines of a bicolon. If we label the members of this parallelism in respect to the key motifs of creation as,

Reprinted with permission from *Iraq* 45 (1983) 43–45.

A = Gods
B = Creation
C = Mankind
D = Decreeing of fate
E = Prescription of work to mankind,

then we obtain a synonymous parallel, A B C D E // A B C D E. Let us further note that in part one, the creation is more abstract than in part two. The significance of part two is that procreation is introduced to mankind so that in the future the gods will no longer have to replenish mankind by creating new creatures. Human beings now clearly become self-propagating entities.

The Akkadian epic, *Atrahasis*, too, has two successive parallel accounts of the creation of man. The first is more abstract than the second and the second is more specific than the first. But both make the same point—that man created of clay is destined to work. The double-creation story in Atrahasis is the background for the early history of mankind which leads to the disastrous great flood.

Here again the organization of the two parallel creation episodes in Atrahasis is like that of a bicolon. Applying the same set of labels used for the "Enki and Ninmah" story, we obtain a parallel pattern, A B C D E // D A B C E.

Clearly many similarities between these Mesopotamian narratives and Genesis, chapters 1 and 2 will be noted. The parallelistic nature of the two biblical creation stories can be schematically presented in the configuration, A B C D E F G // A D B G C E F. The creation narrative in the first chapter begins with Elohim (A) ⟦text continues on p. 174⟧.

Enki and Ninmah ⟦44⟧

1–3 Introduction: A long time ago . . .

4–44 Part I: Creation of Mankind (General)
4–8 Theogony: Goddess bearing gods, division of labour
9–10 Work of gods
11 Complaint of gods against hard labour
12–14 Enki, the creator, sleeps
15–16 Gods weep, blame Enki for their grief, Enki sleeps
17–23 Nammu, Enki's mother, who bore gods, appeals to Enki to create "substitutes" for worker gods
24–28 Enki wakes up and ponders his mother's wish

29–36 Enki says to Nammu that the creature she wants will be made from clay
The Sigensigdu will help nip off the clay and form it; Ninmah will be Nammu's companion; other goddesses stand by
37–43 Nammu will decree the fate of the creature; Ninmah will impose work on mankind
44 Gods rejoice

45–51 Transition: Enki's feast for Nammu and Ninmah; all gods praise Enki

52–141 Part II: Creation of particular individuals (Specific)
52 Enki and Ninmah become drunk
53–57 People-making contest is proposed; one to create and the other to decree fate
58–78 Ninmah begins; she creates from clay six creatures with physical weaknesses. Enki decrees fate for them
58–61 (1) One with weak arm—court officer
62–65 (2) One with blinking eyes—singer
66–68 (3) One with weak feet—?
69–71 (4) One with uncontrollable semen emissions—makes safe
72–74 (5) One barren—appointed to harem
75–78 (6) One sexless individual—court officer
79–82 Ninmah finishes, Enki begins;
83–87 First creature = female; Enki impregnates her
88–91 Second creature = Umul, "My day is far" (with ADK, a baby; cf. Ziusudra, Utanapištim or Um-napištim-rūqi); he looks sick
92–94 Enki asks Ninmah to decree fate; Ninmah cannot
95–101 Umul's defects enumerated . . . "The man you fashioned is neither alive nor dead. He cannot carry anything!"
102–111 Enki's response: "I've decreed the fate for all your creatures . . ."
112– Ninmah's speech (Broken)
–125 Someone is cursed
126–129 Enki's laments
129–139 Enki tells Ninmah to hold Umul in her lap. The man has Enki's "form" and he will be a pious man. Enki's penis is praised

140–141 Coda: Ninmah could not rival Enki; Enki is praised

Atrahasis I 1–351

1–4	Introduction: A long time ago, "When the gods were man . . ."
5–245	Part I: The First Creation of Mankind (General)
5–6	The Anunnaki make the Igigi work; division of labour
7–38	Work of gods; administrative and labour classes
39–69	Complaint of the Igigi against Enlil; the Igigi call for a war
70–83	Enlil is frightened; Nusku tries to calm him
84–100	Anu and Enki are summoned together with the Anunnaki
101–185?	Anu advises Enlil to find out the cause for the uproar, but the Igigi make themselves responsible collectively for the rebellion because of the excessive workload
186?–191	Anu gives a solution to the problem, that is, to ask Bēlet-ilī/ Mami/The Mother-womb to create offspring (*li-gim*?-*ma*?-*a*)
192–234	Mami with the help of Enki creates mankind (*lullû*) from the flesh and blood of a slain god, mixed with clay
235–243	Mami completes her task and imposes labour on man
244–245	Gods rejoice
246–248	Transition: Mami is praised; her name is called Bēlet-kala-ilī
249–351	Part II: The Second Creation of Mankind in Seven Pairs; Marriage, Procreation and Work (Specific)
249–271?	Enki and Mami come to the house of destiny to create seven pairs of people by snipping off clay
272?–276	Marriage is instituted (text broken badly)
277–282	The ten-month gestation period is established by Mami
283–295	Mami performs midwifery and childbirth is perfected
296–304	Mami is praised for instituting marriage and childbirth. Nine days of rejoicing is decreed and Mami's other name, Ištar, is now changed to Išhara
305–351	The people begin to labour for gods; "With picks and spades they built the shrines. They built the big canal banks. For food for the people, for the sustenance of the gods"

Genesis 1–2

1:1	Introduction: "In the beginning . . ."
1:2–2:3	Part I: The First Creation of Mankind (General)
1:2–13	Preparation for creation of moving creatures, by the creation of stationary objects in three stages
1:14–19	Reflection of theogony and division of labour; creation of the first set of moving objects, namely, the sun and the moon to rule the day and night
1:20–23	Creation of the second set of moving creatures; fish and birds
1:24–27	Creation of the third set of moving creatures; animals and people; God creates man in his own image; male and female are created
1:28	Work for people is defined; " . . . subdue it (the earth) and have dominion over the fish of the sea, and over the birds of the air and over every living thing . . ."
1:29–31	Food is provided for their sustenance. They are blessed to be prosperous on the earth
2:1–3	The establishment of the sabbath; the seventh day
2:4	Transition: *tôl*[e]*dôt* of the heavens and earth
2:5–25	Part II: The Second Creation of Mankind: Adam and Eve (Specific)
2:5–6	A long time ago, "and every shrub of the field before it was on the earth . . ."
2:7	Man/mankind, Adam, whose moral weakness provides the drama to the story, is created from the dust of the ground
2:8–14	Plants are grown in the garden
2:15–17	Man's work is to till and keep the garden
2:18–20	Animals are created; man named them
2:21–25	Eve, the special woman, who later on is to be honoured with the title "the Mother of All the Living" is created. Eve "with the help of YHWH" (reflection of the divine consort motif?) gives birth to Cain in the story immediately following (4:1)

⟦45⟧ creating the non-human creatures, including the plants (B), then he creates the animals (C), and finally, mankind (male = D, female = E). Furthermore, he blesses mankind to be abundantly procreating (F) and assigns them the task (G) to rule over the animals. In chapter two, the sequence of creation is disturbed, but the same motifs recur, as Adonay Elohim (A) creates man (D), then he grows the plants (B) in the garden in order to put man there to work (G). Next, he creates the animals (C) and finally the woman (E); thereupon, the man and woman recognize themselves as sexual beings (F).

In summary, one thing I may say is that there were more than a thousand years of literary tradition preceding the compilation of the biblical narrative during which the double creation story is used to preface the early history of mankind that climaxed in the great flood.

The Rivers of Paradise

E. A. SPEISER

⟦473⟧ Although the Paradise of the Bible was manifestly a place of mystery, its physical setting cannot be dismissed offhand as sheer imagination. To the writer of the account in Gen 2:8ff., in any case, and to his ultimate source or sources, the Garden of Eden was obviously a geographic reality. The fantasy in this instance is the unintentional contribution of interpreters, both ancient and modern.[1] In their efforts to locate the site, countless prospectors have roamed over many regions of the earth. The garden and the rivers that circumscribe it have been sought in such places as Armenia and Transcaucasia, Ethiopia, India, and Mongolia. And as A. H. Sayce noted some sixty years ago, even Australia and the North Pole have had their credulous advocates.[2] In short, the storied delights of Eden have been made to cover a multitude of aberrations.

Various recent findings justify a fresh survey of the problem. The relation of the biblical Urgeschichte ⟦'primeval history'⟧ to its Mesopotamian analogues has been clarified on many counts. Our knowledge of the geographic history of Lower Mesopotamia has been substantially advanced in the past few years. And above all, our understanding of the cultural attainments of the ancient Near East in general has been greatly

Reprinted with permission from *Festschrift Johannes Friedrich zum 65. Geburtstag am 27. August 1958 gewidmet* (ed. A. Moortgat et al.; Heidelberg: Carl Winter, 1959) 473–85; reprinted in *Oriental and Biblical Studies: Collected Writings of E. A. Speiser* (ed. J. J. Finkelstein and M. Greenberg; Philadelphia: University of Pennsylvania Press, 1967) 23–34.

1. Cf. especially Friedr. Delitzsch, *Wo lag das Paradies?* (1881); A. H. Sayce, *Dictionary of the Bible I* (1898), 643ff.; S. R. Driver, *The Book of Genesis*, 8th ed. (1911), 57–60; W. F. Albright, "The Mouth of the Rivers," *AJSL* 35 (1919), pp. 161–95, and "The Location of the Garden of Eden," *AJSL* 39 (1922), 15–31. See also U. Cassuto, *Genesis: From Adam to Noah* (1953), 75–79 (in Hebrew).

2. *Loc. cit.*

improved. All this has a bearing, in one way or another, on the site of the biblical Paradise.

It is well to bear in mind in this connection that "the important question about any statement contained in a source is not whether ⟦474⟧ it is true or false, but what it means."[3] To put it differently, the problem is basically one of methodology: does the issue lend itself to a conclusion consistent with all the known facts in the case? I believe that it does. The pertinent details, however, are at once too numerous and too diffuse to be duly developed at this time. The alternative is to concentrate on the salient points and list them schematically as so many links in a progressive chain of reasoning.[4]

(1) The biblical data on the subject either are a valid point of departure, or they are not. The narrative states explicitly that the garden was planted in the east (v. 8), and that the four rivers involved had a common meeting place in a single body of water (10). Those who regard the two unidentified streams, the Pishon and the Gihon, as fictional need waste no time speculating about the site of Eden as a whole. But when the existence of the pair is conceded, it is fallacious to look for the Pishon in India, far from the meeting place of the Euphrates and the Tigris, and to locate the Gihon in Ethiopia, which was surely not east of either Mesopotamia or Palestine. One simply cannot have it both ways.

(2) It does no good to argue, as has often been done, that the ancients had weird notions of geography. When the account before us received its present form, hardly later than the 10th century B.C., Israel had just witnessed, under David, its maximum geographic expansion. By that time, Western Asia, the Nile Valley, and the Aegean had long had many mutual ties. Centuries before, the commercial center of Ugarit benefited from contacts with all these regions. A millennium earlier, there were trade relations between Mesopotamia and the Indus valley; the same is true of Egypt and Mesopotamia at the very dawn of history. Even primitive ⟦475⟧ prehistoric centers like Jarmo managed to obtain obsidian from distant places. There is a vast difference between drawing a reasonably accurate map of a country and dumping the Nile in the Persian Gulf. The chances are that no ancient caravan ever strayed that far from its intended objective.

(3) The source of most of our geographic troubles with the biblical Paradise is the mention of a land called *Cush* in Gen 2:13. Normally, the Bible understands by that term the region of the Upper Nile, cuneiform

3. R. G. Collingwood, *The Idea of History* (1946), 260.

4. Such an approach has long been characteristic of Professor Johannes Friedrich, to whose honor this paper is a small token contribution.

Kus/šu, Kas/ši, Eg. *K*ʾ*š*. But there was also another, and wholly unrelated, Cush; the Nimrod fragment (Gen 10:8–12) connects this homonym unmistakably with Mesopotamia, by assigning it to the father of the hero who is said to have founded a number of Babylonian and Assyrian capitals.[5] This particular Cush, then, is the eponym of the Kassites, Akk. *Kaššû*; its Nuzi form *Kuššu-*[6] and its Greek derivative *Kossaîoi*, actually contain the same vowel as the biblical name. Now the Kassite rule over ⟦26⟧ Babylonia had ended by the 12th century. It was bound to be remembered locally for some time afterwards. But how many authors in first-millennium Palestine would be familiar with this footnote to distant history? The narrator of the Urgeschichte—or at least his sources—knew about it, to judge from the Nimrod account and our present passage; for only a Kassite context can accord with the phrase "in the east" of Gen 2:8. The Samaritan version, too, would seem to reflect the same tradition, for it renders Gihon, the name of the river of Cush, by *ʾAsqop*, evidently the Choaspes, modern Kerkha. With everyone else, however, it was the Ethiopian Cush, naturally enough, that immediately came to mind. Hence LXX translates the present instance as Ethiopia; and Josephus, Jubilees, the new Genesis Apocryphon,[7] and various other ancient sources go on to identify the Gihon with ⟦476⟧ the Nile.[8] Nor could modern scholarship be blamed at first for its ready acceptance of older opinion, especially before the discovery of the form *Kuššu-*, which was used by next-door neighbors at a time when the Kassites were still very much in power. Today, however, no such excuse can be advanced any longer for detouring both Nimrod and the Gihon all the way to Ethiopia.[9]

(4) The river names Pishon and Gihon could only add to the confusion. They were bound to be etymologized as something like "the Gamboler" and "the Gusher" respectively; the latter, moreover, is actually found as the name of a spring near Jerusalem (e.g., 1 Kgs 1:33). Besides, each of these streams is described in the present passage as *sōbēb* its given land, the Heb. participle being interpreted to mean "encompassing, encircling." Now a stream with a playful name and the ability to

5. Cf. my paper on "In Search of Nimrod," *Eretz-Israel* 5 (1958), 32*–36* ⟦reprinted here, pp. 270–77⟧.

6. With the Hurrian adjectival suffix *-ḫi*; for the occurrences see E. R. Lacheman, *BASOR* 78 (1940), 21f.

7. N. Avigad and Yigael Yadin, *A Genesis Apocryphon* (1956), 32.

8. The old rabbinical authorities were fully aware that this interpretation ran counter to the explicit *miqqedem* "in the east" of Gen 2:8. This is why they took the word to mean "in the past"; cf. L. Ginzberg, *Legends of the Jews* 5 (1925), 13f.

9. It should be emphasized, however, that ever since the appearance of Delitzsch's monograph (see fn. 1) a small group of scholars has held to the equation of the present Cush with the Kassites.

encircle a whole country does not inspire confidence in its genuineness. It belongs in Cloud-Cuckoo-Land. Small wonder, therefore, that rabbinic tradition had the four rivers represent honey, milk, balsam, and wine.[10] Yet this is not much more fanciful than the other attempts, old and recent, to identify the Pishon with the Ganges or the Indus.[11] Furthermore, the names of the first two rivers of Eden may merely be secondary and Hebraized forms, just as the other two found their way into Greek in the guise of the Tigris[12] and the Euphrates. As for the accompanying *sbb*, the primary meaning of the verb is not so much "to circle," as "to turn." One of its established uses, therefore, is "to pursue an irregular path," hence "to wander." This is still clear from the passage in 2 Kgs 3:9 *wayyāsobbū derek šibᶜat yāmīm*, which tells us that the three kings in question "wandered for seven days," and not that they went around in circles for a whole week. The same sense, incidentally, suggestive of a winding course, is conveyed by Aram. *seḥar*, the equivalent of ⟦477⟧ Heb. *sbb*. The Genesis Apocryphon shows this use repeatedly, once even with the very Gihon of our present text.[13] And "to turn, twist, meander" is precisely what any normal river will do.

(5) With Cush and its river thus restored to their required eastern location, the theoretical limits of Eden begin to assume manageable proportions. By the same token there emerges this significant fact: the stated order of the last three out of a total of four Paradise rivers—i.e., the Gihon, the Tigris, and the Euphrates—is east to west. This is exactly the opposite of what one would expect from an Israelite vantage point; for from that direction the first one would be the Euphrates, which for that very reason is not infrequently described simply as "the river" (Gen 31:21; Exod 23:21; Num 22:5, etc.), or "the great river" (Gen 15:18; Deut 1:7; Josh 1:4). And with three positions thus assured, there is the inherent probability that the remaining stream—the Pishon—would have to be sought still farther east, and presumably not too far from the Gihon. Accordingly, the same uniform sequence should apply also to the central river of Eden itself, which ought thus to be the most easterly of all. The original narrator, therefore, of the account before us has to be visualized as looking from the Persian Gulf inland.

It would seem to follow, then, that the "four heads" of which the text speaks (v. 10) are meant to be viewed upstream rather than down, some-

10. Cf. Ginzberg, *op. cit.* 1 (1909), 132. Islamic tradition followed suit.

11. Cf. Sayce (fn. 1).

12. Derived from an indigenous term which appears as *Idigna* in Sum., *Idiglat* in Akk., *Ḥiddeqel* in Heb., *Deqlat* in Aram., and *Dijlat* in Arab.

13. Col. xxi 15.

thing that very few authorities appear to have realized.[14] Yet both Akkadian and Hebrew usage support such a view. Thus Akk. *ina rēš Uqnê* stands for "on the upper Kerkha." [15] And A. Ehrlich has pointed out that the Hebrew term for the lower course, of a stream is *qāṣê* (cf. Josh 15:5, 18:19); hence *rōš* must ⟦478⟧ refer to the opposite end, the upper course or headstream.[16] Now S. N. Kramer has shown independently that to the poets and priests of Sumer it was the Persian Gulf that gave the Tigris and the Euphrates their annual overflow, rather than the invisible thaws in far off Armenia.[17] Strong tidal action in the region of the delta, which has left a salt wedge all the way to modern Qurna,[18] may well have helped to foster this ancient illusion.

(6) The biblical text itself contains two semantic trailmarkers that point unambiguously to the land and lore of Sumer. One is the geographic term Eden, which hardly can be separated from Sum. e d i n "plain." The other is the *ʾēd* of Gen 2:6, the term for the groundwater that first irrigated the land. Whether one derives the word, with W. F. Albright, from i d "river," or from a . d e . a (Akk. *edû*) "ground flow," as I have recently advocated,[19] its origin would be Sumerian in any case. Near the head of the Persian Gulf lay the celebrated Dilmun which, as Kramer has shown, was "the land of the living," a place that knew neither sickness nor death, a garden of the gods—or in a word, Paradise. The same general region also bore the name of *pī nārāte* "the mouth of the rivers" (sometimes reduced to "the mouth of the two rivers").[20] Through it access could be gained to the abode of Ut(a)-napishtim, whom the gods had placed there after the Flood, to share in the boon of immortality.[21] The area was thus plainly a favored spot of ancient legend and literature.

Another clue that deserves special mention in the present context is furnished by sacred architecture. Perhaps the most venerated type of Sumerian sanctuary was the reed shrine, the basic "Gotteshaus" ⟦'house of the god'⟧ of W. Andrae's pioneering study on the subject.[22] Now the

14. So Sayce *loc. cit.*; also J. W. Dawson, *Modern Science in Bible Lands* (cited in Driver's *Genesis*, 58, fn. 1).

15. Cf. H. Tadmor, *JNES* 17 (1958), 138.9′.

16. *Randglossen I* (1908), 9.

17. In his paper on "Dilmun, the Land of the Living," *BASOR* 96 (1944), 28, fn. 42.

18. Cf. P. Buringh, "Living Conditions in the Lower Mesopotamian Plain in Ancient Times," *Sumer* 13 (1957), 35.

19. " *ʾEd* in the Story of Creation," *BASOR* 140 (1955), 9–11.

20. Cf. *BASOR* 96, 27f.

21. Gilg. Ep. XI 196.

22. *Das Gotteshaus und die Urformen des Bauens im alten Orient* (1930).

characteristic type of construction that the modern inhabitants of [[479]] the same region—the so-called Marsh Dwellers or Ma^cdān—employ to this day is similarly based on a reed technique. The latest photographs of contemporary buildings[23] cannot but call to mind immediately the selfsame motifs on archaic Sumerian seals and reliefs. It is worth noting in passing that the Marsh Dwellers are a society apart, so much so that their neighbors often question whether the Maᶜdān should at all be regarded as Arabs. We thus have here an immemorial tradition that had a profound spiritual effect on the oldest inhabitants, and has remained very much alive down to the present.

(7) There is no need, then, to stray far from the Persian Gulf in search of the Garden of Eden. The biblical text was not anticipating an aquatic Nephelococcygia. What the narrative calls for is an extensive body of sweet water, with ample areas of vegetation dotted through it, and with four sizable rivers fanning out from there upstream. All these conditions, moreover, should be applicable to the past, the 10th century B.C. at the latest. To be sure, hydrographic features in the soft alluvium of Lower Mesopotamia have been far from stable through the ages. Nevertheless, recent technical studies[24] have made it probable that, contrary to all previous calculations, the area from modern Amara eastward must always have contained reedy marsh and shallow lagoon, in the past even more so than today. Much of it appears to have been a sweet-water spur of the Persian Gulf,[25] a shallow lake into which numerous rivers descended, among them the as yet unmerged waters of the Tigris and the Euphrates. Significantly enough, aerial photographs still show traces of ancient cultivation under the present northwest reaches of the Persian Gulf.[26]

(8) What is the bearing of these data on the identification of the [[480]] Pishon and the Gihon? The one definite result is that, at the time when the narrative before us originated, neither of these rivers could have had its estuary very far from the mouths of the Tigris and the Euphrates. This in itself is an appreciable gain, in view of the geographic anarchy that is implicit in so many of the attempted solutions of the question. If one wishes, however, to be even more specific, the choice is as yet by no means self-evident, even though the range has been vastly reduced. The most likely solution should be among one of the following:

23. Cf. Gavin Maxwell, *People of the Reeds* (1957).

24. See especially G. M. Lees and N. L. Falcon, *Geographical Journal* (1952), 24ff.

25. Cf. fn. 18. This may explain why Akkadian sources sometimes refer to that region as *Nār marratum* "Bitter River."

26. Buringh, *loc. cit.*, 36.

(a) Gihon-Diyala and Pishon-Kerkha. This presupposes, in line with recent hydrographic studies, that the mouth of the Diyala was at the time considerably farther east than it now is. There is no question that the Diyala winds through much of what was once Kassite territory, or one of the two widely separated regions which the Bible designates as Cush. In that case, the Pishon would have to be equated with the Kerkha, a river that comes down from the heart of the Iranian plateau. It so happens that Assyrian records mention Median gold;[27] on the other hand, the Havilah of our passage was a non-distinctive geographic designation, being applied in the Table of Nations to more than one place (cf. Gen 10:7, 29), so that an Iranian namesake is not out of the question. More suggestive, perhaps, is the mention of the *šōham*-stone as one of the products of the Pishon territory. If the Pishon was indeed the Kerkha, then its cuneiform name was *Uqnû* (the lapis lazuli river). Now the biblical term for lapis has yet to be pointed out. It can hardly have been *sappīr,* since sapphire is a different type of blue stone. One the other hand, it is worth noting that *šōham* was the only type of stone used in the decoration of the ephod (e.g., Exod 25:7). Since lapis would be the corresponding decorative material in Mesopotamia, and since neither the [[481]] meaning nor the etymology of *šōham*[28] has been determined, there is a good chance that the term referred to lapis.[29] There is the further circumstance that *šōham* is almost invariably accompanied by the word for "stone," which is very rarely the case with other mineral-names in Hebrew; the same is true, of course, of lapis lazuli itself, and probably also of the Sumerian equivalent z a . g ì n.[30] Now just as the Pishon is said to come from a country known for its *šōham*-stone, the Kerkha originates in a land from which lapis was imported in antiquity. What is more, the Assyrian name for the Kerkha was *Uqnû* "the Blue River," or the same term that was also used for lapis. None of this adds up to conclusive proof. But there is at least a fair possibility that the biblical reference to the Pishon in connection with the *šōham*-stone showed an awareness of the native name *Uqnû.* If these combinations stand up, we shall then have not only a positive equation of the Pishon with the Kerkha but also of the *šōham*-stone with lapis lazuli.

(b) Gihon-Kirkha and Pishon-Karun. In favor of this assumption is the known propinquity of the Kerkha and Karun estuaries and the further fact that all four Paradise rivers would then have converged within

27. R. Campbell Thompson, *A Dictionary of Assyrian Chemistry and Geology* (1936), 58.

28. The often adduced Akk. *sāmtu* "red stone" does not have the same sibilant.

29. It is interesting to note that Job 28:16 mentions *šōham* together with sapphire, which may suggest similarity while precluding actual identity.

30. Thompson, *op. cit.*, 129.

the compass of the shallow lake area. Another favoring argument would be the Samaritan version's apparent identification of the Gihon with the Choaspes/Kerkha. On the other hand, however, the Kerkha would seem to be placed too far from Kassite territory, unless the biblical statement is taken to allude to the Iranian homeland of the Kassites. When it comes to the Pishon, there is little to choose between the Karun and the Kerkha for purposes of geographic comparison.

(c) Gihon-Kerkha and Pishon-Wadi er-Rumma. The latter, or one ⟦482⟧ of the other now dry wadis that slope down from the south, would have to be identified with the Pishon if it is deemed necessary to locate the pertinent land of Havilah in Arabia. Gold is known to have been imported from Arabia as far back as the time of the Royal Tombs of Ur. Furthermore, geographers now estimate that the old shore of the Persian Gulf lay farther to the south,[31] indicating deeper penetration into that quarter in ancient times. It remains to be shown, however, that any of the present wadis was sufficiently active during the period in question to constitute a sizable and perennial river. And if *šōham* was actually lapis, Arabia's stake in the matter would have to be given up.

To sum up, the above discussion has not produced anything like a Treasure Island[32] map of Eden, for all the reported gold of Havilah. What I have tried to show is that the biblical text, the traditions of ancient Mesopotamia, the geographic history of the land at the head of the Persian Gulf, and the surviving building practices in that marshy country point jointly to an older garden land, richly watered, and favored by religion and literature alike—the kind of Paradise, in short, that local tradition still locates at the confluence of the Euphrates and the Tigris. Accordingly, the physical background of the biblical Garden of Eden outlines a real, though remote and atypical, sector of the ancient Near East.

31. Buringh, *loc. cit.*, 37.

32. For mythical accounts of fabulous treasures cf. the Copper Scroll from Qumran; see the discussion by J. T. Milik, *Bibl. Arch.* 19 (1956), 60–62, with parallels from Josephus and some Islamic sources; see also S. Mowinckel, *JBL* 76 (1957), 261–65.

King Lists of the Old Babylonian Period and Biblical Genealogies

Abraham Malamat

⟦163⟧ Biblical genealogies—especially the ethnographic tables in Genesis and the tribal genealogies assembled mainly in the first nine chapters of 1 Chronicles—represent a unique historiographical genre within the literature of the ancient Near East.[1] Only at the start of the Islamic period did Arab chronographers create such broad genealogical tables, encompassing northern and southern Arabian tribes, dwarfing in extent even their biblical archetypes.[2]

An extraordinary document containing the full genealogy of the Hammurapi dynasty (henceforth GHD), recently published by J. J. Finkelstein,[3] prompts a reassessment in this field. The Old Babylonian

Reprinted with permission from *Journal of the American Oriental Society* 88 (1968) 163–73.

1. On genealogies in the Bible in general, see the biblical dictionaries s. v.: e.g., *The Interpreter's Dictionary of the Bible* II, 1962, pp. 362ff. (R. A. Bowman); *Encyclopaedia Biblica* III, 1958, cols. 663ff. (Y. Liver; in Hebrew), with bibliographical references there. For the various interpretations of Israelite tribal genealogies, see W. Duffy, *The Tribal-Historical Theory on the Origin of the Hebrew People*, 1944. Cf. also L. Ramlot, "Les généalogies bibliques," *Bible et Vie chrétienne* 60 (1964), 53ff.

2. The basic treatment of these genealogies in relation with their biblical antecedents is still W. Robertson Smith, *Kinship and Marriage in Early Arabia*², 1903. Cf. also the most recent studies on Arabian genealogies: J. Obermann, "Early Islam," in *The Idea of History in the Ancient Near East*, 1955, especially pp. 242ff. and 290ff.; W. Caskel, "Die Bedeutung der Beduinen in der Geschichte der Araber," *Arbeitsgemeinschaft für Forschung des Landes Nordrhein-Westfalen*, Heft 8, 1953; idem, *Ǧamharat an-nasab—Das genealogische Werk des Hišām ibn Muḥammad al-Kalbi* I–II, 1966.

3. "The Genealogy of the Hammurapi Dynasty," *JCS* 20 (1966), 95–118 (hereinafter cited by page number only); for specific points see also the bibliographical references there.

king list, together with the upper part of the Assyrian King List (henceforth AKL),[4] now provides further insights into the essence and structure of biblical genealogies. Moreover, examination of lineage systems among present-day primitive tribal societies, which have been the subject of intense anthropological study in recent years, may give a clearer picture of genealogical patterns in the ancient Near East, in spite of the different historical and sociological contexts, and especially as those societies are of an entirely illiterate nature.[5]

We should note, *a priori*, the parallel and the divergent features in the genealogical schemes of the Bible and the Mesopotamian king lists, for they define the possibilities of comparative discussion. Whereas the king lists are of an obvious vertical construction, biblical genealogies are spread out on a horizontal plane as well, exemplified for instance by the twelve tribes stemming from Jacob. Only the latter, a two-dimensional pattern, can form a true family tree, revealing a genealogical panorama of a single tribe or of an entire group of peoples. The Bible, followed by the Arabian genealogists, often resorts to accommodating female elements, wives or concubines, mothers or daughters, elements which naturally have no place in strictly vertical lineages of societies basing on agnatic descent.

⟦164⟧ Vertical, one-dimensional patterns record only "genealogical depth" and sequence of generations, while the two-dimensional pattern forms points of segmentation; that is, it encompasses nodal eponyms from which stem several descendants who in turn may act as founding ancestors of peoples, tribes and clans, such as Terah, Abraham, Isaac, Jacob, and his twelve sons, in the Bible. This segmentation, with its wide range of primary and secondary lineages, is the foremost concept in the genealogical positioning of the individual and in the ascertaining of kin-

4. The first real comprehension of the upper portion of AKL was achieved by B. Landsberger, "Assyrische Königsliste und 'Dunkles Zeitalter,'" *JCS* 8 (1954), 33ff. and 109ff. (hereinafter cited only by page number); for two subsequent comprehensive investigations, cf. F. R. Kraus, "Könige, die in Zelten wohnten," *Mededelingen der koninklijke Nederlandse Akademie van Wetenschappen* (Afd. Letterkunde, N. R. 28, No. 2), 1965; H. Lewy, "Assyria (2600–1816 B.C.)," *CAH* I, Ch. XXV (rev. ed.), 1966, pp. 17ff. For the two full copies of AKL extant, cf. I. J. Gelb, *JNES* 12 (1954), 209ff.

5. However, a conclusive study of this facet must be left to a combined effort with modern anthropology, for within the present discussion only casual steps have been taken in this direction. Illuminating comparative material may be gleaned from investigations of, for instance, African peoples; cf., *inter alia*, E. E. Evans-Pritchard, *The Nuer*, 1940 (especially Ch. V); M. Fortes, *The Web of Kinship among the Tallensi*, 1949 (Chs. I and II); I. Cunnison, *The Luapula Peoples of Northern Rhodesia*, 1959 (Ch. IV). Cf. also L. Bohanan, "A Genealogical Charter," *Africa* 22 (1952), 301ff.; and E. Peters, "The Proliferation of Lineage Segments in Cyrenaica," *Journ. Royal Anthr. Inst.* 90 (1960), 29ff.

ship, whether on a broad ethnographic plane or within a more restricted tribal circle. Hence, the king lists are particularly relevant to the study of only the vertical genealogies in the Bible. However, superimposition of the two diverging Mesopotamian lineages, Babylonian and Assyrian, renders a somewhat two-dimensional picture, thus enabling us to approach the other genealogical patterns as well.

It is now evident that the vertical genealogical compositions in the Bible stem from archetypes current among West Semitic tribes from the Old Babylonian period (and possibly earlier), antedating those of the Bible by hundreds of years. The Babylonian king list under discussion dates to the reign of Ammiṣaduqa (1646–1626 B.C., according to the middle chronology used in the present paper), the penultimate ruler of the Hammurapi dynasty. But Landsberger (pp. 109ff.) has convincingly shown that even the upper part of AKL, preserved only in the final redaction of the list as a whole, is the work of scribes of the Old Babylonian period, more precisely of the West Semitic dynasty of Shamshi-Adad, an older contemporary of Hammurapi. Moreover, these royal genealogies were composed in a technique similar to that known in the Bible, of fictitiously linking historical personages to earlier eponyms in fact representing names of an artificial character, such as tribes or geographical entities—as demonstrated by Finkelstein concerning GHD, and Kraus for AKL.

What is more, comparison of the Babylonian and Assyrian king lists, headed by essentially identical putative eponyms, indicates a common genealogical tradition, whether historically based or of mere scribal deduction—one most likely shared by early West Semitic tribes in general. A similar consciousness of common ancestors is evident in the genealogical tables of Genesis, many of the peoples living along-side Israel being assigned within the same family tree as Israel itself. The external evidence now lends support to the assumption that the genealogical traditions contained in Genesis reflect beliefs actually current among these peoples, notions which consciously upheld their common ancestry and not the products of fancy or the pride of Israelite scribes. The self-centered Israelite approach is apparent only in its tendency to place the Israelite line at the center of the family tree, whereas the other peoples derive from it as secondary branches. (The Table of Nations in Genesis 10, which does not include Israel at all, is a matter for separate consideration.)

The upper part of AKL is divided into three sections, the first two of which will concern us in the present paper. At the start, seventeen names are given with the concluding formula "total of 17 kings who dwell in tents," followed by ten names summarized by the phrase "total of 10 kings who are ancestors." As Landsberger has proved (pp. 33f.), this latter group is to be regarded as the "Ahnentafel" of King Shamshi-Adad. In contrast, GHD lists the generations in an uninterrupted line; at the end of the list of fictitious and historical kings, however, three *palū's* (i.e., "eras" or "dynasties") are given by name (in historical sequence, reading): the *palū* of the Gutians, the *p.* of the Haneans, and the *p.* of the Amorites—to which all the generations listed are to be redistributed, as demonstrated by Finkelstein (pp. 103–13).

Yet, to arrive at the very nature of these genealogies and to derive the most instructive lesson for the parallel biblical patterns as well, a structural analysis is called for, comparing the two king lists, Babylonian and Assyrian. Such analysis reveals four successive groups, distinct in their historiographical character and functional aim, which we may here term: (a) the genealogical stock, i.e., the common antecedent generations; (b) the determinative line, i.e., the specific descent of a people or dynasty; (c) the table of ancestors, the actual pedigree of (d) a concrete historical line or dynasty. These, in principle, accord with the structure of the biblical genealogies, yet such segments are not formed into a single continuous line, but are scattered in the Bible.

The Genealogical Stock

Group (a)

⟦165⟧ Group (a) includes the names at the top of the two royal lists which derive from a common basis, as Finkelstein has attempted to demonstrate. The two texts differ in order of names and in several major or minor textual variants, which are, in part, the result of faulty transmission. Moreover, the cumbersome names of the first three lines of GHD prove each to be compounded forms of two originally separate names corresponding to pairs of names in AKL. Accepting Finkelstein's analysis, the first nine to eleven names are common to both lists.[6] This is the genealogical depth of many lineages in ancient times, even as in some modern tribal societies.[7]

6. In AKL, the problematic entries are Emṣu and ḪARṣu (Nos. 7–8) which seem to be variants of a single name corresponding to Namz/ṣū of GHD (No. 8); and Zuʾabu and Nuabu (Nos. 11–12), which may or may not be equated with Zummabu and Namḫū of GHD (Nos. 10–11) (see Finkelstein, pp. 98–99). As the last equation (Nuabu-Namḫū) seems especially doubtful, the latter names are possibly to be ascribed to group (b), and would then reveal a standardized pattern of ten generations in the genealogical stock (see below).

7. For a 10-generation depth among the Bedouin east of Damascus, cf. Caskel, *Die Bedeutung*. . . (above, n. 2), p. 7; for a constant 11 generations among the Bedouin of Cyrenaica (though their history may be traced as far back as the 11th century A.D.), cf.

This genealogical stock is an apparently artificial composition of personal names (such as Adamu) and appellatives or even tribal names (the most obvious examples are Ḫanū/Ḫeana and Dit/dānu) and toponyms (such as possibly Madara and Namzū), presented as putative eponyms. Most have definite affinities, whether ethnic or geographical, or even linguistic (especially the GHD forms), with the West Semitic peoples. Such lists may have been transmitted orally among these tribes as mnemotechnic accounts, such as parallelled in modern tribal genealogies; they could even have been some sort of desert chant, as suggested by Finkelstein concerning the first six names (p. 112). The fictitious stock could have easily been absorbed into the general genealogical scheme, mainly because of the fluidity in usage of personal names, tribal names and toponyms, a universal phenomenon especially frequent among West Semitic peoples in the Old Babylonian period.[8] In order to lend an authentic ring to this putative list, it was built around approximately ten generations, as a sort of retrojection of the optimal ten-generation pattern of real lineages, as found in the "Ahnentafeln" ⟦'pedigree'⟧ of the Babylonian and Assyrian kings, appearing later in both AKL and GHD (see group [c], below).

The character and make-up of this group immediately brings to mind the scheme of the Hebrew line (*tōledōt* ⟦'generations'⟧) from Shem to Terah or Abraham (Gen 11:10–26), surely to be regarded as the genealogical stock of the people of Israel, which was held in common with several other related peoples. Quite a separate matter is the genealogy from Adam to Noah (Genesis 5), comprising the universal ancestors of the antediluvian generations, beyond the realm of actual history. The compiler of GHD was also aware of an earlier era (*palū*), but he saw no need to enter its generations into his list (cf. line 32), they being of no relevance for the historical reality of the West Semitic tribes. Interestingly enough, the biblical name of the progenitor of mankind, Adam, is paralleled by the second name in AKL,[9] and possibly the fourth in GHD. This name may have actually been borrowed from early West Semitic genealogical concepts and applied in the Bible at the beginning of the primordial line,

M. Gluckman, *Politics, Law and Ritual in Tribal Society*, 1965, p. 272 (citing Peters, *op. cit.* [above, n. 5]), and pp. 271–275 for African (quoting several works mentioned above, n. 5) and other tribal lineages of 10- to 12-generation depth.

8. J. R. Kupper. *Les nomades en Mésopotamie au temps des rois de Mari*, 1957, pp. 215ff., gives several examples including Numḫā (compare Namḫū, GHD No. 11), a West Semitic tribal and geographical name, as well as an element in personal names.

9. As alluded to by A. Poebel in the initial treatment of AKL: *JNES* 1 (1942), 253. For the personal name Adamu in the Old Akkadian period, see I. J. Gelb, *Glossary of Old Akkadian*, 1957, p. 19, and in the Old Babylonian period, C. J. Gadd, *Iraq* 4 (1937), 35.

out of etymological considerations; for in Hebrew *ʾādām* is also the generic term for "man," there being a play on the word *ʾadāmā* "ground" in Gen 2:7—"And the Lord God formed man (*ʾādām*) of the dust of the ground (*ʾadāmā*)." The ante- and postdiluvian lines (i.e., Adam and of Shem, respectively), symmetrically arranged to a ten-generation depth, are undoubtedly the product of intentional harmonization and in imitation of the concrete genealogical model (cf. Mishnah Aboth 5:2).

Though according to the Massoretic version the line from Shem to Abraham embraces ten generations, there are various indications of possible ⟦166⟧ minor fluctuations in the original scheme of this group.[10] On the one hand, Shem or Abraham, or possibly both, were not initially included within the genealogical stock. The former may have been appended as a heading to join the Hebrew line to the Table of Nations and the primordial accounts in Genesis, Arpachshad having originally headed the list. We may also assume that the list in fact concluded with Terah, to whom the Bible ascribes a line (*tōledōt*) of his own (Gen 11:27), whereas his three sons, Abraham, Nahor, and Haran, the father of Lot, were conceived of as the founding ancestors of individual lineages. On the other hand, the Septuagint (cf. also Luke 3:35) inserts an additional link between Arpachshad and Shelah—Kenan, a tradition also reflected in the Table of Nations in the Book of Jubilees (8:1ff.).

Moreover, the name Arpachshad is linguistically and ethnographically puzzling, and differs from the other names in Shem's line, which are short and comprised of a single name element. We most likely have here a fused form of two names, just as with the initial entries in GHD, the parallel becoming even more obvious if we assume that Arpachshad once stood at the head of the line. Indeed, already in ancient times (cf. Jubilees 9:4; Josephus, *Antiquities* I, 6:4) there was a tendency, shared by modern exegetes, to identify the second element in Arpachshad with Chesed, the Chaldeans.

Like its Mesopotamian archetype, the line of Shem also contains a mixture of appellatives, tribal names, and toponyms, all in the guise of patriarchal eponyms. Among the appellatives we may include Shem, for its meaning in Hebrew, as in the Akkadian cognate, is simply "name," or "reputation," "posterity."[11] Most likely appellative, too, is Peleg, "a divi-

10. For particulars on this line, which is attributed to the P source, like most of the Pentateuchal genealogical records, cf. the commentaries, especially O. Procksch, *Die Genesis 2–3*, 1924, pp. 492ff.; B. Jacob, *Genesis*, 1934, pp. 304ff.; and U. Cassuto, *From Noah to Abraham* (English ed.), 1964, pp. 250ff.

11. The suggested derivation of Shem from Shumer (with the final syllable silent), reintroduced by S. N. Kramer, *Studia Biblica et Orientalia* III (Analecta Biblica 12), 1959, pp. 203f., does not seem plausible.

sion," at least on the basis of the etymology given in the Bible—"for in his days was the earth divided (*niphlĕgā*)" (Gen 10:25), though there has been an attempt to relate the name with *Phalga* on the middle Euphrates, a place name known from Hellenistic times. The outstanding tribal name is Eber, a personification derived from the gentilicon *ᶜibrī*, "Hebrew" (see below, n. 14), and surely not the other way around. Another possible tribal name is Reu, a compound form of which, Reuel, constitutes a sub-tribe in the genealogy of Edom (Genesis 36 passim), as well as of Midian (Num 10:29; LXX Gen 25:3).[12]

The three last links in the line of Shem—Serug, Nahor and Terah—stand out as topographical entries, all three signifying locations in the Balikh region and attested in neo-Assyrian documents as Sarūgi, Til-Naḫiri, and Til-(ša)-Turaḫi.[13] Only the city Nahor/Naḫur was known as an important political center already in the 19th–18th centuries B.C. in texts from Cappadocia, Chagar Bazar and, above all, in the Mari documents, where it appears as a focal point of West Semitic tribes, as well. The proximity of the three sites to Haran associates these eponyms with the ancestral home, according to biblical tradition, of the Hebrews; this is the special significance of their insertion within the genealogical stock.

As with the Mesopotamian parallel, here too, putative compilation was facilitated by onomastic and toponymic affiliation; that is, identity of personal, clan or tribal names, and of geographic locations, a phenomenon common enough in the Bible, as well. Thus, the name Eber, which in the Israelite mind had a geographic connotation associated with *ᶜēber hannāhār*, "beyond the river," where "in days of old your fathers lived" (Josh 24:2), is found in the Bible also as a clan or personal name (Neh 12:20; 1 Chr 5:13; 8:12, 22). Again, Nahor serves both as the eponym of the Nahorites (Gen 22:20–24), and as the name of the "city of Nahor" (Gen 24:10). Moreover, this phenomenon is clearly displayed ⟦167⟧ in the account of the genealogy of Cain, relating of the founding of the first city, that Cain "called . . . after the name of his son, Enoch" (Gen 4:17). But Enoch is also the name of a clan in the tribe of Midian (Gen 25:4), as well as in the tribe of Reuben (Gen 46:9). The same is true in many other instances, such as the name Dan, which is eponymic, tribal

12. In the latter connection, W. F. Albright, *CBQ* 25 (1963), 5f., has shown that Reuel is the Midianite clan-name of Hobab, and not the name of his actual father.

13. Cf., in addition to the commentaries mentioned in n. 10 above, W. F. Albright, *From Stone Age to Christianity*², 1957, pp. 236f., and R. de Vaux, *RB* 55 (1948), 323f. On Nahor, in the cuneiform sources as well as in the Bible, see A. Malamat, *Encyclopaedia Biblica* V, s.v. cols. 805ff. (Hebrew). The component *Til-* in these and other place-names of the Neo-Assyrian period, may be an Aramean-Assyrian appendage to older names of sites which had been re-established in this period.

and topographic, in the last instance applied to the town of Laish after its conquest by the Danites: "And they called the name of their city Dan after the name of Dan their father, who was born unto Israel" (Judg 18:29).

However, comparison of the Mesopotamian and the biblical genealogical stocks is of special interest concerning the respective eponyms Ḫanū and Eber, both representing actual historic entities well-known even to the later redactors of the lists. The insertion of these eponyms among the antecedent generations undoubtedly represents a prevailing attitude on the antiquity of these tribes, as GHD actually indicates in ranking "the *palū* of the Haneans" earlier than "the *p.* of the Amorites," and implies an awareness of putative relation with subsequent entries. However, this latter does not necessarily have bearing on true ethnic kinship of subsequent generations, as GHD may serve to show. Whereas the Shamshi-Adad dynasty of Assyria in effect likely stemmed from the Hanean tribal association, this does not hold for the Babylonian dynasty, which was closely related with the Amnānu and Yaḫruru tribes, as indicated in its determinative line in GHD (group [b]) and various other sources. Yet, these latter tribes, as is evidenced in the Mari documents, were part of a tribal association other than the Haneans: their oftimes rivals, the Yaminites (see below note 17).

Thus, the mention of the eponym Ḫeana (Ḫanū) in the lineage of the kings of Babylon conflicts with actual ethno-historic reality. But the compilers of GHD took no objection to this obvious discrepancy, indicating the actual contrast only by accommodating the determinative Babylonian line (group [b]) within the *palū* of the Amorites, as against the *palū* of the Haneans, which embraces the latter part of the genealogical stock (group [a]), from Ḫeana on.

The above conclusions are instructive concerning the relation between the eponym Eber and the concept "Hebrew." Eber, too, may have in reality been linked with only this branch or that, and did not necessarily envelop *all* the generations following it. Indeed, the empiric use of the term "Hebrew" (which occurs some thirty times in the Bible) is of a definite ethnic nature, applying only to the people of Israel, as has rightly been noted by several scholars dealing with this problem.[14] Moreover, as widely recognized, this term is specifically used to denote the Israelites as such in their confrontation with other peoples (thus against the Egyptians, Philistines and Canaanites). Hence, anyone as-

14. Among others, B. Landsberger, *Kleinasiatische Forschungen* 1 (1930), 329ff.; de Vaux, *op. cit.* (above, n. 13), 337ff.; and especially M. Greenberg, *The Hab/piru*, 1955, pp. 91ff. The various proposed etymologies of the term ᶜ*ibrī*, and its even more intricate relationship with Ḫab/piru-ᶜApiru (cf. the bibliography in the last mentioned work), are beyond the scope of the present paper.

suming that the biblical term "Hebrew" embraces a circle wider than the Israelites alone, a view based mainly on the appearance of the eponym Eber six generations prior to Abraham, must bear the *onus probandi.*

The other descendants of Eber, such as the Nahorites or even the "sons" of Lot, were not necessarily considered as actual Hebrews, whether by self-definition or otherwise. The direct grafting to Eber of far-away tribes of the South Arabian region, represented by Joktan and his descendants in the Table of Nations (Gen 10:25ff.), is elusive. The only eponym expressly bearing the designation "Hebrew" is Abraham. Much has been speculated regarding the precise meaning of the phrase "Abram the Hebrew" (Gen 14:13), but even with all the shades of meaning attributed to this phrase,[15] its major intent is obviously to single out Abraham as the founder of the determinative line (group [b]) of the Israelite genealogy. There is no indication that any other people related to Abraham but not of the direct Israelite line was "Hebrew" (i.e., the "sons" of Keturah, the Ishmaelites and the Edomites).

⟦168⟧ This state of affairs is similar to the Mesopotamian context: Shamshi-Adad was regarded as a Hanean in contrast to the kings of Babylon, just as the rulers of the local dynasty at Mari actually adopted the titulary "King of Ḫana," while the rulers of the Old Babylonian dynasty at Uruk were apparently referred to as kings (of the tribe) of Amnānu, as attested in regard to two of them.[16] Thus finds expression the concept of the specific determinative line. We cannot be far off in assuming that, had we possession of the genealogical tables of the two latter dynasties (i.e., of Mari and Uruk), Ḫanū would most likely be found among the earlier eponyms (group [a]) in both, in spite of the ethnic affinity of the Uruk dynasty. Another parallel use of the terms "Hanean" and "Hebrew" is revealed in their application in a geographical-territorial context,

15. The two most recent major studies are W. F. Albright, "Abram the Hebrew," *BASOR* 163 (1961), 36ff., regarding *ʿibrī*, like Egyptian *ʿApiru*, as a 'donkey driver', 'caravaneer'; and especially N. A. van Uchelen, *Abraham de Hebreeër*, 1964, which reviews the history of interpretation of our passage, from LXX on, van Uchelen himself stressing the military aspect of the term here, typifying Abraham as a warrior-hero. This same facet is interestingly also often found in the term Ḫana of the Mari documents. E. A. Speiser regards Genesis 14 as a Hebrew adaptation of an Akkadian source, seeing in Abraham a Ḫabiru warrior; see his *Genesis*, 1964, pp. 102ff.

16. I.e., Sīnkāshid and one of his grandsons (either Sīngāmil or Ilumgāmil); see A. Falkenstein, *Baghdader Mitteilungen* 2 (1963), 22ff. Moreover, an obscure passage in a letter of king Anam of Uruk to Sīnmuballiṭ of Babylon (col. III, l. 40—*ibid.*, pp. 58, 62, 70) evidently points to a special connection between Uruk and the Amnānu. However, Falkenstein has raised doubts as to whether the Uruk dynasty truly stemmed from the Amnānu, or for that matter whether it was West Semitic altogether. Cf. also the review of the above by F. R. Kraus, *BiOr* 22 (1965), 287ff.

signifying the main areas of ultimate sedentation of these originally nomadic tribes. Thus, the Mari documents refer to the middle Euphrates region as "the land of Ḫana" (*māt Ḫana*), whereas in the Bible the land of Canaan (or a part thereof) is once called "the land of the Hebrews" (Gen 40:15).

The Further Genealogical Line

Group (b): The Determinative Line

We include in this group the generations bridging the common genealogical stock with the tables of ancestors; in the Mesopotamian lists these determine the pedigrees culminating in the founders of the West Semitic dynasties in Babylon and Assyria (i.e., Sumuabum and Shamshi-Adad, respectively). Finkelstein has convincingly shown that, while the pedigree of Sumuabum actually starts with Ipti-yamūta (No. 14), the latter's two "ancestors," Amnānu and Yaḫruru (Nos. 12 and 13), serve to determine the national affiliation of the Babylonian line (pp. 111–112). As already noted, these latter were West Semitic, basically nomadic tribes; thus, if we were to label the Babylonian lineage up to Ipti-yamūta, in terms employed by AKL, the phrase "total of 13 kings who dwell in tents" would be most appropriate.

The determinative Babylonian line may illuminate the controversial subject of the origin and meaning of the term DUMU.MEŠ-*yamina*, i.e., "sons of the South," found in the Mari documents, and there only, as a designation for a broad tribal confederation, the Amnānu and Yaḫruru comprising its main elements.[17] The grafting of the Babylonian table of ancestors to the latter tribes indicates that Yaminite groups had become entrenched in southern Mesopotamia already long before Yaḫdunlim (c. 1825–1810 B.C.) and Shamshi-Adad (c. 1815–1782 B.C.)—the respective founders of the West Semitic dynasties in Mari and Assyria. In Babylon the Yaminites achieved political independence some three generations prior to the above rulers, namely, in the days of Sumuabum (c. 1894–1881 B.C.), whereas at Uruk the special ties of the Amnānu with the ruling dynasty go back to the time of king Sīnkāshid (c. 1865–1833 B.C.; see above, n. 16). Thus, it would seem that the term DUMU.MEŠ-*yamina*, used

17. On this tribal association and its sub-groups, see Kupper, *op. cit.* (above, n. 8), ch. II: "Les Benjaminites." It should be noted that Amnānu and Yaḫruru together are explicitly designated as Yaminites only in ARM III, 50, ll. 10–13 (and not in the oft-quoted passage in *ARM* I, 42, ll. 30–31), as is the former alone in Yaḫdunlim's Foundation Inscription, col. III, ll. 6ff. (in ll. 17 and 21 DUMU-*mi-im* surely represents an abbreviated form of the term Yaminites). See my "Aspects of Tribal Societies in Mari and Israel," *XVe Rencontre assyr. internat.*, Université de Liège, 1967, p. 137, n. 1, for the various readings of DUMU.MEŠ-*yamina*.

by the Mari authorities and perhaps even coined by them, may have been applied originally to these tribal units for they had already become a decisive historical factor in the regions to the *south*, from the viewpoint of Mari.[18]

⟦169⟧ As for AKL, the determinative genealogical line embraces, according to our present analysis, the names from Abazu to Apiashal (Nos. 13–17); that is, the last five generations of "the 17 kings dwelling in tents." In contrast to the parallel section in GHD, the names here in AKL are obscure and not of a tribal character, but rather seem to be proper names. They are unknown from any other source, except for the name Ushpia (No. 16), mentioned in late Assyrian royal inscriptions as an early Assyrian king who founded the national sanctuary in the city of Ashur.[19] It is doubtful whether Ushpia was inserted in the list, as suggested by Mrs. H. Lewy, in order to indicate the transition from nomadic life to permanent settlement in Ashur, for he is definitely included among the "kings dwelling in tents," and he is not even the last of these. More probably, an early historical Assyrian king was purposely inserted here in the determinative line of AKL in order to lend it further authenticity.

Group (c): Table of Ancestors

While in GHD the table of ancestors may be deduced only indirectly, on the basis of the seeming authenticity of the personal names preceding Sumuabum, in AKL this group appears as a separate section concluding with the rubric "10 kings who are *ancestors*" (see above, p. ⟦185⟧). In the latter list, however, the generations are given in reverse order; that is, in ascending generations. In reality, we should detach the first generation from this table, i.e. Apiashal (son of Ushpia), whose name is not West Semitic, in contrast to all the other names in this group, for he also appears earlier in the genealogical list (No. 17) and is repeated here only to tie up with the former section. Shamshi-Adad should then be

18. Admittedly, the Yaminites as such are referred to throughout the Mari documents as being only in the regions to the north and west of Mari, where they were still pursuing a (semi-)nomadic life. In contrast to important groups of urbanized Yaminites to the south, these gained mention in the documents through their continual conflict with the Mari authorities. On the other hand, A. Parrot, in *Abraham et son temps*, 1962, pp. 45f., has doubtfully suggested that the name Yaminites indicates that this tribal grouping originated in southern Mesopotamia, from whence it penetrated northward at an early period. The DUMU.MEŠ-*simʾal*, i.e., 'sons of the north', were, of course, always located much farther to the north, namely in the upper Habur and Balikh valleys.

19. See Landsberger, p. 109, n. 206. According to H. Lewy, *op. cit.* (above, n. 4), 18f., Ushpia reigned before the mid-third millennium B.C., but the dating of this king to the end of the Third Dynasty of Ur or thereabouts seems preferable; cf. W. W. Hallo, *JNES* 15 (1956), 220f.

appended at the end of the table of ancestors as the tenth name, for this pedigree, beginning now with Ḫalē (No. 18), is actually his (see the Table at the end of this article).

Of special note is the fact that the parallel group in GHD, i.e. from Ipti-yamūta to Sumuabum (Nos. 14–23), also includes exactly ten entries. Thus we may assume that the ideal pattern of an "Ahnentafel" ⟦'pedigree'⟧ was based on a constant genealogical depth of ten generations. From the viewpoint of the genealogical pattern, it was immaterial whether this aim was achieved by means of integrating even fictitious names (such as, possibly, the pair of rhymed names Yakmesi-Yakmeni, Nos. 22–23 in AKL), in the lack of fuller knowledge of actual ancestors; or by means of entries such as Aminu (AKL, No. 26), evidently Shamshi-Adad's brother, not father (who is definitely known as Ila-kabkabu, both from a remark in AKL proper and from other sources), though Aminu apparently preceded Shamshi-Adad to the throne (Landsberger, p. 34).

The nine ancestors of Sumuabum and of Shamshi-Adad, who lived in the 20th and 19th centuries B.C. at places unknown to us,[20] were tribal chieftains who may even have adopted the title "king," like those in the middle Euphrates region mentioned in the inscriptions of Yaḫdunlim from Mari: "7 kings, fathers (*abū*) of Ḫana" (Disc Inscription, col. I, ll. 15–16); and three Yaminite "kings" named with their regal cities and tribal territories (Foundation Inscription, col. III, ll. 4–10). The actual rulers who reigned in the city of Ashur proper during the period of Shamshi-Adad's forebears were accommodated by the compiler of AKL between Aminu and Shamshi-Adad. The first of these, Sulili, is listed as Aminu's son, a seemingly fictitious linkage with the previous section. These kings, most of whom are attested in other sources, should be regarded as a line more or less synchronous with the "Ahnentafel" of Shamshi-Adad, and thus not to be included within his actual pedigree (and consequently omitted in the Table at the end of this article).[21]

20. Only the immediate predecessors of Shamshi-Adad can be assumed to have ruled in the city of Terqa near the confluence of the Habur river; see Landsberger, p. 35, n. 26. This same city may have also been the ancestral home of the Mari dynasty, as indicated by a letter to King Zimrilim urging that the *kispu* rites honoring the manes of his father Yaḫdunlim be performed there (*ARM* III, 40); cf. A. Malamat, "Prophecy in the Mari Documents," *Eretz-Israel* 4 (1956), 76 (Hebrew).

21. For an attempted reconstruction of the two parallel lines, cf. Hallo, *op. cit.* (above, no. 19), 221, n. 9, which we may accept with some reservation: Apiashal and Sulili, respectively opening and closing the Ahnentafel of Shamshi-Adad (Hallo's left-hand column) should be removed to the top of the line of "real" kings of Ashur (Hallo's right-hand column), following Ushpia (cf. Landsberger, p. 33). Mrs. Lewy's conjecture (*op. cit.* [above, n. 4], p. 20) that Shamshi-Adad's Ahnentafel is in fact to be ascribed to Sulili is hardly acceptable.

⟦170⟧ The above analysis clarifies the underlying structure of the royal Mesopotamian genealogies. Tables of ancestors containing ten generations were appended to the universal stock by means of transitional links—our determinative line. Here, the difference in span of the respective determinative lines is highly instructive, five entries in AKL as against two in GHD (or six as against three if the eponyms Nuabu and Namḫū, respectively, are to be detached from the genealogical stock and joined to the following section; see above, n. 6).

This difference of three generations is not, evidently, incidental but rather the outcome of the structure of the genealogical scheme as described, and reflects the true chronological gap existing between the foundation of the two West Semitic dynasties, in Babylon (start of 19th cent. B.C.) and in Assyria (end of 19th cent. B.C.). As Finkelstein has already demonstrated (pp. 109ff.), the two dynastic lists, in spite of the artificiality of many of the names, rely on chronological-historical traditions and on more or less reliable calculations of generations. The surprising chronological harmony between the two lists is evident from the fact that Shamshi-Adad and his Babylonian contemporary, Sīnmuballiṭ the father of Hammurapi, both occupy the same respective numerical positions, that is, the twenty-seventh. However, we have noted above (p. ⟦192⟧) concerning the two dynastic founders, that Sumuabum (No. 23) preceded Shamshi-Adad by some three generations (though he was the fourth king before Sīnmuballiṭ). Now, if the respective scribes of the two lists began their reckoning from one and the same common stock, and since the table of ancestors of the dynastic founders was based on a constant ten-generation depth, the cancelling out of the above chronological discrepancy was achieved by means of appropriate additions to the Assyrian determinative line.

The Royal Genealogies of Israel

In dealing with the generations subsequent to the basic stock, comparative treatment of the data in the Bible and the Mesopotamian archetypes is a more complicated matter, forcing us, *inter alia*, to reconstruct the biblical lineages from scattered materials, sometimes even resorting to sources of a narrative nature. The determinative lineage defining the people of Israel comprises the series of the three Patriarchs—Abraham, Isaac and Jacob, whereas, e.g., Abraham-Isaac-Esau specifies the Edomites, and the eponyms Haran and Lot, the Ammonites and the Moabites, respectively. But intramural Israelite usage demands an additional eponym following the basic patriarchal scheme, representing one of the twelve tribes, such as Judah, Benjamin, etc., to complete the determinative line.

Ultimately, these four generations determine each and every Israelite lineage.

However, these individual lineages, which are to be regarded as the "tables of ancestors," are of a problematic character. On the one hand, the initial generations represent, as a rule, a graduated, intra-tribal classification—sub-tribe, clan, family. On the other hand, the lineages are normally selective, telescoping generations here and there similar to modern tribal genealogies, and thus depriving them of true chronological value.[22] A case in point is the lineage of Moses (third generation from Levi—Exod 6:16–20) as against that of his younger contemporary Joshua (ninth, or possibly tenth, generation from Joseph—1 Chr 7:22–27).

For sake of comparison with GHD and AKL, we must ascertain as closely as possible the ideal genealogical model within the corpus of biblical genealogies. There seems to be no more suitable parallel than the lineage of David, founder of the venerable dynasty of Judah, which was surely compiled and transmitted with the utmost care.[23] Whereas David's line of successors is given in 1 Chronicles 3, his "table of ancestors" may easily be recognized as a distinct entity among the many branches of the tribe of Judah (see 1 Chronicles 2:5, 9–15). The same "table of ancestors" has been ⟦171⟧ appended to the Book of Ruth as well (4:18–22).[24] Both of these sources seemingly derive from an earlier genealogical document, as implied also in the heading "Now these are the line (*tōledōt*) of Perez" (Ruth 4:18) to the lineage: Perez (the son of Judah)-Hezron-Ram-Amminadab-Nahshon-Salmon (Salma)-Boaz-Obed-Jesse-David.

It is most interesting that, here again, a "table of ancestors" contains exactly ten generations, even though this depth is much too shallow to fill the time-span between the "Patriarchal period" and the time of David.[25] This discrepancy is also apparent from the fact that Nahshon son of Amminadab is placed in the fifth generation before David, whereas accord-

22. See the recent pointed remarks of D. N. Freedman, in *The Bible and the Ancient Near East* (ed. G. E. Wright), 1961, pp. 206f., and K. A. Kitchen, *Ancient Orient and Old Testament*, 1966, pp. 54ff., both citing various examples, especially from the Exodus-Numbers cycle.

23. A similar practice is found among modern tribal lineages, e.g. the Luapula of Rhodesia where the royal line is preserved at a 9-generation depth, as against the telescoped commoner lineages which embrace only 4 to 7 generations; cf. I. Cunnison, History and Genealogies in a Conquest State, *American Anthropologist* 59 (1957), 20ff. (especially p. 27).

24. See the commentaries on Chronicles by J. W. Rothstein-J. Hänel, *Das erste Buch der Chronik*, 1927, pp. 18, 44; W. Rudolph, *Chronikbücher*, 1955, p. 16; J. M. Myers, *I Chronicles*, 1965, pp. 13f.; and on Ruth by W. Rudolph, *Das Buch Ruth*, 1962, pp. 71f.

25. But note some 20 generations from Levi to Samuel, David's older contemporary, in the fuller, though suspicious, genealogy of Heman in 1 Chr 6:18–23 (= 33–38 in the English version).

ing to biblical tradition he was a tribal head of Judah in the days of the Exodus (cf. Exod 6:23; Num 1:7, 2:3; 1 Chr 2:10), some two hundred fifty years before David. Moreover, in keeping with the abovementioned principle of gentilic classification, the compiler of this table resorted in the first two or three generations to eponyms personifying well-known tribal groups within Judah (Perez, Hezron and possibly also Ram).

In short, David's table of ancestors is largely an artificial construction formed on an ideal, traditional model, as befitting a royal lineage. David's lineage (group [c]) links up with the eponym Judah in the determinative Israelite line (group [b]), which in turn is tied to the genealogical stock (group [a]), i.e., the line of Shem. Indeed, the entire reconstructed genealogical line, like the continuous Mesopotamian king lists, is brought forth in the New Testament, within the pedigree of Jesus, which was traced back through David (from Abraham to David in Matt 1:3–6, and from David to Adam, in ascending order, in Luke 3:31–38).

As with the Davidic dynasty, the Bible gives the genealogy of the house of Saul, the first Israelite king, of the tribe of Benjamin. Yet Saul's "table of ancestors" has been preserved only in an incomplete form, and then in two conflicting traditions. His immediate ancestors are included in an appendix to the genealogy of the tribe of Benjamin in 1 Chr 8:29ff., with a duplicate, but slightly tampered-with version in 1 Chr 9:35ff.[26] The latter gives the line as: Jeiel ("the father of [the city of] Gibeon")-Ner-Kish-Saul. The linkage of the house of Saul with the Israelite settlement in Gibeon is strange in itself, for Saul's family stemmed from the city of Gibeah of Benjamin. This tie is seemingly artificial, as evidenced also in the Massoretic text of 1 Chronicles 8, an apparently more reliable version where Ner is lacking among the sons of the "father of Gibeon" (v. 30). Ner appears only in v. 33, at the head of Saul's line.

Another genealogical tradition, fuller and more revealing, opens the cycle of the Saul stories in 1 Sam 9:1.[27] Unlike the genealogical lists, and as in narrative and historiographical usage, the sequence of generations here ascends, like the table of ancestors of Shamshi-Adad; that is, "Kish (father of Saul), son of Abiel, son of Zeror, son of Bechorath, son of Aphiah, son of a (Ben)-jaminite." Here, the name of Ner, father of Kish and grandfather of Saul, has been omitted, as against the list in

26. See the commentaries on Chronicles in the previous note: Rothstein-Hänel, pp. 165ff.; Rudolph, pp. 80f.; Myers, p. 62.

27. In addition to the references in n. 25, where the relation between the two traditions is dealt with, see S. R. Driver, *Notes on the Hebrew Text of the Books of Samuel*², 1913, pp. 68f.; M. Z. Segal, *The Books of Samuel*, 1956, p. 65 (Hebrew).

Chronicles and the fragment of the family record of Saul (1 Sam 14:50–51).[28] It is also difficult here to draw the dividing-line between Saul's actual ancestors and the fictitious eponyms personifying sub-tribal groups within Benjamin. Yet it is almost certain that Bechorath, the fifth generation (including Ner) before Saul, already represents Becher, one of the major Benjaminite clans (Gen 46:21; 1 Chr 7:6, 8; and cf. 2 Sam 20:1).[29] However, Bechorath's father ⟦173⟧ Aphiah, who is otherwise unknown, could hardly be the immediate link with the eponym Benjamin. The unusual formulation "Aphiah, son of a (Ben)jaminite (*ben* ᵓ*îš yĕmînî*)" would indicate that at least one antecedent (the unnamed "Benjaminite") is missing before reaching the determinative line.

A comparative table of the parallel genealogical structures underlying the Israelite and Mesopotamian royal lines[30] is given on page ⟦199⟧.

28. This last passage can only read as translated in the King James Version and rightly interpreted by Rudolph, *Chronikbücher* (above, n. 24), p. 81: "And the name of the captain of his (i.e., Saul's) host was Abner, the son of Ner, Saul's uncle; and Kish was the father of Saul; and Ner the father of Abner was the son of Abiel." That is, Abner (and not Ner) was Saul's uncle and the brother of Kish, and Abner and Kish both were sons of Ner and grandsons of Abiel. Any other interpretation would require textual emendation.

29. Thus already B. Luther, *ZAW* 21 (1901), 55; and Segal, *loc. cit.* (above, n. 26). One of Becher's sons, Ahijah (1 Chr 7:8), is possibly to be identified with the abovementioned Abiel (with an exchange of the theophoric element).

30. Another interesting point in GHD possibly bearing on the Bible can only be noted here. Finkelstein has shown that the final passage in GHD, dealing with mortuary offerings for the manes of royal ancestors, etc., gives the raison d'être for the entire document. The text seems to have been inherently involved in the *kispu* ceremonies honoring the past generations of the royal line, held on the day of the new moon (pp. 113ff., 117). In 1 Samuel 20, it is related that Saul held a feast on the new moon (vv. 5, 18ff.), while David was to have returned to Bethlehem, his home, to participate in family sacrifices (vv. 6, 29). Could these gatherings, held at ancestral homes, have been the occasion on which genealogical accounts were employed to invoke the names of dead ancestors, as has been assumed for the *kispu* ritual held by the Babylonian and Assyrian dynasties?

Comparative Structural Table of Royal Genealogies

	Babylonia	Assyria	Israel	
	(Sumuabum)	(Shamshi-Adad)	(David)	(Saul)
	(GHD)*	(AKL)		
Group (a) Genealogical Stock	Ara(m/Ḫarḫar) (1)	Ṭudiya (1)	Shem	
	Madara (2)	Adamu (2)	Arpa//chshad	
	Tu(b)ti(ya) (3)	Yangi (3)	(Kenan)	
	(Y)amuta/Atamu (4)	Sa/i/uḫlamu (4)	Shelah	
	Yamqu (5)	Ḫarḫaru (5)	Eber	
	Suḫ(ḫa)la(m)ma (6)	Mandaru (6)	Peleg	
	Ḫeana (7)	Emṣu (7)	Reu	
	Namz/ṣū (8)	ḪARṢu (8)	Serug	
	Ditānu (9)	Didānu (9)	Nahor	
	Zummabu (10)	Ḫanū (10)	Terah	
	Namḫū (11)	Zuʾabu (11)		
		Nuabu (12)		
Group (b) Determinative Line	Amnānu (12)	Abazu (13)	Abraham	
	Yaḫrurum (13)	Bēlū (14)	Isaac	
		Azaraḫ (15)	Jacob	
		Ušpiya (16)		
		Apiašal (17)		
			Judah	Benjamin
Group (c) Table of Ancestors	Ipti-yamūta (14)	Ḫalē (18)	Perez	—
	Buḫazum (15)	Samanu (19)	Hezron	—
	Su-malika (16)	Ḫayanu (20)	Ram	X (a Benjaminite)
	Ašmadu (17)	Ilu-mer (21)	Amminadab	Aphiah
	Abi-yamūta (18)	Yakmesi (22)	Nahshon	Bechorath
	Abi-ditan (19)	Yakmeni (23)	Salma	Zeror
	Ma-am(?)-x-x-x (20)	Yazkur-ēl (24)	Boaz	Abiel
	Šu-x-ni(?)-x (21)	Ila-kabkaku (25)	Obed	⟨Ner⟩
	Dad(banaya[?]) (22)	Aminu (26)	Jesse	Kish
	Sumuabum (23)	Shamshi-Adad (27)	David	Saul
Group (d) Historical Line	(Sumulaʾē) (24)	(etc.)	(etc.)	(etc.)
	(Zābium) (25)			
	(Apil-Sīn) (26)			
	(Sīn-muballiṭ) (27)			
	(Ḫammurapi) (28)			
	(etc.)			

*(Cf. Finkelstein, p. 114).

The Old Testament Genealogies in Recent Research

ROBERT R. WILSON

I

⟦169⟧ Although the general public tends to regard the OT genealogies as unnecessary parentheses in the biblical text, biblical scholars have always been intrigued by them. This scholarly interest is not a modern phenomenon, but one which has its roots in the biblical period itself. Genealogical concerns can be seen in the apocrypha and pseudepigrapha (Tob 1:1–2; Jdt 8:1; cf. 9:2; Jub 4:1–33), in the NT (Matt 1:1–17; Luke 3:23–38), and finally in rabbinic reflections on the genealogies of the biblical and postbiblical periods (*b. Pesaḥim* 62b; *b. Kiddushin* 71a, b; *Genesis Rabbah* 71:9; 98:11). After the turn of the era, both Jewish and Christian scholars debated the authenticity of extrabiblical genealogies but were more or less in agreement about the nature of the OT genealogies and about their historical accuracy.[1] These genealogies were viewed as generally accurate sources which might safely be used to reconstruct the history of Israel in the biblical period. This strong faith in the historical reliability of the genealogies persisted until the rise of modern biblical criticism in the nineteenth century. Thus as late as 1869 Heinrich Ewald argued that the genealogies in Genesis were originally drawn from historically accurate pre-Mosaic sources and then were used

Reprinted with permission from *Journal of Biblical Literature* 94 (1975) 169–89.

1. Examples of rabbinic genealogical discussions may be found in the Mishnah, *Eduyoth* 8:7; *b. Kiddushin* 69a–71a; and *Genesis Rabbah* 82:11. On the historical accuracy of Jewish genealogies, see Josephus, *AgAp* 1:7; *Life* 1.

as the framework for later narrative expansions. Similarly, he wrote of the genealogies in Chronicles: ". . . we have every reason to ascribe them in their earliest form to public records, the most reliable source possible."[2]

This monolithic view of the nature of the OT genealogies was shattered by the biblical critics who worked during the last half of the nineteenth century. The criticisms of the traditional view came from two directions. First, during this period extrabiblical material was for the first time systematically brought to bear on the OT genealogies. The last half of the nineteenth century was a period of extensive exploration in the Near East, and as ancient Near Eastern documents began to accumulate, scholars discovered an increasing number of ⟦170⟧ parallels between newly discovered mythological texts and the early portions of Genesis. Therefore Ignaz Goldziher and others suggested that at this point the biblical text was dependent on common Near Eastern mythological traditions and that the genealogies in Genesis were simply part of the early "mythological stage" of Israelite religion.[3] Another possibility was suggested by the anthropological data which was being collected during this period. W. Robertson Smith, Bernhard Stade, and others pointed out that genealogies are frequently used in tribal societies to express social and political relationships between tribes. These genealogies are not attempts to write history but are simply reflections of social conditions at the time they were composed. If ancient genealogies are similar to modern ones, then the OT genealogies are of no use in reconstructing the history of Israel.[4]

At the same time that Near Eastern texts and anthropological data were beginning to cast doubt on the historiographic worth of the genealogies, a second attack was made by the newly developing theories of literary and form criticism. Julius Wellhausen, in his attempt to divide the OT text into literary sources, noted that much of the genealogical material appears in P and in the work of the Chronicler, both of which come from a fairly late period in Israel's national life. Even the earliest genealogies, those of the Yahwist, can be dated no earlier than the

2. *The History of Israel* (London: Longmans, Green, 1869), 1. 81, 263.

3. Ignaz Goldziher, *Mythology among the Hebrews and Its Historical Development* (London: Longmans, Green, 1877) 278; W. O. E. Oesterley and T. H. Robinson, *A History of Israel* (Oxford: Clarendon, 1932), 1. 53.

4. W. Robertson Smith, *Kinship and Marriage in Early Arabia* (2d ed.; London: Black, 1903) 1–39; B. Stade, *Geschichte des Volkes Israel* (Berlin: G. Grote, 1887), 1. 27–30; H. Guthe, *Geschichte des Volkes Israel* (Tübingen: Mohr, 1904) 1–2. Scholars who held this position seem not to have considered the possibility that the OT genealogies might be used to study Israelite social history.

Davidic period. Wellhausen, therefore, concluded that extensive genealogies were created in Israel only at a late date and that they were, therefore, worthless as sources for the reconstruction of early Israelite history. Of the genealogies in Chronicles he wrote: "One might as well try to hear the grass growing as attempt to derive from such a source as this a historical knowledge of the conditions of ancient Israel." [5]

Since the time of Wellhausen and Robertson Smith, OT scholars have generally accepted the conclusions of these early biblical critics and until recently have made only two major refinements in their genealogical views. First, many scholars have been willing to admit that the OT genealogies *may* in fact contain old material which *may* be of value to the modern historian. In America W. F. Albright, in particular, has held this view. Albright often refers to the use of genealogies among the Arabs and points to the amazing accuracy with ⟦171⟧ which some Arab groups memorize and transmit oral material. Therefore, according to Albright, there is no reason not to believe that some of the OT genealogies are potentially valuable historiographic sources.[6]

A second major refinement in Wellhausen's position has come from Martin Noth, who argues that in dealing with the OT genealogies we must distinguish between *primary genealogies*, or genealogies in the strict sense, and *secondary genealogies*. According to Noth, a primary genealogy is one which once existed apart from the narrative in which it is now found. On the other hand, a secondary genealogy is one which had no existence *as a genealogy* outside the narrative in which it appears. Rather it is composed of names which were originally associated with their own narrative traditions. These independent traditions were secondarily joined by placing their chief characters in a genealogical framework. Thus Noth believes that the Pentateuch does contain some genealogies which antedate their narrative settings and which are therefore potential historiographic sources. However, other pentateuchal genealogies are simply literary constructs fabricated by the biblical writers in order to link literary units.[7] At this point Noth moves beyond Wellhausen by recognizing that genealogies may have literary functions, even though the genealogies themselves are not reflections of actual events or conditions.

Nevertheless, it is important to recognize that Albright and Noth have simply refined the views of older scholars. Albright has once again

5. *Prolegomena to the History of Ancient Israel* (Edinburgh: Black, 1885) 215, 308–33. Cf. his *De gentibus et familiis judaeis quae 1. Chr. 2.4. enumerantur* (Göttingen: Dieterich, 1870); and E. Meyer, *Die Israeliten und ihre Nachbarstämme* (Halle: Niemeyer, 1906) 444.

6. *From the Stone Age to Christianity* (2d ed.; Garden City: Doubleday, 1957) 72–76, 238–43; *Yahweh and the Gods of Canaan* (Garden City: Doubleday, 1968) 53–109.

7. *A History of Pentateuchal Traditions* (Englewood Cliffs, NJ: Prentice-Hall, 1972) 214–19.

brought anthropological and Near Eastern evidence into the discussion in order to support the historiographic value of the genealogies, but he has not made a fresh, thorough study of this material. Noth has extended the tradition-critical work of earlier scholars, but he has not systematically re-examined the characteristics of genealogies in either oral or written texts. It is therefore fair to say that during the first half of this century there has been little progress in the study of the OT genealogies, and in fact the genealogies have generally been ignored. Scholars still accept modified versions of the views of Wellhausen, and Robertson Smith's Arabic parallels are still cited when comparisons with anthropological material are made.[8]

Now, after almost half a century of neglect, the OT genealogies seem again to have attracted the attention of biblical scholars. In the past five years, three important studies of biblical and Near Eastern genealogies have been made, and additional treatments have been promised for the near future. The first of ⟦172⟧ these studies to appear was Marshall D. Johnson's *The Purpose of the Biblical Genealogies.*[9] Although the author is a NT scholar and thus primarily concerned with the genealogies of Jesus in the Gospels, he nevertheless devotes almost a hundred pages to the OT genealogies. Johnson subjects many of the OT genealogies to a literary analysis and reaches the following conclusions:

1. Many of the OT genealogies (Genesis 10; 19:36–38; 22:20–24; 25:1–6, 12–16; 36) serve to demonstrate the relations between Israel and neighboring tribes by tracing all the groups involved back to a common ancestor.
2. Some OT genealogies, particularly those in the "Toledoth Book," are used to link originally independent traditions about Israel's origins.
3. Certain genealogies (Genesis 5; 11:10–27; Ruth 4:18–22) are used as literary and historical bridges to span gaps in the traditions used by the biblical writers.
4. Genealogies such as those in Genesis 5 and 11 sometimes function as a basis for chronological speculations.
5. Several of the tribal genealogies in 1 Chronicles 2–8 are apparently constructed from military census lists, a fact which demonstrates the use of genealogies for political purposes.

8. A few scholars still believe the genealogies to be important historiographic sources and use them uncritically to reconstruct Israelite history. See, for example, S. Yeivin, *The Israelite Conquest of Canaan* (Istanbul: Nederlands Historisch-Archaeologisch Instituut in het Nabije Oosten, 1971).

9. Subtitle: *With Special Reference to the Setting of the Genealogies of Jesus* (SNTSMS 8; New York/London: Cambridge University, 1969).

6. Some genealogies in 1 Chronicles and Ezra-Nehemiah seem to have been used by office-holders to legitimate their offices. Also involved in these passages may be a postexilic attempt to demonstrate the racial purity of Israel and to express a continuity between preexilic and postexilic Israel.[10]

In some respects Johnson's conclusions have clear connections with previous studies of the OT genealogies. Like Robertson Smith, Johnson recognizes the sociological functions of some genealogies (points 1 and 6 above), and he agrees with Noth in seeing some of them as links between originally separate traditions and literary units (points 2 and 3 above). Following Wellhausen, Johnson concludes that Israelite genealogical interests developed primarily in the postexilic period, although he does not follow Wellhausen in drawing historical inferences from this fact. At the same time Johnson demonstrates that some genealogies may well have been authentic historical documents (point 5 above).

Yet in spite of the similarities between Johnson's views and those of earlier scholars, the fact remains that he has advanced the study of the OT genealogies in two major ways. First, he has recognized the diversity of genealogical functions within the OT literature. Unlike many of his predecessors, who attempted to force all the OT genealogies into the same functional mold, Johnson has suggested convincingly that at the literary level the genealogies function in a number of different ways. This means that future studies of the genealogies may not generalize about their function or their value as historiographic sources. Rather, each genealogy must be considered individually. ⟦173⟧ Second, Johnson has at least begun the task of analyzing in detail the literary structure of the OT genealogies. Although he subordinates structural analysis to the determination of literary function and although it is possible to question individual points in his structural analysis, he has clearly moved beyond earlier studies, which did not consider genealogical structure at all.

However, despite the strengths of Johnson's work, it does exhibit a number of weaknesses. Perhaps because of the length and focus of his study, he does not submit the OT genealogies to a thorough form-critical or tradition-critical analysis. Although he protects himself against this criticism by limiting his study to the *literary* contexts of the genealogies, the fact remains that a thorough exegetical analysis needs to be made. Included in such an analysis should be a study of both oral and written genealogies to determine if oral and written genealogies have the same

10. Ibid., 77–82.

forms and functions. Until now the formal and functional similarity of oral and written genealogies has been assumed but not demonstrated. In addition, Johnson fails to utilize extrabiblical material in his study. He seldom refers to possible ancient Near Eastern parallels to the OT genealogies, and when he mentions standard texts, such as the Assyrian and Sumerian king lists, he is heavily dependent on secondary literature. Similarly, Johnson uses no recent anthropological material. Like most of his predecessors, he simply cites Robertson Smith. Yet it is clear that if scholars are to continue to refer to Near Eastern and anthropological parallels in their treatments of the OT genealogies, then these extrabiblical texts must be studied thoroughly and their value for the study of the OT material must be assessed. Finally, Johnson has not considered the implications of his work for the question of the historiographic value of the genealogies.

In spite of the deficiencies of Johnson's work, it is likely that his book would have remained the definitive treatment of the OT genealogies, had additional comparative material not come to light. In 1966 J. J. Finkelstein published an important Akkadian text which he called "The Genealogy of the Hammurapi Dynasty."[11] The tablet, which was written on behalf of Ammiṣaduqa, a member of the Amorite dynasty of Hammurapi, dates from the Old Babylonian period and thus is not far removed from the dates traditionally assigned to the Hebrew patriarchs. The first portion of the text contains a list of names which are not explicitly related genealogically. However, the last nine names in the list are those of the immediate predecessors of Ammiṣaduqa. From other sources it is known that some of these names were genealogically connected, and for this reason Finkelstein inferred that the whole list was intended to be the royal genealogy of Ammiṣaduqa. The genealogy stretches backward from Ammiditana (GHD 28), the father of Ammiṣaduqa, through the known members of the Hammurapi dynasty to Sumuabum (GHD 20), the founder of the dynasty. In turn, Sumuabum's name is preceded by names presumably belonging ⟦174⟧ to even earlier ancestors. Although the names immediately before Sumuabum are broken or otherwise unknown, Finkelstein was able to identify the names in the first ten lines of the text. GHD 9–10 contain the names Amnānu and Yaḫrurum, which are elsewhere attested as the names of tribes belonging to a confederation to which the Hammurapi dynasty was related. More important, the first eight lines of the text contain names which are simply conflated or mangled forms of names appearing in the first section of the Assyrian

11. "The Genealogy of the Hammurapi Dynasty," *JCS* 20 (1966) 95–118 (hereafter GHD).

King List.[12] According to the AKL these names belonged to "kings who dwelled in tents," and it is generally recognized that the kings of Assyria, and in particular Šamši-Adad I, traced their ancestry back to these tent-dwelling kings.[13] Included among them is Ḫanū (AKL i 5), who appears in the GHD as Ḫeana (GHD 4) and who is undoubtedly the eponymous ancestor of the Ḫanean tribes, with which Šamši-Adad I is known to have been connected.[14] The GHD thus shows that both the Assyrian and the Babylonian kings in this period included among their ancestors the same group of nomadic kings.

However, the text in its present form is not simply a king list composed for historiographic purposes. After the name of Ammiditana (GHD 28), the last king mentioned in the list, the text gives the following four summary statements apparently intended to refer to the preceding list of names: "the dynasty (BAL/*palū*) of the Amorites, the dynasty of the Ḫaneans, the dynasty of Gutium, the dynasty not recorded on this tablet" (GHD 29–32).[15] Members of these dynasties, together with other royal and non-royal dead and those shades who have no one to perform mortuary rites for them, are then invited to partake of food- and drink-offerings and to bless Ammiṣaduqa, who is responsible both for the offerings and for the text. These concluding lines suggest that the tablet was used in the context of *kispu*-offerings to the dead and that the names on the tablet were invoked as part of these rituals.[16]

The importance of the GHD for our understanding of the OT genealogies ⟦175⟧ is obvious. When taken together with the early portion of the AKL, the GHD shows that genealogies, which are not commonly found in Mesopotamia, were used by Old Babylonian tribal groups having Amorite connections. The biblical patriarchs are also traditionally

12. For a discussion of these names, see Finkelstein, "Genealogy of the Hammurapi Dynasty," 97–103. In the following discussion, references to the Assyrian King List are to the "Khorsabad King List" published in I. J. Gelb, "Two Assyrian King Lists," *JNES* 13 (1954) 209–30. A translation of the Assyrian King List (hereafter AKL) may be found in *ANET* 564–66.

13. B. Landsberger, "Assyrische Königsliste und 'Dunkles Zeitalter,'" *JCS* 8 (1954) 33–34; F. R. Kraus, "Könige, die in Zelten wohnten," *Mededelingen der koninklijke Nederlandse Akademie van Wetenschappen,* Afd. Letterkunde, ns 28/2 (1965) 131–40; W. W. Hallo, "Zāriqum," *JNES* 15 (1956) 221; J. J. Finkelstein, "Genealogy of the Hammurapi Dynasty," 104.

14. Ibid., 111; cf. J.-R. Kupper, *Les nomades en Mésopotamie au temps des rois de Mari* (Paris: "Les Belles Lettres," 1957) 1–46; D. O. Edzard, *Die "zweite Zwischenzeit" Babyloniens* (Wiesbaden: Harrassowitz, 1957) 37–39.

15. Finkelstein's interpretation of these summary statements ("Genealogy of the Hammurapi Dynasty," 103–13) raises a number of problems which cannot be treated here. For a brief discussion of the issues, see W. G. Lambert, "Another Look at Hammurabi's Ancestors," *JCS* 22 (1968) 1–2.

16. J. J. Finkelstein, "Genealogy of the Hammurapi Dynasty," 113–16.

connected with the Amorites, and the OT places a number of genealogies in the patriarchal period.[17] One might, therefore, conclude that the GHD, the early portion of the AKL, and the patriarchal genealogies in the Pentateuch are all manifestations of an Amorite custom of using genealogies for political and social purposes.[18] If this is so, then obviously the question of the nature and historiographic worth of the OT genealogies must be re-examined.

The relevance of the GHD for the study of the OT genealogies was quickly pointed out by Abraham Malamat.[19] Working with the GHD and the AKL and drawing from time to time on contemporary anthropological studies of genealogies in tribal societies, Malamat attempted to demonstrate the formal and functional similarities between the OT genealogies and their ancient Near Eastern counterparts.

Malamat argued that the genealogy in the GHD has a formal structure similar to that of the genealogy of Šamši-Adad I in the opening sections of AKL and that both of these king lists have a formal structure similar to the one found in the reconstructed genealogy of Israel. According to Malamat, all three genealogies have four basic parts. The first part, which he called the "genealogical stock," is composed of artificial or traditional names, more or less arbitrarily linked, together with tribal and geographical names. In the two Near Eastern texts, the genealogical stock consists of the names which the texts have in common: the eleven names in GHD 1–8 and the names of the first twelve of the seventeen tent-dwelling kings in AKL i 1–7. In these cases the genealogical stock contains from nine to eleven names and is thus similar to genealogies in living societies, which frequently have a standard depth of about ten generations.[20] In the biblical material Malamat compared the ten-generation genealogy of Shem in Gen 11:10–26 and also suggested that the "dynasty not recorded on this tablet" mentioned in the GHD might correspond to the antediluvian genealogy of Adam in Genesis 5.

The second part of the genealogies Malamat called the "determinative line." ⟦176⟧ In the GHD this section includes Amnānu and Yaḫrurum

17. W. F. Albright, *Yahweh and the Gods of Canaan*, 80–81; J. Bright, *A History of Israel* (2d ed.; Philadelphia: Westminster, 1972) 77–92; R. de Vaux, *Histoire ancienne d'Israël* (Paris: Gabalda, 1971) 194–201. For a critique of the traditional view, see S. Herrmann, *Israel in Egypt* (London: SCM, 1973) 23–24, 29–31, 36–37.

18. W. W. Hallo, "Antediluvian Cities," *JCS* 23 (1971) 62–63; W. W. Hallo and W. K. Simpson, *The Ancient Near East: A History* (New York: Harcourt Brace Jovanovich, 1971) 74–75.

19. "King Lists of the Old Babylonian Period and Biblical Genealogies," *JAOS* 88 (1968) 163–73 ⟦in this volume, 183–99⟧.

20. The exact number of names composing the genealogical stock of the king lists depends on the way in which certain conflated names are divided and on which names are considered "authentic."

(GHD 9–10), which, according to Malamat, serve to link the next name in the list, Iptiyamuta (GHD 11), the founder of the Old Babylonian dynasty of Sumuabum, with the genealogical stock. In the AKL the determinative line includes the names of the last five of the seventeen tent-dwelling kings (AKL i 7–9). In Israel the determinative line consists of Abraham, Isaac, Jacob, Judah, and Benjamin, although a single genealogy linking all of these names and only these names is never found in the OT.[21]

Malamat called the third part of the genealogies the "table of ancestors." This group is not clearly marked in the GHD, but Malamat argued that it included the names from Iptiyamuta (GHD 11) to Sumuabum (GHD 20). Sumuabum was the founder of the Hammurapi dynasty and probably used his table of ancestors to link himself with the earlier genealogies. In the AKL the table of ancestors includes the names mentioned in AKL i 11–20, which in AKL i 21 are called "ten kings who are ancestors." This section of the AKL was originally the genealogy of Šamši-Adad I, whose name now appears in AKL i 39. It is probable that Šamši-Adad, like Sumuabum, used the genealogy to link himself with earlier kings. Malamat also pointed out that after certain minor adjustments, the tables of ancestors in the GHD and in the AKL both contain ten names. Again, this has anthropological parallels, and Malamat concluded that the ideal pattern of an Amorite genealogy was based on a constant genealogical depth of ten generations. A similar pattern is found in Israelite royal genealogies. In David's table of ancestors, now found in 1 Chr 2:5, 9–17 and Ruth 4:18–22, a genealogy of ten names is traced from David back to Perez, the son of Judah. The biblical writers also preserved portions of a genealogy of Saul (1 Chr 8:29–33; 9:35–39; 1 Sam 9:1; 14:50–51), although the versions of the genealogy differ with respect to the number and relation of Saul's ancestors. Malamat found these variations disturbing, but he managed to reconstruct a ten-generation royal genealogy for Saul by leaving three of the slots blank and arbitrarily settling a disputed genealogical relationship.

The GHD in its present form contains a fourth group of names following Sumuabum's table of ancestors, and the AKL follows Šamši-Adad's table of ancestors with a long list of the kings who ruled in Assyria. This fourth group Malamat called the "historical line" and argued that it would have consisted of the immediate ancestors of any king who wished to graft his own genealogy onto that of his predecessors.

21. The genealogy can easily be reconstructed from the relevant chapters in Genesis or from 1 Chr 1:28, 34; 2:1–2. It is important to note, however, that even in 1 Chronicles the names are part of several complex genealogies.

Malamat cited no examples of such royal genealogies in Israel but claimed that it is possible that they once existed.[22]

As an extension of his work on "vertical" genealogies, Malamat has recently examined the "horizontal" genealogies or family trees in the OT.[23] Drawing ⟦177⟧ heavily on recent anthropological studies of tribal genealogies, he notes that family trees in the OT, like their modern counterparts, may have social, political, economic, or religious functions. However, all of his biblical examples of such genealogies deal with their political or geographical functions. Thus Malamat suggests that the genealogy of Nahor (Gen 22:20–24) relates geographical and tribal entities in Mesopotamia and Canaan, whereas in other OT genealogies the migration and merging of tribal segments are indicated by the movement of names within a genealogy or the shifting of names from one genealogy to another. Such migrations probably lie behind the various groupings of the descendants of Jacob in the OT, and as a result these variant genealogies can be used to reconstruct the process of the settlement of the Israelite tribes in Palestine. These genealogies can also be used to uncover the social and political structures of the tribes involved.[24]

Malamat's analysis of the biblical and Near Eastern genealogies seems already to have had an impact on biblical scholarship. In a recent article Thomas C. Hartman follows Malamat in suggesting a connection between the genealogies in Genesis and the Amorite genealogies found in the GHD and in the AKL.[25] After mounting a number of arguments against the theory that Genesis 5 and 11 are dependent upon the Sumerian King List, Hartman turns his attention to the fact that both Genesis 5 and the Sumerian King List record ten antediluvians, a fact which has been used by E. A. Speiser and others to argue that at this point Genesis has been influenced by the Sumerian tradition. Hartman correctly rejects the alleged parallel on the grounds that different texts of the King List mention different numbers of antediluvian kings. The number varies from seven to ten, and it seems impossible to speak of a consensus in the king-list tradition. Hartman then considers the GHD and Malamat's interpretation of it and suggests that the ten-generation antediluvian genealogy in Genesis 5 may have been influenced by

22. "King Lists," 165–73 ⟦186–98 in this volume⟧.

23. "Tribal Societies: Biblical Genealogies and African Lineage Systems," *Archives européennes de sociologie* 14 (1973) 126–36. This article also contains a restatement of the conclusions of his earlier work on the structure of the GHD, the AKL, and the "vertical" genealogies in the OT. See particularly "Tribal Societies," 129, 134–36.

24. Ibid., 131–34.

25. T. C. Hartman, "Some Thoughts on the Sumerian King List and Genesis 5 and 11B," *JBL* 91 (1972) 25–32.

Amorite genealogical practices. He concludes: "The possibility seems real, indeed, that the number of ten antediluvians is more closely tied to this West Semitic (Amorite) penchant for a ten-generation pattern than it is to inspiration arising from the Sumerian King List, as Speiser earlier suggested."[26]

The above survey of recent scholarship suggests that Malamat's analysis of the biblical and Near Eastern genealogies may have a good bit of influence on ⟦178⟧ future research in this area. For the first time Malamat has brought ancient Near Eastern evidence into the picture systematically and thus has shed some light on the form and function of genealogics in the biblical world. In addition, he has taken some tentative steps in the direction of using contemporary anthropological data, a move which clearly advances the discussion beyond the work of Robertson Smith.

However, Malamat's work has three major weaknesses which must be carefully examined. First, he makes no real contribution toward a solution to the problem of the historiographic value of the biblical genealogies, the problem which has plagued scholars since Wellhausen. Malamat's work on the Israelite royal genealogies seems to imply that at least portions of those genealogies may be fabrications, but he also discusses the variants in the genealogical traditions in such a way as to indicate that he considers it possible and indeed important to reconstruct the one historically accurate version. Similarly, his work on family trees in the OT implies that although the names in them represent tribes or tribal segments and not individuals, the genealogies themselves are accurate statements of political and geographical relationships. Thus underlying Malamat's work seems to be the assumption that the OT genealogies are relatively reliable historiographic sources. This assumption should not be accepted without further investigation.

Second, it should be noted that Malamat's analysis of the vertical genealogies in the OT consists almost entirely of reconstructions. Nowhere in the OT is there a coherent genealogy stretching from Shem to David such as the one which Malamat reconstructs. Of the individual genealogies which he discusses in his original article, only the genealogy of Seth and the genealogy of David actually exist in the form in which Malamat presents them. The genealogy of Saul must be reconstructed and stretched to fit the ten-generation pattern, and nowhere in the texts

26. Ibid., 29–30. A similar interpretation is considered by C. Westermann (*Genesis* [BKAT 1; Neukirchen-Vluyn: Neukirchener Verlag, 1966–] 8–24, 463–64, 474–80), whose discussions of the genealogies in Genesis are far more sophisticated than the treatments of earlier commentaries. However, a full assessment of Westermann's genealogical views must await the completion of his commentary ⟦full edition pub. 1974–82⟧.

are Abraham, Isaac, Jacob, Judah, and Benjamin linked in the same genealogy. It is methodologically incorrect to reconstruct a long genealogy and then to demonstrate that this artificial construction has the same structure as two Near Eastern king lists, which in fact seem to have been the pattern for the reconstruction in the first place.

Finally, and most important, Malamat's interpretation of both the anthropological and the Near Eastern evidence which he uses is open to question. In order to indicate the nature and scope of the problems involved, it will be necessary to explore briefly the form and function of the oral genealogies recorded by contemporary anthropologists and to re-examine in detail the genealogies in the AKL and the GHD.[27]

II

Although it is impossible here to make a thorough study of the anthropological ⟦179⟧ evidence, we may at least summarize the available data.[28] On the basis of form, oral genealogies may be divided into two general categories. When a genealogy expresses more than one line of descent from a given ancestor, then it exhibits segmentation or branching. This type of genealogy may be called a "segmented genealogy." In contrast, when a genealogy expresses only one line of descent from a given ancestor, then it exhibits no segmentation and may be designated a "linear genealogy." This formal distinction is quite important, for the function which a genealogy may have is directly related to its form.[29]

Both segmented and linear genealogies possess two other important formal characteristics. First, both exhibit depth. By definition segmented genealogies must have a depth of at least two generations, while linear genealogies exhibit depth as their most important formal feature. Although in theory the depth of a given genealogy should be limited only by the memories of the people who preserve it, in practice oral genealogies are strictly limited in depth. Segmented genealogies, when they are used to express the social structure of tribal societies, rarely

27. The discussion which follows is based on my Ph.D. dissertation, "Genealogy and History in the Old Testament" (Yale, 1972 [Ann Arbor: University Microfilms]). A revised version of the dissertation will be published under the title *Genealogy and History in the Biblical World* ⟦this volume was released by Yale University Press in 1977⟧.

28. The following summary is based on the few available studies of Arabic tribes and on a large number of African tribal studies. For a more thorough treatment, see my dissertation, "Genealogy and History," 12–67.

29. A. Malamat ("King Lists," 163–64 ⟦184–85 in this volume⟧; "Tribal Societies," 126–27) points to these two formal categories when he distinguishes "horizontal" genealogies (family trees) from "vertical" genealogies. However, he does not make the distinction consistently in his work and does not deal systematically with the relation between genealogical form and function.

stretch beyond ten to fourteen generations and in most cases are less than five generations in depth.[30] In addition, the depth of a given genealogy may vary from recitation to recitation depending on the purpose for which the genealogy is being cited. Linear genealogies sometimes exceed the depth usually found in segmented genealogies and may reach a depth of nineteen generations. However, like segmented genealogies, linear genealogies are rarely this extensive.[31] Thus the anthropological literature provides no grounds for assuming the existence of a "standard" genealogical depth in tribal genealogies.

⟦180⟧ The second major formal feature of oral genealogies is fluidity. The form of the genealogies may change rapidly, sometimes within the space of a few days or weeks, and it is common for names to be added or lost and for genealogical relationships to change.[32] In some cases this fluidity has functional significance. It reflects actual or desired changes in the domestic, political, or religious ties between individuals and groups. When segmented genealogies are used to express such relationships, then the genealogies must change when the relationships change, or else the genealogies will no longer be useful. On the other hand, genealogical fluidity may have no functional significance, and in

30. For examples of genealogies having a depth of ten to fourteen generations, see M. Fortes, *Kinship and the Social Order* (Chicago: Aldine, 1969) 167; E. E. Evans-Pritchard, *The Nuer* (Oxford: Clarendon, 1940) 108; M. Fortes, *The Dynamics of Clanship among the Tallensi* (London: Oxford University, 1945) 31; P. Mayer, *The Lineage Principle in Gusii Society* (London: Oxford University, 1949) 9; J. Middleton, *Lugbara Religion* (London: Oxford University, 1960) 8; and H. Kuper, *An African Aristocracy* (London: Oxford University, 1947) 111. For examples of five-generation genealogies, see J. R. Goody, *The Social Organization of the Lo Wiili* (London: Her Majesty's Stationery Office, 1956) 65; P. C. Lloyd, "The Yoruba Lineage," *Africa* 25 (1955) 240–47; and S. F. Nadel, *A Black Byzantium* (London: Oxford University, 1942) 30–33.

31. For discussions of the depth of linear genealogies, see A. I. Richards, "The Political System of the Bemba Tribe—North-Eastern Rhodesia," in *African Political Systems* (eds. M. Fortes and E. E. Evans-Pritchard; London: Oxford University, 1940) 99; H. Kuper, *An African Aristocracy*, 111, 232; I. M. Lewis, *A Pastoral Democracy* (London: Oxford University, 1961) 4, 11, 128; S. F. Nadel, *A Black Byzantium*, 45; P. C. Lloyd, "The Yoruba Lineage," 244; and J. Goody, *Succession to High Office* (Cambridge: Cambridge University, 1966) 49.

32. For discussions of the various types of genealogical fluidity, see M. J. Meggitt, *The Lineage System of the Mae-Enga of New Guinea* (New York: Barnes & Noble, 1965) 54–67; E. L. Peters, "The Proliferation of Segments in the Lineage of the Bedouin of Cyrenaica," *Journal of the Royal Anthropological Institute* 90 (1960) 29–53; I. Cunnison, *Baggara Arabs* (Oxford: Clarendon, 1966) 112; A. I. Richards, "Social Mechanisms for the Transfer of Political Rights in Some African Tribes," *Journal of the Royal Anthropological Institute* 90 (1960) 182–83; L. Bohannan, "A Genealogical Charter," *Africa* 22 (1952) 301–15; E. E. Evans-Pritchard, *The Nuer*, 199–200; M. Fortes, *The Dynamics of Clanship*, 35–36, 40, 51–53, 106; I. Cunnison, *The Luapula Peoples of Northern Rhodesia* (Manchester: Manchester University, 1959) 108–11; P. C. Lloyd, "The Yoruba Lineage," 244–45; and I. M. Lewis, *A Pastoral Democracy*, 147–48.

fact fluidity may be encouraged when the names involved lose their function. This type of fluidity is found both in segmented and in linear genealogies, but it is particularly common in the latter. By virtue of its form a linear genealogy can have only one function: it can be used only to link the person or group using the genealogy with an earlier ancestor or group. The actual number of names in the genealogy and the order of those names play no role in this function, and for this reason names are frequently lost from linear genealogies, and the order of the names which remain sometimes changes.[33]

The fact that fluidity in oral genealogies has various causes means that whenever genealogical fluctuations are observed, an attempt must be made to determine whether or not they have functional significance. It may not automatically be assumed that genealogical changes reflect actual changes in the structure of the relationships which the genealogies express.

When oral genealogies are actually used by a society, they may have a number of functions. For the purposes of our discussion we may distinguish three general areas of social life in which genealogies may be employed.[34] First, genealogies may function in the domestic sphere. In societies where domestic groups are organized on the basis of kinship, the language of kinship, in the context of genealogies, is frequently used to express interpersonal relationships. In most cases kinship-terminology in the domestic sphere indicates actual biological ⟦181⟧ ties, but it is not unusual for such terminology also to be used to express status, economic, or geographical relations. Thus when genealogies function in the domestic sphere, they relate individuals to other individuals and groups within the society and define social rights and obligations. Genealogies which are used in this way are usually segmented, and their form must change constantly to mirror the changing shape of the domestic social structure.[35]

33. Discussions of fluidity due to a loss of function may be found in E. H. Winter, *Bwamba* (Cambridge: W. Heffer & Sons, [n.d.]) 211; M. Fortes, *The Dynamics of Clanship*, 35; J. Middleton, *Lugbara Religion*, 8; and E. E. Evans-Pritchard, *The Nuer*, 199–202.

34. The following schema is an adaptation of categories developed by H. Befu and L. Plotnicov ("Types of Corporate Unilineal Descent Groups," *American Anthropologist* 64 [1962] 313–27) and M. Fortes (*Kinship and the Social Order*, 72).

35. L. Bohannan, "A Genealogical Charter," 314–15; M. Fortes, *The Web of Kinship among the Tallensi* (London: Oxford University, 1949) 7–19; E. H. Winter, *Bwamba*, 211–13; M. Fortes, *Kinship and the Social Order*, 99, 167–68; I. Cunnison, *Baggara Arabs*, 86; E. L. Peters, "Some Structural Aspects of the Feud among the Camel-Herding Bedouin of Cyrenaica," *Africa* 37 (1967) 261–82; P. and L. Bohannan, *Tiv Economy* (Evanston: Northwestern University, 1968) 83–88; M. D. Sahlins, "The Segmentary Lineage: An Organization of Predatory Expansion," *American Anthropologist* 63 (1961) 322–45.

A second area in which genealogies may function is the politico-jural sphere. In this case the genealogies may be either segmented or linear. If a society does not have a monarchical form of government, it may be organized politically along real or fictitious kinship lines. When societies are structured in this way, the political and legal relationships between groups are frequently stated in genealogical terms, with the result that a segmented genealogy becomes an expression of the political structure. The form of such genealogies must change as the political structure changes, or they will become useless for political purposes.[36] On the other hand, if a society has a monarchical form of government, the political system is not likely to be organized along kinship lines, and for this reason segmented genealogies in such societies do not usually have political functions. However, monarchies frequently employ linear genealogies to support the political claims of individual office-holders and to control access to hereditary offices. When fluidity appears in these linear genealogies, it is usually due to the fact that the names involved have lost their function or that variant genealogies are being used polemically to advance claims to status or power.[37]

The final social area in which genealogies may function is the religious sphere. In this case the genealogies may be either segmented or linear and, particularly in the case of segmented genealogies, must be fluid in order to mirror religiously significant changes in the social structure.[38]

⟦182⟧ In any given society, genealogies may function in more than one of the three spheres mentioned above. Therefore, it would be possible for a society to have a number of apparently conflicting genealogies, each of which could be considered accurate in terms of its function. The structure of the society for political purposes may well be different from the structure of the society for domestic or religious purposes, and for this reason genealogies functioning politically may be different from genealogies functioning in other spheres. It would be a mistake to ask which

36. M. Fortes and E. E. Evans-Pritchard, *African Political Systems*, 6–7; J. Middleton and D. Tait (eds.), *Tribes without Rulers* (London: Routledge & Kegan Paul, 1958) 1–3; R. Cohen and J. Middleton, *Comparative Political Systems* (Garden City: Natural History Press, 1967) x–xiv; I. Cunnison, *The Luapula*, 33; E. E. Evans-Pritchard, *The Nuer*, 5–6; I. Cunnison, *Baggara Arabs*, 97–98; L. Bohannan, "A Genealogical Charter," 308–11.

37. M. Gluckman, "The Kingdom of the Zulu of South Africa," *African Political Systems* (ed. M. Fortes and E. E. Evans-Pritchard) 35–37; M. Fortes, *Kinship and the Social Order*, 162, 165, 167–68; Richards, "Social Mechanisms," 181–88; Max Gluckman, *Order and Rebellion in Tribal Africa* (London: Cohen and West, 1963) 84–109.

38. M. Fortes, *The Dynamics of Clanship*, 19, 31; R. Firth, *Social Change in Tikopia* (London: Allen & Unwin, 1959) 227–29; M. Wilson, *Communal Rituals of the Nyakyusa* (London: Oxford University, 1959) 8–17, 40, 70–78; A. I. Richards, "Social Mechanisms," 188.

of the conflicting genealogies is historically accurate. All of them are accurate when their differing functions are taken into consideration.[39]

An analysis of genealogical function is thus crucial for an accurate understanding of any given genealogy, for often the function of a genealogy is intimately related to its form. When one changes, the other is likely to exhibit corresponding changes. Certain genealogical functions require particular genealogical forms, and some forms can have only a limited range of functions. All studies of genealogies must therefore consider the full range of possible genealogical functions in addition to treating genealogical form.

Keeping in mind this discussion of oral genealogies, we may now return to the genealogies in the AKL and the GHD. On purely formal grounds the AKL may be divided into four sections. The first section contains a list of seventeen names which are not genealogically linked with each other in any way. This list is followed by a summary statement which marks the end of the first section and indicates that these initial names are those of "seventeen kings who dwelled in tents" (AKL i 10).

The second section of the AKL records the names and kinship-connections of ten kings, and in this way a linear genealogy having a depth of eleven generations is formed. However, in contrast to the remainder of the AKL, which moves from early kings to more recent ones, the genealogy traced in this section of the list begins with the name of the king who was last in the historical sequence and moves *backward* to the name of the king who was historically first in the royal line. This king is also listed as the seventeenth of the tent-dwelling kings and in the second section is called the son of the sixteenth king in the first section of the list. The second section of the AKL is concluded with the remark that the section contains the names of "ten kings who are ancestors" (AKL i 21).

The third section of the AKL enumerates six kings, although kinship-connections are given only for the first, who is said to be the son of the first king mentioned in section two. A summary statement which is no longer intelligible marks the end of section three (AKL i 25–26).

The final section of the AKL contains the names of the remaining seventy-seven kings in the list and gives the number of years each of these kings ruled. ⟦183⟧ For most of these kings, kinship-connections are also given, and in this way a number of expanded linear genealogies are formed. These genealogies sometimes reach a depth of ten generations (AKL iv 9–27), although most of them are only around five generations in depth (AKL i 27–38; ii 9–18, 28–34, 36–43; iii 1–9, 11–16, 34–45; iv 1–8).

39. On this point, see the extensive discussion in I. Cunnison, *Baggara Arabs*, 10, 60, 104–13, 165, 213–18.

The genealogies in the AKL exhibit some of the same formal and functional characteristics which we have already examined in our discussion of oral genealogies. Like oral genealogies, the genealogies in the AKL are limited in depth. They are usually not much deeper than five generations and rarely stretch beyond ten generations. Still, within this range there is enough variation to indicate that the compilers of the genealogies had no preconceived notion of a "standard" genealogical depth.

In addition, the genealogies in the AKL exhibit a great deal of formal fluidity, just as oral genealogies do. An interesting example is found in AKL iii 1–10, where the descendants of Enlil-naṣir II are listed in the following sequence; Enlil-naṣir II, Aššur-nirari II, Aššur-bel-nišešu, Aššur-rim-nišešu, Aššur-nadin-aḫḫe II. According to the AKL, these kings ruled in unbroken succession, and each was the son of his predecessor. This picture, however, does not agree with the one presented by the genealogical notices preserved in various royal inscriptions. These notices suggest that Aššur-nirari II was the brother of Enlil-naṣir II, rather than his son, and that Aššur-bel-nišešu, Aššur-rim-nišešu, and Aššur-nadin-aḫḫe II were all brothers and sons of Aššur-nirari II.[40] There is no reason to believe that this inscriptional evidence is inaccurate, and so on the surface it would appear that the AKL has re-arranged the correct genealogical relationships and presented a warped genealogy. However, when the functions of the genealogies in the two different types of texts are taken into account, the reason for this genealogical fluidity becomes clear. The form of the genealogy has changed because its function has changed. While in the royal inscriptions the genealogies are intended to legitimate the rulers who cite them, the AKL is interested in tracing the sequence of kings who ruled in Assyria. In this sequence, kingship normally passed from father to son, particularly in the latter portions of the list, and this fact led the compiler of the list to use the idiom of genealogy to express the progress of kingship. In the process he sometimes imposed the father-son relationship on names to which it did not actually apply, but seen in the context of the function of the AKL the genealogies are accurate.[41]

An even more striking example of fluidity can be seen in the second section of the AKL. We have already noted that the order of the names in this section is the reverse of the one found in the remainder of the list. While the rest of the AKL moves from ancient kings to more recent

40. These genealogies have been reconstructed by B. Landsberger, "Assyrische Königsliste," 43.

41. This phenomenon is also frequently found in oral king lists. For examples, see D. P. Henige, "Oral Tradition and Chronology," *Journal of African History* 12 (1971) 378–83.

ones, the genealogy in ⟦184⟧ section two traces a line from a recent king to an earlier one. This unexpected reversal indicates that this genealogy was once a separate entity which was inserted into its present context by a compiler who did not bother to reverse the order of the names to agree with the normal progression of the king list.

The original function of the second section of the AKL was first pointed out by B. Landsberger, who suggested that it was in fact the royal genealogy of Šamši-Adad I, whose brother and father are both named in the first line of the genealogy (AKL i 11).[42] Šamši-Adad probably used the genealogy to provide himself with a royal lineage in order to justify his seizure of the throne from Erišum II (cf. AKL i 39–ii 1). The AKL also preserves a portion of the genealogy of Erišum II, and it is even possible that the genealogy of Šamši-Adad was created as a polemic against the genealogy of the legitimate king.

When the genealogy of Šamši-Adad was added to the AKL, a number of genealogical dislocations occurred. Šamši-Adad (AKL i 39) was separated from his brother (AKL i 11) by nineteen other kings. The father of Šamši-Adad was mentioned twice (AKL i 11–12, 39), and the son of Šamši-Adad's brother (AKL i 22) was separated completely from his father's genealogy and placed in a separate section of the list. Finally, the names of the last two tent-dwelling kings were duplicated (AKL i 9, 19–20), and the entire genealogy of Šamši-Adad was allowed to remain without being reversed to make it agree with the normal sequence of the king list.

The apparent genealogical disarray of this portion of the AKL can easily be explained when the function of the list is taken into account. The genealogy of Šamši-Adad originally served to link him with earlier rulers, perhaps even with the tent-dwelling kings, and was intended to justify his claim to the Assyrian throne. However, the genealogy no longer functioned in this way when it became a part of the AKL. The compiler of the king list was interested in tracing the sequence of kings who ruled in Assyria. In this sequence Erišum II was followed by Šamši-Adad I, so his name was separated from the rest of his genealogy and added after the name of Erišum II. This move left the compiler with the problem of what to do with the rest of Šamši-Adad's genealogy. It could not be inserted before Erišum II, for he was preceded on the throne by his immediate ancestors, all of whom were legitimate kings. The compiler therefore placed the genealogy before the ancestors of Erišum II and treated the ancestors of Šamši-Adad as a group of early kings only

42. "Assyrische Königsliste," 33–34. Landsberger's suggestion has been accepted by most scholars.

slightly less ancient than the tent-dwelling kings. The compiler's editorial work thus gave rise to the genealogical dislocations which we have already noted. In this case genealogical fluidity was encouraged because the genealogies involved lost their original function. In the context of the king list the names originally contained in the genealogies acquired the function of tracing the development of Assyrian kingship. In this new setting, genealogical connections played no necessary role; so some of them disappeared entirely, and others were radically altered.

⟦185⟧ Although the GHD in its present form contains no kinship-terms and so cannot be considered a genealogy, some of the names in the text do exhibit the same sort of fluidity which we have seen in oral genealogies and in the AKL. This fluidity is clearest in lines 1–8, where a comparison with the AKL is possible. So, for example, the names in the two lists appear in different sequences. GHD 1 contains a pair of names which do not appear in the AKL until line 3, while the two names in AKL i 5 have been split apart in the GHD and appear in lines 4 and 7. These differences in sequence suggest that although the Babylonian and Assyrian dynasties included among their ancestors the same group of nomadic kings, there was no consensus as to the order or genealogical relations of those kings. An even more significant example of fluidity is seen in the way in which some of the names in GHD 1–8 have been garbled. GHD 1–3 present names which have been conflated, while the parallel names in the AKL are paired but distinct. This type of conflation is common at the oral level, and it is possible that the early names in the GHD and the parallel names of the tent-dwelling kings in the AKL were once part of an oral genealogy or list.[43]

The original function of the early portion of the GHD cannot easily be determined, but we may still draw a few tentative conclusions. The fact that both the Babylonian and Assyrian kings began their ancestral lists with the same group of nomadic kings strongly suggests that both royal lines considered themselves to be related to each other through this group of early kings. If so, then the names of the nomadic kings were perhaps originally in the form of a segmented genealogy which functioned politically to relate various tribes and lineages. The Babylonian segment of the genealogy would presumably have begun with Amnānu or Yaḫrurum (GHD 9–10), the ancestors of two groups which are known to have been connected with the Hammurapi dynasty, and the Assyrian segment of the genealogy would have begun with Ḫeana/

43. J. J. Finkelstein, "Genealogy of the Hammurapi Dynasty," 112; F. R. Kraus, "Könige, die in Zelten wohnten," 123–24; A. Malamat, "King Lists," 165. ⟦in this volume, 187⟧

Ḫanū (GHD 4; AKL i 5), the eponymous ancestor of the Ḫanean tribes with which Šamši-Adad I is known to have been connected. Both segments would have then been linked through a common ancestor. However, because of the fluidity in the parallel portions of GHD and AKL, it is now impossible to reconstruct this hypothetical segmented genealogy in any detail or even to be sure that these two texts preserve all the names originally involved in it.

Even if the names now contained in the early portions of the GHD and the AKL were once part of an oral or written segmented genealogy, it is also possible that segments of the genealogy were used in linear form. We have already suggested that the second section of the AKL contains a genealogy of Šamši-Adad I and that this genealogy was used to support the king's claim to power. It is possible that a major portion of the list of tent-dwelling kings was also part of this polemical genealogy. If this is the case, then it is not difficult to suppose that a similar linear genealogy was in use among the Babylonians. It ⟦186⟧ is worth noting that Šamši-Adad I and Hammurapi were contemporaries and engaged in a struggle for political dominance. Therefore there may be political significance in the fact that both kings apparently justified their right to rule by tracing a genealogy back to the same group of nomadic kings. However, on the basis of the available evidence it is impossible to determine the exact structure of the Babylonian royal genealogy or to identify the king who first used it.

Regardless of the original form and function of the names in the GHD, their present form and function are clear. The names are presented in the form of a list, and no kinship-connections are mentioned. We have already indicated that this list probably functioned in the context of the *kispu*-offering, which involved gifts of food and drink to the dead. If our reconstruction of the text's early history is correct, then a genealogy which once functioned in the political sphere functioned in its new setting in the religious or cultic sphere. This change in function may also explain the omission of kinship-terms in what was once a genealogy. In the context of the ritual the actual genealogical relations of the kings were no longer important. Rather it was necessary only to include all the ancestors in the list, either by invoking their names or by mentioning the category to which they belonged. Because the genealogy had ceased to function, it disappeared from the text, and even the well-known genealogical relationships of the immediate predecessors of Ammiṣaduqa were not recorded. In addition, the shift in function may have encouraged the fluidity which we have observed in the text, for the precise order of the names was unimportant in their new setting.

III

In the light of the above discussion we must re-evaluate the work of Malamat and those who depend on him. Our survey of oral genealogies indicates that although Malamat has correctly perceived some of the formal and functional parallels between modern and ancient genealogies, he has not fully taken into account the nature of fluidity in oral genealogies or the importance of examining the relation between genealogical fluidity and function. Oral genealogies do indeed seem to be limited in depth and rarely exceed ten generations, but enough variations still exist to prevent ten generations as a "standard" genealogical depth. Similarly, segmented oral genealogies are frequently used to express domestic, political, and religious relationships, and when they are used in this way, they often exhibit fluidity as their functions change. However, each example of genealogical fluidity must be analyzed to determine its significance. It may not automatically be assumed that each genealogical change indicates a corresponding political or geographical change, nor may it be assumed that where conflicting genealogies exist one is necessarily "accurate" while the others are not. In fact, all the versions of a genealogy may be accurate in the light of their functions.

Similarly, our analysis of the AKL and the GHD calls into question the four-part structure which Malamat claims ancient Near Eastern genealogies possessed. ⟦187⟧ We have seen that the AKL and the GHD in their present forms do not function as genealogies, although both texts contain names which were probably once incorporated in genealogies. Therefore, the present structures of the AKL and the GHD may not accurately reflect the shape of linear genealogies in the Old Babylonian period. When genealogies change or lose their functions, concomitant formal changes sometimes occur. It is possible that some of the formal features of the AKL and the GHD are linked to the present functions of these texts and have little to do with previous genealogical functions.

The problems involved in using the present forms of the AKL and the GHD to reconstruct in detail the structure of Amorite genealogies become clear when Malamat's four-part schema is re-examined. Malamat's first structural category, the genealogical stock, has no formal basis in either the AKL or the GHD. Rather it consists of the names which are common to both texts. In the AKL these names are part of a larger group which the compiler of the text designated tent-dwelling kings, and there is no indication that he recognized any formal divisions within that group. In the same way, in the GHD the names of the genealogical stock are simply part of a much longer list. In addition, we have suggested that originally these shared names may not have been in linear form but may have been part of a segmented genealogy, the original shape of which is now unclear. If the names then became part of linear genealogies, the exact form of these genealogies too is unknown. It cannot be assumed that the AKL and the GHD in their present form reflect these underlying genealogies.

Similar problems exist with respect to Malamat's second category, the determinative line. In the AKL the determinative line is said to consist of the last five of the tent-dwelling kings (AKL i 7–9). However, the beginning of this group is not clearly marked, and there is no indication that the compiler of the king list recognized a distinction between this group and the preceding one. The conclusion of the determinative line is clearly indicated by a summary statement (AKL i 10), which separates the tent-dwelling kings from the following genealogy of Šamši-Adad I (AKL i 11–20). This division, however, is the work of the compiler and does not seem to have been originally a part of Šamši-Adad's genealogy itself. The last two of the tent dwelling kings also appear as the two earliest ancestors in the genealogy (AKL i 19–20), where they are not distinguished from the remainder of the names. If the genealogy has not been altered by the compiler of the AKL, then it would appear that the author of the original genealogy recognized no division between these two early kings and Šamši-Adad's more immediate ancestors. The relation between the genealogy and the remainder of the tent-dwelling kings is uncertain. It is possible that the genealogy included the names of all of the tent-dwelling kings before it became a part of the AKL, but it is also possible that most of the tent-dwelling kings were added by the compiler of the AKL.

In the GHD Malamat's determinative line contains only two names, Amnānu and Yaḫrurum (GHD 9–10). However, the GHD provides no formal grounds for separating these names from the surrounding names. Amnānu is the first ⟦188⟧ name in the GHD not shared by the AKL; so it is conceivable that this name originally marked the beginning of a Babylonian genealogy or the beginning of the Babylonian segment of a larger segmented genealogy, although there is no clear evidence on the exact position of the name within this hypothetical genealogy. The only reason for separating Yaḫrurum from the following names is the observation that it is the last demonstrably tribal name in the list.[44] Again, there is no evidence that this sort of distinction would have been made by the author of an underlying genealogy.

44. For a discussion of the relation of Amnānu and Yaḫrurum to the remaining names in the GHD, see J. J. Finkelstein, "Genealogy of the Hammurapi Dynasty," 111–12.

Malamat's third category, the table of ancestors, is clearly marked in the AKL. The king list separates the genealogy of Šamši-Adad I from the remainder of the list by means of the summary statements in AKL i 10, 21. This genealogy probably traced at least eleven generations of ancestors rather than ten, as Malamat suggests, although we have already seen that its original form may have been somewhat different from the one found in the AKL. In the GHD the table of ancestors is said to stretch from Iptiyamuta (GHD 11), the first name following Yaḫrurum, to Sumuabum (GHD 20), the founder of the Hammurapi dynasty. There are no formal grounds in the list for this division, and in particular there is no reason to end the table of ancestors with Sumuabum. If some sort of genealogy does lie behind this portion of GHD, there is now no way to determine the role of these names in that genealogy. Therefore, it would be hazardous to suggest that the names formed a genealogical segment having a depth of ten generations.

We must conclude, then, that although Malamat has made a strong case for the existence of genealogies among the Amorites, he has not supplied enough evidence to support his claim that those genealogies had a stereotypical ten-generation depth or a standard four-part structure. This conclusion must also cast doubt on his analysis of the royal genealogies in Israel.

IV

The above survey of current genealogical research has several implications for future studies of the OT genealogies. First, future research must take into account anthropological evidence. Until recently treatments of the OT genealogies have tended to generalize about them and to posit for them forms and functions which are never actually found in the genealogies used by modern tribal societies. Malamat's work and the brief sketch of anthropological data included above suggest that these tendencies can be avoided if hypotheses about the OT genealogies are developed against the background of contemporary living genealogies. The anthropological material reveals that genealogies have a number of complex forms and functions which must be considered in interpreting the biblical genealogies. In this way biblical scholars can avoid assuming the existence of rigid genealogical patterns.

⟦189⟧ Second, future research must recognize the relationship between genealogical form and function. Both the anthropological data and the Near Eastern texts which we have examined indicate a close connection between these two factors. Therefore, studies of the OT genealogies must consider the influence of function on form and the limitations which form sometimes imposes on function. Similarly, an attempt must be made to place apparent formal contradictions in a functional context.

Finally, the old question of the historiographic value of the OT genealogies must be re-examined. Although we have seen no anthropological evidence indicating that genealogies are created for the purpose of making a historical record, genealogies may nevertheless be considered historically accurate in the sense that they frequently express actual domestic, political, and religious relationships. They are, therefore, potentially valuable resources for the modern historian. However, the nature of genealogy requires that the question of historiographic worth be asked in each individual case, for only in this way can the complexities of genealogical form and function be taken into account. In dealing with the issue of the historiographic value of genealogy, no generalizations are possible.

The Incantation Series *Bīt Mēseri* and Enoch's Ascension to Heaven

Rykle Borger

⟦183⟧ The fact that Sumerian and Akkadian elements appear in the biblical primeval history is quite rightly no longer doubted, despite the extent to which problems remain in points of detail and despite the frequency with which it has been necessary in the course of time to abandon linkages that were all too hastily made.

The model example is the biblical Flood account, for which such linkages have been well known ever since George Smith brought to light the eleventh tablet of the Gilgamesh Epic and a flood fragment from the Atrahasis Epic 100 years ago. Further material has been added through the years to the Mesopotamian flood traditions, and one now finds in Lambert and Millard's *Atra-Ḫasis* all that is needed in order to do justice to the question.[1]

A further example is the passage from the Sumerian Enmerkar Epic discovered a few years ago by S. N. Kramer, which clearly represents the source of the tradition of the Babylonian confusion of languages in Gen 11:1–9.[2] Concerning the Babylonian background to the story of the Tower of Babel, it is also appropriate in this context to mention the article by W. von Soden.[3]

Abridged with permission from "Die Beschwörungsserie *Bīt Mēseri* und die Himmelfahrt Henochs," *Journal of Near Eastern Studies* 33 (1974) 183–96. Translated by V. Philips Long; the translation has been reviewed and approved by Prof. Borger.

1. W. G. Lambert and A. R. Millard, *Atra-Ḫasis: The Babylonian Story of the Flood* (Oxford: Clarendon, 1969); see also Lambert, "A New Look at the Babylonian Background of Genesis," *JTS* 16 (1965) 287–300. ⟦Reprinted in this volume, pp. 96–113.⟧

2. S. N. Kramer, *JAOS* 88 (1968) 108–11.

3. W. von Soden, "Etemenanki vor Asarhaddon nach der Erzählung vom Turmbau zu Babel und dem Erra-Mythos," *UF* 3 (1971) 253–63.

In Lambert and Millard's publication there is an excellent summary of the cuneiform materials that pertain to the antediluvian history of mankind and that may be compared to Genesis 4 (J source) and 5 (P source).[4]

The so-called Sumerian King List, from the beginning of the second millennium, enumerates a list of antediluvian rulers, all of whom were believed to have had enormously long reigns.[5] With respect to the number, order, and lengths of reign of the individual rulers, the various texts exhibit significant differences,[6] but one can draw up the following list of rulers as representative:

1. Alulim of Eridu
2. Alalgar of Eridu
3. Enmenluanna of Badtibira
4. Enmengalanna of Badtibira
5. Dumuzi of Badtibira
6. Ensipazianna of Larak ⟦184⟧
7. Enmeduranki of Sippar
8. Ubar-Tutu of Shuruppak
9. The Sumerian flood-hero Ziusudra (Xisuthros) of Shuruppak

A similar list is found at the beginning of a sort of world chronicle from the library of Assurbanipal (seventh century).[7]

Another list is found in an Uruk text that J. J. A. van Dijk has published.[8] Presented at the beginning of this text are, in addition to seven antediluvian kings (Ajalu = Alulim to Enmeduranki, inclusive), seven antediluvian sages (abgal = *apkallu*) presumed to have lived under these kings: U-An, U-An-dugga, Enmedugga, Enmegalamma, Enmebulugga, An-Enlilda, and Utuabzu. The continuation of this text, which we shall

4. Lambert and Millard, *Atra-Ḫasis*, 15ff. and 25ff. The only necessary addition to this summary, apart from the unpublished material to be handled below, is A. L. Oppenheim's discovery in a Neo-Assyrian state letter of a reference to the first king, Alulim: *BASOR* 97 (1945) 26–27.

5. A. L. Oppenheim, "Babylonian and Assyrian Historical Texts," *ANET*, 265–67.

6. See the synopsis in J. J. Finkelstein, *JCS* 17 (1963) 44ff.

7. K.11261 + K.11624 (Lambert and Millard, *Cuneiform Texts* 46 Nr. 5) + K.12054 (unpublished, join by Lambert) (+) L. W. King, *Chronicles concerning Early Babylonian Kings*, vol. 2, 46–56, col. I (also the unpublished duplicate 79-7-8, 333 + 339, which I identified). ⟦See now the edition by Lambert in the Festschrift for F. M. Th. de Liagre Böhl, *Symbolae Biblicae et Mesopotamicae . . .* (Leiden: Brill, 1973) 271–75 and 280.⟧

8. J. J. A. van Dijk, *XVIII. vorläufiger Bericht über die . . . Ausgrabungen in Uruk-Warka* (ed. H. J. Lenzen; Berlin, 1962) 44ff.

designate the "Uruk List" in what follows, enumerates later kings and their scholars (*ummannu*). The text dates from 165 B.C.[9]

Finally, the Hellenistic priest Berossos has also transmitted the names of the antediluvian rulers.[10] Like the Uruk List, Berossos informs us of the names of the antediluvian sages.[11] Van Dijk has provided a detailed treatment of the correspondences between his list and Berossos and in the process has also noted where individual antediluvian sages are attested elsewhere in the cuneiform literature.[12]

Among the antediluvian rulers, apart from the flood hero and Dumuzi, Enmeduranki of Sippar is the most distinctive figure. Among the Babylonians and the Assyrians, he was regarded as the Father of Soothsaying (extispicy), as described in detail in the ritual text K.2486 + K.3646 + K.4364 (with duplicates), recently treated by Lambert in his article about "Enmeduranki and Related Matters."[13] In the same article Lambert has brought another text into association with Enmeduranki and interpreted it as an inscription of Nebuchadnezzar I, although both names appear only where they have been restored in gaps in the preserved text material. Lambert translates lines 7–10 as follows: "[Nebuchadnezzar], king of Babylon . . . , distant scion of kingship, seed preserved from before the flood, offspring of [Enmeduranki], king of Sippar, who set up the pure bowl and held the cedar-wood (rod), who sat in the presence of Shamash and Adad, the divine adjudicators." In August 1971, as I was looking through unpublished bilingual texts in the Students' Room of the British Museum, I happened on a text (K. 6088) in which I recognized the name Enmeduranki. I showed the fragment to Lambert, who was working in the same room. Lambert recognized immediately that the fragment belonged to the text ⟦185⟧ that he had treated and that it also splendidly confirmed the names Enmeduranki in line 9 and Nebuchadnezzar in line 7, which he had restored.[14] Thus, the tradition of the soothsaying antediluvian ruler from Sippar was still so strong in Babylon in the twelfth century B.C. that King Nebuchadnezzar I appropriated him as his ancestor. The city of Sippar was the residence of the sun-god

9. The only cuneiform reference to the sage Aḫiqar is found in lines 19–20; see ibid., 51–52.

10. See P. Schnabel, *Berossos* (Leipzig and Berlin, 1923) 261ff.; F. Jacoby, *Die Fragmente der griechischen Historiker,* III C (Leiden, 1958) 374ff.

11. See Schnabel, *Berossos,* 253–54, 261ff.; also (less fully) Jacoby, *Die Fragmente,* 369–70, 375–76.

12. Van Dijk, op cit., 47ff. See further Lambert, *JCS* 16 (1962) 73–74; as well as W. W. Hallo, *JAOS* 83 (1963) 174ff. and *JCS* 23 (1970–71) 62.

13. Lambert, *JCS* 21 (1967) 126–38.

14. ⟦See his new treatment in *Compte Rendu XIXe Rencontre Assyriologique Paris 1971* (published Paris, 1974) 434–40.⟧

Shamash, who is also explicitly put forward in the aforementioned ritual text as Enmeduranki's patron deity.

Wherever Berossos has been read, the striking relationship between the Mesopotamian tradition with its antediluvian rulers[15] and the biblical tradition with its ten antediluvian patriarchs has been recognized. The discovery of the Sumerian King List, however, brought a "merciless collapse" to many a fanciful conjecture.[16] What remained, apart from the evident connection of Ziusudra with Noah, was for all intents and purposes only the link between the seventh antediluvian patriarch, Enoch, and the (according to most sources seventh) antediluvian ruler Enmeduranki. Even this equation has repeatedly been contested.

Of the nine descendents of Adam named in Genesis 5, apart from Noah, only Enoch is provided with some particulars. Gen 5:24 states: "Enoch walked with God; then he was no more, because God took him away." This looks like a meager remnant of a mythological story. In Heb 11:5 this verse is repeated and interpreted as follows: "By faith Enoch was taken from this life, so that he did not experience death; he could not be found, because God had taken him away. For before he was taken, he was commended as one who pleased God." Compare this verse with Ecclesiasticus 44:16: "Enoch pleased the Lord and was carried off to heaven, an example of repentance to future generations," and 49:14 (16): "No one on earth has been created to equal Enoch, for he was taken up from the earth."[17] In Jude 14–15, "Enoch, the seventh from Adam" is cited as a visionary. As is well known, it was as a visionary that Enoch played an important role in the apocalyptic literature, whether merely on the basis of Gen 5:24 or also in connection with traditions now lost to us. The book of *Enoch* crystallized around his figure.[18] See also *Jub.* 4:16–26,[19] as well as the *Genesis Apocryphon* from Qumran.[20]

It is no wonder, then, that the seventh from Adam is compared with the seventh Sumerian primeval king, the visionary Enoch with the

15. According to Berossos there were ten antediluvian rulers.

16. H. Zimmern, *Zeitschrift der deutschen morgenländischen Gesellschaft* 78 (1924) 24; contra B. D. Eerdmans, *The Religion of Israel* (1947) 128.

17. ⟦*Translator's note*: Translations are from the NEB.⟧

18. E. Kautzsch et al., *Die Apokryphen und Pseudepigraphen des Alten Testaments,* 2.217–310; cf. O. Eissfeldt, *Einleitung*[3], 836ff.; R. H. Pfeiffer, *History of New Testament Times,* 75ff. and 539.

19. Kautzsch, *Apokryphen,* 31–119.

20. J. A. Fitzmyer's edition, *The Genesis Apocryphon of Qumran Cave 1: A Commentary* (2d ed.; BibOr 18/A; Rome: Pontifical Biblical Institute, 1971) 52ff. A monograph about Enoch was written by the Norwegian historian of religion H. Ludin Jansen: *Die Henochgestalt: Eine vergleichende religionsgeschichtliche Untersuchung* (Oslo, 1939), to be used with caution. ⟦A recent monograph about Enoch: H. S. Kvanvig, *Roots of Apocalyptic* (Neukirchen-Vluyn, 1988). See also Armin Schmitt, *Entrückung—Aufnahme—Himmelfahrt* (Stuttgart, 1973).⟧

prognostic Enmeduranki, the one who died when 365 years old (which possibly admits of a solar allusion) with the favorite of the Mesopotamian sun-god. The weightiest argument against the suggestion that Enmeduranki be regarded as a prototype of Enoch was the circumstance that in the surviving texts there is no word of Enmeduranki ascending or being taken up to heaven. And so it is also no wonder ⟦186⟧ that C. Westermann in his Genesis commentary (publication in progress) rejects the dependence of Enoch on Enmeduranki as unproven and instead considers a possible correspondence to the Mesopotamian sage Adapa.[21] The material was, indeed, insufficient to afford indisputable identification.

Assumption into heaven is well attested in the Old Testament, the best-known cases being those of Enoch and Elijah. A cuneiform parallel to the assumption of Enoch can be found at the end of the flood story in the Gilgamesh Epic: "'Hitherto Utnapishtim has been but human. Henceforth Utnapishtim and his wife shall be like unto us gods. Utnapishtim shall reside far away, at the mouth of the rivers!' Thus they took me and made me reside far away, at the mouth of the rivers."[22] For the ascension motif, the cuneiform literature offers two examples, in the story of Adapa and in the legend of Etana.[23] Also to be included is the "Etiological Myth of the 'Seven Sages,'" treated by E. Reiner. In lines 1′–4′ (and rev. 8′–9′) of this Sumero-Akkadian text we read (according to the translation of Reiner): "[Adapa,] the purification priest of Eridu [. . .] who ascended to heaven."[24]

Thus we return to the "seven sages," with whom we are already familiar from the Uruk List and the communications of Berossos. The Uruk List provides only the seven names and the dates, but Berossos, whose dates differ in part from those of the Uruk List, provides us with more details. We are told of hybrid beings, half-fish, half-human (the Akkadian word is *kulullu*), which are supposed to have arisen in primordial time out of the sea in order to bring culture to humanity.[25] The best known of these fish-shaped sages is the first, named Oan or Oannes = Sumerian U-An(na) = Akkadian *Ūm-Anu*, etc.. In the cuneiform literature the designation "Adapa" is appended a few times to this name.[26] On

21. ⟦See now C. Westermann, *Genesis* (3 vols.; BKAT 1/1–3; Neukirchen-Vluyn: Neukirchener Verlag, 1974) 1.358; English trans.: *Genesis 1–11* (Minneapolis: Augsburg, 1984).⟧

22. E. A. Speiser (trans.), "The Epic of Gilgamesh," *ANET,* 95.

23. Idem, "Adapa," *ANET,* 101–3; idem, "Etana," *ANET,* 114–18.

24. E. Reiner, "Etiological Myth of the 'Seven Sages,'" *Or* n.s. 30 (1961) 1ff. Her reasons for restoring the name Adapa (and not Etana) are presented on pp. 6–7 of her article.

25. See, e.g., the depictions in H. Gressmann, *Altorientalische Bilder,* fig. 525; (C. J. Gadd, *The Stones of Assyria* [London, 1936] 139 no. 30); B. Meissner, *Babylonien und Assyrien* I (Heidelberg, 1920) plates 196 and 213; J. B. Pritchard, *ANEP,* fig. 706; and A. Parrot, *Assur* (Paris, 1961) fig. 82.

26. See van Dijk, *XVIII. vorläufiger Bericht,* 47–48; and Lambert, *JCS* 16 (1962) 73–74.

this basis one might infer that Oannes and Adapa are identical or have been equated. It is difficult to believe, however, that the wise "son" of the god Ea, known from the "Myth of Adapa," who in Eridu engages in fishing and in the Adapa fragment D line 12′ is designated 'human offspring', should have been of all things a fish. In reality, the name Adapa has apparently sometimes been used as an appellative with the meaning 'sage'.[27] The repeatedly suggested identification of Oannes and the god Enki/Ea has never been proved and must be regarded as most unlikely. An allusion to these seven sages is found also in the Epic of Erra: "Where are the seven sages, the pure *purādu*-fish, who like Ea, their lord, are endowed with sublime wisdom . . . ?" The *purādu*-fish is a kind of giant carp, Arabic *bizz*.[28] So the verse fits perfectly with the communications of Berossos ⟦187⟧. In a Sumerian temple hymn the "seven sages" are associated with the city Kuar-Eridu. The "seven sages of Eridu" are mentioned in the incantation series *maqlû*, II 124, V 110, and VII 49.[29] In tablet I, I 19 and tablet XI 305 of the Gilgamesh Epic (*ANET*, 73 and 97) the "seven counselors" are listed as the founders of the city of Uruk. The "seven sages in an incantation ritual," who are described in the passage translated by Ebeling, *ATAT* (Gressmann), 147, differ widely from our fish-shaped seven antediluvian sages and have different names ⟦for a recent edition of this passage see now Wiggermann, *Mesopotamian Protective Spirits* (Groningen, 1992) 6ff. lines 44–65⟧.

The treatment of the Myth of the Seven Sages by Erica Reiner is excellent. Still, the text in its fragmentary state of preservation remained rather unclear. Fortunately, the "little hope that we will ever find more ample material dealing with the *apkallus*"[30] has now in part been fulfilled, and that not only through the Uruk List, which was shortly thereafter published by van Dijk. In Uruk a text was recently discovered that has been identified by the expedition's epigrapher, E. von Weiher, as a duplicate restoring much of the "myth" in question. Through this discovery the important beginning of the text has been in large measure recovered. Independently of these developments, I identified several fragments from the Nineveh Library of King Assurbanipal as duplicates of the text in question, so that also in this manner it was possible to reconstruct the

27. For references see Lambert, ibid., and *AfO* 19 (1959–60) 64, II 72 (with duplicate Sippar 851, II 15′, unpublished copy by Geers; the lexical entry quoted by Lambert in his note to II 72 is registered in CAD A/I 102 s.v. *adapu* B = 'wise'; see also below, note 37). See also S. Parpola, *Letters from Assyrian Scholars* (Kevelaer: Butzon & Bercker, 1970) no. 117, 8.

28. L. Cagni, *L'epopea di Erra* (Rome, 1969) tablet I 162. For a drawing of *bizz*-fishes, see Meissner, *Babylonien und Assyrian* I, plate 92.

29. See Sjöberg, *The Collection of the Sumerian Temple Hymns* (Locust Valley, 1969) 25 no. 10 139 (with commentary p. 79); and G. R. Meier, *Die assyrische Beschwörungsammlung Maqlû* (Berlin, 1937, with supplement *AfO* 21 [1966] 70–81) respectively.

30. Reiner, "Etiological Myth," 10.

text's beginning almost completely. Both the Uruk text and the material from Nineveh confirmed Reiner's perspicacious suggestion that her text represented a portion of the Incantation Series *bīt mēseri*.[31] According to the Nineveh material, her text belongs to the third tablet of this series.

At this juncture it seems a good idea to summarize the textual situation of the series in question. Those who are not primarily Assyriologists can, of course, skip over this second part of my exposition without loss.

⟦Pp. 187 bottom–192 top of the original article are here omitted. A comprehensive edition of the series *bīt mēseri* will be published in the author's forthcoming book, *Sumerisch-akkadische Bilinguen*. The author has now updated this article to include his most recent references and translations.⟧

I will now cite in translation several passages from the beginning of tablet III of *bīt mēseri* ('House of Confinement'), making use of the new material now available. In so doing I will also bring to bear the ritual tablet in reconstructing the text.

The first "incantation" to be cited here (Reiner lines 1′–31′ with additions ⟦forthcoming edition lines 250–90⟧) pertains to the "seven statues (that is, depictions?) of the *purādu*-fish-sages (?), which are painted with plaster and black paste, drawn on the side of the chamber on the wall," and it reads as follows:

Incantation. U-Anna, who accomplishes the plans of heaven and earth,
U-Anne-dugga, who is endowed with comprehensive understanding,
Enmedugga, for whom a good destiny has been decreed,
Enmegalamma, who was born in a house,
Enmebulugga, who grew up in a pasture land,
An-Enlilda, the conjurer of the city of Eridu,
Utuabzu, who ascended to heaven,
the pure *purādu*-fishes, the *purādu*-fishes of the sea, the seven of them,
the seven sages, who originated in the river, who control the plans of heaven and earth.
Nungalpiriggaldim, the wise (King) of Enmerkar, who had the goddess Innin/Ishtar descend from heaven into the sanctuary,[32]

31. Ibid., 5 n. 3.

32. This information is also found in the Uruk List, lines 3–4; see van Dijk, op. cit., 49. Erica Reiner has detected an additional mention of this action in K. L. Tallqvist, *Maqlû*, part 2, p. 96, K.8162, line 2′ (+ K.10357, line 10′, copy by Geers): [N]un-gal-pirig-gal-dím-ma$^{?}$-ke$_4$$^{?}$ Nun-pirig-gal-abzu-NUN-KI-NA.ke$_4$.

Piriggalnungal, who was born in Kish, who angered the god Ishkur/Adad in heaven, so that he allowed neither rain nor growth in the land for three years,
Piriggalabzu, who was born in Adab/Utab, who hung his seal on a "goatfish"[33] and thereby angered the god Enki/Ea in the fresh water sea, so that a fuller struck him dead with his own seal,
fourthly Lu-Nanna, who was two-thirds a sage, who drove a dragon out of the Temple E-Ninkiagnunna, the Innin/Ishtar Temple of (King) Shulgi,
(altogether) four sages of human descent, whom Enki/Ea, the Lord, endowed with comprehensive understanding.

Only a little of the adjoining incantation, which applied to the "seven statues of the sages made of consecrated tamarisk wood", is preserved ⟦forthcoming edition, lines 296–321 with new additions; we now know that the same sages are mentioned here as in *ATAT,* 147⟧.

The next "incantation" (Reiner rev. 1′–9′ with additions ⟦forthcoming edition, lines 324–31⟧) applied to "seven statues of the kneeling sages made of consecrated tamarisk wood, which stand at the foot of the bed":

[Incantation. U]-Anne-dugga, for whom a good destiny has been decreed ⟦193⟧,
[NN], who was born in a house,
[NN], who was imbued with wide understanding,
Enki- . . . [. . .], who with respect to the plans of heaven and earth is perfect,
Anne-padda, who grew up in a pasture land,
Utuabzu, who ascended to heaven,
An-Enlilda, the conjurer of Eridu.

The final "incantation" to be quoted here (Reiner rev. 12′–15′ ⟦forthcoming edition, lines 334–37⟧) applied to the "[seven statues (i.e., depictions?)] of the sages made of plaster, which are drawn in the corners and on the inside of the gate," is badly preserved. The text reads as follows: "[Incantation. Enmedikud, for whom a good destiny has been decreed], Enmedug(? or Enmegalam?), who stands in a house, [. . .] on whom [. . .] was bestowed, Enme?-Enlille?, the conjuror of Eridu, [. . .], who directs the cult, An-Enlilda, Anne-padda, [. . .], Utuaabba, who descended from heaven."

33. The sacred animal of the god Enki/Ea.

When one compares these three listings of seven sages with one another, one is confronted by various problems. Just as in the case of the antediluvian kings, the names and the order of the antediluvian sages are apparently quite variable. The second listing offers a different order and in part also different names from the first, and the third listing differs even more markedly. Evidently three different traditions are here combined in one text.

In the Nineveh material the names of the first listing are broken off, except for [U]-Anna (no. 1) and [U-Anne-dug]ga (no. 2), but the descriptions are preserved. It seemed quite reasonable to assume that the names of this listing coincide with those of the Uruk List. Therefore I have confidently restored the sixth and seventh names of the first listing, in accordance with the Uruk List, from the last two names of the second listing, although there they have changed place, along with their epithets. Further support for these restorations is the fact that An-Enlilda is also designated the "conjurer of Eridu" in another text.[34] The Nineveh material enabled me not only to draw the conclusion that it was Utuabzu who went into heaven,[35] but also that this Utuabzu who had ascended to heaven was, according to one of the *bīt mēseri* traditions, the seventh of the antediluvian sages. The new Uruk text shown to me by E. von Weiher ⟦and later published by him in his book *Spätbabylonische Texte aus Uruk* II (Berlin, 1983) no. 8⟧, removed the last uncertainty that attended this reasoning; it showed that the first *bīt mēseri* tradition does in fact coincide precisely with the Uruk List. According to the Uruk List and to Berossos, this Utu-abzu[36] was contemporary with the seventh antediluvian ruler, Enmeduranki of Sippar.

So now we know that according to a well-attested Mesopotamian tradition, the seventh and last antidiluvian sage, Utuabzu, a contemporary of the seventh antidiluvian ruler, Enmeduranki, ascended to heaven. From this tradition one may arrive at surprising conjectures with respect to the figure of the seventh Old Testament patriarch, Enoch. The possibility that Enmeduranki as predictor of the future and as the seventh ruler of the primeval period was a prototype of Enoch receives unanticipated support. *The mythological conception of Enoch's ascension to heaven derives, however, from Enmeduranki's counselor, the seventh antediluvian sage, named Utuabzu*![37]

34. See van Dijk, op. cit., 48b sub no. 6.

35. This conclusion followed unambiguously from my indirect join K.5119 rev. (+) K.13506.

36. In Berossos, "Utu-abzu" is changed to "Anodaphos": the name means 'One-born-in-the-fresh-water-sea'.

37. Noteworthy is the fact that, as we have seen, in *bīt mēseri* section II, line 29′ in Reiner rev. 15′ ⟦now line 337⟧ there stands at the end of the listing of seven sages a certain

⟦194⟧ Though cautious exegesis of the account of the assumption of Enoch in Gen 5:24 would not necessarily lead to the notion of an ascension into heaven (Utnapishtim was also not assumed into heaven), the Genesis passage, on the basis of the clear formulation of the cuneiform material, can now safely be interpreted in this sense. The cuneiform accounts of the various antediluvian and postdiluvian sages represent remains of more comprehensive mythological conceptions and narratives, just as the account of Enoch in the biblical Primeval History is a sparse remain of a larger legend.

It is not very important for us to know the exact time the series *bīt mêseri* as a whole originated, since there can hardly be any doubt that the accounts treating the seven antediluvian and four postdiluvian sages are dependent on Sumerian tradition. Enoch is, then, with Noah, the second among the list of heroes of the faith in Hebrews 11 to turn out to be ultimately a Sumerian figure.

⟦Pages 194b–196 have been omitted.⟧

"Utuaabba [i.e., 'One-born-in-the-sea'] who descended from heaven." See the previously mentioned lexical entry quoted by Lambert, *AfO* 19 64 lower right = CAD A/I, s.v. *adapu* B: "Ù-tu-a-ab-ba = *a-da-pu*" (above, note 27). This remarkable counterpart to Utuabzu is not otherwise attested, as far as I know.

The "Table of Nations" (Genesis 10): Its General Structure and Meaning

J. Simons

⟦155⟧ Following a discussion of a single verse in the Biblical Table of Nations (v. 19), published in an earlier issue of this series,[1] we propose in these pages to submit some remarks and suggestions regarding the structure and meaning of this equally puzzling and attractive biblical chapter as a whole. We are concerned here with matters of principle rather than with a solution of the many individual problems involved and our study will include a somewhat new, though admittedly tentative, interpretation of the basic ideas underlying the Table of Nations.

Little need be said by way of an introduction about former efforts with similar aims, since the volume of recent literature on the subject is meagre in the extreme, especially if compared with the uninterrupted flow of books and articles dealing with other outstanding chapters of the Book of Genesis, such as that on the Tower of Babel (Genesis 11) or the Invasions of the Northern Kings (Genesis 14), to say nothing of the Creation Narratives (Genesis 1–3). In fact, many annual lists of Biblical literature are without any reference to the Table of Nations. To a ⟦156⟧ certain degree this may be due to the fairly wild theories attempted in earlier works, especially Fr. Hommel's *Ethnologie und Geographie des Alten Orients* and the first volume of E. Meyer's *Geschichte des Altertums*, both of 1926, which have left the impression that on a subject of this nature there is more a lack of solid arguments than of confident assertions.

Reprinted with permission from *Oudtestamentische Studiën* 10 (1954) 155–84.

1. *OTS* 5 (1948) 92ff.

More recently[2] I know of no more than three studies dealing with the entire chapter, but on two of them, both published in 1947, I have not been able to lay hands. They are (1) a study in Bulgarian by B. N. Piperov which appeared in the *Annals of the University of Sophia* under the (translated) title "The Ancient Ethnography of the East according to the Bible: Genesis 10, 1–30," and (2) a booklet by S. Wagner on *Die Stammtafel des Menschengeschlechtes.*[3] The third, the only available comprehensive treatment of the subject, may be seen in the fifth chapter of G. Hölscher's *Drei Erdkarten: Ein Beitrag zur Erforschung des hebräischen Altertums.*[4] Leaving aside those publications which only deal with one or some of the approximately 70 names contained in the Table of Nations I may usefully add three other studies covering one of its three main sections, viz., Fr. Schmidtke, *Die Japhetiten der biblischen Völkertafel*; E. Dhorme, "Les Peuples issus de Japhet, d'après le chapitre X de la Genèse"; and chap. 1 of ⟦157⟧ Aarre Lauha's *Zaphon, Der Norden und die Nordvölker im Alten Testament.*[5] Of course, all commentaries on the Book of Genesis, large and small, include some sort of discussion of the Table of Nations but few are really helpful or of outstanding originality. Two may be singled out for special recommendation, viz., P. Heinisch, *Das Buch Genesis,* which offers a number of sound observations of a general nature, and B. Jacob, *Das erste Buch der Tora "Genesis,"*[6] which goes into considerably more detail, although in his treatment of Genesis 10, more perhaps than anywhere else, the author indulges in questionable efforts to present the entire Genesis as a work *aus einem Guss* ⟦'from a single casting'⟧ and is at pains to explain all apparent irregularities or secondary additions to the text as due to presumably intentional and specially profound meanings.[7]

2. Among still earlier works I should like to mention, even now worth reading, Th. Arldt's essay on "Die Völkertafel der Genesis und ihre Bedeutung für die Ethnographie Vorderasiens" (*WZKM* 30 [1917–18] 264–317).

3. S. Wagner, *Die Stammtafel des Menschengeschlechtes* (2d ed.; Saarbrücken, 1947).

4. Presented to the Heidelberger Akademie der Wissenschaften during the War but published in 1949 as the proceedings of the years 1944–1948 (*Sitzungsberichte* 1944–1948, no. 3).

5. Schmidtke, *Die Japhetiten der biblischen Völkertafel* (Breslauer Studien z. hist. Theologie 7; 1926); E. Dhorme, "Les Peuples issus de Japhet, d'après le chapitre X de la Genèse," *Syria* 13 (1932) 28ff.; Aarre Lauha, *Zaphon, Der Norden und die Nordvölker im Alten Testament* (Annales Academiae Scientiarum Fennicae B49; Helsinki, 1943).

6. P. Heinisch, *Das Buch Genesis* (Bonn, 1930); B. Jacob, *Das erste Buch der Tora "Genesis"* (Berlin, 1934).

7. Merely to prevent the reader from repeating my own initial mistake, mention is made here of A. Herrmann's book *Die Erdkarte der Urbibel* (Braunschweig, 1931). Contrary to the suggestion conveyed by its title, this book, when finally traced, turned out not to deal with the geographical contents of the biblical Genesis as a whole or of chapter 10 in particular, but with those of the Book of *Jubilees.* The fact, surprising at first sight, that references to this book are rare and that none is included in the closing chapter of Hölscher's

⟦158⟧ We shall best begin with some remarks on what may be called the general strategy in attacking the mysteries of Genesis 10, since the question of strategy or method illustrates from the outset the special difficulties of the subject. There are two equally obvious modes of procedure, either of which is commonly tried but suffers from the same disadvantage, viz., that, properly speaking, the results of one method must be known before the other can be successfully applied. One might start the study of the Table of Nations with a diligent scrutiny of all individual names of peoples, lands, cities and islands included in the list, in order to extract from their identifications its general structure and meaning. But in doing so we come across too many items, which cannot be identified at all or with sufficient certainty, for discovering anything more about the nature of the list than what is also *prima facie* evident, viz., that is consists of three main sections. The principle obstacles against further progress along this line turn up in the section of Shem. As long as the leading principle of the tripartition of the list and therefore also the ideas which link together the various elements within each of the three sections, are unknown we have little to go on as regards Arphaxad (v. 22) and shall look about in vain for some identification of Lud (v. 22) suitable to be matched with Elam, Asshur and Aram, while the last named is also likely to remain a rather vague element. We shall be surprised to meet in this section the name of Asshur which has turned up once before (v. 11), and that in such a commendable context as Nineveh and Calah. Further, we shall be left ⟦159⟧ with the awkward fact that the section of Shem which starts in Irân and Mesopotamia, ends up in South Arabia, specifying there, moreover, the largest number of elements. Conversely, whoever takes as his starting-point for interpreting the Table of Nations its *prima facie* apparent division into three sections, either ethnographically or geographically distinct from one another, and endeavours on this basis

Drei Erdkarten, which deals precisely with *Die Karte des Jubiläenbuches,* is after all easily explained by its actual contents. The author lays down the strange proposition that the geographical chapters 8 and 9 of the Book of *Jubilees,* or as it is sometimes called the *Leptogenesis,* do not constitute a midrashic paraphrase of the biblical Table of Nations, written slightly before or after the beginning of the Christian era. The Book of *Jubilees,* the author maintains, must be rather considered "*eine ältere Redaktion der Priesterschrift*" ⟦'an older redaction of the Priestly document'⟧, indeed "*älter als die Quellen der Genesis*" ⟦'older than the sources of Genesis'⟧ and dating from the period of King Solomon (pp. 3, 32, etc.). More than that: instead of the Book of *Jubilees*' being "*eine späte Bearbeitung der kanonischen Genesis,*" ⟦'a late revision of the canonical Genesis'⟧, Herrmann's study intends to prove "*besonders auf geographischem Wege, dass, abgesehen von den makkabäischen Zutaten, eher das Umgekehrte zutrifft*" ⟦'especially regarding geography, but apart from the Maccabaean ingredients, the opposite applies'⟧ (p. 3). Not only the doubtful merits of this theory, but also the fact that Herrmann's book deals with Genesis 10 only for the purpose of illustrating the priority of the Book of *Jubilees* justify its exclusion from further consideration in connection with our subject.

to identify and to locate all individual names, is even more sure to get stuck before making much headway. This is clearly the case, if the tripartition is understood in the far too modern and scientific ethnographic sense. What can be done, in this supposition, with Canaan coupled with Mizraim in the section of Ham (v. 6), or where to find for Phut (v. 6) something ethnographically fitting in with Mizraim as well as with Canaan? Even less can be done in the main group of Shem (v. 22), which would now be a group of "Semites," with Elam, and the door will be closed on the identification of Lud with the non-Semitic Lydians of Asia Minor, although no other reasonable possibility turns up to replace it. The interpretation of the tripartition of the Table of Nations as being of a geographical nature, though naturally more sound in the case of a document of such antiquity, has to face the fact that the section of Ham (via Cush) as well as the section of Shem (via Eber) leads to Arabia and even has to incorporate some identical elements of its population (Sheba and Havilah). It also calls up the aforementioned difficulty that the section of Shem starts in Western Asia but ends in South Arabia, which looks like a travesty of a geographical distribution. This view would also have to explain why the Elamites have been classed in the group of Shem (v. 22), whereas the Madai whose home is likewise in Irân, are assigned to the section of Japheth (v. 2). The difficulties against an unqualified geographical ⟦160⟧ classification increase whenever this is coupled with the idea of a geographical order or consistently maintained direction along the lands and peoples specified. This, in my opinion, is an outstanding defect in Hölscher's interpretation of the Table of Nations, a leading principle of which is a uniform east-west succession of all elements making up the three sections. For this principle he has to place Canaan west of Phut, which he identifies, and rightly so, with Libya. Consequently he is induced to explain the name Canaan as referring to "das Gebiet der Punier um Kartago" ⟦'the territory of the Punic peoples around Carthage'⟧,[8] doubtless a surprising extension of the geographical horizon of the Old Testament. In a similar way Hölscher arrives at a strained interpretation of the Madai who, coming after Gomer and Magog in the section of Japheth (v. 2), have to be pushed further to the west "Er [the author of the Table of Nations] denkt also offenbar nicht speziell an das eigentliche Medien, sondern an die Ausdehnung der 'medischen' Herrschaft über Klein-Asien" ⟦'he therefore apparently does not think specifically of the actual Medes, rather of the expansion of the "Median" hegemony over Asia Minor'⟧. This is how he manages to link up this element with the next, still more westerly item of the list, viz. Javan or Ionia. Tubal and Meshech which are mentioned after Javan, cause even greater embarrassment

8. Hölscher, *Drei Erdkarten*, 53.

requiring a still more violent solution. After stating that at the author's time these peoples were settled on the shores of Pontus, i.e., not at all west of Ionia, nothing remains but to conclude: "Er [the author] scheint sich die Wohnsitze von Tûbâl und Mešek wesentlich westlicher vorzustellen" ⟦'He appears to present the abode of Tûbâl and Mešek essentially westerly'⟧.[9] This amounts to making against the author an imputation of gross error, in order to save a presupposed principle of interpretation. But such a manner of reasoning, I believe, is itself an error of method or at any rate permissible only if the assumed principle justifies itself through its smooth applicability ⟦161⟧ in all other instances. Hölscher, for that matter, does not shrink from charging the author of the Table of Nations, in spite of his evident acquaintance with the world in which he lived, with an even greater blunder as regards Lud (v. 22). Convinced that this name can mean nothing else than "Lydia" but on the other hand cannot possibly refer to the Lydian kingdom of Asia Minor ("da dieses unbedingt dem Gebiete Japhets zugeteilt sein müsste" ⟦'that this certainly must be assigned to the territory of Japheth'⟧), Hölscher goes in search of another Lud, which by virtue of his east-west principle has to be found somewhere west of Elam, Asshur and Arphaxad, and finally turns out to be "die palästinisch-syrische Küste und ein Teil der westlichen Inselwelt" ⟦'the Palestinian-Syrian coast and a port of the western archipelago'⟧.[10] Hölscher himself was the first to be surprised at such a conclusion, which, indeed, is bare of every shred of documentary support. "Die Verteilung der Erdvölker ist sehr konstruktiv" ⟦'The distribution of the nations of the earth is very constructive'⟧, he says, but on his *Abb. 2*, "Lud" figures impudently in the neighbourhood of Jaffa. How, we ask, can the author of the Table of Nations, whom until the contrary is proved we like to think of as settled in Palestine, entertain such an idea? Is it possible, perhaps, that Hölscher without saying so has been thinking of Alt's "Reich von Lydda" ⟦'kingdom of Lydda'⟧? Whatever the answer to these questions, we must point out that Hölscher's "Lud" has not found a place east of Aram, as it should have done according to logic. On the whole, we have the impression that Hölscher has allowed his east-west principle to be forced upon him by the main group of Shem alone, the first element of which, Elam, is indeed the one most easterly situated and is followed by Asshur which lies west of it.

What has been said may suffice to illustrate the inherent difficulties of the two usual forms of strategy in attacking the problem of the Table of Nations. Of course, we are ⟦162⟧ not thereby entitled to the *a priori* assertion that another method of approach is bound to yield better re-

9. Ibid., 56.
10. Ibid., 51.

sults and will provide an adequate insight into the structure and meaning of Genesis 10, which should be here as for any other pericope the ultimate goal of interpretation. But we do feel justified in stating that some other starting-point is a *conditio sine qua non* for reaching or approaching that goal and that only in a second stage the problem of Genesis 10 should be tackled by the inductive or deductive method.

There is at present a more or less general and undoubtedly justified opinion that the interpretation of any biblical pericope, also a pericope of the Pentateuch, should not begin with an operation on the text. However, Genesis 10 must be considered a special case, the nature of which warrants such a procedure. Indeed, we are dealing here with an enumeration or a list of names, and it is well known that no other type of literature is more than this in the habit of eliciting interpolations and additions or glosses which again in due time finish by slipping into the text. This observation applies in a special way in the case of a genealogical list of names, which is the stylistic form of the Table of Nations. For this reason it seems safe enough to assume *a priori* that the contents of Genesis 10 are probably made up of an original nucleus and a smaller or greater number of secondary elements. If this is so, it will be considered methodically justified, when in search of the author's original intention and arrangement, to try before anything else to isolate as far as possible what seems to constitute the hard core of the Table of Nations. This is not saying that all other ingredients of the chapter must necessarily be pushed aside as adulterations of the author's mind or plan. But it would seem to be a matter of sound caution to be aware of the possibility that all secondary elements ⟦163⟧ together may have obscured or distorted it and that one or more such additions may be frankly out of harmony with the author's conception and render our insight into his mind impossible as long as they are being maintained as integral parts of his picture. Consequently, it is our first task in regard to the Table of Nations to trace all such elements, certain or probable, and to do so in the first instance by a careful consideration of the text itself, making use only in the second place of its partition into three sections and of its unquestionably, or with reasonable certainty, identifiable individual names.

We have no hesitation in saying that the prospects in this direction are not particularly promising if only certainties are being allowed for. But it is only fair to add that the same can be said with respect to nearly all that in the Book of Genesis has to do with geography or topography. Moreover, it seems possible to point to at least one paragraph of Genesis 10 as certainly not belonging to its original draft, viz., the Cush-Nimrod passage in the section of Ham (vv. 8–12). It is true that some commentators consider even this passage a genuine part of the Table of Nations. Jacob finds not so much as a difficulty in the association of Cush-

Ethiopia with the cities of the Assyrian and Babylonian empires, seeing that as far as Genesis 11:9, all peoples of the earth are supposed to live together.[11] Jacob seems to forget, however, that Genesis 11 merely intends to explain, historically or theologically, a dispersion of the human race which Genesis 10 has already presented as an accomplished fact. Some others look upon the Cush-Nimrod passage as not really an addition to the original text, because in their view the biblical name of Cush has a much larger meaning than is usually attributed to it. "The name of Cush in the Old Testament," says E. G. H. Kraeling, ⟦164⟧ "often includes Arabia as well as Ethiopia and the region of Chaldea can without difficulty be described as belonging to Cush."[12] The former of these two propositions is, to say the least, exaggerated[13] and the second has no foundation whatever, except Genesis 10 itself which is *sub iudice* ⟦'under discussion'⟧ . The Cush-Nimrod passage is taken as a real dissonant element but from the hand of the author of the Table of Nations himself, not of a glossator or interpolator, by all those who explain its insertion as due to a reminiscence of the Mesopotamian Kashshu, occasioned by the name Cush: this would have provoked the sudden jump from an African people to Mesopotamia and its great historic cities. So Hölscher[14] and long before him especially E. Meyer,[15] who adds that the author's abrupt transition from Africa to Asia is merely an error. As Nimrod, the son of Cush, is quite at home in Libya (the name of Nimrod is "ganz gewöhnlich" ⟦'completely at home'⟧ there), the transfer of Cush via Nimrod to the Accadian world was as unnecessary as mistaken. In our opinion it is considerably simpler and also safer to see in the nature of the Cush-Nimrod passage itself convincing evidence that it is not a genuine part of the Table of Nations. This narrative digression is out of tune with the remainder of the chapter. Notice especially in this respect the introductory *wayyĕhî*-formula. Also, with the enumeration of Accadian cities, inclusive of some Assyrian ones, and the allusion of ⟦165⟧ v. 11 to the chronological priority of the Babylonian to the Assyrian Empire we find ourselves transferred to a fully historical and relatively recent period, whereas it was the author's manifest intention to acquaint us with a dispersion of the sons of Noah which took place in times long past. Even the very fact

11. Jacob, *Das erste Buch,* 283–84.

12. E. G. H. Kraeling, "The Origin and Real Name of Nimrud," *AJSL* 38 (1921–22) 217–18.

13. A very small number of texts mentioning Arab Cushites are more easily accounted for as due to the African penetration into the peninsula across the Red Sea and Bâb el-Mandeb. Only "Cushan" of Hab 3:7 is certainly and exclusively Arab but distinguishes itself through the termination -an, which is typical of many Arab ethnographical names (Midian, Dedan, etc.). It can therefore not be treated as a mere equivalent of Cush.

14. Hölscher, *Drei Erdkarten,* 42–43.

15. E. Meyer, *Die Israeliten und ihre Nachbarn,* 448; *Gesch. d. Alt.* 1, 48.

that this paragraph introduces a number of city-names into the Table of Nations makes a rather strange impression after all that precedes, nor should it be overlooked that, e.g., Asshur and Nineveh belong ethnographically and historically to the same unit. Finally we draw attention to a stylistic peculiarity which by itself constitutes a next-to-decisive argument for the secondary character of the Cush-Nimrod passage. After v. 7 has informed us who were the "sons of Cush," exactly in the same way as has been done in vv. 3–4 with regard to the divisions and subdivisions of Japheth, v. 8 belatedly comes forth with yet another son of Cush, viz., Nimrod. The fact that he is introduced by a *jalad*-formula does not wipe out or obscure the awkward *soudure* ⟦'welding'⟧ but, if possible, rather accentuates it. For all these reasons we feel convinced that vv. 8–12 are a posthumous addition to the Table of Nations, and in view of the improbable link these verses establish between African Cushites and Mesopotamian cities we have no hesitation in considering this particular addition an error as far as its insertion into the Table of Nations is concerned. Consequently it should not be taken into account in our search for the true structure and meaning of this document.[16]

⟦166⟧ The second item in the section of Ham to which we want to draw attention and which, it seems, does not belong to the genuine text of Genesis 10, are vv. 16 to 19 inclusive. To start with v. 19, we observe that it is a boundary description, viz., of Canaan, while, moreover, this name is taken here in a markedly different and much more narrow sense than in v. 15 (and v. 6), where it stands for the whole of the territory between the Euphrates and Egypt. The nature of the verse and its use of the name Canaan are enough to make its presence seem suspiciously strange in our Table of Nations. Perhaps both facts together warrant its definite rejection as a genuine element of the chapter, which in view of the dissimilarity between the two Canaans is more of a gain than of a loss. Elimination of v. 19 would almost certainly entail that of v. 30, where we meet a similar boundary description for the territory of a subdivision of Shem, viz., Joqtan-tribes of Arabia. Probably the case of the

16. The elimination of vv. 8–12 from the Table of Nations is, of course, not a solution of the notorious Nimrod problem. The question remains how somebody could be tempted to link up an African people (Cush) with the name of a hero (Nimrod) who in his eyes evidently belongs to Mesopotamia and the Accadian world; and further: which is the historical or mythological personality of that world hiding behind the name of Nimrod. Kraeling's suggestion deriving Nimrod from Babylonian EN-MARAD or NIN-MARAD = lord of—the city of—Marad (see his article on "The Origin and Real Name of Nimrud," 214ff.) is ingenious. But quite apart from the annexe theory on the Cushites (see above, pp. 163–64) it leaves room for doubt. It should be noticed that the "lord of Marad" is not known for having been a hunter and a founder of cities, the qualities ascribed to Nimrod by Genesis 10. If the "lord of Marad" is identical with Ninib, it must be observed that this god was the subjugator of the great Tigris but not a hunter.

two verses is completely identical, although v. 19 which lists very well known city names, deals more manifestly with a point of provincial interest, i.e., "a Palestinian affair." The contents of both verses specifying a number of boundary cities, scarcely any of which plays a part in world history, are a long way off from the grand panorama which Genesis 10 sets out to unfold, viz., the breaking ⟦167⟧ up of human unity and the fateful parting of the ways which took place after the death of Noah.

As for the paragraph preceding v. 19, it is easily seen that here, too, we are deviating into small fry, a collection of names, which moreover are implicitly contained already in Sidon and Heth and should therefore have been presented as subdivisions, not as elements on a level with them. Indeed, Sidon stands, here and in many other texts of the Old Testament, for the whole of Phoenicia (cp. Deut 3:9; Josh 13:4, 6; Judg 3:3; etc.), while in accordance with the usage of the Assyrian texts from the 9th to the 7th century B.C., not unknown also in the Old Testament itself (Josh 1:4), Heth represents the block of Aramaic principalities in Northern Syria. Furthermore, "Arkite," "Sinite," "Arvadite," "Zemarite" and "Hamathite" (vv. 17b, 18a) are indeed in outward appearance *nomina gentilicia* ⟦'names of nations'⟧, but this is hardly more than camouflage: in point of fact all these elements constitute a single geographic and ethnographic block, so that we are really dealing here once more with an enumeration of cities. It also strikes one that in this paragraph alone we meet *nomina gentilicia* in the collective singular, and as far as these five city names are concerned, this peculiarity is doubtless due to the fact that they follow after a number of tribal names (vv. 16, 17a) which everywhere else turn up in this form. Now, these tribal names—Jebusite, Amorite, Girgasite and Hivite—constitute the hard core of a cliché-list of pre-Israelite peoples of Palestine and Syria which usually includes also the Canaanites and the Hittites and sometimes also the Sidonians. By way of a tentative hypothesis, therefore, we should like to suggest the following course of events. The mention of Canaan, Sidon and Heth—we leave out of consideration, for the time being, the question of the ⟦168⟧ authenticity of v. 15 itself—has provoked the insertion of the Jebusite, Amorite, Girgasite and Hivite. These having been added, somebody has not been able to resist the temptation to lengthen still more this series of names and has done so by attaching a group of Syrian city names superficially adapted to the purpose by being put into the same form of *nomina gentilicia* in the collective singular.

More will have to be said, at a later stage, of the section of Ham with a view to simplifying the structure of the Table of Nations and reducing it to its essential features, but first let us turn now to the section of Shem, that of Japheth being too sober to admit much criticism taken by itself.

The most striking feature of the section of Shem as we now have it, is the preponderance of a single subdivision, the Joqtanides, who constitute a group of South Arabian tribes, as is evident from a sufficient number of identifiable or at least well known names (Hazarmaveth, Uzal, Sheba, Ophir, Havilah). Turning up five stages away from Shem himself, this group represents only a relatively small fraction of the "sons of Shem." In spite of this, the subdivision of Joqtan lists not less than thirteen specified elements or exactly one more than all other previously placed members of the section of Shem taken together. Is such a disproportionate preoccupation with South Arabian tribes really intelligible as a genuine characteristic of the original Table of Nations? Should we not rather explain it as an addition due to somebody particularly well informed on this outlying corner of the world or perhaps to a scholar who happened to be in possession of a list of tribes living there and thought fit to enrich our document with a dozen names from it? It has often been said that the exceptional length and detailed specification of the "sons of Shem" is ⟦169⟧ caused by the fact that in the eyes of the Israelite author of the Table of Nations this section was of overriding importance as leading straight to the people of Israel itself. However, it cannot be denied that the branch of "sons of Shem" which the Table of Nations selects for special and detailed treatment and which alone causes the exceptional length of the section of Shem, is precisely that which does not lead to Abraham and Israel. For this purpose the author should have selected instead of the line of Joqtan, the son of Eber, that of his brother Peleg. As a fact the line of Peleg is continued, outside the Table of Nations, in chapter 11, where it is shown how Abraham descends from Shem via Peleg, Eber, Salah and Arphaxad. The extensive list of Joqtanides also shows itself in a strange and, if we are not mistaken, positively suspected light, if we recall to mind that this subdivision of South Arabian tribes is linked with a main group (v. 22), all recognizable members of which have their home in Western Asia. So the Joqtanides break every sort of unity and unifying principle in the section of Shem, which can be thought of, also that of geographical coherence. We need hardly stress that the manner in which the Joqtanides are linked with the peoples of Western Asia, has nothing to do with ethnographic history: if any link of this nature ever existed between this part of the world and the Arabian peninsula, it was the fact that the latter's periodically overflowing reservoir of people provided the former with repeated fresh waves of settlers, not *vice versa*.

It remains to point out that the elimination of the long list of Joqtanides has the added advantage of doing away with the second duplication of names disfiguring the Table of Nations in its present form, so that Havilah and Sheba are met with only as "sons of Cush" (v. 7). Surely, this ⟦170⟧ must be considered an advantage, because even if the author of an ancient document of this nature is credited with a fair degree of naivete, it remains psychologically difficult to understand how he can have intercalated heedlessly the same link in two different chains. It would be difficult to admit such a strange proceeding also in the supposition that he was interlacing two pre-existent documents.[17]

It may well be that in the view of many the preceding remarks are inadequate to establish the secondary character of the list of Joqtanides, but they do suffice to warrant at least grave suspicion. To this is added that the hypothesis of the list of Joqtanides as a secondary paragraph would at the same time explain the discrepant nature of the opening verse of the section of Shem (v. 21). After the pattern of the two preceding sections, Japheth and Ham, that of Shem should really begin with v. 22: the *bĕnê-shem* ⟦'descendants of Shem'⟧ were the following. Instead of this we now have an opening verse in which among all divisions and subdivisions of Shem a single group is selected for special attention and stress is laid on its link with the common ancestor, viz., the group of Eber ("Shem is the father of the *bĕnê-ᶜeber* ⟦'descendants of Eber'⟧"); in others words, exactly that link of the chain by means of which the Joqtanides are attached to the section of Shem. This verse and that which finally brings the *bĕnê-ᶜeber* themselves on the stage (v. 25), also are the only ones using the passive form *jullad* ⟦'were born'⟧.[18] Finally, there is the fact, admittedly of limited account but not wholly ⟦171⟧ negligible, that the equivalent of v. 21 is completely lacking in the Table of Nations in the first chapter of Chronicles.

The idea alluded to above that, in order to be a harmoniously built-up and worded Table of Nations, the section of Shem should begin with the enumeration of the *bĕnê-shem* in v. 22, introduces yet another consideration. It is, indeed, fairly easy to extract from the present text of Genesis 10 a basic plan which as such would give full satisfaction because of its harmonious structure and reads as follows:

v. 1 (or 1a): general introductory formula:

vv. 2–5 { enumeration of Japheth peoples, in *bĕnê*-formulae;
closing clause of the section;

vv. 6, 7, 20 { enumeration of Ham peoples, in *bĕnê*-formulae;
closing clause of the section;

17. Viz., J and P. Of course, the point would have to be judged differently in the case of a mere juxtaposition of two documents, but this, at any rate, is out of the question here.

18. Verse 1b which has the same form, is usually considered a case by itself, not on the same level with v. 1a.

vv. 22, 23, 31 { enumeration of Shem peoples, in *běnê*-formulae; closing clause of the section;
v. 32: general final clause.

Such would be a model of a Table of Nations in the accepted, genealogical and personifying form, in which, therefore, besides all elements dealt with above there would be also no place for (1) vv. 13–14, (2) v. 24, that is to say: those elements which do not conform to the *běnê*-formula but use some form of *jalad* ⟦'begot'⟧ instead. It is true that, e.g., Jacob discerns in the alternation of *běnê* and *jalad*, especially *jullad*, a deliberate plan and the expression of a more-or-less profound intention on the part of the author: *jalad* would have been chosen wherever a descendant of the first generation had to be introduced; *jullad* would express the additional ⟦172⟧ subtle nuance of fertility, not being childless. He also says: "Von *běnê* wird zu *jalad* übergegangen, und letzteres in allen den Fällen beibehalten, wo wir uns engeren Beziehungen zu Israel und den speziellen Genesiserzählungen nähern" ⟦'The construction with *běnê* changes to the construction with *jalad*, the latter being preserved in all cases where there is a closer relationship to Israel and in the special Genesis narratives'⟧.[19] We confess that the subtle special meaning of *jullad* escapes us. Both other considerations are of a questionable nature. How, we may ask, does Jacob know that, e.g., between Mizraim on the one side and the Ludim, Anamim, etc., of v. 13 on the other, exists the relation of father and sons, where we are not in a position to identify most of the latter? Whether a close or less close relationship to Israel and to the narratives of the Book of Genesis has been a leading principle in the author's selection of names and peoples, might be studied in detail, but the statement does not at first sight carry conviction. For instance, is that relationship so much closer in the case of Nimrod (v. 8) than of Cush (v. 6)? And if the author lets himself be guided by the factor of greater or lesser importance for Israel and the Book of Genesis, why did he fail to include in his list of peoples the Ammonites, Moabites, Edomites and several others? No doubt, the people of Israel were considerably more interested in several of these tribes than in a dozen tribes of Arabia such as the Joqtanides. As a matter of fact, this particular consideration makes little sense except in the supposition—which is Jacob's—that the whole of Genesis is the result of a single, comprehensive and systematically developed literary project.

We do not go to the point of contending that these considerations—that (1) the alternation of *běnê* and *jalad*, (2) the fact that all names

19. Jacob, *Das erste Buch*, 274.

introduced by the *jalad*-formula seem to break in upon the harmonious structure of the Table of Nations, and (3) the fact that in some cases the *jalad*-formula introduces ⟦173⟧ elements which are suspect—prove the undoubtedly secondary character of all elements not included in our above model Table of Nations. There is no doubt, however, that they warrant a question-mark in every case, all the more justified, because the elimination of all parts of the text which we have endeavoured to discredit, coincides with the dissection of Genesis 10 usually arrived at on the basis of a distinction between the documentary sources J and P, as may be seen, e.g., from the synoptic columns printed in Cheyne's *Le Livre de la Genèse* (pp. 150–51).

Any reader who feels unable to share our doubts and criticisms may still agree that the suggested skeleton text represents the nucleus of the biblical Table of Nations, and consequently also agree with the proposition that the investigation into the essential contents, structure and meaning of the document should at least start with the consideration of the *bĕnê*-elements. In this spirit we shall now continue our discussion of the Table of Nations, at the same time paying attention more than before to some individual names and identifications.

Theoretically speaking it is certainly not impossible that one or other of the *bĕnê*-series included in the Table of Nations has been enriched with spurious names, once more with the possible consequence that such accretions do not fit into the author's original framework and hamper our overall interpretation of the document. Indeed, there is at least one individual name, the expulsion of which would be very welcome, if there is a good argument for it, viz., Lud in v. 22. Although in the main group of Shem, Arphaxad continues to be an enigmatic name, there is every possibility ⟦174⟧ that in some way or other it represents the region and people of South Mesopotamia, as it is preceded by Elam and Asshur and followed by Aram which as a geographical term can best be understood in the sense of Aram-Naharaim (cp. Judg 3:10; Hos 12:13). That South Mesopotamia would otherwise be absent from the Table of Nations (Babel in the Cush-Nimrod passage stands little or no chance of being authentic), is almost another argument by itself, while Schrader's suggestion that Arphaxad has to do with Chaldea (perhaps "borderland of C."; Ar. أُرْفَةٌ = boundary) may also carry some weight. Assuming this localisation of Arphaxad the main group of Shem appears to correspond more or less to what is now often called the "Fertile Crescent," a belt of territories which an Israelite author might very well have envisaged as a single unit, viz., as a circle of lands and peoples which as a chain of mountains, everyone of them far greater than Israel itself, cast their shadow from the north upon this small country. This unit would find an excellent counterpart in the section of Ham, grouping all territories below the "Fertile Crescent" which, moreover, together constitute the historic unit of the pharaonic empire. That is to say, the areas mentioned in the genealogy of Ham included Ethiopia (Cush), Egypt (Mizraim), Libya (we shall return to this identification of Phut) and Canaan (or Syria-Palestine). If the areas referred to in the Shem genealogy included a number of Arabian tribes (whether or not an authentic element of the Table of Nations) in the Fertile Crescent, or South Mesopotamia, together the two sections would comprise the Egypt of the Pharaohs. In this way already two out of the three sections of the Table of Nations would turn out to be intelligible and it would not be difficult to complete the picture by a similar idea underlying the section of the "sons of Japheth." But: the suggested interpretation of the main group of Shem is thwarted by the inclusion of Lud, a name which cannot reasonably be explained except as referring to the Lydians of Central Asia Minor, mentioned ⟦175⟧ elsewhere under the same name in a list of northern peoples (Isa 46:19). Indeed, geographically speaking, the country and the people of Lydia would, as Hölscher says, have to be ranged with the Japhethites and find its place there immediately before Javan or Ionia.[20] Chronologically the Lydians of Asia Minor are likewise rather out of place in their present position, since all other names in the main group of Shem represent lands and peoples of venerable antiquity. As far as we know, however, the history of Lydia starts only with the dynasty of the Mermnades, whose first representative was King Gyges (683–652). The American excavations at Sardis seem to have established that the site of the Lydian capital down to 900 B.C. was not even inhabited, so that a Lydian kingdom of some importance probably did not come into being until a considerably later date.[21]

Perhaps the interpretation of the main group of Shem as roughly the equivalent of the "Fertile Crescent" in the sense suggested above, coupled with that of Ham as uniting the component parts of the Egyptian empire which is the traditional anti-pole of the leading power in the "Fertile Crescent," is sufficiently attractive to eliminate the geographically and chronologically disturbing element of Lud. Personally we feel more inclined to do so, because the main group of Japheth seems likewise to contain a geographically and, though to a lesser degree, also chronologically discordant name, the elimination of which would reveal a basic idea underlying this third section such as to confirm the proposed interpretations of the other two or at any rate in perfect harmony

20. Hölscher, *Drei Erdkarten*, 51.

21. J. H. Jongkees, *Jaarbericht Ex Oriente Lux* 4, esp. pp. 234f.

with them. The name referred to is that of the Madai. It is of some importance to note that ⟦176⟧ this name stands for the Persians rather than for the Medes proper. A specific mention of the Medes with the consequent exclusion of the Persians, founders of a great empire after the Assyrians and Babylonians, would be a matter for surprise. Moreover, it is well known that contemporary authors, such as Herodotus and Thucydides, refer to the Persians by the name of Medes (Μῆδοι, μηδίζειν, etc.) and that the same practice occurs, though more incidentally, in the Old Testament itself (Isa 13:17; 21:2; Jer 51:11, 28; elsewhere "Medes and Persians" form a single unit: Esth 1:3, inter alia; cp. also Dan 8:20: the ram with two horns). Now, if the Madai of the Table of Nations really refer to the Persian empire, it should be noticed that such an element belongs to practically the same late period as the kingdom of Lydia, the latter coming to an end in the battle between its King Croesus and Cyrus the Great, the founder of Persian supremacy (546 B.C.). It is true that the late origin of Persia as a great political factor contrasts less sharply with the other members of the main group of Japheth than is the case for Lydia in the group of Shem. The first "generation" of Japhethites includes several peoples whose names repeatedly occur in the writings of the great prophets, especially Jeremiah and Ezekiel. Nevertheless, the Persian empire is of a still later date.[22] More striking and more objectionable, however, is the presence of the Persians among the "sons of Japheth" from a geographical point of view, since the region including Susa and Persepolis combines far more easily with the countries of the "Fertile Crescent" ⟦177⟧ than with the far off Japhethites, and also because beside the mention of Elam in the section of Shem there is no use for the Persians in another section, both Susa and Persepolis being situated in the region which was previously called Elam.

If, therefore, we leave aside the Madai, all well known and some less definitely identifiable names collected under the heading of Japheth suggest that this section of the Table of Nations is meant to answer the idea of a second, outer circle of peoples and territories in the north-east, north and north-west, which rounds off the horizon of the world at that time. The Table of Nations as a whole would thus reveal a distinct general plan, and it is only right to add that without any plan, whether good or bad, scientifically correct or ingenuously naive, a document of this nature could not have been produced. The basic plan of our document

22. The case would be slightly different if the Madai of the Table of Nations were exclusively the Medes, whose independent kingdom dates from about 700 B.C. But as has been said, this supposition is fairly improbable. Both Medes and Persians are, of course, mentioned as ethnic elements in Assyrian texts of the 9th century B.C.

would turn out to be a geographical grouping of names, in which ethnographically heterogeneous elements, such as Elamites and Assyrians, Cimmerians and Ionian Greeks, Canaanites and Egyptians, may stand side by side. The author's plan divides the *oikoumenè* ⟦'humankind'⟧ of his time into three superimposed blocks, each of which has its own unifying principle. Below and penetrating to the very heart of his *mappa mundi* ⟦'map of the world'⟧—is not the land of Canaan the centre of the world?—we have the section of Ham: four main territories bordering on each other and once united under the sceptre of the Pharaohs. Above this block we have the principal lands of the "Fertile Crescent," each of which is in turn a major political and threateningly expansive power, with Elam and Aram-Naharaim on the flanks, Asshur and Babel (Arphaxad) in the centre. Finally on top of this comes the still more remote outer belt of regions and peoples, which never came into very close contact with ⟦178⟧ Israel and were but vaguely known there, a belt running from the Caspian Sea and the border of the Caucasus in the north-east (Tubal, Meshech and the half-mythical Magog) via Lake Urmia[23] and the Lake of Van in Armenia (Gomer), Togarma or *Tilgarimmu* of the cuneiform tablets (now Gürün on the upper course of the river Halys) to the western extremity of Asia Minor (Javan). After this the list of Japhethites is continued still further to the west by a number of islands and peninsulas. Perhaps the first island is Tiras, mentioned already in v. 2, since this name recalls to mind the Tursha, one of the so-called Sea-peoples, or (and?) the Tyrseni or Tyrrheni turning up in Greek texts in connection with Lesbos, Imbros, Samothrace, Athos and others down to the 5th century B.C. Kittim and Rodanim (MT: Dodanim) of v. 4 are fully known as representing Cyprus and Rhodes. Elishah might be close to the shore of Asia Minor, where, e.g., Strabo knew the island of 'Ελαιουσσα, or the name may on the basis of other considerations be thought to refer to the Peloponnesus. Tarshish could in every hypothesis be reached only by sea and was far away.

Besides an intelligible general plan and a logic tripartition the foregoing considerations would also result in a striking formal unification of the types of names listed in the Table of Nations: with two exceptions of the second line, Kittim and Rodanim, all names of lands and peoples would have been treated as individual personal names without any admixture of *nomina gentilicia* on *-i* or *-im*.[24]

23. On the whole we feel more inclined to see in Ashkenaz the name of the Scythians settled near Lake Urmia than an indication of the Phrygians (advocated more recently, e.g., by Hölscher).

24. Of course, Mizraim does not belong to this category.

In our interpretation of the Table of Nations as well as ⟦179⟧ in several incidental remarks we have hitherto supposed that the name of Phut in the main group of Ham refers to Libya. As this is a point of considerable importance we shall end with a note on the problem of this name, in preference of all others which may call for further comment.

The identification of biblical Phut with Punt (*pwn.t*), the incense-bearing country of Egyptian fame, though much advertised, has, we believe, not completely satisfied anybody. Materially it is highly improbable, since according to the more common opinion of Egyptologists Punt lies below Bâb el-Mandeb (Somaliland) and this is beyond the horizon of ancient Israel. Even for Egyptian pharaohs and adventurers Punt was a daringly remote country and it may also well be asked why a distant region which Egyptians of the 18th and 19th dynasties managed to visit occasionally, should have a place in the biblical Table of Nations. Phonetically the identification of Punt and Phut is next to impossible, not only because of *n* in the former but also because of the emphatic *ṭ* in the latter against *t* in Punt which, moreover, does not belong to the root of the name but is a feminine ending.

Of course, the alternative identification of Phut with Libya does not emerge from any similarity of names. On the contrary, although we are satisfied that this view, which is first expressed by the Greek and Latin versions of the Old Testament, is practically certain, we can offer very little to explain why Phut means the same country as that which after the example of the Greeks we now call Libya.[25] It must be added that in any case Phut is but one ⟦180⟧ of the biblical names for Libya, as in a number of texts we meet the transparent name of Lub or Lubim: Dan 11:43, 2 Chr 12:3, 16; according to several authors also Ezek 30:5;[26] and finally Nah 3:9 which will have to be looked into more specially, since this text mentions the Lubim side by side with Phut.[27]

25. There is only the Coptic name ΦΑΙΑΤ mentioned by Hölscher, which according to Peyron, *Lexicon Copticum*, 266, stands for Libya (*Drei Erdkarten*, 26 and n. 1). Flavius Josephus commenting on the biblical Table of Nations informs us that Libya was founded by a certain Φούδης or Φούτης, after whom its people were called Φοῦτοι (*Ant.* 1.132). But it is doubtful whether this statement is based on anything more than the Septuagint's rendering of Puṭ by Libya in several texts (not in the Table of Nations which merely transliterates Φουδ).

26. I rather believe that in this text (v. 5b) the change of Chub into Lud (coming after Phut in v. 5a) is not to be recommended, in spite of some support which the suggestion derives from the Septuagint. Perhaps the correct reading would be *wĕkhôl bĕnê*. ⟦'and all the sons of'⟧.

27. We observe that the Lehabites of the Table of Nations (v. 13) can be left out of consideration. Against many (recently also Koehler: "probably = Lubim") we maintain not only that this identification is phonetically hazardous but also that Gen 10:13 enumerates a

Nevertheless, the interpretation of Phut in the Table of Nations as Libya is strongly supported by various arguments, first of all because after the elimination of Punt no other name representing something on a level with Cush, Mizraim and Canaan can be advanced. On the other hand, the inclusion of Libya in the Table of Nations, side by side with the three just mentioned, is most natural, not to say in the nature of things more than unexpected and out of place. We have put forth another argument for it in our general interpretation of the Table of Nations, in which Phut helps to explain the combination of the four members making up the main group of Ham. Besides these arguments taken from the Table of Nations itself others can be found elsewhere. We have mentioned before ⟦181⟧ the fact that the ancient Greek and Latin versions usually render Phut by "Libyans" (Jer 46:9; Ezek 27:10; 30:5; 38:5)[28] and the other fact that Flavius Josephus explains this by the name of the founder of Libya. The Book of *Jubilees* paraphrasing the text of Genesis 10 explicitly locates Phut west of Egypt (Mizraim), although the value of this argument is rather impaired by the location of Cush east of Egypt (9:1). Lastly, the Old Testament itself mentions on four different occasions the presence of Phutian mercenaries in foreign armies: of Egypt (Jer 46:9), of Tyre (Ezek 27:10), of Gog (Ezek 38:5) and of Nineveh (Nah 3:9). As improbable as this would sound in the supposition Phut = Punt, it is intelligible and plausible, historically speaking, for Phut to represent Libya, especially in the first case, since Libyan mercenaries are a frequently recurring theme in Egyptian texts and pictures. On the other hand the idea of troops from Punt serving in the Pharaoh's army is without any documentary support whatever and can hardly be entertained in view of the distance and the nature of that region. In Ezek 38:5 and Nah 3:9 Phutian mercenaries appear side by side with those from Cush, a quite intelligible combination if Phut is Libya.

The text of Nahum, however, is usually quoted as a decisive argument against this identification, because, as we have said before, it mentions Phut as well as the Lubim or Libyans. The conclusion would be that the two names must represent distinct ethnic elements. Clearly this argument has no conclusive force if we are dealing here certainly or even possibly with two names for the same people. ⟦182⟧ In this case Nah 3:9

---

number of otherwise unknown and manifestly unimportant ethnic elements in or near the Nile Valley. For the same reason we are not inclined to identify the Ludim of the same verse with those of v. 22 and to follow the example of Cheyne (*Le Livre de la Genèse,* 149) and some others who for this reason eliminate the Ludim of v. 13 from the text.

28. The only exceptions, besides Gen 10:6, are Isa 46:19 where the LXX has Φουδ against MT פול and Nah 3:9 to be discussed presently.

would rather provide the best possible argument in favour of the identification of Phutians and Lubim. The fact is that in the first half of Nah 3:9 we do have such a duplication of names: Cush-Mizraim. Hitherto, whenever we have replaced Cush by a more modern name, we have used the term Ethiopia. This term, however, must not be understood in its present sense (the empire of Haile Selassie) but approximately in that of the authors of classical antiquity referring to everything below Egypt as Αἰθιωπία. It should also be kept in mind that in ancient times Egypt proper ended and Cush-Ethiopia began at *Aswân*, not at *Wâdy Halfa*.[29] In spite of this clear geographical distinction, the two names are not kept strictly apart in the Old Testament which, probably as a result of the Nubian domination of the Nile Valley during the 25th dynasty (712–663), sometimes speaks of Ethiopia and Egypt almost *per modum unius* ⟦'as one entity'⟧ mentioning these names in strictest parallelism (Ps 48:32; Isa 20:3, 4, 5). In some texts Ethiopia practically stands for Egypt. Taharka, ruler of the whole of the Nile Valley and residing at Memphis, is called "King of Ethiopia" (2 Kgs 19:9; Isa 37:9). Ezekiel prophesies that "a sword shall come upon *Egypt*, and there shall be anguish in *Ethiopia*, when the slain fall in *Egypt*" (30:4; cp. also v. 9). In the same manner of speaking, "the flood of Egypt" (Amos 8:8; 9:5) or "the rivers of Egypt" (Isa 7:18) can equally well be called "the rivers of Ethiopia" (Isa 18:1; Zeph 3:10). In these and similar sentences the two names are practically interchangeable in spite of the undeniable fact (without which no poetic duplication of names is possible) that ⟦183⟧ some distinction between them is still being felt. If this applies to the two names in the first half of Nah 3:9, it is safe to say that the two names of Nah 3:9b, Phut and Lubim, cannot be interpreted as representing two adequately distinct countries or peoples as far apart as, e.g., Somaliland and Libya. Parallelism demands a relation between Phut and Lubim verging on complete coincidence.[30]

Having drawn special attention to Nah 3:9 we may add a few words on the much-discussed reading and translation of this verse. In the first place we notice that the word קֵצֶה ⟦'end'⟧ or the formula אֵין קֵצֶה ⟦'without end'⟧ when used to express the idea of "endless," "numberless," "measureless" or similar things, occurs nowhere else in the Old Testament without a following preposition לְ ⟦'to, for'⟧ and a specification of the matter which is said to be endless, etc. (cp. Isa 2:7a and b; Nah 2:10;

29. Ezek 29:10 should be read and translated: "from Migdol to Syene, to the border of Cush".

30. While it is easy to see what made possible the interchangeability and at the same time the juxtaposition and implied distinction of Mizraim and Cush, we have no such clue as regards Phut and Lubim. Possibly in this case the difference between them is merely ethnographic, while a geographic unity provides the basis of their assimilation.

3:3). As a matter of fact such a complement is in the nature of things and intrinsically indispensable. This is one reason for suggesting that in Nah 3:9b, too, the preposition ל should be inserted between אֵין קֵצֶה and פוט and that the two terms should be coupled together, reading therefore לְפוט. In the second place there is the fact that the Greek version of Nah 3:9 is manifestly based on a Hebrew reading of this nature, since it renders ואֵין קֵצֶה פוט by καὶ οὐκ ἔστιν πέρας τῆς φυγῆς ⟦'and there is no end of phuge'⟧. And not only that, but the Greek text unmistakably supposes a Hebrew reading with ל, as φυγή is but the Greek rendering of Hebrew פֶּלֶט or פַּלֵט = flight. In other words, the translation originates from ⟦184⟧ the consonants פ, ל, ט which make up לְפוט except that the first two (ל, פ) have been taken in inverse order, either through the translator's or more probably a Hebrew copyist's mistake.[31] Restoring ל to its proper place we obtain for Nah 3:9 a text made up of two perfect parallel *stichoi*, either of which includes two names treated as synonyms, and a translation which reads:

> Ethiopia and Egypt were thy (?) strength,
> Phutians were numberless and Lubim thy helpers.

Or perhaps better:

> Ethiopia and Egypt were thy (?) strength,
> Phutians and Lubim without number were thy helpers.

As can be seen from the place of the *athnach*, the equilibrium of the second line has been upset at any early date, but the corruption of the text still betrays itself by the asyndetic beginning of what is now the second half of 9b. The וְ of וְאֵין should be transferred to before (לְ)פוט.

31. Hölscher (*Drei Erdkarten*, 27 n. 7) also expresses a vague suspicion of this course of events ("plt?"), though without making any effort at a further explanation.

Genesis 10: Some Archaeological Considerations

D. J. WISEMAN

⟦14⟧ The so-called "Table of Nations" in Genesis 10 has long roused the interest of students in various branches of scholarship. There has been a general tendency among Old Testament scholars who, consciously or otherwise, follow Dillmann and Driver in considering the chapter "an attempt to show how the Hebrews supposed they were related through their 'eponymous ancestor' Shem to the other principal nations." Since the names mentioned are not considered as real individuals the list is interpreted as having a primitive ethnological arrangement and as neither a scientific classification of the races of mankind nor an historically true account of their origins which it places about 2500 B.C. The chapter is thought to conform to a geographical knowledge current through trade about the seventh century B.C., by which time a number of the place names are referred to by Jeremiah, Ezekiel and in Assyrian inscriptions. Exponents of this school of thought, following their view of its late composition, are forced to draw attention to seeming omissions in the lists (e.g. Moab, Ammon, China, India). There are, of course, many variations on this view expressed by individual scholars to some of which I shall refer. Professor Albright has recently opted for about 1000 B.C. as the date of composition, but his reasons are, so far as I know, as yet unpublished. The ⟦15⟧ place and general purpose of this chapter within Genesis are more generally agreed. The Hebrew historian gives us sufficient introduction in the brief compass of Genesis 1–9 in which

Reprinted with permission from *Faith and Thought* 87 (1955) 14–24.

he narrows the focus from the universe to the Flood, and in the small space of chapters 10–11 covers the long period from the Flood to Abraham. In accordance with his practice the author condenses large periods of history by the use of historical lists (*toledoth*). The text of Genesis 10 is in little doubt since we have a duplicate with few but important variations in 1 Chr 1:4–23.

The Arrangement of the List

The list is divided according to the sons of Noah—Shem, Ham and Japhet—and as such continues the genealogies from Gen 5:32, but thereafter (v. 2), in accordance with the method observed in Genesis, it notes first those branches not so intimately concerned with the narrative and thus leads to the line which is the subject of the subsequent history, i.e., the order is Japhet, Ham and Shem, Ham perhaps being considered closer to Shem through Cush, Mizraim and Canaan. The main divisions of the table are clear: (1) the descendants of Japhet (vv. 2–5); (2) the descendants of Ham (vv. 6–20); and (3) the descendants of Shem (vv. 21–31). Each of these divisions ends with a descriptive "catch-phrase" (vv. 5, 20, 31) which is reminiscent of the colophon, a literary device typical of Babylonian and Assyrian literature. The purpose of a colophon is to summarize the preceding narrative and form a link with subsequent texts which bear the same or a similar ascription and which were originally recorded on separate documents. A comparison of these phrases, together with the final colophon or sentence added after the three separate lists have been brought together (v. 32), reveals the intent of their compiler. The omission of these verses in 1 Chronicles 1 supports this view that they are not part of, but comments on, the lists. For the phrase, "These are the sons of Japhet," expected in v. 5 (which some scholars would insert on the assumption of textual corruption by comparison with vv. 20, 31), we read, "From these separated off the islands and coastlands of the nations" (so *goyim* is to be translated elsewhere in this chapter; cf. v. 32). This might be a reference to additional territory, such as the European coastlands of Greece which were populated from Asia Minor. The term *meʾelleh* ("from these") can be interpreted only as a separation from the main (parent) body (cf. Gen 2:10; 25:23; Judg 4:11). For the moment it is sufficient to notice that the *common* catch-phrase begins after the purpose and content of each list with the words "in/with their land" and "with/in their nations" (each is governed by the preposition *beth*); and "with reference to their language (tongue)" and "with reference to their family relationship" (each expression being governed by the preposition *lamedh*). In each colophon the order of these terms varies and may be significant in showing the emphasis placed on each in the list. [[16]] Each has in common the feature that they end with the term "in their nations"; that is, the lists include within each branch units which have national affiliations. The list of sons of Japhet would, according to this view, emphasize the territorial or geographical ("with their lands") and the linguistic ("with their tongues") more than family relationships. Those of Ham and Shem deal more with tribal relationships and languages than with geographical relationships. In these it will be observed that the statements giving geographical detail (vv. 10–12, 19, 30) are introduced as explanations or expansions of the genealogical elements in the list. Whether or not this be the true explanation of the formation of these lists it cannot be denied that these "colophons" correctly state that each list contains elements of geography, linguistics and physical affinities. All these are essentially combined in any appreciation of "ethnology" according to ancient Near Eastern thought. Failure to appreciate the mixed nature of these documents has sometimes led to unwarranted criticism. To follow a merely geographical division (i.e., the sons of Japhet as the northern races, Ham as the southern and Shem as the central) requires some of the facts to be ignored, e.g., southern tribes such as the sons of Joktan are listed under Shem. Nor can they be simply linguistic groupings; e.g. Elamite (v. 22) so far as it can be traced is a non-Semitic language. Moreover all attempts to trace existing languages back to these three parent groups have failed and in most cases the earliest texts found in the area are pictographic and therefore there is no certainty to which group they may belong. The confusion of tongues has been further complicated by borrowings and other influences which, combined with insufficient historical data for many languages, make it at present impossible to formulate more than theories on this difficult subject. The most common views of this chapter are that it is either an early "ethnological" or late geographical survey. There is, however, little evidence given here to aid the study of physical anthropology. Too little is known of the racial types in the limited areas here mentioned for any continuous picture to be drawn. There is therefore a tendency to rely for "anthropological conclusions" on such linguistic evidence as can be recovered, but since this is scanty the chapter is seldom mentioned in modern works. It could be argued that the terms for "families" (*mishpahoth*) may not be used in early Biblical Hebrew to denote a physical relationship so much as a group of persons who are *subordinate.* Compare the only other word probably from the same root, *shiphhah,* used of a maidservant or one in an inferior position (Gen 16:1; 2 Kgs 4:2, etc). The word is used somewhat loosely for "clan" or any national subdivision, whether Hebrew or not, or even of animals. Since the etymology and range of this word are still uncertain, too much weight cannot be put upon this but it may point to inter-group relations other than physical and perhaps the result of influence or conquest is covered in this chapter—e.g., Semitic domination ⟦17⟧ of non-Semitic Elam (v. 22). Early ancient Near Eastern texts (especially Babylonian) frequently use the terms of family relation to denote merely political relations between nations; "brother" being freely used for allies or equals, "father" by a dependent of a more powerful nation and "children" in the case of a major nation of its dependents. This does not apply, of course, to each case in Genesis 10, but should evoke caution in interpreting possible ethnological connections dogmatically.

A further caution seems to be needed since some investigators object to the use of personal names to denote either a nation or place. A study of Near Eastern city names shows that many are named after their individual founder, whether he be thought of as a god or a mortal. Larger territories usually take their name from the principal city, or from the name given to the most numerous or powerful group of inhabitants, who themselves are often called after a prominent ancestor or leader. There can therefore be no objection on these grounds, to nations or places in chapter 10 being named as "sons" or to the seeming interplay of individuals, places and generic terms. I personally believe that the tradition of these relationships, where they are listed in the genealogical manner ("begat"), goes back to initial physical relationship, e.g., that the founder of the tribe of Seba was a person of that name, son of Cush, and that his name was retained to describe the line of his descendants, each of whom had his individual name. In the only *direct* reference to cities they are said to have been *built* or their geographical location is precisely given (vv. 10–12, 19–30). In all other places undoubted city names are used only as gentilic, i.e., to denote their inhabitants (e.g., vv. 16–18). The only such conclusion, then, from a survey of the arrangement of the list is that it contains both geographical, linguistic and ethnographical data. An appreciation, if not a verbal expression, of this fact has guided most investigators to analyze the list *seriatim.* Few have, however, followed H. Rawlinson's comprehensive work *The Origin of Nations* (1877) in trying to bring together data on individual references.

The Line of Japhet

In a comprehensive survey of the first list enumerating the sons of Japhet, E. Dhorme (*Les Peuples issus de Japhet,* 1932) shows that "the Bible groups under Japhet all those neighbours of Phoenicia, N. Syria and E. Mesopotamia who were non-Semitic in physiognomy, language and custom." He argues that the descendants of Yawan (Ionians) spread from Cyprus to Rhodes and Tartessos, while the sons of Gomer (Cimmerians) spread northward, colonizing Scythia, where they later met with the Tibarenians (Tubal) and Mushki (Meshek). The Medes, also linked with Japhet, joined up with Persia and the Eastern countries. On the sea borders Tiras (the Etruscans) were pirates until later they settled on the Tyrrhenian coast.

⟦18⟧In general, recent archaeological discoveries, and especially the inscriptions found, support the view that the Japhetic list covers the northeastern Mediterranean–Anatolian region. The Cimmerians (Gomer) and Scyths (I/Ashguzai–Ashkenaz)[1] first appear as settlers in Eastern Anatolia, having crossed the Caucasus some time before the eighth century to infiltrate into Urarṭu (Armenia) but, since they do not move into the "Fertile Crescent" until the next century, no early direct reference is necessary or is made to them by the Assyrian or Hebrew historians (Ezek 38:1–2, 6). Similarly the Medes do not rise to world power until the sixth century but this does not mean that they were not known earlier as an Aryan group inhabiting the Lake Van area. Shalmaneser III (859–824 B.C.) mentions them with Parsua (later Persians) in a way that implies that they are the normal (old) inhabitants of the area. It has been common to deny the existence of Ionians before the eighth century B.C. but there now seem to be undoubted references to them as *ymʾn* in the Ras Shamra texts (thirteenth century B.C.). Tubal or Tabal, east of Cilicia, was annexed to Assyria in 837/836 B.C. and is probably the same as the Hittite Tipal and the earlier Tibar district through which Naram-Sin passed *c.* 2200 B.C. The neighbouring area of Meshek (*Mushki*) was already well known to Assyrian writers in the time of Tiglath-pileser I (*c.* 1116–1090 B.C.). Tiras was linked with the sea peoples by the Egyptians at least by *c.* 1220 B.C., since it is mentioned in a stela of Menephtah (*tw-rw-šʾ*) and men named *ty-w-rʾ-s* of the sea are depicted in Anatolian headdress among the captives of Rameses III (1198–1167 B.C.). There seems every reason then to agree with Dhorme's identification of Tiras with the Etruscans.

The next generation is represented by the sons of Gomer. As already mentioned, the Ashguzai (Ashkenaz) are linked with the Cimmerian (Gomer) influx of peoples into Eastern Anatolia. Riphath remains unknown although identified by some with Bithynia or Paphlagonia. The form of the name would agree with a location near the Black Sea and relate him with the early Cimmerians, Scythians and thus with Tubal and Meshek. Togarmah has been the subject of a number of theories, the

1. L. Piotrovicz, *L'invasion des Scythes*, 477.

most reasonable being an equation with Tagarama in the Carchemish district of the Upper Euphrates mentioned by the Hittite king Mursilis II in the fourteenth century B.C.

The grandsons of Japhet by Yawan are listed as Elisha (Alashia), a name for Cyprus which is frequently found in cuneiform documents in the eighteenth century B.C. (e.g., at Alalakh) and which is linked with *ymʾn* in the Ras Shamra texts. Recent excavations at Enkomi-Alassia in Cyprus show that *c.* 1200 B.C. the "Mycenaean" group there was displaced by a non-Semitic people who are believed to be the Philistines en route for Palestine. Tarshish can be variously identified with sites on the southern coast of Asia Minor, Sardinia and Spain where there is evidence ⟦19⟧ for a Tartessos (the name may mean something like "iron-works"). Recent interpretations show that a "ship of Tarshish" carried metal ore and that the name Tarshish is to be found at a number of Near Eastern mining centres. It would seem therefore that one of these Anatolian sites (even Tarsus?) may be referred to here. Similarly Kittim denotes similar coastal areas East of Rhodes (Rodanim, 1 Chr 1:7; so Samaritan and Septuagint read for Dodanim in Gen 10:4). If we then take the sentence, "from these were the islands of the nations separated off," it would imply that the more westerly Greek mainland and islands were later peopled from the Anatolian mainland, which accords with such little evidence as we yet have for the complex question of the origin of the Greeks.

The Sons of Ham

There is now general agreement over the location of the countries founded or taking their name from the sons of Ham—Cush (Nubia–Ethiopia), Mizraim (Upper and Lower Egypt), Phut (Libya) and Canaan. Despite ingenious attempts, made in a previous paper on this subject to the Victoria Institute,[2] archaeology does not furnish evidence that the Hamites are "ethnically Semites" who spring from the area of Kish (near Babylon). Nor does Ham designate in a general way the native stock in Babylonia and Arabia. A study of Near Eastern civilizations shows that the earliest traces in Egypt are of a non-Semitic people probably directly influenced, and even founded, by the non-Semitic Sumerians of Babylon and that it was a similar people who were the first inhabitants of Canaan. Verse 7 groups the sons of Cush who are to be identified with South Arabian tribes (and places) on both sides of the Southern Red Sea area across which there is now known to have been an early and

2. G. R. Gair, "The Places and Peoples of the Early Hebrew World," *Journal of Transactions of Victoria Institute* 68 (1936).

active sea traffic. That the peoples of this area were correctly considered as a mixture of both Hamitic and Semitic folks is acknowledged by the repetition of some names (e.g., Havilah on the African coast) also under Eber (Semitic nomads). In these areas which were later overrun by Semites there still survive elements in the language and customs which are "Hamitic." The Hebrews themselves imply that Babylonia, Aram, Hittites and Canaan influenced the development of their language.[3] Finds such as early pottery, seals and statuary known to be "Sumerian" have been found in each of the areas listed under Ham.

The list of Hamites goes into more detail when the Babylonians and Assyrians are mentioned, for they were to play an important part in Hebrew history. The method of presentation now differs perhaps because the narrative is more expanded. The early civilization of Mesopotamia is ⟦20⟧ described first as the kingdom of Babylon belonging to Nimrod. The cities of his kingdom are significantly Babylon, Erech (Warka) and Agade. These, with Eridu and Ur, are some of the earliest cities in which civilization began and whose earliest occupations are in part known to us. Babylon was so extensively reconstructed by Nebuchadrezzar in the seventh century that our knowledge of its beginnings rests upon early documents found in other cities. It had previously been the centre of power under Hammurabi (1792–1750 B.C.) and even earlier was the seat of the worship of the sun-god. Erech (Warka) has been excavated by the Germans (1936–1939, 1954), who have unearthed there examples of the earliest writing, pottery and other arts which have led to the levels being styled "Early Dynastic" or "Early Literate" period (dated *c.* 3000 B.C.). The earliest finds at Djemdat Nasr near Babylon are somewhat later and in turn are followed by those at Eridu near the Persian Gulf. A theory once propounded that Erech, written Unuk or Urug in Sumerian, might be the first city mentioned in the Bible, founded by and named after Enoch, and that Irad, Enoch's son, might be the founder of Eridu, may be correct (Gen 4:17–18). We know of early Agade only from early texts but by the time of its hero king Sargon (*c.* 2300 B.C.) it was the military centre of the whole of Mesopotamia. Calneh has been considered as (1) an old name for Nippur (another Early Dynastic site); (2) a site in the Habur region identified with the Sangara district, i.e., Shinar (Isa 10:9); while (3) a large majority of Hebraists, perhaps influenced by these uncertain identifications, now interpret it as "all of them" (*kullanah*) and thus find a term to include the many other early settlements otherwise unmentioned! Others argue that Shinar stands for the Southern Babylonian plain. This is by no means certainly proved, though likely if "in the

3. E.g., G. R. Driver, *Problems of the Hebrew Verbal System,* 151.

land of Shinar" qualifies all the cities and not just Calneh. "From that land (referring to Shinar) went forth Asshur" (v. 11), whose name, as belonging to a god, was given both to the land of Assyria and to the oldest city in it. Ninevah and Calah (modern Nimrud) near Mosul have been excavated and soundings or observations at the lowest (earliest) levels show the presence of remains (e.g., Ninevite pottery) which can be dated back to the Djemdet Nasr period, that is soon after the founding of Erech.

Excavation at other Assyrian sites shows that civilization, as early brought here, has close affinities with the southern kingdom (e.g., Obeid pottery). Rehoboth, "city square," and Resen (Ras Ain?) have led to varied explanations—the most probable, despite its seeming fantasy and ingenuity, being that made by G. Dossin.[4] He thinks that while translating these early lists from Sumerian into a Semitic language a scribe has merely translated some of the rarer names. *Rehoboth-ᶜir* he interprets as the equivalent of ASH-UR since ASH is Sumerian for the *ribatu*, "square," and UR equals *uru*, "city." By this means Assur, the ⟦21⟧ earliest known Assyrian city, is to be found in our lists. Resen he finds to be an early name for Assur also. By a similar early transposition of languages he finds Babylon in Arpachshad (v. 22). We shall return to this question in discussing the occurrence of Asshur in the list of Shem's sons. Important to an understanding of the Hamitic list is the certainty resulting from archaeological discoveries that the earliest inhabitants and languages of both Babylonia and Assyria were, contrary to popular belief, non-Semitic. The civilization before 2600 B.C. in both is "Sumerian" and the racial types found are not true Semitic. There is a direct cultural link between Assyria, Babylonia and Egypt which extended to their polytheistic religious ideas. Sidney Smith believes the Assyrians originated among the western nomads in the Habur region which was noted for its hunting and which he, with others, believes to be the Shinar of Genesis 10. At this point it may be worthy of note that Lutz suggests that Nimrod may be the Hamitic god Nergal, whose Egyptian name means "the mighty hunter." After briefly listing a number of non-Semitic groups which include the Ludim (also mentioned under Shem), and Caphtor (Crete?) and other non-Semitic sea-coast dwellers in the Nile Delta, the Hamitic list gives details of Canaan.

The pre-dispersion area of Canaan is correctly given as from Gaza and Gerar to Sidon. The eastern border being marked by Sodom and Gomorrah, this section at least must pre-date the destruction of these two cities in the early Patriarchal period (1900–1700 B.C.), for no archaizing

4. *Muséon.*

reference would make sense to a later reader. The omission here of Tyre must also point to a date earlier than its founding in the thirteenth century, for thereafter until the sixth century it was a powerful factor in Palestinian history. Excavations at Ras Shamra (Ugarit) and neighboring Alalakh show that the population of Syria was largely Hurrian (Horite) in the same period and spoke that language, which is non-Semitic and akin to those known to us from the countries listed under Japhet. Canaan is referred to in these cuneiform texts as an area roughly corresponding to Gen 10:19. A further mixture of races in later Canaan resulted from Arameans penetrating southwards probably almost in the time of Abraham; but, as subsequent Hebrew history clearly shows, the native (Hamitic) population was never completely extinguished. By the thirteenth century this Semitic influence was markedly increased, and is soon reflected in the Hebrew history after the Exodus; but of this the present description of Canaan makes no mention, being therefore probably much earlier. Of the eleven groups of inhabitants mentioned as descendants of Canaan, five ⟦sic⟧ are known from early texts or excavations (Sidon, Jebus, Amurru, and Hamath) while the remainder are known only from the Old Testament narrative. As with the sons of Japhet, archaeology, so far as it has revealed evidence, corresponds with the Genesis 10 list and, as the colophon in v. 20 implies, shows that the list contains both ⟦22⟧ geographical, linguistic and ethnographical data which are to the ancient mind inseparable if not indistinguishable.

The Descendants of Shem

The list of Shem's issue contains difficulties apart from obscurities in identification (e.g., Arpachshad, Lud). So far as we know, Elam was originally a non-Semitic people. The groups entitled Aram and Eber, the nomads west of the Euphrates in what was later called *mat ebiru* ("the land across [west of] the River"), were always, according to our present discoveries, Semitic in language and racial type. Similarly the sons of Joktan, insofar as they are identifiable, are Semitic tribes inhabiting Southern Arabia, the Hadramaut (an area described in v. 30), and across the Red Sea, where they lived alongside peoples of Hamitic extraction. The only difference among the sons of Eber was probably between those who were semi-nomadic and cultivated irrigated land (*palgu–Peleg*) and the pure nomads (Eber). Asshur as son of Shem may denote the Semitic element which moved north to overspread the Sumerian civilization already established there by descendants of Ham under a leader of the same name. If this is so the capital city of Asshur itself may one day be found to be of Semitic origin (though present discoveries do not support this) and all theories which seek to find its name in the Ham list are unnecessary. Since, however, Elam like early Asshur is of non-Semitic foundation most scholars have been led to view this list as purely geographical ("the central group"). This tenet cannot be sustained, since places or peoples in the same general area have been already listed under Ham, e.g., the cities of Babylonia and Assyria (east of Aram and west of Elam, vv. 10–12), and Lud also has been included in that same genealogy. Another prevalent opinion is that the list includes those nations or areas which were early dominated by Semites, but if this were the case one would expect, for example, the inclusion of Canaan and the exclusion of Elam which never totally succumbed. The simplest solution is to believe that Semites early penetrated Elam even though they were later not the dominant racial and linguistic group, whereas in "Hamitic" Assyria (and Babylonia=Arpachshad?) they later inherited the Sumerian culture. From *c.* 2000 B.C. onwards the whole of the "Fertile Crescent" from the Persian Gulf to Canaan became semitized. Although a few centuries later there were incursions by the Kassites (of the same stock as non-Semitic Elam) and by the Hittites (Indo-Aryans from the area of Japhet) these were temporary dominations only. All this would fit in with the general picture given us in this chapter of Semites occupying a limited area at first. This area was, at the time the list was compiled, wider than Shinar which seems to be the initial home of the "Sumerian" group. Before the time of the confusion of tongues (Gen 11:2), the Sumerians seem to have moved there from the East (the Iranian plateau).

⟦23⟧The above survey accords with evidence which, if increased by future archaeological research, may eventually show that the three dominant language-groups in the ancient Near East were the Semitic, Hamitic (Sumer-Egypt), and the Japhetic (Indo-Aryan), typified by Hurrian and Hittite.

The Geographical Horizon of the Early Hebrews

The general, if confusing, picture we have gathered from a survey of these three groups of peoples of the earliest Near East can be a little clarified by examining the potential and actual knowledge of geography possessed by the inhabitants.

The predominant features of Sumerian civilization is that men dwelt in large walled cities. Archaeological investigation has produced no proof for a gradual evolution from village to town and then city. This means that they were industrialists and exported their varied wares, while importing other things necessary for their economy. Thus we find

Sargon of Agade in *c.* 2300 B.C. on long expeditions into Asia Minor seeking for valuable raw materials. His successors Naram-Sin and Gudea of Lagash have also left us detailed records of similar journeys to collect metals, wood and stone from the areas how identified as Anatolia and Syria. In even earlier periods the results of trade between these earliest inhabitants of Babylonia can be traced in India (Mohenjo-Daro and Harappa) and in Egypt. One of the earliest Sumerians, Enmerkar, has left us the detailed text of his complex business relations with the land of Aratta, bordering on the Iranian plain. The literary evidence for this early trade is supported by the discovery of archaic Sumerian type vessels near Asterabad (N. Persia) while even farther off in Anau (Turkestan) figures, models, vases, copper work, seals and beads of the same period attest Sumerian trade or influence. Similarly in the West even the jewelry of Early Crete speaks of some contact with Ur and Kish, and other goods of this epoch have found their way to the Aegean Islands, the Anatolian coasts and even as far as Macedonia. Well before the Agade dynasty there is literary evidence of the merchant colonists from Mesopotamia working at Kanish in Cappadocia. With an increasing number of cuneiform texts we can now follow in some detail the numerous journeys taken by messengers or caravans in the 19th–17th centuries between Egypt–Canaan–Anatolia–Assyria–Babylonia and Elam. One detailed tablet published by Professor A. Goetze in 1953 gives the daily stages travelled by a merchant (*c.* 1750 B.C.) from Larsa (near Erech) via Assur, Nineveh and up into Anatolia as far as Kanish (less than 150 miles from the Black Sea) before returning via the Euphrates and Habur river routes. The diary nature of this document could well be compared with the detailed entries of Moses' itineraries in Numbers and Deuteronomy. Texts from Ur in the same period give details of a sea trade mainly in ivory, gems and spices ⟦24⟧ between that city and Dilmun (Bahrain) and other places on the Arabian coast (Ophir). They travelled to India itself if we can judge by the seals, ivories and other objects found at Ur. It will be obvious from these references, which could be multiplied, that before *c.* 2000–1800 B.C. the flow of trade, and therefore of merchants and their supporting caravans and military expeditions, is abundantly attested by contemporary documents and implies a knowledge of the very area outlined in Genesis 10. It would not be unreasonable to assume that the information in this chapter could therefore be known to Abraham himself.

Similar evidence from Egyptian archaeology shows how in Early Dynastic times that country colonized Byblos in Syria and boats from the Delta anchored in Cycladic ports. Their land trade-routes stretched towards Nubia (Cush), the Red Sea coasts and along the North African coast beyond the Libya (whence Crete [Caphtor] was founded), as far as

Spain. Soon after the end of the Old Empire (*c.* 2400 B.C.) there were expeditions into Sinai (Pepi II) doubtless to exploit its mineral deposits, and Nubia was colonized. Contacts with, and knowledge of, Asia via Syria would be strengthened by the coming of the Asiatic Hyksos *c.* 1730 B.C. About this time the early Indo-Aryan Hurrians are also found established in North Syria and as far east as the Tigris. A few found their way to Egypt. Thus contact with the east, in addition to a known steady liaison with Babylonia, was established. It is certain from the Tell El-Amarna tablets that Pharaoh's court in 1483–1380 B.C. was receiving letters and reports from allies in and near their newly conquered Asiatic lands, the Mitanni, Babylon and Elam, and would in this way have a wide and detailed geographical knowledge. Even before this the Egyptian painters distinguished the various races (including Negroids). Since, however, we know that the spread of civilization in Africa (as in Europe and across Inner Asia) did not come until later it is not surprising that Genesis 10 should be silent on these points. It may well be that, even if information of the early beginnings of these distant peoples had reached the highly-developed centres of civilization in the ancient Near East, the compiler who brought the three lists together, adding his own note in v. 32 sought to confine attention to the so-called "white" races. It is becoming increasingly clear that the geographical information in Genesis 10 could have been available to the Egyptian court when Moses received his education there in the fifteenth or fourteenth century B.C.

The Name of Babylon

I. J. Gelb

⟦1⟧ It is generally assumed that the Greek name Babylōn for the well-known capital city of Babylonia, as well as the Biblical Bābel, Arabic Bābil, Egyptian BBR, are all derived from some such Akkadian form as *Bāb-il(im)* "Gate of God," or *Bāb-ilān(i)* "Gate of Gods."[1] Some scholars claim, moreover, that the Akkadian form is a direct translation of Sumerian *Ka-dingirra*,[2] which, too, means "Gate of God."

While no objections can be raised against the translations of the Akkadian and Sumerian forms—as they are quite obvious—we must question at once the derivation by translation of the Akkadian form *Bāb-ilim* from a Sumerian *Ka-dingirra*, since parallels to it are lacking in the entire field of Sumero-Akkadian geographic nomenclature. We may quote dozens of Mesopotamian geographic names, such as Ur, Uruk, Eridu, Nippur, Larsa, Lagaš, Sippar, Kiš, Hursag-kalamma, Šuruppak, Adab, Isin, Akkad, Gudua, Barsip, Dilbat, Marad, Akšak, Išnun, Aššur, Ninua, and nowhere shall we find a case of an old Sumerian name replaced by a name translated into Akkadian.

Before we shall try to give a new interpretation of the origin of the nature of Babylon we should go over the oldest sources referring to this city.

Reprinted with permission from the *Journal of the Institute of Asian Studies* 1 (1955) 1–4. ⟦Publisher's note: misplacement and misnumbering of the footnotes in the original publication, beginning at note 11, has been corrected in this reprint.⟧

1. F. Delitzsch, *Wo lag das Paradies?* (Leipzig, 1881) 212f.; F. Hommel, *Ethnologie und Geographie des alten Orients* (Munchen, 1926) 298, 307; A. Baumstark in Pauly-Wissowa, *Real-Encyclopadie der classischen Altertumswissenschaft* IV (1896) 2667ff.; O. Schroeder in Eber's *Reallexikon der Vorgeschichte* I (1924) 308; E. Unger in *Reallexikon der Assyriologie* I (1932) 333f.; R. Campbell Thompson in *The Cambridge Ancient History* I (1928) 503ff.

2. Cf. Baumstark and Unger quoted in note 1.

The oldest occurrence of Babylon is found in a date of Šar-kali-šarrī (about 2224–2199 B.C.), referring to the laying of the foundations of the temple of Anunītum and Aba in KĀ-DINGIR KI.[3]

⟦2⟧ The economic sources of the 3rd Dynasty of Ur (about 2100 B.C.) are full of references to a city spelled uniformly, as in the preceding Sargonic period, KÀ-DINGIRKI.[4] Three cases, reading *ki* PA.TE.SI KA-DINGIR-*ma*^{KI}-*ta* "from the ensi of Babylon,"[5] *bal* PA.TE.SI KÀ-DINGIR^{KI}-*ma* "the tenure of office of ensi of Babylon,"[6] and *kas* PA.TE.SI KÀ-DINGIR^{KI}-*ma* "the beer of the ensi of Babylon"[7] are important since they show clearly that KÀ-DINGIR stands for a form ending in *-m*. This form can hardly be anything else than Akkadian *Bāb-ilim*.

Besides the three clear cases with the phonetic indicator *-ma*, indicating the pronunciation *Bāb-ilim*, there are two or three doubtful cases with the phonetic indicator *-ra*. They are KÁ-DINGIR.RA-šè[8] and KÁ-DINGIR-*ta*[9] or KÀ-DINGIR.RA.[10] Since the 22 cases quoted in n. 4 occur regularly with the determinative KI one may wonder whether the sign(s) RA/TA in the examples above are not due to a miscopy. But even if they are right they do not indicate the pronunciation *Ka-dingirra* but should be interpreted as part of the logogram to be read in Akkadian, of the type found in Sargon LUGAL KALAM.MA^{KI} = Sargon *šar mātim* (*Publications of the Babylonian Section* V 34 ii, iii, vii, etc.), DINGIR-TI.LA and *Su*-TI.LA (*Harvard Semitic Series* X, pp. xxxvii and xxxiii), *I-LI*-TAB-BA (*ibid.*, p. xxxiii), and TE.NA-DINGIR=*Paluh-ilim* (all discussed in my *Old Akkadian Writing and Grammar*, p. 28).

Once it is established that the oldest form of Babylon attested in the written sources is Akkadian *Bāb-ilim* and not Sumerian *Ka-dingirra*, we may go into the problem of whether the form *Bāb-ilim* is actually the oldest form of the name of this city.

Here we may pose the following question: How does such a name as *Bāb-ilim* with the meaning "Gate of God" fit into the general nomenclature of ancient Mesopotamia?

Firstly, we must note that Akkadian geographic names are quite rare in the ancient sources and that they do not begin to appear ⟦3⟧ in larger numbers until after the period of the 3rd Dynasty of Ur. Secondly,

3. Thureau-Dangin, *Die sumerischen und akkadischen Königsinschriften* 225.

4. *Textes cunéiformes du Louvre* II 4679; 5491; 5482 iv; V 6041 ii; *Yale Oriental Series* IV 65; etc. (altogether 22 times), always with the determinative KI.

5. *Yale Oriental Series* IV, 66 rev.

6. *Ibid.*, No. 74.

7. Chiera, *Selected Temple Accounts* . . . 3 ii.

8. *Analecta Oriental*⟦ia⟧ VII 157 rev; *Mémoires de* 12 *Délégation en Perse* X 121.

9. *Analecta Orientalia* VII 162.

10. As corrected (or miscorrected?) *ibid.* 49.

composed as they are with such elements as *āl-* "city," "settlement"; *bīt-* "house," "estate"; *dimat-* "district"; *dūr-* "fortress"; *maškan-* "threshing ground"; *uṣar-* "court" (or the like); the Akkadian geographic names fit perfectly into general onomastics as we have it represented in various areas of the Near East.

Such a name as *Bāb-ilim* "Gate of God," does not fit into our knowledge of ancient oriental onomastics, and consequently we must raise doubts as to whether *Bāb-ilim* actually represents the oldest form of this city. It may be argued with some force that the name *Bāb-ilim* represents a secondary form due to popular etymology of some pre-Akkadian and pre-Semitic form. For this earlier name I would suggest the form *Bābil* attested 15 times in the following Ur III texts:

1. ŠÁ TIR Ba-bil-la[11]
2. TIR Ba-bil-la[12]
3. NI.DUB A.ŠAG$_4$ GIŠ.TIR Ba-bil-la[13]
4. So much ŠE Ba-zi GIŠ.TIR Ba-bil-la[14]
5. ŠÀ GIŠ.TIR Ba! (wr. UR)-bil-la^{KI} [15]
6. "Au bosquet de Ba-bil-la^{KI} " [16]
7. "Compte de laine des [moutons] due patési, provenant du ka-si GIŠ-tir Ba-bil-la-ki" [17]
8. "Compte de peaux de moutons, de šú-dul, de lú (gunu) al-zi-ra: brulé? ba-giš-gi (bi)l au bosquet de Ba-bil-(ki)" [18]
9. So many GURUŠ from TIR Ba-bil^{KI} among workers from Nina^{KI}, Til-sir-ra^{KI}, Gir-su^{KI}, PAP+E.ZAG.(HA^{KI}), Hu-ku-bu-BÌ.(RU)^{KI}, and Ki-éš^{KI}.[19] ⟦4⟧
10. ŠÀ GIŠ.TIR Ba-bil-la^{KI} [20]
11. ŠÀ GIŠ.TIR Ba-bil-la[21]

11. *Cuneiform Texts* III 17, No. 14597 rev.
12. *Ibid.* VII 14 i.
13. *Ibid.* IX 39 ii.
14. *Harvard Semitic Series* IV 23 rev. i.
15. *Inventaire des tablettes de Tello* III 5344 rev.
16. *Ibid.* IV 86, No. 8017, transliterated only.
17. *Ibid.* V 56, No. 9865, transliterated only.
18. *Ibid.* V 62, No. 9986, transliterated only. This may not be a geographic name, cf. *ibid.* Pl. 42, No. 6949 and *Zeitschrift für Assyriologie* XII 261, No. 4.
19. *Ibid.* V Pl. 53, No. 9258 i, evidently identical with *ibid.* V, No. 9441.
20. *Ibid.* V 6943 rev.
21. Barton, *Haverford Library Collection* I Pl. 44, No. 206.

12. ÈA-dam-dun TIR Ba-bil-la[22]
13–14. NI DUB TIR Ba-bil-la-ta[23]
15. Hired slave-girls TIR Ba-bil^{KI}[24]

The attested forms *tir Babilla* and *tir Babil* can mean nothing else than "the forest of Babil," as actually translated by the scholars in the examples quoted above (Nos. 6, 8, 12). For that reason the reading *giš*-TIR-*bil-laki* (No. 10) and the comparison with German "Neuwald,"[25] based on insufficient evidence, have to be corrected in accordance with other parallel texts.

Since six of the texts listed above (Nos. 5–10) were excavated in the ancient site of Lagaš, since the month names found in the texts[26] represent the calendar of Lagaš, which means that the texts may be presumed to come indirectly from that city, and since the forest of Babil occurs in No. 9 in company with such well-known sites in the area of Lagaš as Nina and Girsu, we can draw the conclusion that the forest of Babil is situated in the area of the Sumerian city Lagaš.

In conclusion, we may say that the existence of the forest of Babil in the area of Lagaš presupposes the existence of the element *babil* which was used for several geographic names in Sumer. That element, whatever its meaning and ultimate origin, may have lain at the basis of the name of the city, which through a process of popular etymology appears as *Bāb-ilim* in the earliest extant written sources. Such secondary formations are not uncommon in ancient times. Suffice it to mention here the Ur III names of the Assyrian city *Urbilum, Arbilum,* which appears later as *Arba-il(u)* "Four-gods" (= modern Erbīl), and of the Assyrian city *Ninua* "Nineveh," which is written in later periods as if the name were identical with that of the old Sumerian city of *Nina* "the Fish-City."

22. Nies, *Ur Dynasty Tablets* 58 v interpreted by Nies 52 as "temple of the new grove at Adamdun."

23. Pinches, *The Babylonian Tablets of the Berens Collection* Nos. 31 and 32.

24. *Revue d'assyriologie* X 65, No. 106.

25. L. Oppenheim, *Catalogue . . . of the Wilberforce Eames Babylonian Collection* 107f.

26. SU.NUMUN (No. 3), EZEN.LI, SI_x (No. 11) = EZEN.$^{d}LI_9.SI_x$ (No. 14), and GUD.DU.NE.SAR.SAR (No. 13).

In Search of Nimrod

E. A. Speiser

⟦32*⟧ The figure of Nimrod has claimed attention almost from the moment that a reference to this hero's exploits strayed into Genesis 10. "The mighty hunter before the Lord" has himself been the object of ceaseless chase. Greek, rabbinical and Islamic sources echo the pursuit of this elusive target.[1] Modern scholarship has taken up the task with redoubled vigor. Yet the prey remains at large.

The ancient attempts to run down Nimrod may not quite range from A to Z, but they do happen to include Amraphel as well as Zoroaster. It is the moderns, however, who really have roamed far and wide in their efforts to explain the hero and his name. Among the diverse suggestions that have been offered, we find gods (Marduk,[2] Ninurta[3]), demigods (Gilgamesh,[4] Lugalbanda[5]), as well as sundry mortals (Amenophis III/*Nimmuria*,[6] Ben-Hadad/*Bir-adda*).[7] Syria, Egypt, and even Libya,[8] aside

Reprinted with permission from *Eretz-Israel* 5 (1958) 32*–36*; this article was also previously reprinted in *Oriental and Biblical Studies: Collected Writings of E. A. Speiser* (ed. J. J. Finkelstein and M. Greenberg; Philadelphia: University of Pennsylvania Press, 1967) 41–52.

1. For the rabbinical and Greek references cf. the extensive material cited in Louis Ginzberg's *Legends of the Jews* V, 199ff.

2. First proposed by Josef Grivel, *TSBA* 3 (1874), 136ff.; cf. also J. Wellhausen, *Die Composition des Hexateuchs*, 309f., and T. G. Pinches, *Scribner's Dictionary of the Bible* III, 552f.

3. P. Jensen and A. Ungnad, cf. *OLZ* 20, 359, n. 2.

4. Based on the older reading of the name as Izdubar; cf. George Smith, *TSBA* 1, 205, and Paul Haupt, *Das Nimrodepos.*

5. Presupposing an assumed *Nu/En-marad-da*; cf. A. Deimel, *Orientalia* 26 (1927), 76ff., and E. G. Kraeling, *AJSL* 38 (1922), 214ff.

6. For this suggestion by Kurt Sethe cf. G. von Rad, *Das erste Buch Moses*, 122.

7. T. K. Cheyne, *Encyclopaedia Biblica*, col. 3417–19.

8. Eduard Meyer, *Israeliten und ihre Nachbarstämme*, 1906, 448.

from Mesopotamia, are among the lands that have been asked to give asylum to Nimrod's prototype. It can be seen at a glance that the participants in these academic sweepstakes comprise some of the most distinguished authorities on the ancient Near East to appear in the past seventy years, not to mention contemporary orientalists.

The first step in a constructive review of the problem should be to reduce the area of search by discarding leads that have proved or can be proved to be false. Gilgamesh and Lugalbanda, e.g., were adduced on faulty onomastic grounds. And the African entries—even though they may carry the endorsement of such illustrious men as Eduard Meyer and Kurt Sethe—lean heavily on the erroneous notion that biblical Cush, here listed as Nimrod's father, always refers to Ethiopia. It is now well known that this name is ambiguous, in that it may point either to the Upper Nile valley or to Mesopotamia. In the latter usage the name corresponds to Akk. *Kaššû* (*Nuzi Kušš-*),[9] Greek *Kossaîoi* (Kassites/Cossaeans).[10]

All assumptions, moreover, of an extra-Mesopotamian origin of Nimrod have another serious fault in common. They are predicated on the outright rejection of the entire traditional account, including the specific details which it contains. ⟦33*⟧ Yet to dismiss, say, the geographic content of the Nimrod passage as so much aetiology or popular fancy is to persist in the kind of scepticism that modern discoveries have confounded time and again. In the instance before us there is sufficient internal evidence to stamp the physical background of the story as authentic. For in so far as they can be identified at all, the cities assigned to Nimrod bear out the author's knowledge of his setting: each was a prominent Mesopotamian centre, and each served as a major capital at one time or another. This is true of Ashshur,[11] Calah, and Nineveh in Assyria, and is equally true of Babylon, Erech, and Akkad[12] "in the land

9. It is wholly immaterial in this connection whether the Nuzi form is based on an eponymous deity or not; cf. K. Balkan, *Die Sprache der Kassiten*, 1954 (*AOS* 37), 109. That this form is wholly independent of the name of the Hurrian moon-god *Kušuḫ* follows conclusively from the nature of the underlying sibilants (cf. my *Introduction to Hurrian*, 34 and contrast Balkan, 31f.). The ethnicon is written with *-šš-/s*, whereas the deity is characterized by *š-/z* (single writing). The important thing is that the Nuzi form reflects an *u*-vowel, as does bibl. *kuš*.

10. For an inescapable reference to the land of the Kassites, see Gen 2:13.

11. Although the syntax is ambiguous at this point, the text surely cannot have intended to exclude Ashshur as a city. If Gen 10:11 is interpreted by many to mean "From that land he [Nimrod] went forth to Ashshur and built Nineveh" etc., nothing further needs to be done. Since stylistic requirements, however, favour the rendering "went forth Ashshur," the alternative would be to assume an ellipsis and understand the clause to mean "he went forth and built Ashshur."

12. Albright's proposal, improving on a suggestion by A. Poebel, to read *kullānā* for *kalnē* and render "all of them" (*JNES* 3 [1944], 254f.) is so plausible that it has been widely acclaimed

of Shinar" (Sumer). Now a source familiar with these facts, a source aware of the transient glories of Calah or Uruk or Akkad, would scarcely have credited the building and control of these places to an Amenophis who reigned long before Calah was founded and never even got close to Babylonia or Assyria. Here, in short, is no spurious display of ill-assorted information. What we have instead is a literary piece sketched against a solid backdrop of history and geography. The home of this tale is Mesopotamia. The same must hold true also of its hero and his name.

The Nimrod account, then—Gen 10:8–12—should not be condemned without a fair trial. An unprejudiced approach to it promises worthwhile dividends. For instance, we know that the hero of our all too brief tale was active throughout the length and breadth of the land. Yet his activities were strictly mundane, no matter how heroic their scope. Nimrod's domain embraced both Assyria and Babylonia. His prowess as a hunter was to become proverbial. These are, to be sure, extraordinary achievements, but they are not of themselves supernatural. In other words, although of heroic stature, Nimrod was not a divine being. Accordingly, it should have been apparent from the start, even without benefit of linguistics, that Nimrod was not to be confused with Marduk. By the same token, however, there is likewise no warrant for equating the hero with Ninurta, for all that the latter was the god of the chase as well as of war, and bore a name that agrees with Nimrod. For if the biblical account has any value at all, Nimrod was clearly a mortal.

Similarly, a re-evaluation of the biblical tale is capable of yielding valid chronological limits which could then be tested independently. The lower terminus is necessarily the date of the actual passage itself. Now it so happens that this particular portion of the Table of Nations is assigned by the critics, with virtual unanimity, to the "J" source. On this basis, therefore, the Nimrod passage cannot be later than the turn of the tenth century B.C.E. The upper terminus, on the other hand, is provided by the mention of Calah, this being the latest known city listed in this connection. According to a statement in the annals of Ashurnasirpal II (iii, 132), Calah was founded by a Shalmaneser. Theoretically this could refer to one of two of Ashurnasirpal's ancestors by that name: either Shalmaneser II (ca. 1028–1017),[13] or Shalmaneser I (ca. 1272–1243). The younger of these, however, was a shadowy figure whose brief reign was not distinguished for any notable enterprise, whereas his older

by most subsequent commentators; contrast, however, A. S. Yahuda, *JBL* 65, 325f. There is scarcely room for a freak like *Calneh in such company as Babylon, Uruk, and Akkad.

13. The dates of Middle Assyrian rulers are still subject to minor adjustments. For the sake of convenience I have adopted the absolute dates given by E. Weidner in *AfO* 15, 101.

namesake had proved to be an outstanding ruler in every way. It is not surprising, therefore, that the founding of Calah is generally ascribed to Shalmaneser I. On this basis the date of Nimrod has to be placed in the first half of the thirteenth century at the earliest.

Accordingly, if there is a kernel of truth behind the legend of Nimrod, his historical prototype should fulfill the following conditions. His ⟦34*⟧ date must fall somewhere between the thirteenth and the eleventh centuries. He must have been a famous king whose domain included Babylonia but centered about Assyria; for the fact should not be overlooked that to an eighth-century Judean the land of Nimrod was synonymous with Assyria (Mic 5:5). The name of this Mesopotamian, moreover, should have some tangible relation to that of Nimrod. Above all, the man himself must have had in him the stuff of which legends are made.

Given this set of prerequisites, we do not have far to look for the solution of the problem. There is but one Assyrian king who meets every one of these requirements. Indeed, all of them seem to be made to order for him, and him alone. He is known to history as Tukulti-Ninurta I.

The high point of Tukulti-Ninurta's long and eventful reign (ca. 1246–1206) was unquestionably his conquest of Babylon. The Kassite ruler of this great traditional centre was carried off to Ashshur, as was also the statue of the national god Marduk. The victor could now add to his other titles that of "King of Sumer and Akkad." It was the first time in history that an Assyrian held sway over all of Babylonia. Such an achievement was not to be repeated until five centuries later, under Tiglath-Pileser III. Small wonder, therefore, that these two awesome milestones came to loom large in the minds of Mesopotamians and were highlighted as late as Hellenistic times.[14] But the desecration by Tukulti-Ninurta of the venerated temple of Marduk was bound to shock religious sensibilities throughout the conqueror's realm. This may well have been the reason for the brooding restlessness that marked the latter half of Tukulti-Ninurta's career. The king sought relief in feverish building activity, mostly in his capital city of Ashshur, but also elsewhere, and specifically in Nineveh. Eventually he built himself a new capital a short distance from tradition-ridden Ashshur. And it was within the shining walls of Kār-Tukulti-Ninurta, soon to become a ghost city, that the builder met his death, hemmed in by rebel forces under the command of his own son.[15]

Here, then, was a forceful and independent ruler, resolute and ruthless, enormously successful, yet obviously a prey to dark impulses—in

14. See below, n. 31.

15. Cf. E. F. Weidner, *AfO* 13, 109f.; W. von Soden, *Herrscher im alten Orient*, 1954, 68ff.

many ways a prototype of Israel's Saul. That he could inspire fierce loyalty as well as implacable hatred is proved by an epic, obviously the work of a contemporary poet, describing in an exalted style and with rich imagery the events that led up to the fratricidal war with Babylon. This epic has no close parallel in all the literature of Mesopotamia.[16] Its nearest analogues have to be sought among the poetic works of the Bible. If Tukulti-Ninurta's life was sufficient inspiration for such a composition, his tragic death could only enhance his standing with posterity and help to superimpose legend upon history.

It should now be immediately apparent how well the slim data about Nimrod fit into the much richer background of Tukulti-Ninurta. In both instances we are confronted with famous rulers whose authority extended over the whole of Mesopotamia. The biblical fragment, incidentally, gains in import as soon as v. 10 is given the only possible logical rendering of "The mainstays (*rēšīt*)[17] of his kingdom were Babylon and Erech and Akkad, all these being (*wᵉkullānā*)[18] in the land of Shinar." Any heir to these three ancient dynastic centres would indeed by "King of Sumer and Akkad." Let us recall further that Ashshur and Nineveh are cities in which building works of Tukulti-Ninurta have been directly attested, while Calah was founded by that same king's father and was, moreover, a city holy to Ninurta, the king's protective deity.[19] Lastly, the Cushitic connections of Nimrod which the biblical account reflects gain a measure of support from the fact that Tukulti-Ninurta reigned within the Kassite ⟦35*⟧ period and crowned his political career with a victory over a Kassite ruler.

The one important feature of the Nimrod story for which there is no counterpart in the known records of Tukulti-Ninurta is the celebrated hunting motif. But the extant material cannot be expected to be exhaustive.[20] Besides, the Assyrian's very name carries of itself a plausible reason for the hunting element in the story. The god Ninurta, of course, was himself a famous hunter and patron of hunters; it is to him that Tiglath-Pileser I gives credit for his own prodigious hunting feats (Prism iii, 57). And it is on this very count, as much as on linguistic grounds, that schol-

16. E. Ebeling, *MAOG* 12/2; cf. v. Soden, *op. cit.*, 69ff. [Add now W. G. Lambert, *AfO* 18 (1957), 38ff.]

17. See already v. Rad, *loc. cit.*, 122. That the Heb. term can mean "choicest" as well as "first" is, of course, independently attested. But the "beginning of his kingdom" results in an incoherent context whereas the "main/best parts of his kingdom" (cf., e.g., Deut 33:21; Jer 49:35) is immediately intelligible.

18. See above, note 12.

19. Cf. H. Lewy, *JNES* 11 (1952), 267.

20. Cf., however, note 34.

ars have equated Nimrod with Ninurta, even though this comparison can scarcely be regarded as feasible any longer.

In passing, it may be of interest to point out that the Nimrod fragment in Genesis has been described independently as a survival of what had once been a full-bodied epic tale.[21] Now literary treatments of historical personalities will often overdraw the exotic at the expense of the familiar, or substitute the fictional for the factual. The various legends about Sargon and Naramsin are ample indication of such tendencies.[22] In any case, there are more ways than one to account for the hunting motif in Nimrod.

There remains, finally, the problem of the name *Nimrod* as against *Tukulti-*^{d}*Ninurta.* Herein lies probably the crux of the whole question, i.e., the reason why this particular comparison has not been pressed to date. The answer may not be apparent at first glance. Nevertheless, it is neither complex nor far-fetched. What is more, it leads to a substantial amount of further evidence which bids fair, in turn, to clinch the identification that has here been advocated.

When one deals with proper names, one sometimes tends to forget that long forms tend to be replaced by shorter ones, especially when they are used familiarly or have been transplanted from their native soil. To stay within the biblical and Akkadian fields,[23] I need call attention only to *Baladan* (*blʾdn*),[24] the name of Merodach-Baladan's father (2 Kgs 20:12; Isa 39:1), and *Belteshazzar* (*bltšʾṣr*), the Babylonian name of Daniel (Dan 1:7, etc.). There can be little doubt that these are abbreviated forms, the initial element—in these instances Nabû, Marduk, Nergal, Bēl, or the like—having been sloughed off (cf. esp. Dan 4:5). The process may have taken place on foreign soil, but it could likewise have happened at home; cf. *Aḫa-iddin*: ^{d}*Nergal-aḫa-iddin* or *Šuma-iddin*: ^{d}*Marduk-šuma-iddin*, *Bēl-aḫḫē*: ^{d}*Ninurta-bēl-aḫḫīšu*, and many others.[25] In these particular examples the dropped initial element happens to be the divine component. But in such examples as: *Āmur-rabūt-Adad*: *Rabūt-Sin* or *Ṭāb-šār-*^{d}*Šamaš*: *Šār-Aššur* the theophorous part has been left intact. In *Itti-Ea-balāṭum*: *Itti-Ea*, the

21. See U. Cassuto, *From Noah to Abraham*, 2nd ed. 1953 (in Hebrew), 136ff.

22. Cf. H. G. Güterbock, Die historische Tradition, *ZA* 42, 24ff.; E. A. Speiser, in *The Idea of History in The Ancient Near East*, 1955 (*AOS* 38), 54ff.

23. I may be permitted, however, one outside example because it is both instructive and unfamiliar. In the Italo-American dialect heard on the Atlantic Seaboard, the name *Atlantic City* often becomes *Niksi'ri*, which is easily explained as soon as it is realized that the starting point is not the full name but the abbreviated form "(*Atlan*) *nik-City*' ".

24. As a matter of fact, all that the native sources tell us about Marduk-apla-iddina (II) is that he was *mār Yakina*, i.e., either son or descendant of one *Yakinu*; cf. R. P. Dougherty, *YOR* 19, 44ff.

25. Cf. J. J. Stamm, *Die Akkadische Namengebung*, 1939, 111ff.

final part has been given up.[26] If there is any single principle behind these abbreviations, it would seem to be that the shortened form should be self-sufficient: *Baladan* (*aplam-iddina*) still makes sense as "he has granted a son"; but **Āmur-rabūt* "I beheld the majesty of" could not survive independently, which is why the shortened form had to dispense with the verb and not the divine element, thus becoming *Rabūt-Sin* "the majesty of Sin."

The full name *Tukulti-ᵈNinurta* is obviously a mouthful. If it was to be simplified, the element to be dropped was *tukulti*, since "the trust of" is a homeless form by itself. The result would thus have to be *Ninurta* alone. Such residual forms of personal names are not common, to be ⟦36*⟧ sure, in Mesopotamian records, yet they do occur; cf., e.g., *Marduku* and *Aššur* as names of persons.[27] In foreign use, however, any original hesitancy to misapply divine names in this fashion would readily disappear. In other words, *Tukulti-ᵈNinurta* would give way to Ninurta > Nimrod.[28]

The suggestion just advanced is not completely speculative. For as a matter of fact, Tukulti-Ninurta I found his way into one known literary tradition in a similarly abbreviated form. I refer to the *Ninus* of the Greek sources. That this is a literary figure is immediately apparent from the many fabulous achievements for which he has been given credit. His composite character, moreover, has recently been brought out by H. Lewy,[29] who has also shown that there is no sound basis for regarding Ninus simply as the eponymous hero of Nineveh.[30] But to restrict Ninus to some of the features of Šhamshi-Adad V and Sennacherib alone—as Dr. Lewy has done—is to stress only a part of the story, and a secondary part at that. Berossos, whose competence as a historian has been vindicated time and again, implies that Ninus was the first Assyrian to rule Babylonia, and that his reign was separated from that of Phul (*Pūlu*/Tiglath-Pileser III) by the reigns of 45 Babylonian kings.[31] In other words, the original Ninus could be none other than Tukulti-Ninurta I.[32] Diodorus Siculus hints at much the same thing by stressing

26. *Ibid.*, 116.

27. *Ibid.*, 117, n. 3.

28. The Heb. form *Tiglath-pileser* for Tukulti-apal-ešarra III does not refute the above contention since it is found in historical accounts (2 Kgs 15:29; 16:7, 9) whereas *Nimrod* came in through literary channels. Yet even the great bearer of that royal name found it expedient—although for political reasons, to be sure—to assume the much simpler name of *Pūlu* in his capacity as king of Babylon. Did the sound of the middle element—*apal*—contribute in any way to the choice of the otherwise unrelated *Pūlu*?

29. *JNES* 11 (1952), 264–70.

30. *Ibid.*, 270.

31. See P. Schnabel, *Berossos*, 267 (39a)—the identity of Ninus being vouched for in this instance by the mention of Semiramis—and cf. *ibid.*, 151f. See also F. Cornelius, *AfO* 17, 295.

32. Cornelius, *loc. cit.*; cf. v. Soden, *Herrscher*, 69.

that Ninus' first campaign was directed against Babylonia;[33] for this was likewise Tukulti-Ninurta's most fateful achievement, clearly recorded in the historical works of Assyria and Babylonia and commemorated, besides, in a unique Assyrian epic. It should be noted in this connection that Ninus was also renowned for his encounters with the lion and leopard.[34] Accordingly, the Greek form of the name cannot simply be traced back to Nineveh, a city whose connection with Tukulti-Ninurta was no more than incidental. The source of *Ninus* has to be the name of his Assyrian prototype, or some element thereof, hence its divine component *Ninurta.* The association with Nineveh would be a secondary embellishment. All in all, the Greek sources would seem to have arrived at their Ninus by the same process that gave the Bible its Nimrod, both being based on a hypochoristic form of Tukulti-Ninurta.

We have, then, before us two distinct legendary figures, each descended from the same historical personality. The evidence would appear to be compelling enough as it is. But there is still a further link, one which assumes added interest and importance in the light of the foregoing discussion. Ninus and Nimrod are no strangers to each other. Various ancient sources connect the two directly.[35] The most noteworthy of these is Berossos, who is quoted as stating explicitly that "the Assyrians identify this Ninus with Nimrod."[36] If there was a loophole in the chain of evidence adduced thus far,[37] this last link should close it very effectively.

33. Cf. H. Lewy, *JNES* 11 (1952), 298.

34. See the comment and references in Layard, *Nineveh and Its Remains* II, 431f.

35. Cf. Ginzberg, *Legends of the Jews* V, 201f. Note, moreover, the material in Layard, *op. cit.*, 222f.

36. Apollonius, *Fragmenta,* 59; Layard, *loc. cit.*

37. No special significance attaches, of course, to the fact that the site of ancient Calah bears the modern name of *Nimrud,* since other Mesopotamian sites are similarly linked with the same vivid hero. Nevertheless, all such occurrences add up to an impressive reminder that the appeal of Nimrod carried over undiminished into Islamic times, especially in the land which tradition has steadfastly maintained as his home.

The "Babel of Tongues": A Sumerian Version

SAMUEL NOAH KRAMER

[[108]] In his memorable contribution to biblical cuneiform research, the Anchor Bible *Genesis*, E. A. Speiser analyses with characteristic acumen, learning, and skill the Mesopotamian background of the "Tower of Babel" narrative, and comes to the conclusion that it "had a demonstrable source in cuneiform literature" (pp. 74–76). This paper will help to corroborate and confirm Speiser's conclusion by bringing to light a new parallel to one of the essential motifs in the "Tower of Babel" theme—the confusion of tongues.

Oxford's Ashmolean Museum still has in its tablet collection thirty-odd unpublished cuneiform tablets and fragments dating from the early post-Sumerian period inscribed with Sumerian literary works, some of which were no doubt composed during the Third Dynasty of Ur.[1] The majority of the pieces come from the Anglo-American excavations in Kish (1923–1932); the remainder form part of the Weld-Blundell collection purchased from antiquity dealers.[2] All are now being copied by the Oxford cuneiformist, Oliver Gurney, and will be published in due course with an introduction by the writer.

Some ten of the Ashmolean tablets and fragments are inscribed with hitherto unknown compositions.[3] The rest are of considerable importance

Reprinted with permission from *Journal of the American Oriental Society* 88 (1968) 108–11.

1. For the dating of the Sumerian literary material, cf., e.g., Falkenstein, *SAHG* 11ff.; Kramer, *The Sumerians* 168ff., and Hallo, *JAOS* 83:167ff.

2. The texts from both sources have been published primarily in the *OECT* volumes.

3. Among the more noteworthy of these are (1) a collection of four letters: the first is from a king to one of his officials; the second is a letter to the god Utu from some important individual in Larsa, depicting the bitter suffering of the city at the hands of Elam, Subir, and the Su-people, and pleading for deliverance; the third is a letter to Rim-Sin lamenting the destruction of Larsa; the fourth is a letter probably addressed to the goddess

for the restoration of broken parts of compositions long known.[4] One of these is a fragmentary tablet of 27 lines, copied by Gurney, that helps to restore a "Golden Age" passage known in part for the past quarter century, and provides us with a Sumerian version of the "Babel of tongues" motif.[5] This passage consisted of 20 lines, but ⟦109⟧ only the first 14 lines were well preserved, and those read as follows ⟦a copy of the tablet is found on p. 110 of the original article, but is not reproduced here⟧:[6]

139. Once upon a time there was no snake, there was no scorpion,
There was no hyena, there was no lion,
There was no wild(?)[7] dog, no wolf,
There was no fear, no terror,
140. Man had no rival.
In those days, the lands Šubur (and) Hamazi,
Harmony-tongued(?) Sumer, the great land of the decrees of princeship,
Uri, the land having all that is appropriate(?),
The land Martu, resting in security,
145. The whole universe, the people in unison(?),
To Enlil in one tongue. . . .

Ninisinna, pleading for the welfare of Larsa and its king Sinidinnam; (2) a hymnal prayer to Ninisinna for Larsa and Sinidinnam; (3) a collection of prayers for Iddin-Dagan addressed to the gods Ninisinna, An, Enlil, and Ninlil (in that order; by far the longest is the prayer to Ninisinna), each ending in the obscure phrase a-mu-zu (cf. *UET* VI[1] 93–94 for a collection of prayers for Šulgi that end in the same phrase).

4. Among these are: (1) Three school-practice letters of the type described in *UET* VI[2] 3–4 (comment to Nos. 173–183); (2) a tablet inscribed with lines 65–119 of the "Lamentation over Sumer and Ur" (cf. for the present *UET* VI[2] 1 comment to Nos. 124–134); (3) a four-column tablet inscribed with the Nidaba hymn published in *OECT* I plates 36–39 (cf. *SAHG* No. 7 and *BiOr* 11: 172); (4) the lower half of a rather poorly preserved four column tablet inscribed with the "Instructions of Šuruppak" (cf. for the present *UET* VI[2] 3, comment to Nos. 169–171).

5. This passage is part of the epic tale "Enmerkar and the Lord of Aratta" that I published in 1952 as a University Museum Monograph. The poem is concerned with a struggle for power between the Sumerian hero Enmerkar, and an unnamed ruler of the as yet unidentified city-state Aratta, situated somewhere in Iran. The "Golden Age" passage is part of an address to the en of Aratta designed to persuade him to let himself become a vassal of Enmerkar, and to have his subjects bring down gold, silver, and semi-precious stones in order to build for him sundry shrines and temples, and especially the Abzu-temple of Enki's city, Eridu.

6. The line numbering is that of the "Enmerkar and the Lord of Aratta" monograph.

7. More literally, perhaps, "the princely dog," or perhaps even "the Sumerian dog" (as contrasted with ur-nim "the Elamite dog"); for ur-SÈ = ur-gi.(r) cf. now Gordon in *JCS* 12: 72ff. and Falkenstein in *ZA* 57: 81, comment to line 23.

Then a-da[8] the lord, a-da the prince, a-da the king,
Enki a-da the lord, a-da the prince, a-da the king,
a-da the lord, a-da the prince,[9] a-da the king. . . .

The meaning of the first eleven lines of this passage was quite clear; they portrayed those happy golden days of long ago when man, free from fear and want, lived in a world of peace and prosperity, and when all the peoples of the universe, as represented by Šubur-Hamazi, Sumer, Uri (the later Akkad), the Martu, worshipped the same god, the leading deity of the Sumerian pantheon, Enlil. To be sure, the verb in line 146 was missing, but it was not unreasonable to surmise that it was something like "gave promise" or "spoke." However, this line contained the phrase "in one tongue" that was tantalizingly ambiguous; it could be taken literally, in which case the meaning would be that all the peoples of the universe spoke the same language, or it could be regarded as a figurative expression for unanimity, that is, all mankind was "of one heart" in acknowledging the supremacy of Enlil. Moreover lines 147–149 that concerned Enki, the Sumerian god of wisdom, were left hanging in mid-air, altogether unintelligible in the context, since the remainder of the passage was largely destroyed.

All this is now cleared up by the Ashmolean tablet[10] that provides us with the missing verb in line 146—it turns out to be "spoke" rather than "gave praise" as I had surmised[11]—and fills in virtually all of lines 150–155, so that the second part of the "Golden Age" passage (lines 147–155) can now be meaningfully translated as follows:

8. This enigmatic word was translated (with some qualms) by "father" in the monograph, that is as if a-da stood for ad-da. But as has been pointed out to me verbally by several scholars, this rendering is quite unjustified and it is preferable to leave it untranslated for the present.

9. The Ashmolean text has the variant -e for NE in this line, which indicates that en-NE is to be read en-ne and nun-NE is to be read nun-ne; that is, the two complexes consist of a noun followed by the subject elements -e (in a-da-lugal-la, where the final -a is presumably for -àm, there is no subject element since -àm cannot be followed by a grammatical element). Note, however, that the combination of a final n and the subject element is regularly written with the sign NI rather than NE.

10. The indications are that this was an exercise tablet written by a student who was not yet overly proficient in the scribal art. Thus, for example, in line 4 (= line 139 of the Enmerkar monograph) he writes ŠUL for the expected SU in the complex su-zi-zi-i; in line 5 he writes ZU for SU in gaba šu-gar; in line 6 he writes ZU-bir$_4$ for su-bir$_4$. In all these cases there is a bare possibility that some dialectal phonetic or orthographic variant is involved, but certainly nothing but carelessness and incompetence is involved in the writing of NA for KI following ZU-bir$_4$ (line 6), or KI for NA in nam-nun-na(!)-ka (line 7) or U for KUR in kur(!)-me-te-gál-la (line 8), or KI for NA in gi$_6$-ù-na(!)-ka (line 26).

11. The verb is ḫé-en-na-da-ab-dug$_4$ (the nuance intended here by the infix -da- remains uncertain for the present).

147. Then a-da the lord, a-da the prince, a-da the king ⟦p. 110 is here omitted⟧
Enki ⟦111⟧ a-da the lord, a-da the prince, a-da the king,
a-da the lord, a-da the prince, a-da the king,
150. Enki, the lord of abundance, (whose) commands are trustworthy,
The lord of wisdom, who understands the land,
The leader of the gods,
Endowed with wisdom, the l[ord] of Eridu,
Changed the speech in their mouths, [brought(?)] contention into it,
Into the speech of man that (until then) had been one.[12]

Our new piece, therefore, puts it beyond all doubt that the Sumerians believed that there was a time when all mankind spoke one and the same language, and that it was Enki, the Sumerian god of wisdom, who confounded their speech. The reason for this fateful deed is not stated in the text; it may well have been inspired by Enki's jealousy of Enlil and the universal sway over mankind that he enjoyed.[13]

Turning now to Gen 11:1–9, the first verse reads (in Speiser's translation): "The whole world had the same language and the same words," that is the Hebrew redactors of the Bible, like the Sumero-Akkadian

12. The Sumerian for these lines can now be restored to read:

147. u$_4$-ba a-da-en a-da-nun a-da-lugal-la
^{d}en-ki a-da-en a-da-nun a-da-lugal-la
a-da-en-e a-da-nun-e a-da-lugal-la
150. ^{d}en-ki en-ḫé-gál-la-[du]g$_4$-ga-zi
en-geštug-ga ig[i-g]ál-kalam-ma-ke$_4$
mas-su-dingir-re-e-ne-ke$_4$
geštug-ge-pà-da e[n]-eridu^{ki}-ga-ke$_4$
ka-ba eme ì-kúr en-na mi-ni-in- . . .
eme-nam-lú-lu$_6$ aš ì-me-[a]

To be noted is the following: For the obscure a-da (lines 147–150), cf. note 8. For the variant -e (for -ne) in line 149, cf. note 9. In line 150, text C (plate XIV of the Enmerkar monograph) has only one dug$_4$. In line 151, the restoration igi-gál was suggested by Hallo. In line 164, the crucial en-na has nothing to do with the en-na that is usually rendered "as long as"; it is the en-na which is found as a parallel to nu-še-(ga) in line 131 of the Enḫeduanna hymnal prayer (cf. *UET* VI^2 10–11, comment to Nos. 107–110; a definitive edition of the text prepared by Hallo and van Dijk is soon to appear as a publication of the Yale University Press), and in line 17 of the reverse of *BE* XXIX No. 4. Finally, the new text makes it clear that there was one line too many in the restored text on p. 14 of the Enmerkar monograph, that is, there are only 5 lines between lines 150 and the line there numbered as 156, but which is actually 155.

13. For the assumed rivalry between Enki and Enlil, cf. my comment in *Aspects du Contact Sumero-Akkadian* 276 and note 22. Note, too, that in the Išme-Dagan hymn *TRS* XV 9 line 7, the initial complex ^{d}en-ki-^{d}en-ki parallels the initial ^{d}a-nun-na-ke$_4$-ne of the

mythographers, believed that there was a time when all men spoke the same tongue. Moreover, to judge from the second verse: "As men migrated from the east they came upon a valley in the land of Shinar and settled there," they were of the opinion that the inhabitants of Sumer, (or Sumer-Akkad)[14] originally spoke one and the same language, a view which no doubt goes back to cuneiform literary sources. On the other hand the Biblical explanation of the confusion of tongues that interprets the sky-reaching ziggurat as a product of man's deep-rooted hybris and as a threat to the gods, is quite different from our Sumerian version, and is undoubtedly a product of the Hebrew religious imagination and moralistic temperament.[15] Even so, the central motif was probably the same in both versions, that is, the "confounding" of tongues came about as the result of rivalry, except that in the Sumerian case this was between god and god, and in the Hebrew, between god and man.[16]

---

preceding line; it is not unlikely, therefore, that ^{d}en-ki-^{d}en-ki stands for the *Igigû* (usually written nun-gal-e-ne). If so, we may surmise that in the time of Išme-Dagan there was current a myth revolving about a struggle between the Enki-gods (that is, the *Igigû*) and the An-gods (that is the *Anunnakû*, who are specifically stated to be the children of An) in which the *Igigû* were victorious. This might explain why in later days, the *Igigû* were at times considered as the heaven-gods while the *Anunnakû* (or at least some of them) became Nether-World gods. For different views and for the difficulties, complexities, and ambiguities involved in the *Anunnakû-Igigû* problem, cf. von Soden, *CRRA* XI 102–111; and Falkenstein and Kienast in *Studies in Honor of Benno Landsberger*, 127–158.

14. For the etymology of Shinar, cf. Poebel, *AJSL* 48: 26.

15. The Biblical story-teller was no doubt inspired to invent his moralistic explanation by the two-fold aspect of the Babylonian ziggurat: (a) the high-rise, sky-reaching appearance of the structure in its prime, that could be interpreted as a threat to the gods and their power, and (b) its melancholy and pathetic appearance when in a state of disrepair and collapse (which was not infrequent), that could be viewed as a punishment by the angered gods (or Jahweh) for man's over-reaching ambition. The Mesopotamian, on the other hand, far from viewing the ziggurat as an outgrowth of man's rivalry with, and antagonism to, the gods, actually deemed it to be a bond between heaven and earth, man and god, and attributed its ruin and decay to the inscrutable will of the gods and their incontestable decisions.

16. A tiny fragment in the University Museum very recently identified provides the missing last signs of line 154 as -gar-ra (presumably for -gar-ra-àm); the rendering "brought" should read "set up."

Part 2

Literary and Linguistic Approaches

Theme in Genesis 1–11

D. J. A. Clines

The Nature of "Theme"

[[483]] Most recent studies of theme in the Pentateuch turn out to be investigations of the theme of the individual sources of the Pentateuch. Even though the chorus of dissent from the classic four-source analysis is swelling,[1] most scholars still believe that the Graf-Wellhausen theory is the best we have,[2] and articles and books are being written on "The Kerygma of the Yahwist,"[3] *The Yahwist. The Bible's First Theologian,*[4] "The Elohistic Fragments in the Pentateuch,"[5] "The Kerygma of the Priestly Writers,"[6] and so on.

The aim however of this article is to enquire about the theme of a unit of Pentateuchal text, Genesis 1–11, considered in and by itself. Almost everyone acknowledges that disparate materials went into the fashioning of Genesis 1–11, and most believe they can distinguish at least the major blocks of those materials. But my primary concern here is with the text in its final form,[7] asking, "What is the theme of Genesis 1–11 as

Reprinted with permission from *Catholic Biblical Quarterly* 38 (1976) 483–507.

1. So, e.g., D. B. Redford, *A Study of the Biblical Story of Joseph (Genesis 37–50)* (VTSup 20; Leiden: Brill, 1970); R. N. Whybray, "The Joseph Story and Pentateuchal Criticism," *VT* 18 (1968) 521–8; S. Sandmel, "The Haggada within Scripture," *JBL* 80 (1961) 105–22; M. Kessler, "Rhetorical Criticism of Genesis 7," in *Rhetorical Criticism. Essays in Honor of James Muilenburg* (ed. J. J. Jackson and M. Kessler; Pittsburgh: Pickwick, 1974) 1–17 (16f.).

2. So some time ago H. H. Rowley, *The Changing Pattern of Old Testament Studies* (London: Epworth, 1959) 12: "If a more satisfactory view can be found, I will eagerly accept it"; similarly more recently W. Richter, "Urgeschichte und Hoftheologie," *BZ* 10 (1966) 96–105 (96).

3. H. W. Wolff, *Int* 20 (1966) 131–58, originally published in *EvT* 24 (1964) 73–97.

4. P. F. Ellis, *The Yahwist. The Bible's First Theologian* (London: Chapman, 1969).

5. H. W. Wolff, *Int* 26 (1972) 158–73, originally published in *EvT* 27 (1969) 59–72.

6. W. Brueggemann, *ZAW* 84 (1972) 397–414.

7. On such terms of reference, see J. F. A. Sawyer, "The Meaning of בצלם אלהים ('In the Image of God') in Genesis I–XI," *JTS* 25 (1974) 418–26 (418f.), and for a similar undertaking see M. Fishbane, "Composition and Structure in the Jacob Cycle (Gen 25:19–35:22)," *JJS* 26 (1975) 15–38.

it stands?" G. von Rad has already pointed us in the direction of such a concern in some comments he made on Genesis 2–3 [[484]]:

> Reconstruction of the original texts . . . is not the primary task of exegesis . . . No matter how much a knowledge of the previous stages of the present text can preserve us from false exposition, still there is no question that the narrative of chs. 2f., in spite of certain tensions and irregularities, is not a rubble heap of individual recensions, but is to be understood as a whole with a consistent train of thought. Above all else, the exegete must come to terms with this existing complex unity.[8]

I should like to apply that approach to Genesis 1–11 as a whole.

Since my subject is the *theme* of Genesis 1–11, a few remarks about what I mean by "theme" are in order. My understanding of "theme" can best be presented by distinguishing "theme" from similar terms: "intention," "motif," "plot," and "subject."

"Theme" is both *narrower and broader* than "the intention of the author." It is narrower in that it may express only one aspect of an author's intention. That intention may be, variously, to influence a particular historical situation (e.g., of controversy), or to meet a psychological need on the author's part, or even to make money or gain prestige. "Theme" could only refer to that aspect of the author's intention that is expressed in the shape and development of the literary work. But "theme" is broader than "author's intention" in that it cannot always be stated adequately in terms of what the author had consciously in mind: on the one side, authors do not necessarily formulate the theme of their work even to themselves (see further the last paragraph of this section), and on the other, the reader is under no constraint to make his statement of theme in terms of the author's intention (rather than in terms of the work) when he has no access to that intention apart from the work itself.

"Theme" is *broader* than "motif" or "topos"[9] or "typical scene"[10] or "narrative pattern"[11] or "theme" in the sense used by Parry and Lord in

8. G. von Rad, *Genesis* (rev. ed.; Philadelphia: Westminster, 1972) 75. Von Rad, however, did not follow his own principle when he came to expound Genesis 6–9, where he dealt with the J and P material separately.

9. R. Scholes and R. Kellogg, *The Nature of Narrative* (New York: Oxford University, 1966) 27, define a *topos* as consisting of a narrative and a conceptual element; e.g., a combination of (narrative) motif of a hero's descent to the netherworld and a (conceptual) "theme" of the search for wisdom.

10. As in W. Arend, *Die typischen Scenen bei Homer* (Berlin: Weidmann, 1933); B. Fenik, *Typical Battle Scenes in the Iliad: Studies in the Narrative Techniques of Homeric Battle Description* (Wiesbaden: Steiner, 1968).

11. As the term has been used by my colleague D. M. Gunn, "Narrative Patterns and Oral Tradition in Judges and Samuel," *VT* 24 (1974) 286–317 (see especially 314 n. 2).

⟦485⟧ their studies of South Slavic epic[12] and adopted by other students of techniques of oral composition. It relates to larger units than do these other terms. I am concerned with theme in the sense of the theme of whole work; one could not speak of the motif or typical scene of a work. Even a recurrent motif[13] does not necessarily constitute a theme. Theme and motif are of the same substance, however, for the theme of a pericope may become a motif of a larger work into which the pericope is incorporated.

"Theme" is *deeper* than "plot." "Plot" may be defined as a kind of story, namely, a story with the emphasis on causality;[14] "theme" tends to conceptualize plot, to focus its significance, and state its implication; it may be said (in a narrative work) to be "plot with the emphasis on meaning."

To discern the "theme" of a work is a *more perceptive* undertaking than to discover its "subject." Both theme and subject may be answers to the question, "What is the work *about*?" But to identify its subject is merely to classify, while to discover its theme is to see "the attitude, the opinion, the insight *about* the subject that is revealed through a particular handling of it,"[15] that is, to *understand* the work more deeply than knowing its "subject." Theme of course arises out of the subject, but because it is a matter for deeper perception its identification is more complex and involves more subjective considerations than does an enquiry about the "subject." In a literary work, unlike a scientific or technical work, theme is not usually explicit.

Four further questions about theme are relevant to the present study:

(i) Can there be more than one theme in a literary work? I think not. When different, divergent, or contradictory themes emerge other than the theme the critic has first identified, he has to adapt his statement of the theme to take account of them. There may indeed be different *levels* on which theme is sought, identified, and articulated. Thus a novel whose theme is the declining fortunes of a family may also be seen

12. A. B. Lord defined theme as "a recurrent element of narration or description in traditional oral poetry" ("Composition by Theme in Homer and Southslavic Epos," *TAPA* 82 [1951] 71–80 [73]), and elsewhere as "groups of ideas regularly used in telling a tale in the formulaic style of traditional song" (cited from Scholes and Kellogg, *Nature of Narrative* 26).

13. E.g., the theme of expulsion in Genesis 1–11 (Adam, Cain, the tower-builders).

14. "A plot is . . . a narrative of events, the emphasis falling on causality. 'The king died and then the queen died' is a story. 'The king died, and then the queen died of grief' is a plot. The time sequence [sc. of the story] is preserved, but the sense of causality overshadows it" (E. M. Forster, *Aspects of the Novel* [Harmondsworth: Penguin, 1962; originally published, 1927] 93f.).

15. R. and M. Thompson, *Critical Reading and Writing* (New York: Random House, 1969) 15.

as developing the theme of ⟦486⟧ the decay of a society or an empire. If both themes can be shown to belong to the intention of the writer, a statement of the novel's theme would have to express the author's sense of the relationships between the family and the society. But if the latter theme was not consciously part of the author's intention and identified only as the "deep structure" of the plot, we are dealing with theme on quite another *level*, on which to speak also of the author's theme would be out of place. Unity of theme is a function of the unity of the literary work.[16] Of course, in the case of a work like Genesis 1–11, which is self-evidently a composition from other works, the possibility exists that it has no unity and no unified theme. So a second question arises:

(ii) How can the existence of a given theme in a literary work be demonstrated? There is no way of *demonstrating* a theme to everyone's satisfaction. The only formal criterion for establishing a theme is: the best statement of the theme of a work is the statement that most adequately accounts for the content, structure and development of the work. To state the theme of a work is to say what it means that the work is as it is.

(iii) How can theme be discovered? I know of no technique for exposing an implicit theme apart from trial and error. Since theme arises from subject, is a conceptualization of plot, and is of the same substance as motif, the critic has already defined for him an area within which to move. All he can do then is to examine likely candidates. That is the method I propose following in this study of theme in Genesis 1–11.

(iv) One more preliminary question raises itself: Does our theme need to have been in the mind of the author? Not necessarily. "Theme" is an item from the conceptual equipment of the literary critic, and not necessarily of the creative artist. The function of enquiry about theme is orientation to the work. The author needs no orientation to his own work, and he may not conceptualize its theme. If theme encapsulates the meaning of the work, the theme and the work are created together in the author's mind. It is the critic or reader, looking for a way into the work, for what makes this work the work it is and not another, and for what makes it hang together, who needs to think about theme. None of this is to say that an author cannot or does not perceive the theme of his

16. Cf. the definition of "theme" offered by W. F. Thrall and A. Hibberd, *A Handbook to Literature* (New York: Odyssey, 1960) 486, as "the central or dominating idea in a literary work . . . the abstract concept which is made concrete through its representation in person, action, and image in the work" (cited from D. L. Petersen, "A Thrice-Told Tale: Genre, Theme and Motif," *BR* 18 [1973] 30–43 [36]).

work or that he is not in many cases far better able to state the theme of his work than any of his readers or critics. All I ⟦487⟧ am asserting is that we do not need to assure ourselves that such and such a theme could have been present in the mind of the author or conceptualized by him before we allow the possibility that such and such is the theme of the work.

Suggested Themes

A Sin—Speech—Mitigation—Punishment Theme

The first theme to be considered is realized in the plot or story pattern of the major narratives of Genesis 1–11. G. von Rad has pointed out how the narratives of the fall, Cain and Abel, the "sons of God," the flood and Babel each exhibit a movement from (a) human sin to (b) divine punishment to (c) divine forgiveness or mitigation:

> God reacts to these outbreaks of human sin with severe judgments . . . [Yet] the Yahwistic narrator shows something else along with the consequences of divine judgment . . . Each time, in and after the judgment, God's preserving, forgiving will to save is revealed.[17]

Although von Rad does not state the theme in quite this fashion, he obviously understands the theme of these narratives to be: whenever man sins, God's response is just, yet gracious; he punishes, yet he forgives. Since these are narratives about the human condition, and not about historical actuality, the theme is an affirmation about the character of God's relationship with mankind.

At this point two questions arise: (i) Can the narrative pattern exemplified in these narratives be differently, or better, analyzed? and (ii) Are the *narratives* of Genesis 1–11 an adequate basis for establishing the theme of Genesis 1–11 as a whole?

To (i) we can reply, first, that Claus Westermann's analysis of the narrative pattern[18] brings to light another significant element. He observes that there always intervenes between the act of sin and the act of punishment a divine *speech* announcing or deciding the penalty. Accordingly he draws up the following table ⟦488⟧:

17. Von Rad, *Genesis* (rev. ed.) 152f.

18. C. Westermann, "Arten der Erzählung in der Genesis," in *Forschung am Alten Testament* (Munich: Kaiser, 1964) 9–91 (47).

	I. *Sin*	II. *Speech*	III. *Punishment*
1. Fall	3:6	3:14–19	3:22–24
2. Cain	4:8b	4:11–12	4:16b
3. Sons of God	6:1–2	6:3	—
4. Flood	6:5	6:7	7:6–24
5. Babel	11:4	11:6–7	11:8–9
6. (Canaan)	9:22	9:24–25	—

Westermann very properly sees a theological significance in this recurrent element of the divine speech. It means, he says, first that God's acts of judgment are always related to a particular sin and so are the very opposite of arbitrary; secondly that there is but one God, who is responsible for woe and weal alike; and thirdly that it is the character of that God to be a judge and to hold himself responsible for detecting and punishing human sin.

But, secondly, we observe that Westermann does not include within his analysis the important element of mitigation, to which von Rad has drawn attention. And neither Westermann nor von Rad has noted that this element of mitigation or grace occupies a significant place in the pattern of these narratives: it is always to be found after the speech of punishment and before the act of punishment. That is to say, God's grace or "forgiving will to save" is not only revealed "in and after the judgment," as von Rad says,[19] but even *before* the execution of judgment. The structure of the narratives may then be exposed thus:

	I. *Sin*	II. *Speech*	III. *Mitigation*	IV. *Punishment*
1. Fall	3:6	3:14–19	3:21	3:22–24
2. Cain	4:8	4:11–12	4:15	4:16
3. Sons of God	6:2	6:3	?6:8, 18ff.	?7:6–24
4. Flood	6:5, 11f.	6:7, 13–21	6:8, 18ff.	7:6–24
5. Babel	11:4	11:6f.	?10:1–32	11:8

To observe that all the narratives of the primeval history conform to a pattern does not destroy the individuality of the narratives, but rather highlights it. Some significant differences exist among the various exemplifications of the overall pattern. In nos. 1 and 2 it is individuals who sin

19. Von Rad, *Genesis* (rev. ed.) 153.

and are punished, in 3–5 it is communities. 1 and 2 contain the element of God's investigation of the crime, while in 3–5 the sins are public and in 3 and 5 God only needs to "see" the crime (6:5, 12; 11:5). In 1 and 2 the same persons sin, are punished, and are partly relieved of the severity of their ⟦489⟧ punishment. In 3 more than those who have sinned are punished, and it is uncertain whether there is any mitigation.[20] In 4 the vast majority of those who have sinned are punished and the mitigation operates only for one man and his family;[21] in 5 all those who have sinned are punished, and there is no direct mitigation. These variations are not insignificant. Where God's relationship with individuals is concerned, his dealing can be highly personalized (note especially the differing punishments for the three protagonists of the fall story). But where a whole community's relationship with God is involved, the operation of justice in punishment can sometimes be undifferentiated, as in the sons of God episode, where all mankind's life-span (or, the period before the flood) is shortened because of the sins of the sons of God and the daughters of men, but sometimes differentiated, as in the flood story, where Noah escapes. In each case, however, except perhaps for the last, there is an outworking of the basic pattern of sin—speech—mitigation—punishment. Can this pattern, then, form the basis for a statement of the theme of Genesis 1–11?

That brings us to our question (ii): can the narratives alone form an adequate basis for establishing the theme of Genesis 1–11 as a whole? It is indeed correct that the theme of a narrative work often emerges from a consideration of its plot or narrative pattern, or, as could in principle be the case here, from a narrative pattern repeated in every episode of the narrative. But can the plot of the narratives of Genesis 1–11 account for the presence of the creation account (Genesis 1), the genealogies (4:17–26; 5; 11:10–26), and the table of nations (10)? I think not. If "theme" is a statement of the content, structure and development of a work, as I have suggested above, the "sin—speech—mitigation—punishment" pattern, significant though it is, can only be called a recurrent motif in the primeval history, and not the unifying theme of Genesis 1–11 as a whole. G. von Rad himself, we should note, spoke only of the

20. Westermann, *Forschung*, 56, sees a mitigation in the fact that the punishment is *only* a shortening of life; but this view is unlikely since no hint is given in the narrative that the punishment could have been more severe. If the sons of God episode is closely connected with the Flood narrative, the element of mitigation can be seen in the deliverance of Noah.

21. On the question whether Noah is regarded as typical of his generation or as "righteous" only in view of God's deliverance of him, see W. M. Clark, "The Righteousness of Noah," *VT* 21 (1971) 261–80; A. N. Barnard, "Was Noah a Righteous Man?" *Theology* 84 (1971) 311–14.

"*Yahwistic* Primeval History" when developing his "sin—punishment—mitigation" schema. Although he regarded the Yahwistic scheme as the foundation of the final canonical shape of Genesis 1–11, he did not directly express his understanding of the significance of Genesis 1–11 in its final form, and so falls short of his own excellent goal of understanding the work "as a whole with a consistent train of thought"[22] ⟦490⟧.

A Spread-of-Sin, Spread-of-Grace Theme

Statement. Another element in G. von Rad's understanding of the theme of Genesis 1–11, which I have left aside hitherto for the sake of our analysis of themes, is the theme of the "spread of sin," to which corresponds increasingly severe punishment, and a spread of "grace" on God's part.[23] That is: (i) From Eden to Babel by the way of the sins of Cain, Lamech, the "sons of God," and the generation of the flood, there is an ever-growing "avalanche" of sin, a "continually widening chasm between man and God." There is a movement from disobedience to murder, to reckless killing, to titanic lust, to total corruption and violence, to the full disruption of humanity. (ii) God responds to the extension of human sin with increasingly severe punishment; from expulsion from the garden to expulsion from the tillable earth, to the limitation of human life, to the near annihilation of mankind, to the "dissolution of mankind's unity." (iii) Nevertheless, these are also stories of divine grace: God not only punishes Adam and Eve, but also withholds the threatened penalty of death; he not only drives out Cain, but also puts his mark of protection upon him; not only sends the flood, but saves the human race alive in preserving Noah and his family. Only in the case of the Babel narrative does it appear that the element of "grace" is lacking—a subject to which we shall return in section III below ⟦"A Statement of Theme"⟧.

Development. Such a statement of the theme of Genesis 1–11 is initially open to the same objection as was raised above: it speaks only to the *narratives* of these chapters. However in the case of this theme there is the possibility that it can be extended to parts of Genesis 1–11 outside

22. *Genesis* (rev. ed.) 75.

23. *Genesis* (rev. ed.) 152f.; cf. also his *Theology of the Old Testament* (tr. D. M. G. Stalker; Edinburgh: Oliver and Boyd, 1962) I, 154ff. Similarly already H. Gunkel, *Genesis* (6th ed.; Göttingen: Vandenhoeck und Ruprecht, 1964) 1, noting themes of human sin, God's wrath, God's grace; and J. Skinner, *A Critical and Exegetical Commentary on Genesis* (ICC; 2d ed.; Edinburgh, T. and T. Clark, 1930) 2, who thought that the units of the primeval history were arranged "with perhaps a certain unity of conception, in so far as they illustrate the increasing wickedness that accompanied the progress of mankind in civilisation."

the main narratives, i.e., that it can account for the content, development and shape of the material as a whole.

(i) *The creation account* (Genesis 1). The connection of this chapter with the spread of sin theme becomes clear if we accept the perspective of D. Kidner: he sees Genesis 1–11 as describing "two opposite progressions: first, God's orderly creation, to its climax in man as a responsible and blessed being, and then the disintegrating work of sin, to its first great anticlimax in the corrupt world of the Flood, and its second in the folly of Babel."[24] That is, ⟦491⟧ the theme of the spread of sin is only the negative aspect of the overall theme—which remains yet to be defined. We may take this insight further and observe that the pattern according to which creation proceeds in chap. 1 is in fact the positive aspect of the sin-judgment motif: here it is a matter of obedience followed by blessing, not sin followed by curse. So, for example, light comes into being in prompt obedience to the word of God (1:3), whereupon the divine judgment is pronounced: God saw that it was good. The chapter as a whole moves towards "blessing," first upon the living creatures (1:22), then upon man (1:28), and finally upon the seventh day (2:3). Genesis 1 is thus the positive counterpart to the remainder of the primeval history (though the remainder is not unrelieved gloom).

(ii) *The genealogies* (Gen 4:17–26; 5; 11:10–26). Since the kind of theme appropriate to Genesis 1–11 is obviously theological, we may wonder whether the genealogies can in any way be integrated with the overall theme of these chapters. The genealogies have indeed not usually been thought to serve some theological function, but have often been regarded simply as ancient material reproduced here only because of the chronological relationship of their contents to the narratives of Genesis 1–11.[25] Yet there are some clues in the narrative sections of Genesis 1–11 which point to the validity of a theological interpretation of the genealogies; that is, to the likelihood that the final author of the primeval history intended them to express some theological purpose.

The first clue lies in some statements about the multiplication of the race. In 1:28 the procreation of the human race stands under divine command and blessing: "And God blessed them, and God said unto them, Be fruitful and multiply, and fill the earth." To the same effect are

24. *Genesis* (Tyndale Old Testament Commentaries; London: Tyndale Press, 1967) 13.

25. Cf., e.g., M. D. Johnson, *The Purpose of the Biblical Genealogies with Special Reference to the Setting of the Genealogies of Jesus* (SNTSMS 8; Cambridge: University Press, 1969) 14, 26ff., who distinguishes between the genealogies of J and P, finding in the genealogies of J no particular purpose beyond showing the "interrelation of a certain number of tribes," but in P certain theological purposes, notably to set the stage for the emergence of the chosen people and to trace the narrowing of the line down to Aaron.

the statements by Eve at the birth of Cain and Seth: "I have gained (or, created) a man with the help of Yahweh" (4:1),[26] and "God has appointed for me another child" (4:25). Just as the birth of Eve's children is a token of the divine aid, so the whole growth of the human family witnessed by these genealogies is to be viewed under the sign of the divine blessing.[27]

⟦492⟧ The second clue to the theological significance of the genealogies is provided by their form. No reader of Genesis 5, to take one example, fails to be impressed by the recurrent phrase "And he died," which baldly and emphatically concludes the entry for each of these antediluvians. The whole movement of the regular form of these notices is toward death. The form is:

1. When A lived x years, he begat B.
2. A lived after the birth of B y years, and had other sons and daughters.
3. All the days of A were z $(x + y)$ years.
4. And he died.

Items 3 and 4 are logically unnecessary. They add nothing to the information given in items 1 and 2. Their function is to emphasize a finality about each of these lives; though possessed of an excess of vitality by ordinary human standards,[28] these men also die. The thrust of the Genesis 5 genealogy is toward death, even though human life continues.

A further hint of progression toward death may be given by the diminishing life-spans attributed to the personages of the primeval history. While the antediluvians usually live 800 or 900 years,[29] the generations after the flood live ever shorter lives, from 600 years for Shem (11:10) to 205 for Terah (11:32).[30] This decline may perhaps be seen as a deterio-

26. On the precise significance of the phrase, see most recently I. M. Kikawada, "Two Notes on Eve," *JBL* 91 (1972) 33–7.

27. So C. Westermann, *Genesis* (BKAT 1/1; Neukirchen: Neukirchener Verlag des Erziehungsvereins, 1966) 24.

28. Even in the eschatological age pictured in Isa 65:20, 100 years is the normal span of life.

29. The two exceptions are Enoch (365 years) and Lamech (777 years). It seems undeniable that both these figures have a symbolic significance: the 365 years of Enoch correspond to the number of days of the solar year, Enoch's counterpart (the seventh) in the Sumerian King List being Enmeduranki, king of Sippar, the centre of sun-worship (cf., e.g., E. A. Speiser, *Genesis* [AB; New York: Doubleday, 1964] 43). Lamech's 777 years are presumably to be related to the "sword-song" of the Lamech of 4:24: "If Cain is avenged sevenfold, truly Lamech seventy-sevenfold."

30. The progressive decline, both for antediluvians and postdiluvians, is most consistent in the Samaritan version, but the text-critical value of this version at this point is dubious. A similar progressive decline is apparently exhibited in a portion of the Sumerian King List relating to the first six kings of Kish (they reign 1200, 900 [variant 960], 670, 420, 300,

ration of man's "original wonderful vitality, a deterioration corresponding to his increasing distance from his starting point at creation . . . thus Genesis 5 describes something like a 'transitional period, during which death caused by sin broke the powerful resistance of primitive human nature.' "[31]

⟦493⟧ As for the genealogical material of chap. 4, its function within the primeval history becomes clearly visible when it is viewed from the perspective of the spread of sin theme. The Cainite genealogy of 4:17–24 has the same dialectic significance as the Sethite genealogy of chap. 5.[32] In chap. 4, while the genealogy appears on the surface to be a list of the founders of the arts of civilization (the city, cattle-breeding, music, metal-working),[33] and was perhaps originally transmitted as such, it is made clear by the point to which the progress of civilization reaches, namely Lamech's tyrannous boast (4:23f.), that this has been a progress in sin as much as in civilization.[34] In the seven generations of the line of Cain, history has seen a "progress" from an impulsive act of murder to a deliberate reign of terror. But, by affixing the beginning of a Sethite genealogy (4:25f.) to the Cainite list, the author of Genesis 4 has affirmed that the world of men is not totally given over to the Cainite life-style. Even while the race of Cain is increasing in congenital violence, he means to say, elsewhere there is a line of men who have begun to "call on the name of Yahweh" (4:26).

Thus, whatever may have been the origin of the genealogies or their original function, the present form of Genesis 1–11 permits us to interpret them as displaying a theological purpose analogous to that outlined by von Rad for the narratives. Here also in the genealogies there is in

---

240 years), though the parallel with Genesis 5 has recently been held to be merely fortuitous (T. C. Hartman, "Some Thoughts on the Sumerian King List and Genesis 5 and 11B," *JBL* 91 [1972] 25–32 [30 n. 19]). We might compare also Hesiod's picture of history as a declining succession of metals (*Works and Days* 1.148) as further evidence of an ancient conception of history as a decline.

31. Von Rad, *Genesis* 69f., quoting F. Delitzsch. A connection with the "tree of life" of chap. 3 as the explanation of the longevity of the patriarchs is however too fanciful.

32. The fact that the two genealogies derive from different sources, according to the usual analysis, is not relevant to our present concern with the final form of the text.

33. We may perhaps compare with the Cainite genealogy the list of the Seven Sages of antediluvian times who appear in Mesopotamian texts to be the founders of the arts of civilization; cf. J. J. Finkelstein, *JCS* 17 (1963) 50 n. 41; and E. Reiner, "The Etiological Myth of the Seven Sages," *Or* 30 (1961) 1–11.

34. Cf. T. E. Fretheim, *Creation, Fall and Flood. Studies in Genesis 1–11* (Minneapolis: Augsburg, 1969) 101; and J. L. McKenzie, "Reflections on Wisdom," *JBL* 86 (1967) 1–9 (6): "The culture myths have been woven into a sequence of events in which the progress of culture marches with the growth of human pride and wickedness."

the monotonous reiteration of the fact of death, which increasingly encroaches upon life, a pessimistic note which corresponds to the narrative theme of the continuing spread of sin. But as in the narratives, history is not simply a matter of sin and punishment; where sin abounds, grace much more abounds. Even though the divine grace is experienced not in dramatic acts of deliverance, as it is in the narratives, but in the steady silent expansion of human life, it is the divine grace all the same. To the grace that appoints for Eve another child to take the place of the dead Abel is owed also the furtherance of mankind's growth throughout the genealogy of Genesis 5; and to the grace that preserves the human race through the dramatic rescue of Noah and his family from the flood is due also the repeopling of the earth after the flood (Genesis 10) ⟦494⟧.

(iii) *The Table of Nations* (Genesis 10). It is a remarkable feature of the structure of the primeval history that the Table of Nations (chap. 10) is located not after the story of the tower of Babel (11:1–9) but before it. Since chap. 10 recounts the "spreading" (*pārad*, vv. 5, 32) or "scattering" (*pûṣ*, v. 18) of men, "each with his own language" (v. 5, cf. vv. 20, 31) it would seem more logically placed after 11:1–9 where the "scattering" (*pûṣ*) of men "over the face of all the earth" and the division of languages is narrated.

A thematic explanation for this dischronologization is ready to hand in the "spread of sin, spread of grace" theme as we have been developing it. If the material of chap. 10 had followed the Babel story, the whole Table of Nations would have to be read under the sign of judgment; where it stands it functions as the fulfillment of the divine command of 9:1 "Be fruitful and multiply, and fill the earth," which looks back in its turn to 1:28. All this means that the final author of the primeval history understands that the dispersal of the nations may be evaluated both positively (as in chap. 10) and negatively (as in chap. 11). Since Babel, mankind stands under both the blessing and the curse of God; the division of the peoples and their languages is both a token of the divine judgment and a natural concomitant of man's fulfillment of the divine command and so part of the divine "blessing" (9:1). With this ambivalence in the relationship of God with man the primeval history comes to a conclusion. The final author or redactor of the primeval history has, by the sequence in which he has arranged his materials on the dispersal of mankind, made the same theological point as have the narratives and genealogies in the preceding chapters: that though the judgment of God rests upon men as sinful, they experience not only his judgment but also his grace.

Criticism. So far the statement of the "spread of sin" theme with which this section began has proved productive of insight into material which von Rad did not himself connect with the theme. But next we should consider whether there are any difficulties in regarding the "spread of sin" as the unifying theme of these chapters.[35]

(i) While it is readily granted that a "spread" of sin and an intensification of punishments from Adam to Cain and from Cain to the generation of the ⟦495⟧ flood is clear, it may well be asked whether any such extension or intensification can be discerned with the flood and the Babel narratives are compared. Can the theme of Genesis 1–11 properly be said to be the increasing spread of sin when the last exemplification of the theme, the Babel story, depicts neither a sin so drastic as that which brings on the flood nor a punishment so severe and universal as the flood?[36]

This issue will depend to some extent on how precisely the sins of Gen 6:1–4 and 11:1–9 are understood. It is possible, for example, to interpret the sin of the "sons of God" in 6:1–4 not, as is commonly thought, as the unnatural mixing of the divine and the human, but as a sin of violence on the purely human plane.[37] Then, if the sin of the "sons of God," which is partly if not wholly the cause for the flood, is perhaps not so fundamental as some interpreters have claimed, the sin of the tower builders may not be so trivial as at first sight appears. Their sin may be seen not as a mere expression of human self-importance and self-reliance, but as an act of *hybris*, matched in its defiance of God only by the first sin in the garden; like the eating of the forbidden fruit the tower-building may be an assault on heaven, an attempt at self-divinization.[38] Such an interpretation is confirmed by the fact that, so understood, the primeval history

35. I leave aside the criticism of I. Soisalon-Soininen ("Die Urgeschichte im Geschichtswerk des Jahwisten," *Temenos* 6 [1970] 130–41) that there is no need to attribute any theological plan to the Yahwistic primeval history and that his traditional material effectively determined its own position in his narrative (brother-murder must follow creation of primeval pair; flood that almost annihilates mankind must follow genealogy of mankind's multiplication and story of its motivation, the angel-marriages and so on). On one level that may be so; but we are here considering whether the work (of Yahwist or final redactor) has any conceptual theme beyond a merely "logical" development.

36. So R. Rendtorff, "Genesis 8:21 und die Urgeschichte des Yahwisten," *KD* 7 (1961) 69–78 (75); W. M. Clark, "The Flood and the Structure of the Pre-Patriarchal History," *ZAW* 83 (1971) 184–211 (206); Fretheim, *Creation, Fall and Flood* 20.

37. That is, that the "sons of God" are dynastic rulers; cf. M. G. Kline, "Divine Kingship and Genesis 6:1–4," *Westminster Theological Journal* 24 (1962) 187–204; F. Dexinger, *Sturz der Göttersöhne oder Engel vor der Sintflut?* (Vienna: Herder, 1966). I would want to add that they are *also* (semi-) divine beings, like Gilgamesh, two-thirds god and one-third human (Gilgamesh I ii 1; *ANET* 73b).

38. "Man's attempt to overstep the bounds of creatureliness" (Fretheim, *Creation, Fall and Flood* 123). On the theme of *hybris,* see P. Humbert, "Démesure et chute dans l'A. T.": *maqqēl shāqēd* (*La Branche d'Amandier. Hommage à Wilhelm Vischer* [Montpellier: Graille, Castelnau, 1960] 63–82).

would exhibit the common literary technique of *inclusio*, with the final episode in the story of human sin repeating and balancing the first.

But if the sin of the generation of the flood is not necessarily more heinous than that of the tower-builders, is the scattering of mankind a more severe punishment than the flood? It may be replied that in two ways at least the scattering is more drastic than the flood. First, the flood left no permanent mark on humanity; though the generation of the flood was destroyed, mankind was preserved, and continued to grow. The scattering of mankind is, however, of lasting effect. There are no survivors of Babel. Secondly, what is destroyed at Babel is the community of mankind as a family; hitherto, as the genealogies have witnessed, mankind is one family, ⟦496⟧ and the flood has only accentuated that fact by making one family in the narrowest sense of the word co-terminous with humanity. But the punishment of Babel divides men irrevocably from one another (as did also the first sin in its own way); now mankind is no longer one "people" or "kin-group" (*ʿam*, 11:6), but "nations" (10:32).

In sum, this criticism of a theme of spread of sin from the fall to Babel can be met by a more exact interpretation of the significance of the flood and Babel narratives.

(ii) Another criticism of the spread of sin theme from Eden to Babel arises from the opinion that it is Gen 8:21 (at the close of the Yahwistic flood narrative) and not the Babel story that brings the primeval history to a close. In his influential study,[39] Rolf Rendtorff claims that this verse should be translated: "I will no longer curse the earth," or "I will no longer regard the earth as cursed, and treat it as such." It is not that God will not *again* curse the earth, but that at 8:21 the period of the curse uttered by God in 3:17, "Cursed is the ground because of you," is concluded. "From now on it is no longer curse that rules the world, but blessing. The time of the curse is at an end, the time of blessing has arrived."[40] Some who have followed Rendtorff's view have expressed the contrast rather less starkly. Thus W. M. Clark says, "The power of that initial curse to work disruption is limited,"[41] and T. E. Fretheim writes: "The idea of blessing . . . is here introduced for the first time (v. 22). Since the beginning of man's sin the curse has been predominant in the created order of things, leading to the catastrophe of the Flood. This will not continue to be the case. Now blessing stands alongside of the curse and begins to have its beneficial effects on the earth, breaking down the effects of the curse (3:17). This is made concretely evident for

39. See note 36 above.
40. Rendtorff, *KD* 7 (1961) 74.
41. Clark, *ZAW* 83 (1971) 207.

the first time in the following story (in J) of Noah and his vineyard."[42] If this view is correct, there is of course no point in seeking for a theme of Genesis 1–11, since those chapters do not form a literary unit.

The view of Rendtorff and his followers, however, does not appear to me to be well-founded in its central contention.[43] The curse that will not again come upon the ground (8:21) is not the curse of 3:17. There the curse upon the ground is that it will bring forth thorns and thistles; and that curse is not ⟦497⟧ said in 8:21 to be lifted, nor is it easy to see how the Yahwist, or any author, could have claimed from his own experience that it had been lifted. In 8:21 the curse has been the smiting of the earth with a flood. It is true, as Rendtorff points out,[44] that the introduction to the flood story does not specifically view the flood as a "curse," but that is not a very strong counter-argument to the plain structure of 8:21. Here the clause "I will not again curse the earth" seems clearly parallel to "I will not again smite all living beings,"[45] as God has done by means of the flood. There is indeed a verbal connection between 3:17 and 8:21 ("Cursed is the ground because of [*baᶜăbûr*] thee" and "I will not curse the ground because of [*baᶜăbûr*] man"), but the content of the two passages is different, and we are dealing simply with the repetition of a verbal motif which takes on new light in different settings.[46]

A further weakness in the view that 8:21 ends the period of the curse lies in its interpretation of the narrative of Noah's vineyard (9:20–27). According to W. M. Clark, that narrative "does not convey the idea that wine relieves the toil of mankind, but rather is a verification that the curse has been lifted off the ground which can henceforth produce vineyards, a symbol of fertility."[47] But this is to misunderstand the clear connection between the vineyard story and the birth-oracle of Noah in 5:29: "Out of the ground which Yahweh has cursed this one [Noah] shall bring us relief from our work and from the toil of our hands"; that is, the "relief out of the ground" is the discovery of the cultivation of the

42. Fretheim, *Creation, Fall and Flood* 113.

43. For an independent examination of Rendtorff's view, reaching similar conclusions, see O. H. Steck, "Genesis 12:1–3 und die Urgeschichte des Jahwisten," in *Probleme biblischer Theologie Gerhard von Rad zum 70. Geburtstag* (ed. H. W. Wolff; Munich: Kaiser, 1971) 525–54 (527–42).

44. *KD* 7 (1961) 70.

45. *loᵓ-ᵓōsip lĕqallēl ᶜôd ᵓet-hāᵓădāmâ* parallel to *lōᵓ-ᵓōsip ᶜôd lĕhakkôt ᵓet-kol-ḥay.*

46. For a parallel, cf. 3:16 "your desire [the rare word *tĕšûqâ*] shall be toward your husband, but he will rule (*māšal*) over you," with 4:7 "[sin's] desire (*tĕšûqâ*) is toward you, but you will ruler (*māšal*) over it." There is no connection of substance between the content of these passages. For another parallel, see n. 48 below.

47. Clark, *ZAW* 83 (1971) 208; cf. Rendtorff, *KD* 7 (1961) 74.

vine and the making of wine.[48] The curse is not lifted from the ground, but even the cursed ground can produce some comfort and enjoyment for man. The pattern of punishment relieved by divine grace is visible here too, though it is not as explicitly spelled out as it is in some of the longer narratives.

It may finally be objected to the view of Rendtorff, especially as developed by Clark, that the remainder of J's post-flood primeval history cannot ⟦498⟧ be satisfactorily interpreted as belonging to an age of blessing rather than of curse. What immediately follows the story of Noah's drunkenness is not blessing but curse—the curse of Canaan (9:25ff.). And even though there is contained in this curse a blessing on Shem and Japheth, the first explicit blessing in J, as Clark says (though not the first in the primeval history as it now stands; cf. 1:22, 28; 2:3; 5:2; 9:1), the structure of vv. 25ff., which begin with "Cursed be Canaan," and in which each blessing is followed with "And let Canaan be his slave," shows that attention is focused on Canaan and the curse rather than the blessing. Furthermore, it is difficult to see how Clark can interpret the vineyard and Babel narratives as a "recapitulation of the events prior to the flood . . . a story of sin on the individual level followed by a story in which sin threatens to reach cosmic dimensions again" without understanding them as developing a "spread of sin" theme, which is hardly appropriate for the age of blessing.[49]

It seems incorrect, therefore, to regard Gen 8:22 as marking the major turning-point in the Yahwist's primeval history; the "spread of sin" both includes the flood and extends beyond it.

(iii) A quite different suggestion which would cast doubt on the "spread of sin" as the unifying theme of Genesis 1–11 is that of W. Brueggemann in his study, "David and His Theologian."[50] He argues that the sequence of episodes in the J material of Genesis 1–11 is "dependent upon the career of the sons of David in the quest for the throne."[51] The four stories of sin in Genesis 3–11 (Adam and Eve; Cain and Abel; Noah and the Flood; the Tower of Babel) corresponds to the four major episodes of the Succession Narrative (David and Bathsheba; Amnon and

48. H. Holzinger, *Genesis* (Kurzer Hand-Commentar zum Alten Testament; Freiburg: J. C. B. Mohr, 1898) 60f.; Gunkel, *Genesis* 55; Skinner, *Genesis* 133f. The observation made by U. Cassuto, *Commentary on Genesis* (Jerusalem: Magnes Press, 1961) I, 303, that the roots of "relief," "work," and "toil" (*nḥm, ᶜśh, ᶜṣb*) in 5:29 occur in the same sequence in 6:6, does not destroy the connection of substance between 5:29 and 9:20. 6:6 provides another example of verbal mimicry to add to those mentioned above (n. 46).

49. It may also be objected that the strongly marked element of mitigation in Genesis 3–8 makes it inappropriate to label this an age of the curse.

50. *CBQ* 30 (1968) 156–81.

51. Ibid., 158.

Absalom; Absalom and David; Solomon and David). *Prima facie*, if this is so, the structure of Genesis 1–11 is essentially (at least as far as the J material is concerned) shaped by the course of history and not by a conceptual theme such as "the spread of sin."

Brueggemann is indeed able to point to many striking correspondences of language and motif between the primeval history and the Succession Narrative. But two considerations make his view rather unlikely, in my judgment:[52] (i) The correspondence between Absalom's rebellion and the flood story is not very strong,[53] as Brueggemann himself candidly acknowledges;[54] ⟦499⟧ and one major disruption of the pattern spoils the argument about sequence, which is crucial to the present discussion. Even if some narratives in Genesis 1–11 are reflections of the Davidic history, the sequence of those narratives is not clearly dependent upon it. (ii) Striking parallels of motif and language can also be traced between the Succession Narrative and other sections of J,[55] and a special relationship with Genesis 1–11 cannot be claimed.[56]

Furthermore, even if there is a sequential correspondence between the two works, there is no clear evidence that the Davidic narrative is prior to the primeval history, nor that the telling of the David story has not been influenced—in its selection of episodes and in its language—by the primeval history.[57] It is unnecessary, therefore, to regard Brueggemann's view, stimulating though it is, as an obstacle to uncovering a conceptual link between the narratives of Genesis 1–11, namely the "spread of sin" theme.

To summarize this point: The theme of the spread of sin accounts for the vast majority of the content of Genesis 1–11. It is visible, not just

52. For another critique, see Clark, *ZAW* 83 (1971) 201f.

53. Being confined to motifs of wickedness which is punished, but from which Yahweh delivers Noah/David and makes a new beginning.

54. Ibid., 167 and n. 45.

55. T. Klaehn, *Die sprachliche Verwandschaft der Quelle K (2 Sam. 9ff.) der Samuelisbücher mit J des Heptateuchs* (Borna-Leipzig: Noske, 1914); J. Blenkinsopp, "Theme and Motif in the Succession History (2 Sam XI 2ff.) and the Yahwist Corpus," VTSup 15 (1966) 44–51.

56. From another point of view, a relationship between the primeval history and Jerusalem court traditions in general—not specifically David material—has been claimed by W. Richter, "Urgeschichte und Hoftheologie," *BZ* 10 (1966) 96–105.

57. Even if the Davidic narrative is historically reliable—a view that seems much less certain now than in 1968 when Brueggemann's article was published—(cf., e.g., the role of traditional story-telling elements within it; see D. M. Gunn, "Traditional Composition in the 'Succession Narrative,'" *VT* 26/2 [1976])—the conception of the work and the choice of material from the doubtless greater bulk of Davidic material available could well follow a traditional or developmental sequence such as is displayed in the primeval history. Brueggemann's case depends on the assumptions that the David story is "(a) historically reliable, and (b) chronologically prior to the other piece" (*CBQ* 30 [1968] 158 n. 17).

in the narratives, but also in other literary types in these chapters. It is more than probable that, even if this suggested theme alone does not adequately express the thrust of Genesis 1–11, its pervasiveness ensures that it will have to be taken into account in any statement of theme in the primeval history.

A Creation—Uncreation—Re-Creation Theme

We have already noted that the flood episode has given rise to some criticism of the "spread of sin" theme. While those criticisms can be met, the fact remains that the flood narrative does not function simply as yet a [[500]] further stage in the development of human sin, but imports concepts of "end" and "re-creation" into the primeval history.[58] When chap. 1 is also taken into consideration, some case can be made out for suggesting that the theme of the primeval history is "creation—uncreation—re-creation."

It is very plain that the flood is represented not just as a punishment for the sin of the generation of the flood, but as a reversal of creation—"uncreation," as Joseph Blenkinsopp has put it: "The world in which order first arose out of a primeval watery chaos is now reduced to the watery chaos out of which it arose—chaos-come-again."[59] While Genesis 1 depicts creation as largely a matter of separation and distinction, Genesis 6f. portrays the annihilation of distinctions. If in Gen 1:6ff. a firmament is established to keep the heavenly waters from falling upon the earth except in properly regulated measure, 7:11 has the "windows of heaven" opening to obliterate this primal distinction. Similarly, the distinction between the lower waters and the earth in 1:9 is done away with by the breaking forth through the earth of the "fountains of the great deep" (7:11). The binary nature of created existence gives way to the formlessness of the *tōhû wābōhû* before creation. And significantly, the destruction follows much the same sequence as the creation: earth, birds, cattle, wild animals, swarming creatures, man (7:21).

Re-creation occurs, in the first place, by the renewed separation of sea and land: the waters recede from and dry up from the earth (8:3, 7, 13). Then comes the renewal of the divine order to living beings to "breed, be fruitful, and multiply" (8:17). There follows God's guarantee of the binary structure of existence: seedtime and harvest, cold and heat, summer and winter, day and night are re-established (8:22). Finally, the creation ordinances are reannounced, albeit in somewhat altered form

58. See also D. J. A. Clines, "The Theology of the Flood Narrative," *Faith and Thought* 100 (1972–73) 128–42.

59. Blenkinsopp, in J. Blenkinsopp *et al., The Pentateuch* (Chicago: ACTA, 1971) 46f.

(9:1–7),[60] the separation of sea and land—a fundamental element in the creative process (1:9ff.)—is assured (9:8–17), a mankind begins to be re-created (by procreation, chap. 10), and to fill the earth at God's command (10:32).[61]

As for the intervening material of Genesis 1–11 between creation and flood, when it is viewed from the perspective of the theme "creation—uncreation—re-creation" new understandings emerge. Chief among them is the recognition that chaps. 3–6 are not simply the story of human sin matched by divine grace, but the story of the undoing of creation. The flood is ⟦501⟧ only the final stage in a process of cosmic disintegration which began in Eden. While chap. 1 views reality as an ordered pattern which is confused by the flood, chaps. 2–3 see reality as a network of elemental unions which become disintegrated throughout the course of the narrative from Eden to the flood.

Thus, in Genesis 2, as in Genesis 1, reality has a binary structure; but here creation has not proceeded by distinction and separation, but by the forging of bonds: between man and soil, man and the animals, man and woman, man and God. In chap. 3 the relationship of harmony between each of these parts is disrupted. The communion between God and the man who breathes God's breath (2:7) has become the legal relationship of accuser and defendant (3:9ff.); the relationship of man and woman as "one flesh" (2:24) has soured into mutual recrimination (3:12); and the bond of man (*ʾādām*) with the soil (*ʾădāmâ*) from which he was built has been supplanted by "an alienation that expresses itself in a silent, dogged struggle between man and soil"[62] (3:17ff.); the harmonious relationship of man with beast in which man is the acknowledged master (2:19ff.) has become a perpetual struggle of intransigent foes (3:15). In Genesis 4 another union, of twin (?)[63] brothers, which might have been expected to be paradigmatic of human friendship,[64] is broken by the ultimate act of enmity, murder. Cain is further alienated from the soil, by being driven out from the tillable earth (4:11), and the

60. See Clines, *Faith and Thought* 100 (1972–73) 138f.

61. Traditional source analysis, assigning 8:3, 7, 13a, 22 and parts of chap. 10 to J and 8:13b, 17; 9:1–17 and parts of chap. 10 to P, fails to observe how deeply imprinted this element is upon the whole text in its final form.

62. G. von Rad, *Genesis* (rev. ed.) 94.

63. Does not our text of Gen 4:1f., in which one conception but two births are spoken of, already imply this interpretation, common in rabbinic exegesis? Cf. Ps.-Jonathan *in loc.*; Ber. R. xxii.2; TB San 38b. Even Skinner, *Genesis* 103, acknowledges that this "may very well be the meaning."

64. It is no disproof of this belief that the Cain and Abel story belongs to the well-known folktale type of "the hostile brothers" (cf. Westermann, *Genesis* 428ff.). Such stories are popular just because they are contrary to expectation, like tales of "the unlikely hero."

bond between man and the soil is further loosened. The disintegration of the most intimate bond of all—of man with the divine breath (2:7)—first sets in with the murders by Cain and Lamech (4:8, 23), broadens its scope with the successive deaths of each descendant of Adam in the genealogy of chap. 5, and reaches its climax with the simultaneous death of all mankind in chap. 7. The destruction of mankind is significantly expressed in language reminiscent of creation: Yahweh determines that he will "blot out man whom I have created" (6:7), whereupon "all in whose nostrils was the breath of the spirit of life" (*nišmat-rûaḥ ḥayyîm*) died (7:22), an echo of Yahweh Elohim's breathing into man's nostrils the "breath of life" (*nišmat ḥayyîm*) (2:7). With this, the creation of man is undone.

⟦502⟧ The movement towards uncreation viewed as the dissolution of unities begins again directly after the flood. Ham's incest with his mother—if that is the significance of 9:20–27[65]—strikes at the bond between man and wife (2:23f.), and the scattering of mankind after the building of Babel (11:9) is a potent symbol of the disintegration of mankind's unity. Man's tendency has not been changed by the flood: the "imagination of man's heart is evil from his youth" (8:21) as much after the flood as before it.

There can be little doubt that the theme "creation—uncreation—re-creation" is firmly fixed in Genesis 1–11, and needs to be taken into account in our general statement of the theme of the work.

A Statement of Theme

There seem to be two ways in which the insights about theme gained from considering the foregoing suggestions can be incorporated into a general statement of the theme of Genesis 1–11. The theme of these chapters may be said to be, either:

(a) Mankind tends to destroy what God has made good. Even when God forgives human sin and mitigates the punishment sin continues to spread, to the point where the world suffers uncreation. And even when God makes a fresh start, turning his back on uncreation forever, man's tendency to sin immediately becomes manifest. Or:

(b) No matter how drastic man's sin becomes, destroying what God has made good and bringing the world to the brink of uncreation, God's grace never fails to deliver man from the consequences of his sin. Even

65. So F. W. Bassett, "Noah's Nakedness and the Curse of Canaan," *VT* 21 (1971) 232–7; though cf. also G. Rice, "The Curse that Never Was," *JRT* 29 (1972) 5–27 (11ff.) for criticism of this view.

when man responds to a fresh start with the old pattern of sin, God's commitment to his world stands firm, and sinful man experiences the favor of God as well as his righteous judgment.[66]

Each of these readings does justice, I hope, to the perspectives of our foregoing discussion. But their thrust is in quite opposite directions. How can we decide between these statements?

At this point two issues that have been ignored up to this point have to be brought into the discussion: (i) What is the precise terminus of the primeval history? and (ii) What is the relationship of the theme of Genesis 1–11 to the theme of the Pentateuch?

(i) Although we have been able to speak previously rather loosely of "Genesis 1–11," here the exact terminus of this literary unit becomes critical. If ⟦503⟧ it concludes with the last narrative of these chapters (11:1–9), some color is lent to von Rad's claim (rather strongly expressed) that the absence of the mitigation element in the Babel story means that "the whole primeval history . . . seems to break off in strict dissonance" and that the question arises: "Is God's gracious forebearance now exhausted; has God rejected the nations in wrath forever?"[67] A sharp disjunction can then be made between universal history (Genesis 1–11) and "salvation history" (Genesis 12 onward), with the themes of the two units being set in contrast: universal history leads only to judgment, whereas the narrowing of vision to Abraham opens the way for an era of blessing, that is, for salvation history. Our statement (a) of the theme of the primeval history would thus appear to be appropriate.

However, it is most significant that there is no clear-cut break at the end of the Babel story. Clearly the Abraham material begins a new section of the Pentateuch, but the precise beginning of the Abraham material—and therewith the conclusion of the pre-Abrahamic material—cannot be determined.[68] In the final form of Genesis there is at no point a break between primeval and patriarchal history—11:10 (descendants of Shem) resumes from 10:21–31 (family of Shem) and is directed toward 11:27–30 (Abram and Sarai). Where there is a developed transitional passage from the one unit to the other, the probability of their being set in opposition thematically is minimized. If the patriarchal history unfolds the fulfillment of the blessing promise (12:2f.), the more positive reading of the theme of the primeval history [statement (b) above], with which it is integrated, is to be preferred. The patriarchal

66. Cf. similarly Brueggemann, *CBQ* 30 (1968) 175f.

67. Von Rad, *Genesis* (rev. ed.) 153.

68. Hence, I suppose, von Rad's indecisiveness on this question. On p. 152 of his *Genesis* (rev. ed.) we find the Babel story is the end of the primeval history, on p. 154 the "real conclusion" is 12:1–3, and on pp. 161ff. 12:4–9 is included in the primeval history.

narratives then function as the "mitigation" element for the story of mankind's dissolution at Babel.[69]

(ii) If we broaden our focus beyond Genesis, and consider the function of the primeval history within the Pentateuch as a whole, again I would suggest that the theme of Genesis 1–11, as expressed in statement (b) above, is closely parallel to the theme of the Pentateuch. Broadly speaking, the theme of the Pentateuch may be said to be: in spite of Israel's propensity to sinfulness, it experiences not only God's judgment but also his determination to save. Thus despite the patriarch's deceitfulness and faithlessness, for which they suffer danger and exile, the promise of progeny is fulfilled, and ⟦504⟧ despite Israel's rebellions, for which they suffer a generation's delay in entering the land and the death of their leader, they stand, at the end of the Pentateuch, on the brink of the fulfillment of the promise. That can only be a provisional, and doubtless over-ambitious, attempt to formulate the theme of this vast work, but in so far as it is an appropriate formulation it corresponds well to our reading of the theme of its initial eleven chapters. Genesis 1–11, therefore, works out on the plane of universal history the same theme that is developed in the Pentateuch as a whole.

It may finally be as well to make some remarks about what has and what has not been achieved by attempting to state the theme of Genesis 1–11. The reader may well wonder whether the seemingly banal, or at least rather unexciting, conclusion to which our quest for theme has led us has been worth the journey. Yet the very banality of statements of "themes," of whatever literary work, is evident proof of what they are not: they are not themselves literature, and they are not in any sense substitutes for the work itself. While they may point to the essential message of the work, they do not make the work a disposable packaging to be thrown away once the theme or the point has been extracted. At best their function is to orient the reader to the work, or at least to one critic's reading of the work; at most they serve to guide the reader away from possible misconceptions about the work; and one of their greatest values is when they convince the reader—as hopefully may happen in the present case—that the work *is* a literary work, and not a rag-bag or a scissors-and-paste job. In the end the quest for theme is only really successful if it returns the reader to the text.

69. Von Rad's view of the relation of the primeval and patriarchal histories is essentially similar (*Genesis* 154); my criticism of his exposition is principally that he over-dramatizes the significance of the Babel story, finding tension where none exists.

Historical Setting and Literary History

Up to this point our quest for theme in Genesis 1–11 has been pursued entirely within the boundaries of the text itself in its final form. No consideration has been given to the historical setting of the work or to its literary pre-history. This procedure does not imply any objection in principle to the relevance of such considerations, even though there are some literary critics who assert that a literary work is autonomous and must be understood independently of the circumstances of its origin.[70] Rather, since ⟦505⟧ in the case of the Pentateuch we have little hard evidence concerning its historical and literary origins, we do better, I think, to rest the weight of our study largely upon what we do have—the work itself—however subjective our understanding of it has to be, than upon hypotheses, however much they deal with "objective" data like dates and sources.

Nevertheless, if our reasoned intuitions about the theme of the work fit with current hypotheses about Pentateuchal origins, well and good; that may provide some confirmation of our proposal about theme. Ultimately, of course, our proposal about theme stands or falls with its applicability to the work itself.

I assume, following K. Elliger,[71] W. Brueggemann,[72] and others,[73] that the Priestly work belongs to the period of the exile as a message to the exiled, and I would argue further, that the Pentateuch as a whole relates to the same situation. It would not, however, affect the argument significantly if the more common date for the Pentateuch—the fifth

70. So E. Staiger, *Die Kunst der Interpretation* (4th ed.; Zürich: Atlantis, 1963); cf. M. Kessler, "Narrative Technique in 1 Sm 16, 1–13," *CBQ* 32 (1970) 543–54 (544); J. Blenkinsopp, "Stylistics of Old Testament Poetry," *Bib* 44 (1963) 352–8 (353); and for an extreme expression of this point of view, M. Weiss, "Wege der neuen Dichtungswissenschaft in ihrer Auswendung auf die Psalmenforschung," *Bib* 42 (1961) 255–302 (259). Cf. also R. E. Palmer, *Hermeneutics. Interpretation Theory in Schleiermacher, Dilthey, Heidegger, and Gadamer* (Evanston: Northwestern University Press, 1969) 246f.: "One's interest is in 'the thing said' itself, not in [the author's] intentions or personality. In the text a 'reality' is brought to stand. In the Garden of Eden scenes in *Paradise Lost,* a reality is brought to stand; one is not deeply interested in whether Milton actually had these feelings, nor does one really care whether Adam and Eve 'actually' had them, for in them something deeper and more universal is coming to expression: the possibilities resident in being, lighted up now for a moment in their truth."

71. "Sinn und Ursprung der priesterschriftlichen Geschichtserzählung," *ZTK* 49 (1952) 121–43.

72. "The Kerygma of the Priestly Writers," *ZAW* 84 (1972) 397–414 (398, 409 n. 38).

73. E.g., A. Eitz, *Studien zum Verhältnis von Priesterschrift und Deuterojesaja* (Heidelberg Diss., 1970) (cf. *ZAW* 82 [1970] 482). The recent study of A. Hurvitz, "The Evidence of Language in Dating the Priestly Code," *RB* 81 (1974) 24–56, arguing for a pre-exilic date for P, seems to rest on too narrow a base.

century—were adopted, and the work were interpreted as addressed to diaspora Jewry before the time of Ezra.

Most significantly, the Pentateuch concludes with Israel outside the promised land, but on the brink of entry under a new leader. This is exilic Israel's situation before the return. Genesis through Numbers incorporates Israel's canonical traditions of God's relationship with Israel, while Deuteronomy, a farewell discourse in the mouth of Moses, relates those traditions to Israel's present existence by declaring Israel, even on the eve of fulfillment, to be still open to the possibility of curse as well as of blessing.

Read from this point of view, Genesis 1–11 also takes on new light. The primeval history is not just about the nations, nor about God and man, but is heard in exile as a story of God and Israel. The dispersion of the nations (chap. 11) is Israel's own diaspora, the flood is the uncreation of Israel's life at the destruction of Jerusalem, the judgments of God upon primal sin are his righteous judgments upon sinful Israel. But the movement towards life and ⟦506⟧ salvation which the primeval history evidences is a word of hope to the exiles, a remnant is saved alive through the disaster of uncreation, a divine promise guarantees that such disaster will not recur, and an unbroken line stretches from the moment of dispersion to the summons "Go forth . . . to the land . . . ; I will make of you a great nation" (12:1f.). Although sin is congenital even in a re-created Israel, God's commitment to Israel stands as firm as the promise to Noah (so also Isa 54:9f.). Thus the traditional material of Genesis 1–11 not only is bound together by a unifying theme, and not only realizes *in parvo* the theme of the Pentateuch, but also speaks to a historical situation.

Our historical-critical inclinations compel us to ask one more question: *Whose* is the theme of Genesis 1–11? Clearly it is the final redactor who has worked out the theme we have attempted to discern, but he has been using traditional materials. Assuming the essential correctness of the usual analysis of J and P in Genesis 1–11, the theme-element "Creation—uncreation—re-creation" comes from the P source (Genesis 1; 6–8 [*partim*]; 9), though the sequence creation—flood—re-creation is as old at least as the Atrahasis epic.[74] P does not depict in narrative episodes the human movement towards uncreation; for him it suffices to observe: "The earth was corrupt in God's sight . . . and God saw the earth, and behold it was corrupt, for all flesh had corrupted their way upon the earth" (6:11f.). For P, of course, the genealogy of chap. 5 does not signify the

74. See A. R. Millard, "A New Babylonian 'Genesis' Story," *Tyndale Bulletin* 18 (1967) 3–18 ⟦in this volume, 114–28⟧; Clark, *ZAW* 83 (1971) 184–88.

encroachment of death upon life; to him death is a natural part of life, not the result of sin. Only when his genealogy follows the Yahwist's account of the origin of death (2:17; 3:19) does it take on that significance. From the Yahwist, we may be sure, comes the theme-element of the "spread of sin." The narratives of the primeval history are his,[75] and so especially is their sequence. Particularly if both Genesis 3 and the Cain and Abel story were previously told as tales of the *first* sin, and were first linked by him, his ordering of the narratives will have been in conformity with the theme of his work: the spread of sin cannot defeat, or, has not defeated, the purposes and blessing of God.[76] I take it that the narratives of the Yahwist's primeval ⟦507⟧ history are older than his work. The fact that they have in common a narrative pattern, the "sin—speech—mitigation—punishment" pattern discussed earlier, is not surprising; this may well be a narrative patterning from oral tradition.

The theme of Genesis 1–11, then, from the point of view of the history of tradition, is an amalgam of which the main elements correspond to the layers of the tradition. The amalgam, however, is a new unity, which makes sense and has a meaning independent of the meanings of its sources as they may be uncovered by literary archeology.

75. Cf. M. Noth, *A History of Pentateuchal Traditions* (Englewood Cliffs, N.J.: Prentice-Hall, 1972) 237f.

76. While Wolff, *Int* 20 (1966) 131–58, may well be correct in reading the Yahwist's work as addressed to the Israel of David and Solomon, and in focusing on the theme of blessing, I am not convinced that the Yahwist is proclaiming a message about Israel's responsibility to be a channel of blessing for the nations (e.g., p. 155), since the alternative interpretation of Gen 12:3 seems far preferable; see B. Albrektson, *History and the Gods. An Essay on the Idea of Historical Events as Divine Manifestations in the Ancient Near East and in Israel* (Lund: Gleerup, 1967) 78–81.

The Earth in Genesis 1

DAVID TOSHIO TSUMURA

⟦17⟧ The initial state of the earth is described in Gen 1:2 as *tōhû wābōhû*. This expression is traditionally translated into English as "without form and void" (RSV) or "formless and empty" (NIV). It was translated by various Greek phrases: ἀόρατος καὶ ἀκατασκεύαστος "invisible and unformed" (LXX); κένωμα καὶ οὐθέν "an emptiness and a nothing" (Aquila); θὲν καὶ οὐθέν "a nothing and a nothing" (Theodotion); (ἐγένετο) ἀργὸν καὶ ἀδιάκριτον "(became) unworked and indistinguishable" (Symmachus).[1] All but Symmachus rendered it in an abstract sense, though the Hebrew expression seems to have had a concrete sense originally.[2]

Etymology of **thw*

The term *tōhû* probably means "desert" or "waste" in Deut 32:10 where it appears in parallel with *ʾereṣ midbār* "a desert land." Until recently its etymology has been explained in the light of Arabic *tîh*, which Lane defined "desert or waterless desert in which one loses his way."[3] However, the Arabic term, with a second weak consonant, does not explain the final long /û/ of Hebrew *tōhû*. The Ugaritic term *thw* might be a better candidate for a possible cognate of the Hebrew term.

Reprinted with permission from David Toshio Tsumura, *The Earth and the Waters in Genesis 1 and 2: A Linguistic Investigation* (JSOTSup 83; Sheffield: Sheffield Academic Press, 1989) 17–23 and 30–43.

1. J. W. Wevers, *Septuaginta: Genesis* (Göttingen: Vandenhoeck & Ruprecht, 1974), 75.
2. See below.
3. E. W. Lane, *AEL*, 326, cf. also 323, where he lists *tûh* "desert." Cf. W. F. Albright, "Contributions to Biblical Archaeology and Philology," *JBL* 43 (1924), 365, who also cites Aram, *twh*, "be distracted."

Ugaritic

⟦18⟧ The term *thw* appears in the following Ugaritic text which reads:

14) *p np.š . npš . lbim* 15)*thw.*
hm . brlt . anḫr 16)*b ym.*
And my appetite is an appetite of
the lion(s) in/of the desert(s)
or a desire of the dolphin(?) in the sea.
(KTU 1.5 [UT 67]:I:14–16)[4]

The same phrase appears also in one of the mythological texts published in *Ug.* V (1968), 559–60: *lbim thw* (Text 4, 1.3–4).

A. Caquot, M. Sznycer and A. Herdner (1974) explain *thw* in the light of Hebrew *tōhû* and Arabic *tîh* "desert,"[5] following R. Dussaud, C. H. Gordon, H. L. Ginsberg and U. Cassuto.[6] On the other hand, E. L. Greenstein (1973), W. Johnstone (1978), J. C. de Moor (1979) and R. J. Clifford (1987)[7] follow W. F. Albright, T. H. Gaster, G. R. Driver, J. Gray, J. Aistleitner and A. Jirku who connect the term *thw* with Arabic *hawiya* "to desire" and analyze it as a verbal form.

However, instead of *thw* in *Ug.* V, 559–60, Dietrich-Loretz-Sanmartín (1975) read *thwt*:

1) *w yᶜny . bn* 2)*ilm . mt.*
npšm 3)*npš . lbim* 4)*thwt.*
w npš 5)*anḫr b ym.*
And the god (lit. son of gods) Mot answered:
"Now my appetite is an appetite of
the lion(s) in/of the desert(s),
an appetite of the dolphin(?) in the sea."
(KTU 1.133[604]:2–5)

4. In this ⟦article⟧, Ugaritic texts are cited by *KTU* text number with Gordon's *UT* text number in square brackets.

5. A. Caquot, M. Sznycer and A. Herdner, *TO*, 241, n. *m.*

6. Also J. C. L. Gibson, *CML*², 68 and 159: "waste."

7. E. L. Greenstein, "Another Attestation of Initial ẖ > ʾ̱ in West Semitic," *JANES* 5 (1973), 157–164; W. Johnstone, "Lexical and Comparative Philological Contributions to Ugaritic of Mythological Texts of the 24th Campaign at Ras Shamra," *Ug.* VII (1978), 117; J. C. de Moor, "Contributions to the Ugaritic Lexicon," *UF* 11 (1979), 640; R. J. Clifford, "Mot Invites Baal to a Feast: Observations on a Difficult Ugaritic Text (CTA 5.i = KTU 1.5.1)," in D. M. Golomb (ed.), *"Working with No Data": Semitic and Egyptian Studies Presented to Thomas O. Lambdin* (Winona Lake, Eisenbrauns, 1987), 57, n. 6.

They take both *thw* and *thwt* as nouns from **hwy* (// Heb. **ʾwh*) and translate *thwt* as "Gier, Verlangen" like Hebrew *taʾăwāh* "desire, appetite."[8] ⟦19⟧ Certainly the form *thwt* cannot be a verbal form from **hwy*. Yet, their view that *hm brlt* is a gloss to *thw* and corresponds in KTU 1.133:4 to *wnpš*, also a gloss, is not convincing. The particles *hm* and *w* should be taken as indicating the beginning of the second colon and as introducing terms, *brlt* or *npš*, which correspond to those in the first colon: *npš* or *npš*.[9]

Based on KTU 's reading, B. Margalit (1980) and G. del Olmo Lete (1981, 82) explained *thwt* (KTU 1.133[UT 604]:4) as a variant form of *thw*, i.e., a feminine or plural form of *thw*, and again supported the view that Ugaritic *thw* is a cognate of Hebrew *tōhû*.[10]

Contextually, *lbim thw*(*t*) "the lion(s) in/of the desert(s)" corresponds well to *anẖr b ym* "the dolphin(?) in the sea," since *npš* and *brlt* are a well-known idiomatic pair (e.g., KTU 1.18:IV:25, 36–37, 1.19:II:38–39, 43–44). As for the image of hungry animals, it is interesting to compare it with that in Jer 5:6, where *ʾaryēh miyyaʿar* "a lion from the forest" corresponds to *zĕʾēb ʿărābôt* "a wolf of the desert" in a parallelism. In the Ugaritic texts, the land animal, *lbim thw*(*t*), and the sea animal, *anẖr b ym*,[11] seem to constitute a merismatic pair[12] and express the comprehensiveness of the voracious appetite of the god Mot in the Ugaritic mythology.[13]

In the light of the above, it is probable that Ugaritic *thw* is a cognate of Hebrew *tōhû* and that both have the common meaning of "a desert." If so, they are most probably ⟨qutl-⟩ pattern nouns (<*/tuhwu/) from the common (West) Semitic root **thw*.[14]

8. M. Dietrich-O. Loretz-J. Sanmartín, "Beiträge zur Ugaritischen Textgeschichte (II): Textologische Probleme in RS 24.293 = Ug. 5, S. 559, NR. 4 und CTA 5 I 11*–22*," *UF* 7 (1975), 537 follows Greenstein, "Another Attestation of Initial ẖ > ʾ̱ in West Semitic," 160, n. 20, who suggested a possible interchange of *ʾ*/*h* in Hebrew *ʾwh* and Ugaritic *hwy*.

9. See Clifford, "Mot Invites Baal to a Feast," 58f. for a recent discussion of the '*p* . . . *hm* . . .' structure in lines 3–10.

10. B. Margalit, *A Matter of "Life" and "Death": A Study of the Baal-Mot Epic* (CTA *4-5-6*) (Neukirchen-Vluyn: Neukirchener Verlag, 1980), 97; G. del Olmo Lete, *MLC*, 635 and "Notes on Ugaritic Semantics V," *UF* 14 (1982), 60.

11. Cf. Akk. *nāḫiru* "whale" as a "sea-horse" (*sīsâ ša tâmti*) in *CAD*, N/1 (1980), 137. Also note that in a certain text, VAT 8917 rev. 11–13, *ilibu* (anše.a.ab.ba [lit.: 'horse of the sea']) "dromedary" is identified with the ghost of Tiāmat (*eṭemmu tiāmat*) and appears in parallel with *serrēmu* (anše.eden.na [lit.: 'horse of the plain']) "wild ass," the ghost of Enlil; cf. A. Livingstone, *MMEW*, 82.

12. Olmo Lete, *MLC*, 635 notes that *thw* "estepa, desierto" is antonymous to *ym*.

13. Cf. Hab 2:5. See A. Cooper, "Divine Names and Epithets in the Ugaritic Texts," *RSP* III (1981), 395.

14. J. Huehnergard, *UVST*, 287 and 84: "*/tuhwu/ 'wasteland'."

"Chaos"?

⟦20⟧ Since the earliest times many translators have felt that the meaning "desert" is unsatisfactory for the content of Gen 1:2, as reflected in the various Greek versions. Hence, English translations such as "formlessness," "confusion," "unreality," "emptiness" (BDB) or "nothingness" have been suggested on a contextual basis. And it has been asserted that the term *tōhû* "should, according to all analogies, mean something like 'chaos'."[15]

Though Albright's etymological explanation that *tōhû* should be regarded as "a blend between *bōhû* and *tehôm*, from which the initial *t* was borrowed" is no longer tenable, his conclusion that the phrase *tōhû wābōhû* signifies a "chaos" and *tōhû* is referring to "chaos as a watery deep, or tehom, in the Mesopotamian sense"[16] is shared by many modern scholars. For example, Cassuto thinks that the phrase *tōhû wābōhû* refers to the "terrestrial state" in which "the whole material was an undifferentiated, unorganized, confused and lifeless agglomeration." He assumes in Gen 1:2 existence of a watery chaos, in which "water [was] above and solid matter beneath, and the whole a chaotic mass, without order or life."[17] Thus, the expression *tōhû wābōhû* in v. 2 is taken as signifying the primordial "chaos," which means not simply "emptiness," like Greek χάος "empty space,"[18] but also "disorder" or "disorganization," and stands in direct opposition to the "creation."

Before discussing the biblical usages of the term *tōhû*, the etymology of the term *bōhû* and a possible extra-biblical usage of *tōhû wābōhû* will be discussed in the following sections.

Etymology of **bhw*

Arabic

⟦21⟧ The Hebrew term *bōhû* occurs only three times in the Bible, always with *tōhû*. Its etymology has been explained by the Arabic *bahiya* "to

15. Albright, "Contributions to Biblical Archaeology," 365; also F. M. Cross, *Canaanite Myth and Hebrew Epic: Essays in the History of the Religion of Israel* (Cambridge, Mass.: Harvard University Press, 1975), 323.

16. Albright, "Contributions to Biblical Archaeology," 366.

17. U. Cassuto, *From Adam to Noah* [Part I of *A Commentary on the Book of Genesis*] (Jerusalem: Magnes, 1961, 1944 [orig.]), 23. B. K. Waltke, "The Creation Account in Genesis 1:1–3. Part III: The Initial Chaos Theory and the Precreation Chaos Theory," *BS* 132 (1975), 225–228 interprets the phrase *tōhû wābōhû* as referring to "the chaotic state . . . before the creation." Also G. J. Wenham, *Genesis 1–15* (Word Biblical Commentary 1; Waco: Word Books, 1987), 16: "the dreadfulness of the situation before the divine word brought order out of chaos is underlined."

18. Gk. χάος "empty space," from χαίνειν, "gape, yawn" (cf. the Norse *Ginunga Gap*). Cf. Albright, "Contributions to Biblical Archaeology," 366.

be empty" (BDB).[19] This Arabic term is used to describe the "empty" or "vacant" state of a tent or house which contains nothing or little furniture or goods.[20] Thus, it has basically a concrete meaning rather than an abstract meaning such as "nothingness" or "emptiness."

Akkadian

Albright suggested that the Akkadian term *bûbûtu*, "emptiness, hunger," came from **buhbuhtu* and is a possible cognate of the Hebrew *bōhû*.[21] However, *CAD* B (1965), 301–302 does not list "emptiness" as the meaning of *bubūtu* A, only giving translations "famine, starvation, want"; "hunger"; "sustenance" for the term. *AHw*, 135 suggests simply "Hunger" for the meaning of *bubūtu*. For a different term *bubuʾtu*, the root of which is **bwʿ* rather than **bhw*, *CAD* B, 300 gives the meanings, "inflammation, boil, pustule."[22] Neither of these Akkadian terms is cognate of the Hebrew *bōhû*.

Phoenician

It has been suggested that the term *bōhû* is associated with a Phoenician divine name Βάαυ, the goddess of "night,"[23] which is mentioned by Philo of Byblos. According to Albright, the divine name Βάαυ "shows that the original form of the noun was **báhu*, like Arab. *bahw*; **buhw* has changed ⟦22⟧ *a* to *u* under the influence of the labials."[24] Cassuto admits this possibility.[25] Certainly it is phonologically possible to posit an original "Canaanite" form */báhwu/ for both Hebrew *bōhû*[26] and Phoenician */bah(a)wu/, which was seemingly represented in Greek script as *ba-a-u*. However, there is no evidence that the Hebrew term had any connection with the Phoenician divine name, except for their possible common derivation from the root, **bhw*.

19. Lane, *AEL*, 260.

20. Lane, *AEL*, 269f.

21. Albright, "Contributions to Biblical Archaeology," 366.

22. Cf. A. R. Millard, "עלץ 'to exult'," *JTS* 26 (1975), 89 comparing Akkadian *bubuʾtu* with *bûʿāʾ*, *bûʿătāʾ* "abscess" (< *bûaʿ* "to swell, to rejoice").

23. As E. Ebeling noted more than half a century ago, this DN and Heb. *bōhû* have nothing to do with the Sum. goddess Baʾu; cf. Ebeling, "Baʾu," *RlA* 1 (1928), 432. See also Albright, "Contributions to Biblical Archaeology," 366, n. 7; Cassuto, *From Adam to Noah*, 22.

24. Albright, "Contributions to Biblical Archaeology," 366.

25. Cassuto, *From Adam to Noah*, 21f.

26. Cf. **báhwu/* > /búhwu/ > /búhu̯u/ > /búhū/ > /bṓhū/. See below p. 24 ⟦not reprinted here⟧, however, for a possible original form */bíhwu/ from a Ugaritic example written syllabically.

Egyptian

If, as recent studies show,[27] the material for Philo's cosmogony originated in Egypt, the divine name Βάαυ might have come from an Egyptian word such as *bꜣ.w*.[28] However, even if this should be the case, it is not likely that Hebrew term *bōhû*, with the consonant /h/, is related to these Egyptian terms.

Recently Görg suggested that *tōhû* and *bōhû* should be explained by other Egyptian terms, *thꜣ* "abweichen" ⟦'to depart'⟧, "verfehlen" ⟦'to miss'⟧ and *bhꜣ* "kopflos fliehen" ⟦'to flee precipitously'⟧.[29] However, his etymological argument is almost purely speculative. For one thing, there is no evidence for the existence of the nominal forms *t(e/u)hꜣ́ǎw. ˘t* and *b(e/u)hꜣ́ǎw. ˘t*. Moreover, their suggested meanings, "Ziellosigkeit" ⟦'aimlessness'⟧, "Vergeblichkeit" ⟦'uselessness'⟧ and "Flüchtigkeit" ⟦'transience'⟧, "Nichtigkeit" ⟦'nothingness'⟧, are pure guesses, especially "Vergeblichkeit" and "Nichtigkeit." Furthermore, no hendiadic combination of them is attested in Egyptian. So it is highly speculative to think that the pair, "haltlos und gestaltlos" ⟦'unstable and shapeless'⟧ refers to "Negativeigenschaften des hermopolitanischen Chaos" ⟦'negative qualities of the Hermopolite chaos'⟧.

Hebrew

Westermann recognizes only a stylistic variation between *tōhû* and *tōhû* ⟦23⟧ *wābōhû*. According to him, "בהו is added only by way of alliteration" and "when תהו and בהו occur together there is no real difference in meaning."[30] However, if *bōhû* were added simply as an "alliteration" to *tōhû*, it would be difficult to explain why the conjunction *wā* is used to connect these two terms. Moreover, *tōhû* and *bōhû* seems to be a traditional word pair, which can appear as a parallel word pair (A//B), as in Isa 34:11, or as a juxtaposed phrase (A and B), as in Gen 1:2 and Jer 4:23.

Thus, in the light of the above discussion, Hebrew *bōhû*, though still lacking definite etymology, seems to be a Semitic term based on the root

27. R. A. Oden, Jr., "Philo of Byblos and Hellenistic Historiography," *PEQ* (1978), 126.

28. J. Ebach's position that Βάαυ comes from the plural form of Egyptian Ba (*bꜣ.w*) is rejected on a phonological basis by Görg, who suggests that "Bāu" should be connected with Egyptian *bjꜣ* "heaven" or *bjꜣ.w*; cf. M. Görg, "*Tohû wabohû*—ein Deutungsvorschlag," *ZAW* 92 (1980), 431–434. However, *bjꜣ* is no better than *bꜣ.w*.

29. Görg, "*Tohû wabohû*—ein Deutungsvorschlag," 433f.

30. C. Westermann, *Genesis*. I. Teilband: Genesis 1–11 (BKAT I/1; Neukirchen-Vluyn: Neukirchener Verlag, 1974), 143 [ET 103]. ⟦In the following footnotes, numbers in double brackets are original footnote numbers.⟧

**bhw* and possibly a cognate of Arabic *bahiya* "to be empty." ⟦pp. 24–29 omitted⟧

. . . .

Uses of Hebrew *tōhû* and *tōhû wābōhû*

tōhû

⟦30⟧ The term *tōhû* occurs twenty times in the Old Testament, eleven of which are in Isaiah. The uses of the term can be classified into three groups: from the concrete meaning "desert" to the abstract "emptiness." According to Westermann, they are:[31]

(1) "desert": "the grim desert waste that brings destruction"
—Deut 32:10; Job 6:18, 12:24 = Ps 107:40;

(2) "a desert or devastation that is threatened"
("eine Öde oder Verwüstung, die angerichtet wird")
—Isa 24:10, 34:11, 40:23; Jer 4:23;
"the state which is opposed to and precedes creation" ⟦31⟧
—Gen 1:2, Isa 45:18; Job 26:7;

(3) "nothingness"[32] —1 Sam 12:21 (twice); Isa 29:21, 40:17, 41:29[!], 44:9, 45:19,[33] 49:4,[34] 59:4.

"desert" The first group of the texts (1) certainly describes *tōhû*, which is synonymous with "a desert land" (Deut 32:10), as "the wasteland" where caravans perish (Job 6:18) and as "a trackless waste" where people wander (Job 12:24, Ps 107:40). Thus, the term refers to the actual desert as "a wasteland."

"emptiness" As for the third group (3), the term *tōhû* seems to refer to a situation which lacks something abstract that should be there, such as worth, purpose, truth, profit and integrity. The term *tōhû* is used in an abstract sense in these passages where it appears in parallel with other abstract nouns such as *ʾayin* (or *ʾāyin*) in Isa 40:17 and 23,[35] *rîq* "empty" in 49:4 and *ʾepes* "nothing" in 41:29. The idols and the idol makers are also condemned as *tōhû* which is in parallel with the phrase *lōʾ-yôʿîlû*

31. ⟦65⟧. Westermann, *Genesis* I, 142f. [ET 102f.].

32. ⟦66⟧. "It should be noted that in none of these passages does 'nothing' or 'nothingness' indicate the existence of a material 'nothing'; it is contrasted rather with meaningful existence" (Westermann, *Genesis* I, 143 [ET 103]).

33. ⟦67⟧. Isa 45:19 should be classified as (2). See below, pp. 34ff. ⟦319–21⟧, for a detailed discussion.

34. ⟦68⟧. Not in ET, but in the German original.

35. ⟦69⟧. However, Westermann classifies this verse as the second group (2).

or *bal-yôᶜîlû* "unprofitable, worthless" in 1 Sam 12:21 and Isa 44:9.[36] In two passages, the term *tōhû* refers to words of the unrighteous, i.e., "false testimony"[37] in Isa 29:21 and "empty argument" (NIV) in 59:4.

In this regard, the term in this category would be better understood as "a lack" or "emptiness" rather than "nothingness." Moreover it should be noted here that this abstract use of *tōhû* seems to be typical of Isaiah and that the only other usage in this sense is in 1 Sam 12:21, referring to idols in ⟦32⟧ a similar fashion to Isa 44:9. Furthermore, it is significant to note that the term in this sense is never used with nouns such as "earth" (*ʾereṣ*) and "city" (*ᶜîr*).

"desert-like state". In all but one[38] of the passages classified in Westermann's group (2), the term *tōhû* is used for describing the situation or condition of places such as earth, land or city. Let us examine each passage in detail.

Isa 24:10

nišběrāh qiryat-tōhû
suggar kol-bayit mibbôʾ

The city of chaos is broken down,
every house is shut up so that none can enter. (RSV)
The ruined city lies desolate;
the entrance to every house is barred. (NIV)

The entire chapter of Isaiah 24 talks about the Lord's devastation of the earth. The beginning and the end of the opening section, vv. 1–3a, refer to the earth which will be "completely laid waste" (YHWH *bôqēq hāʾāreṣ // hibbôq tibbôq hāʾāreṣ*) and thus comprise an *inclusio.* In v. 12, "the city is left in ruins, its gate is battered to pieces" (NIV), the desolation of a city is mentioned in terms, *šammāh* and *ᶜîr,* different from those in v. 10 where the term *tōhû* signifies a "desert-like" (or "desolate") state of a city, *qiryāh. Thus, *tōhû* here is almost equivalent of *šammāh.*[39]

Job 26:7

nōṭeh ṣāpôn ᶜal-tōhû
tōleh ʾereṣ ᶜal-bělî-māh

36. ⟦70⟧. E. J. Young translates *tōhû* in Isa 44:9 as "unreality" and explains that the word "suggests an absence of all life and power," *The Book of Isaiah III* (NICOT; Grand Rapids: Eerdmans, 1972), 172.

37. ⟦71⟧. E. J. Young, *The Book of Isaiah II* (NICOT; Grand Rapids: Eerdmans, 1969), 322: "deceit." He explains that "תּוֹהוּ prob. signifies 'lies and falsehoods, anything that is vanity and not based upon truth' " (p. 329).

38. ⟦72⟧. Isa 40:23 belongs to the third group, as noted above.

39. ⟦73⟧. See below p. 39 ⟦324–25⟧ on *šěmāmāh* (Jer 4:27).

He stretches out the north over the void,
  and hangs the earth upon nothing. (RSV)
He spreads out the northern 'skies'[40] over empty space;
  he suspends the earth over nothing. (NIV)

⟦33⟧ Westermann thinks that the term *tōhû* here is "the direct opposite of creation," though he avoids translating *tōhû* as "chaos" here. However, the two verbal forms from *nṭh "to stretch, spread" and *tlh "to hang, suspend," seem to require concrete objects. The term *tōhû*, which is in parallel with "a place where there is nothing" (*bĕlî-māh*), not with an abstract concept "nothing" or "nothingness" as in the case of the third group (above), would have a concrete meaning. Hence, a translation like "a desert-like place" or "an empty place" might be suggested for *tōhû* in this context.

If the term *ṣāpôn* (cf. Isa 14:13) should be originally a place name "Zaphon,"[41] it may possibly stand, like Ugaritic *ṣpn*,[42] for a high mountain in this context and the idea that the Lord stretches out the high mountains, i.e., the high places of the earth,[43] over an empty place could correspond to the Lord's suspending the earth over a place where there is nothing (*bĕlî-māh*), i.e., an empty place. Thus, the following transition might be suggested:

He stretches out the high mountains over an empty place,
he suspends the earth over a place where there is nothing.

Isa 45:18

lōˀ-tōhû bĕrāˀāh
lāšebet yĕṣārāh

he did not create it a chaos,
he formed it to be inhabited (RSV)[44]
  he did not create it to be empty,
  but formed it to be inhabited. (NIV)

40. ⟦74⟧. Cf. Isa 40:22: "He stretches out the heavens like a canopy" (NIV).

41. ⟦75⟧. M. H. Pope, *Job*³ (AB 15; New York: Doubleday, 1973), 180; cf. J. J. M. Roberts, "Ṣāpon in Job 26:7," *Bib* 56 (1975), 554–557.

42. ⟦76⟧. Cf. *Ug.* V (1968), 44 on RS 20.24 where *ḫuršan ḫazi* "Mount Ḫazzi" corresponds to *ṣpn* in the alphabetic divine list (*KTU* 1.118:4; cf. 14).

43. ⟦77⟧. Cf. N. H. Tur-Sinai, *The Book of Job: A New Commentary* (Jerusalem: Kiryath Sepher, 1967), 380f.: "the floating land."

44. ⟦78⟧. "He did not create it a waste,
But formed it for habitation." (JPS)

Taking *tōhû* as "chaos," Westermann explains that *tōhû* here is "the direct opposite of creation."[45] However, *tōhû* here is contrasted with *lāšebet* in the parallelism and seems to refer rather to a place which has no habitation, like the term *šĕmāmāh* "desolation" (cf. Jer 4:27; Isa 24:12), ⟦34⟧ *ḥārēb* "waste, desolate"[46] and *ᶜăzûbāh* "deserted."[47] There is nothing in this passage that would suggest a chaotic state of the earth "which is opposed to and precedes creation."[48] Thus, the term *tōhû* here too signifies "a desert-like place" and refers to "an uninhabited place." The verse might be better translated as follows:

> Not to be a desert-like place he created it;
> to be inhabited he formed it.

It should be noted that *lōᵓ-tōhû* here is a resultative object, referring to the purpose of God's creative action. In other words, this verse explains that God did not create the earth so that it may stay desert-like, but to be inhabited. So, this verse does not contradict Gen 1:2, where God created the earth to be productive and inhabited though it "was" still *tōhû wābōhû* in the initial state.[49]

Isa 45:19

> *lōᵓ bassēter dibbartî*
> *bimqôm ᵓereṣ ḥōšek*
> *lōᵓ ᵓāmartî lĕzeraᶜ yaᶜăqōb*
> *tōhû baqqĕšûnî*

The term *tōhû* here has been interpreted in basically two ways, in a concrete (locative) sense and in an abstract sense. For example, "Seek me in chaos" (RSV); "Look for me in the empty void" (NEB); "in a wasteland" (JPS); "Look for me in an empty waste" (NAB). On the other hand, NIV translates *tōhû* as "in vain," thus suggesting an abstract sense. A similar interpretation has been given by Westermann, who translates *tōhû* as in "im Öden (oder im Nichtigen)" ⟦'in the wastelands (or in nothingness)'⟧ and explains "*Tōhū*, meaning nothingness, that which is empty,

45. ⟦79⟧. Westermann, *Genesis* I, 142 [ET 103].

46. ⟦80⟧. Note the Akkadian cognate, *ḫarbu* "wasteland" and its verbal use in the following passage: *erṣetu šî iḫarrumma ana arkat ūmē uššab* "that land will become waste but it will be (re-) inhabited thereafter" (CT 39, 21:168, SB Alu—cited by *CAD*, Ḫ [1956], 87). Also Ezek 28:19.

47. ⟦81⟧. See below p. 39 ⟦324–25⟧ on Jer 4:23ff. for these terms.

48. ⟦82⟧. Westermann, *Genesis.* I, 142 [ET 103].

49. ⟦83⟧. See below pp. 41ff. ⟦326–28⟧.

can also have the sense of 'futile' ('das Sinnlose')—the meaning would then be, 'Seek me in vain' ('Umsonst suchet mich')."[50]

⟦35⟧ All of them understand the syntax in the same way, following MT's punctuation and taking *tōhû* as an adverbial phrase which modifies the verbal phrase *baqqĕšûnî*, thus as part of the direct speech. LXX similarly takes *tōhû* as a part of the direct speech. On the other hand, Symmachus' translation leaves some ambiguity in its understanding of the syntax of *tōhû*.[51]

Those who take the term *tōhû* in an abstract sense assume that *tōhû* corresponds to *bassēter* "in secret" (or "secretly") and hence means "in vain" or the like. *BHS*'s suggestion to read בְּתֹהוּ here seems to take this position. However, the term *tōhû* usually has such an abstract meaning when it appears in parallel with the abstract nouns with a similar meaning such as "nothing" or "emptiness" as noted above.

It may be that *tōhû* is just a part of the sarcastic expression *tōhû baqqĕšûnî* "In vain seek me!" (cf. NIV) and has no grammatical correspondence with any preceding phrase. However, since the two verbal phrases *dibbartî* and *ʾāmartî* correspond to each other, *tōhû baqqĕšûnî* "In vain seek me!" could be taken as a direct object of *dibbartî* too. Thus, "Not in secret I spoke. . . 'In vain seek me!' " However, such an understanding is the least suitable to the context.

The most natural explanation structurally would be that *tōhû* is in parallel with *bimqôm*[52] *ʾereṣ ḥōšek* "in a land of darkness." In other words, *tōhû* without a preposition directly corresponds either to *ʾereṣ ḥōšek* or to *ḥōšek* and, in the last colon, an element corresponding to *bimqôm* or *bimqôm ʾereṣ* is ellipsized. The former may be supported by the fact that *tōhû* basically means "desert." On the other hand, the latter might be supported by a similar expression, though in a reverse order, *tōhû wābōhû* // *ḥōšek* (Gen 1:2) and *tōhû wābōhû* // *ʾên ʾôr* "no light" (Jer 4:23) as well as *tōhû* // *ḥōšek* (Job 12:24–25).[53] In this case, the term *tōhû*, ⟦36⟧ corresponding directly to *ḥōšek* "darkness," probably means "desolation."

50. ⟦84⟧. C. Westermann, *Das Buch Jesaja: Kapitel 40–66* (Göttingen, 1966) [ET: *Isaiah 40–66* (London, 1969)], 140 [173]. Cf. also Young, *The Book of Isaiah III*, 210: "In vain seek ye me"; M. Dijkstra, "Zur Deutung von Jesaja 45, 15ff.," *ZAW* 89 (1977), 221: "Suchet mich vergebens" ⟦'Seek me in vain'⟧.

51. ⟦85⟧. For a detailed discussion, see D. T. Tsumura, "*tōhû* in Isa. xlv 19," *VT* 38 (1988), 361–364.

52. ⟦86⟧. *bimqôm* "in (lit. in the place of)" here functions almost as a compound preposition like *bĕtôk* or *baʾăšer*. Also cf. *bimqôm ʾăšer* in Hos 2:1, 2 Sam 15:21, etc.

53. ⟦87⟧. Note that vv. 24a–25b constitute the so-called "AXYB Pattern," in which v. 24a and v. 25b are in a distant parallelism, while v. 24b and v. 25a constitute an "inserted" bicolon; cf. D. T. Tsumura, "'Inserted Bicolon', the AXYB Pattern, in Amos I 5 and Psalm IX 7," *VT* 38 (1988), 234–236. In this structure, it is clear that *tōhû* and *ḥōšek* are a parallel

It is thus probably correct that the term *tōhû* is not to be included in the direct speech, since the verbal phrase *dibbartî*, like *ʾāmartî*, seems to take *lĕzeraʿ yaʿăqōb* as an indirect object and *baqqĕšûnî* as a direct object, i.e., direct speech. If *dibbartî* should take *tōhû baqqĕšûnî* as a direct object, the term *tōhû* would become a redundant element in a structure such as "I did not speak . . . in a land of darkness, 'In a waste land / in a land of desolation (*tōhû*) seek me!' "

Our new translation would be as follows:

I did not speak in secret,
  in a land of darkness,
I did not say to Jacob's descendants
  (in a land of) desolation,[54] 'Seek me!'

tōhû wābōhû

Jer 4:23

23)rāʾîtî ʾet-hāʾāreṣ wĕhinnēh-tōhû wābōhû
wĕʾel-haššāmayim wĕʾên ʾôrām
24)rāʾîtî hehārîm wĕhinnēh rōʿăšîm
wĕkol- haggĕbāʿôt hitqalqālû
25)rāʾîtî wĕhinnēh ʾên hāʾādām
wĕkol-ʿôp haššāmayim nādādû
26)rāʾîtî wĕhinnēh hakkarmel hammidbār
wĕkōl-ʿārâw nittĕṣû
mippĕnê Yhwh *mippĕnê ḥărôn ʾappô*

⟦I looked at the earth,
  and it was desolate and empty;
And at the heavens,
  and their light was gone.
I looked at the mountains,
  and they were quaking;
  and all the hills were rocking.
I looked and there was no man;
  and all the birds of the sky had fled.

---

word pair. This has never been noticed by commentators: e.g., Tur-Sinai, *The Book of Job*, 218f.; Pope, *Job*[3], 95; S. R. Driver and G. B. Gray, *A Critical and Exegetical Commentary on the Book of Job* (ICC; Edinburgh: T. & T. Clark, 1921), 120; E. Dhorme, *A Commentary on the Book of Job* (London: Thomas Nelson & Sons, 1967), 180; R. Gordis, *The Book of Job* (New York: Jewish Theological Seminary of America, 1978), 141.

54. ⟦88⟧. Or "(in) a desolate place."

I looked: the fruitful land was a wilderness;
and all its towns were in ruin—
Because of the Lord,
Because of His fierce anger. (JPSV)]]

It is often asserted that Jer 4:23–26 pictures a return to the primeval chaos. For example, Bright says that "the story of Genesis 1 has been reversed: men, beasts, and growing things are gone, the dry land itself totters, the heavens cease to give their light, and primeval chaos returns. It is as if the earth had been 'uncreated.' "[55] McKane also expresses a similar [[37]] view in his recent commentary. He thinks that this signifies the "return to the chaos which prevailed before the world was ordered by Yahweh's creative acts."[56] He even says that "According to v. 23 there has been a collapse of cosmic order and an invasion by the power of chaos."[57]

However, this view is greatly influenced by the interpretation of the phrase *tōhû wābōhû* as "chaos" in Gen 1:2 and is not based on the contextual analysis of Jer 4:23ff. itself.

There is certainly no question about the similarity in the terms and phrases between Jer 4:23ff. and Gen 1:2ff. However, it is not so certain as some scholars assume whether the former is patterned after or "modelled on" the latter.

For example, Fishbane[58] finds in Jer 4:23–26 the same order of creation as in Gen 1:1–2:4a and assumes a "recovered use of the creation pattern" in this Jeremiah passage. According to him, the order of creation reflected in Jer 4:23–26 is as follows: *tōhû wābōhû*–"light"–"heavens"–"earth" (:"mountains," "hills")–"bird"–"man"–"his fierce anger." However, the actual order of terms and phrases mentioned in Jer 4:23ff. is as follows: ["earth"–*tōhû wābōhû*] // ["heavens"–"light"], "mountains" // "hills," "man" // "bird," and ["fruitful land"–"desert"] // "towns." Fishbane thinks that the difference in "the order of creation" in the cases of "earth" → "heavens" and "man" → "bird" in Jer 4:23ff. does not disprove his case, because "the synthetic parallelism progresses from below to above in all cases" and "there is no one fixed order to these traditional pairs."

55. [[89]]. J. Bright, *Jeremiah* (AB 21; New York: Doubleday, 1965), 33.

56. [[90]]. W. McKane, *A Critical and Exegetical Commentary on Jeremiah*, Vol. I (ICC; Edinburgh: T. & T. Clark, 1986), 106. Cf. also B. S. Childs, *Myth and Reality in the Old Testament* (London: SCM, 1960), 42 and 76; H. Wildberger, *Jesaja*, 2. Teilband: Jesaja 13–27 (BKAT X/2; Neukirchen-Vluyn: Neukirchener Verlag, 1978), 920; R. P. Carroll, *Jeremiah* (London: SCM, 1986), 168.

57. [[91]]. McKane, *Jeremiah* I, 107.

58. [[92]]. M. Fishbane, "Jeremiah IV 23–26 and Job III 3–13: A Recovered Use of the Creation Pattern," *VT* 21 (1971), 152.

However, it should be noted that not all the terms of the Jeremiah passage appear in the Genesis passage. Moreover, the order is not the same in both passages despite Fishbane's explanation. For one thing, the "earth" in Jer 4:23 should be compared with the "earth" in Gen 1:2, since both are described by the same phrase *tōhû wābōhû*. If this is the case, his suggestion to reverse the order of "earth" → "heavens" to "heavens" → "earth" so that the order might be the same as that of Gen 1:3ff. is without support.

Also, "light" in Jer 4:23 refers to the light of the "heavens" and it should be compared rather with "luminaries" of the sky in Gen 1:14. Fishbane ⟦38⟧ thinks that *ʾôr* "light" in Jer 4:23 should be connected with *ʾôr* which was created on the first day in Genesis account. On the other hand, McKane explains *ʾôr* as referring to the "luminaries" of the sky, like *mĕʾōrōt* (Gen 1:14).[59] Holladay takes *ʾôr* (Jer 4:23) as "light" rather than "the light-giving sun and moon and stars," but says: "In Genesis 1:3–5 the creation of light is not associated specifically with the heavens but is thoroughly appropriate here."[60] Thus he notes the difference between Gen 1:3–5 and Jer 4:23.

Recently, Kselman noted that "The chiastic *thw wbhw* // *ḥšk* [in Gen 1:2] is echoed in Jer 4:23 (*thw wbhw* // *ʾyn ʾwrm*), a poem modelled on Gen 1."[61] Thus he also takes the similarity in the two parallel pairs as a result of the direct relationship between the two documents. However, the similarity between Gen 1:2 and Jer 4:23 exists only in the similar phrases, "darkness" *ḥōšek* (Gen 1:2) and its *negated antonym* "no light" *ʾên ʾôrām* (Jer 4:23) as well as *tōhû wābōhû*,[62] but not in the subject matter, or referents. In other words, in the Genesis passage it is "earth" // *tĕhôm* that is referred to; in Jeremiah, "earth" // "heavens."

Moreover, the nature of relationship between the two referents in Gen 1:2 is different from that in Jer 4:23. In the latter it is merismatic, or contrastive; in the former it is hyponymous.[63] While in Gen 1:2 only the "earth," which was totally covered with *tĕhôm*-waters, is the subject matter, in Jer 4:23 the whole universe, "the heavens and the earth," is the topic of concern. In the light of the above discussion, it is rather

59. ⟦93⟧. Cf. McKane, *Jeremiah* I, 107.

60. ⟦94⟧. W. L. Holladay, *Jeremiah 1: A Commentary on the Book of the Prophet Jeremiah Chapters 1–25* (Philadelphia: Fortress, 1986), 165.

61. ⟦95⟧. J. S. Kselman, "The Recovery of Poetic Fragments from the Pentateuchal Priestly Source," *JBL* 97 (1978), 164, n. 13: "a poem modelled on Gen 1; cf. M. Fishbane, *VT* 21 (1971), 151–67."

62. ⟦96⟧. See above pp. 35f. ⟦320–21⟧ on a word pair, *tōhû* and *ḥōšek* in Isa 45:19 and Job 12:24–25.

63. ⟦97⟧. See below pp. 67–72 ⟦not reprinted here⟧ for a detailed discussion of a hyponymous relation between the "earth" and *tĕhôm*.

difficult to assume that Jer 4:23–26 is patterned after or "modelled on" the creation story in Gen 1:1–2:4a.

Let us place the passage Jer 4:23–26 in a wider literary context and view it in connection with vv. 27–28 where Yahweh's speech is mentioned.[64] For one thing, what Jeremiah saw in vv. 23–26 should be closely related to what Yahweh said in vv. 27–28. ⟦39⟧

27) *kî-kōh ʾāmar YHWH*
šĕmāmāh tihyeh kol-hāʾāreṣ
wĕkālāh lōʾ ʾeʿĕśeh
28) *ʿal-zōʾt teʾĕbal hāʾāres*
wĕqādĕrû haššāmāyim mimmāʿal
ʿal kî-dibbartî zammōtî
wĕlōʾ niḥamtî wĕlōʾ-ʾāšûb mimmennāh
⟦For thus says the LORD:
The whole earth will become a desolation,
But I will not make a total destruction.
For this the earth will dry up,
The heavens will be dark above—
Because I have spoken, I have planned,
And I will not relent or turn back from it.⟧

Holladay rightly notes that v. 28 corresponds with v. 23 and says, "Here the expression nicely dovetails with the extinguishing of the light of the heavens in v. 23. In a way the whole cosmos is in mourning for itself."[65] Thus, he notes the correspondence between *ʾên ʾôrām* ⟦their light is gone'⟧ (v. 23) and *qdr "to be dark" (v. 28). However, he does not discuss the other correspondence, i.e., *tōhû wābōhû* and *ʾbl "to dry up," with regard to the "earth" in these verses.

From the structural analysis of vv. 23–28 as a whole, it is noteworthy that the word pair "the earth" (*hāʾāreṣ*) and "the heavens" (*haššāmayim*) appears in this order both in the beginning (v. 23) and at the end (v. 28) of this section, thus functioning as an *inclusio* or a "framing" for the section. In other words, "(The earth is) *tōhû wābōhû*" // "(the heavens) are without light" in v. 23 corresponds to "(The earth) will dry up" (*ʾbl) // "(the heavens) will be dark" (*qdr) in v. 28. Here, the phrase *tōhû wābōhû*

64. ⟦98⟧. Wildberger, *Jesaja* 2, 920 treats Jer 4:23–28 as closely related to Isa 24:4 which mentions the "earth" which "dries up" (*ʾābĕlāh*) and the "whole world" which "withers" (*ʾumlĕlāh*).

65. ⟦99⟧. Holladay, *Jeremiah 1*, 168.

corresponds to the verbal phrase "to dry up"[66] and suggests the "aridness or unproductiveness" of the earth. This is in keeping with v. 27 which mentions that "the whole earth will become a desolation"[67] (*šĕmāmāh tihyeh kol-hāʾāreṣ*).

As for the second half of v. 27, *wĕkālāh lōʾ ʾeʿĕśeh*, various suggestions have been made. Most recently, it has been translated as "and I will make its destruction complete" (McKane)[68] or "and none of it shall I (re)-make" (Holladay),[69] by slightly changing the MT reading. On the other ⟦40⟧ hand Bright has translated the MT as it is: "though I'll make no full end,"[70] thus taking *kālāh* as "full end."[71] However, *kālāh* here as well as in Nah 1:8[72] seems to refer to "total destruction," i.e., destruction brought about by a flood, like *gamertu* ⟦'totality'⟧ which was brought about by *abūbu* "a flood" in the Babylonian Flood story.[73] Thus, the Jeremiah passage mentions a destruction brought about by the lack of water, not by the flood water. This is in keeping with our explanation which takes *tōhû wābōhû* as signifying "aridness or unproductiveness" of the earth.

Since without v. 23 there would be no reason to compare the Jeremiah passage with the Genesis creation story,[74] we might conclude that the two single verses, Jer 4:23 and Gen 1:2, simply share a common literary tradition in their use of *tōhû wābōhû*, which, according to the Jeremiah context, refers to a "desert-like" state of the "earth."

Isa 34:11

wîrēšûhā qāʾat wĕqippôd
wĕyanšôp wĕʿōrēb yiškĕnû-bāh

66. ⟦100⟧. Cf. KB: II *ʾbl* "to dry up" Jer 12:4, 23:10, Amos 1:2 and *CAD*, A/1 (1964), 29f.: *abālu* B "to dry up, dry out"; *AHw*, 3: *abālu* "(aus)trocknen" which is sometimes used for *šadû* and *eqlu*.

67. ⟦101⟧. Cf. Exod 23:29, Isa 1:7. Note the term *šĕmāmāh* "desolation" has its synonymous variants *ḥārēb* "waste, desolate" (Jer 33:10, cf. 32:43) and *ʿăzûbāh* "deserted" (Zeph 2:4; Isa 62:4; Jer 4:29, cf. 4:27). For Zeph 2:4, see L. Zalcman, "Ambiguity and Assonance at Zephaniah II 4," *VT* 36 (1986), 368.

68. ⟦102⟧. McKane, *Jeremiah* I, 108.

69. ⟦103⟧. Holladay, *Jeremiah 1*, 166.

70. ⟦104⟧. Bright, *Jeremiah*, 33. Bright adds the following comment: "the land will indeed be a waste, but it will not be the 'full end' described in vss. 23–26."

71. ⟦105⟧. Cf. "complete destruction" (BDB, 478).

72. ⟦106⟧. For this verse, see my article "Janus Parallelism in Nah 1:8," *JBL* 102 (1983), 109–111.

73. ⟦107⟧. AH III v 42–44, cf. II viii 34 and III iii 38. Cf. Lambert and Millard, *AH* 158 [a note on II viii 34].

74. ⟦108⟧. Carroll thinks that "the poem could be a meditation on the creation story . . . ," while rejecting Fishbane's view. See Carroll, *Jeremiah*, 169.

wĕnāṭāh ʿālêḥā qaw-tōhû
wĕʾabnê-bōhû

⟦Jackdaws and owls will possess it;
Great owls and ravens shall dwell there.
He will measure it with a line of desolation
And with weights of emptiness.⟧

The motif of "desolation" or "Verlassenheit"[75] can be also found in Isa 34:11 where *tōhû* and *bōhû* appear in parallel expressions, i.e., "the line of *thw*" (*qaw-tōhû*) // "the stones of *bhw*" (*ʾabnê-bōhû*). The text has been again connected with Gen 1:2 and it is often explained, for example, as "Yahweh had reduced the country for ever to a place just like chaos, to a real *tōhū-wābōhū* (cf. Gen. 1:2)."[76] However, as Wildberger rightly says, "Aber wie die Stelle aus dem Jeremiabuch zeigt, braucht die Schöpfungserzählung ⟦41⟧ von Gn 1 nicht vorausgesetzt zu sein" ⟦'But, as the passage from the book of Jeremiah shows, the creation narrative need not be assumed to be from Genesis 1'⟧,[77] Isa 34:11 simply means that "the land will become a desolation and waste so that it can no more receive inhabitants."[78] From the context of the Isaiah passage it is rather difficult to see any direct connection with Genesis creation story. It seems that Isaiah inherited the same literary tradition as Jer 4:23 and Gen 1:2 in describing the desolateness of the earth or land by *tōhû* and *bōhû*.

Let us summarize what we have concluded in the above discussion: the term *tōhû* means (1) "desert," (2) "a desert-like place," i.e., "a desolate or empty place" or "an uninhabited place" or (3) "emptiness"; the phrase *tōhû wābōhû* has a similar meaning and refers to a state of "aridness or unproductiveness" (Jer 4:23) or "desolation" (Isa 34:11).

Having studied the etymology and Biblical usages of the term *tōhû* as well as the expression *tōhû wābōhû*, it is now time to place this expression in the Genesis context.

tōhû wābōhû in the Framework of Genesis 1

The Earth in a Bare State

In light of the above, it would be very reasonable to understand the phrase *tōhû wābōhû* in Gen 1:2 as also describing a state of "unproduc-

75. ⟦109⟧. H. Wildberger, *Jesaja*, 3. Teilband: Jesaja 28–39 (BKAT X/3; Neukirchen-Vluyn: Neukirchener Verlag, 1982), 1346.

76. ⟦110⟧. Kaiser, *Isaiah 13–39: A Commentary* (London: SCM, 1974), 359.

77. ⟦111⟧. Wildberger, *Jesaja*, 3, 1346. Here he changes his previous view on the Jeremiah passage. Cf. *Jesaja*, 2, 920.

78. ⟦112⟧. Young, *Isaiah* II, 438, who, however, holds that the prophet Isaiah took language from Gen 1:2.

tiveness and emptiness,"[79] though the context suggests that this was the initial state of the created earth rather than a state brought about as a result of God's judgment on the earth or land (cf. Jer 4:23; Isa 34:11). In this regard, the earth which "was"[80] (*hāyĕtāh*) *tōhû wābōhû* signifies the earth in a "bare" state, without vegetation and animals as well as without man.

Day 3 (Climax) and Day 6 (Grand Climax)

⟦42⟧ This interpretation of *tōhû wābōhû* (lit. "desert-like and empty") as describing a bare state, i.e., "unproductive and uninhabited" state, of the earth fits the literary structure of the entire chapter.

As the discourse analysis of this section indicates, the author in v. 2 focuses not on the "heavens" but on the "earth" where the reader/audience stands, and presents the "earth" as "still" not being the earth which they all are familiar with. The earth which they are familiar with is "the earth" with vegetation, animals and man. Therefore, in a few verses, the author will mention their coming into existence through God's creation: vegetation on the third day and animals and man on the sixth day. Both the third and the sixth day are set as climaxes in the framework of this creation story and the grand climax is the creation of man on the sixth day.[81]

This literary structure[82] might be expressed as follows:

Gen 1:2	The *earth* as unproductive and uninhabited (*tōhû wābōhû*)		
[DAY 1]	light and darkness	[DAY 4]	"sun" and "moon"
[DAY 2]	two waters	[DAY 5]	fish and birds
[DAY 3]	*earth* and seas vegetation	[DAY 6]	animals and man on the *earth*

Thus, the "not yet productive" earth becomes productive when God says *tadšēʾ hāʾāreṣ dešeʾ* "Let the land produce vegetation" (v. 11) on the third day; the "empty," i.e., "not yet inhabited," earth becomes inhabited

79. ⟦113⟧. See also Tur-Sinai, *The Book of Job*, 381: "in Gen 1:2 . . . [*tōhû*] describes the barrenness of the earth before anything grew on it."

80. ⟦114⟧. Andersen, *SBH*, 85 thinks that Gen 1:2a means "the earth had become (or had come to be) . . . " as a circumstance prior to the first fiat recorded in Gen 1:3.

81. ⟦115⟧. Cf. Wenham, *Genesis 1–15*, 6; B. W. Anderson, *Creation versus Chaos: The Reinterpretation of Mythical Symbolism in the Bible* (Philadelphia: Fortress, 1967, 1987 [reprint with Postscript]), 187f. and 191. Young notes that the definite article is used only with the ordinal number "6" in this chapter; see E. J. Young, *Studies in Genesis One* (Phillipsburg: Presbyterian and Reformed, n.d.), 99.

82. ⟦116⟧. Wenham, *Genesis 1–15*, 6f.; I. M. Kikawada and A. Quinn, *Before Abraham Was: The Unity of Genesis 1–11* (Nashville: Abingdon, 1985), 78, suggest that the first three days [regions] correspond to the second three days [corresponding inhabitants].

when he says *tôṣēʾ hāʾāreṣ nepeš ḥayyāh* "Let the land produce living creatures" (v. 24) and *naʿăśeh ʾādām bĕṣalmēnû kidmûtēnû* "Let us make man in our image, in our likeness" (v. 26). Therefore it is by God's fiats that the "unproductive and empty/uninhabited" earth becomes productive with vegetation and inhabited by animals and man.[83] The story of creation in ⟦43⟧ Gen 1:1–2:3 thus tells us that it is God who created mankind "in his image" and provided for him an inhabitable and productive earth.

In conclusion, both the biblical context and extra-biblical parallels suggest that the phrase *tōhû wābōhû* in Gen 1:2 has nothing to do with "chaos" and simply means "emptiness" and refers to the earth which is an empty place, i.e., "an unproductive and uninhabited place." Thus, the main reason for the author's mentioning the earth as *tōhû wābōhû* in this setting is to inform the audience that the earth is "not yet" the earth as it was known to them. As Westermann notes, "creation and the world are to be understood always from the viewpoint of or in the context of human existence."[84] In other words, to communicate the subject of creation to human beings it is impossible to avoid using the language and literary forms known to them. In order to give the background information, the author uses experiential language in this verse, to explain the initial situation of the earth as "not yet."

83. ⟦117⟧. B. Otzen, "The Use of Myth in Genesis," in B. Otzen, H. Gottlieb and K. Jeppesen, *Myths in the Old Testament* (London: SCM, 1980), 39, thinks that "the background of [Gen 1:11f.] is the ancient mythological idea of the 'Earth Mother' who 'gives birth' to the products of the soil." It should be noted, however, that in Genesis 1 animals are also the products of the earth and that the existence of both plant life and animal life on the earth is the result of the divine fiats. Note also that there is no single myth in the ancient Near East which treats both plants and animals as the products of the earth.

84. ⟦118⟧. Westermann, *Genesis* I, 145 [ET 104]; also O. Kaiser, *Die mythische Bedeutung des Meeres in Ägypten, Ugarit und Israel* (BZAW 78; Berlin: Alfred Töpelmann, 1959), 13; W. H. Schmidt, *Die Schöpfungsgeschichte der Priesterschrift: Zur Überlieferungsgeschichte von Genesis 1:1–2:4a und 2:4b–3:24.* 2., überarbeitete und erweiterte Auflage (Neukirchen-Vluyn: Neukirchener Verlag, 1967), 86, n. 3.

"Male and Female He Created Them": Genesis 1:27b in the Context of the Priestly Account of Creation

PHYLLIS A. BIRD

⟦129⟧ In the history of biblical interpretation and dogmatic speculation, Gen 1:26–28 has proved remarkably fecund as a source of exegetical and theological reflection. Literature on the passage is now boundless, but shows no sign of ceasing or abating, despite the appearance in recent decades of several exhaustive treatments of the text and the existence of substantial consensus among biblical scholars.[1] The reason ⟦130⟧ for

Reprinted with permission from *Harvard Theological Review* 74 (1981) 129–59.

I would like to thank Frank M. Cross for his comments on the MS and William L. Moran for advice on the Akkadian transliterations and translations.

1. It is impossible to list even the major works on the passage. For the history of modern exegesis, however, two studies require special note: Paul Humbert, "L''*imago Dei*' dans l'Ancien Testament" (*Études sur le récit du paradis et de la chute dans la Genèse* [Mémoires de l'université de Neuchâtel 14; Neuchâtel: Secrétariat de l'université, 1940] 153–75), and Ludwig Koehler, "Die Grundstelle der Imago-Dei-Lehre, Gen 1:26" (*ThZ* 4 [1948] 16–22). Recent detailed exegetical treatments of the Priestly creation account as a whole, with compilations of the most important literature, are offered by Claus Westermann, *Genesis* (BKAT 1/3; Neukirchen-Vluyn: Neukirchener, 1968) 203–22, esp. 203–4; and Werner H. Schmidt, *Die Schöpfungsgeschichte der Priesterschrift* (WMANT 17; 3d ed.; Neukirchen-Vluyn: Neukirchener, 1973). Subsequent specialized literature includes the following: Bernhard W. Anderson, "Human Dominion over Nature," *Biblical Studies in Contemporary Thought* (ed. M. Ward; Somerville, MA: Greeno, Hadden, 1975) 27–45; James Barr, "The Image of God in the Book of Genesis—A Study in Terminology," *BJRL* 15 (1968) 11–26; "The Image of God in Genesis—Some Linguistic and Historical Considerations," *Ou Testamentiese Werkgemeenskap van Suid-Afrika: Proceedings of the 10th Meeting, 1967* (1971) 5–13; "Man and Nature—The

the perpetual fascination of the passage lies in the nature and limits of the text. The verses contain a fundamental, and unique, statement of biblical anthropology and theology—presented in a terse and enigmatic formulation. A rare attempt within the OT literature to speak directly and definitively about the nature of humanity in relation to God and other creation, the statement is at once limited in its content, guarded in its expression, and complex in its structure. As a consequence, philologist and theologian are enticed and compelled in ever new contexts of questions and understandings to explore anew the meaning and implications of creation "in the divine image"—for it is this striking and unique expression, above all, that has dominated the discussion.

A legacy of the long and intense theological interest in the *imago dei* ⟦'image of God'⟧ has been an atomizing and reductionist approach to the passage, in which attention is focused on a single phrase or clause, severing it from its immediate context and from its context within the larger composition, a fixation and fragmentation which has affected exegetical as well as dogmatic discussion. A further legacy of this history of speculation has been the establishment of a tradition of theological inquiry and argument with a corresponding body of knowledge and norms separate from, and largely independent of, exegetical scholarship on the same passage.[2] The rise of a biblical science distinct from dogmatic the-

---

Ecological Controversy and the Old Testament," *BJRL* 55 (1972/73) 9–32; Gerhard Hasel, "The Meaning of 'Let Us' in Gen 1:26," *AUSS* 13 (1975) 58–66; "The Polemic Nature of the Genesis Cosmology," *EvQ* 46 (1974) 81–102; Norbert Lohfink, "'Seid fruchtbar und füllt die Erde an!' Zwingt die priesterschriftliche Schöpfungsdarstellung in Gen 1 die Christen zum Wachstumsmythose?" *BK* 3 (1975) 77–82; Oswald Loretz, *Die Gottebenbildlichkeit des Menschen. Mit einem Beitrag von Erik Hornung: Der Mensch als 'Bild Gottes' in Ägypten* (Munchen: Kösel, 1967); Tryggve N. D. Mettinger, "Abbild oder Urbild? 'Imago Dei' in traditionsgeschichtliche Sicht," *ZAW* 86 (1974) 403–24; J. Maxwell Miller, "In the 'Image' and 'Likeness' of God," *JBL* 91 (1972) 289–304; John F. A. Sawyer, "The Meaning of *bĕṣelem ʾĕlōhîm* ('In the Image of God') in Genesis I–XI," *JTS* 25 (1974) 418–26; Norman Snaith, "The Image of God," *ExpTim* 86/1 (1974) 24; Phyllis Trible, *God and the Rhetoric of Sexuality* (Philadelphia: Fortress, 1978) 1–30.

A fuller listing of titles would reveal even more clearly how discussion of Gen 1:26–28 has concentrated on the *imago dei* and the first person plurals of the divine address in v. 26. More limited interest has been shown in the imperatives of v. 28, esp. in recent literature concerned with the ethical issues of population, reproduction and ecology. Relatively little attention has been given to the specification of male and female in v. 27b, with the exception of recent feminist literature or literature generated in response to feminist critique of the OT's androcentric anthropology. Most of the latter is of a relatively popular nature and while of considerable importance for the question of hermeneutics, has contributed little in the way of new exegetical insight.

2. Cf. Karl Barth's criticism of the neglect of the text by theologians who regularly cited it, a practice which he traces back into the early church (*Church Dogmatics* [hereafter *CD*] 3/1

ology resulted in a dual history of scholarship on the passage with little significant dialogue between the respective specialists.[3] To the biblical ⟦131⟧ exegete, the interpretation of the theologian appears frequently strained, sometimes false, and often simply unrecognizable as commentary upon the text.[4] While biblical scholars may feel compelled to challenge or accommodate dogmatic claims or assess current theological interpretations of the text, theologians appear for the most part content simply to "touch base" with the biblical passage, dismissing or ignoring the technical exegetical literature. There may be good reason to ignore or decry restrictive interpretations and proprietary claims of biblical specialists, but absence of dialogue can hardly be viewed as a healthy state for theology. How, in the present organization and functioning of the disciplines, such needed dialogue can take place, is not clear, however, though ventures from both camps would seem to be essential.

An underlying concern of this essay, focused by examination of the literature on Gen 1:26–28, is the question of the relationship between text-critical or historical-exegetical interpretation and constructive interpretation in theology. I am convinced that collapse of the distinction between historical and constructive tasks is fatal, not only to the integrity of the scriptural witness, but also to the credibility of theology. The two tasks describe or relate to distinct modes or moments in the work of theology, however they may be united in the interpretive art of individual

---

[Edinburgh: T. & T. Clark, 1958] 192–93). On the legacy of a problematic anthropology derived from Gen 1:27 in the earliest period and determinative for later discussion, see also Karl Ludwig Schmidt, "Homo imago Dei im Alten und Neuen Testament," *Der Mensch als Bild Gottes* (ed. Leo Scheffczyk; Darmstadt: Wissenschaftliche Buchgesselschaft, 1969) 17–20.

3. The origins of an OT exegetical tradition distinct from the dominant philosophical and theological tradition and generally critical of it are usually traced to Theodor Nöldeke ("צלמות und צלם," *ZAW* 17 [1897] 183–87) and Hermann Gunkel (*Genesis* [HKAT 1; Göttingen: Vandenhoeck & Ruprecht, 1901]). Their interpretation of the "image" as a physical resemblance, confirmed by the word studies of Humbert (*Études*) and Koehler ("Grundstelle"), became the basis of subsequent OT discussion. Cf. Johann Jakob Stamm's review of the history of OT scholarship in "Dei Imago-Lehre von Karl Barth und die alttestamentliche Wissenschaft," *Antwort* (Festschrift K. Barth; Zollikon-Zürich: Evangelischer, 1956) 84–96. OT treatments of the passage often take up the older theological and philosophical views as a part of the history of scholarship and/or to show their inadequacy (see, e.g., Westermann, *Genesis* 1/3, 205–6, and Loretz, *Gottebenbildlichkeit*, 9–41). Theologians, as heirs to the dominant tradition of speculation, more commonly confine their discussion within it, showing little recognition that an independent exegetical tradition has emerged alongside it. See, e.g., the articles collected under the heading, "Die systematische Durchdringung," in the volume edited by Scheffczyk (*Der Mensch als Bild Gottes*, 331–525).

4. See, e.g., Mettinger, "Abbild oder Urbild?" 410. Cf. Stamm, "Die Imago-Lehre von Karl Barth," 94.

scholars. But isolation of the tasks and lack of a critical methodology for relating them appear to me equally disastrous for theology.

The problem may be illustrated by reference to Karl Barth's widely influential treatment of the *imago* ⟦'image'⟧ passage.[5] His critique of a history of speculation divorced from exegesis—or of speculation construed as exegesis—is apposite and appealing:

> We might easily discuss which of these and the many other similar explanations is the finest or deepest or most serious. What we cannot discuss is which of them is the true explanation of Gen 1:26f. For it is obvious that their authors merely found the concept [of the *imago dei*] in the text and then proceeded to pure invention in accordance with the requirements of contemporary anthropology, so that it is only by the standard of *our own anthropology*, and not according to *its* anthropology and on exegetical grounds, that we can decide for or against them.[6]

⟦132⟧ Appealing too is Barth's conversance with contemporary OT scholarship and his attempt to incorporate that understanding is his work. Yet his own interpretation of the passage is as problematic as any that he criticizes—and for the same reason. Despite close reference to the biblical text as his primary source, he has failed to discern *its* anthropology—and theology—and has advanced only a novel and arresting variation of the classical trinitarian interpretation, an interpretation characterized by the distinctly modern concept of an "I-Thou" relationship, which is foreign to the ancient writer's thought and intention at all three points of its application (God in the relationship within the Godhead, humanity in the relationship between the sexes, and God and humanity in relationship to each other).[7] At its most fundamental level Barth's exegesis fails to understand the grammar of the sentences he so ingeniously manipulates.

The most serious problem with Barth's impressive theological creation, however, is not its provocative thesis, which must ultimately be judged on internal grounds of adequacy and truth, nor his understanding of the key texts, which can and must be challenged by biblical scholars. It is the fact that his work is so widely accepted as definitive exegesis, obviating or impeding independent access to the text. Approval of the

5. *CD* 3/1. 183–206.

6. *CD* 3/1. 193.

7. Dietrich Bonhoeffer appears to have been the first to interpret the *imago dei* ⟦'image of God'⟧ in terms of an *analogia relationis* ⟦'relational analogy'⟧ in which the male-female duality is the defining human relationship (*Schöpfung und Fall* [Munich: Kaiser, 1933] 29–30). It is Barth's development of the idea, however, as a keystone of his anthropology (*CD* 3/1. 194–95), that has made it—and its faulty exegesis—such a widely influential notion.

theological construction is taken as validation of the exegesis.[8] Barth's synthesis of exegetical and constructive tasks is attractive in demonstrating the rich possibilities of a theology in close conversation with the biblical text, but it is a dangerous synthesis insofar as it becomes a substitute, rather than a model, for continuing dialogue between theologian and biblical scholar.

I have cited Barth's treatment of Gen 1:26–28 because of the justice of his critique, because of his laudable effort to ground theology in exegesis informed by current biblical scholarship, because of the prominence ⟦133⟧ and popularity of his interpretation (at least in secondary theological literature), and because of the unacceptability of his exposition to most OT exegetes.[9] Barth's attractive, but mistaken, interpretation of the meaning of sexual distinction in Gen 1:27 has served as a catalyst for this reexamination of the neglected clause in the Priestly account of the creation of *adam* and has served to focus the question of the relationship between historical and constructive theology, both of which may claim the title "exegetical." But the question of meaning which impels the study has arisen elsewhere. It is feminist theology, or the feminist critique of traditional theology and exegesis, that has made necessary a new look at the passage and forged the encounter with Barth.[10]

8. See, e.g., the argument of Clifford Green ("Liberation Theology? Karl Barth on Women and Men," *USQR* 29 [1974] 221–31), who quotes with general approbation a critique of Barth's exegesis in 3/1 (esp. 183ff., 289ff.) by Paul Lehmann ("Karl Barth and the Future of Theology," *RelS* 6 [1970] 113): "[This] elaborate interpretation . . . offers an impressive correlation of ingeniousness and arbitrariness, which allows Barth to ascribe insights and affirmations to ancient writers which, as historical human beings they could not possibly have entertained." Green qualifies this assessment, however, with the following statement: "This criticism does not, in my view, apply to Barth's reading of the *imago Dei*, which is liberating for women and men alike" (225). Green's argument appears typical of much recent literature, which concerns itself with the consequences or implications of the idea (e.g., is it liberating or not?), but does not question or examine its exegetical base.

9. See, e.g., the critique of Stamm ("Die Imago-Lehre von Karl Barth," esp. 94). Cf., however, Friedrich Horst ("Face to Face" The Biblical Doctrine of the Image of God," *Int* 4 [1950] 259–70), who follows closely Barth's argument concerning the *analogia relationis* (266–67).

10. By "feminist" theology or critique I refer to that work which is characterized by an awareness that traditional theology and biblical interpretation have been dominated, in one way or another, by "patriarchal" or androcentric perspectives, values and judgments. Awareness of this persistent bias has led to various attempts to expose, explain, and reinterpret texts that have traditionally carried the patriarchal message and to identify, where possible, sources which qualify or contradict it. These efforts differ considerably in methodology, attitude toward the tradition and its authority, and knowledge for the relevant disciplines and scholarly tools. Much is the work of amateurs, for the origins of the critique and new constructions were almost entirely "outside the camp"—precisely because those within the scholarly guilds lacked the necessary experiential base, or, for other reasons of restricted environment, failed to recognize the problem.

For critics of a biblical and theological anthropology which ascribed to women an inferior or derived nature, Gen 1:27 has emerged as a text upon which a corrective anthropology of equality might be built. Barth's interpretation of the passage has had particular appeal because of his attempt to ground a relationship of mutuality between the sexes in a corresponding relationship within the Godhead itself. Feminist theology turned to Barth, whether to embrace or attack his views, because his exegetical approach to theology required him to take account of the prominent attention given to sexual distinction in both of the biblical accounts of human creation.[11] But the search that led to Barth must ⟦134⟧ return to the text. The rationale for our reexamination of the passage is this: a new socio-theological context, characterized by new questions, perceptions and judgments, requires a new statement of the meaning of the passage in its primary OT context—even if this be largely a restatement of older findings and arguments. The result, I believe, is more than a restatement, though few of the elements are entirely novel.

The argument of this essay may be summarized as follows. Gen 1:27 must be understood within the context of vv. 26–28, and this complex within the larger structure of the Priestly creation account. V. 27 may not be isolated, nor may it be interpreted in relation to v. 26 alone; vv. 27–28

11. The ambivalence of feminist response to Barth may be attributed to a number of factors, including selective reading of an extensive and complex treatment of the relationship of the sexes and dependence on an inadequate English translation. Most criticism has focused on his discussion of order in the male-female relationship, developed in relation to NT texts and Genesis 2 (*CD* 3/4). The notion of "ontological subordination" ascribed to Barth on the basis of this reading has become a commonplace, though Green ("Liberation Theology," 222–23 and 229) argues that the expression cannot be attributed to Barth and that it misconstrues his intention—and language. Cf. Mary Daly, *Beyond God the Father* (Boston: Beacon, 1973) 3, 22; Linda L. Barufaldi and Emily E. Culpepper, "Androgyny and the Myth of Masculine/Feminine," *Christianity and Crisis* 33/6 (16 April 1973) 69; and Sheila Collins, "Toward a Feminist Theology," *The Christian Century* 89 (2 August 1972) 797–98.

A serious problem involves the key term *ungleich.* Barth characterizes the duality of I-and-Thou in Gen 1:26–27 as a "correspondence of *unlike*" (*CD* 3/1. 196; = "Entsprechung des Ungleichen" [*KD*, 220]), but appears to spell this out in his discussion of Gen 2:18–25 as a relationship of inequality ("*unequal* duality" [*CD* 3/1. 288]) (Joan Arnold Romero, "The Protestant Principle: A Woman's-Eye View of Barth and Tillich," *Religion and Sexism* [ed. Rosemary R. Reuther; New York: Simon and Schuster, 1974] 324). However, the German adjective is identical in both passages ("ungleiche[n] Zweiheit" [*KD* 3/1. 329]) and means to negate the idea of "sameness," not "equality," in the pair (Green "Liberation Theology?" 229, n. 14).

For feminists who have been able to read Barth's exposition of the *analogia relationis* in Gen 1:27 apart from—or over against—his treatment of the male-female relationship in other contexts, the possibilities it suggests for a new appreciation and evaluation of human sexual distinction have been attractive. See, e.g., Paul Jewett, *Man as Male and Female* (Grand Rapids: Eerdmans, 1975) esp. 33–48, and Emma Justes, "Theological Reflections on the Role of Women in Church and Society" (*Journal of Pastoral Care* 32 [1978]) 42–54.

form an expanded parallel to v. 26, in which 27b is a plus, dependent upon and preparatory to the following statement in v. 28 and dictated by the juxtaposition in vv. 27–28 of the themes of divine likeness and sexual reproduction. The specification of human sexual distinction and its position in the text are determined by the sequence of themes within the account and by the overall structure of announcement and execution report within the chapter. Our understanding of the place and function of this specification in the account dissociates the word of sexual distinction, specifically sexuality, from the idea of the divine image, and from the theme of dominion, and associates it with a larger theme of sustainability or fertility running throughout the narrative of creation. A general contribution of this investigation is a clearer articulation of the relationships among the several statements about *adam* (image, dominion, sexuality, blessing) and a clearer statement of the meaning and function of each within the Priestly account of creation. The analysis concludes with an attempt to spell out the consequences and implications of this understanding for the theology of P, for a comprehensive OT anthropology, and for contemporary theological anthropology ⟦135⟧.

The Priestly Account of Creation: Overall Structure and Themes

The Priestly account of creation is an exceedingly compressed account, marked by a repetitive structure of announcement and execution report (*Wortbericht* and *Tatbericht*). But it is also comprehensive in its intention and design, attempting to identify, locate and describe in their essential features all of the primary elements and orders of creation. The author has chosen his terms with care, from names to descriptive statements.[12] As von Rad has rightly emphasized, only what is essential is here; nothing

12. I assume for Gen 1:1–2:3 a unified work by a priestly editor/author active in and during the Babylonian exile, who edited an already existing Israelite creation account (perhaps extant in multiple variants, or supplemented by material from other traditions) to form the opening chapter of a great history of beginnings reaching from creation to the death of Moses and climaxing in the revelation/legislation at Sinai. Whether the author/editor was a single or corporate "individual" is irrelevant to the argument of this essay. The two essential assumptions of my analysis are (1) that the present (final) edition of the material displays a unified overall conception characterized by recognizable stylistic and theological features and forms part of a larger whole displaying similar literary and theological characteristics, and (2) that the present form of the composition in Genesis 1 is the result of a complex history of growth, stages of which are apparent in the received text, but can no longer be isolated or fully reconstructed.

I agree with Werner Schmidt (*Schöpfungsgeschichte*) that the framing structure of *wayyōʾmer ʾĕlōhîm* ⟦'and God said'⟧ + *wayĕhî-kēn* ⟦'and it was so'⟧ and the *Wortberichte* as a whole belong to the final editor and give evidence of selection, shaping and expansion of older material. I am less certain about the recovery of the underlying tradition or of the relationship of *Wortbericht*/Announcement to *Tatbericht*/Execution Report. I retain the terms

is accidental or included merely because it stood in the received tradition.[13] Though bound in significant measure to the items, order and conception of process found in older creation accounts of the ancient Near East and circulating in Israelite tradition, the Priestly author has selected from the tradition and shaped it to carry his own message. And though the history of the Priestly composition is itself complex, and final design and wording is governed by a unified conception and purpose and the account set as the lead statement in a ⟦136⟧ larger historico-theological work. Thus every assertion and every formulation in this highly compact and selective account warrants careful attention and questioning with regard to its origin and meaning. How does it function within the Priestly composition? Why was it included? Is it unique to P, a new idea, or a new formulation? Was it present in essentially the same form in older tradition or does it represent an alteration of the tradition, a substitution, or a reformulation?

Because descriptive statements are so limited in P's account, the two which amplify the report of *adam*'s creation are immediately striking:

(27aβ) *bĕṣelem ᵓĕlōhîm bārāᵓ ᵓōtô*
(27b) *zākār ûnĕqēbâ bārāᵓ ᵓōtam*

(27aβ) in the image of God he created him;
(27b) male and female he created them.

The parallel construction invites the question of how the two clauses are related. But other questions impose as well. Why does 27aβ repeat the content of 27aα? What is the relationship of v. 27 to vv. 26 and 28? And why of all that might be said about *adam* does the author choose to emphasize their bisexual nature, using language employed elsewhere by P to characterize the animal orders but omitted from their description

---

to refer not to independent literary compositions, or traditions, but to literary features of the final composition. Anderson's insistence on the stylistic unity of the Priestly creation account and his attention to the controlling patterns of the final form of the text ("A Stylistic Study of the Priestly Creation Story," *Canon and Authority in Old Testament Religion and Theology* [eds. George W. Coats and Burke O. Long; Philadelphia: Fortress, 1977] 148–162, esp. 151) represents a welcome shift from earlier dissecting approaches; however, I do not think that his analysis invalidates much of Schmidt's observations and explanations of disparity between *Wort-* and *Tatberichten.* I find it necessary, in any case, to posit a prehistory of Israelite usage; Genesis 1 is in my view neither a "free" composition nor a direct response to any known Mesopotamian or Canaanite myth, despite clear evidence of polemical shaping (cf. Hasel, "The Polemic Nature of the Genesis Cosmology," and Victor Maag, "Alttestamentliche Anthropogonie in ihrem Verhältnis zur altorientalischen Mythologie," *Asiatische Studien* 9 [1955] 15–44).

13. Gerhard von Rad, *Genesis. A Commentary* (Philadelphia: Westminster, 1961) 45.

in Genesis 1? The answer to all of these questions lies in an analysis of the structure of vv. 26–28 as a whole and of the place and function of these verses within the overall structure of Gen 1:1–2:3 and the larger Priestly work.[14]

The primary concerns of the Priestly creation account are two: (1) to emphasize the dependence of all of creation on God—made explicit in the framing structure that marks each stage of creation: "God said . . . and it was so,"[15] and (2) to describe the order established within creation—as an order determined by God, from the beginning.[16] Secondary or subordinate concerns are evident in emphasis on the permanence, or maintenance, of the created cosmos and its orders, and in [[137]] anticipation of the history which will be played out within it, a history centering upon *adam* and initiated in the final, climactic word of creation and blessing.

26. *wayyō*ʾ*mer* ʾ*ĕlōhîm*
*na*ʿ*ăśeh* ʾ*ādām bĕṣalmēnû kidmûtēnû*
*wĕyirdû bidgat hayyām ûbĕ*ʿ*ôp haššāmayim*
*ûbabbĕhēmâ ûbĕkol-hā*ʾ*āreṣ*
ûbĕkol-hāremeś hārōmēś ʿ*al-hā*ʾ*āreṣ*

27. *wayyibrā*ʾ ʾ*ĕlōhîm* ʾ*et-hā*ʾ*ādām bĕṣalmô*
bĕṣelem ʾ*ĕlōhîm bārā*ʾ ʾ*ōtô*
*zākār ûnĕqēbâ bārā*ʾ ʾ*ōtām*

28. *wayĕbārek* ʾ*ōtām* ʾ*ĕlōhîm*
*wayyō*ʾ*mer lāhem* ʾ*ĕlōhîm*
*pĕrû ûrĕbû ûmil*ʾ*û* ʾ*et-hā*ʾ*āreṣ wĕkibšūhā*
*ûrĕdû bidgat hayyām ûbĕ*ʿ*ôp haššāmayim*
ûbĕkol-ḥayyâ hārōmeśet ʿ*al-hā*ʾ*āreṣ*[17]

14. Vv. 29–30 are an essential part of P's statement about the nature and role of *adam* within the created order and form a significant link with the later P complex, Gen 9:1–3, bringing to the received tradition a peculiar interest of the final Priestly writer (Schmidt, *Schöpfungsgeschichte,* 152–53; cf. Westermann, *Genesis,* 227–28; Sean E. McEvenue, *The Narrative Style of the Priestly Writer* [Rome: Biblical Institute, 1971] 66–71; and Miller, "In the 'Image' and 'Likeness' of God," 299–304). We omit consideration of these verses here because they constitute a distinct unit and lack any connection, direct or indirect, to 27b, which is the focus of this investigation.

15. The full series is found only in the LXX. Cf. Anderson, "A Stylistic Study," 152.

16. The theme of order and the specification of orders cannot be reduced to cultic interest, though elements of that are present. Nor can it be subsumed under the needs of *adam,* though the account is certainly anthropocentric. It is rather a broad and fundamental theological concern, which may properly be characterized as "scientific" in its interest and observations.

17. Textual variants are few and of minor significance for our analysis. LXX has a conjunction (*kai* [['and']]) between *bĕṣalmēnû* [['in our image']] and *kidmûtēnû* [['according to

26. And God said:
    "Let us make *adam* in our image, according to our likeness,
    and let them have dominion over the fish of the sea and
      the birds of the air,
      and the cattle and all the earth
      and everything that creeps upon the earth."
27. And God created *adam* in his image,
    in the image of God he created him;
    male and female he created them.
28. And God blessed them,
    and God said to them:
    "Be fruitful and multiply and fill the earth and subdue it,
    and have dominion over the fish of the sea and the
      birds of the air
      and every living creature that creeps upon the earth."

Image and Dominion

The order described in Genesis 1 is progressive, structured as a twofold movement oriented toward the earth and culminating in *adam*.[18] The crowning species in this account is defined, uniquely, in terms of a dual relationship or identity, a relationship to God and to coinhabitants of earth. Humanity, according to this statement, is created ⟦138⟧ "like God"[19] and with dominion over other creatures. The two statements of v. 26 must be understood in conjunction; in P's construction they belong to a single thought complex. Nature or design in creation is related to function and status, or position: the firmament is to divide the waters, the luminaries are to give light (and in their specific identity as planets, to mark time and seasons, etc.), and humankind is to rule over the realm of creatures.[20] The presupposition and prerequisite for this rule is the

---

our likeness'⟧ in v. 26 and reads only the second *bĕṣelem* ⟦'in the image of'⟧ in 27a (see discussion below), while individual MSS and versions assimilate the singular and plural object pronouns or eliminate *bārāʾ ʾōtô* ⟦'he created him'⟧ in 27aα. LXX also renders more uniform parallel lists and formulas repeated with variation in MT (28b // 26b; 28aα // 22a). See commentaries.

18. Anderson, "A Stylistic Study," 154–59.

19. The basic meanings of the terms *ṣelem* and *dĕmût* are "representation" and "likeness" (see further below). The prepositions, which are used synonymously, create parallel and synonymous adverbial clauses which describe the manner and end of construction (*adam* is "modeled" on *ʾĕlōhîm* and is consequently a model of *ʾĕlōhîm*). The intention is to describe a resemblance of *adam* to God which distinguishes *adam* from all other creatures—and has consequence for *adam*'s relationship to them.

20. For the understanding of *wĕyirdû* ⟦'let them have dominion'⟧ . . . as a purpose or result clause, see, *inter alios*, Schmidt, *Schöpfungsgeschichte*, 127 ("damit sie herrschen"); NEB

divine stamp which sets this creature apart from all the rest, identifying *adam* as God's own special representative, not simply by designation (command), but by design (nature or constitution)—i.e., as a representation of God.[21] The notion of the divine image serves here to validate and explain the special status and role of *adam* among the creatures.

⟦139⟧ The adverbial modifier *bĕṣelem-* ⟦'in the image'⟧, further qualified by *kidmût-* ⟦'according to the likeness'⟧ in v. 26,[22] describes a

("to rule"); Snaith, "The Image of God," 24; and Westermann, *Genesis*, 216. The function of *wĕyirdû* as specification of purpose or consequence has been understood in a number of different ways, often as a direct explication of the image, or of creation in the divine image (cf. von Rad, *Genesis*, 57; Snaith, "The Image of God," 24). Westermann observes that specification of purpose or goal is a characteristic feature of accounts of human creation (*Genesis*, 218).

21. Westermann has correctly emphasized the adverbial character of *bĕṣalmēnû kidmûtēnû* ⟦'in our image, according to our likeness'⟧ (*Genesis*, 214), basing his analysis on the consensus of recent scholarship which rejects the *b*-essentiae interpretation and recognizes the essentially synonymous meaning of the two phrases, whose interchangeable prepositions must have the meaning "according to," "nach" (so LXX [*kata* for both] and Vg ["ad" for both]) (*Genesis*, 201; cf. Sawyer, "The Meaning of *bĕṣelem ʾĕlōhîm*," 421; Mettinger, "Abbild oder Urbild?" 406–7; Miller, "In the 'Image' and 'Likeness' of God," 295). This grammatical analysis leads Westermann to argue that the text "macht nicht eine Aussage über den Menschen, sondern über ein Tun Gottes" ⟦'does not make a statement concerning humanity, but rather concerning God's action'⟧ (*Genesis*, 214). But the alternatives are too exclusively drawn. What describes the act or mode of construction cannot be excluded from an understanding of the product; i.e., construction (as process and design) determines or affects construction (as product or result). Surely the Priestly writer intended to characterize *adam* by this formulation, to specify more closely the essential nature of humanity, while avoiding direct description. P intends a comparison between God and *adam*, but he intends it to be indirect. The prepositions guard against identity, even the identity of an image or icon. Strictly speaking, *adam* is not the image of God (so rightly Westermann) nor one possessing the divine image, but only one who is like God in the manner of an image or representation.

Since *bĕṣelem ʾĕlōhîm* ⟦'in the image of God'⟧ describes, indirectly, the nature of *adam*, it characterizes all humankind in all time and not simply the original act, or specimen, of creation. The stamp of divine likeness must therefore be understood to be transmitted not through repeated acts of God but through the process by which the species is perpetuated in its original identity, viz., through procreation (Gen 5:3).

22. So correctly Koehler ("Grundstelle," 20–21), building on Humbert (*Études*, 163); the qualifying character of *kidmût* is suggested by its position as the second term (Sawyer, "The Meaning of *bĕṣelem ʾĕlōhîm*," 421) as well as by its common lexical meaning and use. As an abstract term, whose very meaning suggests approximation, it weakens or blurs the outline of the preceding concrete term. *Dĕmût* ⟦'likeness'⟧ is used by P's contemporary, Ezekiel, in the same sense of qualified resemblance that it has in Genesis 1; and it is employed elsewhere by P, alone (in 5:1), where the specific content or connotation of *ṣelem* ⟦'image'⟧ is not required or desired. *Ṣelem*, in contrast, is the specialized and unique term, "defined" by its use in Genesis 1.

Miller's argument for the priority of *dĕmût* ("In the 'Image' and 'Likeness' of God," 299–304) is not convincing. *Dĕmût* belongs to the final P edition of Genesis 1 and occurs

correspondence of being, a resemblance—not a relationship nor an identity, even partial identity. And it is a resemblance described in terms of form, not of character or substance.[23] *Ṣelem* ⟦140⟧ as a metaphor for

alone in 5:1, which is a purely P construction, creating a bridge between the creation story (traditional material shaped by P) and the genealogical framework of the primeval history. There, in 5:1–2, the essential content of 1:26–28 is recapitulated in P's own terms—with the addition of the naming motif that prepares for the transition from collective *adam* in Genesis 1 and 5:1–2 to the representative individual, Adam, who heads the genealogy of 5:3ff.

23. See Humbert (*Études*), Koehler ("Grundstelle"), and n. 34, below. *Ṣelem* in P's use is neither the crudely or naively literal image assumed by those who fail to recognize the determining metaphor, nor the description of a conversation partner or counterpart. Recognition that the term is basically concrete in its meaning has not stopped commentators from asking wherein the resemblance lies and from drawing on other OT texts, as well as modern psychology, for their answers. Thus, e.g., Koehler sought the resemblance in *adam*'s "upright stature" ("Grundstelle," 20), while others endorse a more general physical resemblance, noting, however, that Hebrew thought treated the individual as a psycho-somatic unity, thereby excluding the notion of merely external correspondence (so, e.g., Gunkel: "das Geistige [ist] dabei nicht ausgeschlossen" ⟦'the spiritual is not rendered out of the question by this'⟧ [*Genesis*, 99]; cf. von Rad [*Genesis*, 56] and Westermann [*Genesis*, 207–8]). For many interpreters influenced by Barth, the correspondence suggested by the metaphor is spelled out as a relational correspondence describing a capacity and need for relatedness, including communication. Thus Stamm sees the meaning of the *imago* as "Partnerschaft und Bündnisfähigkeit" ⟦'partnership and capacity for alliance (or relationship)'⟧ (*Die Gottebenbildlichkeit des Menschen im Alten Testament* [Theologische Studien 54; Zollikon-Zürich: Evangelischer, 1959] 19), while Horst would have it describe a special capability of intercourse with God ("Face to Face," 267), making *adam* "the vis-à-vis (*Gegenüber*) of God in the same manner as the woman, in Gen 2:20, is a helpmeet 'as over against' (*im Gegenüber*) the man" (265). This argument is faulty on a number of grounds. There is no similarity in language or idea between the *kĕneged* ⟦'fitting helper'⟧ of Gen 2:18, 20 and the *bĕṣelem-/kidmût-* of 1:26. And it is obvious from the (secondary) use of *ṣelem* in 5:3 and 7:6 that it does not describe a quality of relationship or even precondition of relationship. P is not concerned with communication between Adam and Seth, but with the preservation of an essential likeness of the species through successive generations. Cf. also the critique of Victor Maag ("Alttestamentliche Anthropogonie," 34).

In response to continuing attempts to spell out the content of the image, James Barr has recently argued that the term *ṣelem* was deliberately chosen for its opaque etymology and ambivalent connotations as the best term available in Hebrew to describe a likeness without giving it a particular content ("A Study in Terminology," 18, 20–21; cf. "Some Linguistic and Historical Considerations," 12–13). Recent literature has also stressed the fact that the notion of humans as godlike creatures, created according to a divine model or prototype and standing in a special relationship to the gods, is not unique to Israel, but is a widely shared notion, though implications of this likeness may be spelled out in quite different ways. The concept, in this analysis, is an inherited one for P, whose problem was to fit it to Israelite theology and exclude as far as possible false understandings which may have accompanied it (Maag, "Sumerische und babylonische Mythen von der Erschaffung der Menschen," *Asiatische Studien* 8 [1954] 96–98; cf. "Alttestamentliche Anthropogonie," 36–37; Westermann, *Genesis*, 212–13; and Loretz, *Gottebenbildlichkeit*, 63–64).

likeness is concrete, formal, holistic—and "empty," lacking specific content, and thus an ideal term for P, who employs it with changing connotations in changing contexts (cf. 5:1, 3 and 9:6). Here, in its primary and initial use, its content or implications must be spelled out, and that is the contribution of *wĕyirdû* ⟦'let them have dominion'⟧. The *ṣelem ʾĕlōhîm* in Genesis 1 is, accordingly, a royal designation, the precondition or requisite for rule.

The interpretation of the expression as a royal motif is not simply dependent, however, on the context of its use in Gen 1:26. Though the term *ṣelem*, by itself, lacks specific content, the phrase *ṣelem ʾĕlōhîm* appears to derive its meaning from a special association with the royal ideology of the ancient Near East.[24] It is true that OT uses of *ṣelem* do not point to such a thesis, nor does the OT's ideology or lexicon of kingship.[25] If a royal image lies behind the use of *ṣelem* in Gen 1:26–27, it must rest on an idea or expression of kingship found outside of preserved Israelite sources. That appears to be supplied by evidence from Egypt, where the idea of the king as "image" of the god is a common one, finding expression in a rich and diverse vocabulary of representation which describes the pharaoh as image, statue, likeness, picture, etc., of the deity (usually the chief, creator god).[26] However, ⟦141⟧ the expression in Egyptian royal usage is closely linked to the idea of the pharaoh as the incarnation

24. The first scholar to read the expression of Genesis 1 as the adaptation of a royal title or designation appears to have been Johannes Hehn in 1915 ("Zum Terminus 'Bild Gottes,' " *Festschrift Eduard Sachau* [ed. Gotthold Weil; Berlin: Reimer] 36–52). Hehn's lead has been followed by von Rad (*Genesis*, 58); Wildberger ("Abbild," 245–59, 481–501); and Schmidt (*Schöpfungsgeschichte*, 137–48), *inter alios*.

25. It is often noted that *ṣelem* and *dĕmût* are not used in the OT to speak of the king. Anderson stresses the contrast between Genesis 1 and Psalm 8 precisely in respect to royal language and theology ("Human Dominion," 39), though he allows that "vestigial remains" of a royal theology can be seen in Genesis 1, especially in "the motif of the image of God which entitles Man to have dominion over the earth" (36).

26. See esp. Hornung, "Der Mensch als 'Bild Gottes' in Ägypten," in Loretz, *Die Gottebenbildlichkeit des Menschen*, 123–56; and Eberhard Otto, "Der Mensch als Geschöpf und Bild Gottes in Ägypten," *Probleme biblischer Theologie* (ed. H. W. Wolff; Munich: Kaiser, 1971) 334–48. Schmidt and Wildberger both draw upon Egyptian texts to suggest parallels, and a source, for the expression in Gen 1:26, 27. Of particular interest to Schmidt is the "democratized" usage found in the wisdom literature, in which a title that originally designated, and distinguished, the king is "extended" to humanity as a whole, and associated more particularly with their creation (cf., e.g., "The Instruction of Merikare," *Schöpfungsgeschichte*, 139). This evidence, combined with a more limited occurrence of the same expression in Mesopotamian royal designations, suggested a common ancient Near Eastern royal ideology. That the expression of Gen 1:26–28 was anchored in this tradition was made virtually certain, Schmidt argued, by the explicit royal language used in Psalm 8, the only OT parallel to the Genesis 1 account (140).

of the god, the deity's visible form on earth[27]—an idea foreign to Israelite thought. If an Egyptian root for the expression is to be sought, it is the wisdom tradition, with its reference to general humanity and its language of analogy rather than representation, that offers the closest parallels.[28]

Evidence from Mesopotamia is more limited, but appears closer to the Priestly usage in language, conception, and time. One text of Middle-Assyrian provenance and three of Neo-Assyrian and Neo-Babylonian date employ the identical cognate expression, *ṣalam*-DN ⟦'image of DN'⟧, as a designation of the king.[29]

1. (KN) *šūma ṣalam Enlil dārû*
   He (KN) is the eternal image of Enlil [MA][30]
2. *šarru bēl mātāti ṣalmu ša* ᵈ*Šamas šū*
   The king, the lord of the lands, is the very image of Shamash [NA]
3. *abūšu ša šarri bēlīya ṣalam* ᵈ*Bēl-ma šū*
   u šarru bēlī ṣalam ᵈ*Bēl šū* ⟦142⟧
   The father of the king, my lord, was the very image of Bel,
   and the king, my lord, is likewise the very image of Bel [NA][31]

27. Otto, "Der Mensch als Geschöpf und Bild Gottes," 344–47; and Hornung, "Der Mensch als 'Bild Gottes' in Ägypten," 147–51. Otto distinguishes the royal usage sharply from the use of similar (in some cases identical) expressions to describe the relationship of nonroyal figures to the god or gods. The royal usage implies—and depends upon—a notion of identity, he insists, while the nonroyal usage describes only a form of analogy. The distinction lies in the ancient and fundamental Egyptian distinction between royal theology and (general) anthropology (344).

28. So, apparently, Hornung ("Der Mensch als 'Bild Gottes' in Ägypten," 150), who notes that the expression appears in the wisdom tradition prior to and independent of the royal usage. Neither Otto nor Hornung recognize a development within the complex Egyptian usage which could be described as the "democratizing" of an original royal concept and designation.

29. The following texts are cited in *CAD* (nos. 2–4) and *AHW* (all under the heading of "transferred meanings," with the translation "likeness"/"Abbild."

30. From a fragment of the Tukulti-Ninurta Epic, probably composed not long after the defeat of Kashtiliash IV (1232–25) (W. G. Lambert, "Three Unpublished Fragments of the Tukulti-Ninurta Epic," *AfO* 18 [1957] 38–51; and William L. Moran, private communication). The statement occurs in a hymn of praise to the Assyrian king, which compares him to a god in his stature (1.16; Moran, citing *AHW* 374b; cf. Lambert, 51) and birth (1.17) and proclaims his exaltation to a position next to Ninurta himself (1.20):

18. He is the eternal image of Enlil, who hears what the people say, the "Counsel" of the land.

....

20. Enlil, like a physical father (*kīma abi ālidi*) exalted him (*ušarbīšu*) second to (*arki*) his firstborn son [i.e., Ninurta] (Lambert, 50–51).

31. Nos. 2 and 3 are from petitions of the court astrologer Ada-šumu-uṣur to Esarhaddon and his son Ashurbanipal, respectively (Simo Parpola, *Letters from Assyrian Scholars to the*

4. *šar kiššati ṣalam* [d]*Marduk attā*
   O King of the universe, you are the image of Marduk [NB][32]

Akkadian *ṣalmu* ⟦'image'⟧ exhibits the same range of meaning as its Hebrew cognate, designating in its basic use a statue (in the round), a likeness or representation, usually of a deity or king, especially as set up in a temple as a visible sign and manifestation of the living god or person. It may also describe a relief or drawing, again usually of a king or deity. In transferred uses the basic idea of a likeness is maintained, with emphasis on resemblance, correspondence and representation.[33]

Kings Esarhaddon and Assurbanipal, Part I [= AOAT, 5/1; Kevelaer: Butzon & Bercker; Neukirchen-Vluyn: Neukirchener, 1970] nos. 143 [= ABL 5] r 4ff. [pp. 112–13] and 125 [= ABL 6] 17f. [pp. 98–100]; cf. Leroy Waterman, *Royal Correspondence of the Assyrian Empire,* Parts 1 and 3 [Ann Arbor: University of Michigan, 1930–31]). In no. 2 the writer draws an analogy with the sun god (Shamash) who, he says, stays in the dark only half a day. The king, he urges, should not remain indoors for days on end, but like the Sun, whose image he is, come out of the dark (Parpola, 113). No. 3 belongs to a profession of loyalty to the new king. Both texts are a courtier's words of adulation, but the terms of exaltation are hardly his invention.

32. From a Babylonian astrological report (= R. C. Thompson, *The Reports of the Magicians and Astrologers of Nineveh and Babylon in the British Museum,* 2 [London: Luzac, 1900] no. 170 r 2). The text appears to liken the king to Marduk in his display of anger—and reconciliation—toward his servants (Moran, private communication; cf. Thompson, *Reports,* lxii; and Ernst Weidner, *OLZ* 15 [1912] 319).

33. *CAD/AHW*: *ṣalmu*; BDB: *ṣelem.* The notion of representation goes beyond that of a representative in suggesting a measure of identity, or an essential correspondence. Such identity, however, is not identity of substance or being, but of character or function (and power), for the image is always a copy, not a double or derivative; it is of different material or kind than the original. The image stands for the original, which it reproduces and shows forth. The term is basically concrete. It does not refer to an idea, nor does it describe a model, pattern or prototype (*contra* Mettinger, "Abbild oder Urbild?" esp. 411). Since *ṣalmu/ṣelem* describes a formal resemblance and holistic representation, the particular attributes of the original which the *ṣelem* may be intended to manifest must be determined by contexts of use.

In Mesopotamia, the most common use of the term is to designate the statue of a god or king, while the largest class of metaphorical usage describes an individual as the "statue/image" of a god. In four of the five examples cited in *CAD* and *AHW,* the one designated *ṣalmu* of the god is a king. The fifth example describes a conjuror priest and belongs to a twofold identification, of word and person, which serves to emphasize the truth and efficacy of his conjuration: *šiptum šipat* [d]*Marduk āšipu ṣalam* [d]*Marduk*: "The conjuration (recited) is the conjuration of Marduk, the conjuror is the very image of Marduk" (*AfO* 14 150. 225f. [*bīt mēsiri*]) (cited from *CAD*). In both royal and priestly designations the human representative is viewed above all as one possessing the power and authority of the god, whether for weal or woe. No "democratized" usage of the expression is attested in Akkadian sources; "likeness" to the god belongs only to the god's special representative(s).

⟦143⟧ The passages cited above use the expression *ṣalam*-DN figuratively to designate one who, according to Mesopotamian royal ideology, is understood to be a special representative of the god or gods, possessing a divine mandate to rule, and hence divine power, but who is himself neither deity nor divine—except in the limited terms of election and exaltation.[34] In these texts the designation of the king as "image of the god" serves to emphasize the godlike nature of the king in his ruling function and power.[35]

But this usage, despite close affinity to the Priestly formulation, is hardly its source. Though our primary clues to the meaning of the language and constructs of Genesis 1 must be sought in Akkadian and Egyptian texts, their origin is presumably in neither, but in a still unknown "Canaanite" tradition. That silent source must have incorporated and mediated both Mesopotamian and Egyptian influences, but it appears to have stood closer to the former in its basic language and thought. To the extent that the Genesis creation account may be viewed as an alternative, or counter, myth, either in its original Yahwistic formulation or in its final Priestly edition, the elements with which it most clearly compares and contrasts are found in traditions known from Mesopotamia. Since the final editing of the work is also located there, a polemical reading of the account may be suggested, even if the terms of the polemic do not originate with the final composition.[36]

34. Henri Frankfort, *Kingship and the Gods* (Chicago: University of Chicago, 1948) 215–61, 295–312, esp. 237, 307, 309.

35. Franz M. T. Böhl ("Das Zeitalter der Sargonide," *Opera Minora* [Groningen/ Djakarta: Wolters, 1953] 403) found expression of the idea of the king as image of the god not only in the term *ṣalmu*, but also *ṣillu*, which he translated "Schattenbild" (403). The meaning of the term in his key text (ABL 652 = Parpola, *Letters*, no. 145) is disputed, however, as is the meaning of the proverb cited in the text (cf. *Böhl*, "Der babylonische Fürstenspiegel," MAOG 11, 3 [1939] 49; Frankfort, *Kingship*, 407, n. 35; and Parpola, *Letters*, 113). The final line appears, nevertheless, to contain a clear expression of the king's likeness to the god, in this case using the term *muššulu* (<*mašālu* "to be similar" [*CAD*]), a term corresponding to Hebrew *dĕmût* (cf. Wildberger, "Abbild," 254):

šarru šu [*k*] *al*! *muššuli ša ili*
The king is the perfect likeness of the god

(Parpola, *Letters*, 113; cf. Böhl, "Fürstenspiegel," 49; and "Zeltalter," 403).

36. Polemical features of the account have been widely noted, often in relation to the dominant Mesopotamian creation myth, *Enuma Elish* (see, e.g., Maag, "Alttestamentliche Anthropogonie," 31–41, esp. 37; cf. Hasel, "The Polemic Nature of the Genesis Cosmology"). The Babylonian exile surely encouraged sharpening of the distinctive elements of Israelite theology, cosmology—and anthropology—in relation to the views of the surrounding culture. But Israel's dialogue with "foreign" culture did not begin there. Israel's theology was constructed from the beginning in dynamic critical appropriation of the religious

⟦144⟧ The genius of the formulation in Gen 1:26 may be seen in its use of a common expression and image of Mesopotamian (-Canaanite) royal theology to counter a common image of Mesopotamian (-Canaanite) anthropology, viz., the image of humanity as servant of the gods, the dominant image of Mesopotamian creation myths.[37] The language that describes the king is chosen by the author of Genesis 1 (perhaps under influence of Egyptian wisdom tradition) to describe humanity as a whole, *adam qua adam* ⟦'humanity as humanity'⟧, in its essential nature. The expression of Genesis 1 is unique in the OT, determined, we would suggest, by the genre and context of composition. But the idea of the royal status of *adam* is not; it is prominent in Psalm 8, where the language of coronation is combined with the language of dominion to describe the distinctive status and role of humanity in creation. In our understanding, *ṣelem* and *RDH* ⟦'have dominion, rule'⟧ belong to a single complex of ideas and describe a sequence of thought which parallels exactly the twofold statement of Psalm 8.

The Unique Creature

The special interest of God in this culminating act of creation and ordering is registered at a grammatical and lexical level by a shift in the word of announcement from intransitive verbal forms or verbs of

---

heritage of Canaan and confrontation with the recurrent challenge of competing local and foreign cults and myths. The origins of the Priestly creation account and many of the features that characterize it as a counter myth must be placed during the monarchy rather than the exile.

The significance of the Akkadian cognate equivalents to the unique OT expression, *ṣelem ʾĕlōhîm* lies in their close association with the royal theology and their distribution in time; the usage spans the period from the origin of the Israelite monarchy and its temple cult to the seventh and sixth centuries, when the temple traditions received their final form. Past emphasis on the latter period as the significant period of cultural interchange, and polemic, may be attributed to the dating of P—and to the dates of the extant parallels. The one early example among our citations, and the one in which the expression is most clearly part of a consciously articulated royal theology, was not published until 1957. Thus Böhl could argue in 1953 ("Zeit der Sargonide," 403) that the idea of the king as image of the god was a new and distinctive feature of the Neo-Assyrian royal theology.

37. See, esp., *Enuma Elish* 6.34–35. The tradition that humankind was created to serve the gods, and thus free them from their onerous labor, is much older, however, as may be seen from *Atraḫasis* 1.194–97:

194 You are the birth-goddess, creatress of mankind
195 Create *Lullu* that he may bear the yoke,
196 Let him bear the yoke assigned by Enlil,
197 Let man carry the toil of the gods!

(W. G. Lambert and A. R. Millard, *Atra-ḫasis* [Oxford: Clarendon, 1969] 56–57).

generation to an active-transitive verb, and from third person to first person speech. The verb *ᶜāśâ* ⟦'do, make'⟧, which has heretofore been used only in the execution reports, to emphasize the divine activity, is now taken up into the announcement itself. The becoming of *adam* is inconceivable ⟦145⟧ apart from God's own direct action and involvement; the willing of this creation requires divine commitment.

The structure of the final word also differs from that of the words that describe the other orders of living things. For them no purpose or function is announced or reported.[38] And each order is referred to an already existing element of earth (land and water) and its locus and proximate source. In contrast, *adam* is assigned a function or task by the very word of announcement, a task defined in relation to the other creatures and to the earth, which is its habitat but not its source.[39] Humanity is also distinguished from other orders of life by its direct and unmediated dependence upon God. For *adam,* habitat is neither source of life nor source of identity.[40]

The *Wortbericht* ⟦'announcement'⟧ emphasizes the exalted, isolated position of *adam* within the created order, as one uniquely identified with God and charged by God with dominion over the creatures. Yet the full account insists that *adam* is also creature, sharing both habitat and constitution with the other orders of animal life. The creation of humankind stands in the overall structure of the Priestly creation account as an amplification and specification of the creation of the land animals, and the two acts of creation together comprise a single day's work. This classification of *adam* with the other creatures of earth has required an adjustment in the account of the sixth day's work, for the formula of blessing which speaks of the filling of earth (parallel to the filling of the seas in v. 22) cannot be addressed to two orders occupying the same

38. The designation of the plants as food in vv. 29–30 is a secondary and subordinate theme and differs in structure from the purpose clauses or compound sentences of vv. 6, 9, 14–15, and 26. The specifications, "bearing seed" and "producing fruit," in v. 11 do not describe a purpose or function, but introduce the theme of fertility as a subtheme of the word about nature (see below).

39. The notion of task or function is suggested by the verbal form of the clause; the meaning of the verb itself, however, points to an emphasis on status and power as its primary message rather than exercise of a responsibility of function (see below).

40. P avoids, or counters, by this formulation not only the primitive notion of humankind "sprouting" from the ground (cf., e.g., "The Myth of the Pickax" and "The Myth of Enki and E-engurra"), but also the more elevated, but likewise unacceptable, notion of humanity as a mixture of earthly and divine substance (clay and blood [—or breath?]; cf. *Atraḫasis, Enuma Elish* [and Genesis 2]). Nor is *adam* conceived in this formulation as a fallen god, but rather by original design as the "God-like" one among the creatures.

space. The expected blessing of the land animals has accordingly given way to the blessing of *adam*, the supreme land creature.[41]

⟦146⟧ The combination of events on the sixth day suggests that *adam* is to be understood as a special type or species of earth creature. In contrast to *adam*, all other life is described in broad classes, with subclasses or species (*mîn*) recognized but not named.[42] Thus grasses and fruiting plants represent the primary classes of vegetation, each with its myriad individual species, while "fish," fowl, cattle, and creepers describe comparable classes of animal life. *Adam*, however, is an individual, at once species and order, a creature among creatures yet apart from them and above them.

Sexual Distinction and Blessing

The word that most clearly locates *adam* among the creatures is the blessing of v. 28 and the specification which immediately precedes and prepares for it: *zākār ûnĕqēbâ bārāʾ ʾōtām* ⟦'male and female he created them'⟧. But the theme articulated in these coordinated clauses reaches beyond the world of creatures addressed by the word of blessing to include all life. For P, there is a corollary to the idea that all of creation is derived from God and dependent upon God. It is the idea of the permanence and immutability of the created orders. For living things, with their observable cycles of life, permanence must be conceived in dynamic terms, as a process of replenishment or reproduction. Thus for each order of living thing explicit attention is given to the means by which it shall be perpetuated. That is the meaning of the cumbersome and seemingly unnecessary specification that both classes of vegetation were created bearing seeds—i.e., equipped to reproduce their kind.[43] And that is the

41. Schmidt, *Schöpfungsgeschichte*, 147. Cf. Westermann, *Genesis*, 196. That the blessing of the land animals is to be understood as included in the blessing given to *adam* seems unlikely in view of the expansion of the latter blessing to include the subjugation of the earth (*wĕkibšūhā* ⟦'and subdue it'⟧). Equally unlikely is the notion that the land creatures receive their blessing through *adam*, or that they receive no blessing, since the "renewal" of the blessing after the flood addresses both classes—separately: Noah and sons in 9:1 and the animals in 8:17 (including birds as land-based creatures—a combination of classes treated as distinct in Genesis 1) (196). What this shows is a selective and flexible employment of categories and formulas, varied according to changing situations and need (e.g., omitting the sea creatures in 8:17).

42. Eduard König, "Die Bedeutung des hebräischen *mîn*," *ZAW* 31 (1911) 133–46. Cf. Schmidt, *Schöpfungsgeschichte* 106–7, 123; Westermann, *Genesis*, 174–75. The differentiation of plant and animal life into species or types does not find a correspondence in the sexual differentiation of humankind, described in v. 27 (*contra* Schmidt, *Schöpfungsgeschichte*, 107, n. 1). See below.

43. Cf. Maag, "Alttestamentliche Anthropogonie," 39.

meaning of the blessing that imparts to all creatures the power of reproduction: "Be fruitful and multiply and fill the earth/waters."

While the immediate intention of this word in its expanded form (including *milʾû* ⟦'fill'⟧) is surely to describe the filling of an empty earth through the multiplication of original specimen pairs,[44] there may be ⟦147⟧ another intention as well, a polemical one. For P, the power of created life to replenish itself is a power given to each species at its creation and therefore not dependent upon subsequent rites or petitions for its effect.[45] The emphatic and repeated word which endows life with the means and the power of propagation undercuts the rationale of the fertility cult—and in yet another manner deposes and annihilates the gods; for the power to create life and to sustain it belongs to God alone, who incorporates the means of perpetuity into the very design and constitution of the universe,[46] and the power to rule earth and its creatures is delegated to *adam*. Thus the gods are denied all power, place and function by this account, whether to create, renew or rule.

Adam is creature, who with all other created life is given the power of reproduction through the word-act of creation, receiving it in the identical words of blessing addressed first to the creatures of sea and sky

44. The terms used to describe each order and class are all singular collectives ([*dešeʾ*] ⟦'vegetation'⟧ *ʿēśeb* ⟦'plant'⟧ *ʿēṣ* ⟦'tree'⟧, [*šereṣ*] ⟦'swarming things'⟧], *nepeš ḥayyâ* ⟦'living creatures'⟧, *ʿôp* ⟦'flying creatures'⟧, *bĕhēmâ* ⟦'cattle'⟧ *remeś* ⟦'creeping things'⟧ *ḥayĕtô-ʾereṣ* ⟦'wild beasts'⟧, *ʾādām* ⟦'human-kind'⟧) with the exception of *tannînīm*, a plural used to create a comparable class designation for the creatures of the sea. Each class is understood as an aggregate of species (*mîn*), which could conceivably be represented by individuals of each type (cf., e.g., Gen 2:19, where *adam* is a single individual—and also representative of the species). But the theme of reproductive endowment enunciated in the blessing assumes sexual differentiation and hence pairs as the minimal representation of each species. In fact, the image of a pair as the model of a species is so common that it needs no special articulation, especially in such a terse account. It is only where a particular need for clarification or emphasis arises that the assumption must be made explicit—as in 1:27, and 7:9 and 16. See below.

45. Maag's recognition of the polemical function of the repeated statement concerning the seed and his linking of this to the blessing of the creatures ("Alttestamentliche Anthropogonie" [1955] 39) seems to have been lost in the subsequent literature. I discovered it only after arriving at a similar understanding. My characterization of the polemic (below) is admittedly overstated. I mean thereby to suggest implications, and possible ancient readings of the text, which lie below the surface message and may escape the modern reader.

46. The blessing of fertility, as Westermann correctly notes, is not a separate or supplemental act, but one which completes the act of creation for the living creatures (*Genesis*, 192). The reason that the power of reproduction is conveyed in a blessing and not simply described as a feature of their constitution, as in the case of the plants, may lie in a recognition that unlike the "automatic" reproduction of plants, animal reproduction is a matter not simply of design, but also of will or of power to realize its end. The blessing activates the latent capacity and directs it toward its goal.

(v. 22). It is in relation to this statement that the specification, "male and female he created them," must be understood. The word of sexual differentiation anticipates the blessing and prepares for it. And it is an essential word, not because of any prehistory which related a separate creation of man and woman,[47] but because of the structure of the Priestly account and the order of its essential themes. Sexual constitution is the presupposition of the blessing of increase, which in the case of the other creatures is simply assumed. In the case of *adam*, however, it cannot be assumed, but must be specially articulated because of the statement that immediately precedes it.

⟦148⟧ The word about *adam* is twofold in both *Wortbericht* ⟦'announcement'⟧ and *Tatbericht* ⟦'execution report'⟧ ; it identifies humanity by nature or constitution and by position or function. And the primary word about the nature of *adam*, and the sole word of the *Wortbericht*, is that this one is like God, created in resemblance to God as an image or representation. This audacious statement of identification and correspondence, however qualified by terms of approximation, offers no ground for assuming sexual distinction as a characteristic of *adam*, but appears rather to exclude it, for God (*ʾĕlōhîm*) is the defining term in the statement. The idea that God might possess any form of sexuality, or any differentiation analogous to it, would have been for P an utterly foreign and repugnant notion. For this author/editor, above all others in the Pentateuch, guards the distance between God and humanity, avoiding anthropomorphic description and employing specialized terminology (e.g., *bārāʾ* ⟦'created'⟧) to distinguish divine activity from analogous human action.[48] Consequently, the word that identifies *adam* by reference to divine likeness must be supplemented or qualified before the blessing of fertility can be pronounced; for the word of blessing assumes, but does not bestow, the means of reproduction.

47. So Westermann, *Genesis*, 220–21.

48. The *naʿăśeh* ⟦'let us make'⟧ of v. 26 has long troubled commentators mindful of the deliberateness and precision of P's language, especially in referring to the Deity. In view of the control exercised by P over the final composition and especially evident in the *Wortbericht*, the plural formulation cannot be regarded as a "slip" nor as an undigested remnant of tradition. For though the expression depends ultimately upon the tradition of the divine council, in its Yahwistic and monotheistic adaptation, it appears also to have been *selected* by P as a means of breaking the direct identification between *adam* and God suggested by the metaphor of image, a way of blurring or obscuring the referent of the *ṣelem*. Cf. the *ṣelem ʾĕlōhîm* of v. 27aβ, which has a similar function in respect to the preceding *ṣalmô* ⟦'his image'⟧ (see below). The plural *ʾĕlōhîm* has a useful ambiguity here (v. 27). It is not, however, to be viewed as suggesting a collectivity of male and female deities to which the male-and-female *adam* would correspond (*contra* Loretz, *Gottebenbildlichkeit*, 68).

The required word of qualification and specification is introduced in v. 27b. *Unlike* God, but *like* the other creatures, *adam* is characterized by sexual differentiation.[49] The parallel clauses of v. 27aβb form a bridging ⟦149⟧ couplet between the primary and emphasized statement concerning the divine likeness, introduced in the *Wortbericht* (26) and repeated as the lead sentence of the *Tatbericht* (27aα), and the pronouncement of the blessing of fertility (v. 28)—a new theme found only in the *Tatbericht.* It recapitulates the word about the image, in an emphatic yet qualifying manner, and adds to it the word of sexual distinction:

bĕṣelem ʾĕlōhîm bārāʾ ʾōtô	⟦'in the image of God he created him;
zākār ûnĕqēbâ bārāʾ ʾōtām[50]	male and female he created them'⟧

49. The specifying clause, "male and female he created them," must not be understood as distinguishing humans from other creatures or as giving to human sexual distinction a special meaning. In the economy of the Priestly writer's account it is mentioned here only out of necessity (see below). The same specification, in the same terms, *zākār ûnĕqēbâ* ⟦'male and female'⟧ is made elsewhere with reference to the animals—and for a similar reason of clarification and emphasis. In the Priestly account of the flood story, the author wishes to make clear that the "two of every sort" of animals that are to be brought into the ark constitute a minimal pair, capable of reproduction, and thus he specifies, *zākār ûnĕqēbâ yihyû* ("they shall be male and female" [Gen 6:19]; cf. 7:9).

The Priestly writer has chosen his terms, as well as their placement, with care. *Zākâr* ⟦'male'⟧ and *nĕqēbâ* ⟦'female'⟧ are biological terms, not social terms—as *ʾîš* ⟦'man'⟧ and *ʾiššâ* ⟦'wife'⟧ in 2:22–24. Harmonizing of the creation accounts of Genesis 1 and 2 has affected the translation as well as the interpretation of the terms in 1:27, especially in the German tradition, where the rendering "Mann und Frau" (Westermann, *Genesis,* 108; Schmidt, *Schöpfungsgeschichte,* 127, *inter alios*) or "Mann und Weib" (Gunkel, *Genesis,* 103; Zürich Bible, 1942; "Luther Bible," rev. ed., 1964; *inter alios*) is common. Westermann seems to have fallen prey to the subtle persuasion of this traditional rendering, for despite his caution against overloading the interpretation of the clause, he avers: "Wohl aber ist hier ausgesagt, dass der zu zweit geschaffene Mensch sowohl im Verstehen menschlicher Existenz wie auch in den Ordnungen und den Institutionen des menschlichen Daseins also ein *zur Gemeinschaft bestimmter* gesehen werden muss" (*Genesis,* 221; emphasis added) ⟦see Westermann, *Genesis 1–11* (London: SPCK/Minneapolis: Augsburg, 1984), 160, for Eng. trans.⟧.

50. Most recent analyses of vv. 26–28 recognize a complex history of growth resulting in repetitions, expansions, and substitutions in the present text. There is little consensus, however, about primary and secondary elements or stages of growth or editing. Consequently, understandings of how the component parts fit together to make their statement differ considerably. E.g., Schmidt concludes that pre-P tradition is found only in vv. 26–27a—and no longer in pristine form. Within this material he finds that 27a gives the impression of particular antiquity (*Schöpfungsgeschichte,* 148–49). Westermann sees the present text as overloaded with "repetitions" (including 26b and 27aβ as well as *bĕṣalmô* ⟦'in his image'⟧ in 27aα), which he eliminates from his reconstructed text (*Genesis,* 198–99). The text which he creates by this surgery ("Lasst uns Menschen machen, / nach unserem Bild, uns ähnlich: // Und Gott schuf die Menschen, / er schuf sie als Mann und Frau", 198–99) is the text which Barth's exegesis requires, but which the MT with its deliberate qualifications does not allow. ⟦See Westermann, *Genesis 1–11,* 143, for Eng. trans.⟧

The two parallel cola contain two essential and distinct statements about the nature of humanity: *adam* is created *like* (i.e., resembling) God, but *as* creature, and hence male and female.[51] The parallelism of the two ⟦150⟧ cola is progressive, not synonymous. The second statement adds to the first; it does not explicate it.[52]

Expansion and Conflation in the Tatbericht

The position of the specification of humanity's bisexual nature is dictated by the larger narrative structure of the chapter and by the themes it must incorporate. Here, following the pattern of the preceding acts or episodes, the *Wortbericht* conveys the essential content of the word about the order (viz., created according to divine likeness and given dominion), and the *Tatbericht* repeats it. And here, as in the parallel account of the sixth act of creation, the *Tatbericht* is expanded by a word of blessing, introducing the subtheme of sustainability alongside the primary theme of order. But in vv. 27–28 the introduction of the word of blessing, with its

---

I recognize, with most commentators, a history of growth in the tradition behind the present text, but I do not think the stages can be identified or isolated with any precision. I would regard the couplet in 27a as the work of a single author, more specifically, the final editor, and view the seemingly awkward or redundant *bĕṣelem ʾĕlōhîm* as a deliberate qualification of the preceding *bĕṣalmô*, perhaps employing a phrase from an earlier stage of the tradition. The repetition of *bĕṣelem* with its significant variation in 27aα and β has an important theological purpose. The reflexive singular suffix of 27aα requires that the image be referred directly to God, the sole and single actor, and not to a lower order of divine beings (*contra* Gunkel [*Genesis*, 98], *inter alios*). It thus "corrects" the impression of a plurality of deities which might be suggested by the plurals of v. 26. But *bĕṣelem ʾĕlōhîm* qualifies the masculine singular antecedent by repetition of the name, which in its third-person formulation gives both precision and distance to the self-reference. With its ambiguous plural form and its class connotation, *ʾĕlōhîm* serves, as the plurals of v. 26, to blur the profile of the referent.

51. The shift from the collective singular (*ʾōtô* ["him"]) in the first colon to (collective) plural (*ʾōtām* ["them"]) in the second is significant. The author relates the notion of the divine image only to an undifferentiated humanity as species or order and thus takes pains to use the singular pronoun in both clauses of 27 employing *ṣelem*, despite the fact that the plural has already been introduced in the verb (*wĕyirdû* ⟦'and let them have dominion'⟧) of the preceding verse.

52. *Contra* Barth, who sees 27b as a "geradezu definitionsmässige Erklärung der Gottesebenbildlichkeit" ⟦'perfectly well-defined explanation of the image of God'⟧ (*KD* 3/1. 219). Cf. Trible (*God and the Rhetoric of Sexuality*, 16–21), who finds in the parallelism of v. 27 a metaphor in which "the image of God" is the tenor and "male and female" the vehicle (p. 17). This interpretation rests on a faulty syntactical analysis which isolates v. 27 as a unit of speech/thought. The metaphor is the creation of the interpreter. Schmidt, who judged 27b a secondary addition on grounds of vocabulary, style, and meter, noted that apart from Gen 1:27 and 5:1–2 the themes of divine image and sexuality are associated nowhere else, either in the OT or the ancient Near East (*Schöpfungsgeschichte*, 146–47). He failed to recognize, however, why the two are juxtaposed here.

clarifying prefatory note, has broken the connection between image and dominion articulated in v. 26. In the expanded execution report, the word which conveys dominion is joined directly to the preceding words of blessing, creating an extended series of imperatives, all apparently governed by the rubric of blessing (*wayĕbārek ʾōtām* ⟦'and blessed them'⟧ [v. 28])—and all apparently conditioned by the dual qualification of bisexual nature and divine resemblance. Such a reading of vv. 27–28, however, which treats the series of words addressed to *adam* as homogeneous and relates both statements of nature (God-like and bisexual) to the whole series without discrimination, ignores the interpretive clues contained in the *Wortbericht* and in the parallel construction of v. 22. Fertility and dominion belong to two separate themes or concerns: one, the theme of nature with its subtheme of sustainability (fertility), the other, the theme of order with its interest in position and function. The word of sexual distinction pertains only to the first, and has relevance or consequence in P's theology only for the first.

⟦151⟧ There is no message of shared dominion here,[53] no word about the distribution of roles, responsibility, and authority between the sexes, no word of sexual equality. What is described is a task for the species (*kibšūhā* ⟦'subdue it'⟧ and the position of the species in relation to the other orders of creatures (*rĕdû* ⟦'dominion over'⟧). The social metaphors to which the key verbs point are male, derived from male experience and models, the dominant social models of patriarchal society. For P, as for J, the representative and determining image of the species was certainly male, as 5:1–3, 9:1, and the genealogies which structure the continuing account make clear.[54] Though the Priestly writer speaks of

53. *Contra* Anderson ("Human Dominion," 43) and Trible (*God and the Rhetoric of Sexuality*, 19), *inter alios*. Anderson rightly argues that "dominion is given to mankind as a whole," finding in this collective understanding a clear expression of the "democratization" of the royal motif (42). But then he explicates "mankind as a whole" to mean "man and woman." "Here," he notes, "the priestly view departs from royal theology in Egypt, for it is not said that Pharaoh *and* his wife represent together the image of God." Psalm 8 stands much closer to the royal theology, he argues, in that "'man' is spoken of in the singular and no reference is made to male and female" (43). Both contrasts are false, however, since the specification of male and female relates neither to dominion nor to the image. The "Egyptian pattern" of male representation is continued unqualified in the biblical tradition of Genesis 1 as well as Psalm 8. See below.

54. When P moves from protohistory (creation) to "history" his view of humankind is limited to the male actor or subject. Thus *adam* becomes Adam and is renewed in Noah and his sons, not Noah and his wife. The blessing of fertility is addressed in 9:1 to the men alone, with no mention of the wives, who as necessary helpers in the task of maintaining the species are explicitly noted in the enumeration of those entering the ark. The pointed reference to the unnamed wives of Noah and of his three sons in 7:7 and 7:13 has the same function as the specification of "male and female" in 1:27. This theme of reproductive capability also finds expression in the phrase, "other sons *and daughters*," incorporated into

the species, he thinks of the male, just as the author of Psalm 8. But maleness is not an essential or defining characteristic. Against such reduction or confusion of attributes the word of bisexual creation stands as guard, even if it provides only a minimal base for the anthropology of equality.

The theme of sexuality (reproduction) has a limited function in this account. And the words which introduce it are bracketed within the *Tatbericht.* The divine address, initiated in the blessing of fertility, moves beyond the idea of increase to climax in the independent theme of dominion, resuming the thought and expression of the announcement in v. 26.[55] But the resumption in v. 28 appears to contain an ⟦152⟧ expansion, extending *adam*'s dominion from the rule over the realm of creatures to subjugation of the earth. The expression *wĕkibšūhā* ⟦'subdue it'⟧ forms a bridge in the present text between the word of increase and the word of sovereignty. In subject matter it appears linked to the latter, suggesting that *RDH* ⟦'have dominion, rule'⟧ might be understood as an elaboration or specification of *KBŠ* ⟦'subdue'⟧.[56] Grammatically, however, it is an extension of the blessing, with an object and function distinct from that of the following verb, and must consequently be distinguished from the theme of dominion articulated by *RDH.*

The theme of divine blessing, specifically blessing of increase, is a key interpretive element within the larger Priestly work, located at strategic points in the account and formulated according to the particular demands of each situation. The vocabulary is neither fixed nor unique to P, though the root pair *PRH* ⟦'be fruitful'⟧ + *RBH* ⟦'multiply'⟧ forms a constant core of his usage and may be seen as a signature of his work.[57] Outside of P, or dependent usage,[58] the closest parallels are

---

the summarizing statement of each generation of P's otherwise all-male genealogical tables (5:4, 7, 10, 13, 16, 19, 22, 26, 30; 11:11, 13, 15, 17, 19, 21, 23, 25). The history in which P's theological interest lies is a history carried by males and embodied in males. Females come into view only where the issue of biological continuity or reproduction is raised.

55. The expansion of the introduction in v. 28 over the parallel in v. 22 may be related to the expanded statement which it introduces. The repetitive *wayyōʾmer lāhem ʾĕlōhîm* ⟦'and God said to them'⟧ following *wayĕbārek ʾōtām ʾĕlōhîm* ⟦'and God blessed them'⟧, in place of the simple *lēʾmōr* ⟦'saying'⟧ of v. 22, is usually explained in terms of emphasis and differentiation: in the case of *adam,* unlike the lower creatures, the divine word has become a word of address, an act of communication. But the twofold introduction may indicate an awareness that what follows is not simply blessing, but rather blessing together with a word conveying authority (Schmidt, *Schöpfungsgeschichte,* 148–49).

56. Cf. Schmidt, *Schöpfungsgeschichte,* 147; and Westermann, *Genesis,* 222.

57. Cf. Westermann, *Genesis,* 192–95; Schmidt, *Schöpfungsgeschichte,* 147–48.

58. P: Gen 1:22; 1:28; 8:17; 9:1; 9:7; [17:6 *PRH* alone (hiph.)]; 17:20 (hiph.); 28:3 (hiph.; Isaac as subject); 35:11; 42:27; 48:4 (hiph.); Exod 1:7. Dependent on P: Ps 105:24 (*PRH* hiph. + *ʿṢM* ⟦'be numerous'⟧ hiph., reflecting Exod 1:7); Lev 26:9 (*PRH* hiph.); Exod 23:30 (*PRH* qal).

found in exilic prophecies of restoration (Jer 3:6; 23:3; Ezek 36:11). In all usage, the word of blessing, whether direct or indirect, past or future, has a particular end or goal related to a particular situation of need; and in the majority of cases it is a territorial goal.[59]

This is explicit in the Patriarchal History, where the language of blessing has been assimilated by P to the older tradition and form of the promise. Here the goal, given by the promise tradition, is possession of the land—a historical as well as a territorial goal.[60] In P's edition of the Primeval History, the language of increase has been adapted to the situation of prehistory and the emptiness of newly created earth in a three-part ⟦153⟧ formula of blessing, repeated in Gen 1:22, 28 and 9:1: *pĕrû ûrĕbû ûmilʾû* . . . ("be fruitful and multiply and fill . . . "). The orientation of the words of increase toward particular time and space is clear from the final term of the formula, *ûmilʾû*, and from the placement of the blessing, addressing creatures classified by habitat (land and non-land creatures) and by "historical" circumstances (Noah and sons after the flood).[61]

The blessing of 1:28, directed to the first, representative specimens of humanity, adds an element lacking in the parallels of 1:22 and 9:1, one which establishes the conditions essential, and unique, to this species for continuing life and for history. The newly formed earth must not only be filled, but also tamed or "harnessed."[62] The author knows that

59. In extra-P usage, *PRH* as a term for human and animal increase, is typically related to possession of (the) land and/or security against foes, with increase understood as the necessary condition or presupposition. Jer 3:16, 23:3 and Ezek 36:11 envision the increase of a remnant which shall again "fill" the land, while Exod 23:30 speaks of Israel's original possession of the land. All of the "historical" uses of *PRH* point to a future or restored Israel, closely associating the ideas of territorial possession and nationhood.

60. That the historical goal may be future as well as past (assuming a programmatic or eschatological dimension to the Priestly Work) does not change this assertion. The promise of P is not open ended. It envisions historical fulfillment.

61. The periodization of the Primeval History is overlooked by Lohfink, when he suggests that the blessing of 1:28 looks to the rise of the various nations and the settlement of their lands ("Seid fruchtbar," 82). He is right, however, in stressing that the imperative of Gen 1:28 is not a general word for all time, but a word that belongs to the situation of origins (80). Thus neither the historic problems of underpopulation or overpopulation are relevant to the interpretation of this word.

The repetition of the blessing in 9:1 focuses on the human species alone, whose history now becomes the subject of the continuing account. This renewed blessing sets in motion the growth which leads to the rise of nations, in which the history of Israel is hidden.

62. The basic sense of the root *KBŠ* is "subdue, bring into bondage" (BDB; preferable to KB: "treten, niedertreten, drücken" ⟦'tread, press'⟧). All uses of the qal, niphal and hiphil are exilic. The oldest usage is in 2 Sam 8:11, a piel, with king David as subject and *haggôyīm* ("the nations") as object. While the image is forceful, attention is directed to the resultant state, as subdued, deprived of (threatening) power, hence "pacified," controlled. Cf. George W.

earth will support human life only when it is brought under control—a condition distinguishing *adam* from the birds and sea creatures, who appear to be sustained by their environment rather than having to win life from it. The agrarian perspective is obvious and is shared with the Mesopotamian author of *Atraḫasis*, who views the task as drudgery, however, not as an act of mastery, a burden imposed upon humanity, not a blessing. It is also shared by the Yahwist, who distinguishes an "original" relationship to earth from the historical one and thus accommodates, in sequential arrangement, both the sense of mastery and the experience of drudgery or servitude. For P, who adapts the views of his cultural ancestors, the presupposition of history and culture is the subjugation of earth, rendering it productive and responsive to a master, *adam*. Because this subjugation is essential to the sustaining of human life it is included in the original blessing.[63]

⟦154⟧ The theme announced by the final imperative, *ûrĕdû* ⟦'have dominion over'⟧ is distinct from that of the preceding "commands," despite the similarity in meaning of the verbs *RDH* ⟦'have dominion'⟧ *and KBŠ* ⟦'subdue'⟧. This theme describes the relationship of *adam* to the other creatures who share the earth. Its concern is order and status, rather than life and growth. Its message of human superiority and sovereignty over the creatures appears independently in the creation hymn, Psalm 8, associated there as here with the idea of humanity's proximity to the divine world, but there without any hint of the theme of increase and subjugation of the earth.[64]

RDH in OT usage describes the exercise of dominion, authority or power over an individual, group or territory (nation), often in contexts that specify harsh or illegitimate rule.[65] The term cannot simply be

---

Coats, "The God of Death, Power and Obedience in the Primeval History" (*Int* 29 [1975] 227–39) esp. 229 ("render productive"); and Barr, "Man and Nature," 63–64 ("work or till"). Most discussions of v. 28 treat this clause under the heading of "dominion" and do not distinguish between *KBŠ* and *RDH*.

63. It is not repeated with the blessing to Noah after the flood, since the blessing there has a new and more limited function. The issue is no longer the preconditions of human life and culture but the history of the nations. See above.

64. Anderson sees this absence of the increase-subjugation motif as the clearest evidence for the independence of Psalm 8, but mistakenly links the theme of dominion to the blessing in Genesis 1 ("Human Dominion," 36).

65. BDB gives as the basic meaning: "have dominion, rule [over . . .]." Cognate usage suggests a prevailing negative connotation: Aramaic, Syriac: "chastise"; Arabic: "tread, trample." In OT usage the verb is often accompanied by qualifying expressions such as *bĕperek* ⟦'with ruthlessness'⟧ or *bĕḥozqâ* ⟦'with force'⟧ (Lev 25:43, 46, 53; Ezek 34:4), *bāʾap* ⟦'in fury'⟧ (Isa 14:6) or by parallel verbs such as *NKH* ⟦'smite'⟧ (hiph.; Isa 14:6), *NŚʾ* ⟦'lord it over'⟧ (hithp.; Ezek 29:15), *NGP* ⟦'strike'⟧ (Lev 26:17), *ʿBD* ⟦'enslave'⟧ (Lev 25:46).

equated with the idea of governing, ruling, or managing, with or without emphasis on a caretaker function or maintenance of harmony and order.[66] And, as is often noted, it is not exclusively, or even predominantly, royal language, though, I have argued, it does describe a royal function or prerogative in Genesis 1. When used of kings, it is usually to describe their subjugation of other nations or peoples,[67] or rule over their own people as though they were foreigners.[68] The term emphasizes superior position and power rather than any particular activity, purpose, or equality of rule.[69] The sentiment expressed by the verb *RDH* in Gen 1:26, 28 is, in fact, very close to that expressed by the distinctively royal and hymnic language of Psalm 8, where the idea of dominion is spelled out as subordination/subjugation ("put all things under his feet," v. 7) and linked to the idea of exaltation. Human superiority over other creation is stressed in both accounts. The primary ⟦155⟧ function of *RDH* in Genesis 1 is to describe *adam*'s place in creation. If there is also a message of responsibility here, it is not dependent on the content of the verb but on the action of God in setting *adam* over the creatures in an ordered and sustaining world.

Summary and Conclusions

If the foregoing analysis is correct, the meaning and function of the statement, "male and female he created them," is considerably more limited than is commonly assumed. It says nothing about the image which relates *adam* to God nor about God as the referent of the image. Nor does it qualify *adam*'s dominion over the creatures or subjugation of the earth. It relates only to the blessing of fertility, making explicit its necessary presupposition. It is not concerned with sexual roles, the status or relationship of the sexes to one another, or marriage. It describes the biological pair, not a social partnership; male and female, not man and wife. The specification is not dictated by any prehistory that told of a separate creation of man and woman. Rather, it is P's own formula-

66. *MŠL* ⟦'rule'⟧ is not chosen here, though it is used to describe the function of the sun and moon in v. 16.

67. 1 Kgs 5:4; Ps 110:2; 72:8; Isa 14:6; 41:2.

68. Ezek 34:4; Lev 25:43, 46, 53.

69. I do not think that Lohfink's interpretation of *RDH* in Gen 1:26, 28 as "domestication" of the animals (including fish and birds!) can be defended, though it rightly grasps the elements of superiority and constraint which color the biblical use of the term ("Seid fruchtbar," 82). *RDH* is appropriate in this context to describe rule over those who are not of the same kind or order and who may be viewed in their created state as potentially hostile. This is not the rule of a "brother" but of a stranger. Cf. Westermann, *Genesis,* 219–20.

tion, dependent upon his overarching theme of the sustainability (fertility) of the created order. It may also serve, secondarily, to link the creation narrative to the genealogically structured history which follows.

These conclusions may disappoint in their largely negative formulation, but they have positive consequence as well. The Priestly writer appears in our analysis as a more consistent and intentional theologian in his treatment of the sexes. And the contemporary theologian-exegete is reminded that the Bible is often quite uninterested in, or unable to comprehend, the questions pressed upon the text from modern perspectives and experiences. To describe and to emphasize the limits of a biblical text is not to dishonor it or depreciate its message, but to give integrity and authority to its voice where it does have a word to speak. Sharpening the contours of a given text or profile of an author brings into our range of hearing a greater variety of voices and enables us to discern more clearly common themes and motifs, as well as dissonances. Questions of context (literary, historical, and theological) acquire greater prominence, prohibiting simple transfer of words from the past into modern contexts. The ancient text in historical analysis presents to the contemporary theologian not simply a vocabulary, a treasury of images and concepts, but also a grammar, or grammars, which are fully as essential to the message as the individual terms.

Emphasizing the literary and historical integrity of the ancient text draws more sharply the line between historical and constructive theology, but it may also enable recognition of affinity between the two disciplines, namely, in attention to process in interpretation. Both biblical and contemporary theology may be seen as creative responses to ⟦156⟧ ever-changing contexts; ancient and modern word share a common dynamism which finds expression in changing forms and images, or in changing content of inherited forms and images. Past answers need not be forced to fit contemporary questions.

The task of the biblical exegete in enabling meaningful conversation with an ancient text is first of all to articulate as clearly and carefully as possible the message/intentions of the ancient author or authors at every stage or level of the tradition at which they are exposed within the relevant literary unit. The second task is to ask where they lead (i.e., what may be implied in them but not fully recognized or elaborated) and how they have been amplified, challenged, or corrected by subsequent or alternative understandings arising within the canon and without. The answers to these latter questions move beyond the primary competence of the biblical scholar, but are essential to the task of appropriating the biblical message. The final task of interpretation for the believer is the task of the theologian (which includes the exegete as theologian) viz., assessment of the truth of the message in the light of all available sources of knowledge and rejection or reformulation of the message in contemporary terms and in relation to contemporary questions and experience. The following is an attempt to take the first steps of generalization, comparison and appraisal of our text within the larger OT context. It does not aim to be comprehensive, but only to suggest some leadings.

In the case of Gen 1:26–28, it seems possible to say the following concerning the consequences or implications of our reading for an understanding of P's anthropology and its place in and contribution to the larger biblical anthropology. (1) The incongruous portrait of P as an equal-rights theologian is removed and Genesis 1 can be read in harmony with the rest of the Priestly work—in which the genealogies that form the essential link between creation and the establishment of the cult know only male names (unlike the older "family" stories incorporated into this lineal framework); in which the cult which represents the culminating word or work of God has no place for women in its service; and in which circumcision is the essential sign of identity for members of the covenant people. Gen 1:27 does not contradict this Priestly view of a special male role in history. (2) Our analysis also removes from P the equally incongruous notion of a correspondence between relationship of the sexes and relationship within the Godhead. For the Priestly theologian who so carefully guards the mystery, singularity and distance of God from creatures, the thought of such a correspondence, albeit analogical, is neither tolerable nor conceivable. (3) The word of sexual distinction in Genesis 1 refers only to the reproductive task and capacity of the species; its consequences for social status and roles are left unspecified. Furthermore, all words of task or ⟦157⟧ position address the species collectively. For the Priestly author of Genesis 1 the division of labor, honor, and responsibility within the human species is not a matter of creation; it belongs rather to history.

Thus the Priestly account of creation contains no doctrine of the equality—or inequality—of the sexes, either explicit or implied. It is, however, an indispensable text for any theology of sexuality, significant for its silence as well as its affirmation. The voice of P is not alone in the biblical story of creation, but must be heard alongside that of J, with attention to their juxtaposition within the canonical context. And though the creation accounts have special importance for theological anthropology as a unique locus of reflection on the essential nature of humanity, their words must be supplemented by the less direct, less conscious and less comprehensive statements and images found in the historical, narrative, prescriptive, and prophetic literature. A full statement of the biblical understanding of human sexuality or sexual distinction must draw on a wider range of literature and relate the Genesis texts to it.[70]

Within that larger assemblage of texts Gen 1:27 contributes the notion, rightly understood if wrongly isolated and absolutized in traditional interpretation, that sex, as differentiation and union, is intended for procreation—a divinely given capacity and power conceived both in terms of blessing and command. But the word that activates the endowment addresses the species, not the individual, and is limited in its application by the setting in which it is spoken, a limitation made explicit in the qualifying amplification, "and fill the earth." It is a word for beginnings, not for all time; and wherever it is repeated it is with a definite, proximate goal in mind. The "command" is neither absolute nor universal.[71] It must be repeated and reinterpreted in changing historical/ecological situations. Yet its basic presupposition—the association of sexuality with procreation—is not repeated and thus stands as a generally relevant word concerning the nature of the species.

P's understanding of sexual reproduction as blessing, in humans as well as animals, is an important contribution to a theology of sexuality. Sex at its most fundamental, biological level is not to be despised or deprecated. It is God's gift and it serves God's purpose in creation by giving to humans the power and the responsibility to participate in the process of continuing creation by which the species is perpetuated. But P's statement is insufficient to guide the process, to give essential ⟦158⟧ directives concerning the circumstances of its use. The concerns of creation, as concerns of nature, must be supplemented by the concerns of ethics to produce an adequate anthropology; and for the latter one must look beyond Genesis 1. For the Priestly account of origins ignores completely the question of the social structuring of roles and of individual and collective responsibility in carrying out the charge addressed to the species. The author may simply have assumed the roles and norms of his day, but he offers no theological rationale for them. P's silence at this point enables the interpreter to move readily into areas where that author had no answers or perceived no questions. In this movement into the areas of P's silence, texts such as Genesis 2–3, which offer differing or supplementary statements and perspectives, must be taken into

70. See my limited attempt to do that in "Images of Women in the Old Testament" (*Religion and Sexism*, 41–88).

71. If the word "command" is too strong, it nevertheless correctly insists that the word is not simply permissive or optative. The questions which then arise are: who is addressed and under what circumstances? Does it bind each individual? or pair? for all time? a reproductive lifetime? etc. Such questions make clear that this statement is insufficient as a guide to practice—if it is properly oriented to the historical situation at all.

account, with the possibility that they may ultimately challenge or qualify the thesis of the initial text.

That is the case with the Yahwistic account of creation, in which the primary meaning of sexuality is seen in psycho-social, rather than biological, terms. Companionship, the sharing of work, mutual attraction and commitment in a bond superseding all other human bonds and attractions—these are the ends for which *adam* was created male and female and these are the signs of the intended partnership. This is not to deny that the help which the woman was intended to give to the man was the help of childbearing (implied in Gen 3:16), but that does not express the full intention of the writer of Genesis 2–3, whose interest also includes the socio-sexual bond. And because the social relationship of the sexes is addressed in this account, the question of equality or status is also addressed, though indirectly. The intended partnership implies a partnership of equals, characterized by mutuality of attraction, support and commitment. The story is *told* from the point of view of the man and is thus clearly androcentric in construction, does not alter this basic tone of the account as a tone of mutuality and equality. But the most explicit statement of the intended equality of man and woman is found in the account of the "fall," J's picture of creation in its historical manifestation. Here the consequence of sin, the disturbance of the original (i.e., intended) relationship between God and creation, is portrayed as the disturbance of the original/intended relationship between the man and the woman. And the sign of this disturbed relationship is this, that while the woman's relationship to the man is characterized by desire, the man's relationship to the woman is characterized by rule. The companion of chapter 2 has become a master. The historical subordination of woman to man is inaugurated—and identified as the paradigm expression of sin and alienation in creation. Thus Genesis 2–3 supplements the anthropology of Genesis 1, but also "corrects" or challenges it by maintaining that the meaning of human sexual distinction cannot be limited to a biological definition of origin or ⟦159⟧ function. Sexuality is a social endowment essential to community and to personal fulfillment, but as such it is also subject to perversion and abuse. Genesis 2–3 opens the way for a consideration of sex and sexuality in history.

There remains a word about the image of Gen 1:26–27. Though the note of sexual distinction does not qualify or explain it, the juxtaposition of the two statements does have consequence for theological anthropology and specifically for a theology of sexuality. Sexuality and image of God both characterize the species as a whole and both refer to *adam*'s fundamental nature; but they do so in different ways. While the image is referred always and only to the species as a whole (*adam*/ʾōtô

⟦'him'⟧—singular, undifferentiated collectivity), sexuality is referred to individuals of the species (*ʾōtām* ⟦'them'⟧—plural, differentiated collectivity). Thus the grammar of the parallel clauses in v. 27 prevents identification or interchange of the defining terms. While P's own image of *adam* as the image of God was surely male, as the terms for task and position (*KBŠ* ⟦'subdue'⟧ and *RDH* ⟦'have dominion'⟧) as well as the note of 5:3 suggest, the carefully guarded language of 1:26–27 does not allow this masculine identification to define the image.

But if the divine image characterizes and defines the species as a whole, it cannot be denied to any individual of the species. To be human is to be made in the image of God. And if to be human means also to be male *or* female (the plural of v. 27 also works against any notion of androgyny), then *both* male and female must be characterized equally by the image. No basis for diminution or differentiation of the image is given in nature. Thus it cannot be altered or denied by history. What belongs to the order by constitution (creation) is immutable and ineradicable. It is essential to human identity. Distinctions of roles, responsibilities or social status on the basis of sex—or other characteristics—are not excluded by this statement. But where such distinctions have the effect of denying to an individual or group the full and essential status of humanity in the image of God, they contradict the word of creation. Contemporary insistence that woman images the divine as fully as man and that she is consequently as essential as he to an understanding of humanity as God's special sign or representative in the world is exegetically sound even if it exceeds what the Priestly writer intended to say or was able to conceive. Like Paul's affirmation that in Christ there is no more "male and female" (Gal 3:28), the full content and implications of the Priestly statement lie beyond the author's ability to comprehend.

Genesis 2:4b–3:24: A Synchronic Approach

JEROME T. WALSH

[[161]] The story of man and woman in the garden of Eden holds eternal fascination for scholar and layman alike. As an object of study, it enjoys an immense bibliography; as a story, it forms part of the literary heritage of Jews, Christians, and Moslems, and is surely one of the world's most widely known tales.

This study of Gen 2:4b–3:24 has a double purpose. Firstly, it is a study of the text: it attempts to identify and interpret certain of the structural patterns in which the text's fascination is rooted. Secondly, it is hoped that, as an experiment in method, the paper may contribute to the continuing dialogue between synchronic and diachronic exegetical perspectives.[1]

Analysis

The action of Gen 2:4b–3:24 unfolds in a series of seven scenes[2] distinguished from one another principally by shifts in *dramatis personae* and changes in literary form.[3]

Reprinted with permission from *Journal of Biblical Literature* 96 (1977) 161–77.

1. Diachronic and synchronic exegesis must not be opposed as rivals but coordinated as complements. Cf. Robert Culley, "Structural Analysis: Is It Done with Mirrors?" *Int* 28 (1974) 167–71; also Martin Kessler's opening remarks in "Rhetorical Criticism of Genesis 7," *Rhetorical Criticism: Essays in Honor of James Muilenburg* (ed. Jared J. Jackson and Martin Kessler; Pittsburgh Theological Monograph Series, 1; Pittsburgh: Pickwick, 1974) 1–2.

2. " 'Szenen' nennen wir diejenigen kleineren Teile einer Erzählung, die durch den Wechsel der Personen, des Schauplatzes oder der Handlung von einander unterschieden sind." Hermann Gunkel, *Genesis* (8th ed.; Göttingen: Vandenhoeck & Ruprecht, 1969) xxxiv.

3. The few vv. of speech within narrative sections (2:16–17, 18, 23; 3:22) and vice versa (3:1a, 9a) pose no difficulties for this division. The situation is different for 3:20 and 3:21,

1. 2:4b–17: a predominantly narrative section whose only active figure is Yahweh God. Man is present in a completely passive role.
2. 2:18–25: a second predominantly narrative section wherein the active role of Yahweh God is supplemented by subordinate activity on man's part. Woman and the animals appear as passive figures.
3. 3:1–5: a dialogue between the snake and the woman.
4. 3:6–8: a narrative with two characters, the woman and the man.
5. 3:9–13: a dialogue involving Yahweh God, the man, and the woman ⟦162⟧.
6. 3:14–19: a monologue of Yahweh God; the snake, the woman, and the man are present as passive figures.
7. 3:22–24: a predominantly narrative section whose only active figure is Yahweh God. The man is present in a completely passive role.

Scene 1: Genesis 2:4b–17

The narrative of the first scene is introduced by a poetic descriptive passage (vv. 4b–6), and interrupted by another descriptive passage (vv. 10–14). The remaining narrative material is structured around five phrases of the format *wayyiqṭōl yhwh ʾĕlōhîm* ⟦'and YHWH God ⟨did⟩ . . .'⟧ (vv. 7, 8, 9, 15, 16).

Genesis 2:4b–6. The opening verses form a poetic introduction consisting of a single line, a quatrain, and another single line.[4] The basic meter is a six-foot line, with variations in the quatrain (2+2+2; 3+3, 3+2, 2+3, 2+3; 3+3).[5]

The opening line functions as a title. The slow tempo (two caesuras, long vowels in the opening phrase, progressive lengthening of each phrase) contrasts with the faster movement of the quatrain (light single caesuras, easy consonant combinations, diminished meter). The strong caesura after *ʾādām ʾayin* ⟦'humanity was not'⟧ (reinforced by the alliteration) retards the flow, emphasizes v. 5bβ (man) over the parallel clause v. 5bα (rain), and brings the quatrain to a close. V. 6 reestablishes

---

which conform neither to scene 6 nor to scene 7, nor to one another. In anticipation of later discussion, both vv. will be treated together with scene 6.

4. This analysis of the poetic structure of vv. 4b–6 complicates the already vexed question of the syntax of the sequence. Against the position that v. 7 is the apodosis must be weighed the formal break between vv. 4b–6 (poetry) and v. 7 (prose). A relatively unexamined hypothesis is to locate the apodosis in v. 6. The latter's independence of the quatrain argues against its being simply coordinate to v. 5a. Further, it will be shown that v. 6 holds a pivotal place in the structure of the whole scene.

5. George Buchanan Gray (*The Forms of Hebrew Poetry* [1915; reprinted, New York: KTAV, 1972] 221–22) recognized the metric character of 2:4b–6; but his scansion, following that of Sievers, is 4 + 4.

the six-foot meter and is unified by a continued ʾ-alliteration. The unity of vv. 5–6 is further marked by the final words *ʾereṣ* ⟦'earth'⟧ (vv. 5aα, 5bα, 6a) and *ʿădāmâ* ⟦'soil', 'ground'⟧ (vv. 5bβ, 6b).[6]

Genesis 2:7–8. Vv. 7–8 form a unit marked by the verbal inclusion *wayyîṣer... ʾet-hāʾādām* ⟦'formed man'⟧ ... *ʾet-hāʾādām ʾăšer yāṣār* ⟦'the man whom he had formed'⟧. V. 7 details the formation of man, v. 8 depicts his establishment in a garden.[7] These vv. are written in poetic prose, the dominant style of the entire Eden account. Poetic characteristics (regular meter, parallelism, alliteration) are especially marked in the couplet vv. 7aβb.

Genesis 2:10–14. V. 10 consists of three descriptive clauses with durative predicates (participle, *yiqṭōl* of past, *wĕqāṭaltî* of past). Vv. 11–14 comprise a series of nominal and participial clauses describing the rivers of the world and their geographical locations. The passage breaks the narrative flow of the scene, and has long been recognized as intrusive. Certainly vv. 10b–14 reveal ⟦163⟧ no connection with their context. V. 10a, on the other hand, contains the idea of the garden in Eden (v. 8), and a number of striking parallels to v. 6.[8] Its function can be determined only in terms of the overall structure of the scene.

Structural Unity. The scene is structured around a triad of motifs: vegetation, water, man. The nonexistence of all three is stated in v. 5. In vv. 6–8, first water (the *ʾēd*),[9] then man, then vegetation (the garden)

6. The absence of *ʾădāmâ* in v. 5aβ is dictated by style and content. Its presence would overdo the parallelism of v. 5a and produce doggerel. It would also weaken the correlation of *ʾādām* ⟦'man'⟧ and *ʾădāmâ* both of which appear for the first time in v. 5b.

7. There is a further structural technique that integrates the two verses. V. 7b is a conclusion, a synthesis, of the two clauses of v. 7a (cf. Ernst Haag, *Der Mensch am Anfang* [Trier Theologische Studien 24; Trier: Paulinus Verlag, 1970] 14; and Claus Westermann, *Genesis* [BKAT 1/1; Neukirchen-Vluyn: Neukirchener Verlag, 1966–74] 276, 283). V. 8b bears a somewhat similar relationship to vv. 7b and 8a, though the comparison is obviously limited.

8. "Regarding v. 10 it should be noted that it resembles v. 6 both in its phrasing and in its external construction, and also—which is most important—in its connotation. What is stated in the earlier verse concerning the waters of the deep . . . —that is, the waters of the springs and rivers—is repeated here with reference to this specific river. . . . We are thus told here about the garden what we were told there about the earth in general, namely, that irrigation was effected by water flowing from the earth." U. Cassuto, *A Commentary on the Book of Genesis* (2 vols.; Jerusalem: Magnes, 1961) 1. 114–15.

9. Augustin Bea (*De Libris Veteris Testamenti.* II: *De Pentateucho* [2d ed.; Rome: Pontificio Instituto Biblico, 1933] 148–49); E. F. Sutcliffe ("Notes on Job, Textual and Exegetical," *Bib* 30 [1949] 77–78); Ernst Haag (*Der Mensch am Anfang*, 8, 13); *et al.* read v. 6 as subordinate to v. 5bβ: "There was no man to till the ground and raise the flowing waters from the earth to irrigate the whole surface of the ground." (So E. F. Sutcliffe in "Genesis," *A Catholic*

appear. Vv. 9–15 repeat and embellish the triad: vegetation (trees in the garden; two specific trees); water (the river of Eden [v. 10a]; ultimately the rivers of the world [vv. 10b–14]); man (established in the garden as *ᶜōbēd* ⟦'to till'⟧ and *šōmēr* ⟦'to tend'⟧).

Vv. 6 and 16–17 are examples of prolepsis, a narrative technique found throughout the passage (cf. 2:25; 3:8, 20). Structurally, they stand at the end of the unit to which they belong, and relatively independent within it; their content introduces a point of narrative tension which will be resolved only in a subsequent section. V. 6, independent of the quatrain, ends the poetic introduction (vv. 4b–6). Yet by introducing water (in opposition to v. 5bα), it points ahead to vv. 7–8 where vegetation and man will also make their appearance. Vv. 16–17, independent of the vegetation-water-man pattern that structures the entire scene, brings the scene to a close on a note of suspense that will not be taken up again until 3:1.

Scene 2: Genesis 2:18–25

The second scene begins with a deliberation preliminary to the narrative action (v. 18). The narrative is in two parts (vv. 19–20, 21–24), each comprising acts of God, an act of man, and a non-narrative line. V. 25 concludes the scene.

Genesis 2:18. The opening verse presents the situation of imperfection whose rectification will be the theme of the entire scene. The divine deliberation is in poetic prose; its gravity is emphasized by the ponderous 4 + 4 meter and the marked dominance of long *ô* sounds.

Genesis 2:19–20. The acts of God are presented as a complex unity (the full *wayyiqṭōl yhwh ᵓĕlōhîm* ⟦'and YHWH God ⟨did⟩ . . .'⟧ phrase is used only once); the narrative flow is broken after the divine acts by a nominal clause (v. 19b) and after the man's response by an inverted *qāṭal* (v. 20b).

Genesis 2:21–24. Here, the acts of God are detailed in two parts, each introduced by a *wayyiqṭōl yhwh ᵓĕlōhîm* phrase. The only interruptive element is the ⟦164⟧ single word *wayyîšān* ⟦'and he slept'⟧ in v. 21a. V. 22's rather involved word order throws into strong relief the single word *ᵓiššāh* ⟦'woman'⟧, which appears here for the first time.

The man's speech in v. 23 is the second example of pure poetry in the Eden account. As in 2:4b–6, the basic meter is a six-foot line (2+2+2; 3+3). The couplet is unified by the appearance of *zōᵓt* ⟦'this

---

Commentary on Holy Scripture [London: Thomas Nelson and Sons, 1953] 184). This reading of the syntax is forced and unnecessary.

one' (fem.)⟧ in three highly emphatic positions. The two lines, however, are very different in character. The three phrases of v. 23a are three bursts of emotion. The two caesuras and difficult pronunciation[10] emphasize each phrase separately. V. 23b, on the other hand, is more "intellectual" both in form and content: it is a decree of naming, involving a word-play and an elaborate chiastic structure.[11]

Structural Unity. The opening deliberation identifies man's solitude as undesirable; Yahweh God proposes to create a "matching helper" to correct the situation. The two narrative units which follow recount respectively the failure and the success of this project. They are parallel to one another in structure; but the elements of the second unit are doubled, thus emphasizing the successful actions.

The first unit opens with a set of divine actions; the second unit describes two sets of divine actions (vv. 21, 22), the second of which is exactly parallel to that of the first unit. Similarly, where the first unit has a single response on man's part, the second unit has two: v. 23a, the joyful shout of recognition; and v. 23b, the naming, parallel to the man's response in v. 20. The first unit ends with a judgment of failure, which recalls the wording of the proposal in v. 18b (*ᶜēzer kĕnegdô* ⟦'matching helper for him'⟧). The second unit ends with two comments. The first (v. 24) parallels v. 20b, revealing with a gnomic generalization that the problem of man's solitude (v. 18a) has been definitively overcome. The second (v. 25) is relatively independent of vv. 18–24, and brings the entire scene to a close with a prolepsis pointing forward to 3:7.[12]

Scene 3: Genesis 3:1–5

After the opening descriptive sentence (v. 1a), the third scene is an unbroken unit.

10. Each phrase is marked by a repeated consonant: *p* in *happaᶜam* ⟦'at last'⟧; *m* in *ᶜeṣem mēᶜăṣāmay* ⟦'bone of my bones'⟧; *b* in *mibbĕśārî* ⟦'my flesh'⟧.

11. The word-play would become even closer if one were to follow the Samaritan Pentateuch and the LXX in reading *mēᵓîšāh* ⟦'from her man'⟧ for *mēᵓîš* ⟦'from man'⟧. Since the improvement of the pun is more easily explained than its weakening, the MT is to be retained.

12. The frequent occurrence of prolepsis in the Eden account adds likelihood to the suggestion of Luis Alonso Schökel that v. 24 too points forward to the next chap. "Está descripción del amor futuro, a dos versos de la aparición de la serpiente, adquiere resonancia de presentimiento: el varón podrá abandonar para adherirse e identificarse; Adán, que no tiene padres, ¿podrá abandonar a su Creador por seguir a su mujer?' "Motivos Sapienciales y de Alianza en Gen 2–3," *Bib* 43 (1962) 307.

Genesis 3:1b. The snake's first speech is a statement, not a question. Nowhere else in the OT does *ʾap kî* have interrogative force. It is here an expression of surprise ("Indeed! To think that . . . !"). The woman's response is not an answer but a correction[13] ⟦165⟧.

Genesis 3:2–3. The woman's speech recalls the divine command of 2:16–17, but with three paraphrases. Two seem to be innocent embellishments, since they play no part in the subsequent narrative (the addition of "fruit" and the addition of "nor touch it"). The third paraphrase (*pen-tĕmūtûn* ⟦'lest you die'⟧ for *môt tāmût* ⟦'be put to death'⟧) offers the point of departure for the snake's second speech.

Genesis 3:4–5. The explanation of the snake's syntactically unusual retort (*lōʾ môt tĕmūtûn* ⟦'you will not be put to death'⟧) is disputed. Some see it as a direct reference to God's words in 2:17;[14] others explain it simply on the basis of the woman's statement.[15] The solution is beyond syntax: the snake's words are clearly intended to answer the woman's, and they just as clearly recall to the ear the original divine prohibition, which the woman has inexplicably paraphrased.

The last part of the snake's speech contains two ambiguities. The word *kēʾlōhîm* could mean Yahweh God (for the name Yahweh is absent throughout this dialogue) or "gods." The participle *yōdĕʿê* ⟦'knowers of'⟧ could modify *ʾĕlōhîm* (in either acceptation), or it may be predicative after *wihĕyîtem* ⟦'you will be'⟧. Both these ambiguities are ultimately irreducible; but the ambiguity itself is of importance for the structure of the scene.

Structural Unity. The introduction establishes the motif of the scene as the snake's cleverness. The snake's opening gambit is to present himself to the woman as ill-informed and needing correction. His cleverness becomes clearer in his second speech; the snake reveals the extent of his knowledge only gradually. By oblique references to the wording of 2:16–17 (*lōʾ môt tĕmūtûn* ⟦'you will not be put to death'⟧ . . . *kî bĕyôm ʾăkolkem mimmennû* ⟦'as soon as you eat of it'⟧ . . . *yōdĕʿê* ⟦'knowers of'⟧ [v. 2:17; *haddaʿat* ⟦'knowledge'⟧] *ṭôb wārāʿ* ⟦'good and bad'⟧), he shows himself

13. Cf. E. A. Speiser, *Genesis* (AB; Garden City, New York: Doubleday, 1964) 23; also John Skinner, *A Critical and Exegetical Commentary on Genesis* (2d ed.; ICC; Edinburgh: T & T Clark, 1930) 73.

14. For example, GKC §113v; Westermann, *Genesis*, 254; Haag, *Der Mensch am Anfang*, 56. Haag's explanation is forced: "Die Schlange leugnet also nicht die Tatsache des Sterbens, sondern die Geltung des göttlichen Verbotes" ⟦'The serpent does not deny the fact of death but rather the validity of the divine prohibition'⟧.

15. So Paul Joüon, *Grammaire de l'Hébreu Biblique* (Rome: Institut Biblique Pontifical, 1923) §123o; Skinner, *Genesis*, 74–75; Cassuto, *Genesis*, 1. 145–46.

to know what God really said; he claims to know what God is really thinking; finally, he reveals a mysterious knowledge couched in delphic ambiguity.[16]

The snake has, in this scene, uncompromisingly pitted his knowledge against God's. At the end of the first scene, the question was, "To eat or not to eat?" And this question meant, "To die or not to die?" At the end of this scene, the question has become, "To eat or not to eat?" that is, "To believe the snake or to believe God?"

Scene 4: Genesis 3:6–8

The fourth scene is an uninterrupted narrative unit. Vv. 6–7 have a strongly marked metric structure; v. 8 is transitional to the following scene ⟦166⟧.

Genesis 3:6–7

wattēreʾ hāʾiššâ	*kî ṭôb hāʿēṣ lĕmaʾăkāl*	
wĕkî taʾăwāh-hûʾ lāʿênayim	*wĕneḥmād hāʿēṣ lĕhaśkîl*	
wattiqqaḥ mippiryô wattōʾkal	*wattittēn gam-lĕʾîšāh ʿimmāh*	*wayyōʾkal*
wattippāqaḥnāh ʿênê šĕnêhem	*wayyēdĕʿû kî ʿêrummim hēm*	
wayyitpĕrû ʿălēh tĕʾēnâ	*wayyaʿăśû lāhem ḥăgōrōt*	
⟦When the woman saw	that the tree was good for eating	
and a delight to the eyes	and that the tree was desirable as a source of wisdom	
she took of its fruit and ate.	She also gave some to her husband with her	and he ate.
Then the eyes of both of them were opened	and they perceived that they were naked	
and they sewed together fig leaves	and made themselves loincloths.⟧	

These two vv. are the center of the entire narrative; this position is reflected in their rich, complex array of poetic devices. Metrically, the verses comprise a couplet (2+3, 3+3), a single line (3+4), and another couplet (3+3, 3+3); the concentric structure highlights the single line (v. 6b) wherein the sin is recounted. Further, the departure from the basic 3+3 meter tends to emphasize the final word of the line.

16. "The fascination of this statement is in its lack of restriction, its intangibleness; it is intentionally mysterious, and after it has brought the thoughts of man into a definite direction, it is again open on all sides and gives room to all whispering secret fantasies." Gerhard von Rad, *Genesis: A Commentary* (2d ed.; London: SCM, 1963) 87.

The full richness of v. 6b can be appreciated only in the context of the preceding vv. Scenes 3, 4, and 5 consist of an unbroken series of narrative *wayyiqṭōl*s. The tempo of the narrative, however, changes notably. Vv. 1–5 are in dialogue, a slow-moving narrative form; the subordinate nominal clauses of v. 6a retard the action still more. Suspense is built up about the woman's reaction to the choice with which she was faced in v. 5.

V. 6b releases the tension with a rush: first the woman, then her husband, eat of the fruit; the account of the sin takes only 8 words. The actions of the woman are described with breathtaking rapidity; three *wayyiqṭōl*s in four words. Yet the extremely difficult pronunciation (six doubled consonants in the four words, all of them voiceless plosives) forces a merciless concentration on each word. Suspense about the man's response to the woman's initiative is created by the unnecessarily long phrase *gam lĕʾîšāh ʿimmāh* ⟦'also to her man with her'⟧ (two of three words semantically superfluous). The *m*-alliteration and the long final *āh*'s retard the line and isolate the final word. Thus the sonant structure reinforces the metric effect noted above and puts the final, critical deed—the man's acquiescence in sin—in a highly emphatic single word: *wayyōʾkal* ⟦'and he ate'⟧.

Structural Unity. Beyond the carefully constructed meter and sound patterns of vv. 6–7, the unity is integrated by a motif-triad introduced proleptically in v. 5. The triad "eating, seeing (eyes), knowing" structures the snake's promise (v. 5), the woman's deliberation (v. 6a), and finally the sin itself and its immediate results (vv. 6b–7a).

V. 8 is transitional between scenes 4 and 5. It is attached to scene 4 by its narrative form and its characters; but it prepares the imminent reentrance of Yahweh God in v. 9, and the point of departure for his question, viz., man's flight and concealment.[17]

Scene 5: Genesis 3:9–13

The fifth scene continues unbroken the series of narrative ⟦167⟧ *wayyiqṭōl*s that began in 3:1. In itself, the scene is a single unit, a dialogue comprising three interrogations by Yahweh God, the first two answered by the man, the third by the woman.

Genesis 3:11–12. Only here does the divine interrogation consist of two questions. They are not, however, two separate questions, the first of which remains unanswered. They are two attempts to discover the same information; the second simply spells out what is implicit in the first.

17. The expression of the subject in v. 8b is another transitional device (cf. note 37 below). This expression in turn allows the use of the singular verb (Joüon §150q; GKC §146f).

The involved word order of the second question has the effect of isolating and emphasizing the operative word, *ʾākāltā* ⟦'Did you eat?'⟧. Exactly the same technique and emphasis are found in the man's answer, where the emphatic word is *wāʾōkēl* ⟦'and I ate'⟧.[18]

Genesis 3:13. The woman's response, like the man's in v. 12, ends with *wāʾōkēl.* Emphasis and isolation are not achieved here by complex word order, but by an almost all-inclusive alliteration (*h, n,* and *š*) that integrates the preceding words of the woman's speech and separates them from *wāʾōkēl* ⟦'and I ate'⟧.

Structural Unity. Beyond the motif word *ʾkl,* two chains of ideas structure this dialogue. First, the events recounted retrace those of the previous scene: hearing God in the garden and hiding (v. 8); the discovery of nakedness (v. 7); eating of the fruit (v. 6). Second, the characters mentioned retrace the story back through scene 3: the man (v. 6b), the woman (v. 6a), the snake (vv. 1–5).

Scene 6: Genesis 3:14–19

The divine monologue sets out in three sections of unequal length the punishments due to the snake (vv. 14–15), the woman (v. 16), and the man (vv. 17–19). The punishments themselves are expressed in poetry.

The scene ends with two isolated narrative lines (vv. 20, 21).

Genesis 3:14–15. The punishment of the snake is introduced by an allusion to his crime; the phrase is not part of the poetic structure. The punishment itself comprises a couplet (2+2+3, 2+2+2) and a triplet (2+3, 2+2, 3+3).

The first line of the couplet proclaims a curse; the line moves slowly and heavily because of the piling up of doubled consonants (in each word except the first). The first two stichs of the triplet too move very slowly, here because of the abundance of long vowels.

Genesis 3:16. The punishment of the woman, despite its clearly poetic flavor, is difficult if not impossible to scan satisfactorily.[19] The whole unit is integrated by the ending *-ēk* ⟦'you' fem.⟧ in four metrically significant positions (perhaps carried through by the final *bāk* ⟦'over you'⟧).

18. The dialogue begins to identify the speakers from v. 12. This is perhaps because the man here introduces the woman, to whom Yahweh God's next question will be addressed. The introduction of a third participant was a complicated format for ancient literature.

19. The strong tendency to hear two stresses on *ʿiṣṣĕbṓnēk* ⟦'your labor pangs'⟧ *wĕhērōnēk* ⟦'your child-bearing'⟧ and *tĕšûqātēk* ⟦'your desire'⟧ results in an anomalous 2+2+2, 3, 2+2+2. Yet alternative schemas result in highly unbalanced syllable count.

Genesis 3:17–19. The punishment of the man is introduced by a lengthy and detailed statement of his crime. The punishment is described in a series of balanced poetic lines (3+4; 3+3; 2+2; 2+2+2; 2+2). The last two lines (v. 19aβb) ⟦168⟧ involved a chiasm with three elements: the root-syllable *šûb* ⟦'return'⟧ an *ʾel* ⟦'to'⟧ phrase, and a *kî* ⟦'for, because'⟧ clause.[20]

Structural Unity. The triad man-woman-snake noted in the preceding scene provides the general framework of this scene as well. The sequence, however, is reversed, and the three units connected by inverted *qāṭal*s instead of by *wayyiqṭōl*s. The result is to suspend the narrative flow and to rule out chronological succession as an organizing principle of the scene.

Within this general framework, the punishments themselves have a very intricate structure.

Each decree imposes two punishments, one involving an essential life function, the other a relationship. The snake is cursed in his mode of locomotion—simply to move from one place to another will require grovelling. He is punished too in regard to the woman whom he misled: the relationship of trust he so painstakingly effected will become undying enmity. The woman's motherhood is burdened with severe pain; her relationship with her man as his "matching helper" will be frustrated of ultimate fulfillment.

The arrangement of these first two units is due to the influence of the snake-woman-man structural triad: unit 1, the snake: (a) locomotion; (b) the snake and the woman; unit 2, the woman: (a) child-bearing; (b) the woman and her man; unit 3, the man. In the case of the man, the two punishments are interwoven. The pain of insufficiency and labor will burden man's eating (vv. 17bβ,[21] 18b, 19aα); his relationship with the

20. The structural parallelism of the *kî* clauses suggests that they have similar syntactic value. V. 19b may be analyzed as a subordinate causal clause followed by a *waw apodoseos* in a major conclusion (cf. Joüon §176e, o). The translation would then be:

> Until you return to the earth,
>   since from it were you taken;
> Since dust you are,
>   to dust shall you return.

The words thus form the climactic decree of the monologue of judgement.

21. Skinner says of the form *tōʾkălennâ* ⟦'you shall eat of it'⟧: "The government of direct acc. seems harsh, but is not unexampled: see Jer. 36:16 [*sic*; read 36:15]." (*Genesis*, 84, note). On the other hand, this may well be an example of a primitive energetic form without suffix, a common occurrence in Ugaritic and a sporadic one in Hebrew. Cf. Cyrus H. Gordon, *Ugaritic Textbook* (3 vols.; Rome: Pontifical Biblical Institute, 1965) 1. 72–73; and David N. Freedman, "Archaic Forms in Early Hebrew Poetry," *ZAW* 72 (1960) 102 (with further references), 106–7.

earth is cursed[22]—it will be intractable to his cultivation, and will eventually reclaim him who was made from it (vv. 17bα, 18a, 19aβb).

Further, the two punishments of each unit are mutually involved. Because the snake is doomed to crawl on the ground, his head and mankind's heel are both apt—each as target and each as weapon—for their never-ending strife. Woman's yearning for her husband and his domination over her will have as its most profound result her motherhood, with its frequent and severe pain. The intractability of the earth is the direct cause of man's burdensome labor to [[169]] eke out minimal sustenance. The interrelationship is most clearly revealed here in vv. 17–19 by the interweaving of the two punishments. In the preceding units the influence of the snake-woman-man framework has resulted in a separation and ordering of the punishments that conceal their mutual involvement.

The scene ends with two narrative vv. (20, 21) which have no structural connection with the rest of scene 6.[23]

Scene 7: Genesis 3:22–24

The final scene consists of a deliberation (v. 22) and consequent action (vv. 23–24). Although there is an unbroken sequence of narrative *wayyiqṭōls* from v. 20, the unnecessarily repeated subjects in vv. 22 and 23 reveal the beginnings of new units.

Genesis 3:22. The v. is grammatically incomplete. The effect is to underline its character as a divine deliberation rather than as a pronouncement directed to a hearer.[24]

Structural Unity. The principal source of unity for the scene is that of theme, the exiling of man from the garden. The three verses are related as deliberation about and execution of this plan. Beyond this, a series of verbal links connects each verse with the others: vv. 23 and 24 contain the phrase *gan-ᶜēden* [['garden of Eden']]; vv. 22 and 24 contain the phrase *ᶜēṣ haḥayyîm* [['the tree of life']]. Vv. 22 and 23 are linked by

22. Hebrew *baᶜăbûrekā* is not to be understood here as causal ('because of you', i.e. 'because of your sin') but as relational ('in regard to you'). The *ʾădāmâ* [['ground, soil']] is not cursed absolutely, but only insofar as it impinges upon the existence of *hāʾādām* [['the man']].

23. On a scale which transcends Gen 2:4b–3:24, v. 3:20 is of course a proleptic reference to 4:1. But the function of both verses within the Eden account must be sought on the level of the account as a whole.

24. Speiser's unconvincing attempt to avoid anacolouthon by translating *wĕᶜattâ pen* [['and now lest']] as 'what if' is thus unnecessary. Westermann also obscures the deliberative character of the line when he translates *wayyōʾmer yhwh ʾĕlōhîm* [['and YHWH God said']] in 2:18 as "und Jahwe Gott dachte" [['and YHWH God thought']] but in 3:22 as "und Jahwe Gott sagte" [['and YHWH God said']].

the unusual process of repeating common verbs from the first verse (*yšlḥ* ⟦'stretch out'⟧ and *lqḥ* ⟦'take'⟧, both qal) in less common forms and derived meanings in the second (*yšlḥ* ⟦'banished'⟧, piel; and *lqḥ* ⟦'taken'⟧, pual).

Structural Unity of Genesis 2:4b–3:24: Concentric Pattern

The basic structural principle of the Eden account is the concentric arrangement of its scenes. The pattern involves *dramatis personae,* themes, and in some cases, internal structural elements of each scene. Scene 4 is the climax and turning point of the narrative.

Scenes 1 and 7. Only Yahweh God and the man appear in these scenes; in both, the man is a passive figure.

The scenes differ notably in length, but correspond in theme. Scene 1 recounts the formation of man, and culminates in his establishment in the garden. Scene 7 recounts his exile from the garden and return to "the earth from which he was taken"—verbally recalling 2:15, but more profoundly an allusion to 2:7a. An interesting parallel in detail is that both man's installation in the garden and his eviction from it are recorded twice in their respective scenes.

A series of words and phrases occurs only in these two scenes—the cumulative effect is an impressive vocabular inclusion: *miqqedem* ⟦'east of'⟧, *ᶜēṣ haḥayyîm* ⟦'tree of life'⟧, (*gan-*)*ᶜēden* ⟦'garden of Eden'⟧, *ᶜbd* ⟦'till'⟧, *šmr* ⟦'guard'⟧ ⟦170⟧.

Scenes 2 and 6. Only these two scenes involve all four characters: God, the animal(s),[25] the man, the woman. In both scenes, God is the principal actor.

Each scene deals with relationships: the authority of man over the animals contrasts with the eternal hostility between the snake and mankind; woman's aptness as "matching helper" is doomed to become a frustrating dynamic of yearning and domination. Each scene, as will be shown, involves an ordering of creation.

Structurally, each scene ends with two lines that are independent of the rest of the scene. The lines themselves are parallel: 2:24 and 3:20 deal with woman's destiny as wife and mother respectively;[26] 2:25 and 3:21 introduce and conclude the development of the motif of "nakedness."

25. The collective "animals" of scene 2 are represented by the snake in scene 6. He is established as their narrative individualization in 3:1.

26. Formally, 3:20 finds a better parallel in 2:23—both are namings of the woman by the man. But 2:23 is a naming based on *origin.* The deeper parallel lies in the content and future-orientation of 2:24 and 3:20. Woman is the final and perfect solution to the problem of man's solitude (2:24); woman's motherhood extends to a universal posterity (3:20).

Scenes 3 and 5. Scenes 3, 4, and 5 constitute the core of the narrative. An unbroken series of *wayyiqṭōl*s unifies the three scenes across the changes of characters and setting.

Scene 1
narrative
Yahweh God, the man
from *ʾădāmâ* to garden
vocabulary

Scene 7
narrative
Yahweh God, the man
from garden to *ʾădāmâ*
vocabulary

Scene 2
narrative
Yahweh God, man, woman, animals
relationships among the creatures
2:24–25

Scene 6
monologue
Yahweh God, woman, snake
relationships among the creatures
3:20–21

Scene 3
dialogue
the snake, the woman
eating from the tree
three statements

Scene 5
dialogue
Yahweh God, the man, the woman
eating from the tree
three questions-and-answers

Scene 4
narrative
the woman and her husband
eating from the tree
concentric structure of scene

⟦171⟧ The parallelism of scenes 3 and 5 is antithetic. In scene 3, the snake initiates and dominates a dialogue with the woman. In scene 5, Yahweh God initiates and dominates a dialogue with the man (and, briefly, with the woman). The dialogue consists of three statements in scene 3, three questions-and-answers in scene 5.

Thematically, both dialogues are concerned with the eating of the fruit. The snake gradually reveals to the woman "the truth" of what will happen when she eats it; in so doing, he pits himself against God. In scene 5, Yahweh God gradually learns from the man (and woman) the truth of what has happened, that they have eaten; in so doing, he discovers the role the snake has arrogated to himself.

Scene 4. At the center of the narrative stands the account of the humans' sin. More precisely, the concentric structure of scene 4 itself reveals that the man's sin—the single word *wayyōʾkal* ⟦'and he ate'⟧—is the turning point of the entire Eden account.

Structural Unity: Other Patterns

The narrative lines that end scenes 2 and 6 mark the major structural divisions in the narrative: the breaks between introduction (scenes 1–2), action (scenes 3–6), and epilogue (scene 7).

Scenes 1 and 2. The two introductory scenes have closely parallel internal structures. The opening line of each scene (vv. 2:5, 18) sets out the lack whose suppliance is the theme of the scene's narrative. The action begins with the programmatic phrase *wayyîṣer* [-*ī*-] *yhwh* *ʾĕlōhîm* ⟦'YHWH God formed'⟧ (vv. 2:7, 19). Two action complexes follow in each scene (vv. 7–8, 9 and 15; 19–20, 21–24), the second in each case more detailed than the first. Both scenes end with a proleptic final line (vv. 16–17, 25).

Scene 6. As the final scene of the action, and last major scene of the entire narrative, scene 6 draws together all the threads of the entire account. There is little in the scene that has not been introduced earlier.

We know of the snake that he is the cleverest of the beasts; he is to be accursed among them, crawling upon the earth from which he and they were made. His enticements tempted the woman and through her the man; the snake is doomed to eternal strife with her and, through her, with all mankind, her seed.

Of the woman we know that she is man's "matching helper"; her relationship with him is henceforth to be marred by incomplete fulfillment. The motherhood of the woman has not been mentioned before.

Of the man we know that he is earth's natural tiller (2:5b); the earth will be unproductive for him. He is made from the dust of the earth; he will return to his source. The privilege and prohibition that was his in the garden concerned eating, he will eat sparely and only after much pain and labor. Instead of an abundance of fruit trees he receives as food the wild plants that are the natural result of his tillage (2:5a).

Conclusion

Analysis reveals that the apparently "artless" story of man and woman in the garden of Eden has in fact structures and intricate patterns of organization that involve even minor details of the text. Moreover, the patterns so interlock that the deletion of any part of the text (except, perhaps, 2:10b–14) ⟦172⟧ would have significant repercussions for the whole passage.

These structures are the framework within which the development of motifs, images, etc., takes place, and the context within which that development must be understood.

Application

The "meaning" of a work of literature is communicated as much by the structure of the work as by surface "content."[27] This section of the study attempts to illustrate this critical principle by using the structures analyzed in section I to interpret two selected narrative components of the passage: locale and character relationships.

Each component will be examined in turn. The first step is to isolate the relevant indications in the text. Each of the components undergoes a change in the course of the narrative, and in each case development takes place according to a coherent pattern. The second step is to identify this pattern by comparing the data with the structures analyzed in section I. Finally, we will make suggestions about the significance to be attached to each component.

Locale

The Data. Scene 1 begins on the *ʾădāmâ* where man is formed. A garden is planted to the east, and the action moves into the garden. Scene 2 contains no local indications at all. The setting of scene 3 is likewise unspecified, but the woman's phrase "the tree which is in the middle of the garden" implies a certain distance from that tree. Scene 4 takes place at the tree, and therefore in the middle of the garden. At the end of scene 4, the man and his wife leave that place to hide among the trees of the garden. Scenes 5 and 6 contain no further local indications. In scene 7 the action moves from the garden back to the *ʾădāmâ* from which man was taken.[28]

The Pattern. Local movement in the Eden account follows the concentric pattern of scene arrangement. Scene 4 alone takes place in the middle of the garden. The dialogues of scenes 3 and 5 are bivalent—they are set away from the middle of the garden, but focus attention on the tree that is located there. Scenes 2 and 6 are presumably inside the garden, but are not further specified. Scenes 1 and 7 involve movement between the garden and the *ʾădāmâ* outside.

The Interpretation. Two essentially different kinds of movement must be distinguished in the Eden account; each has its own narrative effect.

27. René Wellek and Austin Warren, *Theory of Literature* (3d ed., Harmondsworth: Penguin Books, 1963) 139–41.

28. There is no "eastward" movement in scene 7. The cherubim are stationed to the east of the garden (unless *miqqedem* here simply means 'in front of'). This is not necessarily because the man was exiled in that direction, but because the way of approach to the garden led from the east.

In scenes 1 and 7, a boundary is crossed: movement is from one "space" to another. Scenes 2–6 take place within the garden and involve movement toward and away from a center point ⟦173⟧.

Scenes 1 and 7. The two "spaces" between which the man moves in these scenes are "the garden" and "the *ʾădāmâ* from which he was taken." The *ʾădāmâ* outside the garden is distinguished from that within[29] by its correlation to the *ʾādām* ⟦'man'⟧. It is *ʾădāmâ* of his origin (2:7, 15), and therefore the *ʾădāmâ* of his destiny (3:19). It is his *ʾădāmâ*, his own proper world by contrast with the garden.[30] Space and time within the garden are not those of man's world, and events that occur inside the garden are not of that world's history. Human history begins only with man's return to his own *ʾădāmâ*, his own world—already a sinner, faced with pain, labor, and death.

The Eden account is an etiology of the human condition—formed by God, deformed by man's own deed; but it presents this picture of the human condition as true from the first moment that man steps onto the stage of history.

Scenes 2–6. The movement within the garden relates the story to the literary topos of the "quest for the center." The symbolism of "the center" is a mythological universal: it is the locus of "absolute reality, sacred power, and immortality."[31] This holds true of the center of the garden of Eden as well. But in almost every other particular the Eden account is a systematic reversal of the "quest for the center," calculated to produce a contrary literary effect.

In the standard myths, supernatural powers hostile to man surround the center with obstacles and guardian monsters to thwart his access—the quest is for heroes only. In Genesis, Yahweh God's goodwill and concern are evident throughout the account. The divine prohibition is for man's own protection. There is no obstacle beyond this prohibition, and no guardian but man himself. The attainment of the center requires neither endurance nor courage; all man need do is betray the divine trust. Thus the grandeur of the heroic achievement is transformed into the sordidness of a sin of disloyalty.

29. There is *ʾădāmâ* inside the garden; see 2:9 and probably 2:19 as well.

30. The garden is not planted for man's benefit, as is often suggested (e.g., by von Rad, *Genesis*, 76; Haag, *Der Mensch am Anfang*, 22; Westermann, *Genesis*, 283; *et al.*). Man does indeed benefit from it, but his position in the garden is a tenancy rather than a sinecure. Furthermore, if the garden were planted for man, why was it planted at some distance from him (*miqqedem* ⟦'from the east'⟧ 2:8) rather than around him? And why were trees forbidden and in fact dangerous to him planted in the middle?

31. Mircea Eliade, *Patterns in Comparative Religion* (London: Sheed and Ward, 1958) 380.

The reversal carries through into the effect the tale has on its hearer. A hero epitomizes what is best in man, and the hearer naturally identifies with him. The hearer shares vicariously the hero's quest, his victory, his glory. The resultant sense of ennoblement awakens in the hearer a desire to imitate in his own life the admirable qualities exemplified by the hero. In the Eden account, the hearer identifies with the *ʾādām* as prototype and ancestor of the race. He thus becomes inextricably enmeshed in the man's sin and shares his sense of shame. This awakens in him the desire to disassociate himself from the sinful characteristics he sees at work in the man, and to seek to remove them from his own life ⟦174⟧.

Character Relationships

Two levels of character relationships must be carefully distinguished. Firstly, characters are principal, secondary, tertiary, etc. The criteria for such an identification are essentially formal: e.g., the principal character is the one who acts or speaks first or most in a given scene. Secondly, characters may be related to one another as equals or as superior and inferior (in the broadest possible acceptation). Here the criteria are material: the nature of the characters' actions is more to the point than their number. The two levels often coincide; indeed, making a character the principal in a scene is a standard device for establishing his superiority over other characters present. But the contrary is conceivable, and the distinction must be kept in mind.

Our concern here is with the second level—relationships of equality or superiority/inferiority; the first level will be discussed only when it illuminates the second.

The Data. Scene 1. Yahweh God "forms" the man, transfers him from place to place, and "commands" him. Yahweh God's superiority is clear.

Scene 2. The introduction of the animals and the woman leads to a more complex situation. Yahweh God "forms" and "brings" the animals; he puts the man to sleep and changes his bodily constitution; he "builds" and "brings" the woman. His superiority is universal. Man in his turn names the animals and the woman. He has authority over them.[32]

32. There is an essential difference between the man's relationship to the woman and that to the animals; this is shown by 2:23a, and by the quality of the name she is given in v. 23b. The narrative attributes a dignity to woman's role which is in sharp contrast to the actual practice of Israelite society. But it is not accurate to say that "the narrative treats woman as an equal and a partner of man" (John L. McKenzie, "The Literary Characteristics of Genesis 2–3," *TS* 15 [1954] 559; similarly, Claus Westermann, *The Genesis Accounts of*

The relationship between the animals and the woman is neither direct nor directly expressed. The woman is superior to the animals not in authority but in the perfect way she answers the man's need for companionship. This relationship is implied in the man's responses. The man names the animals, and finds them inadequate to be his "matching helper." He names the woman too, but only after uttering a jubilant cry of recognition: "This is the one at last!"

Scene 2 therefore establishes a type of hierarchy among the characters: Yahweh God is supreme; the man is the highest of the creatures, with the woman closely associated but subordinate to him; least of all are the animals ⟦175⟧.

Scene 3. The levels of "principal character" and "superiority" do not coincide. The snake is the principal—he initiates the dialogue and he has two speeches to the woman's one. But the deeper question is left open. The snake attempts to act as the woman's superior by advising and influencing her, but the scene ends with no indication of her response to the snake's initiative.

Scene 4. The woman eats the fruit, thus resolving the unanswered question of scene 3. She has accepted the snake's guidance. She in turn "gives" the fruit to the man. Her initiative influences him to follow her lead. The woman's superiority over the man is further pointed up by the phrase *ʾîšāh ʿimmāh* ⟦'her man with her'⟧. To this point, the man has consistently been *hāʾādām* or *ʾîš* (2:23–24), 'the human' or 'man'. Here, unnecessarily, he becomes '*her* man/husband'. She had been named for her derivation from him; now he is designated in terms of his relationship to her. She had been created his 'matching helper'; now he is identified as 'with her'—an adjunct.[33]

Creation [FBBS; Philadelphia: Fortress, 1964] 28; Henricus Renckens, *Israel's Concept of the Beginning* [New York: Herder and Herder, 1964] 225; *et al.*).

The woman is built to fill man's need; she is presented to him for approval; he recognizes in her a "matching helper" to answer his solitude. There is no concern for the woman's needs, her reaction to the man, or her fulfillment. There is not the slightest implication of mutuality. Contrast the Ewe legend from Togo which Westermann offers as a parallel: "In the beginning God fashioned a man and set him on the earth; after that he fashioned a woman. The two looked at each other and began to laugh, whereupon God sent them into the world." (Westermann, *Genesis*, 316, citing J. G. Frazer; Frazer's text cited here from Theodor H. Gaster, *Myth, Legend, and Custom in the Old Testament* [New York: Harper & Row, 1969] 15.)

33. The effect of the phrase's appearance here would be seriously weakened if *ʾîšāh* ⟦'her man'⟧ were to be read in 2:23. Thus internal evidence supports the textual judgment made above (n. 11).

The use of *ʾîšēk* ⟦'your (fem.) man'⟧ in 3:16 is an allusion to the *ʾîšāh* of 3:6.

Scene 5. In scene 5, Yahweh God is the principal character; the man is secondary, and the woman tertiary. This ordering is not perfectly reflected in the character relationships. The man professes fear of Yahweh God; the man and the woman come out of hiding at his summons, and submit to his interrogation. Yahweh God is superior to them. The remaining relationships are ambiguous. When questioned, the man pleads the woman's influence over him. He does so however in the perfect (*nātĕnāh* ⟦'she gave'⟧ and recalls at the same time (but also in the perfect: *nātattâ* ⟦'you gave'⟧) the order originally established by God.[34] Similarly, the woman pleads the snake's influence, but she too does so in the perfect and characterizes that influence as deception.

Scene 6. All four characters are present in the scene. Yahweh God shows his superiority over each of the others by decreeing punishment for them and their descendants. Man's superiority over the woman is explicitly stated in the woman's punishment—"he shall have dominion over you"—and visible in the act of naming (3:20).

The relationship of the man and the woman to the snake is less clearly described. Only in 3:15 is this relationship spoken of explicitly, and the strife that is there ordained is of uncertain outcome.[35] It is the snake's humiliation among the other animals that implicitly involves his other relationships. The physical lowness to which he is cursed is in itself a form of inferiority. But ⟦176⟧ beyond the simple question of height, the snake is humiliated by being forced to eat the *ʿāpār* ⟦'dirt, dust'⟧, reminder of the humble origins of the man at whose feet he crawls. His curse also affects his struggle with the woman's seed. The battle is no less deadly for it, but it is carried out on the terms of "head" versus "heel"—terms whose inequality involves at least humiliation if not positive disadvantage.

Scene 6 thus establishes the following order: Yahweh God is supreme; the man has dominion over the woman; lowest of all is the snake.

34. The *ʿimmādî* ⟦'with me'⟧ of 3:12 recalls the woman's original position *kĕneged* ⟦'fitting for'⟧ the man, and at the same time alludes to the reversal of that position in the *ʿimmmāh* ⟦'with her'⟧ of 3:6. The changing polarities of the man-woman relationship are reflected in these expressions of physical accompaniment. This tends to support the thesis that 2:24 is another example of prolepsis (see n. 12).

35. The identification of 3:15 as promising ultimate victory to the woman's seed is without adequate foundation in the text. The same verb is used for the snake's and the man's attacks; whatever meaning is attached to it, it cannot be used to imply victory for one or for the other. The distinction between a deadly attack on the snake's head and a merely injurious attack on the man's heel loses force when we remember that "probably . . . all serpents were thought to be poisonous" (F. S. Bodenheimer, "Serpent," *IDB* 4, 289b).

Scene 7. Yahweh God transfers the man from place to place; the man is completely passive before him.

The Pattern. Character relationships follow the concentric pattern of scene arrangement. Scenes 1 and 7 are simple: only Yahweh God and the man are involved, and the superiority of Yahweh God is unequivocally set forth. Only scenes 2 and 6 present all four characters, and both order them identically: Yahweh God, the man, the woman, the animal(s). Scenes 3 and 5 leave many ambiguities unresolved; in this way they act as transitional scenes between the order established in scenes 2 and 6 and that established in scene 4. In scene 4 alone the woman appears as the man's superior.

The Interpretation. Only scenes 2–6 involve change in the pattern of character relationships. Scene 2 establishes an order: God, man, woman, animals. Scene 3 introduces a serious disturbance into that order. The snake invites the woman to accept him as her guide and familiar, and, under his influence, to dismiss the authority of God. In other words, he offers her a new order wherein he has exchanged places with God. The scene ends with no resolution.

Scene 4, therefore, involves this larger context. Even though only the woman and the man are present in the scene, the woman's act of eating has the effect of ratifying the snake's proposal. His promises prevail, and God's prohibition is forgotten. The inversion of the original order thus begun proceeds to infect the community of man and woman itself. The woman takes the initiative and offers "her husband" the fruit. By accepting, he completes the inverted chain of influence: snake, woman, man, God.

Scene 5, like scene 3, introduces tension. Yahweh God, assuming the continuing validity of the old order, addresses himself to the man. The new order is revealed as the man defers to the woman and she to the snake. In scene 6, Yahweh God reacts to the revelations of scene 5. His reestablishment of the God, man, woman, animal order is not however a simple return to the original state. The harmony of that state has been irretrievably lost; like the garden itself, it does not belong to man's world. Outside the garden, the relationships between creatures will be burdened with frustration and strife.

The effect of this development is to identify the process of temptation, sin, and punishment with the disestablishment and restoration of the whole created order. The central word of the entire narrative is at once the man's sin ⟦177⟧ and his acquiescence in and affirmation of the perverted chain of influence it achieves.

This identification of sin with a reversal of the created order is not a historical statement but a theological one.[36] Narratively, the story deals with origins; but on a deeper level, every hearer identifies with this "man and his woman" not filially but personally. The sin depicted is not simply the first sin, it is *all* human sin; it is *my* sin. And I who hear the tale am forced to acknowledge that my sin too has cosmic dimensions; my sin too is an attack on creation and an establishment of moral chaos.

Conclusions

(1) On a literary level, Gen 2:4b–3:24 is a highly structured unit. The principal pattern is a concentric arrangement of seven scenes, each of which is itself tightly organized. The entire narrative focuses on the single word *wayyōʾkal* ⟦'and he ate'⟧ in 3:6.

(2) Although the passage is narrative in form, it communicates effectively on other planes as well. Our limited study of narrative components has brought to light three such "messages":

a. anthropological: Man, not God, is responsible for human sinfulness and its consequences; nevertheless, these realities are present from the first moment of human history.
b. moral—theological: Human sin has cosmic dimensions. No matter how petty or private the deed may seem, it is a violation of the sacred at the heart of reality; and it involves a rejection of the whole divinely established order of creation.
c. parenetic: There is nothing exhilarative or exciting about sin; it is easy, ignoble, and ultimately profitless.

(3) This study has also been an experiment in methodology. As such it has attempted to identify and interpret significant structural patterns in the literary fabric of the passage. Synchronic and diachronic methods of analysis are, of course, complementary; a thorough exegesis of the passage would involve examination from both points of view.

36. This flows from the earlier discussion of locale. It is further indicated by the restriction of the inverted order of influence to the actual moment of sin itself. As soon as the action leaves the middle of the garden, the human couple become "the man and his wife" once more (3:8b). The interrogation of scene 5 shows that God's authority is in reality undiminished, even if the humans' responses leave their subjective commitment ambiguous.

Genesis 2–3: The Theme of Intimacy and Alienation

Alan Jon Hauser

⟦20⟧ The narrative in Genesis 2–3 is one of the better-known pieces of Western literature, largely because it has the ability to focus the reader's attention on key issues relating to man's existence. The writer has artfully woven his story, using a limited number of characters and objects to present in brief but moving form the story of man's fall. Any attempt to make a complete analysis of this writer's work would be a major undertaking, especially when one considers the complexity of issues such as the role and identity of the serpent, or the form and function of the knowledge that woman so strongly desires. In this study I have a fairly limited goal: to analyze the writer's development of the two-dimensional theme of intimacy and alienation. These are my words, not his, but it is my conviction that they clearly express a major motif the writer has used to focus and integrate his narrative. As I analyze this motif, I will pay special attention to the ways in which the writer leads his audience, by means of numerous literary devices, to experience the shattering of the closely-knit created order and the onslaught of that divisiveness which both writer and reader know to be a part of their everyday life.

Of necessity, this study will fall into two parts. The first will treat the development of the theme of intimacy in Genesis 2. The second will analyze the theme of alienation as it unfolds in Genesis 3.

Reprinted with permission from *Art and Meaning: Rhetoric in Biblical Literature* (ed. D. J. A. Clines, D. M. Gunn, and A. J. Hauser; Journal for the Study of the Old Testament Supplement Series 19; Sheffield: JSOT Press, 1982) 20–36.

I

In ch. 2 the writer weaves several components into an intimate picture of harmony, with all revolving around man, the first and central element in the created order. These components are: the ground (*hʾdmh*); the Lord God (*yhwh ʾlhym*); the garden (*hgn*) and its trees (*kl ʿṣ*); the animals; and woman [[21]] (*ʾšh*). A study of select verses from this chapter will show in detail how the writer has used various stylistic devices to convey the theme of intimacy.

Verse 7

wyyṣr yhwh ʾlhym ʾt hʾdm (then the Lord God molded man). The verb *yṣr* (to form, mold) underlines the intimacy between God and man. God does not simply create man or bring him into being: he takes pains with him, just as a potter would in forming a fine vessel. Man is therefore most special.

ʿpr mn hʾdmh (dust from the ground). This phrase points to man's close association with the ground: *ʾdm* [['man, Adam']] is taken from *ʾdmh* [['ground']]. The Hebrew mind viewed the similarity of sounds, as here with the words *ʾdm* and *ʾdmh*, as a key to the interrelatedness of the persons, objects, or concepts embodied in the words. In subsequent verses the writer will develop this association of man with the ground, as when God causes trees to grow out of the ground to provide food for man (2:9, 16), or when God forms animals out of the ground as companions for man (2:19). Furthermore, the phrase *ʿpr mn hʾdmh* [['dust from the ground']] forms an *inclusio* with 3:19. Man is formed by God from the dust of the ground (2:7): after man has disrupted creation he must return to the ground as dust (3:19). Significantly, even though *ʾdmh* is used repeatedly in chs. 2 and 3, 2:7 and 3:19 are the only two points where *ʾdmh* [['ground']] and *ʿpr* [['dust']] are directly associated with one another. As a result, the statement of consequences in 3:19 harks back directly to the time of beginning, making more poignant man's fall.

wypḥ bʾpyw nšmt ḥyym wyhy hʾdm npš ḥyh (and he breathed into his nostrils the breath of life, and man became a living creature). In addition to further developing God's closeness to man during the act of creation, these words stress through repetition the gift of life that man has received. In a fashion reminiscent of Hebrew poetry, the writer parallels *nšmt ḥyym* (breath of life) with *npš ḥyh* (living creature). The rest of ch. 2 continues to stress the gift of life, life which is created for the benefit of man and in order to provide him with companionship. It is in 3:19 that the gift of life is withdrawn; thus, the life-death sequence forms a further link between 2:7 and 3:19.

Verse 8

The garden is created for man. The writer emphasizes this fact by having God plant it immediately after man receives life, and by having God set the man in the garden immediately after it is planted.[1] *wyśm šm ʾt hʾdm ʾšr yṣr* (and there he set the man whom he had formed). It would have been adequate for the writer to say, "And there he set the ⟦22⟧ man." He chooses, however, to add the last two words, using the identical verb (*yṣr* ⟦'formed'⟧) from v. 7, so that he may again stress the close association between man and God.

Verse 9

God causes the trees to grow *mn hʾdmh* (from the ground). Man, who himself was taken from the ground, is able to enjoy through sight and taste the produce God has brought forth for him from the ground. Here man's enjoyment of the trees through sight and taste is part of God's plan. This sets the stage for 3:6, where enjoying the tree in the midst of the garden belongs to the sequence of disruption.

Verse 15

Man's closeness to the garden is again stressed. He lives in harmony with it, having the responsibility of caring for it, even while he enjoys its fruit (v. 16). The verb *ʿbd* (to till, care for) points back to v. 5, where there were as yet no plants, because there was no man to till (*ʿbd*) the ground. Now, however, it is appropriate that God has planted trees in the garden: there is a man to care for them.

Verse 18

The writer now turns to the element of creation closest to man. He tells us this not only by using the programmatic clause, "It is not good that man should be alone," but also by means of the phrase *ʿzr kngdw* (a companion corresponding to him, a helper like him). The writer also makes his point by means of a word play: although man is part of the created order, in close harmony with God and the garden, for which he cares (*ʿbd*: v. 15), he is alone (*lbd*), lacking a close companion, someone to care for him. The fact that a suitable companion is not found immediately, but only after prolonged effort by God, helps to emphasize the closeness to man of the ultimate companion, woman.

1. The creation of the garden for man is further stressed by the repetition in v. 15 of the idea that God placed man in the garden, specifically using the verb *nwḥ* (to place, to cause to settle).

Verse 19

Like man, the animals are formed (*yṣr*) from the ground (*ʾdmh*). The writer thus represents God as attempting to create a companion for man who is as much like him as possible, being formed in the same way and being taken from the same source. This sets up the failure at the end of v. 20, where none of the animals proves acceptable as man's companion. In light of this failure, woman, who is the appropriate companion, must be seen to be very close to man.

Verses 19–20

The writer places great stress on the naming of the animals by man. Three times the verb *qrʾ* (to name) is used, and the noun *šm* (name) is used twice. The writer does not have God name the animals, because the man must examine each thoroughly and discern for himself a companion. This is stressed by the clause *wybʾ ʾl hʾdm lrʾwt mh yqrʾ lw* (and he ⟦23⟧ brought them unto the man, to see what he would name them). This clause, the two lists naming categories of animals God has created (vv. 19 and 20), and the clause *wkl ʾšr yqrʾ lw hʾdm npš ḥyh hwʾ šmw* (and whatever the man named each living creature, that was its name), all serve to elongate the process of man's careful scrutinizing of the animals. The writer has chosen to employ this repetition so that the last phrase in v. 20 will be even more emphatic: *wlʾdm lʾ mṣʾ ʿzr kngdw* (but there was not found for man a companion like him). Despite God's efforts to make the animals as much like man as possible, the long search is fruitless, and man is still alone. Man's being alone is especially stressed by the repetition of the phrase *ʿzr kngdw* (a companion like him) from v. 18, which described the beginning of the search.

Verse 21

God now causes a deep sleep to fall upon man, because the creation of a companion for man literally requires that God take a part of man himself: *wyqh ʾḥt mṣlʿtyw* (and he took one of his ribs). The animals, like man, were taken from the ground, but this does not give them the closeness to man which woman will possess. The closing up of the wound with flesh (*bśr*) enables the writer to anticipate the end of the scene in v. 24 where man and woman are described as one flesh.

Verse 22

The writer repeats the phrase "the rib which he had taken from man" in order to stress again the intimate connection between man and woman. *wybn* (and he built): the writer uses the verb *bnh* in order to stress the uniqueness of woman's creation; for whereas God formed (*yṣr*) man and the animals from the ground, he builds up woman from man's rib. While *bnh* normally means "to build," in this context it carries the connotation of "building up," since from a small part of man God fashions a companion for him.

wybʾh ʾl hʾdm (and he brought her to the man). These words echo God's bringing the animals to man in v. 19. The writer deliberately parallels the wording in the two scenes so that the reader will keep the former scene in mind, and thereby focus on the contrast between woman, who indeed is man's *ʿzr kngdw* (companion like him), and the animals, which are not. This phrase also suggests the way in which a father brings to a man his bride (cf. Gen. 29:23), thereby preparing the reader for v. 24.

Verse 23

The writer uses this short piece of poetry to bring to a climax the search for man's *ʿzr* (helper). The demonstrative pronoun *zʾt* (this)[2] is used three times in order to single out woman emphatically as *the* one who is suited to be man's ⟦24⟧ companion. The poetry begins with man exclaiming *zʾt*, as if he has been watching a long parade of nominees and now suddenly sees the right one. The next word, *hpʿm* (at last, finally), strengthens the image, declaring man's exasperation over the long wait. The second use of *zʾt*, at the beginning of line two, again accentuates woman as she receives a name indicating her closeness to man. The final *zʾt*, at the end of the short poem, forms a neat *inclusio* with the opening word, recalling man's earlier word of joy upon having at last found his companion. It also serves to emphasize for a third time woman's suitability as the writer repeats, in language closely parallel to v. 22, the fact that woman is taken from man (*mʾysh lqchh zʾt*).[3]

ʿṣm mʿṣmy wbśr mbśry (bone of my bone and flesh of my flesh). This phrase is often used in the OT to express intimate family ties, as in Gen 29:14; Judg 9:2; 2 Sam 5:1, 19:12–13. In such cases, a common ancestry is assumed. Here, however, woman is literally man's bone and flesh (see the writer's earlier setting of the stage in v. 21). The writer knew that the special twist he was putting on the common phrase would seize the attention of his reader and therefore stress even more the intimacy of man and woman.[4] Furthermore, *ʿṣm* (bone), because of its vocal similarity to

2. The writer could have used *hwʾ* (she) in some or all of the instances where *zʾt* is used, but that would have reduced the emphasis on woman provided by the demonstrative pronoun. On the use of *zʾt* for emphasis, see Ludwig Koehler and Walter Baumgartner, *Lexicon in Veteris Testamenti Libros* (Leiden: Brill, 1958) 250.

3. See also the use of the verb *lqḥ* in v. 21.

4. See the discussion of Umberto Cassuto, *A Commentary on the Book of Genesis: Part I* (Jerusalem: Magnes Press, 1961) 135–36.

ʿzr (companion), calls to the reader's attention the fact that woman, who is *ʿṣm* of man's *ʿṣm*, ⟦'bone'⟧, is also man's *ʿzr*.

lzʾt yqrʾ ʾšh (for this will be called "woman"). As with the animals, man names the woman, except that in this case he clearly perceives the *woman* to be his *ʿzr kngdw* (companion like him). The writer does not specifically use that phrase here. Rather, he employs a word play between *ʾšh* (woman) and *ʾyš* (man) to make his point. While there is no etymological relationship between the two words,[5] the phonetic similarity makes a "common sense" case for the closeness between man and woman. Thus, while man's observation of each animal led him to give each a name, so his perception of woman causes him to give her a name closely akin to his.

Verse 24

Again the writer makes his point about woman being one flesh with man. As close as man is to his parents, who have given him life, he will be even closer to his wife, to whom he will cleave (*dbq*), and with whom he will become one flesh. But in this first instance the relationship is even closer, since the writer is clearly alluding to v. 21, where the first woman is taken directly from man.[6] Thus, the theme of alienation in ch. 3 becomes even more tragic in light of this special oneness ⟦25⟧ of the first man and woman.

Beginning with v. 24, the word is not simply "woman," but rather "his woman." While the root word in Hebrew, *ʾšh*, is the same as that used in vv. 22–23, the sense of the passage makes "his wife" a better translation.

Verse 25

The reference in v. 24 to being one flesh does not refer only to sexual relations (nor does it exclude them). In v. 25 the sexual overtones are more pronounced. Throughout the OT there is basically a reserved attitude towards nakedness, with it being presumed that one's nakedness is, with only rare exception, to be shielded from the eyes of others. To expose someone's nakedness was to lay them bare before the world, to make them open and vulnerable, in a most thoroughgoing sense (Gen 42:9, 12; Isaiah 20; Ezek 16:22, 39; 23:22–35; Hosea 2). It often means to expose one to shame (1 Sam 20:30; 2 Sam 10:4–5; Isa 47:3; Nah 3:5). Clearly, one's nakedness was seen as a very personal thing, a key to one's innermost self. It is for this reason that the phrase "to expose the naked-

5. E. A. Speiser, *Genesis: Introduction, Translation, and Notes* (AB; Garden City, N.Y.: Doubleday, 1964) 18.

6. It is precisely this point which allows the writer to stress in v. 24 the fact that man and woman become one flesh.

ness of . . . " is often used to refer to sexual intercourse (Leviticus 18; 20), wherein two people open themselves to one another in the most complete way possible. Thus, in v. 25 man and his wife stand naked before one another, expose themselves completely to one another, and are not ashamed.[7] Their vulnerability causes no anxiety, and their intimacy is complete. This sets the stage for ch. 3, where the intimacy is disrupted, as expressed in part through the urgent need of man and woman to cover up their nakedness.

II

As we move into ch. 3, the writer dramatically shifts the course of his narrative. The world of harmony and intimacy becomes a world of disruption and alienation. The sudden introduction of the serpent[8] alerts the reader that he is entering a new stage of the narrative, as does also the format of the opening words, which may be translated "Now the serpent was. . . . " The word *ʿrwm* (cunning) also presents a new element, one which is accentuated by the writer's word play between it and the similar-sounding *ʿrwmym* (naked) from the previous verse. The nakedness of man and woman had given expression to their intimacy. Now, however, the cunning of the serpent injects into the created order a disruptive feature which grows until it reaches a climax in vv. 12–13. The intimacy of ch. 2 dissolves in a rapid sequence of events. ⟦26⟧

Verses 1–6

In the encounter between woman and the serpent, the writer subtly but firmly continues to stress the intimacy between man and woman. Throughout vv. 1–6, plural verbs are used when the serpent addresses woman, as though man were also being addressed (e.g., v. 5 *whyytm kʾlhym*, and you will be like God), plural verbs are used to summarize God's command concerning the fruit of the trees (e.g., v. 3 *lʾ tʾklw*, you shall not eat),[9] and woman in speaking of herself and man uses a plural verb (v. 2 *nʾkl*, we may eat). The writer's use of these plural verbs[10] implies that man

7. The writer stresses their standing in each other's presence both by using *šnyhm* (the two of them) and by specifically mentioning each, *hʾdm wʾštw* (the man and his wife).

8. The inverted word order, with the noun *hnḥš* (the serpent) coming first, places even greater emphasis on the serpent.

9. This despite the fact that woman has not yet been created when man alone receives the command from God in 2:16–17.

10. Interestingly, almost all these plural verbs are second person masculine, even when woman alone is addressed (vv. 4–5). The writer thus makes it impossible for the reader to think of woman apart from man in vv. 1–6.

and woman are one, that they cannot be dealt with or addressed apart from one another. When woman eats the fruit of the forbidden tree, her first act thereafter is to give some to man, and the writer further stresses the intimacy by using the phrase *lʾyšh ʿmh* (to her husband with her). While the intimacy between man and woman continues to be stressed in the opening verses of ch. 3, it will soon dissolve into open animosity between the two (especially in vv. 12–13).

But if the intimacy between man and woman continues in vv. 1–6, other elements of the intimate world described in ch. 2 are already being torn apart. In a series of steps, the serpent moves woman from correcting the serpent's false statement about God's command, to doubting God's truthfulness, craving the forbidden fruit, and desiring to be wise like God. The intimacy with God is being destroyed by the serpent's cunning even before woman eats of the fruit.

Thus, in vv. 1–6 the writer has artfully woven together his themes of intimacy and alienation. The intimacy of man and woman, the most complete form of intimacy described in ch. 2, temporarily continues as a remnant of the harmonious world of ch. 2, even while the disruption between God and his creatures grows at a rapid pace.

The writer has used the verb *ydʿ* (to know) to strengthen the image of alienation. It is first used at the beginning of v. 5, where the woman is told, "God knows that when you eat of it, your eyes will be opened." The tone of this statement is that God is deliberately withholding information, desiring to keep his creatures in their place. Thus, woman is led to doubt God. Furthermore, the writer is using a word play, for at the end of v. 5 there is the phrase "knowing good and evil." Both forms of *ydʿ* are participles. One might loosely paraphrase the sense of this word play as follows: "God knows that . . . you will know good and evil (and he doesn't want you to know!). This use of ⟦27⟧ *ydʿ* in v. 5 sets the stage for the knowledge that is actually received in v. 7.

The writer also stresses the divine-human alienation by means of the clause *whyytm kʾlhym* (and you will be like God) in v. 5. It is noteworthy that, unlike Genesis 1, which stresses the intimacy between God and man by man's being made in the image and likeness of God, Genesis 2–3 stresses this intimacy by means of God's great care in the creation of man and man's companion. Although God forms man and breathes into him the breath of life, man is different from God, and has a clearly-defined place as God's creature (as in 2:16–17, 18, 21–22). Thus, any human desire to be like God places the creature in rebellion against his creator. He becomes estranged from God.

Beginning in v. 5, the writer places great stress on the motif of seeing. Woman is told that their eyes (*ʿynykm*) will be opened if they eat the fruit of the tree (v. 5). She saw (*wtrʾ*) that the tree was good for food (v. 6), and that it was a delight to the eyes.[11] It is therefore ironical that after the fruit has been eaten (v. 6), man and woman desire that *they* not be seen. Although the tree was a delight (*tʾwh*) to the eyes (v. 6), the "eye opening" experience they have after eating the fruit is anything but delightful, and there now is an attempt to cover up (vv. 7–11). The writer uses this fear of being seen as a key means to express the alienation that destroys the harmony of ch. 2.

The writer has devoted only a bare minimum of words to the act of eating, and even a majority of these words are used to indicate that man and woman take part in the act together.

Verse 7

Here the writer's interweaving of the themes of intimacy and alienation continues. As a result of their eating, both man and woman have their eyes opened. While they experience this together,[12] the knowledge they have gained separates them. They can no longer tolerate being naked in one another's presence. Since, as noted earlier, one's nakedness is a key to one's innermost self, man and woman are pulling apart from one another: their intimacy is no longer complete.

The clause, "Then the eyes of the two of them were opened," is rather surprising, given all the seeing that has taken place in the previous verses. The writer is using this clause to express the dramatic change that has come about as a result of the forbidden act. As a consequence of their rebellion against God, the man and woman see things very differently. The writer has also stressed this change by means of the word play on *ydʿ* (to know). While knowing had appeared very attractive in v. 5, ⟦28⟧ now man and woman know that they are alienated from one another, and they make clothes.

The influence of alienation is not yet complete. There is a remnant of togetherness, as indicated by the plural verbs describing the making of clothes, and by the plural *lhm* (for themselves).

Verses 8–10

God has been absent since 2:22, his absence being part of a deliberate pattern by the writer. In ch. 2 God and man had been quite intimate,

11. This wording parallels 2:9, except that in 3:6 there is the additional clause, "and that the tree was to be desired to make one wise." The addition of this clause in 3:6 helps contrast the situation there, where disruption is breaking into the created order, with earlier conditions where the created world was in harmony.

12. As indicated by the phrase *ʿyny šnyhm* (the eyes of the two of them). It should further be noted that the verbs throughout v. 7 are plural, continuing the patterns of vv. 1–6, where the plural verbs indicate the oneness of man and woman.

but the chapter closes by stressing the complete intimacy of man and woman (vv. 23–25), and God recedes into the background. In ch. 3 God continues to be absent as the forces of disruption are turned loose. His reappearance in v. 8, however, brings the theme of alienation to its climax. Thus, not only does God create the most complete form of intimacy (2:22); he also brings out into the open all the divisive consequences of man's rebellion (3:9–13).

Upon hearing God, man and his wife hide themselves (*wytḥbʾ*) in the midst of the trees of the garden. This act, their mutual hiding from God, is the last remnant of the "togetherness" of man and woman. Hereafter they act as individuals, and the plural verbs of vv. 1–8 are absent. Similarly, the phrase "the man and his wife" (*hʾdm wʾštw*) is the last time the two words are used in relation to one another to express intimacy. The complete phrase appears earlier in 2:25, and singly the words "his wife" (*ʾštw*) and "her husband" (*ʾyšh*) appear in 2:24 and 3:6, respectively. This usage, along with the stress in 2:23–24 on man and woman being one flesh, is in stark contrast to the way man refers to woman in 3:12.

The phrase *btwk ʿṣ hgn* (in the midst of the trees of the garden) points back to v. 3. Woman had told the serpent that they were forbidden to eat the fruit of the tree in the midst of the garden (*hʿṣ ʾšr btwk hgn*). But she and her husband did eat of it. Thus, by using the same words (slightly rearranged) in v. 8 the writer again brings to the reader's attention the offense that unleashed the forces of disruption and alienation, and now causes man and woman to hide from the presence of God (*mpny yhwh ʾlhym*), with whom they formerly had been intimate. The writer is also being ironical: man and woman eat of the fruit of the tree in the midst of the garden in order to be like God (v. 5); now, as a consequence of their eating, they hide from God in the midst of the trees of the garden.[13] They sin by means of a tree; yet, they must hide among the trees. Thus, they cannot escape what they have done. Indeed, from this point on, everywhere ⟦29⟧ man and woman turn they encounter as symbols of alienation what had formerly been elements of the created world of harmony.

Significantly, in v. 9 God does not address man and woman together, but rather calls to man (*wyqrʾ yhwh ʾlhym ʾl hʾdm*). To stress further that God is speaking to man alone, the writer adds *wyʾmr lw* (and he said to him), and *ʾykh* (where are you?), the latter having a second person mas-

13. As noted above, there was great stress on the delight of seeing in vv. 5–6, whereas in vv. 7–11 man and woman cannot bear to be seen, either by God, or by one another.

culine singular ending.[14] The writer is thus suggesting, as he soon will stress more bluntly (v. 12), that man and woman no longer are one.

Man's response (v. 10) to God's question emphatically stresses man's aloneness. Verse 8 had begun by stating, "and they heard (*wyšmᶜw*) the sound (*qwl*) of the Lord God walking in the garden (*bgn*)." In v. 10 the words *qwl*, *gn*, and the root *šmᶜ* are repeated, so as to underline the parallelism between vv. 8 and 10. This makes the singular form of *šmᶜty* (I heard) in v. 10 stand out all the more in contrast to the plural form of v. 8. Thus, in v. 8 man and woman hear together; in v. 10 man has become alienated to the point that he now perceives himself to have heard alone. Man's alienation is further underlined by the final verb *wʾḥbʾ* (and I hid myself), which contrasts with the plural *wytḥbʾ* of v. 8. The writer also stresses man's aloneness through the singular verb *wʾyrʾ* (and I was afraid) and through the phrase *ky ᶜyrmʾnky* (because I was naked).

While the contrast between the plural forms of v. 8 and the singular forms of v. 10 stresses the alienation of man from woman, the writer also emphasizes man's alienation from God. Man hears God's voice in the garden, and is afraid. God heretofore has been very intimate with man, forming him from the dust of the ground, planting the garden for him, forming animals for him from the ground, and building up woman from the rib taken from man's side. All this, however, is now gone, as man fears the very one who has given him life and his world. Man is afraid, "Because I am naked," and he hides himself. As noted earlier, one's nakedness was seen as a key to one's innermost self; as a consequence, being comfortably naked in another's presence was a sign of real intimacy. But now man must cover up, since he fears having God see him as he is.

Verse 11 stresses man's act of rebellion against God, which more than anything else is what he wishes to hide. It was after his eating that man became conscious of his nakedness, of his alienation. The writer uses God's questions to recall that for the reader: "Who told you that you were naked? Have you eaten of ⟦30⟧ the tree of which I commanded you not to eat?" The double use of the verb *ʾkl* (to eat) focuses the reader's attention even more sharply on the act, since this is the same verb used three times in v. 6 to describe the act.[15] Furthermore, the writer's emphasis on the fact that *God* commanded man not to eat of the tree helps stress even more man's alienation from God. The writer also continues to underline man's alienation from woman by having God address

14. See A. E. Cowley (ed.), *Gesenius' Hebrew Grammar as Edited and Enlarged by the Late E. Kautzsch* (Oxford: The Clarendon Press, 1910) 256.

15. Note also the usage in vv. 1, 2, 3, and 5.

man with singular verbs and pronouns. Thus, man stands before God completely alone.

Verse 12

The motif of man's alienation from God and from woman reaches its climax in v. 12. In previous scenes the intimacy between man and woman has been thoroughly developed, especially through the idea that man and woman are one flesh (2:23–25). Furthermore, when woman's relationship to man has been described, she has consistently been referred to as *ʾštw* (his wife; 2:24, 25; 3:8). Now, however, man coldly passes the blame for his deed to "*the* woman" (*hʾšh*):[16] "*she* gave to me" (*hwʾ ntnh ly*).[17] To man she has become an object, not a companion, and the clause *ʾšr ntth ʿmdy* (whom you gave to be with me) points the reader back to an earlier situation of intimacy which no longer exists. The alienation of man from woman is complete.

While God's question in v. 11 called for a simple yes or no answer, man refuses to accept responsibility for what he has done. It is not only woman who is blamed, however, as indicated by the words *ʾšr ntth ʿmdy* (whom you gave to be with me),[18] which closely parallel the immediately following words *hwʾ ntnh ly* (she gave me). Man is clearly saying that God is to blame, since God gave to man the woman who led him astray. Thus, not only has man ceased to see woman as a companion: he also has ceased to see God as a well-intentioned creator who provides man with all good things. The alienation of man from God is also complete.

As previously noted, *ʾkl* (to eat) is used to point to the act of rebellion, most importantly in the twofold usage in v. 11 and in the threefold usage in v. 6. In v. 12 it again serves this function in the clause *hwʾ ntnh ly mn hʿṣ wʾkl* (she gave to me from the tree, and I ate), which closely parallels the wording in v. 6, *wttn gm lʾyšh ʿmh wyʾkl* (and she gave also to her husband with her, and he ate). Furthermore, the double use of *ntn* in v. 12 helps recall woman's giving of the fruit to man in v. 6, and the use of *ʿmdy* (with me) in v. 12 points back to *ʿmh* (with her) in v. 6. Thus, in v. 12 the writer has carefully constructed a ⟦31⟧ number of links with the description of the act of rebellion in v. 6. This is most appropriate, since it is in v. 12 that the consequences of the act are most sharply focused.

16. Prior to 3:12, the writer has used *hʾšh* only in 3:1–6, where he describes the serpent's tempting of the woman.

17. Note the stress that is placed on *hwʾ* (she), both by the fact that it is an added element, not really required in its clause, and by its position at the beginning of the clause, which is opposite to the normal verb-subject word order in Hebrew.

18. The writer has used the longer spelling, *ntth*, as opposed to the shorter *ntt* (see Gesenius, 121, 175), so as to make a more perfect parallel to the subsequent *ntnh*.

Finally, man's concluding word, *wʾkl* (and I ate) points once again to man's aloneness, since the verb is in the singular. This directly parallels the aloneness of woman in v. 13, where her concluding word is exactly the same.

Verse 13

As was the case with man (v. 12), woman refuses to shoulder any blame. She ignores man's claim that she had led him to sin, and instead passes to the serpent the blame for her own deed. Nevertheless, God's question to woman, "What is this that you have done?," underlines the devastating nature of woman's deed. The tone of God's question is, "How could you do such a horrible thing?"[19] The final word *wʾkl* (and I ate), being in the singular, further stresses woman's aloneness and alienation from man.

Verses 14–19

There are a number of ways in which the writer expresses his motif of alienation in the poetry of these verses:

1. As in the previous section (3:9–13), the principal figures are each addressed separately by God. Their relationship to one another is consistently depicted as one of animosity and separation. There will be enmity and strife between the serpent and woman, and between the serpent's seed and woman's seed (3:15), which means all mankind (cf. 3:20). While man and woman remain together, they no longer are intimate in the way they were previously, since man will rule over his wife (3:16), and the woman will desire her husband (cf. 2:24–25).
2. The serpent is singled out from the cattle and the creatures of the field and cursed (3:14), because of what he has done.[20] The writer has stressed the serpent's role in causing alienation by paralleling *ʾrwr ʾth mkl hbhmh wmkl ḥyt hśdh* (cursed are you more than all the cattle and all the creatures of the field) with *ʿrwm mkl ḥyt hśdh* (more cunning than all the creatures of the field) from 3:1. Because the serpent was cunning (*ʿrwm*), leading woman to eat of the fruit of the tree, he is now cursed (*ʾrwr*).
3. Man has become alienated from the ground. Although God formed man from the dust of the ground (*hʾdmh*; 2:7), and from the ground created for man the trees of the garden (2:9) and the animals (2:19),

19. See Cassuto, 158.

20. Note the parallelism of *ky ʿśyt zʾt* (because you have done this) to *mh zʾt ʿśyt* (what is this that you have done?) in v. 13.

man must now cope with a ground that is cursed, that has become his enemy (3:17–19). He must constantly wrestle with it to sustain his life, yet in the end his life must be surrendered to the ground. Thus, although he is one with it in ⟦32⟧ his creation and in his death, he will throughout his life be alienated from his source. As noted previously (see my comments on 2:7), the writer uses *ʿpr* (dust) in conjunction with *ʾdmh* in only two places: 2:7, where God forms man from the dust of the ground and in 3:19, where man's death is described. The writer thus gives the reader a subtle reminder of what could have been, man's ongoing, intimate relationship with God and the ground, even while the writer stresses the devastating consequences of man's rebellion against God.

4. The main verb used to describe man's rebellion against God was *ʾkl* (to eat: cf. 3:1, 2, 3, 5, 6, 11, 12, 13). The writer continues to use this verb in 3:17–19 in order to link the fact of man's rebellion with the consequences that follow. This is most clearly focused in v. 17: because man ate of the tree from which God had forbidden him to eat, the ground will henceforth be cursed, causing man to eat in toil all his days (cf. also v. 19). He will struggle with it, but it will bring forth thorns and thistles (v. 18). Significantly man will eat *ʿśb hśdh* (the plants of the field): now that he has eaten of the tree in the midst of the garden, all the trees of the garden become unavailable to him.
5. The writer employs a word play between *ʿṣ* (tree) and *ʿṣb* (pain). *ʿṣ* has consistently been used to develop the theme of man's rebellion (3:1, 2, 3, 6, 8, 11, 12). Consequently, *ʿṣb*, with its similar sound, reminds the reader of the human rebellion even while describing woman's pain in childbearing (v. 16) and man's toil in raising food (v. 17). The offense of man and woman concerning the *ʿṣ* results in their *ʿṣb*.

Verse 21

The act of "covering up" had earlier symbolized the first awareness of man and woman that they were alienated from God and from one another (vv. 8–11). Now the permanence of that alienation is stressed. The creator, who had made man and woman naked, in the most perfect form of intimacy, covers their nakedness, thereby acknowledging the ongoing nature of the divisiveness which man and woman have brought upon themselves. The fact that he makes for them garments of skins, as compared to the hastily-sewn aprons of fig leaves they had made for themselves, helps to emphasize the permanence of their need to cover up.

The words *lʾdm wlʾštw* (for man and for his wife) hark back to the earlier intimacy described in 2:21–25, but they do so in a melancholy manner. As man and woman's clothing indicates, their relationship to one another will henceforth be quite different from what it was before the fall. The writer emphasizes ⟦33⟧ this by repeating *wylbṣm* (and he clothed them) after *wyʿś . . . ktnwt ʿwr* (and he made . . . garments of skins).

Verse 22

Chapter 2 shows man being given specific roles and functions within the created order, with definite bounds being set for man (e.g., 2:16–17). Most notably, although man is intimate with God, he is clearly subordinate to him (as in 2:18, 21). In 3:22, however, emphasis is placed on man's attempts to be like God. Thus, man has stepped beyond the bounds set for him as creature, desiring instead to make himself creator.

hn hʾdm hyh kʾḥd mmnw ldʿt ṭwb wrʿ (Behold; the man has become like one of us, knowing good and evil). These words echo the serpent's statement to the woman in 3:5, thereby reminding the reader at the close of the account of man's rebellion against his creator. It is not just that man has transgressed the bounds set for him: he threatens the creator's supremacy as creator.

This is especially brought out by the second half of v. 22. Traditionally in the ancient Near East, one of the key boundaries between man and the gods is the fact that man is mortal whereas the gods are eternal (as, for example, in the Gilgamesh epic). In 3:22 God fears that man will attempt to transgress this boundary also (*gm*), since he has already acquired the knowledge of good and evil. Thus, man could attempt to be even more like God (3:5). The writer uses the idea of eating (*ʾkl*) from the tree (*ʿṣ*) of life to parallel man's potential deed with his earlier act (3:1–6, 11–13, 17). God's status as creator is sorely threatened by man, and God takes stringent measures (vv. 23–24) to guard this last divine possession from man.

Verse 23

Man was originally formed from the dust of the ground, and the writer throughout ch. 2 (vv. 7, 9, 19) notes the importance of the ground in the creation of man's world. As noted above, in 3:17–19 the writer stresses man's alienation by emphasizing the antagonism between man and the ground which has been brought about by man's act of rebellion. Verse 23 re-emphasizes that point through the words *lʿbd ʾt hʾdmh ʾšr lqḥ mšm* (to till the ground from which he was taken). Thus, the result of man's alienation from God (v. 22) is man's alienation from the very ground from which God had formed him.

Verse 24

In v. 23 God had sent (*šlh*) man forth from the garden. Verse 24 repeats this for emphasis, only in stronger terms: *wygrš ʾt hʾdm* (and he drove out the man). Man must not have access to the tree of life![21] This leads well into the final image of these two chapters. God places the cherubim and ⟦34⟧ a flaming sword to guard the way to the tree of life. There is now no turning back. Man has striven to be like God, and will always do so. God must take strong measures to see that man is kept in his place. The fact that God must act so decisively to keep his creatures in line re-emphasizes the radical victory of alienation.

Summary

One of the main themes the writer of Genesis 2–3 has used to tie his story together is the motif of intimacy and alienation. This motif is developed in ch. 2 by: the writer's depiction of God's care in forming man from the dust of the ground; God's creation of the garden for man, with its trees growing from the ground and providing man with food; God's forming the animals from the ground in an attempt to create a companion for man; God's creation of a companion for man who is literally a part of man; and the picture of man and woman being one, naked but yet completely at ease in one another's presence. This intimate world of harmony developed in ch. 2 is shattered in ch. 3. Although man and woman have a set place in the created order, the writer pictures woman striving, at the serpent's urging, to become like God, knowing good and evil. Man and woman act together in eating the fruit of the tree, but their intimacy is beginning to be shattered as the writer portrays them making clothes to cover themselves. Furthermore, their striving to be like God in fact results in their being alienated from him: they hide from him. But this is their last act together. God's probing questions expose the alienation of man and woman not only from God, but also from one another. The use of singular nouns and verbs, along with the tendency of man (and subsequently of woman) to blame everyone but himself, shows that the alienation of the various elements of the created order from one another and from God is complete. The poetry of 3:14–19 gives clear expression to this state of alienation, and appropriately presents the picture of man returning to the ground, from which he was taken at the beginning of the narrative. Finally, the permanence of alienation is stressed both by the clothing God makes to cover man and woman's nakedness and by God's decisive measures to keep man out of the garden and away from the tree of life.

21. The word play on *šlḥ* in vv. 22 and 23 helps strengthen this point. God sent man forth (*wyšlḥhw*) from the garden (v. 23) so that he would not stretch out (*yšlḥ*) his hand to take and eat from the tree of life.

Sanctuary Symbolism in the Garden of Eden Story

GORDON J. WENHAM

⟦19⟧ On first hearing, the Garden of Eden story seems to be a simple, straightforward narrative just right for children or indeed adults in a non-literary culture. But a more careful re-reading poses certain intractable problems. Who was right, the LORD God who warned that if man ate of the tree he would die or the snake who denied it? Inherently one expects God's words to be vindicated, but the narrative apparently shows man escaping the threatened penalty at least for 930 years! Another problem concerns the stationing of the cherubim to guard the eastern end of the garden: could not the expelled couple re-enter the garden from some other direction? Again the details of the geography of Eden, with its mention of the four rivers and the gold, seem quite irrelevant to the story. Why were these verses, 2:10–14, included? Do they perhaps betray the hand of scholastic interpolator or redactor interested in ancient geography?

I wish to argue here that these difficulties in the story may be explained if we see it not as a naive myth but as a highly symbolic narrative. The garden of Eden is not viewed by the author of Genesis simply as a piece of Mesopotamian farmland, but as an archetypal sanctuary, that is a place where God dwells and where man should worship him. Many of the features of the garden may also be found in later sanctuaries particularly the tabernacle or Jerusalem temple. These parallels suggest that the garden itself is understood as a sort of sanctuary.

Reprinted with permission from *Proceedings of the Ninth World Congress of Jewish Studies, Division A: The Period of the Bible* (Jerusalem: World Union of Jewish Studies, 1986) 19–25. Transliteration of Hebrew has been altered to conform to the system used in *Journal of Biblical Literature.*

Earlier writers have occasionally made suggestions along similar lines. Genesis Rabbah 16.5 comments on the phrase *leᶜobdâ ûlĕšomrâ* 'to till and keep it' as follows. "Another interpretation is an allusion to sacrifices." On the basis of Exod 3:12 and Num 28:2 it equates man's work in the garden with the offering of sacrifice. Later 21:8 compares the expulsion of man from the garden to the destruction of the temple. Both examples suggest that some ⟦20⟧ early commentators saw the garden as a type of sanctuary, but they did not work out the idea systematically.

Somewhat closer to the interpretation I am proposing is the view of the phenomenologist Mircea Eliade[1] who holds that every sanctuary is in somc way a replica of the divine heavenly abode, and that in worship man seeks to reenact creation. Thus he suggests that the Garden of Eden story with its tree of life at the centre may be a type of later Israelite sanctuary which was regarded too as the source of life. Eliade however has not attempted to demonstrate his views exegetically; they simply form a part of his wider theory.

Most recently David Chilton in *Paradise Restored* (1985) had adumbrated some of the points that occurred to me independently. He noted that the Garden of Eden was apparently entered from the east like later sanctuaries.[2] He also drew connections between the jewels and gold of Eden and the materials used to decorate the tabernacle and priestly vestments that are described in the book of Exodus.[3] He noted also the parallel between the tabernacle menorah and the trees of the garden.[4] Yet though this book is full of remarkable insight into the symbolism of Eden, his ideas are affirmed rather than proved and his symbolic interpretations are by no means comprehensive. He leaves many features in the garden unexplained. I hope closer attention to the actual descriptions and greater comprehensiveness will make a symbolic interpretation more plausible.

To establish that Genesis 2–3 is using sanctuary symbolism, I first propose to list the large number of items in the garden that find parallels in later sanctuaries. Then I shall note some of the features in adjacent chapters that also seem to relate to the theme of worship, and which therefore make a cultic interpretation of Genesis 2–3 more likely. Finally, I shall note some of the implications of a symbolic interpretation for understanding Genesis as a whole, and for views of biblical theology.

First the verbal hints that suggest that the garden should be viewed as an archetypal or ideal sanctuary. The first of these is the verb *hithallēk*

1. M. Eliade, *Patterns in Comparative Religion* (London: Sheed and Ward, 1958) 367–408.
2. D. Chilton, *Paradise Restored* (Tyler: Reconstruction Press, 1958) 29.
3. *Ibid.*, 32–36.
4. *Ibid.*, 44.

'to walk to and fro' (Gen 3:8). The same term is used to describe the divine presence in the later tent sanctuaries in Lev 26:12, Deut 23:15, 2 Sam 7:6–7. The LORD walked in Eden as he subsequently walked in the tabernacle.

⟦21⟧ The second phrase to attract attention is the mention of the *kĕrûbîm* ⟦'cherubim'⟧ stationed east of the garden to guard the way to the tree of life. As Cassuto noted the *kĕrûbîm* must have been stationed here because the garden was entered from the east.[5] He did not however observe that the tabernacle and Jerusalem temple were also entered from the east. That the entrance of the garden was guarded by *kĕrûbîm* is another indication that it is viewed as a sanctuary, for *kĕrûbîm,* Akkadian *kuribu,* were the traditional guardians of holy places in the ancient Near East. In Solomon's temple two *kĕrûbîm* guarded the inner sanctuary (1 Kgs 6:23–28). Two others on top of the ark formed the throne of God in the inner sanctuary (Exod 25:18–22) and pictures of *kĕrûbîm* decorated the curtains of the tabernacle and walls of the temple (Exod 26:31, 1 Kgs 6:29).

The third feature that suggests the garden should be viewed as an archetypal sanctuary is the tree of life, whose fruit gives eternal life. The idea that fulness of life is to be found in the sanctuary is of course a basic principle of the sacrificial law and a recurrent theme of the Psalms. Trees were sometimes planted by the patriarchs at places where they worshipped (Gen 21:33), and were a regular feature of Canaanite and later shrines. More interesting still is the observation of Carol Meyers[6] that the tabernacle menorah was a stylised tree of life, a conclusion she reached on the basis of archaeology and its description in Exod 25:31–35.

Fourthly, the description of Adam's job in Eden, also suggests it is a sanctuary. He was told 'to till it and keep it' *leᶜobdâ ûlĕšomrâ.* The midrash drew attention to passages where these terms were used separately. It did not note though that the only other passages in the Pentateuch where these verbs are used together are to be found in Num 3:7–8, 8:26, 18:5–6, of the Levites' duties in guarding and ministering in the sanctuary. If Eden is seen then as an ideal sanctuary, then perhaps Adam should be described as an archetypal Levite.

The quasi-priestly role of Adam is perhaps suggested by another remark in the narrative. "The LORD God made tunics of skin for them and clothed them" (Gen 3:21). Several times the accounts of the ordination of the priests mention Moses clothing them (Hiphil of *lābaš*) in their tunics ⟦22⟧ (*kĕtōnet*) (Exod 28:41, 29:8, 40:14; Lev 8:13). So once again

5. U. Cassuto, *A Commentary on the Book of Genesis* I (Jerusalem: Magnes Press, 1961) 174.
6. C. L. Meyers, *The Tabernacle Menorah* (Missoula: Scholars Press, 1976).

vocabulary associated with worship in the sanctuary is being used in Genesis. Certainly the law is very insistent that priests approaching the altar must have their privy parts decently covered (Exod 20:23, 28:42), unlike Sumerian priests who officiated naked. Even lay Israelites are urged to exercise discretion in relieving themselves "for the LORD God walks (*mithallēk*) in the midst of your camp" (Deut 23:13–15).

The brief account of the geography of the garden in 2:10–14 also makes many links with later sanctuary design. "A river flows out of Eden to water the garden." Water is of course a powerful symbol of life throughout Scripture, so it is not surprising to have it mentioned in connection with divine sanctuaries. More specifically Ps 46:5 speaks of "a river whose streams make glad the city of God" and Ezekiel 47 describes a great river flowing out of the new Jerusalem temple to sweeten the Dead Sea. Of course one of the rivers of Eden is called Gihon, the name of Jerusalem's spring, but it is doubtful whether the two are identical.[7]

Special mention is made of the "good gold" of Havilah (2:12). If Eden is seen as a super sanctuary, this reference to gold can hardly be accidental for the most sacred items of tabernacle furniture were made of or covered with "pure gold."[8] Furthermore the precious stones, *bĕdōlaḥ* and *šōham*, also suggest associations with later Israelite sanctuaries. The only other biblical reference to *bĕdōlaḥ* is Num 11:7, where manna is compared to it. Exod 16:4 describes the manna as "bread from heaven" and some of it was stored in or beside the ark (16:33). Even more important in the sanctuary were *šōham* stones, whatever their identity may be. They were widely used in decorating the tabernacle and temple and high priestly vestments (Exod 25:7; 28:9, 20; 1 Chr 29:2). In particular two *šōham* stones engraved with the names of the twelve tribes were inset into the high priest's ephod. He then presented them to God when he carried out his duties (Exod 28:9–14).

Finally, the tree of the knowledge of good and evil also evokes associations with later sanctuaries. Here it is irrelevant exactly what is meant by "the knowledge of good and evil."[9] It is sufficient to note that the description of this tree given in 2:9, 3:6 was "pleasant to the sight, good for food and to be desired to make one wise" seems to be echoed in Ps 19:8–9 where the law is described as ⟦23⟧ "making wise the simple,

7. Cf. C. Westermann, *Genesis 1–11* (Neukirchen: Neukirchener Verlag, 1974) 296, and other commentaries *ad loc.*

8. E.g., Exod 25:11, 17, 24, 29, 36.

9. See the commentaries for full discussion. W. M. Clark's suggestion *JBL* 88 (1969) 266–78 that it refers to moral autonomy, i.e., deciding what is right without reference to God's revealed will, fits in with the symbolic interpretation we advocate. To eat this tree is to disregard the law.

rejoicing the heart and enlightening the eyes."[10] The law was of course kept in the holy of holies: the decalogue inside the ark and the book of the law beside it (Exod 25:16, Deut 31:26). Furthermore Israel knew that touching the ark or even seeing it uncovered brought death, just as eating from the tree of knowledge did (2 Sam 6:7, Num 4:20).

These then are the features I have noted within Genesis 2–3 that suggest that the Garden of Eden is seen as an archetypal sanctuary. The surrounding material supports this interpretation. 1:1–2:3 tells of the creation of the world in six days. The parallels in phraseology between the conclusion of the creation account in 1:1–2:3 and the tabernacle building account in Exodus 25–40 have long been noted.[11] Kearney[12] argued that the six commands in the instructions for building the tabernacle corresponded to the six days' creation. More recently Weinfeld[13] argued that God's rest on the first sabbath (2:1–3) corresponds to his resting, i.e., dwelling in the tabernacle. Further that the completion of the "universe parallels the completion of the tabernacle." On this interpretation of Genesis 1 there is a very smooth transition to chapters 2–3. Admittedly there are changes in the symbols used, but all three chapters look forward to the construction of the tabernacle.

Concern with cultic issues[14] is also evident in the stories after Genesis 3. The Cain and Abel story treats the issue of the acceptability of sacrifice. Gen 6:1–4 may well be condemning cult prostitution and sacred marriage rites. Noah is portrayed as an exemplary keeper of the covenant law, observing the sabbath, distinguishing between clean and unclean, and offering a sacrifice effective for all mankind. Finally the tower of Babel is a powerful polemic against the religious claims of Babylon. If then the adjacent sections of Genesis are making points about man's proper approach to worship, it seems likely that Genesis 2–3 should be interpreted in similar fashion.

Further support for such a view arises from the overall purpose of Genesis. The main weight of Genesis falls on the patriarchs: Genesis 1–11 is merely a prologue to the story of redemption beginning in

10. So D. J. A. Clines, "The Tree of Knowledge and the Law of Yahweh," *VT* 24 (1974) 8–14, and P. C. Craigie, *Psalms 1–50* (Waco: Word, 1983) 182.

11. U. Cassuto, *A Commentary on the Book of Exodus* (Jerusalem: Magnes Press, 1967) 476.

12. P. J. Kearney, "Creation and Liturgy: The P Redaction of Exod 25–40," *ZAW* 89 (1977) 375–87.

13. M. Weinfeld, "Sabbath, Temple and the Enthronement of the Lord—The Problem of the Sitz im Leben of Gen 1:1–2:3," *Mélanges bibliques et orientaux en l'honneur de H. Cazelles* (Neukirchen: Neukirchener Verlag, 1981) 501–12.

14. For further discussion see G. J. Wenham, *Genesis 1–15* (Waco: Word, forthcoming) ⟦Word Biblical Commentary, 1987⟧.

chapter 12. But as Clines[15] has observed the promises to the patriarchs are essentially a reaffirmation of the divine ideals for all mankind expressed in Genesis 1–2. The promise of many descendants, for example, enables the patriarchs to fulfil man's primal duty to be fruitful and multiply. Looked at in this light [[24]] the opening chapters of Genesis describe what human life should be like. According to the rest of the Pentateuch worship is of the greatest importance (consider the great bulk of cultic legislation), so it is not surprising to find such interests reflected in Genesis 2–3.

If the Garden of Eden story is meant to be interpreted symbolically in terms of later cultic legislation two conclusions follow. One, the divine threat "in the day that you eat of it you shall die" should also be interpreted symbolically. According to later cultic ritual the sanctuary was the centre of life, because there God was present. To be excluded from the camp of Israel, like the *meṣoraᶜ*, the skin diseased, was to enter the realm of death.[16] And those so afflicted behaved as though mourning someone's death (Lev 13:45–46). Thus the expulsion of Adam and Eve from the garden was in the narrator's view the real fulfilment of the divine sentence. He regarded their alienation from the divine presence as death. But the serpent was a literalist who believed death meant physical death and so he denied that eating the fruit would result in their demise. Though many commentators imply that the serpent was right after all, because God relented and acted more leniently than he had threatened, I suggest this is unlikely. The narrator and his audience must surely have believed that God was in the right and the serpent in the wrong, and this further confirms that the story should be read symbolically. Two, it is usually held that Genesis 2–3 came from the Yahwistic source (J) whereas 1:1–2:3 and the sanctuary regulations in Exodus that explain the symbolism came from the priestly source (P). Whatever the stylistic differences between the sources, our interpretation suggests that ideologically the J and P sources are much closer to each other than is usually held.

15. D. J. A. Clines, *The Theme of the Pentateuch* (Sheffield: JSOT Press, 1978) 78–79.

16. G. J. Wenham, *The Book of Leviticus* (Grand Rapids: Eerdmans, 1979) 177, 201. *Idem, ZAW* 95 (1983) 432–34.

Lamech's Song to His Wives (Genesis 4:23–24)

S. Gevirtz

עדה וצלה שמען קולי [[25]]
נשי למך האזנה אמרתי

כי איש הרגתי לפצעי
וילד לחברתי

כי שבעתים יקם קין
ולמך שבעים ושבעה

Adah and Zillah hear my voice!
Wives of Lamech give ear to my speech!

Because I have slain a man for my wound,
Even a boy for my hurt.

If Cain be avenged sevenfold,
Then Lamech seventy and seven!

The song expresses Lamech's overweening pride, his refusal to suffer any hurt without a severalfold and dire revenge. This expression of arrogant self-conceit and disdain for customary retribution is skillfully reinforced by the poet through a clever manipulation of poetic convention. Following the initial couplet, each of whose three component pairs of parallel terms has been structured entirely in accordance with the Syro-Palestinian poetic tradition, there ensues a rapid and continued disintegration of the tradition of fixed pairs, climaxed in the final couplet with the hero's exaggerated and pretentious claim, which the poet has

Reprinted with permission from S. Gevirtz, *Patterns in the Early Poetry of Israel* (SAOC 32; Chicago: University of Chicago Press, 1963) 25–34.

fashioned by the formulation of a deliberately nontraditional and even outlandish parallelism.

Its age cannot be determined with any certainty, but "the fierce implacable spirit of revenge that forms the chief part of the Bedouin's code of honour"[1] and animates the present poem accentuates its primitive quality, and most scholars concur in assigning it a high antiquity. Study of the names of the hero and his wives lends a measure of support to this conclusion. While the women's names, עדה ⟦'Adah'⟧ and צלה ⟦'Zillah'⟧, are attested in late periods, they are also found as elements ⟦26⟧ of longer proper names in the Old Akkadian period, with צלה being particularly common.[2] The name למך ⟦'Lamech'⟧, it may be suggested, is to be identified with the Old Akkadian names *Lam-kí-um* and *Lam-ki*$_x$-*Ma-rí*.[3] If the latter identification prove correct, then outside the biblical references to this particular individual the only occurrences of this name or name element, למך, are these of the earliest period for which Semitic names are attested.

Beginning his song in conventional manner, the hero addresses his wives:

עדה וצלה שמען קולי
נשי למך האזנה אמרתי

Adah and Zillah hear my voice!
Wives of Lamech give ear to my speech!

Three sets of parallel terms may be distinguished: "Adah and Zillah" // "wives of Lamech," "hear" // "give ear," and "voice" // "speech." Though the first of these, "Adah and Zillah" // "wives of Lamech," does not recur, it may nevertheless be regarded as having been constructed according to the manner of the Syro-Palestinian poets, for the setting of a noun or proper name in parallel formation with a descriptive or identifying word or epithet was a pattern, a regular feature of their style. We cite but one example from Ugaritic and one from Hebrew verse,

UM Krt 135–36:[4]

אֱדמ יתנת! אִ ל
וּאֻשנ אֲ ב אֲ ד מ

1. John Skinner, *A Critical and Exegetical Commentary on Genesis* ("International Critical Commentary" [2d ed.; Edinburgh, 1930]) 120.

2. Cf. I. J. Gelb, *Glossary of Old Akkadian* (*MAD* No. 3 [1957]) 16 (under "Ur III PN's") and 243f. respectively.

3. For references see ibid., 162 (under "LMG?"). On the value *ki*$_x$ (Gelb: *ki*$_4$) for GI$_4$ in Old Akkadian writing, see Gelb, *Old Akkadian Grammar and Writing* (*MAD* No. 2 [2d ed.; 1961]) 90, No. 176, who cites the spelling *wa-ar-gi*$_4$-*um*.

4. Cf. *UM* Krt 277f.

ʾUdm is a gift of *ʾIl,*
And a present of the *father of Man,*

Judg 5:7:

עד שקמתי ד ב ו ר ה
שקמתי א ם ב י ש ר א ל

Until thou didst arise *Deborah,*
Didst arise a *mother in Israel.*

To this very frequently appearing parallel construction may perhaps be applied the designation "epithetic" parallelism,[5] other examples of which will be found below in Study IV ⟦not reprinted⟧.

⟦27⟧ That the verbs "hear" // "give ear" constituted a fixed pair in Hebrew poetry may be inferred from the pair's sixteen additional occurrences in biblical verse with the verbs in this sequence[6] and two with the verbs in reverse sequence,[7] for example

Judg 5:3:

ש מ ע ו מלכים
ה א ז י נ ו רזנים

Hear, O kings!
Give ear, O rulers!

Isa 1:2:

ש מ ע ו שמים
ו- ה א ז י נ י ארץ

Hear, O heavens!
And *give ear,* O earth!

Ps 54:5:

אלהים ש מ ע תפלתי
ה א ז י נ ה לאמרי פי

O God, *hear* my prayer!
Give ear to the words of my mouth!

5. To specify this type of parallelism in Sumerian poetry the term "particularizing" has been employed by Thorkild Jacobsen, *JNES* 12 (1953) 162, n. 5.

6. Num 23:18; Judg 5:3; Isa 1:2 and 10, 32:9; Hos 5:1; Joel 1:2; Ps 17:1, 39:13, 49:2, 54:4, 84:9, 143:1; Job 33:1, 34:2 and 16. Cf. also Exod 15:26 and Deut 1:45.

7. Deut 32:1, Isa 42:23; cf. also Isa 28:23.

The pair "voice" // "speech" may be noted again in

Isa 28:23:

האזינו ושמעו ק ו ל י
הקשיבו ושמעו א מ ר ת י

Give ear and hear my *voice*!
Attend and hear my *speech*!

Isa 29:4*b*:

והיה כאוב מארץ ק ו ל ך
ומעפר א מ ר ת ך תצפצף

And thy *voice* shall be like a ghost from the earth,
And from the dust thy *speech* shall resound,

Isa 32:9:[8]

נשים שאננות קמנה שמענה ק ו ל י
בנות בטחות האזנה א מ ר ת י

O carefree women arise (and) hear my *voice*!
Trusting daughters give ear to my *speech*!

⟦28⟧ With the succeeding bi-colon the poet begins the deliberate breakdown of his tradition. The rejection is not thoroughgoing, for the couplet is composed of two seeming pairs of parallel terms; but the first is odd and not otherwise known, while the second can hardly be construed as a particularly poetic parallelism:

כי איש הרגתי לפצעי
וילד לחברתי

Because I have slain a man for my wound,
Even a boy for my hurt.

The parallelism of איש, "man," or, as it might better be rendered, "someone,"[9] with ילד, "boy," occurs only here and is curious on two counts. Firstly, the regular parallel of איש, "man," in Old Testament verse is בן אדם, "son of Man," as may be seen from its several occurrences,[10] for example

8. In addition cf. Ps 5:2–3 and perhaps also Ps 19:4 and Prov 1:20–21.

9. I.e., as an indefinite pronoun, a meaning it very often bears; cf. Gen 10:5, Exod 25:20, Isa 36:18 (= 2 Kgs 18:33), Job 41:9 and 42:11, etc. For discussion see I. Eitan, *AJSL* 44 (1928) 190.

10. Num 23:19; Isa 52:14; Jer 49:18 and 33, 50:40, 51:43; Mic 5:6; Ps 80:18; Prov 8:4; Job 35:8; and, in prose, 1 Kgs 8:39 (= 2 Chr 6:30). In reverse sequence: Jer 32:19; Ps 49:3, 62:10. Cf. also Isa 51:12, 56:2; Ps 8:5, 90:3; Job 16:21, 25:6.

Num 23:19:

לא א י ש אל ויכזב
ו- ב ן א ד ם ויתנחם

God is not a *man* that he should lie,
Or a *son of Man* that he should repent,

Prov 8:4:

אליכם א י ש י ם אקרא
וקולי אל ב נ י א ד ם

Unto you, O *men*, do I call,
And my voice (is) unto the *sons of Man*,

Job 35:8:

ל- א י ש כמוך רשעך
ול- ב ן א ד ם צדקתך

Thy wickedness concerns a *man* as thyself,
And thy righteousness a *son of Man.*

Secondly, it must surely strike the reader as odd that the poet should deliberately have elected to employ the term "boy," that he should have his hero boast of having slain a mere boy (for discussion of significance of this term in its present context see pp. 30–34 ⟦410–15⟧).

The terms composing the remaining parallelism of the couplet, "wound" // ⟦29⟧ "hurt," are found associated elsewhere in biblical literature but not again in poetic parallelism. For example they occur as the last in the series of propositions comprising the so-called "Law of Talion," Exod 21:23–25:

> If any harm follow then thou shalt give life for life, eye for eye, tooth for tooth, hand for hand, foot for foot, burn for burn, *wound* (פצע) for *wound* (פצע), *hurt* (חבורה) for *hurt* (חבורה),

in Isa 1:6:

מכף רגל ועד ראש אין בו מתם
פ צ ע ו- ח ב ו ר ה ומכה טריה

From the sole of the foot even unto the head there is no soundness in it:
(But) *wound*(s) and *hurt*(s) and raw bruise(s),

and in Prov 20:30:

ח ב ר ו ת פ צ ע תמריק ברע
ומכות חדרי בטן

Hurts of a *wound* cleanse (one) from evil,
And bruises (cleanse one's) inner recesses.

With the final couplet the disintegration of the tradition of fixed pairs of parallel terms is complete:

כי שבעתים יקם קין
ולמך שבעים ושבעה

If Cain be avenged sevenfold,
Then Lamech seventy and seven!

The reference here is to Lamech's ancestor, the first-born son of Adam and Eve, who, having slain his brother, was exiled by God. Fearful of his life, Cain had appealed to God and had been granted the protection of a sevenfold revenge. Lamech vaunts himself even beyond his infamous forebear, and his exaggeration is underscored by the very composition of his pretentious bravado. The parallelism in which this may be seen and which commands our attention is that of the numbers "sevenfold" // "seventy and seven." We have already noted in the preceding study the tradition of number parallelism so common in Syro-Palestinian verse, a tradition which required a gradation of numerals in successive lines such that the figure employed in the second of two parallel lines was one unit larger than that in the first. The significance of this pattern, it was stressed, lay in the "equivalence" of the two numbers. Had the present couplet, therefore, been fashioned after this pattern of Syro-Palestinian number parallelism the sequent of "sevenfold" would of necessity have been "eightfold," or, conversely, the correspondent of "seventy and seven" appearing in the second colon would have had to be "sixty and six" ⟦30⟧ in the first colon. But, had either of these parallelisms been employed, Lamech's meaning would have been that his claim to revenge was as great as that of Cain. And this is the point of the poem and of its nontraditional final couplet: Lamech pretends to an even greater—an exaggerated—measure of revenge and is made to do so through a disproportionate parallelism of numbers.

Additional Note on ילד, "Boy," in the Parallelism איש // ילד

Modern scholars are generally agreed that the lines

For I have slain a *man* for my wound,
Even a *boy* for my hurt,

constitute a synonymous parallelism and that the parallel terms "man" // "boy," therefore, have reference to one and the same individual. The difficulties here, as we have indicated, are two: (1) the parallelism "man" // "boy" is a deliberate rejection of the traditional "man" // "son of Man" parallelism, and (2) the question inevitably arises, why should Lamech boast of having slain a boy, a child?[11] What is eminently clear is that the poet, having deliberately rejected the regular parallel "son of Man," as well as such terms to denote a grown man as אדם, גבר, אנוש, or even בחור, has selected the term "boy" with care—and means precisely what he says. His opponent, his adversary, the object of his act of violence was a boy.

Now there is reason to believe that warriors and, more particularly, war-leaders and heroes in the ancient world were considerably younger than we are wont to imagine. Admittedly, evidence for this belief is largely circumstantial, but enough exists to warrant the assertion.

Among the military figures of classical antiquity about whom clear and relevant evidence is available may be cited Alexander the Great, who, though of scholarly bent and reluctant to follow the military career of his father, was nevertheless in command of the cavalry at the Battle of Chaeronea at the age of eighteen. At nineteen, after his father died, Alexander reconquered all Macedonia and Greece and at twenty invaded Asia. And Hannibal, it is known, was being trained in the art of war at least as early as his ninth year.

From cuneiform sources we learn that Yasmaḫ-Addu, set upon the throne of Mari by his conqueror father, Shamshi-Addu, was evidently very young and hardly, perhaps, out of childhood.[12] Yet the father berates the boy for ⟦31⟧ failing to emulate his older brother who "has made a great name" for himself gaining military victories. Despite his extreme youth, Yasmaḫ-Addu was expected to "act the man" and lead his troops in military expeditions.[13]

11. The RSV's translation of the word here as "young man" only serves to hide, not to solve, the problem.

12. His father refers to him as being a child, e.g., in *ARM* I 85:6: *ù at-ta ṣí-iḫ-re-ta*, "And thou, thou art a child." It may also be worthy of note that Shamshi-Addu arranges a marriage for Yasmaḫ-Addu (*ARM* I 24, 46, 77), since it may indicate that the boy was still under parental authority in such matters and too young to act for himself.

There is, in addition, an enigmatic statement by which Shamshi-Addu chides his son and which may point still further to the latter's extreme youth (*ARM* I 73:43f., 108:6f., 113:7f.): *ṣí-iḫ-re-et ú-ul eṭ-le-et ú-ul šar-tum i-na li-ti-ka.* The editor of the texts, G. Dossin, understands it to mean: "Thou art little, thou art not a man, thou hast no hair upon thy cheek!" For other interpretations of the statement see W. von Soden in *WO* I 193 and *CAD* IV (1958) 407 *b*.

13. *ARM* I 69.

In an Egyptian inscription Ramesses II is said to have been a "chief of the army" when he was "a boy in the tenth year."[14] While the statement may contain an exaggeration, in that the title may have been merely honorific, there is no reason to doubt its essential validity, namely that the young prince had accompanied his father on the latter's military campaigns and been delegated some, perhaps minor, responsibility. By way of analogy we may note that Gideon's son, his first-born, Yether, accompanied his father on the military expedition which resulted in the capture of Zebah and Zalmunnah and that Gideon offered the boy what was no doubt the privilege of executing these enemy chiefs. The youngster did not draw his sword, the text relates, "because he was afraid, because he was yet a youngster."[15] And there is evidence, too, to suggest that Taharqa (biblical Tirhaqa, 2 Kgs 19:9), when he led his Nubian forces in the abortive attempt to stay the Assyrian army under Sennacherib in 701 B.C.E., was probably in his teens.[16]

14. J. H. Breasted, *Ancient Records of Egypt* (Chicago, 1906) III, §288 (line 17).

15. Judg 8:20. It may also be of interest here to recall the words of (General) Othello, the Moor, in Shakespeare's play of that name (Act I, scene iii, lines 81–85, 128–33; italics mine):

> . . . Rude am I in my speech
> And little bless'd with the soft phrase of peace;
> For since these arms of mine had *seven* years' pith
> Till now some nine moons wasted, they have us'd
> Their dearest action in the tented field.
> Her father lov'd me, oft invited me;
> Still question'd me the story of my life
> From year to year—the battles, sieges, fortunes
> That I have pass'd.
> I ran it through, even *from my boyish days*
> To th' very moment that he bade me tell it.

16. From Egyptian sources it is known that the Pharaoh of Egypt at this time was Shabaka, Taharqa's uncle, a fact which has led some to regard the biblical text as being in error (e.g., M. Noth, *The History of Israel* [trans. by S. Godman; London, 1958] 268). But Sennacherib, in that section of the annals concerned with his military activities in Palestine in 701, states that Hezekiah had appealed for help to the kings of Egypt and Ethiopia and that he (Sennacherib) defeated them in the plain of Altaqu (*ANET,* 267f.). The Assyrian has here distinguished between Egypt and Ethiopia, and it is of interest to note that the Hebrew historian has referred to Taharqa not as king of Egypt nor yet as Pharaoh but as "king of Ethiopia," *melek Kush.*

Sometime after 701 Shabaka was succeeded on the throne of Egypt by his nephew Shebitku, who, in turn, was succeeded by his younger brother, Taharqa, in 689. Taharqa ruled for twenty-six years (see most recently, R. Parker, *Kush* 8 [1960] 268–69). In an inscription dated to his sixth year Taharqa relates that as "a goodly youth, a king's brother," he, in the company of other "goodly youths," came north (from Nubia) to Thebes to rejoin his brother Shebitku, who was then the reigning Pharaoh (M. F. Laming Macadam, *The Temples of Kawa* I [London, 1949] Inscr. IV 7f.). In another inscription of "year 6" he tells

⟦32⟧ Another line of argument appears from the observation that marriages in the ancient world (as in many nonurban societies of the modern world) generally took place between people of very young age, people in the middle to ⟦33⟧ late teens. And since the heroes of legend,

---

that he had left his mother in Nubia when he was "a youth of twenty years when [he] came with His Majesty to lower Egypt." He goes on to say that "after an interval of years" his mother came to see him and found him crowned king of Egypt (ibid., Inscr. V 17–18). Macadam is of the opinion that Taharqa came north to join his brother on the throne of Egypt as coregent, that he numbered his regnal years from the start of his coregency, that Shebitku died about five years later, and that "year 6" was, in reality, Taharqa's first year as sole ruler (ibid., 18–20, n. 30). If it be assumed with Macadam that Taharqa became coregent as a youth of twenty, and as it is known that he ruled for twenty-six years, then he would have been forty-six years of age at the time of his death in 664/663 and eight or nine years of age in 701. This calculation has led Macadam (ibid.) to reject the account in 2 Kgs 19:9 as a manifest "mistake."

J. Leclant and J. Yoyotte, however, have argued cogently against Macadam's conjecture of a coregency of the two brothers. They point out that (1) Inscr. V 15 states explicitly that the successor of Shebitku had ascended the throne, had been crowned king, and had received his Horus name only after his predecessor's decease, (2) that Taharqa engaged in royal activities in Nubia and in Egypt from his second year, (3) that royal attributes are accorded him in texts and representations before his "year 6," and (4) that there exist private documents from Thebes dated according to his first years (*Bulletin de l'Institut français d'archéologie orientale* 51 [1952] 24).

The coregency of Taharqa with his elder brother, Shebitku, being now generally regarded as unlikely (cf. *Les peuples de l'orient méditerranéen*. II. *L'Égypte*, par Étienne Drioton et Jacques Vandier [3 éd.; Paris, 1952] 548, n. 1), some interval of time must have elapsed between Taharqa's arrival at Thebes, when he was twenty years of age, and his first year of reign. To compute his age at death in 664/663, then, we must total 20 years (= his age on leaving his mother to join his brother), *x* years (= the interval between his arrival in Thebes and his enthronement in Memphis), and 26 years (= the length of his reign). In that inscription in which Taharqa tells that he was twenty years old when he came north at the bidding of the king, his brother (Inscr. V), he tells also that he "appeared" (i.e., became king) after his brother's death, that his mother came to see him "after an interval of years," and that she found him enthroned as king. It seems reasonable to assume that the visit of the queen mother had been occasioned not alone by the enthronement of her younger son but also by the death of the elder. If this assumption be valid, then the reference to the "interval of years" would correspond to the lapse of time between Taharqa's arrival in Thebes and his enthronement in Memphis, the "*x*" of our computation. The indefinite "interval of years" signifies a minimum of three years. If this minimum number, three years, be taken to be the actual lapse of time, then Taharqa would have been forty-nine years old when he died in 664/663 and twelve or thirteen when he led his (Nubian = "Ethiopian") forces in 701. Since the indefinite "interval of years" can signify more than three years, however the chronology of Taharqa be resolved, it may be said that when he led his troops in the Battle of Altaqu in 701 he was certainly less than twenty years of age and more than twelve, i.e., he was in his teens. [I am greatly indebted to Dr. Edward F. Wente for references to Egyptological data and for several very valuable discussions pertaining to the problems surrounding the reign of Taharqa.]

or warriors of the "heroic age," were frequently unmarried, or married but a short time, the implication inevitably follows that the heroes were in their early teens or younger. Evidence for teen-age marriage is not abundant, but it does exist. *Pirqe Aboth* (v. 24), for example, sets the age for marriage at eighteen, while Rabbinic law forbids parents to give their children in marriage before the age of puberty yet urges them to do so as soon as this stage is reached.[17] And the Assyrian Laws (cf. §43) permit marriage as early as the tenth year. Some evidence for teen-age marriage, moreover, is furnished by the Old Testament. In 2 Kgs 21:19 it is told that Amon was twenty-two years old when he began to reign and that he reigned two years. At the end of that time, at age twenty-four, he was assassinated (v. 23). The rebellion having been quelled, his son Josiah was set on the throne. This son was eight years old when he began to rule (2 Kgs 22:1), a fact which indicates that Amon, his father, was sixteen years of age at the time of Josiah's birth and, therefore, that he married no later than his fifteenth year. In addition, Josiah, it is told, being eight years old when he began to reign and having reigned thirty-one years when he died, was thirty-nine years of age at the time of his death. His son, Jehoahaz, succeeded without incident to the throne at age twenty-three. If the biblical account is here correct, then Josiah was sixteen years old at the time of the birth of Jehoahaz and, as his father before him, therefore, had married no later than his fifteenth year.

Of the principal heroes of Homer's *Iliad,* Achilles is unmarried and Hector, though married, has only an infant child. Concerning Achilles there is, furthermore, a legend extant which relates of the attempt on the part of Achilles' mother to prevent her son from participating in the war against Troy. This she does by having him disguised as a girl and harbored among the young women at the court of Lycomedes. To this court came the "wily" Odysseus on his assignment to locate the hero and, for this purpose, he carried with him a sword hidden among some woven goods. While the girls were engaged in inspecting the apparel, Achilles became engrossed in examining the sword. By this ruse, and this ruse alone, was Achilles' identity revealed and his disguise uncovered. The only age at which such successful deception is possible is before a boy ⟦34⟧ acquires secondary male characteristics, that is to say, before the age of puberty.

In Mesopotamian literature, too, there are indications that military "heroes" were young and unmarried, that military activity preceded marriage. Witness the following excerpt from a Sumerian text referred to by Professor Thorkild Jacobsen as "The Lad in the Desert":

17. Sanh. 76 *b.*

Before the young wife was yet in his arms,
And my mother might raise a (grand-)child on (her) knees;
When (his) father- and mother-in-law had (just) thought of him
And he had acquired them as father- and mother-in-law,
When he was accepted among fellows as a friend,
  when he was merely a young soldier,
(Then) did (the powers) pass sentence upon him,
On the noble young lord,
And his god let the sentence befall him![18]

Extra-biblical examples can, but need not, be multiplied. It may suffice merely to cite two biblical figures who achieved fame for "heroic" physical and military prowess before their respective marriages, Samson and David. Samson's renowned physical exploits, it will be remembered, centered around his attempts at winning a bride, while it was not until David had gained fame as a successful military leader that marriage was proposed for him. In this connection it is highly significant that the Hebrew poet of the "Song of Deborah" should have envisaged the enemy commander's (Sisera's) mother as waiting anxiously for his return (Judg 5:28–30) and not a wife.

Whatever, therefore, may have prompted the poet of Lamech's boast song to substitute for the traditional parallelism "man" // "son of Man" the unique parallelism "man" // "boy," there is no reason to doubt his intention or his meaning. Lamech is proud of his feat, the slaying of a boy, and we must no doubt understand by this a very young warrior, an upstart would-be hero.

18. The translation is that of Thorkild Jacobsen in "Toward the Image of Tammuz," *History of Religions* 1 (1961) 201.

From Analysis to Synthesis: The Interpretation of Genesis 1–11

BERNHARD W. ANDERSON

⟦23⟧ The vitality of biblical scholarship is shown by a disposition to test and challenge working hypotheses, even those that are supported by a broad consensus. Today there are new signals that call for advance, like the rustling of leaves in the tops of the balsam trees, to cite a biblical figure of speech (2 Sam 5:24).[1] The purpose of this essay is to reexamine some old-fashioned views that have constituted the critical orthodoxy of the twentieth century and to look toward the new era of biblical study that is dawning. Attention will focus on the book of Genesis which has been a storm-center of biblical criticism in the modern period. In order to make the task somewhat manageable, however, I shall bracket out the patriarchal history and consider only the primeval history (Gen 1:1–11:26). But even this is too much to deal with; so, within the primeval history, I shall concentrate on the flood story. Everyone will admit that we have more than enough problems to handle within this pericope!

Reprinted with permission from the *Journal of Biblical Literature* 97 (1978) 23–39.

1. Recent examples, *inter alia,* of the new ferment are Hans Heinrich Schmid, *Der sogenannte Jahwist: Beobachtungen und Fragen zur Pentateuchforschung* (Zurich: Theologischer Verlag, 1976) and Rolf Rendtorff, *Das überlieferungsgeschichtliche Problem das Pentateuch* (BZAW 147; Berlin/New York: de Gruyter, 1977).

The Genesis of Genesis

Before coming to the flood story, let us consider briefly the methodological crisis in which we find ourselves. As we look back over the history of pentateuchal criticism in the twentieth century, it is clear that the mainstream of biblical scholarship, as represented by the Society of Biblical Literature, has been concerned with the genetic development of the biblical materials. Otto Eissfeldt's little book, *Die Genesis der Genesis* (1958), the German version of his article on "Genesis" in *IDB*, is symptomatic of the major interest of past generations. In this period the interpretive task has been both analytic and diachronic: analytic in the sense that one dissects the received text into its component parts, and diachronic in the sense that one seeks to understand the genesis of the text from its earliest origin to its final formulation. Thus the source critic begins by analyzing the text into its component "documents" on the basis of criteria applicable to literary texts. As Eissfeldt points out, however, these "narrative threads" have had a prehistory. Accordingly, it is the task of the form critic, following the lead of Gunkel, to venture behind the ⟦24⟧ literary sources into the previous period of oral tradition and to recover the *Urform* ⟦'original form'⟧ of a particular text and its setting in life. Finally, the task of the historian of traditions is to realize Gunkel's goal of presenting a *Literaturgeschichte*, that is, a reconstruction of the whole genetic development from the early phase of oral tradition through the stages of various literary formulations to the end-result of the pentateuch which we have received.

It is not my intention to denigrate this period of scholarship, for it has contributed to our understanding of the depth-dimension of the texts. To borrow a figure of speech used by Gerhard von Rad in his Genesis commentary and employed effectively by Brevard Childs in his commentary on Exodus, the final text must not be read on a flat surface, "superficially," but in a dimension of depth,[2] that is, with sensitivity to the voices of the past—the whole history of traditions—that resound in the final polyphonic presentation. Nevertheless, we ought to be aware of the assumptions that have governed this genetic interpretation. Let me list three of them. First, the early period of tradition, which we seek to recover, is the creative stage of tradition. This was clearly Gunkel's conviction, apparently influenced by romanticism;[3] and it survives in a modified form in von Rad's emphasis on the primacy of the Yahwist's epic which, being based on early creedal formulations, provided the

2. Gerhard von Rad, *Genesis* (2d ed.; Philadelphia: Westminster, 1972) 28.

3. See my introductory essay, Martin Noth, *A History of Pentateuchal Traditions* (Englewood Cliffs: Prentice-Hall, 1972) xviii–xx.

determinative ("canonical") tradition that was accepted basically in the final priestly formulation of the traditions. Secondly, the earliest stages of the transmission of traditions are reconstructed with help from the literary models employed in source or documentary criticism. Tensions in the text, as evidenced by literary style, vocabulary, inconsistencies, and duplications, are transferred from the literary stage to an earlier, preliterary stage. Using these accepted literary criteria, one attempts to reconstruct the prehistory of the written text, that is, "scripture." And thirdly, it has been assumed that the way to understand the combination of strata in the final text is to explore their origin and development. As Eissfeldt's essay on "the genesis of Genesis" indicates, excursions into the prehistory of the text are motivated by a concern for historicity, that is, criticism enables us to make judgments about the historical value of narratives for the time about which they claim to speak or about their place in religious history.[4] This seems to imply that the scriptural text points to a meaning the lies, to some degree, outside of the text: in the history of the ancient world or in the ideas or customs reflected in various circles during the history of traditions.

If I am not mistaken, a new generation of biblical scholars has arisen that wants to move beyond this kind of analysis to some sort of synthesis, beyond a method that is rigidly diachronic to one that gives appropriate weight to the synchronic dimension of the text. Without attempting to survey the whole ⟦25⟧ scholarly scene, let me mention several scholarly impulses that are potentially significant for the study of Genesis.

First of all, let me call attention to the stylistic or rhetorical criticism that was given new impetus by James Muilenburg's presidential address to this society a few years ago on "Form Criticism and Beyond."[5] My esteemed teacher certainly did not intend to throw overboard the substantial contributions of past scholarship, including Wellhausen, in spite of increasing reservations about his kind of historical criticism and Gunkel from whom he learned most. An essay that summarizes his career concludes: "'We affirm the necessity of form criticism'—and that demands appropriate exploration of the prehistory of the text; 'but we also lay claim to the legitimacy of what we have called rhetorical criticism'—and that requires attention to the text itself: its own integrity, its dramatic structure, and its stylistic features."[6]

4. *IDB*, 2. 378–80.

5. *JBL* 88 (1969) 1–18. See further my essay, "The New Frontier of Rhetorical Criticism," in Jared J. Jackson and Martin Kessler, eds., *Rhetorical Criticism* (Pittsburgh: Pickwick, 1974) ix–xviii.

6. "The New Frontier of Rhetorical Criticism," xviii.

This type of study is evidenced in a recent book by J. P. Fokkelman, dealing with various specimens of narrative art in Genesis;[7] and his study, in turn, is influenced by the so-called new literary criticism advocated, for instance, by René Wellek and Austin Warren who call into question scholarly preoccupation with questions of authorship, social context, and prehistory of the text and insist that the proper task of the literary critic is the study of the work itself.[8] Using a vivid figure of speech, Fokkelman writes:

> The birth of a text resembles that of man: the umbilical cord which connected the text with its time and the man or men who produced it, is severed once its existence has become a fact; the text is going to lead a life of its own, for whenever a reader grants it an adequate reading it will come alive and become operative and it usually survives its maker. Whereas the creation of a text is finite, finished after hours, years or centuries, its re-creation is infinite. It is a task for each new age, each new generation, each new reader, never to be considered complete.[9]

Frankly, I must admit to misgivings about some exercises in rhetorical criticism which seem to be purely formal, almost mathematical, and lack a dimension of depth that adds richness to the text. Moreover, some biblical theologians wonder whether this new form of literalism, which disavows interest in historical questions, leads us to a docetic view of revelation, if indeed revelation is considered a meaningful term at all. Despite these reservations, one is compelled to agree that the proper starting-point methodologically is with the text as given, not with the reconstruction of the prehistory of the text which, as Fokkelman observes, is usually "an unattainable ideal." Something more is involved, however, than the ⟦26⟧ epistemological problem that the prehistory of the texts is unknowable in any certain sense. What is at stake is the question, to which Hans Frei has directed our attention, as to whether the narrative can be split apart from its meaning (a hermeneutical presupposition inherited from the 18th century) or whether, alternatively, "the story is the meaning," as he puts it.[10] The beginning and end of exegesis is the text itself—not something beyond it. Given this textual basis, excursions behind the text are appropriate and often illuminating; but, as Amos

7. J. P. Fokkelman, *Narrative Art in Genesis: Specimens of Stylistic and Structural Analysis* (Amsterdam: Van Gorcum, 1975).

8. R. Wellek and A. Warren, *Theory of Literature* (3rd ed.; London: Harcourt, Brace & World, 1963).

9. *Narrative Art*, 3–4.

10. Hans Frei, *The Eclipse of Biblical Narrative: A Study in Eighteenth and Nineteenth Century Hermeneutics* (New Haven/London: Yale University, 1974).

Wilder has reminded us, we should be on guard against "the historicist habit of mind" that "may operate unconsciously to handicap a free encounter with a writing in its final form."[11]

Secondly, recent studies in oral tradition should make us more cautious about basing our study of the depth-dimension of the text on the literary presuppositions which, in the past, have been applied by both source criticism and form criticism (i.e., differences in style and vocabulary, seams and inconsistencies, duplications and repetitions). Field studies in oral tradition, to which scholars like R. C. Culley and recently Burke Long have drawn our attention,[12] challenge the view, near and dear to source and form critics, that it is possible to recover an *Urtradition* ⟦'original tradition'⟧ and even an *Urtext* ⟦'original text'⟧ behind the final, written formulation of the pentateuch as we have received it.

This problem struck me as I was reviewing the work of Martin Noth and Claus Westermann. Careful rereading of Noth's study of pentateuchal traditions[13] will disclose that, although he was in bondage to the literary model of source criticism and could even "out-Wellhausen" Wellhausen in refined source analysis, he was somewhat sensitive to the fluid, dynamic character of the transmission of the traditions, based on major themes and their elaboration. This central thrust of Noth's work has not escaped the attention of Westermann, a consistent form-critic who has carried Gunkel's work to a logical and brilliant conclusion. "Gunkel's new impulse," Westermann observes, "was that he elevated the significance of the preliterary history of the individual narrative"—a narrative that had its own life (*Eigenleben*) and that was governed by "laws other than that of a written text"; but, Westermann insists, Noth fails to stress "the smallest literary units" and their respective forms, and, instead, he concentrates on the major themes of the Israelite tradition that were elaborated and filled out in the course of their transmission.[14]

⟦27⟧ Almost everyone will admit—even conservative scholars like Umberto Cassuto and Benno Jacob—that ancient traditions have been utilized in the final formulation of the pentateuch. The debatable question is twofold: (a) whether these traditions were cast into a *fixed* form,

11. Amos N. Wilder, "Norman Perrin, What is Redaction Criticism?" in *Christology*, Norman Perrin Festschrift (Claremont, CA: The New Testament Colloquium, 1971) 153.

12. Burke O. Long, "Recent Field Studies in Oral Literature and their Bearing on Old Testament Criticism," *VT* 26 (1976) 187–98, who carries forward the discussion of R. C. Culley, "An Approach to the Problem of Oral Tradition," *VT* 13 (1963) 113–25.

13. *A History of Pentateuchal Traditions*, my translation of a basic study first published in German in 1948.

14. Claus Westermann, *Genesis* (BK 1; Neukirchen-Vluyn: Neukirchener Verlag, 1976) 765. See further my reviews of this work; *JBL* 91 (1972) 243–45 and 96 (1976) 291–94.

and (b) whether we are in a position to recover the *Urform* ⟦'original form'⟧ or *Vorlage* ⟦'original'⟧. In the past, scholars have proceeded on the assumption that, as Albert Lord puts it in the context of a study of Homeric texts, poets "*did* something to a fixed text or a fixed group of texts," as though they composed "with pen in hand."[15] This *scribal* view of composition does not do justice to the dynamic of oral performance which involves the role of the narrator, the response of a live audience, and improvisation on traditional materials in various and changing settings. Some of the phenomena which in the past have prompted source or form critical analysis, such as repetitions or inconsistencies, may well be the *stigmata* of oral transmission. Burke Long wisely reminds us that, in view of our limited knowledge of the sociology of ancient Israel and the nature of oral composition, we should be cautious about attempting to reconstruct the original wording or *Vorlage* of a text that comes to us only in its final, written form.[16] I would add a further caveat: since efforts to recover preliterary stages lead us away from the givenness of the text itself into the realm of hypothesis, it is not valid to regard the reconstructed *Urform* as normative for interpretation or as having some superiority to scripture itself. Whatever excursions into the prehistory of the text are possible or necessary, the beginning and end of interpretation is "a free encounter with a writing in its final form" (Wilder).

There is a third scholarly movement which I mention with some hesitance, for I do not claim to understand it fully or sympathetically, and therefore I shall treat it with an undeserved brevity. Structuralism is an invitation to explore the "depth dimension" of biblical texts in a new way: not by analytically juxtaposing various levels of tradition and tracing a genetic development to the final composition, but by exploring the sub-surface unity, coherence, and even dramatic structure at "deep levels" of language that generate the text as it is heard or read. In the view of one of the advocates of this method, Hugh White, it is structural exegesis that lies beyond form criticism and beyond redaction criticism; for the "artistic power" of the narrative art that we have received cannot be accounted for adequately by understanding the text as a function of an ancient *Sitz im Leben*, whether social or cultic, nor can "the large contours of the narrative" be simply the product of "a more or less insensitive redactor of relatively fixed traditional materials." In his judgment, "the enormous role played by the narrator of ancient tales in the formation of the structure and texture of the form of literature" (as emphasized by Lord, Culley, Long, *et al.*) calls for a method that enables us to

15. Albert B. Lord, *The Singer of Tales* (Cambridge: Harvard University, 1960) 11; cf. 57.
16. "Recent Field Studies," 194–98.

penetrate and articulate the deep linguistic and dramatic ⟦28⟧ structure that is implicit in the narrative.[17] Whatever more should be said about structuralism, at least this deserves attention: in contrast to analytic methods of the past, this method attempts to grasp wholes or totalities (*l'attitude totalisante*).

Past Analysis of the Flood Story

Thus various scholarly impulses have moved us away from an excessive preoccupation with the genetic development of the text to exegesis that takes with greater seriousness the style and structure of the received texts and that considers how these texts function in their narrative contexts. In a previous essay,[18] I tried to show that form and content are so inseparably related that attempts to separate out traditions (*Tatbericht and Wortbericht* ⟦'account of actions and account of words'⟧) are not successful. That endeavor was facilitated by the general recognition that the present creation story is homogeneous (P). Now, however, I turn to a pericope, the flood story, about which there is just as great scholarly agreement, only in this case it is agreed that the text is composite (a combination of J and P).

Evidences for the disunity of the story in its present form can be recited easily. (1) Some passages prefer the divine name Yahweh, others Elohim (e.g., 6:13 and 7:1). (2) There are irregularities and inconsistencies: (a) some passages speak about a downpour (*gešem*) lasting forty days and forty nights (7:4, 12, 17a), others of a cosmic deluge (*mabbûl*) whose waters maintained their crest for 150 days (7:11, 24); (b) some passages make a distinction between clean and unclean animals—seven pairs of the former and a pair of the latter (7:2–3), while others speak only of the pairing of every kind of animal (6:19–20). (3) There are instances of parallel or duplicate passages; for instance, the command to enter the ark (6:18b–20) seems to be paralleled in 7:1–3, and the execution of the command (7:5, 7–9), is paralleled in 7:13–16a. (4) Peculiarities of style and vocabulary suggest that the story is not of one piece (see the standard commentaries). In his monumental commentary on Genesis, Hermann Gunkel declared that the analysis of the story into separate sources, J and P, is "ein Meisterstück der modernen Kritik" ⟦'is a masterpiece of modern criticism'⟧. According to him, the redactor had at hand

17. Hugh C. White, "Structural Analysis of Old Testament Narrative," unpublished manuscript (Sept. 1975) 5.

18. "A Stylistic Study of the Priestly Creation Story," in *Canon and Authority: Essays in Old Testament Religion and Theology*, ed. G. W. Coats and B. O. Long (Philadelphia: Fortress, 1977) 148–62.

two full and distinct versions of the flood story, quite similar in structure and sequence. "The Redactor," he averred, "attempted to preserve both accounts as much as possible" and allowed no *Körnlein* ⟦'grain'⟧ to be lost, especially from the priestly version that he highly esteemed.[19]

Since Gunkel's time, there has been a broad consensus regarding this ⟦29⟧ scribal view of the composition of the flood story. Commentators have agreed that the *first step* is to separate analytically the two component parts and to comment on each independently, although—like Gunkel—giving only short shrift to the artistic work presented in the whole, that is, the accomplishment of the "redactor." Take as an example the excellent commentary by the late Gerhard von Rad. In his introduction, von Rad draws attention to Franz Rosenzweig's observation that the underrated siglum "R" (redactor) should be understood to mean *Rabbenu*, "our master," because it is from his hands that we have received the scriptural tradition as a finished product. In this context, however, von Rad jumps immediately to the question of what it means in the Christian community to receive the OT "from the hands of Jesus Christ," *Rabbenu*.[20] True, von Rad stresses the overall thematic unity of the hexateuch in which the themes of the early Israelite credo are elaborated; but in exegetical practice he does not reflect on the final shape of the pentateuchal (hexateuchal) tradition. Hence, in his exegesis of the flood story he comments separately on the isolated J and P versions and even resorts to textual rearrangement to restore the putative original texts.

It is noteworthy that the Jewish scholar, E. A. Speiser, who accepts the view that "the received biblical account of the Flood is beyond reasonable doubt a composite narrative, reflecting more than one separate source," admits to misgivings about "reshuffling the text" in violation of "a tradition that antedates the Septuagint of twenty-two centuries ago."[21] He does not follow up on the possible implications of his caveat, however, but settles for translating the received text with slash marks to indicate J and P sources. It is a fact, of course, that at least since the time of the LXX translation the flood story has functioned in its final form in Judaism and Christianity, rather than in separable traditions lying behind the text; and it is in this form that the story continues to make its impact upon the reader today.

These scholars, though operating within the scholarly consensus of the twentieth century, seem to raise questions about the relative priority of a genetic vs. a synthetic, a diachronic vs. a synchronic approach to the

19. Hermann Gunkel, *Genesis* (HKAT; Göttingen: Vandenhoeck & Ruprecht, 1910) 137. See his brief treatment of the redactor, 139–40.

20. *Genesis*, 41.

21. E. A. Speiser, *Genesis* (AB; Garden City: Doubleday, 1964) 54.

task of exegesis. Claus Westermann, in his massive and impressive commentary on the *Urgeschichte* ⟦'primeval history'⟧, also addresses himself to this issue. At one point he observes:

> To interpret the flood story of J and P separately, as in most commentaries, threatens a neglect of the peculiarity of the narrative form as it has been transmitted to us. It cannot be denied that the formulation of the combined narrative by R represents an important voice of its own, and that the subsequent impact [*Wirkungsgeschichte*] of the flood story is neither that of J nor of P, but that of R.[22]

In exegetical practice, however, Westermann juxtaposes J and P and at times relocates verses for the sake of emphasizing the separate identity of the two ⟦30⟧ sources. In his view, the unity of the flood story lies primarily in a prehistory of tradition that is refracted separately in the two sources. At the conclusion of his commentary, however, he devotes a couple of paragraphs to the work of the redactor whose intention, he maintains, was to preserve the *Mehrstimmigkeit* of the tradition—a musical figure suggesting a polyphonic performance in which each voice sings its own part according to fixed texts. He writes: "R created out of both [i.e., J and P] a new, flowing, self-contained narrative composition" in which the separate voices of J, P, and R are heard; and this was possible because all three shared the same "basic view of the primeval event and of reality."[23]

Westermann's commentary is a laudable witness to the need to go beyond analysis of separate sources to interpretive synthesis, to grasping the text as a whole. Even in this endeavor, however, he falls into the genetic fallacy of the past in that he posits a unity outside of and before the text which, he maintains, may be recovered by a phenomenological exposition of the religious consciousness expressed in ancient myths. The creativity of R(edactor) is evidenced in his ability to combine texts, each of which gives its own variation on the basic mythical datum. The question is whether this view is adequate to account for the final narrative which, to use Westermann's adjectives, is "new," "flowing," and "self-contained." Similar claims for the final composition have been made by others, for instance by Eduard Nielsen, a representative of the Scandinavian circle. "Our present text," Nielsen observes (speaking of the flood story), "is a work of art, composed of different traditions, it is true, but in such a way that a unified work has been the result."[24] If we are dealing

22. *Genesis*, 580.

23. Ibid., 797–98.

24. Eduard Nielsen, *Oral Tradition* (London: SCM, 1954) 102. For his criticism of source analysis of the flood story, see pp. 93–103.

with "a work of art," however, is not the final whole greater—or at least, different—than the sum of its parts? This, it seems to me, is the basic issue. Without denying the legitimacy of excursions into the prehistory of the text in their proper place, the question is whether the present narrative art can be understood and appreciated by a genetic study of its origin and development.

Finally, the symbol R constitutes a special problem.[25] R(edactor) is a shadowy figure, to whom virtually nothing is attributed except the synthesis of discrete traditions, J and P. Gunkel said precious little about this mystery man in his commentary and, as indicated above, Westermann devotes very brief space to him in the lengthy conclusion to his commentary on the *Urgeschichte.* R is merely a synthetic agent; and statements about him are inferences from the fact that traditions have been reworked or reshaped so as to produce a new totality. My own study of the primeval history has corroborated the judicious proposal of Frank Cross that P and R should be ⟦31⟧ merged into one. While accepting the broad results of source criticism, Cross observes that "the Flood story has been completely rewritten by P." "The interweaving of the sources," he writes, "is not the work of a redactor juxtaposing blocks of materials, but that of a tradent reworking and supplementing a traditional story."[26]

This tantalyzingly brief reference to the flood story contains implications that may lead us beyond the rather artificial source analysis of the past. This story is not a mere combination of discrete texts (J juxtaposed to P and conflated by R), according to the usual understanding; rather, we have a story from the priestly circle or "tradent" into which traditional epic material has been incorporated. The priestly version is a reworking and recasting of the story, not just a preservation of past traditions in their *Mehrstimmigkeit.* The re-presentation of the flood story in this elaborated and expanded form is a work of art in its own right, and deserves to be considered in the form in which it is given. We must admit our ignorance about the circumstances of the composition. Was the story the scribal result of retelling in situations of performance? Was it the result of purely literary activity in the time of the exile? There is much that we do not know. However, the important point is that, whatever the history of transmission or whatever the immediate occasion of

25. This has already been observed by Samuel Sandmel in "The Haggada within Scripture," in Sandmel, ed., *Old Testament Issues* (New York: Harper & Row, 1968), esp. 97–98; reprinted from *JBL* 80 (1961) 105–22.

26. Frank M. Cross, "The Priestly Work," *Canaanite Myth and Hebrew Epic* (Cambridge: Harvard University, 1973) 305. See also Samuel Sandmel, "The Haggada within Scripture," 106.

final composition, the priestly "tradent" shaped the story to produce a dramatic effect as a totality.

The Dramatic Movement of the Story

Let us turn, then, to the flood story itself and consider some of the structural and stylistic features that make it a dramatic unity in its present form.

In an important monograph on the priestly work, Sean McEvenue shows that priestly narrative style, far from being pedantic and unartistic, displays rhetorical and structural features that are characteristic of narrative art generally, such as a sequence of panels in which formulaic patterns are repeated. (He uses the homely example of the story of "The Little Red Hen.")[27] With specific regard to the flood story, he maintains that in the P version the narrative builds up dramatically to the turning point reached in 8:1a: "However, God remembered Noah and all the wild and tame animals that were with him in the ark." The narrative, as he puts it, "swells toward the climax" and, after the turning point is reached, moves "toward repose."[28] His stylistic study, it should be noted, is based exclusively on the juxtaposition of J and P components of the story. He maintains that P was "writing from a Yahwist narrative, which he either knew by heart or had in front of him"; and ⟦32⟧ he aims to understand the divergences of P from J—divergences that are all the more striking since "P has stuck so closely to his source."[29] McEvenue, however, does not take the step that we are advocating and that is implicit in his own view that P reworked J tradition, namely, to consider the narrative as a totality in which the priestly tradent has absorbed into his composition elements of old epic tradition.

Since the story in its final form has been shaped by the priestly tradent, McEvenue's observation about the dramatic movement of the P narrative applies also to the story as a whole—as people read it today. Indeed, it is not surprising that the Jewish scholar, Umberto Cassuto, who rejects source analysis,[30] makes a similar observation. According to Cassuto, the story is organized into a series of "paragraphs" that move in

27. Sean E. McEvenue, *The Narrative Style of the Priestly Writer* (AnBib 50; Rome: Biblical Institute, 1971) chap. 1. See further Joseph Blenkinsopp, "The Structure of P," *CBQ* 38 (1976) 275–92.

28. Ibid., 36.

29. Ibid., 27. McEvenue adopts as a working basis K. Elliger's delimitation of P set forth in Elliger's "Sinn und Ursprung der priesterlichen Geschichtserzählung," *ZTK* 49 (1952) 121–42, esp. 121–22.

30. See U. Cassuto, *The Documentary Hypothesis* (Jerusalem: Magnes, 1961).

crescendo toward a climax as the rising waters of chaos lift up the ark on their crest and then, after the turning point in 8:1 ("God remembered Noah"), falls away in decrescendo as the waters of chaos ebb and there is the beginning of a new creation. Of the twelve paragraphs that comprise the story, according to his division, he writes:

> The first group depicts for us, step by step, the acts of Divine justice that bring destruction upon the earth, which had become filled with violence; and the scenes that pass before us grow increasingly gloomier until in the darkness of death portrayed in the sixth paragraph there remains only one tiny, faint point of light, to wit, the ark, which floats on the fearful waters that have covered everything, and which guards between its walls the hope of future life. The second group shows us consecutively the various stages of the Divine compassion that renews life upon earth. The light that waned until it became a minute point in the midst of the dark world, begins to grow bigger and brighter till it illumines again the entire scene before us, and shows us a calm and peaceful world, crowned with the rainbow that irradiates the cloud with its colours—a sign and pledge of life and peace for the coming generations.[31]

Readers who submit to the text of the story in its present form find themselves caught up in this rising and falling movement, corresponding to the tide and ebb of the waters of chaos. At the climax, God's remembrance of Noah and the remnant anticipates the conclusion, where God promises to remember the "everlasting covenant" that signals the beginning of a new humanity and, indeed, a new creation, paralleling the original creation portrayed in Genesis 1. In short, the flood narrative in its present form is composed of a sequence of episodic units, each of which has an essential *function* in the dramatic movement of the whole. The story as a totality deserves attention.

To begin with, notice the immediate context in which the story is placed, namely, the genealogical outline followed by the priestly tradent. Between 6:1 and 9:27 we find a long block of narrative material dealing with Noah's lifetime which has been inserted into the heart of Noah's genealogy as ⟦33⟧ presented in the toledoth document (5:1). In this document the genealogies follow a fixed lineal, rather than ramified, pattern: (a) N lived x years, (b) and he fathered S; (c) after the birth of S, N lived y years; (d) he fathered sons and daughters; (e) the lifetime of N was z years; and (f) then he died. Now, the first two elements of Noah's genealogy (a and b) are found in 5:32, right at the end of a series of excerpts from the toledoth document, namely, (a) Noah lived 500 years, and (b) he fathered Shem, Ham, and Japheth. The conclusion of the genealogy

31. Cassuto, *Commentary on Genesis* (Jerusalem: Magnes, 1964) 2.30–31.

is found in 9:28–9, although the pattern is modified to refer to the flood, the principal event in Noah's lifetime: (c) After the flood Noah lived 350 years; (d) . . . ; (e) the lifetime of Noah was 950 years; and (f) then he died. Whether the Noachic entry in the toledoth document once contained a brief reference to the flood, on the analogy of some editions of the Sumerian King List,[32] cannot be said with confidence. In any case, the narrative material extending from the episodes that deal with the promiscuity of the celestial beings (6:1–4) and the "Sorrow of Yahweh" (6:5–8) to the post-diluvian story of Noah's intoxication and the condemnation of Canaan (9:20–27), is encased within the genealogical frame. According to this sequence, the initial epic material constitutes the prologue to the flood, or as Speiser phrases it, "Prelude to Disaster," and the subsequent material, dealing with Noah's post-diluvian situation, is an epilogue.

The priestly drama proper begins with the transitional passage concerning the *ṣaddîq* ⟦'righteous'⟧ Noah and his three sons, which is formulated in the style of the toledoth document (6:9–10); and at the end of the priestly story we find another transitional passage (9:18–19) which both recapitulates previous elements and prepares for the sequel by saying that the sons of Noah who went forth from the ark were Shem, Ham, and Japheth, and that from them the whole earth was repopulated.[33] In between these boundaries the drama of the flood unfolds in a succession of episodic units, each of which has a definite function in relation to the whole. Let us follow the sequence as it is given to us, at the expense of paying closer attention to details.

(1) The keynote is struck in 6:11–12: violence and corruption in the earth—first announced as an objective fact (v. 11) and then reiterated in terms of God's perception (v. 12). These verses display noteworthy stylistic features, such as the emphasis achieved through repetition, the play upon the verbal root *šāḥat* in three variations ("become corrupt," "spoil," "ruin"), and the climactic use of the particle *kî* ("for") to provide expla-

32. *ANET,* 265–66.

33. Usually these verses are assigned to J, mainly because P has already mentioned Noah's sons by name (6:10; 7:13) and a third mention seems too repetitious, and because the scattering-verb (*nāpĕṣâ*) is found in other passages that must be assigned to C. Westermann (*Genesis,* 650) quotes with approval Gunkel's dictum: "The expression has its *Sitz* in the Babel story." But these arguments are questionable. The argument based on repetition is not strong when dealing with priestly material; and there is no reason why the priestly tradent could not have used the scattering-verb, one that is prominent in his approximate contemporary, Ezekiel. Furthermore, the participial expression "those who went forth [*hayyôṣĕʾîm*] from the ark" (9:18) corresponds to the same formulation in the preceding priestly material (9:10): *yôṣĕʾê hattēbâ* ⟦'have come out of the ark'⟧). In any case, the passage now has a transitional function in the overall narrative.

nation (v. 12b). The ⟦34⟧ discordant note struck at the beginning is resolved at the end with the restoration of harmony and peace in God's creation (9:1–17).

(2) The main action of the drama begins in 6:13–22, introduced by the declarative formula, "Then God said." God's first address, in good priestly narrative style, is structured according to a twofold announcement-command sequence: announcement of God's resolution to destroy (6:13) followed by the command to build the ark (vv. 14–16); repeated announcement of the imminence of the *mabbûl* ⟦'flood'⟧ waters (vv. 17–18), followed by a command that deals mainly with laying away supplies of food for those to be saved (vv. 19–21). This passage concludes with the execution formula: "Noah did this. Just as Elohim commanded him, so he acted" (6:22).

(3) The divine command to load the ark with its passengers is the subject of the next unit in 7:1–10, usually ascribed to J (except for the chronological notation in v. 6). Strikingly, the second divine address is introduced by the declarative formula, "Then *Yahweh* said." Also, the execution of the command is indicated in the formula, "Noah did just as Yahweh commanded him" (7:5), though at the conclusion of the unit (7:9) we find "just as Elohim commanded him." It is incontrovertible, in my judgment, that in this passage the priestly tradent has drawn upon and reworked old epic tradition whose peculiarities are evident in various matters of content (for instance, seven pairs of clean animals and a pair that are not clean, 7:2–3; but cf. 7:8–9), and in turns of speech (e.g., "a male and his mate" rather than "male and female," 7:2; but cf. 7:9).[34] However, the question is whether these phenomena, which we perceive as inconsistencies, actually disturb the structure and movement of the narrative in its final form.[35] I do not see that this is the case. On the contrary, this unit, which is also formulated in a command-execution sequence, advances the motion of the previous unit by showing that the disaster is at hand, only seven days away, and therefore it is time to get on board the ark! In spite of modern views based on alternation in the usage of divine names in the book of Genesis, the priestly tradent seems to have

34. See the commentaries for a treatment of words and phrases characteristic of J and P. It is noteworthy that in the execution passage (7:7–9) it is stated that the animals, clean and unclean, went into the ark by pairs, "two and two." The priestly tradent, who reworked the epic tradition, may have been concerned at this point with the sexual pairing of the animals, not the total number of clean and unclean.

35. The same question is asked by George Coats in his study of the Joseph Story, *From Canaan to Egypt: Structural and Theological Context for the Joseph Story* (CBQMS 4; Washington: Catholic Biblical Association, 1976) 57.

had no compunction about using both names, Yahweh and Elohim, in his reworking of the pre-Mosaic traditions.[36]

(4) The two divine addresses are followed by a unit found in 7:11–16 which source critics have credited to priestly tradition, except for the statement about the forty-day downpour (*gešem*) in 7:12 and the brief anthropomorphic ⟦35⟧ touch in 7:16b, "Yahweh closed him inside." This unit clearly involves repetition, for it resumes and summarizes the earlier narrative, beginning with the point reached in 7:10 of the previous episode ("At the end of seven days the waters of the Flood were upon the earth") and harking back to the command regarding the saving of animals and humans, anticipated in 6:18b–21 and definitely mandated and executed in 7:1–10. The new element in the dramatic movement of the story is the announcement of the manner in which "the waters of the flood" came upon the earth (vv. 11–12). Clearly the priestly tradent sought to rework the received tradition of a violent forty-day rainstorm into his own conception of the *mabbûl* ⟦'flood'⟧ cosmic catastrophe which threatened the earth with a return to primeval chaos. The chief function of this unit, however, is to indicate the inception of the disaster, and this provides the opportunity to rehearse once again the number of those whom God commanded to be saved in 7:13–16a, a passage that harks back to the priestly command passage in 6:18b–21 by way of resumption and inclusion. Notice that the recapitulation of the divine command is indicated once again by the obedience formula: "just as Elohim had commanded him" (7:16a). This is followed by the celebrated sentence, "Then Yahweh closed him inside." Usually this is regarded as a fragment of the J epic because of the usage of the name Yahweh and the anthropomorphism which allegedly is out of keeping with priestly tradition. However, this brief sentence—a snippet of only three Hebrew words (*wayyisgōr* Yhwh *ba*ᶜ*ădô* ⟦'then Yahweh closed him inside'⟧) in a predominantly P context, calls into question the analytical procedure of the past. How does this notice *function* in the received text? Coming after the summarizing recapitulation of the divine command to enter the ark and its execution, these words serve as a final punctuation of the unit and at the same time they anticipate what follows, God's "remembrance" of those who were sealed in the ark—the anthropomorphism stressed in the priestly recension (cf. Exod 2:24–25).

36. Arguments based on the alternation of divine names in Genesis, which appeal to Exod 6:2–3 for support, perhaps need to be reexamined. It is noteworthy that the priestly tradent clearly uses the divine name Yahweh in Gen 17:1 ("Yahweh appeared to Abram, and said to him, 'I am El Shaddai.' "); and he has even hyphenated Yahweh and Elohim in the paradise story.

(5) The storm is now raging, as indicated in the next unit, 7:17–24. This unit is framed within two chronological statements, the first (7:17) stating that the *mabbûl* ⟦'flood'⟧ inundated the earth for forty days (apparently the priestly tradent's reinterpretation of the epic tradition [7:4] to mean the time required for the ark to be buoyed on the waters), and the last (7:24) giving the total duration of the cresting waters, that is, 40 + 110 + 150 days. The swelling of the waters is vividly portrayed by the repeated use of the key words "the waters prevailed" to create an ascending effect.

wayyigbĕrû hammayim (v. 18)
wĕhammayim gābĕrû (v. 19)
gābĕrû hammāyim (v. 20)
⟦'And the waters swelled.
When the waters had swelled.
The waters did swell'.⟧

Source critics find traces of old epic tradition (J) in vv. 22–23, largely because these verses seem to repeat the content of v. 21, "All flesh died that moved upon the earth. . . . " But in the reworking of the tradition, the repetition serves to heighten the dramatic contrast between the perishing of "every human" (v. 21) and the climactic statement, "Only Noah was left [the verb ⟦36⟧ suggests the 'remnant'], and those that were with him in the ark" (7:23b).[37] Thus the narrative swells to a climax, with the ark and its precious remnant tossed on the waters of chaos. "We see water everywhere," Cassuto comments, "as though the world had reverted to its primeval state at the dawn of Creation, when the waters of the deep submerged everything."[38]

(6) The next unit, 8:1–5, brings us to the turning point of the story with the dramatic announcement of God's remembrance of Noah and the remnant with him in the ark. The statement, "God caused a wind to blow over the earth," which recalls the "wind from God" (*rûaḥ ʾĕlōhîm*) of Gen 1:2, introduces by way of contrast the theme of the new creation which becomes explicit in 9:1–17 where the *imago Dei* reappears. Source critics attribute this passage to P, with the exception of the notice about the restraining of the downpour (*gešem*) from the sky (8:2b). This traditional element, however, should not be separated out, for the priestly tradent, as we have already noticed, has absorbed the forty-day rainstorm into his view of a cosmic deluge and into his chronology. The

37. See Martin Kessler, "Rhetorical Criticism of Genesis 7," in *Rhetorical Criticism* (see note 5) 1–17.

38. *Genesis,* 2.97.

effect of the text at this point is to show dramatically that when all seems to be lost, from a human point of view, God's faithfulness makes possible a new beginning.

(7) The decrescendo from the climax is effectively carried out in the next unit, 8:6–14. The first part, the vignette about the release of the birds (8:6–12), is derived from old epic tradition (J). This material, however, should not be detached from its present context, for it now has a definite narrative function, namely, to portray the gradual ebbing of the waters from their crest and the emergence of the dry land, as at the time of creation (cf. 1:9–12). The dramatic action is retarded and extended over a span of time so that the hearer or reader may sense in Noah's experiment with the birds (including his tender treatment of the dove, vv. 8–9!) the wonder of what was taking place. The unit concludes by dating the emergence of the dry land, and therefore the possibility of the earth's renewed fertility, in relation to the New Year, which was also the 601st anniversary of Noah's birth. This wonderful event is indicated in two ways (as in 6:11–12): one in terms of Noah's perception (8:13b) and the other as an objective fact (8:14)—sentences that source critics attribute to J and P respectively.

(8) After the drama of the rising and the falling of the waters, the story returns to a scheme of divine addresses, as at the beginning. Notice that the address in 8:15–19, which is attributed to priestly tradition, is also structured in a command-execution sequence. In this case, the theme is God's command to leave the ark (vv. 16–17), accompanied by a special word that the animals should swarm, be fertile, and increase on the earth, and the fulfillment of that command (vv. 18–19) ⟦37⟧.

(9) Next comes a unit, 8:20–22, dealing with Noah's sacrifice and Yahweh's resolution never again to engage in wholesale destruction but, rather, to maintain the regularities and rhythms on which earthly existence is dependent. It is true that this episodic unit, derived from old epic tradition, harks back to the passage about "The Sorrow of Yahweh" (6:5–8) and forms an inclusion with it.[39] The episode, however, has an important function in its present narrative context. On the one hand, it provides the appropriate sequel to disembarking from the ark, namely, a human act of praise; and, on the other, the divine response to the sacrifice (i.e., Yahweh's resolution) serves as a transition to the final priestly discourse which elaborates God's pledge in the theological perspective intended to govern the whole story.

(10) The final unit, 9:1–17, is also cast in the form of a divine address, though this one is articulated in three parts, each marked by the declarative formula, "Then God said" or variations of it (9:1, 8, 12). In

39. See McEvenue, *Narrative Style*, 28.

the fourth address the narrator rounds off the story by re-sounding tones that were heard earlier. God's promise to establish his covenant with Noah (6:18a) is fulfilled in the "everlasting covenant" (*bĕrît ᶜôlām*)—a covenant that is made, however, not just with Noah but with "every living creature of all flesh that is upon the earth" (9:8–11). God's remembrance of Noah and the remnant in the ark (8:1a) is consummated in his pledge to "remember" his covenant, whose visible sign is the rainbow (9:12–17). And above all, the initial discordant note—violence in God's creation (6:11–12)—is resolved into the harmony of a new creation, as shown by the renewal of the blessing given at the original creation (9:1: "Be fertile, multiply, and fill the earth"), by a restatement of the role of man who is made in the image of God (9:6), and by the creator's pledge, based unconditionally on his faithfulness, that the earth would not be threatened by a return to pre-creation chaos.

The Overall Design

Thus the present flood story, in which the priestly tradent has incorporated old epic tradition into his narrative, discloses an overall design, a dramatic movement in which each episodic unit has essential function. McEvenue attempted to demonstrate that the story displays a chiastic structure—or, as he prefers to put it, "a rough palistrophe."[40] He would have had more success in tracing a symmetrical design had he not restricted his attention to the analysis of P, regarded as a discrete document, and had he concentrated, instead, on the total priestly revision of the tradition. It is indeed striking that the story in its final form flows in a sequence of units toward a turning-point and then follows the same sequence in reverse, as the following outline indicates ⟦38⟧:

Transitional introduction (6:9–10)
. 1. Violence in God's creation (6:11–12)
. . 2. First divine address: resolution to destroy (6:13–22)
. . . 3. Second divine address: command to enter the ark (7:1–10)
. . . . 4. Beginning of the flood (7:11–16)
. . . . . 5. The rising flood waters (7:17–24)
. . . . . . GOD'S REMEMBRANCE OF NOAH
. . . . . 6. The receding flood waters (8:1–5)
. . . . 7. The drying of the earth (8:6–14)
. . . 8. Third divine address: command to leave the ark (8:15–19)
. . 9. God's resolution to preserve order (8:20–22)
. 10. Fourth divine address: covenant blessing and peace (9:1–17)
Transitional conclusion (9:18–19)

40. Ibid., 31.

The first part of the story represents a movement toward chaos, with the hero Noah and the remnant with him as survivors of the catastrophe. The second part represents a movement toward the new creation, with Noah and his sons as the representatives of the new humankind who were to inherit the earth.

As I see it, there is no need to try to harmonize the flood story by denying the irregularities and inconsistencies which source analysis has sought to understand in its own way and according to its presuppositions. The question is whether we are bound exclusively or even primarily by this analytical method. This method demands that we *begin* by analyzing and juxtaposing "sources" or "levels of tradition" under the assumption that by charting the genesis of the text we can best understand the text itself, which is regarded as a conflation of discrete, identifiable traditions, loosely joined together by a redactor. There is an alternative to this analytical method which, I believe, is overdue, namely, to begin by examining the structural unity of the story that we have received from the priestly tradent who is actually *Rabbenu* ⟦'our master'⟧, to recall once again the remark of Rosenzweig. In this case, our first priority would be to understand the text in its received form and to consider what George Coats has termed its "functional unity";[41] and after that we would turn—as our second priority—to an investigation of the prehistory of the text, hoping to find further light on the richness and dynamic of the text that we have received. In regard to the flood story, this set of priorities is dictated by at least two considerations. First, the priestly tradent has absorbed the old epic tradition into his presentation, though under circumstances that are not as yet clear to us; and second, the result of this reinterpretation of the tradition is not a literary patchwork but a story whose overall design and dramatic movement make it a work of art, one that even yet stirs and involves the hearer or reader.

It is not enough, however, to consider the dramatic unity of the story by itself, in isolation. If we are to understand the story theologically, it is equally important to consider how this story functions in its present context in the ⟦39⟧ book of Genesis and specifically within the toledoth scheme used by the priestly tradent to organize the primeval history. When the priestly revision of the story is regarded as a separate pericope, the *ḥāmās* ("violence," "lawlessness") that prompted God's resolve to bring the flood hangs in the air (6:11, 13), and the prohibition against murder in 9:6 is unmotivated. "P's summary statement referring to violence and corruption," Frank Cross observes, "must presume a knowledge of concrete and colorful narratives of the corruption of the

41. *From Canaan to Egypt,* 7–8.

creation. Otherwise, it has neither literary nor theological force."[42] By appropriating the old epic tradition, the priestly tradent has provided a vivid portrayal of the disorder rooted primarily in creaturely freedom, as illustrated in the stories of primeval rebellion in the garden, fratricide in the first family, Lamech's measureless revenge, and the marriage of celestial beings with human daughters.[43] Thus the *Urgeschichte* in its final form displays an overall design: a dramatic movement from the original harmony of creation, through the violent disruption of that order and the near return to chaos, and finally to a new creation under the rainbow sign of the everlasting covenant.

42. "The Priestly Work," 306.

43. See Paul D. Hanson, "Rebellion in Heaven, Azazel, and Euhemeristic Heroes in 1 Enoch 6–11," *JBL* 96 (1977) 195–233, who points out that in old epic tradition (J) the mythic fragment in 6:1–4 serves to illustrate the degeneration of humankind and specifically to highlight two related themes: "the divinely ordained separation of heaven and earth as two distinct realms, and the enforcement of distinct limits upon the human race" (p. 214). Clearly the priestly tradent saw in this enigmatic episode the final evidence of "violence" and "corruption" in God's creation.

The Coherence of the Flood Narrative

GORDON J. WENHAM

⟦336⟧ For more than a century the account of the flood in Genesis 6–9 has been regarded as one of the prime examples of composite narrative in the Pentateuch.[1] Occasional dissenting voices[2] have failed to disturb the general consensus of scholarship that these chapters are composed of two sources J and P. When Genesis 6–9 is dissected into its constituent sources, two new versions of the flood story are produced, which differ both from each other and from the version we now find in Genesis.[3] It is a tribute to the skill of the final redactor of Genesis that he has been able to knit together his sources in such a way that the ordinary reader is often unaware of the composite nature of the present story.

In a recent study of Hebrew syntax[4] F. I. Andersen has questioned the value of the documentary analysis of Genesis at certain points. He argues that in the flood story the division of material into J and P leads to one part of a grammatical construction being assigned to one source and the rest of the construction being ascribed to a different source. For example, Gen 7:6–17, describing the onset of the flood and the entry into the ark, is a single grammatical unit (pp. 124–6), making elaborate use of chiasmus (pp. 119ff.) and epic repetition (pp. 39ff.). Yet verses 7–10, 12, 16b are traditionally assigned to J, and the rest to P.

Reprinted with permission from *Vetus Testamentum* 28 (1978) 336–48. Revised version of a paper read to the Society for OT Study in Oxford, July 1975.

1. H. Gunkel, *Genesis*[7] (Göttingen, 1966), 137.

2. U. Cassuto, *A Commentary on the Book of Genesis* II (Jerusalem, 1964), 34ff. A. Heidel, *The Gilgamesh Epic and OT parallels*[2] (Chicago, 1963), 245ff. E. Nielsen, *Oral Tradition* (London, 1954), 93ff.

3. See C. Westermann, *Genesis 1–11* (Neukirchen, 1974), 532ff.

4. F. I. Andersen, *The Sentence in Biblical Hebrew* (The Hague, 1974).

Andersen comments:

> The significance of this kind of construction has generally escaped literary critics. Either they assign parallel passages to different "sources" as "doublets," thus destroying the fabric of composition; or else they speak disparagingly of its [[337]] tedious redundancy. But if the text is left as it is, and its grammatical structure is taken seriously as serving artistic purposes, more positive conclusions about the integrity of a passage and the solemnity of its style are possible. Sentences from the Flood Epic . . . cut across passages generally assigned to the "J" and "P" documents. . . . This means that if the documentary hypothesis is valid, some editor has put together scraps of parallel versions of the same story with scissors and paste, and yet has achieved a result which, from the point of view of discourse grammar, looks as if it has been made out of whole cloth (p. 40).

These observations do not rule out the possibility that a redactor of Genesis could have used two independent sources to create the present form of the flood narrative, but they underline the fact that, if he did work this way, he has knit the sources together very thoroughly. The purpose of this study is to present three fresh arguments for supposing that Genesis 6–9 is a carefully composed piece of literature, which is more coherent than usually admitted.

The Structure of the Flood Narrative

One mark of the coherence of the flood narrative is to be found in its literary structure. The tale is cast in the form of an extended palistrophe, that is a structure that turns back on itself. In a palistrophe the first item matches the final item, the second item matches the penultimate item, and so on. The second half of the story is thus a mirror image of the first. This kind of literary structure has been discovered in other parts of Genesis,[5] but nowhere else is it developed on such a large scale. This may be partly due to the fact that a flood narrative is peculiarly suited to this literary form.

Gen 6:10 to 9:19 appears to be a palistrophe containing 31 items. It begins and ends with a reference to Noah. Then Noah's sons are named and so on. Particularly striking are the references to days (lines H, I, L, O).[6] The periods of time form a symmetrical pattern, 7, 7, 40, 150, 150,

5. In Genesis 1 see P. Beauchamp, *Création et Séparation* (Paris, 1969), 68ff. In Genesis 17 see S. E. McEvenue, *The Narrative Style of the Priestly Writer* (Rome, 1971), 157ff. On Genesis 22 see R. Lack, *Biblica* 56 (1975), 6.

6. Only the references to days form part of the palistrophe; the 40 days *and nights* (7:4, 12) and the dates do not.

40, 7, 7. The turning point of the narrative is found in 8:1 "God remembered Noah."

This is a palistrophe on a grand scale. Up to a point it is not [[338]] surprising to find one in the flood story. After all, a palistrophic literary structure closely resembles the real-life situation. Noah enters the ark with the animals, and then later they leave it. The waters rise and then fall. In other words the story naturally falls into two halves which ought to resemble each other to some extent. The surface structure of the narrative mirrors the deep structure of the event being described.

Genesis 6:10–9:19

A Noah (6:10a)
B Shem, Ham and Japheth (10b)
C Ark to be built (14–16)
D Flood announced (17)
E Covenant with Noah (18–20)
F Food in the ark (21)
G Command to enter ark (7:1–3)
H 7 days waiting for flood (4–5)
I 7 days waiting for flood (7–10)
J Entry to ark (11–15)
K Yahweh shuts Noah in (16)
L 40 days flood (17a)
M Waters increase (17b–18)
N Mountains covered (19–20)
O 150 days waters prevail ([21]–24)
P GOD REMEMBERS NOAH (8:1)
O′ 150 days waters abate (3)
N′ Mountain tops visible (4–5)
M′ Waters abate (5)
L′ 40 days (end of) (6a)
K′ Noah opens window of ark (6b)
J′ Raven and dove leave ark (7–9)
I′ 7 days waiting for waters to subside (10–11)
H′ 7 days waiting for waters to subside (12–13)
G′ Command to leave ark (15–17[22])
F′ Food outside ark (9:1–4)
E′ Covenant with all flesh (8–10)
D′ No flood in future (11–17)
C′ Ark (18a)
B′ Shem, Ham and Japheth (18b)
A′ Noah (19)

Though a palistrophe is an appropriate form for describing the flood, there are certain features in the story which reflect the large element of contrivance in casting the whole tale into this form. First, though the central section (from the command to enter the ark [G] to the command to leave it [G′]) intrinsically fits a palistrophic ⟦339⟧ structure, this is not true of the section dealing with the situation before the flood (6:10–21) and the closing scene (9:1–19). Yet both passages continue the palistrophe outwards. In the closing scene, "Shem, Ham and Japheth," "the ark," "the flood," "the covenant," and "food" are mentioned in precisely the reverse order to that found in the opening scene. There is clearly an element of artificiality here.

The second unnatural feature of this narrative is to be found in the duration of different phases of the flood, though this is not immediately apparent. The 7 days of waiting for the flood is mentioned twice, and matches the 14 days of waiting for the water to subside. The 150 days of water prevailing correspond to the 150 days of water abating. In other words, the rise of the flood seems to take exactly the same time as its decline, namely 204 days, and these time spans are fitted very neatly into the palistrophe.

But closer examination suggests that some of these time spans are mentioned purely in order to achieve symmetry in the palistrophe. This is most clear in the pair of 7 days at the beginning and end of the sequence. The 7 days waiting for embarkation is mentioned twice (7:4 and 7:10), although only one week of 7 days is involved. I suggest that this week is mentioned twice partly to keep the literary balance[7] with the two weeks of waiting in the ark at the end of the flood (8:10, 12). Here in fact three weeks have been compressed into two, for 8:10 says, "He waited another seven days," which implies an additional 7 days, probably between the raven's departure and the dove's first reconnaissance flight. Another contrived feature of the chronology is found in the central section. For example, the 40 days of flood mentioned in 7:17 seem to form part of the 150 days that the waters prevailed on the earth (7:24). The 40 days in 7:17 balance the 40 days in 8:6, before Noah opened the window of the ark. In short, some of the references to time in the flood appear to have as much a literary as a chronological function. They underline the symmetry of the flood's rise and fall, thereby enhancing the structure of the palistrophe.

What then is the function of the palistrophe? Firstly, it gives literary expression to the character of the flood event. The rise and fall of the

7. Another reason is to draw attention to the exact fulfilment of God's warning (cf. 7:4 with 10, 12, 23).

waters is mirrored in the rise and fall of the key words in its description. Secondly, it draws attention to the real turning point [[340]] in the saga: 8:1, "And God remembered Noah." From that moment the waters start to decline and the earth to dry out. It was God's intervention that was decisive in saving Noah, and the literary structure highlights this fact. This large-scale palistrophe co-exists alongside the smaller literary and syntactic patterns in these chapters noted by other scholars.[8] Similar phenomena are observable in Genesis 1 and 17.[9] Artists must necessarily be concerned as much with the details of a work as with the overall effect.

It should also be pointed out that certain items in the story do not fit the palistrophe exactly. For example, Noah's sacrifice (8:20ff.) does not form part of the pattern. This is inevitable to some extent if the writer was to be faithful to the traditions he had received. He managed to mention the initial 7-day period of waiting twice, and to reduce the final 21 days to 14 for the sake of the palistrophic structure. But there are limits to this process if he was not to alter the contents of his sources as well as their form. Further, if he had achieved total and perfect symmetry, the story might have lost some of its interest. In most works of art perfect repetition and symmetry are not desirable. It is the variation of shape and form against the background of an established pattern that gives the viewer or listener such pleasure. Total formlessness is incomprehensible. Absolute repetitiveness is dull. Our writer avoids both extremes. While the palistrophic structure provides him with a framework which draws attention to the main point of the story, he does not allow it to override his concern to reproduce the contents of his sources faithfully.

The introductory paragraphs are not incorporated into the main palistrophe, but are linked to it in others ways. The first paragraph (6:5–7) tells of God's displeasure at the corruption of the earth. The second (6:8–9) tells how Noah was the one exception who found favour in the eyes of the Lord.

The first paragraph displays a loose form of panel writing,[10] that is, certain key words are repeated in a fixed order.

Genesis 6:5–7

A	The Lord	The Lord	The Lord
B	saw	was sorry	said
C	that	that	
D	man	man	man
E	in the earth (*ʾereṣ*)	in the earth (*ʾereṣ*)	on the earth (*ʾădāmâ*)
F	his heart	his heart	

8. Cf. Andersen, 124–6; McEvenue, 37ff.
9. Cf. Beauchamp, 43ff.; McEvenue, 145ff.
10. For a discussion of this technique see McEvenue, 13ff., 158ff.

⟦341⟧ The important words here are "Yahweh," a verb describing his action, "that," "man," "on the earth," "his heart." The threefold repetition serves to show the intensity of God's reaction to human sin, and prepares the reader for the drastic solution to the problem first hinted at in verse 7.

The first paragraph finds a close parallel in one of the scenes after the flood (Gen 8:21). They are written in two parallel panels.

Genesis 6:5–7 and 8:21

A	The LORD (6:5)	The LORD (8:21)
B	saw	smelled
C	man	man
D	every imagination	imagination
C	his heart	man's heart
D	only evil	evil
E	continually	from his youth
F	blot out (6:7)	destroy
G	man	every creature
H	made (*ᶜāśāh*)	done (*ᶜāśāh*)

Here the literary structure does two things. It binds the opening paragraph into the main narrative, and it puts God's change of mind into high relief. Though man is just as sinful as he was before the flood, God has decided never to destroy the world again.

Gen 6:8 should probably be viewed as opening the second paragraph, not closing the first (so Andersen, pp. 80ff.). Certainly verses 8 and 9 form a tightly knit chain of clauses in chiastic apposition, with Noah[11] alternately subject and predicate. Or these verses may be viewed as a short palistrophe, a pre-echo of the main structure which it immediately prefaces.

Genesis 6:8–9

A Noah
B found favour
C in the eyes of the LORD
D These are the generations (*tôlĕdōt*) of Noah
E Noah was righteous
E′ perfect he was
D′ in his generations (*dōrōt*)
C′ with God
B′ walked
A′ Noah

11. Noah is sometimes referred to by a pronominal suffix.

⟦342⟧ The centre of the pattern this time is: "Noah was righteous. He was perfect." Once again a literary form is being used to underline a theological point.

There are other cross-links between these opening paragraphs and the main section. For example, 6:8–9, "Noah found favour in the eyes of the Lord . . . Noah was a righteous man, perfect in his generations," is echoed in 7:1, "And the Lord said to Noah . . . I have seen that you are righteous before me in this generation." Similarly 6:7, "I will blot out man," is fulfilled in 7:23. Thus, both introductory paragraphs are carefully bound into the main body of the narrative.

Narrative Coherence and Chronology

If the writer demonstrated his literary skill in producing the complex structures we have discussed, did he neglect to produce a coherent tale that is self-consistent when read as a straightforward narrative? It seems unlikely. But, since he has sometimes been charged with failing to combine his sources carefully enough to avoid contradictions within the narrative, let us consider the question afresh.

The first paragraph of the main story (6:11–22) tells how God informed Noah of his intention to destroy the earth. Therefore, Noah is commanded (in the imperative) to build an ark and stock it with food (6:14, 21). In passing he is told (in the indicative) that, when the flood comes, he and his family will board the ark, and he will bring pairs of animals with him to preserve life on the earth (6:18–20).

The second paragraph (7:1–5) deals with the situation after the ark is built. In seven days the flood will come; therefore Noah must now enter the ark, and bring in the animals. Whereas in the previous paragraph this was simply a statement about the distant future after the ark had been built, now a precise command is given: he must bring in seven pairs of clean animals and one pair of each kind of unclean animals. That there was only one pair of unclean animals but several pairs of clean animals explains why certain points are made later in the story. The purpose of the animals' voyage was to preserve life on earth: this is stated three times (6:19, 20; 7:3). Thus, if any of the unclean animals in the ark died, that species would have died out. When the raven, an unclean bird (Lev 11:15), went out to see if there was any dry land, he never returned to the ark. Had the story ⟦343⟧ of the raven ended there, one might have supposed that the raven drowned and became extinct. To explain why ravens are still extant, the narrative goes on to mention that the raven went on flying around till the earth dried out. Conversely Noah's sacrifice of every kind of clean animal and bird would have led to their extinction, had there been only one pair of each in the ark.

A striking feature of the flood narrative is the number of references to time within it. The rise and fall of the flood is exactly chronicled. How many days a particular phase lasted, or the date on which a new phase began, is noted. Yet it is here that some have found difficulty in maintaining the narrative's self-consistency. The data are set out in the diagram below.

The left-hand column lists the events dated by reference to the 600th year of Noah's life. For example, on the 17th day of the 7th month the ark rested on Ararat (8:4). The middle column lists the periods of time mentioned in the story. With the exception of the forty days and nights mentioned in 7:4, 12 they form part of the palistrophic pattern.

The Chronology of the Flood

Date (in Noah's life)	*Period*		*Day of the Week*
	After *7 days* flood came (7:10)	(10.2	Sunday flood announced)
17.2.600	Rain and floods began (7:11)		Sunday
	40 days and nights rain (7:12)	(26?27.3	Thursday? Friday rain ended)
	40 days flood was on earth (7:17)		
	150 days waters strong (7:24)		
	After *150 days* waters abate (8:3)	(15.7	Wednesday)
17.7.600	Ark rests on Ararat (8:4)		Friday
1.10.600	Mountain tops seen (8:5)		Wednesday
	End of *40 days* Noah sends out raven (8:6–7)	(10.11	Sunday)
	Another *7 days* dove's second flight (8:10)	(24.11	Sunday)
	Another *7 days* dove's third flight (8:12)	(1.12	Sunday)
1.1.601	Waters dried up (8:13)		Wednesday
27.2.601	The earth dry: Noah emerges (8:14)		Wednesday

If the periods in the middle column are added up, they do not tally with the dates given in the first column. For example, according to the first column there were three months between the appearance of the mountain tops on the 1st of the 10th month and the water drying up on the 1st of the 1st month. But in the middle column only fifty-four days are explicitly mentioned.[12] There is a discrepancy of at ⟦344⟧ least a

12. As argued above (p. 339) ⟦439–40⟧ 8:10 probably implies a total of 61 days.

month.[13] Nothing is told of what happened in the ark during the 12th month. However, the same may be said about the longer periods between the ark resting on Ararat (8:4) and the mountain tops appearing (8:5), and between the waters drying up (8:13) and the earth drying out (8:14).

This indicates that the writer was not concerned to tell how Noah spent all the time in the ark, so it would be unfair to accuse him of inconsistency simply for failing to mention what happened in the 12th month.

The arrival of the flood presents a quite different problem. There are too many days to fit in between the beginning of the flood on the 17th of the 2nd month (7:11) and the ark resting on Ararat exactly five months later (8:4). That is presumably about 150 days.[14] However, the total number of days mentioned in the middle column comes to 380.

There is no difficulty in halving this figure. The chiastic structure (cf. Andersen, pp. 124ff.) of Gen 7:6–17 shows that the 40 days and nights in 7:12 are the same as the 40 days that the flood was on the earth in 7:17. Similarly the natural way to take the references to the 150 days in 7:24 and 8:3 is that they refer to the same period. Gen 7:24 says: "The waters prevailed for 150 days." Gen 8:3 states that "at the end of 150 days the waters abated." If we assume that the 40 days preceded the 150 days, we have a total of 190 days for the first phase of the flood.

However, it is clear that the author of P,[15] the redactor of Genesis and the translators of the ancient versions[16] understood the 40 days to be included in the 150 days. For example, though the Septuagint adjusts some of the dates to make the flood last exactly a year,[17] it still only allows five months for this phase of the flood. I see nothing in the text to preclude this old understanding of the chronology. McEvenue suggests the 40 days was the time it took for the ark to become seaborne (p. 63). It then floated on the waters for about ⟦345⟧ 110 days before grounding on Mount Ararat. Interpreted in this way there is no self-contradiction within the time-table of the flood narrative.

This interpretation of the chronology of the flood receives independent support from the observations of Jaubert and Beauchamp. The

13. This discrepancy is eliminated in LXX by changing the date in 8:5 to 1.11.600.

14. If the lunisolar year is presupposed, only 147 or 148 days; if the Jubilees calendar, 152 days.

15. If the "40 days" is included in P (McEvenue, p. 24), rather than assigned to a redactor (Westermann, 527).

16. With the exception of the Vulgate, the versions all agree with MT in allowing five months between 7:11 and 8:4. The Vulgate allows 5 months 10 days.

17. Flood begins 27.2.600 (7:11). Waters abate 27.7.600 (8:4). Earth dry 27.2.601 (8:14).

latter plausibly argues that Genesis 1 intends New Year's Day and other important festivals to fall on Wednesday (pp. 113f.). Working on the hypothesis that Genesis uses a calendar akin to that found in the book of Jubilees, Jaubert[18] had already pointed out that certain events in the flood story fall on appropriate days of the week. The flood, like the work of creation which it reversed, began on Sunday. The ark came to rest on a Friday, in order to keep the Sabbath the following day. The other dated events fall on Wednesdays.

Jaubert did not however consider the timing of the events which can be worked out using the number of days each phase of the flood lasted. These other events tend to fall on appropriate days of the week. The flood was announced on a Sunday (7:4, 10). Righteous Noah also kept the Sabbath, and began work again on Sundays. He therefore sent out the birds on Sundays (8:7, 10, 12).[19] Finally, the first 40 days and nights of rain ended on Thursday or Friday. If the latter is intended,[20] it would seem to be another deliberate contrast with the creation story. As the work of creation was begun on a Sunday and was completed on Friday, so the work of de-creation began on a Sunday and ended on a Friday. In these ways even the chronology of the flood story becomes a vehicle for expressing theological ideas. Further, it is a chronology that embraces the whole story, not just parts of it. Thus, the evidence of chronology corroborates that of syntax and literary structure, that the Genesis flood story is a coherent unity.

Mesopotamian Parallels

Finally, the question of the coherence of the flood story may be looked at from a different angle. As is well known, some of the closest parallels to the biblical flood story are to be found in Mesopotamian ⟦346⟧ literature. Exactly how the relationship between the accounts is to be explained is difficult to determine.[21] But that is not the issue here. It is simply that by comparing the biblical account of the flood with the Mesopotamian, we should be in a better position to appreciate the conventions of Near Eastern flood stories. In particular, the Mesopotamian flood story may be compared with the J and P versions, as well as with the combined version in Genesis, with a view to determining which conforms most closely to oriental tradition.

18. A. Jaubert, *La Date de la Cène* (Paris, 1957), 33; cf. E. Vogt, *Biblica* 43 (1962), 212–16.

19. This presupposes the 40 days (8:6) are reckoned inclusively.

20. In Genesis 1 night ("evening") precedes day ("morning"). In 7:12 "days" precede "nights," which could suggest that the 40 days are reckoned exclusively and end on a Friday.

21. See the discussion in Cassuto, 4ff., and Heidel, 260ff.

When the Genesis account is set alongside the fullest Mesopotamian account of the flood, that found in the Epic of Gilgamesh tablet 11, the stories are seen to have a great deal in common. The other Near Eastern accounts of the flood are too fragmentary for a full-scale comparison, but where there are points in common they are noted too. This is not to overlook the many differences between the accounts. These fall into two main categories: major theological differences, e.g., polytheism versus monotheism, or the reason for the flood; and minor details, such as the names of the gods, the names of the flood heroes, the duration of the flood, the size of the ark and so on. The broad outline of the plot is similar in both cultures. At least seventeen features appear in both stories, usually in the same order.[22]

1. Divine decision to destroy mankind	Gen 6:6f. (J); G 14–19; A 2:7:38ff.; 2:8:34; RS 1, 3; S 140ff.
2. Warning to flood hero	Gen 6:13 (P); G 20–23; A 3:1:13–21; RS 12, 14; S 152–160.
3. Command to build ark	Gen 6:14–21 (P); G 24–31; A 3:1:22–33.
4. Hero's obedience	Gen 6:22; 7:5 (P/J); G 33–85; A 3:2:10ff.
5. Command to enter	Gen 7:1–3 (J); G 86–88.
6. Entry	Gen 7:7–16 (P/J); G 89–93; A 3:2:30–51.
7. Closing door	Gen 7:16 (J); G 93; A 3:2:52.
8. Description of flood	Gen 7:17–24 (P/J); G 96–128; A 3:2:53ff.; S 201ff.
9. Destruction of life	Gen 7:21–23 (P/J); G 133; A 3:3:44, 54.
10. End of rain, etc.	Gen 8:2–3 (P/J); G 129–31 ⟦347⟧.
11. Ark grounding on mountain	Gen 8:4 (P); G 140–4.
12. Hero opens window	Gen 8:6 (J); G 135; S 207.
13. Birds' reconnaissance	Gen 8:6–12 (J); G 145–154.
14. Exit	Gen 8:15–19 (P); G 155; A 3:5:30.
15. Sacrifice	Gen 8:20 (J); G 155–58; A 3:5:31ff.; S 211.
16. Divine smelling of sacrifice	Gen 8:21–22 (J); G 159–161; A 3:5:34f.
17. Blessing on flood hero	Gen 9:1ff. (P); G 189–96; S 255–60; RS r. 1–4.

These lists underline the very close parallels between the Mesopotamian and biblical accounts of the flood. This is particularly striking in the case of the combined (J + P) version of the flood in Genesis. Whereas the combined account in Genesis 6–9 has seventeen points in common

22. Epic of Gilgamesh (G) quoted from Heidel; Atrahasis Epic (A), Ras Shamra (RS), and Sumerian (S) flood story quoted from W. G. Lambert and A. R. Millard, *Atrahasis* (Oxford, 1969).

with the Epic of Gilgamesh version, J by itself has twelve points in common with Gilgamesh, and P by itself only ten. The most notable omissions from the J account are the warning to Noah about the flood, the command to build the ark, the grounding of the ark on a mountain, and the disembarkation. The P version also has some notable gaps; there is no divine decision to destroy mankind recorded, no command to enter the ark, no reconnaissance by the birds, no sacrifice and attendant divine approval.

It is strange that two accounts of the flood so different as J and P, circulating in ancient Israel, should have been combined to give our present story which has many more resemblances to the Gilgamesh version than the postulated sources. Perhaps it could be explained by assuming that the J and P versions of the flood story were in their original form much closer to each other than the relics of these sources now suggest. Alternatively, one might suppose that only one source was used by the writer of Genesis, a source presumably similar to the Mesopotamian flood story. Whichever solution is preferred, it underlines our previous argument that the Genesis flood story is a coherent narrative within the conventions of Hebrew story-telling.

Conclusions

The syntax, literary structure, chronology and Mesopotamian parallels all point to the unity and coherence of the account of the flood found in Genesis 6–9. None of these observations is absolutely incompatible with the notion that Genesis 6–9 is compiled from two independent sources. The documentary hypothesis may yet be ⟦348⟧ defended, if one is prepared to posit a most ingenious and thorough redactor who blended J and P into a marvellous and coherent unity.

Yet a simpler and more economical hypothesis would have much to commend it. Three recent studies[23] of other parts of Genesis have suggested that it is better to think in terms of one epic source which has been reworked by a later priestly editor. This type of hypothesis would cover the evidence considered here. It would explain both why the Genesis flood story has so many narrative elements in common with the Mesopotamian, and why it contains literary and syntactic features in common with the rest of Genesis.

23. F. M. Cross, *Canaanite Myth and Hebrew Epic* (Cambridge, Mass., 1973), 293ff.; D. B. Redford, *The Biblical Story of Joseph*, SVT 20 (1970), 251ff.; L. R. Fisher, "The Patriarchal Cycles," in H. A. Hoffner (ed.), *Orient and Occident: Essays presented to C. H. Gordon* (Neukirchen, 1973), 59–65.

The "Tower of Babel" as a Clue to the Redactional Structuring of the Primeval History (Genesis 1:1–11:9)

Jack M. Sasson

⟦211⟧ The "Tower of Babel" is a well known episode in Genesis which concludes the Hebrews' assessment of mankind's history previous to the election of Abraham as the first patriarch of God's chosen people. Immediately afterwards (Gen 11:10ff.) the narrative concerned with that ancestor and with his descendents is introduced by means of a genealogy which links Abraham through Eber, the eponymous forebear of all the Hebrews, with Shem, father of all Semites. In this paper, offered in tribute and affection to a teacher and friend, Cyrus H. Gordon, we will avoid the issues concerned with the unity, derivation, dating, and structure of this narrative;[1] rather, we will discuss the ⟦212⟧ relationship of

Reprinted with permission from *The Bible World: Essays in Honor of Cyrus H. Gordon* (ed. G. Rendsburg, R. Adler, M. Arfa, and N. H. Winter; New York: KTAV and the Institute of Hebrew Culture and Education of New York University, 1980) 211–19.

1. (a) *Unity*: See the discussion in H. Gunkel, *Genesis* (Göttingen, 1969), 92–101; J. Skinner, *A Critical and Exegetical Commentary on Genesis* (ICC; Edinburgh, 1930), 223–231. (b) *Derivation*. The opinions that this tale either depended on direct Mesopotamian prototype (cf. S. N. Kramer, "The Babel of Tongues: A Sumerian Version," *JAOS* 88 [1969], 109–111 ⟦in this volume, 278–82⟧), or that it was written by someone who had knowledge of Mesopotamian practices (e.g., N. Sarna, *Understanding Genesis* [New York, 1966], 70–77) are commonly met with in Biblical scholarship. While in no way wishing to imply that the ancient Hebrew lived in a hermetically sealed environment, I find it as doubtful that the

this episode to the one immediately preceding it, "The Table of Nations"; we shall assess its position in the complex of tales which make up the so-called Primeval History (Gen 1:1–11:9); lastly, we will gauge the import of these two queries for our understanding of the *modus operandi* of the Genesis Redactor/Compiler.

The "Table of Nations," occupying chapter 10, had given the order with which Noah's descendents branched out upon Earth after the Flood "according to their origins and by their nations" (v. 32). The presentation was elaborated in a very intricate manner, providing, at one and the same time, political, historical, genealogical, geographical as well as tribal information.[2] In one case, this listing sought dexterously to explain the presence of *three* separate geographical entities which shared

---

bits of information about Mesopotamia which are found in this tale reflect a real appreciation and understanding of its modes of living, as that the journeys of Gahmuret and Feirefiz, recorded by Von Eschenbach's *Parzival*, accurately recreate life in the Middle and Far East. The audience of such stories simply did not expect to be given a detailed appreciation of foreign regions, but merely to be entertained and edified through references to them. (c) *Dating*. Most date this text by attributing the episode to J. However, I must agree with J. P. Fokkelman, *Narrative Art in Genesis* (Assen, 1975), 44: "Dating this story is not essential in order to understand it; the text forbids dating, as it were, out of inner necessity." (d) *Structure*. Cf. Fokkelman, *op. cit.* 11–45; B. Jacob, *Das erste Buch der Tora: Genesis* (Berlin, 1934), 297–304; I. M. Kikawada, "The Shape of Genesis 11:1–9," *Rhetorical Criticism: Essays in Honor of James Muilenberg* (Pittsburgh, 1974), 19–32; cf., also, *idem.*, "Literary Convention of the Primeval History," *Annual of the Japanese Biblical Institute* 1 (1975), 3–21.

2. (a) *Political*. For example, note how the Canaanite border in v. 19 is described. Despite the obscure לשע ⟦'Lasha'⟧ of this line, as has been noted by commentators, the border thus described matches that of Israel's most ambitious aspirations; cf., B. Jacob, *op. cit.*, 289, who cites Amos 6:14; 1 Kgs 8:25; 2 Kgs 14:25; 2 Chr 7:8; Gen 15:18; Deut 11:24. For Israel, it should be noted, the political boundaries were rarely sketched without theological considerations in mind. (b) *Historical*. Although we might label such endeavors as "pseudohistorical," note how a date for Eber, eponymous ancestor of the Hebrews, is established by recalling that when his son Peleg was born "a chasm opened in the earth." For this interpretation of a difficult verse that is usually translated: "For in his days the earth was divided," see my "A Genealogical 'Convention' in Biblical Chronography?" *ZAW* 90 (1978); 176 n. 4. (c) *Genealogical*. The genealogical pattern followed in this table is that of three horizontal lines which, beginning with Noah, ran 3, 7, 7 deep for, respectively, Yaphet, Ham, and Shem. The total number of descendents amounts to 70, a number symbolic of a "total community" (cf., Genesis 46, and the comments of B. Jacob, *op. cit.*, 296). This number, it should be emphasized, could be obtained only if one recognizes the major role played by the compiler in harmonizing and streamlining the material which he obtained from his J and P sources. (d) *Geographical*. It has been pointed out, e.g., S. R. Driver, *The Book of Genesis* (London, 1926), 113–114, how the children of Noah occupy, with some overlapping, the Northwest, Middle, and Southeastern segment of the Near East known to the Hebrews. (e) *Tribal*. Note the pattern in the listing of (mostly) Arabian tribes as descendants of Cush (v. 7) and Joktan (vv. 26–30).

the same name.[3] Concluding the treatment of each one of Noah's sons, a statement is added clarifying that the blocks of descendents were given "according to their clans (משפחתם), languages (לשנתם); by their lands (ארצתם), and their nations (גויהם)." This summary is commonly regarded by scholars as an insertion of P into a fabric woven by J. The only attempt within the Hebrew traditions at explaining the [[213]] cause of this division into 70 nations, however, is not made until the *succeeding* "Tower of Babel" episode. It has generally escaped exegetical attention how singular is the nature of a literary relationship in which the consequences of the division of mankind ("Table of Nations") *precede* the occasion in which an explanation is offered for that division ("Tower of Babel"). It may be that scholarship has been satisfied to resolve this difficulty by providing those verses in chapter 10 which distinguished mankind according to languages (vv. 5, 20, 31) with an origin (P) which differed from those within Gen 10:1–11:1–9 (J). Occasionally, one meets with an opinion that accuses a redactor of retaining contradictory materials simply because they were available to him.[4]

Yet it might well be worth our while to seek a solution which does not depend so heavily on documentary separation, but one which would retain a healthy respect for the literary sensitivity of redactors. Such an approach might, to be sure, seem to ignore the source divisions so meticulously charted by generations of Biblical scholars. At the outset, therefore, I should state that while it is entirely proper for scholarship to concern itself with the origins and significance of each one of the many units that are identified in the OT; while it is certainly beneficial that it should trace the background of each one of these units by searching for valid parallels from ancient Near Eastern lore; while it is very useful to consider the literary context of even the smallest of Hebrew formulae; it is equally important a task to outline the frameworks of overarching, architectonic structure within Biblical narratives and to seek therein evidence for the theological presuppositions and the hermeneutical perspectives of those redactors who, by gathering the hoary traditions,[5] by sifting from among them those which suited didactic purposes, and by shaping as well as by arranging and welding them in a manner which

3. Note how neatly the compiler solved the problem of homonymous Cush. The *Ethiopian* Cush is listed in v. 6 as belonging to Ham's line; the *North-Arabian* Cush, whence came Moses's wife Zipporah, is divided into its Arabian parts (v. 7), while the *Kassite* Cush is reckoned as father of Nimrod, ancestor of Mesopotamian city-states (vv. 8–12).

4. Cf. C. A. Simpson, "Genesis," *IB* 1, 562.

5. Legends concerning Paradise, the Flood, primordial days and the patriarchs are known to occur in the prophetic and belles-lettres literatures in forms that differ enough from the accounts preserved in Genesis to betray independent origins.

promoted their ideals, created a compilation of Genesis which approximates our very own.[6] We begin our discussion with a short statement on the periodization of history as seen by the Hebrew redactors.

Hebrew chronographers charting the pre-monarchical period used basically two schemes by which to locate events in linear time: (1) a chronology which counted from the moment in the past when the cosmos was created, and reckoned the years by establishing the age of ancestors as they bore ⟦214⟧ descendents important to Hebraic history. Somewhat complex, this scheme permitted infinite difficulties to creep into the transmission of traditions, even when written down (compare, as one instance, the same chronologies as preserved in the LXX and the MT). (2) Another approach, much less likely to be distorted in the course of time by scribal vagaries, was to depend on genealogical structuring: horizontal to demonstrate kinship between tribes, clans, and families; vertical to establish the precise generational slot occupied by specific ancestors. Now for the periods preceding Solomon, that is from Creation to David's reign, the generational span was divided into 4 blocks of time paired into two distinctive types:

a. Creation to Noah [via Seth] .... 10 generations
b. Flood to Abram [via Eber] .... 10 generations
c. Abraham to Exodus [to Moses's sons] ..... 7 generations[7]
d. Abraham to David [reconstructed] .... 14 generations

Within each one of these blocks a powerful theme repeated itself but which, in successive retelling, nevertheless became increasingly particularizing. We shall explore this theme more thoroughly as we concentrate on the block-periods *a* and *b*.

1. From Creation to Noah

This series of episodes occupies Gen 1:1–6:8. It opens with God expressing satisfaction with his labors, but ends with His decision to wipe out his human creation. This block of tales could be divided up into the following segments.

6. Of late, scholars have become increasingly sensitive to this approach. For the latest contribution to the discussion on Genesis 1–11, cf. B. W. Anderson, "From Analysis to Synthesis: The Interpretation of Genesis 1–11," *JBL* 97 (1978), 23–29 ⟦in this volume, 416–24⟧.

7. It may be highly coincidental that Moses's generation, the 26th since Creation, is equivalent to the gematria of the tetra-grammaton (Y = 10; H = 5; W = 6; H = 5).

i. Creation(s) (Gen 1:1–2:14)

We have gathered into one episode narratives that are commonly ascribed to two separate documents. The first, culled from the work attributed to P, may have been developed primarily to confer divine sanction upon an institution, the Sabbath, whose background and original purpose had become lost in primordial antiquity (Gen 1:1–2:4a).[8] We might ⟦215⟧ note, in passing, that at least one other tradition, preserved in Deut 5:12–15, knew of an alternate solution to the same problem. The second creation narrative, beginning with Gen 2:4b, is attributed to J. It is a creation tailor-made to describe the beginnings of man and to underscore the intimate relationship that he had with his Creator. That these traditions were seen as supplementary rather than contradictory is a conjecture that could be bolstered by the finds at Kouyounjik. There, a number of totally different creation narratives were gathered by the Assyrian scribes of Aššurbanipal who, no doubt, conceived of truth as not necessarily conveyed by a single tradition.

ii. Warning and Covenant with Man (Gen 2:15–24)

This episode continues the narrative conceived by J. Man is allowed free movement in Paradise, but is warned of the consequence of eating from the Tree of Total Knowledge (lit. 'good and evil'). The implication is that, by having access to the Tree of Life, man will be repeatedly rejuvenated (hence immortal), but will not be divine in that he will not have total wisdom. In exchange for this requirement, God's covenant with man is conceived as allowing him to have total dominion over the animal world (Gen 2:19–20) and to give him a worthy companion (Gen 2:21–25).

8. On the difficulties in establishing the antiquity and original purpose of the Sabbath, cf. G. Robinson, *The Origin and Development of the Old Testament Sabbath*, unpublished Ph.D. dissertation at University of Hamburg (Hamburg, 1975), and the bibliography gathered by B. E. Shafer in *IDB* Supp. Vol., 761–762. Often met with as explanation for the P creation narrative is that it served as a polemic against the Mesopotamian concepts of creation as found in the *Enuma Elish*. That the last is not a composition which addressed itself primarily to creation, but to the exultation of Marduk and his city Babylon, is one reason to reject such a conjecture. But more seriously perhaps, is the unlikelihood that a Hebrew priest would have access to, or information about, a highly secret account, recounted in the late afternoon, in the holy temple of Marduk, during the Akītu festival. We might perhaps better appreciate the difficulties that any ancient Hebrew would have had in reacting against the literature of his neighbors, when we acknowledge that J. B. Pritchard's *ANET* was not available to him for easy consultation.

iii. The Fall (Genesis 3)

The reasons for man's loss of daily interaction with God are given in this episode, also attributed to J. Once he had broken the covenant by partaking from the Tree of Total Knowledge, man had now become like a god, immortal and totally knowing (Gen 3:22). Ejected from the garden of Eden where his access to the Tree of Life permitted him unending life, man was, however, granted immortality not for an individual, i.e., Adam and Eve, *but for the whole seed* through the gift of birthgiving.[9] It is of interest in that respect to note that woman, who is to bear the brunt of the painful process of rejuvenation, is *never* cursed (verb: ארר) by God as are the snake and (because of Adam) the Earth. Alas, by the time man is old enough to properly enjoy the gifts of Total Knowledge, his days upon earth will end.

iv. Cain and Abel (Gen 4:1–16)

Although the context whence came this tale and the precise meaning of some of its obscure passages remain the subjects of scholarly debate, for the redactor it afforded a singular opportunity to stress ⟦216⟧ the aggressive, all-too-human aspect of man as he commits fratricide. From this point on in the narrative, the gap between God and man will become unbridgeable. (Also attributed to J.)

v. A. Pre-Diluvian Cultural Ancestors (Gen 4:17–26)

The line of Cain, which progresses no further than the 7th generation, is used by the compiler to explain how mankind, no longer in proximity to the divine, established institutions basic to civilization: city dwelling (Cain); nomadism and animal husbandry (Jabal); the arts (Jubal); and craftsmanship (Tubal-Cain). (Attributed to J, also.)

v. B. Pre-Diluvian Eponymous Ancestors (Genesis 5)

The line of Seth is the one which ultimately will populate the Earth. This genealogy, commonly attributed to P (except for v. 29), links Adam to Noah within 10 generations.

9. I am unaware of this proposal elsewhere in scholarly literature. Among its merits is that it does explain God's injunction of Gen 2:17: "As to the Tree of Total Knowledge, you (Adam) should not eat from it; for the moment you eat partake of it, you shall die (מות תמות)." E. A. Speiser's lame explanation for his translation, "you shall be doomed to death," is not convincing; cf. his *Genesis* (AB; Garden City, N.Y., 1964), 16.

vi. The Nephilim (Gen 6:1–8)

Mankind's *hubris,* perhaps spurred by desperation over the loss of privileges accorded to divine beings, leads it to attempt regaining Paradise. This angers God who decides to wipe out his creation. While the origin of this remarkable fragment, attributed to J, who might have used older materials, is obscure—(is it to explain the superhuman aspects of the Nephilim, a race which the Hebrews, against all odds and aided by God, will face and defeat when they enter Canaan [Num 13:33]?)—the compiler used it to set the stage for a new creation. The obscurity of crucial vocabulary (e.g., in v. 3) makes hopeless our task of understanding its 'original' purpose. The coda (vv. 5–8), also attributed to J, may well have belonged to the Flood narrative, but the compiler used it not only to quote God's decision to send a universal Flood, but to indicate that henceforth God's hopes for mankind were to be centered on Noah.

2. From the Flood to Abram (Gen 6:8–11:9)

We shall note how God's hopes for this newer world fade as mankind once again chooses to blur the distinction between the human and the divine.

a. The Flood and Its Aftermath (Gen 6:9–9:22)

The narrative was compiled from materials attributed to J and P. That the Flood sets the stage for a New Creation and World Order is acknowledged by many scholars who note strong similarity, in vocabulary as well as in formulations, with Gen 1–2:4a. Among these we list the following:

רוח ⟦'wind'⟧ 8:1 cf. 1:2
תהום ⟦'deep'⟧ 8:2 cf. 1:2
Separation between waters and dry land 8:13, 14 cf. 1:9
Be fertile and increase for animals 8:17 cf. 1:22
Be fertile and increase for humans 9:1 cf. 1:28 ⟦217⟧
Mastery over animals and plants 9:1–3 cf. 1:28–30
The root שבת ⟦'cease'⟧ 8:22 cf. 2:2

Additionally, it should be noted that the New Order began on: "the six hundred and *first* year, in the *first* month, on the *first* of the month. . . . "

b. Warning (Curse of Reckoning) and Covenant with Man (Gen 9:3–9:17)

In these verses, attributed to P, an injunction (v. 2) is followed by two restrictions: one forbids the eating of animal blood (v. 4), the second the shedding of human blood (v. 6). Sandwiched between is God's reckoning from both kingdoms. The whole is completed by a reiteration of a past blessing. This passage clearly shows the skill in which either P or a redactor stitched together elements which very likely stood separately, by resorting to paronomasia on the root אדם ⟦'earth, man, Adam'⟧. That the warnings may have belonged to narratives which went on to detail the results of violating such directives is plausible, but can no longer be established.

The Covenant with man (Gen 9:8–17) is also attributed to P. This covenant is remarkable in that it does not reveal the terms of agreement between man and deity, but only records the manner by which man may know that that covenant remains in effect.

c. The Curse of Canaan (Gen 9:18–27)

This very complex narrative shows Noah in a different light than has heretofore appeared. That this does not necessarily signify that a 'different' Noah is at stake here can be recognized by comparing the Hebrews' total assessment of his character with that promoted by the Canaanites about El; patriarchal, loving, and wise, he is occasionally totally inebriated.[10] For our purpose, it is essential to note that this episode narrates the manner in which a fallout occurred between brothers. Ham and his son Canaan are now at odds with his brothers Shem and Yaphet.

d. Nations of the Earth (Genesis 10)

This listing, considered as a fusion of P and J materials, is discussed above.

e. The Tower of Babel (Gen 11:1–9)

This episode ends the sequence of narratives which began with the Flood. We note that man's motives and goals are still those which were furthered by *hubris*. We also note how God had to interfere directly with human activities which, once more, were spurred by a desire to blur the lines that separate God from man.

⟦218⟧ With an alternate translation of the notice for the birth of Peleg (Gen 10:25)[11] removing from consideration the slight possibility that it may contain a dating for the dispersion of the human population, we

10. Text first published by C. Virolleaud, *Ugaritica V* (1968), No. 1 (pp. 543–551). Commonly called "the Banquet of El," this text has been repeatedly studied; cf., M. Pope, "A Divine Banquet of Ugarit," in *The Use of the Old Testament in the New and Other Essays: Studies in Honor of William Franklin Stinespring* (Durham, N.C., 1972), 170–203. The connection between this text and the drunkenness of Noah deserves further elaboration.

11. Cf. above, n. 2, section b.

have no directives from the Hebrews about their own temporal place for the Tower of Babel within primeval history. All that we could say is that they conceived this moment to have occurred prior to Abraham's emigration to Canaan, and that the last occurred 75 years into the 10th generation after the Flood. We are therefore encouraged to think that the compiler of these episodes considered the period from the Flood to Abram to span ten generations, thus duplicating the one between the Creation and the birth of Noah. If this point is conceded, then we might be able to note that the episodes culled from Hebraic traditions of early history were conceived in two matching sequences.

From Creation to Noah (10 generations)	*From the Flood to Abram* (10 generations)
i. *Creation(s)* (Gen 1:1–2:14)	a. *The Flood and Its Aftermath* (Gen 6:9–9:2)
ii. *Warning and Covenant with Man* (Gen 2:15–24)	b. *Warning and Covenant with Man* (Gen 9:3–17)
iii. *The Fall* (Genesis 3)	[No equivalent][12]
iv. *Cain and Abel* (Gen 4:1–16)	c. *Curse of Canaan* (Gen 9:18–27)
v. *Mankind's Ancestries* (Gen 4:17–5:32)	d. *Nations of the Earth* (Genesis 10)
vi. *The Nephilim* (Gen 6:1–8)	e. *Tower of Babel* (Gen 11:1–9)

Each one of these sequences describes the manner in which man was removed progressively from the realm of God, in which he initiated fraternal (and hence human) strife, divided into tribal and national groupings, attempted to restore his divine nature or gain access to the divine realm, but was foiled in this by God. In each case, it is the consequence of this *hubris* which launched God into a decision to particularize his relationship with man. In the first case, God destroys mankind, allows it to survive through his choice of Noah, but almost immediately recognizes (Gen 8:21) that His measure ⟦219⟧ was a shade too drastic. It may very well be, as is often ascribed, that the Hebrews' use of the Flood as a punishing instrument was borrowed from Mesopotamian lore or, better, was shared with other folk of Amorite background. But the next sequence and its working out was purely Hebraic in its theological perspective. Distressed by man's repeated attempt to unbalance the cosmological order, and no longer allowing Himself the option of totally annihilating mankind, God finally settles on one individual, uproots him

12. It should not be surprising that the Fall has no equivalent episode in the narrative that stretches from Gen 6:9–11:9, since it depicts the unique occasion in which man was taken away from the realm of God and thus lost his opportunity to be immortal.

from his own kin, and promises him prosperity and continuity in a new land, provided that his descendents do not follow other Gods. This individual, descendent of Eber, is of course Abram the Hebrew. With the first tangible reward for Abram's faith, the birth of Isaac, the story of God's relationship with Israel will be one of repeated disappointments, but also one of ardent reconciliations.

We can now return to the promise made in this paper's title and specify how the Tower of Babel may be considered as a clue to the redactional structuring of episodes found in Gen 1:1–11:9. A series of events which occurred after creation had culminated in an act of human arrogance so overwhelming (Gen 6:1–4) that God chose to destroy man. But He relented and allowed him one more chance. A new series of events (Gen 6:9–11:9) began which *duplicated,* in its consequence rather than in the contents of each individual episode, the previous sequence. Among the individual tales was the Tower of Babel which told of man's recurring act of excessive pride as he desired to storm the heavens, an act which directly caused his dispersal throughout Earth. In placing that tale *after* The Table of Nations, the compiler not only succeeded in recapturing a pattern (Gen 1:1–6:18) with a clear goal and message, but was able to show how the birth of the Hebrew nation occurred at a junction in history crucial to the future relationship between God and man. It is at this point, the Redactor implies, that God, despairing over recalcitrant man but no longer wishing to destroy him, focused His hopes in a covenant with Abra(ha)m, ancestor of the Chosen People.

Index of Authorities

Index of Ancient Sources

Index of Scripture

Deuterocanonical Books

New Testament

Other Related Sources